THE
CROSS
AND
SALVATION

THE
CROSS
AND
SALVATION

FOUNDATIONS OF
EVANGELICAL THEOLOGY

THE DOCTRINE OF SALVATION

BRUCE
DEMAREST

JOHN S. FEINBERG, GENERAL EDITOR

CROSSWAY BOOKS • WHEATON, ILLINOIS
A DIVISION OF GOOD NEWS PUBLISHERS

The Cross and Salvation

Copyright © 1997 by Bruce Demarest

Published by Crossway Books
        a division of Good News Publishers
        1300 Crescent Street
        Wheaton, Illinois 60187

Cover Design: D² DesignWorks

First printing, 1997

Printed in the United States of America

Library of Congress Cataloging-in-Publication Data
Demarest, Bruce A.
   The cross and salvation / Bruce Demarest.
      p.   cm. — (Foundations of evangelical theology ; vol. 1)
   Includes bibliographical references and indexes.
   ISBN 0-89107-937-8
   1. Salvation.   I. Title. II. Series.
BT751.2.D46 1997
234—dc21   96-47760

05   04   03
15   14   13   12   11   10   9   8   7   6   5   4

To the late Frederick Fyvie Bruce,
my mentor at Manchester University,
for the powerful example of
his superb scholarship,
winsome personality,
and godly life.

CONTENTS

PART THREE:

THE APPLICATION OF SALVATION—

SUBJECTIVE ASPECTS

PART FOUR:

THE APPLICATION OF SALVATION—

OBJECTIVE ASPECTS

Why another series of works on evangelical systematic theology? This is an especially appropriate question in light of the fact that evangelicals are fully committed to an inspired and inerrant Bible as their final authority for faith and practice. But since neither God nor the Bible change, why is there a need to redo evangelical systematic theology?

Systematic theology is not divine revelation. Theologizing of any sort is a human conceptual enterprise. Thinking that it is equal to biblical revelation misunderstands the nature of both Scripture and theology! Insofar as our theology contains propositions that accurately reflect Scripture or match the world and are consistent with the Bible (in cases where the propositions do not come per se from Scripture), our theology is biblically based and correct. But even if all the propositions of a systematic theology are true, that theology would still not be equivalent to biblical revelation! It is still a human conceptualization of God and his relation to the world.

Although this may disturb some who see theology as nothing more than doing careful exegesis over a series of passages, and others who see it as nothing more than biblical theology, those methods of doing theology do not somehow produce a theology that is equivalent to biblical revelation either. Exegesis is a human conceptual enterprise, and so is biblical theology. All the theological disciplines involve human intellectual participation. But human intellect is finite, and hence there is always room for revision of systematic theology as knowledge increases. Though God and his word do not change, human understanding of his revelation can grow, and our theologies should be reworked to reflect those advances in understanding.

Another reason for evangelicals to rework their theology is the nature of systematic theology as opposed to other theological disciplines. For example, whereas the task of biblical theology is more to describe biblical teaching on whatever topics Scripture addresses, systematics should make a special point to relate its conclusions to the issues of one's day. This does not mean that the systematician ignores the topics biblical writers address. Nor does it mean that theologians should warp Scripture to address issues it never intended to address. Rather, it suggests that in addition to expounding what biblical writers teach, the theologian should attempt to take those biblical teachings (along with the biblical mindset) and apply them to issues that are especially confronting the church in the theologian's own day. For example, 150 years ago, an evangelical theologian doing work on the doctrine of man would likely have discussed issues such as the creation of man and the constituent parts of man's being. Such a theology might even have included a discussion about human institutions such as marriage, noting in general the respective roles of husbands and wives in marriage. However, it is dubious that there would have been any lengthy discussion with various viewpoints about the respective roles of men and women in marriage, in society, and in the church. But at our point in history and in light of the feminist movement and the issues it has raised even among many conservative Christians, it would be foolish to write a theology of man (or, should we say, a "theology of humanity") without a thorough discussion of the issue of the roles of men and women in society, the home, and the church.

Because systematic theology attempts to address itself not only to the timeless issues presented in Scripture but also to the current issues of one's day and culture, each theology will to some extent need to be redone in each generation. Biblical truth does not change from generation to generation, but the issues that confront the church do. A theology that was adequate for a different era and different culture may simply not speak to key issues in a given culture at a given time. Hence, in this series we are reworking evangelical systematic theology, though we do so with the understanding that in future generations there will be room for a revision of theology again.

How, then, do the contributors to this series understand the nature of systematic theology? Systematic theology as done from an evangelical Christian perspective involves study of the person, works, and relationships of God. As evangelicals committed to the full inspiration, inerrancy, and final authority of Scripture, we demand that whatever appears in a systematic theology correspond to the way things are and must not contradict any claim taught in Scripture. Holy Writ is the touchstone of our theology, but we do not limit the source material for systematics to Scripture alone. Hence, whatever information from history, science, philosophy, and the like is relevant to our understanding of God and his relation to our world is fair game for systematics. Depending on the specific interests and expertise of the contributors to this series, their respective volumes will reflect interaction with one or more of these disciplines.

What is the rationale for appealing to other sources than Scripture and other disciplines than the biblical ones? Since God created the universe, there is revelation of God not only in Scripture but in the created order as well. There are many disciplines that study our world, just as does theology. But since the world studied by the non-theological disciplines is the world created by God, any data and conclusions in the so-called secular disciplines that accurately reflect the real world are also relevant to our understanding of the God who made that world. Hence, in a general sense, since all of creation is God's work, nothing is outside the realm of theology. The so-called secular disciplines need to be thought of in a theological context, because they are reflecting on the universe God created, just as is the theologian. And, of course, there are many claims in the non-theological disciplines that are generally accepted as true (although this does not mean that every claim in non-theological disciplines is true, or that we are in a position with respect to every proposition to know whether it is true or false). Since this is so, and since all disciplines are in one way or another reflecting on our universe, a universe made by God, any true statement in any discipline should in some way be informative for our understanding of God and his relation to our world. Hence, we have felt it appropriate to incorporate data from outside the Bible in our theological formulations.

As to the specific design of this series, our intention is to address all areas of evangelical theology with a special emphasis on key issues in each area. While other series may be more like a history of doctrine, this series purposes to incorporate insights from Scripture, historical theology, philosophy, etc. in order to produce an up-to-date work in systematic theology. Though all contributors to the series are thoroughly evangelical in their theology, embracing the historical orthodox doctrines of the church, the series as a whole is not meant to be slanted in the direction of one form of evangelical theology. Nonetheless, most of the writers come from a Reformed perspective. Alternate evangelical and non-evangelical options, however, are discussed.

As to style and intended audience, this series is meant to rest on the very best of scholarship while at the same time being understandable to the beginner in theology as well as the academic theologian. With that in mind, contributors are writing in a clear style, taking care to define whatever technical terms they use.

Finally, we believe that systematic theology is not just for the understanding. It must apply to life, and it must be lived. As Paul wrote to Timothy, God has given divine revelation for many purposes, including ones that necessitate doing theology, but the ultimate reason for giving revelation and for theologians doing theology is that the people of God may be fitted for every good work (2 Tim. 3:16-17). In light of the need for theology to connect to life, each of the contributors not only formulates doctrines but also explains how those doctrines practically apply to everyday living.

It is our sincerest hope that the work we have done in this series will first glorify and please God, and, secondly, instruct and edify the people of God. May God be pleased to use this series to those ends, and may he richly bless you as you read the fruits of our labors.

John S. Feinberg
General Editor

As many observers of the contemporary religious scene have noted, America has had a powerful Christian heritage. For more than a century this country has been the most spiritually vital and productive nation on earth. Multitudes around the world have looked to America as a beacon of spiritual light, truth, and hope. But in recent years the power and vitality of these spiritual convictions have waned. The torch of truth and hope has flickered and in the closing years of the millennium threatens to be extinguished. Confidence in the Bible and its teachings is ebbing to an all-time low. Time-honored theological convictions have been relegated to the trash-heap of irrelevance. The virtual eclipse of the notion of sin has led to confusion regarding the cross and a clouding of the hope of salvation. The biblical verities of atonement through Christ's work on Calvary and salvation from sin and satanic powers has been supplanted by substitute agendas of psychological wholeness, social adjustment, and simply being a good and loving person. George Barna predicts that America's faith in the new millennium will become syncretistic (not unlike that of OT Israel's religion), embracing themes of love and acceptance from Christianity, self-divinity from Eastern religions, and relationships in community from Mormonism (George Barna, *The Frog in the Kettle* [Regal, 1990], p. 141).

When invited by Crossway Books and Dr. John S. Feinberg, to participate in this theology series, I sensed the need for a clear and comprehensive treatment of the doctrines of the cross and salvation from sin. Unless a person appropriates Christ's saving work holistically in the life, one winds up in a cul-de-sac of disappointment and despair. This study is presented with the hope and prayer that it will make plain and relevant God's glorious plan of salvation, his provision for the human dilemma through Christ's work, and the application of saving grace to the unconverted. Why write another book on the cross and the plan of salvation? Many fine treatises have been written on these themes through the years. And surely the Gospel and the way of salvation through Christ never change. But the human situation is constantly in flux, and new and challenging issues come to the fore that demand biblically faithful answers. When asked why he had labored to write several lengthy tomes, the German theologian and preacher Helmut Thielicke replied that the Gospel needs to be redirected in fresh and compelling ways to each new generation, for modern people are constantly changing their addresses. It is hoped that this book will appeal to college and seminary students seeking clarification of their theological views, to pastors, to motivated Christian laypeople, and to honest seekers of the truth who do not yet embrace the faith.

Apart from the introduction (chap. 1) and the conclusion (chap. 12), the ten chapters that constitute the heart of the book follow a common format. In each of these chapters we *first* seek to define the topic or problem and identify the most important issues needing to be addressed. *Second*, believing that the Spirit of God has been with the church in its pilgrimage through the centuries, we examine the most important ways in which this problem has been understood and lived out historically within the broad framework of Christendom. *Third*, we interpret the data of biblical revelation and construct a statement of the doctrine that is factually accurate and rationally coherent. And *fourth*, we propose meaningful ways in which the reader can apply the realities proposed in practical life and conduct. The conviction here is that a coherent, biblical theology must be lived out in a distinctively Christian lifestyle. It is our hope that this volume will be historically perceptive, biblically faithful, culturally relevant, and experientially viable. Our intention is that it will inform minds, inflame hearts, and motivate hands to practical Christian living.

Appreciation is expressed to the faculty, administration, and board of trustees of Denver Seminary for granting a sabbatical leave that made possible the completion of this work. I am indebted to my colleague in theology, Senior Professor Gordon Lewis, whose interaction over the years has sharpened my perspective on many of these issues. Denver Seminary students, in the daily give and take of theology courses, likewise have stimulated understanding and application of the topics presented in this work. I thank my former teaching assistant, Darius Panahpour, for checking Scripture references and proofing the manuscript. Finally, I am greatly indebted to my wife, Elsie, for her encouragement and sacrifice in the production of this volume. May this and other volumes in the series bring glory to God and contribute to the advancement of his kingdom on earth.

AV	*Authorized Version*
BAGD	*A Greek-English Lexicon of the New Testament,* William F. Arndt and F. Wilbur Gingrich, eds.; rev. by F. Wilbur Gingrich and Frederick W. Danker. (Chicago: University of Chicago Press, 1979)
BDT	*Beacon Dictionary of Theology,* Richard S. Taylor, ed. (Kansas City, Mo.: Beacon Hill, 1984)
CD	Karl Barth, *Church Dogmatics,* G. W. Bromiley and T. F. Torrance, eds. (Edinburgh: T. & T. Clark, 1936-77)
CR	*Corpus Reformatorum,* 101 vols. (Berlin, et al.: C. A. Schwetschke, 1834-1956)
EBC	*The Expositor's Bible Commentary,* Frank E. Gaebelein, ed. (Grand Rapids: Zondervan, 1976-)
EDT	*Evangelical Dictionary of Theology,* Walter A. Elwell, ed. (Grand Rapids: Baker, 1984)
ICC	*The International Critical Commentary,* J. A. Emerton and C. E. B. Cranfield, eds.
ISBERev	*The International Standard Bible Encyclopedia,* G. W. Bromiley, ed., 4 vols. (Grand Rapids: Eerdmans, 1979-88)
JETS	*Journal of the Evangelical Theological Society*
JB	*Jerusalem Bible*
KD	Karl Barth, *Kirckliche Dogmatik,* 4 vols. (Zurich: Theologischer Verlag, 1986-)
JSNT	*Journal for the Study of the New Testament*
LCC	*Library of Christian Classics,* J. A. Baillie, J. T. McNeill, and H. P. Van Dusen, eds., 26 vols. (Philadelphia: Westminster, 1953-69)
LKGNT	*A Linguistic Key to the Greek New Testament,* Fritz Rienecker and Cleon L. Rogers, Jr., eds. (Grand Rapids: Zondervan, 1982)
LW	*Luther's Works,* J. Pelikan and H. T. Lehman, eds., 55 vols. (St. Louis: Concordia; and Philadelphia: Fortress, 1955-76)
NBCRev	*The New Bible Commentary,* D. Guthrie and J. A. Motyer, eds. (London: InterVarsity, 1970)
NCBC	*The New Century Bible Commentary,* R. E. Clements and M. Black, eds.
NCE	*New Catholic Encyclopedia,* F. J. Corley, ed., 15 vols. (San Francisco: McGraw-Hill, 1967)

NDT	*New Dictionary of Theology*, Sinclair B. Ferguson, David F. Wright, and J. I. Packer, eds. (Downers Grove, Ill.: InterVarsity)
NEB	*New English Bible*
NICNT	*The New International Commentary on the New Testament*, Ned B. Stonehouse and F. F. Bruce, eds.
NICOT	*The New International Commentary on the Old Testament*, R. K. Harrison, ed.
NIDNTT	*The New International Dictionary of New Testament Theology*, Colin Brown, ed., 3 vols. (Grand Rapids: Zondervan, 1975-78)
NIGTC	*New International Greek Testament Commentary*, I. Howard Marshall and W. Ward Gasque, eds.
NLBC	*The New Layman's Bible Commentary*, G. C. D. Howley, F. F. Bruce, and H. L. Ellison, eds. (Grand Rapids: Zondervan 1979)
NLCNT	*New London Commentary on the New Testament*, F. F. Bruce, ed.
NPNF	*Nicene and Post-Nicene Fathers*, 2nd series, P. Schaff and H. Wace, eds., 14 vols. (Grand Rapids: Eerdmans, 1952-56)
NRSV	*New Revised Standard Bible*
NTC	*New Testament Commentary*
SCG	Thomas Aquinas, *Summa Contra Gentiles*, 4 vols. in 5 (Notre Dame: Notre Dame University Press, 1975)
SEE	*Spurgeon's Expository Encyclopedia*, 15 vols. (Grand Rapids: Baker, reprint, 1978)
ST	Thomas Aquinas, *Summa Theologica*, 22 vols. (London: Burns, Oates and Washbourne, 1927-35)
TDNT	*Theological Dictionary of the New Testament*, G. Kittel and G. Friederich, eds., 9 vols. (Grand Rapids: Eerdmans, 1965)
TDNTAbr	*Theological Dictionary of the New Testament*, abridged by G. W. Bromiley (Grand Rapids: Eerdmans, 1965)
TDOT	*Theological Dictionary of the Old Testament*, G. J. Botterweck and H. Ringgren, eds., 6 vols. (Grand Rapids: Eerdmans, 1977)
TI	Karl Rahner, *Theological Investigations*, 21 vols. (New York: Seabury, 1947-88)
TNTC	*Tyndale New Testament Commentaries*, R. V. G. Tasker, ed.
TOTC	*Tyndale Old Testament Commentaries*, D. J. Wiseman, ed.
TWOT	*Theological Wordbook of the Old Testament*, R. Laird Harris; Gleason L. Archer, Jr.; and Bruce K. Waltke, eds., 2 vols. (Chicago: Moody, 1980)
WA	*D. Martin Luther's Werke: Kritische Gesamptausgabe* (Weimar, 1883-)
WBC	*Word Biblical Commentary*, David A. Hubbard and Glenn W. Barker, eds.

I

THE PLAN
OF SALVATION

"WHAT MUST I DO TO BE SAVED?"

A C T S   1 6 : 3 0

———□———

INTRODUCTION TO
THE DOCTRINE OF SALVATION

I. THE BIBLE
A BOOK ABOUT SALVATION

The issue of one's future security, if not eternal destiny, is uppermost in the hearts and minds of most right-thinking people. The heart cry of unsaved people who are sensitive to their deepest spiritual needs can only be that posed to Paul and Silas by the Philippian jailor: "Sirs, what must I do to be saved?" (Acts 16:30). It is obvious even to the casual reader that the central message of the Bible concerns the spiritual recovery or salvation of lost men and women. From the *Protoevangelium* of Gen 3:15 to Rev 22:21, Scripture relates the grand story of how God has acted in grace to save his wayward image-bearers.

The OT deals with salvation in a promissory and provisional way. The Hebrew words for salvation shed valuable light on the meaning of this important theological concept. The root *ys'* means to "be broad" or "spacious," suggesting freedom from powers that restrict holistic personal development. The Hebrew verb *yasa'* and its derivatives appear 353 times in the OT. In the Niphal it bears the meaning "be saved" or "be delivered," whereas in the Hiphil it means to "deliver," "give victory," or "save." The nouns *yesu'ah* (sixty-four times), *yesa'* (thirty-one times), and *tesu'ah* (nineteen times) signify "help," "deliverance," "salvation." The preceding verb and nouns are most frequently used in the general sense of deliverance from various forms of distress, danger, or bondage. Thus the word group describes deliverance from Egypt via the Exodus (Exod 14:13, 30; 15:2; Deut 33:29), victory over Israel's enemies (Num 10:9; Judg 6:14-16; Neh 9:27; Ps 44:7), release from exile (Ps 106:47; Isa 46:13; Ezek 34:22), and preservation in times of national peril (Jer 14:8). But given the close connection in the OT between the material and the spiritual, the word group occasionally denotes deliverance from sin and its consequences (cf. Jer 17:14; Ezek 37:23), especially in the Psalms (51:12, 14) and Isaiah (30:15; 52:7; 59:1; 61:10). The literature makes clear that the Lord God, not any human warrior or king, is the only Savior. "I, even I, am the Lord, and apart from me there is no savior" (Isa 43:11; cf. 43:3; 45:15, 21; Hos 13:4). In Isaiah's prophecy "God" and "savior" are synonymous (Isa 45:21; cf. 25:9). All strictly human attempts to confer salvation are futile (Ps 60:11; 146:3). Marshall correctly concludes that in the OT the word salvation is "used in a very broad sense of the sum total of the effects of God's goodness on his people (Ps 53:6)."[1]

In the NT the verb *sozo* (more than 100 times) means to "rescue," "deliver," "save;" the noun *soteria* (forty-nine times) denotes "salvation"; and the personal noun *soter* (twenty-four times) signifies "redeemer," "deliverer," "savior." The word group generally connotes rescue or deliverance from danger, disease, enemies, or bondage (Matt 8:25; 14:30; Mark 5:34; Luke 1:71; Heb 11:7; Jas 5:15). But in the NT the personal, spiritual, and ethical dimension of salvation, implicit in the OT, comes to full light. Thus the Greek word group commonly bears the theological meaning of deliverance from sin, death, and the Devil and the gift of eternal life (Luke 1:69, 77; 18:26; Acts 4:12; Rom 10:9-10; 1 Thess 5:9; Heb 9:28). In the NT God is the Savior (Luke 1:47; 1 Tim 1:1; 2:3; Tit 1:3; 2:10; 3:4), in that the divine Father planned the gift of salvation and sent his only Son into the world on a saving mission. But specifically Jesus is the Savior (Luke 2:11; Acts 13:23; Eph 5:23; Tit 1:4; 2 Pet 1:1, 11; 3:2, 18), because the purpose of his life and death was to recover sinners from their lost condition (Matt 1:21; John 3:17; 12:47). The salvation Jesus brought is primarily personal and spiritual. It is instructive that the Greek name for Jesus, *Iesous*, is a transliteration of the Greek form of the Hebrew name Joshua, which means, "Yahweh is salvation." Christians (Acts 26:28; 1 Pet 4:16), at a minimum, are those who believe in and commit themselves to Jesus as Savior.

The centrality of salvation in the NT is further evidenced by the fact that the burden of the disciples' message, both orally and in writing, was salvation from sin. Thus *Peter*, used of God to launch the Christian movement, boldly proclaimed salvation through the name of Jesus (Acts 4:12;

5:31; 1 Pet 1:3-5). God in eternity past chose his people for salvation (1 Pet 1:1; 2:9), and in time he gave them new life (1 Pet 1:3, 23; 2 Pet 1:4) through their response of faith (1 Pet 1:9, 21). Peter enjoined believers to purify themselves (1 Pet 1:15-16; 2:1, 11; 2 Pet 3:11) through God's enablement (2 Pet 1:3) and so to persevere in God's grace (1 Pet 5:12). *John* taught that the Father sent his only Son to bring the world salvation (John 3:17; 1 John 2:2). Thus Jesus is "the Savior of the world" (John 4:42; 1 John 4:14). According to John, the Father gave to the Son the "sheep" he purposed to save (John 6:37, 39). For their part the "sheep" believe on the Son and obey him (John 10:27, 42). They receive forgiveness and cleansing of sins (1 John 1:7, 9; 2:12) and the gift of eternal life (John 3:16-17, 36; 1 John 2:25; 5:11, 13). The Father and the Son vouchsafe to preserve the "sheep" safe to the end (John 6:39; 10:29). *Paul* declared that in grace (Rom 5:15; 1 Cor 1:4; 15:10; 2 Cor 9:14) God sent his Son into the world to bestow on sinful Jews and Gentiles (Acts 13:26, 46; 28:28) the gift of salvation, viewed as forgiveness of sins (Eph 4:32; Col 2:13), right standing with God (Rom 1:17; 3:21-22; 5:17; Phil 3:9), reconciliation with the Father (Rom 5:10; 2 Cor 5:18-19), and new birth (2 Cor 5:17; Tit 3:5). *Luke* viewed the universal salvation (Luke 1:69, 71, 77; 3:6; 19:9) as redemption from oppression and sin (1:68, 74), particularly the recovery of that which was lost (15:3-32; 19:10). Salvation is predicated upon a spirit of true repentance (13:3, 5). *The writer to the Hebrews* used the word "salvation" seven times, more than in any other NT document. The letter envisages Jesus' saving work as the perfect fulfillment of the OT sacrificial system (Heb 2:3; 5:8-9; 9:28). Via the single self-offering of his body, Christ destroyed Satan (2:14), put away sin (9:26, 28; 10:18), freed those who were in spiritual bondage (2:15), and so brought "many sons to glory" (2:10). The saints are urged to persevere in faith that they may receive all that God has promised (6:12; 10:36). *Jude* upheld the true salvation that came through Jesus Christ against the distorted views of proto-Gnostic false teachers (Jude 4) who will perish in their unbelief (v. 7). To gain salvation Jude stressed the need for correct beliefs (v. 3), prayer (v. 20), and perseverance (v. 21a). Yet he assured believers that God is fully able to preserve them safely to the end (vv. 24-25).

In sum, the word salvation in its theological sense denotes, negatively, deliverance from sin, death, and divine wrath and, positively, the bestowal of far-ranging spiritual blessings both temporal and eternal. God freely conveys these benefits on the basis of the life, death, and resurrection of Jesus Christ the Mediator. Soteriology (from the Greek words *soter* and *logos*) is the theological term denoting the doctrine of salvation, the aspects of which will be discussed in logical order in the subsequent chapters of this volume.

II. HUMANKIND'S NEED
FOR SALVATION

Because of the problem of human sin, the salvation described above is absolutely necessary if one would experience new life in fellowship with God. Scripture is clear in asserting that every last person in the world succumbs to sin (Ps 53:1, 3; Jer 17:9; Rom 3:10, 23; 5:12) and consequently experiences moral corruption, estrangement from God, forfeiture of eternal life, and everlasting punishment.

Consider, first, what Scripture teaches concerning the *present condition* of the lost. The Lord Jesus spoke candidly about the present spiritual condition of unconverted men and women. In conversation with Nicodemus, Jesus implied that those who have not been born again are perishing (*apollymi*, John 3:16). Furthermore, in his encounter with Zacchaeus Jesus said, "the Son of Man came to seek and save what was lost" (*to apololos*, Luke 19:10). The figurative notions of perishing and lostness connote the forfeiture of everything good and utter spiritual ruin. The parable of the lost son (Luke 15:11-32) graphically highlights the spiritual bankruptcy and moral degradation of unconverted rebels against the loving Father. In addition, Jesus described the present condition of the unconverted in the language of judgment or condemnation. The Lord said, "whoever does not believe stands condemned already [*ede kekritai*] because he has not believed in the name of God's one and only Son" (John 3:18). The true believer in Jesus experiences no judgment or condemnation; but the unbeliever has been judged already (perfect tense), and thus stands under the condemnation of the holy God.

The apostle Paul wrote extensively about the present condition of the lost. Paul explained (1) that the unsaved are *spiritually depraved*. To the Ephesian Christians he wrote that formerly "you were dead in your transgressions and sins, in which you used to live when you followed the ways of this world and of the ruler of the kingdom of the air, the spirit who is now at work in those who are disobedient" (Eph 2:1-2). The unsaved, Paul continued, live "in the futility of their thinking. They are darkened in their understanding and separated from the life of God because of the ignorance that is in them due to the hardening of their hearts. Having lost all sensitivity, they have given themselves over to sensuality so as to indulge in every kind of impurity, with a continual lust for more" (4:17-19). (2)

They are *alienated from the life of God*. Paul added, "remember that at that time you were separate from Christ, excluded from citizenship in Israel and foreigners to the covenants of the promise, without hope and without God [*atheoi*] in the world" (2:12; cf. Col 1:21). Cut off from the fellowship and privileges of God's people, the Ephesians prior to their conversion had no life in God, no hope in the present, and no hope beyond the grave. (3) The unconverted are *guilty and condemned*. Unable to keep the law in its entirety, the unsaved dwell under the curse of the law (Gal 3:10). So Paul wrote that "The judgment followed one sin and brought condemnation" (*katakrima*, Rom 5:16), and "the result of one trespass was condemnation [*katakrima*] for all men" (v. 18). And so "we were by nature objects of wrath" (Eph 2:3b). And (4) the unsaved are hopelessly *enslaved by sin, death, and the Devil*. Paul described the unconverted as "controlled by the sinful nature" (Rom 7:5), taken captive and dominated by Satan (2 Tim 2:26; 1 John 5:19), and so as a practical manner of living, "slaves to sin" (Rom 6:16-17, 20). The writer of Hebrews recognized that the unregenerate live in bondage to the fear of death (Heb 2:15).

From careful observation of human behavior the secular Roman orator and politician Cicero boldly asserted that "Man is a disaster!" The French apologist Pascal recognized the pathetic paradox that is man, at one and the same time image of God yet grossly corrupted by sin. "What sort of freak then is man! How novel, how monstrous, how chaotic, how paradoxical, how prodigious! Judge of all things, feeble earthworm, repository of truth, sink of doubt and error, glory and refuse of the universe!"[2] In the same vein the Puritan Joseph Alleine wrote, "O miserable man, what a deformed monster has sin made you! God made you 'little lower than the angels;' sin has made you little better than the devils."[3]

We can say that the merely once-born are "sub-human,"in the sense that they have allowed sin to deform and deface their authentic personhood as image of God. While imprisoned by the Germans, Dietrich Bonhoeffer acutely recognized the descent into barbarism brought about by sin. The Lutheran theologian and martyr wrote, "Only the man who is taken up in Christ is the real man."[4] We must acknowledge the truth that the unsaved are radically fallen and stand under the wrath and condemnation of God Almighty. This situation is true of primitive pagans who practice the devilish rites of heathen religion. (As an aside, the following chapter will deal with the issue of God's kindness and mercy directed to pagan people.) But just condemnation is also true of so-called enlightened and sophisticated western people in their unconverted state.

Consider also Scripture's depiction of the *future condition* of the lost. Certain OT poetic and wisdom texts speak about the wicked perishing or being destroyed (Ps 1:6; 37:20; 49:10; 73:27; Prov 11:10; 28:28). The Kal form of the verb *'abad* in the preceding verses sometimes denotes physical death, but on other occasions it signifies utter spiritual loss or ruin—albeit never extinction of being. The prophet Daniel under inspiration of the Spirit wrote that "Multitudes who sleep in the dust of the earth will awake: some to everlasting life, others to shame and everlasting contempt" (Dan 12:2).

Moreover, the altogether lovely and compassionate Lord Jesus said to the Pharisees who rejected him, "I told you that you would die in your sins; if you do not believe that I am the one I claim to be, you will indeed die in your sins" (John 8:24; cf. 5:28-29). It is significant that Jesus spoke more about the sorrows of hell than of the joys of heaven. The Lord taught that the unrepentant or unsaved would be consigned to *gehenna*, the place of eschatological punishment (Matt 10:28; 23:33; Luke 12:5). He affirmed that hell is a place of conscious torment (Matt 5:22; 18:9; Mark 9:43) and of everlasting duration (Matt 25:41, 46; Mark 9:48). Jesus' saying in Matt 25:46 (cf. 18:8) clearly confirms that "The damned shall live as long in hell as God Himself shall live in heaven."[5] The compassionate Lord candidly described hell as a place of "darkness" (Matt 8:12; 22:13), a fiery furnace (Matt 13:42, 50; cf. 5:22; 13:30; 18:8-9; 25:41; Mark 9:43, 48), and a place where the worm never dies (Mark 9:48).

Paul, in strong and harsh language, wrote that "the Lord Jesus [will be] revealed from heaven in blazing fire with his powerful angels. He will punish those who do not know God and do not obey the gospel of our Lord Jesus. They will be punished with everlasting destruction and shut out from the presence of the Lord and from the majesty of his power on the day he comes to be glorified in his holy people" (2 Thess 1:7b-10a). The apostle firmly believed that those who refuse God's offer of grace will be consigned to perdition, forever beyond the reach of God's love and care.

The apostle John, in a foreboding vision of the future, saw the dead in resurrected bodies standing before the Great White Throne. The books containing the record of human deeds were opened, and each person was judged according to what was written therein. John's concluding words are hauntingly sober: "If anyone's name was not found written in the book of life, he was thrown into the lake of fire" (Rev 20:15). John explained that "The lake of fire is the second death" (v. 14)—i.e., the state of agonizing exclusion from the presence of God (Matt 22:13). Jesus told us that the second death is an event more fearful than the death of the body (Matt 10:28). John then added that "the cowardly, the unbelieving, the vile, the murderers, the sexually immoral, those who practice magic arts, the idolaters and all liars—their place will be in the fiery lake of burning sulfur.

This is the second death" (Rev 21:8). This punishment in hell, or the lake of fire, according to John, will be everlasting (Rev 14:11).

Several Greek words metaphorically connote ultimate spiritual ruin, the loss of everything good, and perdition in hell. One word group consists of the verb *apollymi* (active, to "destroy," "ruin"; passive, "irretrievably perish," "be lost in hell") and the noun *apoleia* ("loss," "ruin"). Jesus said, "wide is the gate and broad is the road that leads to destruction" (Matt 7:13). Both *apollymi* (John 3:16; 10:28; 17:12a; Rom 2:12; 1 Cor 15:17-18; 2 Thess 2:10) and *apoleia* (John 17:12b; Rom 9:22; Phil 1:28; 3:19; 2 Thess 2:3; 1 Tim 6:9; Heb 10:39; 2 Pet 2:1; 3:7) figuratively describe absolute spiritual ruin—namely, eternal perdition in hell, which is the polar opposite of salvation and eternal life. The NT writers also employed the verbs *ptheiro* (to "defile," "corrupt," "spoil," "ruin") in 1 Cor 3:17 and Jude 10, and *diaptheiro* (to "corrupt," "destroy") in Rev 11:18 figuratively of ultimate spiritual ruin in hell. They also described the future ruin of the unsaved by the nouns *pthora* ("decay," "corruption," "ruin") in Gal 6:8, Col 2:22, and 2 Pet 2:12 and *olethros* ("ruin," "destruction") in 1 Thess 5:3; 2 Thess 1:9; and 1 Tim 6:9.

The Puritan Thomas Watson struggled to describe in human words the future state of the lost in hell.

> Thus it is in Hell; they would die, but they cannot. The wicked shall be always dying but never dead; the smoke of the furnace ascends for ever and ever. Oh! who can endure thus to be ever upon the rack? This word "ever" breaks the heart. Wicked men now think the Sabbaths long, and think a prayer long; but oh! how long will it be to lie in hell for ever and ever?[6]

Faithful to revealed truth, the Scottish professor James Denney wrote, "If there is any truth in Scripture at all, this is true—that those who stubbornly refuse to submit to the Gospel, and to love and obey Jesus Christ incur at the Last Advent an infinite and irreparable loss. They pass into a night on which no morning dawns."[7] Such is the horrendous future of sinners who do not experience in life God's gracious salvation.

III. VARIOUS INTERPRETATIONS OF SALVATION

The nature of salvation has been variously interpreted by the different traditions within Christendom. Consider first the traditional *Roman Catholic* understanding of salvation. Rome argues that the visible church, which was founded on Peter (Matt 16:18-19) and transmitted to his successors, the bishops, mediates salvation to its adherents. Catholicism insists that the supernatural benefits of Christ's sacrifice are conveyed physically through the church's sacraments. Assuming the recipient imposes no obstacle to their working, the sacraments mediate saving grace simply because performed in an approved way (*ex opere operato*). The sacrament of baptism is said to remit original sin, impart sanctifying grace, and unite the soul to Christ. The baptized person is justified not legally by the imputation of Christ's righteousness, but as he or she cooperates with the sacramentally infused grace and performs meritorious works. Thus justification, in Catholic thought, merges into what Protestants understand as sanctification. Viewed as personal transformation, salvation is progressively realized throughout the lifetime of the baptized. Apart from a private revelation, assurance of final salvation is not possible, since the perpetration of a single mortal sin would separate the soul from Christ and incur the judgment of final damnation. Catholicism traditionally holds that at the end of one's life residual sin is burned away by the purifying fire of purgatory. On balance Roman Catholic theology is synergistic, stressing the synthesis of divine and human actions; salvation is by grace *and* by works. The Second Vatican Council redefined salvation existentially and broadened its scope to include all non-Christian religionists and even atheists. Contemporary Catholicism thus is quite universalistic in its outlook.

Theological liberalism assumes a number of forms, but a typical liberal understanding of salvation in the American context could be represented as follows. Stimulated by the rationalism of the Enlightenment, liberalism denies supernaturalism, miracles, biblical authority, and other classical doctrines of the faith. The tradition commonly rejects the fall of the race, human depravity, divine wrath, Christ's substitutionary atonement, and the need for definitive, individual conversion. Positing an optimistic, evolutionary view of persons and history, liberals view salvation as the process of perfecting an infantile, but inherently noble, race rather than redeeming a fallen, and inherently sinful, one. On the individual level, salvation amounts to the moral transformation of persons by right conduct and good works stimulated by the teachings and example of Jesus. In this respect theological liberalism simply stated is "a religion of ethical culture."[8] The so-called "social gospel" liberals of the first half of the twentieth century envisaged salvation as a collective reality. They defined salvation as the transformation of human society by education, social change, and political action motivated by the ideals and ethics of Jesus of Nazareth.

Although *Christian existentialism* also embraces a range of opinion, it is united by several common themes. Its focus is anthropocentric rather than theocentric, and it centers on the individual rather than on the group or community. It believes that human existence is estranged from reality by preoccupation with the world of objects, requiring no decision or risk (the 'I-it' relation), rather than the fulfilling world of personal relationships (the 'I-Thou' relation). According to Christian existentialism, persons are estranged from their authentic mode of being and hence suffer alienation, anxiety, and despair. Assent to rational truths, formal creeds, or theological systems does not save; rather it constitutes a cheap faith, even the faith of demons. The faith that saves, Christian existentialists assert, is the act of believing with deep inner passion and radical engagement; it is the faith that gives itself to a life of costly discipleship. Faith commits to the ultimate paradox that Jesus Christ bridged the chasm between the infinite God and sinners. It makes a courageous commitment, in defiance of all reason, to the One who demands that a choice be made between living according to God's demands or one's own pleasure. The result of this costly decision is Christ's presence in the heart and the personal realization of authentic existence—namely, the elimination of anxiety (*Angst*), the forgiveness of sins, the realization of one's full potential, and the transformation of life.

Liberation theology, viewing itself as a faith contextualized for developing societies, is a theology of praxis that relies heavily on the Marxist analysis of culture. The movement advocates a retreat from personal, inward, and spiritual realities to collective, outward, and structural concerns. It generally assumes that all persons are in Christ, but that they have become radically dehumanized by social, economic, and political oppression, which in turn have spawned poverty, illiteracy, violence, and untold human suffering. Liberationists view salvation collectively as the overthrow of unjust and corrupting social structures by revolution and violence, if necessary. They extol the Exodus from Egypt as the primary biblical paradigm of God's liberating action from structural oppression. Liberationists allege that the release of the oppressed Israelites by severe plagues made them whole again and freed them to serve God and others. The agenda of liberation theology thus is congruent with the cry of the black activist Angela Davis, who in the 1960s exclaimed, when handcuffed by the police: "Break these chains and I will be free!" Liberation theology usually makes little place for Christ's atoning work on the cross, faith as belief in the truth and trust in the Savior, and the lostness of those who do not trust Christ. Indeed, it commonly subscribes to the doctrine of universalism, which means that God is saving all people everywhere. As expressed by the Indian theologian M.M. Thomas, liberationists uphold a salvation "not in any pietistic or individualistic isolation, but related to and expressed within the material, social and cultural revolution of our time."[9]

Against Bultmann and the existentialists, *Barthian neoorthodoxy* regards salvation as an objective event and only secondarily as a subjective process. Barth held that Christ objectively wrought salvation for all people by his victory on the cross (the "classic" theory of the Atonement). He argued that Christ at his coming united to himself *humanum*—the entire human race. Thus in Christ's death on the cross the world's sin was judged and in his resurrection the race was vindicated. The justification and sanctification (or conversion) of every person through Christ's death and victorious resurrection represent the outworking of the *covenant* God instituted in eternity past to bring humankind into fellowship with himself. Salvation thus is something God decisively accomplished at Calvary; people have little to contribute to its achievement. Indeed, Barth envisaged faith, repentance, and obedience as *manifestations* of a finished salvation rather than as the means by which that salvation is personally realized.[10] Barth minimized the human responses of faith, repentance, and obedience to avoid introducing into the scheme of salvation by grace what he perceived to be a dangerous works doctrine. Herein Barth's strong reaction against theological liberalism is evident; not man but *God* is the chief actor in the drama of salvation. Given the triumph of grace in the Cross, Barth's formulation of salvation brings us to the vestibule of universalism. All persons are in Christ, Barth held, even though Christ is not in all persons. Formally the unrepentant are justified and sanctified, but existentially they need to awake from their spiritual slumber and experience the salvation Christ accomplished as their Representative.

Evangelical *Arminians* claim that in love God sent Christ into the world for the purpose of saving humankind from the ruin of sin (universal Atonement) and that God desires the salvation of all (1 Tim 2:4; 2 Pet 3:9). They insist that universal, prevenient grace flowing from Christ's cross ("preparing grace") transforms sinners in the first moment of moral light, thereby nullifying the debilitating effects of depravity, restoring moral free agency, and convicting of sin. Thus blessed by prevenient grace and when confronted with the general call to salvation, the unsaved cooperate with God, repent of sins, and trust Christ as Savior. Arminians emphasize that the grace and calling of God are *resistible*, hence sinners may choose to reject Christ and continue in their sins. Arminians understand the doctrine of *election* conditionally as God's decision to save those he foresaw would respond to grace and accept Christ. Corporately, the class of people who believe the Gospel and persevere to the end are designated "the elect."

Many Arminians view *regeneration* synergistically; the new birth occurs as a result of human willing and divine working. Furthermore, some affirm that God wills that *sanctification* be perfected in this life by a second work of grace that is said to eradicate the sinful nature and its desires, fill the heart with perfect love for God, and enable Christians to live without willful sin. This decisive post-conversion experience is designated "entire sanctification," "sinless perfection," and "full salvation." In addition, many Arminians deny the doctrine of the *perseverance of the saints*. They insist that by deliberate sin Christians can renounce their prior faith commitment and thereby fall from the state of grace, forfeit eternal salvation, and be doomed to perdition. The Arminian understanding of salvation thus is synergistic (a "working together"); divine grace and the liberated human will cooperate to bring about salvation. From inception to consummation the unsaved via free will make significant contributions to the outworking of their salvation.

Evangelicals in the *Reformed* tradition believe Scripture to teach that by willful spiritual defection the highest of God's creatures are spiritually dead in trespasses and sins (Eph 2:1). As noted above, Scripture portrays the unconverted as possessing minds darkened to spiritual truth, wills arrayed in enmity against God, affections disordered by sundry lusts, consciences defiled by faithless responses, and hands devoted to every evil work. Holistically depraved sinners have neither the inclination nor the ability to seek God and spiritual life. Hence the initiative in salvation must reside with the sovereign God. God's grace plans, precedes, undergirds, and executes the process of salvation from beginning to end. Reformed Evangelicals thus extol the confession of Jonah after experiencing God's wisdom and goodness: "Salvation comes from the Lord" (Jon 2:9).

The reformational tradition asserts that in eternity past God sovereignly purposed to bestow saving grace upon whom he would, independent of foreseen works. The rest of humanity he left in their self-chosen sin to suffer the just penalty thereof. Those whom God in eternity past graciously chose by the Spirit in time he effectually draws to Christ. One strand of Reformed thinking holds that, subjectively, the Spirit enables the chosen and called to believe the truth in Christ, turn from all known sins, and trust Jesus as Savior and Lord of their lives. God creates in the converted a new spiritual nature—in the sense not of another ontological constitution but as a new set of godly inclinations, desires, and habits. Objectively, the Spirit incorporates regenerated believers into Christ in a vital, spiritual, and indissoluble union, attested by the common "in Christ" motif. The Father then forgives their sins, accepts them as righteous in his sight, and bestows the gift of eternal life. Furthermore, in the lifelong work of sanc-

tification the Spirit progressively mortifies believers' old nature and fortifies the new nature such that they become like Jesus in thought, word, and
deed. Thus God not only declares believing sinners righteous; he effectively *makes* them so by the Spirit. We are saved not merely to gain heaven
but also to live in holiness, truth, and love. Moreover, those whom God
has regenerated, united to Christ, and justified he preserves by the Spirit
to the end. Twice-born people at times disobey God and grieve his Spirit;
but the Lord's sure grip prevents them from falling away finally and completely. Lastly, God will bring salvation to completion at the return of
Christ when pilgrim saints behold the Savior's face and are fully transformed into his likeness. Biblical salvation thus has past, present, and
future dimensions. The born-again person can say with confidence, "I
have been saved, I am being saved, and at Christ's return I finally will be
saved."

IV. THE 'ORDER OF SALVATION'

Scripture reveals that God applies Christ's objective work on the cross progressively by the Spirit through a series of movements. This has led theologians to suggest that God purposefully established a definable order of
salvation. The Lutheran theologians Franz Buddeus and Jacob Carpov in
the first half of the eighteenth century were the first to coin the phrase
"*ordo salutis*" to denote such a sequence. Formulations of the *ordo*
attempt to express the way by which God through Christ imparts salvation to sinners from inception to consummation or from eternity past to
eternity future. Such an ordering scheme may be logical, chronological, or
both. It may involve what God purposes and what he actually accomplishes. It may equally include what God does and what humans do. It
may contain aspects that are declarative and instantaneous as well as those
that are experiential and progressive. According to John Murray, "God is
not the author of confusion and therefore he is the author of order. There
are good and conclusive reasons for thinking that the various actions of
the application of redemption . . . take place in a certain order, and that
that order has been established by divine appointment, wisdom, and
grace."[11] We proceed to summarize the ways in which leading Christian
traditions have represented the order of salvation. Thereafter we will
examine relevant NT passages to make a decision concerning the legitimacy of such an ordering schema and to propose our own arrangement
of the elements of salvation.

The order of salvation in *Roman Catholic theology* is usually expressed in terms of the grace mediated by the church's sacraments. Thus (1) the sacrament of *baptism* (Tit 3:5) imparts supernatural life by regenerating the soul and uniting it with Christ. Water baptism, in addition, is said to remove the guilt and penalty of original sin. Through the sacrament of baptism "Man is made white as a sheet, brighter than snow."[12]

(2) The sacrament of *confirmation* (Acts 8:15-17) strengthens the baptized through a Pentecostal outpouring of the Holy Spirit. By this endowment the confirmed are enabled to witness to Christ and to stand firm in the midst of life's struggles.

(3) The sacrament of the *Eucharist* (Matt 26:26-28) imparts spiritual nourishment as the worshiper feeds on the body and blood of Christ in the transubstantiated wafer. "This sacrament is nourishment. It is for the divine life of the soul what food and drink are for the life of the body. This life, the state of grace, is maintained by it, preserved from ruin, strengthened and augmented."[13]

(4) The sacrament of *penance*, or the "second pardon," remits the guilt and punishment of post-baptismal, mortal sins (apostasy, murder, adultery). The sacrament requires of the penitent contrition for sins, confession, and works of satisfaction (almsgiving, fasting, etc.).

Finally (5) the sacrament of *extreme unction* or *last anointing* (Jas 5:14-16) equips the soul for the final conflict with death and prepares the recipient for the beatific vision of God. This sacrament "gives the grace of a good death, consolation in that depression which comes to so many because of the memory of their sins, and pardon for all sins not yet forgiven in confession."[14]

The order of salvation in *Lutheran theology* seeks to define and distinguish the Spirit's multiple acts of grace without creating an artificial separation one from the other. Elements of the order more or less overlap one another. The following order generally prevails.

(1) *Calling* or *vocation*. God offers forgiveness of sins and right standing with himself through the offer of the Gospel that brings with it sufficient grace for the unconverted to respond to the message.

(2) *Illumination*. The Gospel call universally imparts a certain illumination and quickening that enables the hearer to comprehend the benefits of accepting the Gospel and the consequences of rejecting it.

(3) *Conversion* or *repentance*. This involves the work of the Spirit that leads sinners to remorse for their sins and to knowledge that they may be saved on the basis of Christ's merits.

(4) *Regeneration*. Repentance may result in the kindling of faith in the Gospel and then the transformation known as the new birth.

(5) *Justification*. In response to a person's faith God forgives sins, reck-

ons the perfect righteousness of Christ, and bestows right standing with himself.

(6) *Mystical union.* By this step the believing soul is brought into a supernatural union of love with the triune God.

(7) *Renovation or sanctification.* Assisted by the Spirit, the justified advance in holiness and bring forth the supernatural fruits of the new life.

(8) *Conservation.* Provided that the justified continue to heed biblical warnings about defection and persist in faith, God will preserve them safely to the end. The unbelieving, however, may fall away from grace and forfeit salvation. Christians must not presume on the Spirit's grace.

Arminian theology typically represents the order of salvation as follows.

(1) *Universal, external calling.* God extends the call to salvation to all by a general work of the Spirit on the soul and by explicit Gospel proclamation. Prevenient or "exciting" grace, which allegedly proceeds universally from the Cross, alleviates the effects of depravity, thereby freeing all persons for moral and spiritual action.

(2) *Repentance and faith.* Since every person is transformed by prevenient grace, the human will is capable of freely turning from sin unto Christ. Given the fact that God commands sinners to work out their own salvation (Phil 2:12), conversion is a synergistic activity.

(3) *Justification.* Since God does not declare anyone righteous in principle who is not so in practice, the forensic view of justification (the imputation of Christ's righteousness to believing sinners) often is rejected. Arminians usually define justification as forgiveness of sins that in turn fosters the moral government of the universe.

(4) *Sanctification.* Believers should seek that instantaneous, second-blessing experience by which the Spirit eradicates sin and fills the heart with perfect love for God and others. This second work of grace is denoted "entire sanctification," "Christian perfection," and the "fullness of the blessing." The term regeneration often is used inclusively to embrace the broad movement of salvation from conversion to sanctification.

(5) *Perseverance.* Given their strong emphasis on free agency, many Arminians hold that believers by willful sin may fall completely from the state of grace. The possibility of final apostasy motivates Christians to holiness and constancy of life.

Covenant Reformed theology insists that every aspect of salvation is grounded in the covenant of grace, occurs in union with Christ, and is brought forth by the Holy Spirit.

(1) *Calling.* The general call to trust Christ is issued through the widespread offer of the Gospel. By means of this general call God sovereignly

issues a special calling to the elect. The Spirit facilitates sinners' response to the Gospel by enlightening their minds, liberating their wills, and inclining their affections Godward.

(2) *Regeneration.* Without any human assistance the third person of the Trinity creates new spiritual life, including God-honoring dispositions, affections, and habits.

(3) *Faith.* Having been granted new spiritual life, the elect believe the truths of the Gospel and trust Jesus Christ as Savior. Faith is viewed as a gift and enablement of God, indeed as a consequence of new spiritual birth.

(4) *Repentance.* Here believers grieve for sins committed and deliberately turn from all known disobedience. This response likewise is a divine enablement.

(5) *Justification.* On the basis of Christ's completed work, the Father reckons to believers the righteousness of his Son, remits sins, and admits the same to the divine favor. Justification is the legal declaration of believing sinners' right standing with God.

(6) *Sanctification.* The Holy Spirit works in justified believers the will and the power progressively to renounce sin and to advance in spiritual maturity and Christlikeness. By the process of sanctification God makes believers experientially holy.

(7) *Preservation and perseverance.* The God who has chosen, regenerated, justified, and sealed believers with his Spirit preserves them by his faithfulness and power to the very end. True believers persevere by virtue of the divine preservation.

(8) *Glorification.* God will complete the redemption of the saints when the latter behold Christ at his second advent and are transformed into his likeness.

Evangelicals in the broadly Reformed tradition insist that the whole of salvation, from eternity past to eternity future, proceeds from the grace of God, centers on Christ, and is wrought by the power of the Holy Spirit.

(1) *Election.* Without regard for foreseen human faith or good works, God in eternity past chose from among the lot of fallen humanity some to inherit eternal life.

(2) *Effectual calling.* The Spirit of God illumines the minds and softens the wills of the elect, thus enabling them personally to respond to the external call of the Gospel.

(3) *Belief in the Gospel.* Quickened by the Spirit, the minds of the elect are persuaded of the truths of the Gospel of God's grace.

(4) *Repentance.* Likewise enabled by the Spirit the effectually called despise and turn away from all known sins.

(5) *Trust in Christ.* The effectually called personally commit themselves to Jesus Christ as Savior and Lord of their life.

(6) *Regeneration.* God creates in justified believers new life, defined as the radical reorientation of the dispositions and affections toward God.

(7) *Union with Christ.* The Spirit unites newly born saints with Jesus Christ in a vital, spiritual, and indissoluble union. The NT describes this experiential reality by the familiar "in Christ" motif.

(8) *Justification.* God in turn reckons believing sinners righteous in his sight and bestows upon them the gift of eternal life.

(9) *Sanctification.* By a lifelong process that involves both ups and downs the Spirit of grace gradually transforms true believers into the image of Jesus Christ.

(10) *Preservation and perseverance.* By the application of divine power, God faithfully preserves regenerate saints in faith and hope unto the attainment of eternal life.

(11) *Glorification.* God perfects the final and complete redemption of the believer—body, soul, and spirit—at the *Parousia* of the Lord Jesus Christ.

We now turn to the NT documents to determine if an order or arrangement of the doctrines of salvation can be substantiated. We examine first those texts that deal most comprehensively with the plan of salvation. Consider the following major Scripture passages.

Paul presents a broad outline of the plan of salvation in Rom 8:28-30, popularly known as the "golden circle of salvation." God's *foreknowledge* and *predestination* undergird other aspects of salvation, given here as *calling*, *justification*, and *glorification*. Verses 31-39 affirm the certainty of God's *preservation* of elect believers.

In 1 Cor 1:26-30 Paul gives the order of salvation as God's choosing or *election, calling, union with Christ* ("in Christ Jesus"), *justification*, and *sanctification*.

Paul's order in Eph 1:11-14 is *election* through Christ the Redeemer, *faith* defined as "hope in Christ," *union with Christ, sealing* with the Spirit, and *glorification*, viewed as the final "redemption."

In 2 Thess 2:13-15 the following order is evident: *election* as the act of God's choosing, *belief* in "the truth," *calling* through the Gospel, and *glorification*. Verse 15 upholds the need for *perseverance* in the faith.

In 2 Tim 1:8-10 Paul writes of grace that undergirds *election* viewed as God's saving "purpose," *calling, sanctification* as a "holy life," and future *glorification*, here designated as "life and immortality."

In language drawn from the OT, 1 Pet 1:1-2 delineates the order of salvation as *foreknowledge, election, effectual calling* expressed as "the sanctifying work of the Spirit," *faith* identified as "obedience to Jesus

Christ," and *justification* and *sanctification*, both perhaps implied by the phrase "sprinkling by his blood."

Finally, 2 Pet 1:9-11 discusses *election, calling, justification, perseverance*, and *glorification*.

Many biblical texts, though less comprehensive than the preceding, are nevertheless helpful in the search for a possible ordering of soteriological doctrines. Consider the following scriptural passages.

Tit 2:11-14 refers to saving *grace, sanctification* of life, and *glorification*.

Acts 13:48 gives the order *election* ("appointed for eternal life") and *faith*.

Eph 1:4 refers to *election* through Christ and *sanctification* ("be holy and blameless").

Eph 1:5 cites sovereign *election* through Christ and *adoption* as sons and daughters of God.

Acts 16:14 specifies *effectual calling* (opening the heart) and *faith* (response to the Gospel message).

Acts 26:18 sets forth the order of *effectual calling* ("open their eyes"), *conversion* (including "*faith*"), and *positional sanctification* or *justification*.

John 6:44, 65 gives the order *effectual calling* and coming to Christ in *faith*.

2 Pet 1:2-4 cites the doctrines of *grace, effectual calling, faith, union with Christ* ("participate in the divine nature"), and *sanctification* ("escape the corruption in the world"), although the precise order is less intentional in this text.

1 Thess 5:23-24 presents the sequence as *effectual calling, sanctification*, and *preservation* ("kept blameless").

Many NT texts—e.g., John 5:24; Rom 1:17; 3:22, 26, 28, 30; 4:3, 5, 11, 13; Gal 2:16; 3:6, 8, 11, 24; Phil 3:9—refer to the *faith* that results in *justification*.

John 1:12-13 highlights *faith, regeneration* ("born of God"), and *adoption* ("become children of God"). In this text regeneration precedes adoption into the family of God.

2 Pet 1:5-6, 9 affirms *faith, justification* ("cleansed from past sins"), and *perseverance*.

Rom 5:1-2 (cf. Gal 5:5) presents the sequence as *faith, justification, reconciliation* ("peace with God"), and *glorification* ("the hope of the glory of God").

Gal 3:26-27 depicts *faith, union with Christ* ("baptized into Christ"), and *adoption*.

First John 5:1-5 sets forth the order of *faith, regeneration* ("born of God"), and *sanctification* ("overcomes the world").

First John 2:5-6 (cf. Gal 2:20) describes *faith* ("obeys his word"), *union with Christ* ("we are in him"), and *sanctification* ("walk as Jesus did").

First Pet 1:22-23 affirms *faith* ("obeying the truth"), *sanctification*, and *regeneration*. Faith results in both regeneration and sanctification, although the order of the last two is not explicitly stated here.

First Pet 1:5, 9 identifies *faith*, *preservation*, and *glorification* ("the salvation . . . to be revealed in the last time").

First John 3:5-6 refers to *justification* ("take away our sins") followed by *sanctification* (does not "keep on sinning").

Rom 8:1-2 speaks of *union with Christ* ("in Christ Jesus"), *justification* ("no condemnation"), and *sanctification* ("set me free from the law of sin and death").

First John 3:9-10 describes *regeneration* ("born of God"), *adoption*, and *sanctification* ("cannot go on sinning").

Heb 12:1-11 indicates that *adoption* precedes *sanctification* and *perseverance*.

Rom 8:13-17 gives the order as *adoption* ("sons of God"), *sanctification* ("put to death the deeds of the body"), and *glorification* ("share in his glory").

John 3:3, 5 identifies the particular order of *regeneration* and the attainment of *eternal life* ("enter the kingdom of God").

First Pet 1:3-4 cites *regeneration* ("new birth") and *glorification* ("an inheritance that can never perish, spoil or fade").

Second Cor 5:17-18 describes *union with Christ* through *faith*, *regeneration* ("a new creation"), and *reconciliation*, although the ordering relation is not clearly given.

First Cor 6:17-20 describes *union with Christ* and *sanctification* of life.

Finally, Eph 5:23, 26-27 delineates the order of *union with Christ* (the "body" of Christ image), *sanctification*, and possibly *glorification*.

What shall we conclude about attempts to construct an order of salvation for purposes of systematization and study? In recent years the notion of an ordering of the doctrines of salvation has come under criticism by theologians such as Karl Barth, G.C. Berkouwer, H.N. Ridderbos, and O. Weber. Admittedly, it is difficult to schematize temporally the boundless riches of God's saving grace exercised from eternity past to eternity future. Moreover, it is possible that the *ordo* as a rigid structure may direct our focus away from Christ to an unhealthy psychologizing of salvation (subjectivism). Nevertheless, it remains true that our God is a God of order rather than disorder or confusion. Indeed, the many Scripture texts cited above appear to provide a warrant for conceptualizing the process of salvation in an orderly manner. Within the unity of the plan of salvation it is legitimate to consider various aspects of God's gracious salvation in relation to one another. One's conversion may be sudden and dramatic or so gradual that the person may not know when he or she came to Christ. But a genuine salvation experience will share common doctrinal aspects as certified by the Scriptures.

Granting the legitimacy of the order of salvation, certain qualifications regarding such a formulation must be made. (1) The order of salvation includes things that God does (election, calling, justification, regeneration, etc.) as well as things that humans do (belief, repentance, trust, perseverance). (2) The *ordo* must be viewed as a logical as well as a chronological relation. Conversion, regeneration, union with Christ, and justification occur simultaneously in the moment of decision for Christ, and not successively. (3) Certain aspects of the scheme of salvation are not discrete events but realities that pervade the entire Christian life: e.g., belief, repentance, trust, sanctification, divine preservation, and human perseverance. (4) As Berkouwer and Hoekema point out,[15] aspects of the salvation experience are interactive. Thus faith is active in justification, in sanctification, and in perseverance. Moreover, union with Christ (abiding in him) is essential for sanctification and perseverance. Hence the order of salvation must not be viewed simplistically as a linear sequence of chronological occurrences. And finally (5) every aspect of salvation profoundly focuses on Christ. Thus Christ apportions grace (Eph 4:7). Moreover, saints are elected in Christ (Eph 1:4); they are called to Christ (1 Cor 1:9); they believe the truth about Christ (Rom 10:9; 1 John 5:1, 5); they turn to Christ in repentance (1 Pet 2:25); they are justified by the blood of Christ (Heb 13:12); regeneration takes place in Christ (2 Cor 5:17; Tit 3:5-6); they are united with Christ (Gal 2:20); they are transformed into the image of Christ (2 Cor 3:18); they are kept and preserved by Christ (1 John 5:18); and they will receive the glory of Christ (2 Thess 2:14). Given these significant observations and qualifications, we suggest the following ordering of the various aspects of the salvation wrought by Christ on the cross (Atonement), which constitutes the structure of this volume.

The *Plan and Provision of Salvation* from beginning to end is rooted in God's grace and originates with God's sovereign elective decision for life made in eternity past.

The *Application of Salvation* in its subjective aspects commences with the Spirit's effectual calling and continues in the movements of conversion and regeneration. In its objective aspects the fruit of Christ's work applied to believers includes union with Christ, justification, and adoption into the family of God.

The *Progress of Salvation* is manifested through the Holy Spirit's sanctification or purification of believers' lives and the divine preservation that enables human perseverance to the end.

Finally, the *Perfecting of Salvation* will be realized in the glorification of true believers at Christ's second advent. In this consummation of the entire movement of salvation, Christians will be perfectly conformed to the image of Jesus Christ.

V. THE AUTHOR OF SALVATION

The rich biblical data indicate that salvation is a work of the triune God involving an authentic response on the part of the individual person. On God's side, Scripture depicts the *Father* as the ultimate source, planner, and initiator of salvation. Thus the apostle Paul wrote in Eph 1:3-6: "Praise be to the God and Father of our Lord Jesus Christ, who has blessed us in the heavenly realms with every spiritual blessing in Christ. For he chose us in him before the creation of the world to be holy and blameless in his sight. In love he predestined us to be adopted as his sons through Jesus Christ, in accordance with his pleasure and will—to the praise of his glorious grace, which he has freely given us in the One he loves." James confirmed this initiating role of the Father in salvation, as follows: "Every good and perfect gift is from above, coming down from the Father of the heavenly lights. . . . He chose to give us birth through the word of truth, that we might be a kind of firstfruits of all he created" (1:17-18). Other texts affirming the Father's role as planner and initiator of salvation include 2 Tim 1:9 and 1 John 4:14.

Second, *Christ the Son* provided complete redemption through his obedient life and atoning death. After citing the Father's role in salvation Paul explained the Son's unique contribution in Eph 1:7-12. There he wrote, "In him [Christ] we have redemption through his blood, the forgiveness of sins, in accordance with the riches of God's grace that he lavished on us with all wisdom and understanding" (vv. 7-8). We recall, in addition, the words of an angel of the Lord who said to Joseph, the husband of Mary, "you are to give him the name Jesus, because he will save his people from their sins" (Matt 1:21). The Father effects redemption through Christ, the "one mediator between God and men" (1 Tim 2:5). He is the mediator of the new covenant, whereby the called receive the promised eternal inheritance (Heb 9:15; cf. 8:6; 12:24).

Finally, the *Holy Spirit* applies, makes effective, and preserves the redemption Christ bought to those who believe. Eph 1:13-14 specifies an important work the third person of the Trinity performs in the economy of salvation: "Having believed, you were marked in him with a seal, the promised Holy Spirit, who is a deposit guaranteeing our inheritance until the redemption of those who are God's possession." Lloyd-Jones expressed the saving work of the three persons according to Eph 1:3-14 thusly: "The Father has His purpose, the Son says He is going to carry it out, and He came and did it, and the Holy Spirit said He was ready to apply it."[16] Summing up the diverse functions of the Spirit in salvation, we note that the latter effectually calls (Heb 3:7-8; Rev 22:17), justifies (1 Cor 6:11), regenerates (John 3:5-8; 6:63; Tit 3:5), unites with Christ (1 Cor 12:13), seals (Eph 1:13; 4:30), sanctifies (Rom 15:16; 2 Thess 2:13; Gal 5:16, 25), and provides assurance by his own invincible testimony (Rom 8:16). In addition to Eph 1:3-14, Paul summarized the saving functions of the three persons in Tit 3:4-6. There the apostle wrote, "when the kindness and love of God our Savior appeared, he saved us, not because of righteous things we had done, but because of his mercy. He saved us through the washing of rebirth and renewal by the Holy Spirit, whom he poured out on us generously through Jesus Christ our Savior."

On the human side no person can come savingly to God by the power of their own initiative or on the basis of their own merits, as the Titus text just cited indicates. But men and women, enabled by the Spirit's gracious working, perform their own necessary work. To receive salvation the chosen must believe the Gospel (John 20:30-31), repent of sins (Acts 2:38; Rev 3:3, 19), trust or commit themselves to Christ (Rom 10:9; 2 Tim 1:12), pursue holiness and sanctification of life (2 Tim 2:21; Heb 12:14), and persevere in the way of Christ (Matt 24:13; John 8:31; 1 Cor 16:13-14). Salvation thus is both a work of God and of the individual, where the latter's effort and cooperation is graciously enabled by God. Paul made this point perfectly clear in his exhortation to the Philippian Christians: "continue to work out your salvation with fear and trembling, for it is God who works in you to will and to act according to his good purpose" (Phil 2:12-13).

VI. The Relation of Soteriology to Other Doctrines

Given the organic and inherently coherent nature of biblical theology, we are not surprised to find significant interrelationship between the doctrine of salvation and other Christian doctrines. Consider first the doctrine of *theology proper.* A high estimate of God's sovereignty, love, and grace leads the faithful student of Scripture to ascribe the initiative in salvation to God himself. God in freedom works to bring about his own eternal purpose for the human race. On the other hand, a liberal or deistic understanding of God envisages the Creator as relatively uninvolved in the process of bringing salvation to sinners. According to the latter perspective, the unconverted forge their future by their own moral decisions and actions independently of God.

Reflect also on the doctrine of divine *providence*. The postulate that God is the efficient cause of all occurrences (hyper-Calvinism) leads to the conclusion that the Lord in eternity past sovereignly planned both the salvation of the elect and the damnation of the reprobate. On the other hand, the insistence that God merely extends to the unconverted the promise of rewards and the threat of punishment (Arminianism) places the salvation of the unconverted squarely with themselves. The view that God works by supernatural means to draw some sinners to Christ and for his own good reasons leaves others in their self-chosen state of sin leads to an altogether different outcome (moderately Reformed).

Consider also the doctrines of *anthropology* and *harmartiology*. Acceptance of the Bible's realistic view of the effects of depravity upon the mind, will, and affections (Augustinianism) leads to the conclusion that God himself provides the spiritual dynamic that effectively brings moral aliens to Christ. On the other hand, the view that human nature is not fallen in sin (Pelagianism) eliminates the need for spiritual redemption altogether. According to Pelagians old and new, whatever persons need to do for salvation, they are capable of accomplishing by their own strength. The mediating position that human nature was merely wounded by the Fall (Semi-Pelagianism) envisages salvation as the outcome of a synergistic process of cooperation between God and the unconverted.

Thoroughly pertinent is the doctrine of *Christology*, which deals with the person of Jesus Christ and the work he accomplished. The commonly held modern view that Jesus was a mere man indwelt by divine power and thus our moral example obviates the need for justification and reconciliation predicated on his atoning death at Calvary. Contrariwise, the conviction that Jesus Christ, the God-man, bore the punishment due our sins and so satisfied the demands of a righteous God leads to the classical understanding of the new birth, justification, and reconciliation. Moreover, whether or not Jesus bodily rose from the grave profoundly affects the future resurrection of those who trust him. Likewise his ascension to heaven, session at the Father's right hand, and continuing intercession on our behalf significantly impacts the quality and permanence of the spiritual life we profess to have received.

The doctrine of the *Holy Spirit* likewise impinges upon the quest for salvation. Understood merely as an impersonal power or influence, the Spirit could not convict hardened souls of sin, impart a new nature with heavenly qualities, sanctify the life in the path of holiness, or fortify believers to persevere in the faith. But the Spirit who truly is an intelligent, divine person—even the third person of the Trinity—possesses the infinite wisdom, power, and grace to save, sanctify, and sustain born-again believers to the very end.

The doctrine of *ecclesiology* impinges upon our understanding of Christian salvation. The liberal view that equates the church with the world undercuts the need for supernatural salvation. Evangelical theology, however, envisages the church as the chosen people called out of the godless world and transformed by divine grace. Moreover, our view of the efficacy of the church's sacraments will impact our understanding of how God applies salvation to sinners and causes it to be perfected. The Roman church, for example, claims that the sacraments accomplish their saving work simply because performed by legitimate authority (the *ex opere operato* concept).

Finally, soteriology is relevant to the doctrine of *eschatology*. Personal eschatology deals with the resurrection body, the disposition of persons at the final judgment, and their final state in heaven or hell. A humanistic worldview that denies life beyond the grave takes no account of the glorious future of God's people. Soteriology treats this latter issue under the head of the glorification of the saints. General eschatology considers the grand truths of Christ's return to earth, the inauguration of his kingdom, and the new heaven and new earth. These great realities represent the future blessings of soteriology considered from a corporate point of view. In sum, the close nexus between soteriology and other major doctrines confirms the fact that Christianity is more than a noble ethical system. The way of Christ, in its warp and woof, is the path of salvation itself.

"While We Were Still Sinners"

R O M A N S 5 : 8

□

THE DOCTRINE OF GRACE

I. Introductory
Concerns

Grace is the seed-bed of the entire drama of human salvation. Grace has to do with God in his sovereign goodness entering human history and showering sinful creatures with undeserved favor. Scripture and Christian theology suggest that grace is the source of all material and spiritual blessings. Without God's unmerited favor we would all be lost, both here and in the hereafter. Indeed, without grace life itself would not exist. The fact that the word "grace" occurs some 100 times in Paul's letters alone suggests that the whole of life and salvation is rooted in God's boundless goodness and favor.

A proper consideration of grace is impossible without regard to the contextual issue of sin and its effects upon the individual and society. The nature of the fallen person's capabilities serves as the canvas for the rich portrait of God's saving grace. Thus to appreciate the character of grace we need to consider the Bible's teaching on the nature and consequences of human rebellion.

Reflection on the topic of grace raises several important issues. Foundationally, why does man, as the unique image of God, require the gift of free grace? What have the Fall and sin done that mandate the need for gratuitous favor from God? Can a man or woman—as the highest and noblest of God's creatures—attain salvation without special enablement in part or in whole from the gracious God?

Moreover, how shall we define God's grace? Is grace a quality inherent in God or in humans? If the former, is grace a pseudonym for God himself or possibly Jesus Christ? Should grace be viewed more impersonally as a power or energy from God? Or is grace God's loving self-communication to humans? If the locus of grace is humanward, is grace an entity that is infused in people? In this regard we might ask whether grace is an endowment natural to persons or whether it is a supernatural gift. What, we ask, is the meaning of divine grace?

Furthermore, is grace single and undifferentiated? Or can we legitimately distinguish between common (non-salvific) grace and special (salvific) grace? If the two are distinct, does the latter differ from the former in degree or in kind? If God should give common grace to all, does this necessitate that he must also bestow special grace universally? If the answer to the last question is no, could God be accused of partiality or favoritism?

In the sphere of redemption, is grace the sole efficient cause for a person coming to Christ, or is it only a contributing cause? Does grace alone bring a man or a woman to the experience of salvation? Or does grace accomplish the initial work and the human person subsequently cooperate therewith? Or does the latter perform the initial work and grace thereafter perform an assisting function? The issue at hand is whether salvation involves a monergism or a synergism of grace.

Additionally, we inquire into the role of Jesus Christ in the impartation of grace. Is Christ the unique purveyor of grace, or are there other personalities or systems that convey saving grace? This leads to the question of the extent to which grace is found in non-Christian religions. Are the Buddhist, Hindu, Confucian, and Islamic faiths illumined and informed by grace? If so, to what extent? Do the non-Christian religions mediate to their sincere adherents and worshipers the grace that saves the soul?

II. HISTORICAL INTERPRETATIONS OF GRACE

Discussion of the doctrine of grace has a long history in the reflection of Christian thinkers. The following represent the principal ways in which the grace of God has been understood in the broad Christian tradition.

A. The Natural Capacity for Doing Good (Pelagians & Liberals)

This view is held chiefly by Pelagians, Rationalists, and Liberals. According to Pelagius (d. 419) and his disciples Coelestius (d. 431) and

Julian of Eclanum (d. 455), grace amounts to the natural endowments of conscience, reason, and free will (the ability to choose between good and evil) divinely implanted in humans at their creation. The counter-claim that persons need special assistance from God to be virtuous was said to contradict the created human condition. The Pelagians insisted that for persons to be human they must have the ability to perform what God commands. God at creation gave people the capacity (*posse*) to obey him, but the actual willing (*velle*) and the resultant being (*esse*) are the responsibility of each person. The Pelagians concluded that all humans are able to live sinlessly and obtain salvation by their own powers apart from any special grace from God.

The British monk Pelagius claimed that as the product of God's creation human nature is morally and spiritually sound. Adam's primal sin injured only himself, not his offspring. Since persons are born free of guilt and pollution, they can keep God's commands and live sinlessly by natural powers alone. Hence men and women have no need of special or supernatural grace to obtain eternal life.

Pelagius defined grace in a twofold way. (1) *Internally*, grace is God's act of endowing persons at creation with a rational mind and free will by which to keep his commands, resist the power of evil, and live sinlessly if they choose. Pelagius wrote, "the charity whereby we live righteously and devoutly is not [poured forth] from God into us, but is from ourselves."[1] By willing and performing the good, even the heathen can please God and attain salvation. Pelagius added, "This power of free will we declare to reside in all alike—in Christians, in Jews, and in Gentiles. In all men free will exists equally by nature, but in Christians alone it is assisted by grace."[2] (2) *Externally*, grace consists of the inducements to virtuous living God gives Christians via the law and Christ's example. The natural endowments enable all persons to reach their goal, but the external graces assist Christians to succeed more readily. "While we have within us a free will so strong and steadfast against sinning, which our Maker has implanted in human nature generally, still by his unspeakable goodness, we are further defended by his daily help."[3] Pelagius was accused of heresy and banished from Rome where he had promulgated these views. The church formally rejected his teachings and those of his followers at the Synod of Carthage (418) and later at the Council of Ephesus (431).

In the modern era liberal theologians likewise dismiss the notion of special grace. They view sin not as an offense against God but as an anomaly arising from the struggle between man's evolving, material body and his immaterial spirit. Fundamentally, liberals regard all persons as children of God by birth. Although flawed by the evolutionary process, men and women are capable of forging their own future. Liberals typically view salvation as the triumph of man's higher spirit over his lower, animal nature. Persons achieve this goal by dedicated moral effort stimulated by the example and teachings of Jesus. The paucity of references to grace in liberal theological writings confirms that they judge the operation of special grace unnecessary for the attainment of their moral and social goals.

George Burman Foster (d. 1918), a student of Ritschl and Harnack and a free-thinking University of Chicago theologian, was a liberal Baptist minister who later pastored a Unitarian congregation. Denying many fundamental tenets of the Christian faith, Foster championed the following theological vision: "not supernatural regeneration, but natural growth; not divine sanctification, but human education; not supernatural grace, but natural morality; not the divine expiation of the cross, but the human heroism . . . of the cross."[4]

Shailer Mathews (d. 1941), former dean of the University of Chicago Divinity School, rejected the doctrines of inherited sin and depravity. As a highly evolved creature, man possesses the power of free choice and the ability to ameliorate social evils. Mathews defined salvation as the person ordering his individual life to peace and happiness and society ordering itself to the virtues of justice and fair play. These personal and collective goals are facilitated by the personality of Jesus and the power of his teachings. Because God advances nature and society via evolutionary forces and because humans are morally and spiritually competent, no need exists for supernatural coercion as affirmed by the Reformed doctrine of grace.

Process theology thoroughly dismisses the notion of sovereign and efficient grace. Whiteheadians link the Reformed view of grace with a despotic God. From a panentheistic perspective (where everything is in God but does not exhaust the reality of God), God is said to work from within the natural order rather than from without. Thus grace is not a matter of external coercion on God's part but of internal lure or persuasion toward novelty and wholeness. The Anglo-Catholic theologian Norman Pittenger (b. 1905) defines God as the exemplar energy-event that shapes and is shaped by the cosmic process. Pittenger repudiates the doctrine of inherited human sinfulness. Consequently, God's children possess freedom of choice and the power of self-actualization. "The stuff of which humans are made is *good* stuff and human potentiality remains a *good* potentiality."[5] Pittenger avers that God gives each agent in the natural order its "initial aim" or "initial possibility" by which it freely acts to fulfill itself. God then lures or solicits further development in grace. On this showing, grace represents the cosmic Lover bringing out the best in his children. God's work is not that of "saving" souls but of maximizing human potential. Pittenger insists that God pursues this goal of "healthy and sound human growth"[6] not by coercion but by lure, enticement, and persuasion. "Through his 'tenderness' and by means of his 'lure,' he moves them towards those self decisions which can bring about great and greater good."[7] For Pittenger the impetus in salvation lies with autonomous persons themselves.

Pittenger concludes that the working of divine grace, thus understood, is not restricted to the sphere of Christendom; rather it operates also in the world's great religions—i.e., in Hinduism, Buddhism, Confucianism, Taoism, Islam, and even animism. Liberal Protestantism thus posits a grace that is common and universal, but which is hardly grace in the biblical sense of the term.

B. *The Divine Enablement That Supplements Human Initiatives (Semi-Pelagians & Roman Catholics)*

Influenced by Greek humanism, some early Fathers judged that God gives grace to those who worthily strive after virtue. Hilary (d. 367) made statements that had a Semi-Pelagian ring to them. He claimed that Adam's descendants inherit moral and spiritual weakness rather than depravity and so retain freedom to perform the good. As image of God, the unconverted manifest a desire for God, to which the latter responds at baptism with sanctifying grace. To say that man takes the first step in salvation means that the human soul must advance to meet grace. Hilary wrote, "This is the whole office of our nature that it should desire to incorporate itself into the family of God, and should make the beginning. It is the work of divine mercy to aid the desirous, to uphold the beginners. . . . But the start is from ourselves, that He may perfect the work."[8]

Churchmen such as Vincent of Lerins (d. 434), John Cassian (d. 435), and Faustus of Riez (d. 490) steered a course between Pelagianism and Augustinianism. They rejected the doctrines of effectual grace and unconditional election as incompatible with free will, human responsibility, and the universal offer of salvation. Moreover, operating in a monastic setting, they judged that effectual grace would undermine Christian discipline and foster spiritual sloth. The label "Semi-Pelagian" was first ascribed to the movement by the Formula of Concord in 1577, although advocates have also been known as "Semi-Augustinians." Augustine himself, although strongly challenging their views, referred to the Semi-Pelagians as "brethren of ours."[9]

Semi-Pelagians shared Augustine's view of the seriousness of sin, but they denied that Adam and his offspring suffered holistic depravity.

Human free will was diminished rather than destroyed; consequently sinners are capable of initiating the process of salvation (cf. Matt 7:7-8). In their infirm condition the unconverted bring forth the first desire to please God and exercise initial faith. Against Augustine, the Semi-Pelagians held that faith is not God's special gift to helpless sinners. When individuals produce initial faith, God responds with grace. In sum, the Semi-Pelagians defined grace as the indwelling divine power that illumines the human mind and will thereby increase faith.

John Cassian, a founder of monasticism in Western Europe, argued that Augustine's view of grace would lead to spiritual apathy. Human capacities can initiate spiritual progress, otherwise cherished free will would become a fiction. The first step in salvation is the human act of willing the good; thereafter God responds with assisting grace. Cassian expressed this relationship as follows: "God, when he sees in us some beginnings of a good will, at once enlightens it and strengthens it and urges it on towards salvation, increasing that which he himself implanted, or which he sees to have arisen from our own efforts."[10] Considerable connection exists between Semi-Pelagianism and the monastic disciplines. Thus Cassian wrote, "We insist that God's mercy and grace are bestowed only upon those who labor and exert themselves, and are granted to them that 'will' and 'run.'"[11] He added, "the word of the gospel raises those that are strong to sublime and lofty heights."[12]

Semi-Pelagianism was widespread in the Middle Ages. In the latter part of that period Semi-Pelagianism was advocated by theologians such as Duns Scotus (d. 1308), William of Occam (d. 1349), and Gabriel Biel (d. 1495). Scotus and Occam averred that humans by natural powers alone are able to love God above all else. Said Scotus, "If a man . . . can love a girl or a covetous man love money—all of which are a lesser good—he can love God, who is a greater good. If by his natural powers he has a love for the creature, much more does he have a love for the Creator."[13] Medieval Catholicism held that good works (alms, masses, etc.) performed by free will prior to the bestowal of grace earn a "merit of congruity." Since such works are not perfect, God is not obliged to give any benefit. But in grace God infuses a new nature ("formal righteousness") together with the supernatural power of love. Thereafter good works performed in the state of grace according to the rule of love earn as a reward the "merit of condignity" and eternal life. In the state of grace God gives the reward (eternal life) as our proper due.

The Protestant Reformers charged the Council of Trent with advancing Semi-Pelagianism, in the sense of exalting human achievements above divine grace. Trent held a high view of human ability, maintaining that the will of the unconverted is free to cooperate with prevenient grace. "Free-will, attenuated as it was in its powers, and bent down, was by no means extinguished in them."[14]

Trent's discussion of grace is found in its "Decree on Justification," promulgated at the Sixth Session (1547). Trent disputed the Reformational definition of grace as God's unmerited favor, suggesting rather that grace is a power that assists free human responses. Thus Trent identified (1) the *reception of grace*. Adults are moved by "prevenient" or "assisting grace" and their own free will to exercise faith in Christ and submit to baptism. Thus adults "who by sins were alienated from God, may be disposed through his quickening and assisting grace, to convert themselves to their own justification, by freely assenting to and cooperating with that said grace."[15] Emphasizing the connection between the sacraments and grace, Trent insisted that baptism is the instrumental cause and the beginning of the process of justification. God infuses into the baptized not only justifying grace but also the virtues—faith, hope, and charity—without which a person cannot be perfectly united with Christ and become a member of his body. The Council plainly taught that prevenient grace is not irresistible; human free will may reject the divine offer.

There follows, according to Trent, (2) the *augmentation of grace*. Assisted by grace the baptized keep the commands of God and the church and perform other good works, thereby advancing their justification. Thus justification is "preserved and also increased before God through good works."[16] Trent viewed the consummation of justification, i.e., the attainment of everlasting life, as a reward "to be faithfully rendered to their good works and merits."[17] In some people there may occur (3) the *loss and restoration of grace*. Since God's grace is resistible, at any point in the pilgrimage saving grace may be forfeited by mortal sin. But said grace can be restored in the repentant by the sacrament of penance, which includes the performance of fasts, alms, prayers, and other spiritual exercises. Further grace may be supplied by Mary's exemplary life, her suffering at Jesus' death, and her prayers to her Son in heaven. Additional grace is supplied from the surplus of merits accumulated by the saints.

C. Universal, Undifferentiated Prevenient Grace (Arminians)

Arminian, Wesleyan, and Holiness authorities deny the Augustinian distinction between general and special grace, claiming that these differ in degree rather than in kind.[18] The tradition holds to certain basic assumptions, as follows. (1) Christ died to bring salvation to every person. (2)

God desires the salvation of the entire race (1 Tim 2:4; 2 Pet 3:9). And (3) personal obligation is limited to one's ability to respond. Arminians assert that the grace that flows from Christ's cross is bestowed unconditionally on all people. Prevenient grace erases the debilitating effects of sin on minds, restores moral free agency, convicts of sin, and exerts a Godward influence on hearts. The liberating work of prevenient grace enables the unconverted to cooperate with God (synergism) and respond to the Gospel. By virtue of prevenient grace all people *de facto* exist in a preliminary state of grace. "While all were born sinful, they were also born in grace."[19] Thus the Spirit graciously provides every human with the potential for salvation.

The tradition adds that prevenient grace is not coercive but *resistible* (Acts 7:51); human freedom has the power to embrace or reject the movement of God's grace. The human will, in other words, can override the divine determination. The main features of Arminianism pertinent to the topic at hand are "partial depravity, . . . universal resistible grace, . . . a Semi-Pelagian cooperation of a person with God's grace and the possibility of a true believer falling from grace."[20] Accordingly, some Reformed authorities judge that Arminianism has revived the Semi-Pelagian formulation of grace.

James Arminius (d. 1609) was a Reformed pastor in Amsterdam and later Professor of Divinity at Leiden. Arminius strongly opposed the supralapsarianism of Beza, the head of the Geneva academy, and of Gomarus, his colleague at Leiden. Arminius accepted the reality of human depravity, by virtue of which free will is maimed and lost. "In his *lapsed and sinful state*, man is not capable, of and by himself, either to think, to will, or to do that which is really good."[21] The absence of righteousness he attributed to inherited sin; corruption of nature he ascribed to each person's perverted choices.

Arminius defined grace as God's gratuitous affection that results in the Spirit's perpetual assistance. He criticized the Augustinian distinction between common and special grace. Rather, grace is God's undifferentiated kindness to sinners that effects salvation. Arminius stated that God's grace is *universal*. God gives to all persons "preventing" or "exciting grace" by which they may repent and believe. Sinners' wills are impelled to evil; but given the infusion of universal, sufficient grace, their wills become pliable to the good. "This grace goes before . . . it excites, assists, operates that we will, and cooperates lest we will in vain."[22] Arminius derived the notion of preventing grace from God's justice. It would be unfair of God, he argued, to condemn the majority of humankind who were unable to believe because not visited by grace. Moreover, without the enablement of "sufficient grace" no one could be held accountable for their sins. For Arminius grace is also *resistible*. Free will may embrace God's grace or it may repel it. This is true of unbelievers who may resist the Gospel call (Matt 23:37; Luke 7:30; Acts 7:51) as well as believers who may fall from grace (Gal 5:4; Heb 12:15). Grace, Arminius insisted, is not an omnipotent action of God that cannot be thwarted by free wills.[23]

In 1610 followers of Arminius drafted five doctrinal articles known as the "Remonstrance." Article 4, "Prevenient Grace," reads in part as follows: "Man himself without prevenient or assisting, awakening, following and co-operative grace, can neither think, will, nor do good, nor withstand any temptations to evil; so that all good deeds or movements, that can be conceived, must be ascribed to the grace of God in Christ." The article continues by upholding the resistibility of this prevenient grace: "But as respects the mode of operation of this grace, it is not irresistible, inasmuch as it is written concerning many, that they have resisted the Holy Ghost, Acts 7, and elsewhere in many places."

John Wesley (d. 1791) had a powerful influence on the eighteenth-century evangelical movement in Britain and beyond. He agreed with the Reformational view of grace as God's undeserved favor or free mercy. Yet Wesley appealed to God's love for all people, the universality of Christ's death, and the Father's unlimited offer of salvation. He argued that God in grace must provide all persons with the ability to accept Christ and be saved. Wesley taught that there are two saving movements to grace, the first being prevenient grace—that universal and unconditional benefit of the Atonement. Thus "Salvation begins with . . . *preventing* grace; including the first wish to please God, the first dawn of light concerning his will, and the first slight transient conviction of having sinned against him. All these imply some tendency toward life; some degree of salvation; the beginning of deliverance from a blind, unfeeling heart, quite insensible of God and the things of God."[24] Prevenient grace, in other words, renews sinners' minds, affections, and wills such that they are able to respond to God. An important modality of prevenient grace is the conscience. The preliminary working of grace that is conscience imparts to all people the knowledge of good and evil and awareness of their fallen condition (John 1:9). Wrote Wesley, "in one sense it [conscience] may be termed natural, because it is found in all men; yet properly speaking, it is not natural, but a supernatural gift of God, above all his natural endowments."[25]

Wesley held that a positive response to prevenient grace results in further gifts of grace. "Stir up the spark of grace which is now in you, and he will give you more grace."[26] Wesley described this additional grace as follows: "Salvation is carried on by *convincing* grace, usually in Scripture termed *repentance*; which brings a larger measure of self-knowledge, and a further deliverance from the heart of stone. Afterwards we experience the proper Christian salvation; whereby, 'through grace,' we are 'saved by faith;' consisting of those two grand branches, justification and sanctification."[27] The additional gifts of grace enable awakened sinners to cross the threshold from unbelief to belief. Moreover, God's grace (both prevenient and convincing) does not work invincibly; it restores in persons the freedom either to cooperate with or to resist the Spirit's work. Wrote Wesley, "Arminians hold that . . . any man may resist, and that to his eternal ruin, the grace whereby it was the will of God he should have been eternally saved."[28]

Concerning prevenient grace, Wesley wrote, "The grace or love of God, whence cometh our salvation, is FREE IN ALL, and FREE FOR ALL."[29] Grace is "free for all" in that it blesses all people; hence everyone (conceived in sin) is born in grace. What did Wesley believe about the millions of souls who never heard of Christ? His understanding of prevenient grace led him to assert that Christ secretly works in the souls of those who lack explicit knowledge of the Savior, affording such the opportunity of responding inwardly to his gracious working. "The benefit of the death of Christ is . . . extended . . . even unto those who are inevitably excluded from this knowledge. Even these may be partakers of the benefit of His death, though ignorant of the history, if they suffer His grace to take place in their hearts, so as of wicked men to become holy."[30] Wesley appealed to the account of Cornelius in Acts 10, whose prayers he judged to be a response to the secret working of prevenient grace.

Richard Watson (d. 1833), the first Methodist systematic theologian, judged that for the numerous biblical commands and warnings to have meaning God must restore to sinners the ability to heed them. "As all men are required to do these things which have a saving tendency, we contend that the grace to do them has been bestowed upon all."[31] Thus by a gracious assistance bestowed on all, the Spirit creates in sinners good thoughts, desires, and spiritual tendencies. In particular, universal prevenient grace cancels the deadening effects of original sin and restores ability to respond to Christ. "The doctrine of the impartation of grace to the unconverted, in a sufficient degree to enable them to embrace the gospel, must be admitted."[32] Watson added that persons must also be able to resist universal, saving grace. If freedom to choose Christ and reject him were disallowed, people would not be accountable for personal behavior and the moral government of the universe would be subverted. Watson further stated that by virtue of universal prevenient grace the heathen are supplied with the means of salvation. He believed that virtuous heathen in all ages have been saved apart from written revelation or explicit hearing of the Gospel (Rom 2:7, 10).[33]

The Evangelical Arminians improperly are designated Semi-Pelagians, for according to the latter (1) human nature is wounded rather than spiritually incapacitated, and (2) sinners are capable of taking the first step toward God, grace thereafter assisting. The summaries above indicate that most Evangelical Arminians do not accept these two premises. However, the Semi-Pelagians and the Arminians, each in their own way, do promote a synergistic view of salvation.

D. Grace Identical to Jesus Christ (Barthians)

Karl Barth (d. 1968), the Swiss founder of neoorthodoxy, held a profound view of human sin and the quest for independence from God. Barth insisted that because fallen persons absolutize their own being, they fail to recognize grace and indeed hate grace. But, as we shall see, by virtue of his death and resurrection Jesus Christ has borne man's enmity against grace and overcome it. Christ's redemptive work thus "is the victory of grace over human enmity against grace."[34] Hence a new situation prevails: humans are now open to God and receptive to his grace.

Barth viewed grace holistically as the grace of redemption in Jesus Christ. He regarded the notion of general grace as a fatal error of the Enlightenment and liberal theology. Appeal to a non-redemptive grace in nature and history usurps God's grace in his Son. Barth's point is that there is no grace outside of God's revelation in Jesus Christ. A dynamic rather than a static concept, grace is God working through Jesus Christ to restore the fallen race to its original image and likeness. "God's grace—his grace for our humanity, that kindness, compassion and condescension in which He is our God and as our God befriends us—is Jesus Christ, He Himself and He absolutely alone."[35]

God's grace was actualized in eternity past as his elective decision concerning the human race. In the beginning, before anything existed, God determined to be gracious to humankind through his Son. God in grace decided positively for the human race, purposing to restore it to its original righteousness. "The election of grace is the eternal beginning of all the ways and works of God in Jesus Christ. In Jesus Christ God in His free grace determines himself for sinful man and sinful man for himself. He therefore . . . elects man to participation in his own glory."[36] God's grace reached out to embrace the entire world, such that all persons were elected to life in Jesus Christ.

God's gracious election assumed the form of the "covenant of grace" established between himself and the human race. "His covenant [is] a covenant of grace and His election an election of grace."[37] With an eye to classical Reformed theology, Barth insisted that there are not two covenants (a covenant of works and a covenant of grace). Rather, through the single covenant of grace God entered into partnership with humankind to reconcile the race to himself. Inherent in the covenant was God's gracious decision to become man in Jesus Christ, suffer, and die on the cross. From a modified supralapsarian perspective, Barth argued that God then determined to create a world of people who would receive his grace. "Creation sets the stage for the story of the covenant of grace."[38] Only in this sense did Barth speak of the grace of God in creation, preservation, and providence.

As noted above, the focus of God's elective decision and the content and accomplishment of the covenant of grace is Jesus Christ. Simply put, "He is the miracle of grace."[39] Christ is the form of God's decree, for in eternity past the Father determined that as Son of God he would be the "electing God" and as Son of Man he would be the "elected man." Although fuller discussion will follow in the next chapter, we mention here that Jesus Christ as "electing God" means that he is the *subject* who elects others. And Jesus Christ as "elected man" means that he is the *object* of God's election, the one through whom God works to be gracious. Moreover, Christ is the *content* of the covenant of grace since by his assumption of flesh at the Incarnation he reconciled the errant race to the loving God. "He, the living Jesus Christ, is the circle enclosing all men and every man and closed in Christian faith—the circle of divine judgment and divine grace."[40]

Barth specified several characteristics of the grace just described. (1) It is *sovereign*. Barth emphasized that grace is *God's* offer and *God's* gift. It arises wholly from *his* good will and pleasure, thus negating all synergism. Grace is "God Himself in all His sovereignty. Grace cannot be called forth or constrained by any claim or merit, by any existing or future condition, on the part of the creature."[41] (2) Grace is *free*. The result of God's own decision to be for man, God's favor is unconditioned and unconstrained. "God owes his grace to no one, and . . . no one can deserve it."[42] Barth repeatedly upheld the miracle of free grace. "In all its manifestations, in all its activity, His grace is free grace."[43] (3) God's grace is *irresistible*, in the sense of being wholly effectual. Since man is a being in grace, ultimately he cannot reject the cosmic restoration to the Father. "Grace in itself means primarily that the sin of the creature, the resistance which it opposes to God, cannot check, weaken or render impossible the operation of divine grace. On the contrary, grace shows its power over and against sin."[44] And (4) God's grace ultimately will prove *triumphant*. By virtue of God's eternal elective decision and covenant, the entire world will be conquered by grace despite its flight from God. Wrath may be God's penultimate word, but grace will be his ultimate word. "That Jesus Christ is Conquerer cannot be undone."[45]

Finally, for Barth religion—defined as people's attempt to apprehend God apart from the Word of grace—is "idolatry," "self-righteousness," and "unbelief."[46] This side of the victorious consummation, "Religion is unbelief. It is a concern, indeed . . . it is the one great concern of godless man."[47] As the world's ironic attempt to safeguard itself against God, religion is a degeneration of the true covenant relationship, a surrogate of the true grace of God. In all human striving, religion "is the attempted replacement of the divine work by a human manufacture."[48] Barth held that because blessed by the grace of God in Jesus Christ, Christianity alone is the true religion. "The Church is the locus of true religion, so far as through grace it lives by grace."[49]

E. God's Universal, Saving Self-Communication (Vatican II Catholics)

This view is held by avant-garde Catholics such as Rahner and Boff and by the Second Vatican Council. The Jesuit theologian Karl Rahner (d. 1984) formulated his views within the worldview known as panentheism, which affirms that ontologically all created reality is in God, but that God is not exhausted by finite reality. Accordingly, Rahner denied the classical and scholastic distinction between natural and supernatural orders. He insisted that "nature is in grace" and vice versa,[50] in the sense that grace permeates and informs nature. Hence the concept of "pure nature" is a fiction.

Grace, according to Rahner, is "the self-communication of God to the finite creature, the direct presence of God, the dynamism directed towards participation in the life of God."[51] This dynamic force that orients man's spiritual existence toward God is bestowed on humans universally such that all are transformed by it. Scholastic theologians averred that all people experience only *nature*. Rahner, however, insisted that by virtue of God's universal self-communication all persons experience *grace*. "The grace of God and Christ are present in everything as the mysterious essence of every reality."[52] Grace is profoundly embedded in the fabric of life and history rather than isolated in the church and its sacraments. Thus grace "occurs always in an encounter with the world and not merely in the confined sector of the sacred or of worship and 'religion' in the narrow sense."[53] Since Christ rose from the dead, Rahner expects that grace will succeed and become savingly victorious.[54]

Rahner viewed persons as transcendent beings who by creation are open to the infinite or grace. Human nature "is a nature installed in a supernatural order which it can never leave, even as a sinner and unbeliever."[55] Given this human reality, God's universal will to save and his comprehensive self-communication, the spirit of transformation predisposes all persons to the life of God. This dynamic impulse that orients all people toward the immediacy of God, Rahner called the "supernatural existential." This signifies the supernaturally elevated mode of existence that continually endows all persons with an orientation to grace and a positive drive toward their salvific end. It is "the supernatural capacity which arises from grace and belongs to man in his freedom."[56] Moreover, "This 'supernatural existential,' considered as God's very act of self-bestowal which he offers to men, is universally grafted into the roots of human existence."[57] Rahner added that all who accept their experience of transcendence, who open themselves to the mystery of grace, and who do not deliberately renounce it, in fact believe and are Christians. This is true even in the absence of hearing the Word of God, for a positive human response to grace may be completely unconscious and unreflective.

Rahner judged that non-Christian religionists, or even atheists who lack explicit knowledge of Christ but who follow the leading of grace so-defined, are "anonymous Christians." He wrote, "The anonymous Christians—whether they know it or not, whether they distinguish it from the light of their natural reason or not—are enlightened by the light of God's grace which God denies to no man."[58] Rahner judged that the entire world of religions is an "anonymous Christendom," containing supernatural moments of grace. Thus in the divine wisdom the religions are providentially willed vehicles of salvation. "The history of the world is the history of salvation. God's offer of himself, in which God communicates himself absolutely to the whole of mankind, is by definition man's salvation."[59] Rahner believed that theological formulations represent thematizations of the grace that all people experience implicitly. Rahner's views have exercised considerable influence upon Roman Catholic theology in recent decades.

Leonardo Boff, a Brazilian, Franciscan priest, and liberation theologian, follows Rahner's universalized view of (saving) grace. For Boff, grace signifies God's liberating presence in the world and in all human beings. Thus, "Grace is not a quality of God; it is the essence (*divinitas*) of God."[60]

Because grace is God, it is present in all finite reality (Acts 17:28). Consequently "the world . . . is imbued and suffused with the grace of God."[61] It follows that all persons inescapably live and move in the divine *milieu* of grace. Boff continues that *experientially* humans are capable of erecting obstacles to the personal realization of grace. But *ontologically* humans can never remove themselves from the presence of grace. God's superabundant grace must prevail over human sin and indifference.

Boff adds that the non-Christian religions represent the *ordinary* agents of grace. "The world's religions . . . are vehicles that communicate grace, forgiveness, and the future that God promises to human beings."[62] Boff specifies that Lao-tzu, Buddha, and Gandhi, as well as the writings of Seneca, Marcus Aurelius, and Plato, are vehicles of grace. Thus without any contact with Christianity, every human being engages transforming grace. Christ and his church, however, represent the *extraordinary* vehicle of grace. Boff adds that the decisive encounter with grace occurs at death, when every mortal will be given the opportunity of meeting God and sharing in the divine nature (2 Pet 1:4). Thus through grace-filled moments, either in life or in death, God's loving design for the human race will be realized: the salvation of all his children.

Rahner and Hans Küng significantly influenced the Second Vatican Council. The council affirmed that humans, as spontaneously free beings in the image of God, are "weakened" by sin.[63] Thus pre-Christians can engage God with the assistance of grace. The council merged not only general and special revelation but also general and special grace. From a panentheistic perspective it claimed that grace infuses the whole of nature. Hence grace is a light that enlightens all people (John 1:9) and "a hallowed power which lies behind the course of nature and the events of human life."[64] As people follow the light of grace within, they are united to Christ. "Those who through no fault of their own, do not know the Gospel of Christ or his Church, but who nevertheless seek God with a sincere heart, and, moved by grace, try in their actions to do his will as they know it through the dictates of their conscience—those too may achieve eternal salvation. Nor shall divine providence deny the assistance necessary for salvation to those who, without any fault of theirs, have not yet arrived at an explicit knowledge of God, and who, not without grace, strive to lead a good life."[65] The council anticipated that universal grace will transform all people into a new humanity, which is the body of Christ and the temple of the Holy Spirit. To this Catholic unity belong "all mankind, called by God's grace to salvation."[66] This is true not only of nominal Christians but also of Jews, Muslims, Buddhists, Hindus, and even atheists.

F. The Divine Favor That Sustains Life and Efficiently Leads to Christ (Reformed Evangelicals)

Augustine, most Reformers, and Reformed Evangelicals hold to the reality of both common and special grace. Common grace denotes God's undeserved goodness to every person in the form of his general care. It includes the provision of basic human needs, the restraint of evil, the delay of judgment, and the maintenance of the civil order. Special grace, on the other hand, represents the exercise of God's saving power toward sinners. God enlightens the minds of alienated rebels, quickens their wills, and energizes their affections Godward. Thus inwardly renewed by the Spirit, the recipients of special grace willingly believe the Gospel, repent of their sins, and trust Christ.

Proponents of this view claim (1) that God's saving grace is *prevenient*; it goes before all Christ-honoring spiritual responses. (2) Saving grace is completely *effectual*. God's grace cannot fail, for the Almighty's will and working cannot be frustrated. Special grace invincibly changes the hearts of those the Father has given to the Son. Many modern Calvinists replace the older notion of "irresistible grace" with the idea of "effectual grace." God does not violate the recalcitrant human will; he powerfully changes it from an attitude of unwillingness to willingness. Special grace may be resisted by the elect, but not finally. (3) The focus of special grace is *individual*; it ministers to particular persons at the point of their helplessness and need. And (4) general and special grace are *mediated by Christ's person and work*; apart from Jesus Christ human life and salvation are impossible.

Augustine (d. 430) was converted from a morally profligate life in Manichaeanism that involved a protracted struggle with sin. Later the Bishop of Hippo viewed his own conversion as an exemplar of God's grace in action. In his Christian writings he vigorously opposed Pelagian and Semi-Pelagian views of sin and grace. Citing the multitude of blessings God bestows on all creatures, including sinners, Augustine delineated what later came to be known as common grace. God in his goodness sustains the processes of nature, ensures the availability and variety of foods, maintains the light of human reason, facilitates the development of vocational skills such as medicine, architecture, and agriculture, stimulates artistic achievements such as music and poetry, and regulates the moral order of the universe.[67] Without such universal beneficence, life on our planet would cease to exist.

Initially Augustine held that sinners could prepare themselves for the working of grace. He came to understand, however, that original sin rendered Adam and his descendants spiritually impotent. Corrupted by inherited sin, unregenerate human nature is overcome with pride, egotism, and lust. Although sinners possess significant psychological freedom, they lack moral and spiritual freedom, namely, the power of contrary choice (*libertes*). Sinners can neither will the good nor perform any meritorious work to earn God's favor. "Free will is sufficient for evil, but it is of no avail for good unless it is aided by Omnipotent Good."[68] The unregenerate thus lack the power to come to Christ unless graciously enabled by God himself. "The human will does not attain grace through freedom, but rather freedom through grace."[69] Augustine defined grace as God's gift, through Jesus Christ, of the Holy Spirit, working in the inner life of the elect to restore the disposition or ability to love God and to perform the good.[70] Grace is God the heavenly Physician curing the maladies of sin and restoring sinners to spiritual health.

In his disputes with the Pelagians and Semi-Pelagians, Augustine identified the grace of God as redemptive power. Augustine, as noted, held that God's goodness operates universally in nature. Nevertheless, the grace that saves is beyond nature and its capabilities. Grace, in other words, deals not with the *constitution* of nature (so Pelagius), but with its *cure*. The Bishop of Hippo wrote, "I defend grace, not indeed as opposed to nature, but as that which controls and liberates nature."[71] Augustine thus laid the foundation for the Scholastic dictum, "Grace does not destroy nature, it perfects it."

Since enslaved sinners cannot be restored to God by their own powers, God brings them to Christ through a sovereign work of grace. Divine grace does no violence to the human will. Rather, grace so heals the will, restores it to true freedom, and kindles in it spiritual desires that the person freely cleaves to Christ. With an eye to Pelagius, Augustine wrote that grace is not "by law and teaching uttering their lessons from without, but by a secret, wonderful and ineffable power from within, that God works in men's hearts not only revelations of the truth, but also good dispositions of the will."[72] By the gift of effectual power, grace elicits God-directed and God-honoring human responses. "We indeed work; we observe; we do. But he made us to walk, to observe, to do. This is the grace of God making us good. This is his mercy preventing us"[73] The working of divine grace is summed up in Augustine's famous dictum: "Give what you command, and command what you will."[74]

Augustine described several characteristics of grace, or the divine love in action. (1) It is radically *gratuitous*. Against the Semi-Pelagians, God's redeeming favor is bestowed as a free favor, not in response to any virtuous activity on the part of the sinner. "Grace is not bestowed according to men's deserts, otherwise grace would be no longer grace. Grace is so designated because it is freely given."[75] The sinful human will is incapable of meriting the first grace. (2) Grace is *effectual*. Having purposed to bestow favor on a given person, God's will and working can never be thwarted. "God works in the hearts of men to incline their wills wherever he wills, whether to good deeds according to his mercy, or to evil after their own deserts."[76] All those who have been taught by grace actually come to Christ. And (3) God's grace is *secret* in its working. The blessings of grace "happen through the secret providence of God, whose judgments are unsearchable, and his ways past finding out."[77]

Augustine further categorized grace as preventing and subsequent or as operating and cooperating. Preventing grace (Ps 59:10a) is God mercifully anticipating sinners' needs by changing their hearts by the Spirit. It is the grace that heals sinners spiritually and imparts new life. Subsequent grace (Ps 23:6) is the favor that enables Christians to live righteously. It is the grace that frees from the defilements of sin and that stimulates Christian growth.[78] Augustine elaborated on the preceding pair of terms thusly. Operating grace is God working new life in the unregenerate without their cooperation (Phil 1:6). Cooperating grace is the Spirit assisting the willing and working of the regenerate in the disciplines of the Christian life (Phil 2:12-13). "God operates without us in order that we may will. But when we will and so will that we may act, he cooperates with us. We can, however, ourselves do nothing to effect good works of piety without him either working that we may will, or co-working when we will."[79]

Finally, Augustine linked grace with explicit and objective revelation concerning Christ and the plan of salvation. The bishop restricted saving grace to the sphere of Christendom and specifically to the church and recipients of the sacrament of baptism. In this matter he sided with the familiar dictum of Cyprian (d. 258): "Outside the church there is no salvation."

Martin Luther (d. 1546) sharply opposed Nominalist and Semi-Pelagian optimism regarding the powers of human nature. He rejected the notion that the unconverted, by the exercise of free will, are able to love God, keep the law, and thereby merit saving grace. Rather, inherited sin in Adam's descendants paralyzes the will in matters spiritual and evokes enmity toward God. "On the part of man nothing precedes grace but indisposition toward grace, nay, rebellion against grace."[80] The unconverted will, in fact, can do nothing but sin. Hence Luther wrote, "After the fall free will is a mere name; when it acts according to its ability it commits mortal sin."[81] Thus salvation never is predicated on the sinner's response to or cooperation with, grace.

Against the Roman Scholastics, Luther claimed that grace is not a created quality infused in the soul making it righteous. He held that grace is both a disposition in God and an activity of God. It is God's free kindness, favor, and love to sinners through Jesus Christ that removes sin and guilt and that makes persons pleasing to God. "Grace signifies the favor with which God receives us, forgiving our sins and justifying us freely through Christ."[82] Derivatively, grace is the imputed righteousness of Christ poured into our hearts by the Holy Spirit; it is the state of being justified. Luther firmly rejected the Scholastic divisions of grace ("uncreated" and "created," "operating" and "cooperating," etc.). "Grace is not divisible and is not given piecemeal as are the [spiritual] gifts; but it takes us entirely into God's favor for the sake of Christ, our Advocate and Mediator."[83]

Radical human sinfulness necessitates that God must lend his goodness and power for the maintenance of human existence. Thus the begetting of children, the blessings of family life, the institutions of society, and the maintenance of law and order all derive from God's beneficence. Without using the term itself, Luther acknowledged the reality of what later came to be known as common grace.

But the grace that justifies, God secretly bestows on the elect. "The best and infallible preparation for grace and the sole disposition toward grace is the eternal election and predestination of God."[84] Since grace is God's sovereign gift, human good will or works avail for naught. God imparts justifying grace to sinners gratuitously; hence the unsaved can neither demand nor earn grace. "Grace is given freely to those without merits and the most undeserving, and is not obtained by any efforts, endeavors, or works, whether small or great, even of the best and most virtuous of men, though they seek and pursue righteousness with burning zeal."[85] Luther particularly scorned the Scholastic system of merits. "God has never given anyone grace and eternal life for the merit of congruity or the merit of condignity."[86] Law (with its call for works) and grace (as divine gift) are antithetic one to another. "The law says 'do this,' and it is never done. Grace says, 'believe in this,' and everything is already done."[87] Outwardly human works may appear attractive, but inwardly they are odious to God. Thus "disgrace [*Umgnade*] rather than grace [*Gnade*] comes by the works of the law."[88] "*Sola gratia*" was Luther's battle cry!

Luther insisted that justifying grace is mediated exclusively through Christ and made known through the Gospel. Thus those who lack the Word and who do not know Christ by faith are hopelessly lost. Wrote Luther, "whatever is not Christ is not the way but error, not the truth but a lie, not the life but death."[89]

John Calvin (d. 1564) held that by virtue of original sin minds are darkened to spiritual truth and human wills incapable of responding to God.

In the spiritual realm, Calvin insisted, "the greatest geniuses are blinder than moles!"[90] The debilitating effects of sin ensure that except for special grace sinners can perform no work pleasing to God. Grace, according to Calvin, is God's unmerited favor or beneficence. Calvin distinguished between the "general grace of God" and the "special grace of God."[91] The former accounts for all that is noble and good in humankind short of salvation. Such universal benefits include restraint of evil forces, maintenance of the moral order of the universe, universal religious aspirations, elements of truth in non-Christian philosophies and religions, and the development of the arts, sciences, medicine, and politics. "We ought not to forget those most excellent benefits of the divine Spirit which he distributes to whomever he wills for the common good of mankind."[92] Added Calvin, "all the notable endowments that manifest themselves among unbelievers are gifts of God."[93]

Special grace, on the other hand, represents God's saving mercy, particularly the imputation of undeserved righteousness to the elect. "Scripture everywhere proclaims that God finds nothing in man to arouse him to do good to him, but that he comes first to man in his free generosity."[94] Special grace efficiently illumines the mind and frees the will as the first step toward saving faith, remission of sins, and reconciliation with God. Calvin rejected the notion that God distributes special grace to those he foresaw would make good use of it. Since depraved sinners will only evil, apart from special grace they can perform no spiritual good. Neither do sinners cooperate with the grace of God. As the necessary starting point of every good, divine grace precedes all human effort. Calvin staunchly refused to attribute an ounce of merit to sinners in the attainment of salvation. "Everything good in the will is the work of grace alone. . . . If even the least ability came from ourselves, we would also have some share of the merit."[95]

For Calvin the beneficence of God is summed up in Jesus Christ. "In Him [Christ] alone God the Father is gracious to us."[96] It follows that any philosophy or religion that does not acknowledge the saving grace of Christ is a worthless vehicle of redemption.

The Westminster Confession of Faith (1647), an important standard of British and American Reformed theology, discussed the concept of grace within the framework of the covenant of grace. Grace is God in undeserved kindness entering into a redemptive covenant with elect sinners, making them by sovereign power willing and able to believe. Thus God "frees the sinner from his natural bondage under sin, and by his grace alone enables him freely to will and to do that which is spiritually good" (ch. 9.4). God's grace operates through the appointed Mediator, Jesus

Christ, to whom God gave a people to be his faithful seed. The Confession adds that God's grace, applied by the Spirit, is *sovereign* and *free*. God's favor is bestowed solely according to his good pleasure, not on the basis of anything foreseen in man (ch. 10.2). Moreover, God's grace is wholly *efficacious*. Grace convincingly persuades those given by the Father to the Son to believe and obey the Word as it touches their hearts. God's inviolable elective purpose and covenant of grace ensure this saving outcome.

C.H. Spurgeon (d. 1892) held that depraved descendants of Adam, being dead in sin, are devoid of love for God and destitute of obedience to him. Because sinners are helpless to redeem themselves, salvation derives from God's free favor. Spurgeon acknowledged the reality of common grace, whereby all forms of life are dependent on God for their existence and welfare. But he focused attention on the grace that saves sinners. Thus "Grace is the free favor of God, the undeserved bounty of the ever-gracious Creator against whom we have offended, the generous pardon, the infinite, spontaneous lovingkindness of the God who has been provoked and angered by our sin."[97] God's grace proceeds exclusively through Jesus Christ, the Mediator. "All things come to us through Christ Jesus: he is the golden pipe of the conduit of eternal love, the window through which grace shines, the door by which it enters."[98]

Spurgeon agreed with other Reformed authorities as to the nature of saving grace. (1) Grace is *infinite* in extent. Because we are human and the giver of grace is God, grace is always greater than our sins. Thus "The Lord has as much grace as the whole universe will require, but he has vastly more. He overflows: all the demands that can ever be made on the grace of God will never . . . diminish his store of mercy."[99] (2) Grace is *sovereign*, in that God bestows grace upon whom he will. God often gives grace to those who humanly speaking are the least deserving—the most disobedient, unchaste, ungodly. Conversely, he often withholds grace from those who are outwardly decent, talented, and respected. (3) God's grace is always *free*. It is a gift to be received, not a prize to be earned. "Salvation is not granted to men as the result of anything they are, or do, or resolve to be, but it is the undeserved gift of heaven."[100] And (4) God's grace is unfailingly *effectual*. Abounding grace conquers sinful, human resistance to God's beneficent purposes. The ability to receive God's gifts of grace must be attributed to the Spirit's enablement. Sinners are absolutely dependent on God for the obtaining of grace and for its outcome—the salvation of the soul.

This latter view, which distinguishes between common grace and special grace, best coheres with the biblical data, as the following section will indicate.

III. Exposition of
the Doctrine of Grace

A. The Language of Grace

Our first task will be to identify the meaning of grace in the Old and New Testaments. Our study will show that the concept of God's grace is a very common biblical theme that, in fact, undergirds every facet of human salvation.

GRACE IN THE OLD TESTAMENT. The word "grace" occurs relatively infrequently in the *English* translations of the OT: namely, thirty-seven times in the AV and eight times in the NIV. The root *ḥnn*, found in most ancient Near Eastern languages, signifies gracious attitudes that issue in kindly deeds. The Hebrew verb *ḥānan*, from the root meaning to "bend" or "stoop," in the Qal form means to "show favor," "be gracious," and "act in a kindly manner." Several Hebrew names were derived from this stem: i.e., "Hanani" ("gracious," 1 Kgs 16:1; Ezra 10:20), "Hananel" ("God is gracious," Neh 3:1; Jer 31:38), and "Hananiah" ("Yahweh is gracious," 1 Chron 25:23; Jer 36:12). The verb is used with a human as subject (e.g., Judg 21:22; Ps 109:12; Prov 14:31), but more often with God as subject (e.g., Gen 33:11; 43:29; Exod 33:19b; Ps 67:1; Mal 1:9). God's message to Moses in Exod 33:19b is typical: "I will have mercy [*ḥānan*] on whom I will have mercy [*ḥānan*], and I will have compassion [Piel of *rāḥam*] on whom I will have compassion [Piel of *rāḥam*]." *Ḥānan* is used of God showing mercy or kindness in delivering from foreign exile (Isa 30:18-19; Amos 5:15), in saving from distress or danger (Ps 4:1; 25:16; 31:9; 56:1), and in prayers for healing from sin's defilement (Ps 41:4; 51:1).

The noun *ḥēn* occurs sixty-one times in the OT, occasionally in the sense of "charm" or "beauty" (Prov 1:9; 3:22; 31:30). Its principal meaning, however, is "favor," "grace," or "benevolence," usually manifested by a superior to an inferior. "It denotes the stronger coming to the help of the weaker who stands in the need of help by reason of his circumstances or natural weakness."[101] *Ḥēn* thus denotes favor shown by one person to another. In older versions it often was translated by the formula, "to find favor in the eyes of." Thus Laban found favor in the eyes of Jacob (Gen 30:27), Jacob in the eyes of Esau (Gen 32:5; 33:8, 10, 15), and Joseph in the eyes of Pharaoh's men (Gen 39:4, 21; 50:4). For further examples see Ruth 2:2, 10, 13; 1 Sam 20:29; 27:5; Esth 8:5. *Ḥēn* furthermore signifies favor before God (Prov 3:34; Jon 2:8; Zech 12:10), often expressed by the formula, "to find favor in the eyes of the Lord." Thus Noah (Gen 6:8), Abraham (Gen 18:3), Moses (Exod 33:12-13; 34:9), Gideon (Judg 6:17), and David (2 Sam 15:25) found grace or favor with God in accord with the latter's sovereign plan. According to Esser, "*ḥēn* . . . is used mostly in the sense of God's undeserved gift in election."[102]

The adjective *ḥannûn*, "gracious," occurs thirteen times in the OT. The word is used exclusively as a quality of God (e.g., Exod 34:6; Neh 9:17; Ps 86:15; Joel 2:13).

The noun *ḥesed*, which occurs some 250 times in the OT, signifies "lovingkindness," "favor," or "mercy" and is translated by *eleos* in the LXX. The word in Scripture has a strong relational or covenantal flavor. Thus *ḥesed* "expresses spontaneous goodness or grace in a specific relationship or in ongoing fellowship."[103] In a relation between humans *ḥesed* signifies love bestowed (Gen 20:13) or kindness shown (Gen 40:14; 1 Sam 15:6; Ps 109:12), especially vis-à-vis the poor or needy (Job 6:14; Ps 109:16). Like *ḥēn* it occurs in the expression, "find favor in your eyes" (Gen 19:19; 47:29). In the more common usages with God as subject, *ḥesed* denotes the grace or mercy that guides (Exod 15:13; Ps 143:8), that strengthens (Ps 94:18), that delivers from danger (Gen 19:19; Ps 86:13), that comforts (Ps 119:76), that forgives sins (Num 14:19; Ps 25:7; 51:3), that gives life (Job 10:12), and that saves or redeems (Ps 119:41). *Ḥesed* often is paired with other qualities in humans or God: viz., "righteousness" (Ps 36:10; 103:17; Hos 10:12), "truth" (Ps 40:11), "faithfulness" (Gen 24:49; Ps 57:3; 115:1; Prov 14:22), "goodness" (Ps 23:6), "compassion" (Ps 103:4; Hos 2:19; Zech 7:9), "pity" (Jer 16:5), "mercy" (Ps 25:6; 40:11; 51:1), "justice" (Ps 101:1; Jer 9:24; Mic 6:8), and "salvation" (Ps 13:5; 85:7). *Ḥesed* differs from *ḥēn* in that it stresses favor within a specific relationship and connotes the attitude and action of the stronger or more privileged toward the weaker or less privileged.

The concept of grace is inherent in the Hebrew words *'āhēb* (to "love") and *'aḥªbāh* ("love," "affection"). Grace is God loving, choosing, entering into covenant with, and saving his unworthy people. Thus with respect to the verb *'āhēb*, God loved the patriarchs (Deut 4:37), Israel (Isa 43:4; Jer 12:7; Hos 3:1), believers (Deut 5:10; Jer 32:18), and individuals such as Jacob (Mal 1:2) and Solomon (2 Sam 12:24-25; Neh 13:26). The noun *'aḥªbāh* similarly is used of God's great love for his undeserving people (Deut 7:8; Isa 63:9; Jer 31:3; Zeph 3:17).

The verb *rāḥam* in the Piel means to "have compassion" (Ps 103:13; 116:5) and in the Pual to "find" or "be shown compassion" (Prov 28:13; Hos 14:3). The Piel form is used of God exercising compassion in election

(Exod 33:19), in withholding judgment (Deut 13:17; 2 Kgs 13:23), in restoring Israel to their land (Deut 30:3; Isa 14:1; 54:7), and in forgiveness and salvation (Isa 55:7). The plural noun *raḥᵃmîm* ("tender mercy," "compassion") occurs some forty times in the OT and attests the sensitive, feeling side of God's mercy or grace (Neh 9:19; Ps 77:9; Lam 3:22; Dan 9:9). The objects of God's *raḥᵃmîm* are the alienated or the helpless. The adjective *raḥûm* describes God's mercy or goodness, particularly toward the afflicted (Exod 34:6; Deut 4:31; Ps 103:8). The noun *rāṣôn*—"desire," "pleasure," but more pointedly "goodwill," "favor," or "grace"—connotes the favor that God shows or that persons obtain (Deut 33:16, 23; Ps 106:4; Prov 8:35; 12:2). The word occurs in such expressions as "the time of your favor" (Ps 69:13; cf. Isa 49:8) and "the year of God's favor" (Isa 61:2).

GRACE IN THE NEW TESTAMENT.   The principal Greek word for grace is *charis*, which occurs 155 times in the NT, including some 100 times in Paul's writings. Endowed with a rich heritage in secular Greek, *charis* bears the following meanings in the NT: "grace, gracefulness, graciousness, favor, thanks [and] gratitude."[104] In secular Greek *charis* fundamentally meant qualities that stimulated delight or pleasure—namely, charm, attractiveness, and beauty (cf. Luke 4:22). It also denoted specific acts of kindness or favor, often extended by a dignitary to persons of lesser rank (cf. Acts 25:3). Finally, *charis* signified the response offered to acts of kindness—namely, gratitude or thankfulness (cf. Luke 6:32-34; 17:9; 1 Cor. 15:57). In the secular world *charis* was used of personal qualities and relations between persons. Greek thought was Pelagian in holding that people could attain virtue without the aid of God or the gods. The specific Christian idea of God's undeserved goodness was not present in Hellenistic Greek.[105]

Luke reflects the OT notion of grace as favor with man (Luke 2:52; Acts 2:47; 7:10) and favor with God (Luke 1:30; 2:52; Acts 7:46). Persons of privilege or power extended favor (*charis*) to individuals of lesser social or economic status (Acts 24:27; 25:9). With the coming of Christ, however, the apostles invested *charis* with richer significance than that evidenced in the OT. John expressed this startling new reality as follows: "The Word became flesh and made his dwelling among us. We have seen his glory, the glory of the One and Only Son, who came from the Father, full of grace [*charis*] and truth" (John 1:14). John added, "the law was given through Moses; grace [*hē charis*] and truth came through Jesus Christ" (John 1:17). Subsequent to the Incarnation, *charis* assumed the meaning of God's unmerited favor or merciful kindness in Jesus Christ to lost sinners (Rom 5:15, 17; 2 Cor 9:8; Eph 1:6-8; Tit 2:11). A more complete and nuanced definition of *charis* will be given below. Suffice it to say here that the richness of *charis* in the NT is hinted at by other religious concepts juxtaposed with it: namely, "peace" (*eirēnē*, Rom 1:7; 1 Cor 1:3; 2 Cor 1:2; and most epistolary introductions), "mercy" (*eleos*, 1 Tim 1:2; Heb 4:16; 2 John 3), "kindness" (*chrēstotēs*, Tit 3:4), "love" (*philanthrōpia*, Tit 3:4; *agape*, 2 Cor 13:14), "truth" (*alētheia*, John 1:17), and "knowledge" (*gnōsis*, 2 Pet 3:18).

The verb *charizomai*, to "show favor or kindness, give as a favor, to be gracious to someone, to pardon,"[106] occurs sixteen times in Paul and seven times in Luke-Acts. It is used of humans forgiving others (2 Cor 2:7, 10; Eph 4:32; Col 3:13) and of God giving graciously (Rom 8:32; 1 Cor 2:12; Gal 3:18) and forgiving sinners (Col 2:13; 3:13). The verb *charitoō*, to "give favor" or "bless," depicts believers favored with grace in Christ (Luke 1:28; Eph 1:6). The noun *charisma* ("gift"), found sixteen times in Paul and in 1 Pet 4:10, describes various grace-gifts of God: namely, the gift of salvation (Rom 5:15-16; 6:23), historical privileges given to Israel (Rom 11:29), diverse spiritual endowments (Rom 12:1, 6; 1 Cor 1:7; 12:4, 9, 28, 30-31; 1 Pet 4:10), the gift of office (1 Tim 4:14; 2 Tim 1:6), the favor of providential care (2 Cor 1:11), and the gift of marriage or celibacy (1 Cor 7:7).

B. The Need for Grace

Why do humans, the highest of God's creation and unique image-bearers, require grace for salvation and Christian living? Because sin's terrible tragedy affects all persons through Adam and Eve. Although furnished by God in Eden with abundant physical, aesthetic, social, and spiritual provisions, the first couple heeded Satan's promptings and disobeyed their Creator. By virtue of their determination to live autonomously rather than under their Creator's liberating lordship, Adam and Eve tragically fell from innocency into sin (Gen 3:1-7). This act of disobedience brought upon the first couple guilt (v. 7), estrangement from God (vv. 8-10), a sinful or depraved nature (as each blamed the other, vv. 11-13), and physical death (vv. 3, 19). Instead of enjoying unbroken relationship with God, our first parents became wicked law-breakers and rebels against the Lord of the universe.

Scripture teaches that Adam's sin affected not only himself but all of his offspring. Jesus affirmed as much when he said, "Flesh gives birth to flesh" (John 3:6)—*sarx* indicating fundamental human aversion to God and his holiness. Paul likewise taught the reality of inherited sin in Rom 5:12-19, although we leave the exegesis of this and related texts to the volume in this series on sin. Calvin's verdict enjoys solid biblical support: "All of us, who have descended from impure seed, are born infected with the contagion of sin."[107] In the language of classical theology, the human race prior to the fall was *posse non peccare et mori* ("able not to sin and die"); but after the fall each sinful member is *non posse non peccare et mori* ("not able not to sin and die"). The entire human race is afflicted with objective guilt, alienation from God, and depraved natures that refuse to know, love, and serve the Creator.

Universal sinfulness through Adam has seriously maimed human capacities to actualize the good. As Luther said, "All our faculties are leprous, indeed, are dull and utterly dead."[108] *Intellectually* sinners are unreceptive to spiritual truth. Although the unregenerate know the changing, material world, they fail to grasp the full significance of truth from the changeless, spiritual realm. Paul wrote that unconverted Gentiles "are darkened in their understanding and separated from the life of God because of the ignorance that is in them due to the hardening of their hearts" (Eph 4:18). Again, "The god of this age has blinded the minds of unbelievers, so that they cannot see the light of the gospel of the glory of Christ, who is the image of God" (2 Cor 4:4). See also Rom 8:7 and 1 Cor 2:14. Centuries ago Augustine noted that the unsaved apart from supernatural grace make inadequate sense of changeless, redemptive truth. Lacking the Spirit, their minds are not attuned to spiritual realities.

Volitionally the unconverted consistently exercise their wills against God and his purposes. Peter wrote that reprobates promise the unwary freedom, "while they themselves are slaves of depravity—for a man is a slave to whatever has mastered him" (2 Pet 2:19). Additional biblical testimony concerning spiritual "death" (Eph 2:1, 5; Col 2:13) and servitude to the sinful nature (John 8:34; Rom 6:6, 16-20; 2 Tim 2:26) confirm that the wills of the unsaved are lifeless in spiritual matters. "Free will" in common parlance means that within the constraints of one's nature a person possesses (1) the power of self-determination, i.e., to do what one desires, and (2) the uncoerced ability to choose between alternatives. "Free will" in the theological sense, however, means not only (1) but also the requirement (2) that the person is able to choose between alternatives in the moral and spiritual realm, particularly to love and serve God. But rebellion against God and the habitual practice of sin turn God-given freedom into sinful necessity. Thus in the theological sense the will of the unsaved is bound rather than free. As Augustine wrote, "A man's free will, indeed, avails for nothing, except to sin, if he knows not the way of truth."[109] Compare article 9.3 of the Westminster Confession of Faith: "Man, by his fall into a state of sin, hath wholly lost all ability of will to any spiritual good accompanying salvation."

Emotionally sinners' affections are disordered by the fallen nature, causing them to delight in evil. Reflecting on personal experience, Paul wrote that "we . . . were foolish, disobedient, deceived and enslaved by all kinds of passions and pleasures. We lived in malice and envy, being hated and hating one another" (Tit 3:3). See also Eph 2:3; Gal 5:16; 1 Pet 2:11. Apart from the experience of God's love (John 5:42), the unsaved hate Jesus and the Father (John 15:24; Jas 4:4). *Morally* Paul indicated that sinners "have given themselves over to sensuality so as to indulge in every kind of impurity, with a continual lust for more" (Eph 4:19). The result is that "both their minds and consciences are corrupted" (Tit 1:15). By the continual practice of evil, their "consciences are seared with a hot iron" (1 Tim 4:2, NRSV); hence this primary moral faculty may fail to discriminate between right and wrong.

Depravity *relationally* means that sinners are alienated from their Creator and oppose his purposes and values. Paul reminded the Colossians that "Once you were alienated from God and were enemies in your minds because of your evil behavior" (Col 1:21). See also Isa 59:2 and Rom 5:10. The sweet communion the first pair enjoyed with God in Eden has yielded to the pain and despair of isolation from their Creator and Redeemer. And *behaviorally* the unsaved give themselves to a life of cruel and violent deeds. After rehearsing humankind's rejection of the Creator (Rom 1:18-23), Paul stated that God released the unrepentant to their base impulses (vv. 24, 26, 28). The picture of humanity perpetrating a host of sexual (vv. 26-27) and social crimes (vv. 29-31) is tragic indeed. Peter described the pagan way as "living in debauchery, lust, drunkenness, orgies, carousing and detestable idolatry" (1 Pet 4:3; cf. 2 Pet 2:14). With total realism, Paul wrote that "there is no one who does good, not even one" (Rom 3:12b).

Scripture thus testifies that the unsaved are holistically depraved, in that sin has corrupted every aspect of their being: mind, will, emotions, relationships, and actions. By virtue of their anti-God bias and predilection to sin, the unregenerate, apart from grace, are incapable of turning to God, pleasing God, and saving themselves (cf. Jer 13:23; Rom 8:3, 8). Left to their own resources, sinners degenerate from bad to worse (Rom 1:26-32). This grim human condition, widely attested by revelation and life experience, constitutes the stage for the display of God's marvelous grace.

C. God's Provision of Common Grace

The scriptural data permit us to distinguish between God's common grace operative throughout the creation and his special grace efficient in the salvation of believers. Just as we differentiate between general revelation and special revelation and between a general call and a special call to salvation (see chap. 5), so we distinguish between two forms of grace that differ in kind, not merely in degree. Common grace is the undeserved beneficence of the Creator God expressed by his general care of creation and of all persons everywhere without discrimination (Ps 36:5; 119:64; 136:1-9). The psalmist plainly stated, "The Lord is good to all; he has compassion on all he has made" (Ps 145:9; cf. 33:5). Jesus similarly affirmed, "the Most High . . . is kind [*chrēstos*] to the ungrateful and wicked" (Luke 6:35), and he is also "merciful" (*oiktirmos*, v. 36). Concerning the ordinary blessings of life, James wrote, "Every generous act of giving [*dosis agathē*], with every perfect gift [*dōrēma teleion*], is from above, coming down from the Father of lights" (Jas 1:17, NRSV).

The Creator's general beneficence brings about many positive ends. (1) In common grace God upholds the laws and processes of nature, viz., sunshine, rain, and fructification of the soil (Job 37:13; Ps 65:9a; Matt 5:45; Acts 14:17a). (2) Via common grace God maintains human and lower forms of life in existence (Ps 36:6b; Isa 42:5b; Acts 17:28a). (3) Through grace God supplies temporal needs universally: viz., food, water, and shelter (Gen 27:28; Ps 65:9b; 104:14). These life provisions create in the unsaved a measure of gladness (Acts 14:17b). (4) Through the Spirit God restrains the power of sin (Gen 6:3; Rom 13:1-4; 2 Thess 2:6-7; cf. 1 Sam 16:14). Common grace hinders wickedness from being as destructive as it might otherwise be individually and corporately. (5) Common grace delays or withholds deserved judgment (Gen 8:21-22; Rom 2:4). (6) It facilitates the development of what is true and good in philosophy, the arts, sciences, and technology (Exod 31:2-11; 35:30-35). The contributions of Plato, Shakespeare, Beethoven, Mozart, and Einstein are examples of this. (7) Common grace maintains the social and political order, thus enabling fallen people to live together in mutually helpful relations. (8) Common grace serves to foster harmonious international relations, even among atheists and non-Christians. And (9) God's good gifts are given to sinners as incentives to repentance (Rom 2:4). They demonstrate that God takes no delight in the death of the wicked (Ezek 33:11; 1 Tim 2:4; 2 Pet 3:9). In sum, God's common grace facilitates everything that sustains and enhances life on this fallen planet. Because of it sinners are not as bad as they could be. Common grace, in other words, accounts for the existence individually of "splendid pagans" and corporately of "civic righteousness" in a fallen world.

Abraham Kuyper (d. 1920) of the Netherlands summarized the benefits of this non-saving benevolence as follows: "By His common grace God bridles the evil of fallen human nature, restrains the ruin which sin has produced and spread, and enables even the unregenerated men to do good in the broad, non-redemptive sense. It is the source of the good, the true, and the beautiful which remain, in spite of sin, in human life, even in human life which has not been regenerated."[110] Both Scripture and experience attest that common grace is resistible; hence the deprivation and godlessness that exists in the world. The prophet Isaiah put it well: "Though grace is shown to the wicked, they do not learn righteousness; even in a land of uprightness they go on doing evil and regard not the majesty of the Lord" (Isa 26:10).

D. God's Provision of Special Grace

That universal benefit of God as Creator, denominated common grace, does not save. Common grace functions as the presupposition for special grace in that it creates in the unsaved awareness of God's goodness and their own unworthiness. Special grace, on the other hand, is a benefit of God as Redeemer that effectually imparts salvation (Tit 2:11). Special grace emerges as the fountainhead of all redemptive blessings. Paul wrote, "Grace and peace to you from God our Father and the Lord Jesus Christ. Praise be to the God and Father of our Lord Jesus Christ, who has blessed us in the heavenly realms with every spiritual blessing in Christ" (Eph 1:2-3). Special grace is the *raison d'etre* for the Christian life in its commencement (Eph 2:4-5), its continuation (2 Cor 12:9), and its consummation (1 Pet 1:13). Special grace originates with God the Father (1 Cor 1:3; Eph 1:3, 6; Tit 2:11), is mediated through the saving work of Jesus Christ (Rom 5:15; 1 Cor 1:4; Tit 3:6-7), and is made experientially real through the ministry of the Holy Spirit (Zech 12:10; Heb 10:29).

DIMENSIONS OF SPECIAL GRACE. (1) Foundational to all other aspects is the notion of grace as *an attitude of God* revealed to the undeserving. *Charis* fundamentally connotes God's unmerited favor shown to sinners. As noted above, we unregenerates were against God, but God in his kindness, mercy, and generous love was for us. Paul reflects this basic meaning in Ephesians, where he wrote that God predestined believers "in accordance with his pleasure (*eudokia*) and will—to the praise of his glorious grace" (1:5-6). Juxtaposed with the statement, "it is by grace you have been saved" (2:5), is the affirmation (2:4a) of God's "great love [*agape*] for us" and the fact that he is (2:4b) "rich in mercy" (*eleos*; cf. Tit 3:5). Paul further wrote of "the incomparable riches of his grace, expressed in his kindness [*chrēstotēs*] to us in Christ Jesus. For it is by grace that you have been saved" (2:7-8). This foundational sense of *charis* occurs also in Rom 5:15, 17, 20-21; 2 Tim 1:9; 2:1; Tit 2:11; Heb 12:15.

(2) More specifically, grace is an *action of God* on behalf of undeserving people. God's favor finds concrete expression in terms of his personal activity vis-à-vis unsaved and saved. God shows that he is for us by his activity toward us in Jesus Christ (John 1:14). In this respect grace is God's love in action personwise. Paul acknowledged this dimension when he wrote, "The grace of our Lord was poured out on me abundantly, along with the faith and love that are in Christ Jesus" (1 Tim 1:14). Elsewhere he stated that believers "are justified freely by his grace through the redemption that came by Christ Jesus" (Rom 3:24). "For Paul *charis* is the essence of God's decisive saving act in Jesus Christ, which took place in his sacrificial death."[111]

(3) In particular, grace is the *gift of God* bestowed upon people. Grace connotes God's loving, self-donation (Ps 84:11; 1 Cor 1:3-4). In particular, *charis* signifies (a) the gift of Jesus Christ, the supreme revelation of God's favor (John 4:10; 2 Cor 8:9; 9:15) and (b) the gift of righteousness and salvation (Acts 15:11; Rom 5:15-17; 2 Cor 6:1-2). Beyond the initial bestowal of salvation, grace signifies (c) the gift of God's power at work in the lives of his servants (2 Cor 8:1; 9:14), (d) the gift of apostleship and ministry (Rom 1:5; Gal 2:7-9; Eph 3:2, 7-8; 4:11), (e) the gift of spiritual endowments (Rom 12:6; 1 Cor 12:4, 7-11; Eph 4:7; 1 Pet 4:10); and (f) the final blessedness revealed at Christ's second advent (1 Pet 1:5, 13).

(4) Grace is more finely depicted as the *power of God* at work in persons. Dynamically, grace is the divine influence or energy that achieves God's purpose in lives. Grace as power operates in the unsaved, evoking faith in Christ and delivering from sin and the Devil (Acts 18:27; Rom. 5:20-21). More frequently, the NT portrays grace as a power operative in believers and transforming them into Christ's image, granting victory over sin, energizing for service, and enduing with hope. This is especially prominent in the book of Acts (4:33; 6:8; 14:26; 15:40) and in the Pauline letters (Rom 12:3; 1 Cor 3:10; 15:10b; 2 Cor 1:12; 8:1). Consider Jesus' words to Paul: "My grace is sufficient for you, for my power is made perfect in weakness" (2 Cor 12:9). The Pauline benediction—"the grace of our Lord Jesus (Christ) be with you" (Rom 16:20; 1 Thess 5:28; 2 Thess 3:18; cf. 1 Cor 16:23; Gal 6:18; Phil 4:23)—conveys this sense of powerful enablement. The fact that every letter of Paul begins and ends with

mention of divine grace highlights the centrality of *charis* in the Christian life. The notion of grace as dynamic power is reflected elsewhere in the NT (Heb 4:16; 13:9; Jas 4:6; 1 Pet 5:10; 2 Pet 3:18).

(5) Grace also is *God's method of saving us.* Grace objectified is God's way of justifying sinners by faith in Jesus Christ. Paul wrote that we "are justified freely by his grace [*tē autou chariti*] through the redemption that came by Christ Jesus" (Rom 3:24). In another letter he stated, "it is by grace (*tē chariti*) you have been saved through faith" (Eph 2:8). The datives in the preceding verses are instrumental in force. Paul further wrote, "you are not under law [*hypo nomon*], but under grace" (*hypo charin*, Rom 6:14). The parallelism suggests that Paul's Jewish addressees formerly thought they could operate under the law to attain life, but later they correctly embraced salvation by grace. God's method of justification by grace is antithetical to human attempts to keep the law by self-effort (Rom 11:6; Gal 2:21).

(6) Grace is a *new state or realm entered by faith.* This sense refers to believers' present standing before God, the state of acceptance with God, the new relationship into which we are brought, and ultimately the future state of "eternal glory in Christ" (1 Pet 5:10; cf. 1:13). Paul viewed grace as a new state of affairs for Christians when he wrote, "we have gained access by faith into this grace [*eis tēn charin*] in which we now stand" (Rom 5:2; cf. Gal 5:4).

Finally (7) grace is a *synonym for the Gospel or the Christian salvation.* So rich and diverse is God's unmerited grace that in Scripture it becomes equivalent to "the Gospel," either explicitly (Col 1:5-6) or implicitly (1 Pet 5:12; Jude 4). By a similar enlargement the biblical writers employ grace as a synonym for "salvation" (2 Cor 6:1-2; 1 Pet 1:9-10) or "redemption" (Ps 111:4, 9; 130:7). Special grace is not an *entity* or a *thing* but a multifaceted love and kindness that enters our world relationally to bless and save.

Is grace properly an attribute or quality of God? To what reality does the NT phrase, "the grace of God" (Tit 2:11; Heb 2:9; 12:15) point? We have argued that grace is not an entity or a substance; and since it is predicated of God, it must be an attribute. With respect to its basic meaning (undeserved favor to sinners), it appears that grace embodies an aggregate of attributes, including God's kindness, mercy, love, compassion, freedom, omniscience, and omnipotence. This comprehensive view is preferable to regarding grace as a single attribute or perfection of God.

QUALITIES OF SPECIAL GRACE.   Scripture attests the following qualities of God's unmerited favor or grace. As the outflow of God's nature, grace (1) is absolutely *sovereign*. This implies that the initiative in saving grace is with God and not with humans. As the Lord said to Moses, "I will make all my goodness pass before thee, and . . . I will be gracious [*ḥānan*] to whom I will be gracious, and will show mercy on whom I will show mercy" (Exod 33:19, AV). The Lord of the universe bestows grace according to his sovereign purpose conceived in eternity past (Eph 2:8, 10; 2 Tim 1:9). (2) God's grace is entirely *free*. This means that God is not moved by any external constraint in bestowing grace; he does so freely in accord with his own will. Thus Paul wrote, we "are justified freely [*dōrean*] by his grace" (Rom 3:24; cf. Eph 1:6). The free and unconstrained nature of grace is supported by the fact that grace is a gift, quite undeserved but lavishly given (Rom 5:15-16; Eph 2:8; etc.). (3) God's sovereign and free grace is *abounding* in scope (Neh 9:17; Ps 86:5, 15; Jon 4:2; 2 Cor 9:8; 1 Tim 1:14). Paul used the language of abounding grace in Rom 5:15 (*perisseuō*, to "abound"), 5:17 (*perisseia*, "abundance"), and 5:20 (*hyperperisseuō*, to "abound more exceedingly"). John wrote, "From his fulness we have all received, grace upon grace" (John 1:16, NRSV). For the psalmist, *ḥesed* extends to the heavens (Ps 57:10; 103:11). (4) God's grace is *all-encompassing*. *Charis* embraces a rich variety of mercies. Recall the Petrine phrases, "the God of all grace" (1 Pet 5:10a) and "God's grace in its various forms" (4:10). And Paul, reflecting on saving grace, wrote, "All this is from God" (2 Cor 5:18).

(5) God's grace, moreover, is *sufficient* for any person in any situation facing any need. Paul experienced "weaknesses," "insults," "hardships," "persecutions," and "difficulties" (2 Cor 12:10). Yet the risen Christ said to Paul, "My grace is all you need" (v. 9, NEB). See also 1 Pet 5:10. (6) God's grace *meets people where they are*. *Ḥesed* is near to those who fear God (Ps 85:7, 9; cf. Isa 46:13). Grace precedes the saints in their daily walk (Ps 59:10). As the Lord said to Israel, "When you pass through the waters, I will be with you; and when you pass through the rivers, they will not sweep over you. When you walk through the fire, you will not be burned" (Isa 43:2). Finally (7) grace *endures forever*. God's love and grace are not relegated to the past, nor confined to the present, but continue unabated throughout eternity future. This is confirmed by the common OT refrain, "his love [*ḥesed*] endures forever" (Ps 100:5; 107:1; 136:10-26; Jer. 33:11; etc.). Recall the saying in Isa 54:8: "'with everlasting kindness [*beḥesed 'ôlām*] I will have compassion on you,' says the Lord your Redeemer."

THE EXHIBITION OF SPECIAL GRACE. In addition to biblical words and declarative statements, the reality of grace is conveyed by major events of saving history. The prophet Isaiah wrote (63:7): "I will tell of the kindnesses [*ḥesed*, pl.] of the Lord, the deeds for which he is to be praised, according to all the Lord has done for us—yes, the many good things he has done for the house of Israel, according to his compassion [*raḥᵃmîm*] and many kindnesses [*ḥesed*, pl.]." Grace, in other words, is God's favorable attitude toward people that issues in beneficent actions. Consider examples of the demonstration of grace from the OT history.

(1) Immediately following Adam and Eve's rebellion in Eden, God made a prediction that was an open declaration of his grace. To the serpent God said, "he [the 'offspring' of the woman] will crush your head, and you will strike his heel" (Gen 3:15). The holy God justly could have consigned the human race to eternal perdition. But from the fathomless wealth of his grace God announced the future redemptive sufferings of the Messiah and the defeat of Satan. This gracious announcement in the third chapter of the Bible constitutes the basis of all God's merciful dealings with his people.

(2) God's sovereign choice of Israel to be his special people is a further display of grace. The Lord said to the Israelites, "I will take you as my own people, and I will be your God" (Exod 6:7). Selection of the Hebrews among the peoples of earth for this blessing was based not on any fitness or virtue; rather, it was a sheer act of divine kindness and compassion. Thus Moses said to Israel, "The Lord your God has chosen you out of all the peoples on the face of the earth to be his people, his treasured possession. The Lord did not set his affection on you and choose you because you were more numerous than other peoples, for you were the fewest of all peoples. But it was because the Lord loved you" (Deut 7:6-8a; cf. 4:37; 14:2; Isa 41:9). By sheer grace God said to Pharaoh in the context of the plagues, "I will make a distinction between my people and your people" (Exod 8:23). This gracious choice of the nation Israel was an outcome of God's covenant with Abraham (Gen 12:1-3; 15:1-21; 17:1-21), whereby the Lord pledged to Abraham and his offspring to be their God. In fact, each of the covenants (the Abrahamic, Mosaic, Davidic, and new covenant) involves the promises of undeserved blessings and so "represents God's initiative in grace. No covenant recipient can boast of merit."[112]

(3) Yahweh's powerful deliverance of two million Israelites after 430 years of harsh slavery in Egypt represents a constellation of gracious mercies (Exod 12:31–14:31; cf. Ps 136:10-15). The Lord, the divine "warrior," fought for his ancient people Israel (Exod 14:14; 15:3). Grace was powerfully evident in the provision of the cloud and the fire that guided the path to the sea (13:21-22), in the presence of the "angel of God" before the fleeing throng (14:19a), in the dividing of the waters of the sea (14:16, 21) as Israel was hemmed in by impassible terrain, in their passage on dry

ground between the walls of water (14:22, 29; 15:19b), and in the dramatic destruction of Pharaoh's pursuing forces (14:23-28; 15:19a). Israel viewed this deliverance as an act of grace (Exod 15:13; Deut 4:37; 7:8a) and a salvific event (Exod 14:13; 15:2). Scripture portrays the Exodus redemption as a paradigm of the wider spiritual salvation (Ps 74:2; 107:2; Isa 43:1; Jer 31:11).

Other displays of grace in Israel's history include (4) guidance through the wilderness from the Sea of Reeds to Sinai, including the provisions of quail and bread from heaven and water from the rock (Exod 15:22–18:12; cf. Deut 8:15-17; Ps 136:16-20) as well as guidance from Sinai to the plains of Moab (Num 10:11–22:1). (5) Repeated acts of forgiveness and the withholding of judgment in the face of flagrant sin. Consider God's dealings following the golden calf incident (Exod 32:11-14) and Israel's many acts of disobedience from the time of the Judges to the exile (Ps 106:43-46). And (6) restoration of the Jews following the Babylonian exile. Undeserved mercies include the repopulations under Zerubbabel in 538 B.C. (Ezra 2; Neh 7:6-73), Ezra the scribe in 458 (Ezra 7–8), and Nehemiah in 445 (Neh 2); the rebuilding of the temple and renewal of the temple worship (Ezra 3; 5:1–6:22); and the rediscovery of God's law by Ezra (Neh 8:1-18). Scripture elsewhere depicts Israel's return from captivity as a gracious act of salvation (Isa 26:1-2; 43:1, 5-6; 49:8; Jer 30:11; 31:11; 33:6-8).

We will briefly mention several displays of grace in the NT history. (1) The first, both in time and importance, was the birth of Jesus Christ. In the fullness of time, God's grace became incarnate in the person of his Son. So John wrote, "grace and truth came through Jesus Christ" (John 1:17; cf. 1:14). Grace was manifest in Mary's conception through supernatural agency (Matt 1:18; Luke 1:35); hence the angel called her "highly favored" (Luke 1:28, perfect passive participle of *charitoō*, to "bestow grace," "show favor"). Grace emerged in the name given to Mary's son ("Jesus"), which indicates that "he will save his people from their sins" (Matt 1:21). Grace was further manifest in the angel's warning that Herod sought to kill Mary's infant son (Matt 2:13). Christ's birth truly was the paramount gracious, saving event (Luke 1:68-79; 2:11, 30-32).

(2) The event of Pentecost in A.D. 30 (Acts 2) involved a powerful display of grace. The mighty outpouring of the Holy Spirit with wind and fire (vv. 2-3, 33), the inward transformation of the disciples that caused them to speak in unlearned languages (vv. 6, 8-11), Peter's bold proclamation of Jesus (vv. 14-36), and the Spirit's convicting work that led to the conversion of 3,000 hearers (vv. 37, 41) were miracles of grace. (3) The conversion of Saul, the zealous persecutor of the church, likewise was a

mighty act of grace. Saul was a Pharisee who went from house to house to imprison Christians (Acts 8:3; 9:1-2; 26:10-11) and to persecute, terrorize, and destroy the fledgling church (Acts 9:21; Gal 1:13). Concerning his pre-conversion ragings against God and his people, Paul wrote: "I was once a blasphemer and a persecutor and a violent man" (1 Tim 1:13). But en route to Damascus to apprehend Christians, Saul was supernaturally subdued by the risen Lord Jesus (Acts 9:1-9). In that experience of blinding light Saul was made a new creature in Christ. Later reflecting on that transforming experience, Paul said in 1 Tim 1:13-14 (cf. Gal 1:15), "I was shown mercy," and "The grace [*charis*] of our Lord was poured out on me abundantly." This dramatic transformation from a violent antagonist of Christianity to its outstanding advocate is a powerful testimony to divine grace.

E. *Prevenient Grace*

Much debate surrounds the issue of how God's grace is prevenient to the sinner's first positive response to God. Both Reformed and Arminians agree that grace is prevenient in the general sense that God initiates the first movement in salvation (Ps 80:3; 85:4; Jer 31:18). Wesleyans and Arminians insist that prevenient grace savingly engages all people, whereas the Reformed limit its efficacy to the elect, or the "sheep," given by the Father to the Son. Arminians envisage prevenient grace as that action of the Spirit that mitigates inherited depravity and corruption universally. This "sufficient grace" is said to restore to all sinners the ability to respond to the Gospel call. Since depravity is judged to be neutralized by prevenient grace, Arminians posit an optimistic view of sinners in their empirical condition. The Scripture texts we have adduced earlier in support of real human depravity appear to contradict this claim of restored spiritual ability in sinners universally.

(1) To clarify the meaning of the phrase "prevenient grace," consider Jesus' words to the crowd gathered for the Passover feast (John 12:32): "But I, when I am lifted up from the earth, will draw all men to myself." Jesus' audience included not only Jews but "some Greeks" (v. 20) or non-proselyte Gentiles. The Lord's words suggest that his saving work was intended for both ethnic Jews and Gentiles, as he and his apostles plainly taught in John 10:16, John 11:52, Acts 10:34-35, and elsewhere. In other words, John 12:32 means that "Christ will draw people to himself without regard for nationality, ethnic affiliation or status."[113] (2) Recall Jesus' teaching regarding the Paraclete's ministry in John 16:8: "When he comes, he will convict [*elenxei*] the world of guilt in regard to sin and righteous-

ness and judgment." The verb *elenchō* means "expose," "refute," or "convict."[114] Jesus undoubtedly had in mind here several contrasting ministries of the Spirit. The Spirit helps or assists believers (John 14:16-17, 26) but exposes and convicts the world of the gravity of their sin. There is no hint that this convicting work of the Spirit changes the carnal dispositions of sinners universally. (3) Consider also Tit 2:11, where Paul wrote that "the grace of God that brings salvation has appeared [*epephanē*] to all men." The "grace of God" Paul referred to here is the kindness of God in Jesus Christ (cf. 2 Tim 1:9), not the person of the Holy Spirit. The aorist passive of *epiphainō* points to the past event of Christ's manifestation in history for the purpose of salvation, consistent with Paul's Epiphany Christology described in 1 Tim 3:16. The context of Tit 2:11, moreover, indicates that the condition of the unsaved is thoroughgoing moral and spiritual corruption (cf. 1:15-16).

The ample biblical teaching cited earlier concerning the moral and spiritual depravity of the unsaved likewise argues against the hypothesis that prevenient grace has neutralized inherited sin in pre-Christians. Scripture depicts the unsaved as blind to spiritual truths (1 Cor 2:14; 2 Cor 4:4; Eph 4:18), as "dead" or unresponsive to spiritual concerns (Eph 2:1-3, 5; Col 2:13), as slaves to the law of sin (John 8:34; Rom 6:16-20; 7:25), as haters of the light (Ps 139:21a; John 3:20), and as rebels against God (Isa 30:9; 48:8; Rom 3:11-12). The Bible hardly portrays the unsaved as liberated from the darkening and debilitating effects of original sin. Indeed, the very opposite is the case. It appears that Arminians have introduced their interpretation of prevenient grace to support the universality of Christ's saving work and the freedom of the will in all persons. Consider the judgment of a late British scholar: "This doctrine [of sufficient grace] is evolved in a sincere attempt to do justice to the idea of universality in the gospel; but this avowedly 'sufficient' grace shows itself to be quite 'insufficient' for its purpose."[115]

Prevenient grace as a soteriological concept refers to the grace that works in the elect to illumine their darkened minds, soften their contrary wills, and incline their affections toward Christ and his offer of salvation. This concept is discussed in the following section and more fully in chapter 5.

F. Effectual or Irresistible Grace?

Older Reformed authorities often described God's special grace as irresistible. There is an element of truth in the phrase "irresistible grace," in that no mortal finally can thwart God's sovereign purpose. Scripture indicates that penultimately people can and do resist the Spirit's operation (Acts 7:51; 26:14; Heb 12:25). But ultimately human resistance does not prevail, for the Spirit exerts on the souls of chosen sinners an influence of sufficient grace and power to cause the Father's saving purpose to bear fruit. We suggest that this life-transforming operation of the Holy Spirit be denominated not "irresistible grace" but "effectual grace," "invincible grace," or "indefectible grace." All of us are familiar with the game of tug-of-war. In the spiritual realm, it is not true that God drags sinners into his kingdom against their wills, kicking and screaming. The unwilling do not enter the kingdom of God; only the *willing* do. But God's omnipotent Spirit powerfully moves on sinners' hearts to make those formerly unwilling *willing* to come to Christ. Thus God's grace is "irresistible in the sense that it is efficacious, that once it enters into the life of man it will penetrate his inner being and alter his will."[116]

Scripture amply supports the concept of effectual grace. By grace God causes his Word to take root in lives (Jer 31:33) and bring about meaningful hearing at the spiritual level (John 10:16, 27). Effectual grace, in other words, quickens unbelieving hearts to know and trust Christ. As the Lord said through the prophet, "I will give them a heart to know me, that I am the Lord" (Jer 24:7a). Special grace, furthermore, frees the unregenerate from the bondage of sin (Rom 6:18; 8:2), draws sinners effectively to Christ (John 6:37, 44), and imparts spiritual life to the dead (Eph 2:4-5). In sum, effectual grace enables spiritually impotent sinners to embrace Christ unto salvation (John 6:65). It should be clear from this discussion that effectual grace is prevenient, in the general sense that it precedes sinners' decision for Christ (see section E above). But prevenient grace, as here defined, not only prepares pre-Christians to respond, it actually evokes their Christ-honoring responses (effectual grace). The thrust of the Bible's teaching is that without God's prevenient (i.e., effectual) grace no sinner, in fact, would trust Christ unto salvation.

How shall we understand the relation between effectual grace and human freedom? God's wise and powerful benevolence in action effectively restores forfeited human freedom (defined as the power of contrary choice spiritually) in responsible agents by radically changing the disposition of their sinful hearts. In other words, the personal love-activity of God works compellingly on hearts such that sinners now act freely to welcome Christ in accord with their deepest wishes. We noted above that sinners can be saved only through their willing assent; but effectual grace makes unwilling hearts personally willing and impotent hearts personally potent to respond freely to God's offer of life. Effectual grace, in other words, creates the conditions of knowing, desiring, and willing that are necessary for sinners to be saved. This discussion coheres with the compatibilist view of freedom (as opposed to the indeterminist), whereby the Spirit decisively inclines the human will Godward without forcing it to act against its wishes. For further interaction with this problem of divine sovereignty and human freedom, see the volume on God in this series. In any case, in the discussion of free will and salvation we must avoid two errors of extremes: (1) that alleged human free will is a cause or ground of salvation, and (2) that one is saved by grace apart from an authentic, personal response.

G. Grace in Relation to Law-keeping

Many Jews erroneously thought they could attain salvation by trusting their racial descent from Abraham (Acts 22:3; 2 Cor 11:22) and by attempting to perform the requirements of the law (Luke 18:18; Gal 1:14; Phil 3:5-6). Law (*tôrāh*, *nomos*) variously designates (1) the Pentateuch, or the first five books of the OT (1 Chron 22:12-13), (2) the Mosaic code, with its civil, ceremonial, and moral statutes (Deut 4:5, 8), and (3) generally, all the ordinances, precepts, and commandments enjoined by God in the OT (Ps 1:2; 19:7-9; John 10:34). The NT teaches that as a *method of salvation* grace is opposed to law-keeping. As a means of attaining eternal life, law-keeping has been a complete failure. No mortal has ever gained right standing with God by fulfilling works required by the law. Paul, the cultured Jew, reflected on his personal experience and concluded that righteousness cannot be attained by the works of the law. "Clearly no one is justified before God by the law" (Gal 3:11; cf. Rom 3:20a; Gal 2:21; 3:21). Because righteousness requires performance of the entire law (Gal 5:3; Jas 2:10), the person who violates one point thereof breaks the whole and thus forfeits life (Matt 5:19). Scripture realistically teaches that the sinful heart is incapable of satisfying God's moral requirements and securing right standing before the Judge of the universe (Rom 3:20a; 8:3a, 8). In the words of Paul, the path of law-keeping represents a "law of sin and death" (Rom 8:2). This discussion does not nullify the fact that the law exercises certain salutary functions. Thus the law (1) reveals God's character and will (Lev 19), (2) discloses the depths of human sin (Rom 3:20b; 7:5, 7; 1 Cor 15:56), (3) condemns sin in sinners (Rom 3:19), and (4) points up the need for salvation through God's gracious initiative in Jesus Christ (Gal 3:23-24).

As discussed above, grace signifies God doing for sinners what sinners could never do by their best, unaided efforts. Theologically, grace is God through Jesus Christ performing for the unrighteous "the righteous requirements of the law" (Rom 8:4). From the biblical perspective, grace is completely antithetical to works of the law as a means of attaining salvation (Rom 4:16; 6:14; 11:6; Gal 5:4; Eph 2:8-9). The gracious gift of God is thoroughly opposed to all human striving and merit (Rom 4:4-5). God's grace efficiently conveys salvation, whereas humanly contrived works consistently fall short of the Almighty's righteous requirements. It should be noted that grace is not antithetical to law, per se, for the moral law is a reflection of God's character and is a gift of his goodness. What grace opposes is men and women's futile attempts to gain God's favor by their own strivings.

H. Saving Grace and Non-Christian Religions

Some theologians claim that saving grace is at work in the non-Christian religions. The Anglo-Catholic James A. Carpenter asserts, "If grace is the key to the Christian reality, it has to be in some sense a universal reality, operative at all levels of existence and certainly in the higher reaches of the religious life the world over, however obscured by religious practices and beliefs."[117] Concerning this hotly contested issue, it is imperative that we be guided by clear evidence and not merely by our emotions. The fact is that grace is not a prominent theme in the non-Christian religions, be it animism, Buddhism, Hinduism, or Shintoism. Most of these religions seek to please the higher powers by personal effort, self-denial, or virtuous works. It appears that certain Christian theologians have invested non-Christian religions with more grace (defined as God's unmerited favor) than the religions claim for themselves.

To address this problem we consider four proposals in the form of questions to be tested against the relevant evidence. (1) *Is saving grace present in nature and world history universally?* The missionary writer Don Richardson answers this question affirmatively. Abraham, he argues, was the first recipient of special revelation ("the Abraham factor"), whereas Melchizedek and all godly pre-Abrahamites (Adam, Enoch, Noah, etc.) possessed only general revelation and were saved by its light ("the Melchizedek factor"). For Richardson, general revelation is older than and superior to special revelation. Hence special revelation must bow to general revelation, even as Abraham paid homage to Melchizedek (Gen 14:18-20). The outcome of this theology is the claim that without explicit knowledge of Christ and the Gospel many "low threshhold-of-resistance" people are saved by the light of nature and by "redemptive analogies" (viewed as the product of common grace and general revelation) embedded in their culture. Scripture is clear, however, that God granted many *pre-Abrahamites* special revelation from earliest times—e.g., Adam, Eve, Noah, Enoch, etc.. We concur with the African theologian Tite Tienou that "the enigmatic Melchizedek is a type of special revelation, not general revelation."[118] Biblical texts such as Ps 19:1-4, John 1:4, 9, Acts 14:17; 17:24-28, Rom 1:18-20, and Rom 2:14-15 state that all people acquire rudimentary knowledge of God from the moral law within and from nature and history without. We have shown elsewhere that what general revelation communicates to people universally is limited comprehension of God's existence, character, and moral demands.[119] But sin-darkened rebels quickly reject and distort this non-salvific knowledge (Rom 1:18, 21-23, 28) and worship idols instead of God (1:23, 25). Thus God's common goodness does not save; on the contrary, it renders all persons "without excuse" (*anapologetos*, 1:20). J.I. Packer concludes, "The Bible says that God's general revelation, even when correctly grasped, yields knowledge of creation, providence, and judgment only, not of grace that restores sinners to fellowship with God." He continues, "Non-Christian religions exhibit much that is noble and many insights that are true, but they do not exhibit saving grace."[120]

In Acts 17 Paul ministered to idol-worshipers, Epicureans, and Stoics who possessed only common grace and general revelation and who had never heard of the Christian message. He noted that his audience in the idol-rich city of Athens were "very religious" (v. 22) and that they had erected an altar with the inscription, "TO AN UNKNOWN GOD" (v. 23). In spite of their intense religiosity they had not been reached by saving grace, for the sophisticated Greeks regarded Paul's teaching as new doctrine about a foreign god (vv. 18-19). The apostle insisted that the Athenians must repent (v. 30) and believe (v. 34) the message about the risen Christ (v. 31; cf. 10:36). Common grace prepares the way for the coming of special grace, even as general revelation prepares the way for special revelation (v. 27).

But is it not possible that the unsaved, blessed by common grace, might cast themselves on the mercy of the God they know in part and so be saved? We judge this unlikely, for apart from God's special working on the heart the unconverted are afflicted with sin-darkened minds and an anti-God bias. Quoting the OT, Paul wrote: "there is no one who understands, no one who seeks God. All have turned away, they have together become worthless; there is no one who does good, not even one. . . . There is no fear of God before their eyes" (Rom 3:11-12, 18). We concur with Carl Henry, who said: "The notion that apart from redemptive revelation some persons might repent of sin and throw themselves on the mercy of God has no express biblical support; repentance and faith are gifts of the self-revealing God who has provided a Savior."[121] Thus our answer to the first question reluctantly must be *no*.

(2) *Is saving grace present in human experience universally?* As noted above, Rahner claimed that God and grace penetrate all of nature and impart to it divine life. Blessed by grace and energized by the "supernatural existential" (the dynamic impulse that orientates all persons to Mystery), the human spirit preconceptually apprehends the divine Reality. Thus "Every human being is really and truly exposed to the influence of divine, supernatural grace which offers interior union with God."[122] Rahner added that the person who follows his conscience and accepts his orientation to the Absolute—even though formally an atheist—dwells in a graced state existentially. The person who implicitly reaches out beyond himself in an act of self-transcendence—be he a Buddhist, Hindu, or atheist—is said to be an "anonymous Christian." The latter phrase, Rahner defined as "the pagan . . . who lives in a state of Christ's grace through faith, hope and love, yet who has no explicit knowledge of the fact that his life is orientated in grace-given salvation to Jesus Christ."[123] Salvation, according to Rahner, is by grace; but Christ and grace are implicitly operative in the whole of human experience, including that offered by the world's religions. Thus the entire world, Rahner insisted, is an "anonymous Christendom."

Clark Pinnock expresses his preference for the views of Rahner and the Second Vatican Council. Pinnock defines grace as God's providential presence in all his creatures that directs them to salvation. Saving grace, so defined, is a function of God's general providence. Grace is not restricted to the sphere of Christianity, but is contained in and mediated by the non-Christian religions. Pinnock, in fact, regards the world's major religions as God-ordained systems for mediating grace to their faithful adherents and for advancing God's kingdom purposes.[124] Pinnock is optimistic concerning the salvation of the heathen apart from Gospel proclamation on the basis of common grace. In this way Pinnock argues for the inclusivity rather than the exclusivity of grace.

We judge that Rahner, Vatican II, and Pinnock have overreacted to the Thomistic epistemology by affirming that saving grace penetrates nature, to the end that all persons are embraced and claimed by it. However, Scripture support is lacking for the notion that humankind is efficiently enveloped by the grace that justifies and saves. Rahner's transcendental theology weakens the importance of the cross and minimizes the biblical demands of repentance, faith, and volitional commitment to Christ. It also disregards the determined opposition of atheism and unbelief to the claims of Jesus Christ. Thus our answer to the second question must also be *no*.

(3) *Is saving grace mediated through the message of Christ and the*

Gospel? The clear burden of the NT is that saving grace comes through the person of Jesus Christ. Peter, speaking of God's dealings with Gentiles and Jews, said, "We believe it is through the grace of our Lord Jesus that we are saved, just as they are" (Acts 15:11; cf. John 1:17; 2 Tim 2:1; 1 Pet 5:10; Rev 22:21). And the NT asserts that the same saving grace is contained in the Gospel message (Acts 14:3; Col 1:5-6). This grace of God conveyed by Christ and the Gospel clearly possesses the power to save. As Paul wrote to Titus, "the grace of God that brings salvation has appeared to all men" (Tit 2:11; cf. 3:7). Thus the biblical revelation presents Jesus as the sole and exclusive way to the Father (John 14:6; Acts 4:12; 1 Tim 2:5). For this Christological reason Christianity is not just one way among many; it is "the Way" (Acts 9:2; 19:9, 23). Hence our answer to this third question must be a resounding *yes*.

(4) *Is saving grace mediated through special revelatory disclosures to the individual soul?* Scripture indicates that certain individuals came to God redemptively outside the framework of Israel. The Jewish book of I Enoch indicates that the man Enoch received special revelations concerning the heavenly world. According to Wisdom 4:10 and 15, the saving initiative in Enoch's life originated with the sovereign God. Enoch is "loved by God," and "God's grace and mercy are with his elect." We also appeal to Christ's revelation of himself to Saul en route to Damascus. Hence scriptural precedent, certain contemporary witnesses, and the divine sovereignty and freedom suggest the possibility that Christ may choose to reveal himself specially to a person who has not previously heard the Good News. What is special and different here is not the content of the Gospel message, but the manner in which the message is revealed. Of course, in acknowledging God's freedom to reveal himself savingly to a human soul, we do not legitimize all alleged 'experiences of God.' The reader should note that the view presented is not that of a person casting himself on the mercy of God as a result of his own searchings. The possibility we hold open is that of a supernatural and contentful revelation of Christ to the soul, which elicits the free response of faith and commitment. In such a case the person is saved through personal encounter with Jesus Christ. Our answer to this fourth question, then, is *yes,* in exceptional cases.

In sum, saving grace does not inhere in the world's non-Christian religions. In God's goodness significant elements of truth are found in Buddhism, Hinduism, Shintoism, etc., but not the grace of Christ that redeems the soul. The uniqueness of Jesus Christ and the work he accomplished on the cross are biblical norms that must not be compromised in the name of modernity.

I. Grace in Relation to the Plan of Salvation

As a rich and multifaceted concept, grace is the fountainhead of salvation and a reality present in every aspect of the Christian redemption. The all-encompassing character of grace vis-à-vis salvation is clear in texts such as Eph 2:8 and Tit 2:11.

Specifically, grace undergirds (1) the doctrine of election to life. Paul wrote concerning the core of believing Jews, "there is a remnant chosen by grace" (*kat eklogen charitos*, Rom 11:5; cf. Eph 1:4-6). (2) The doctrine of *effectual calling*. Concerning his life-transforming encounter with Christ near Damascus, the apostle wrote, "God . . . called me by his grace" (Gal 1:15). (3) The doctrine of *faith*. Luke described disciples in Achaia as "those who by grace had believed" (Acts 18:27).

(4) The *forgiveness of sins*. Here we cite the words of Paul: "In him we have . . . the forgiveness of sins, in accordance with the riches of God's grace that he lavished on us with all wisdom and understanding" (Eph 1:7-8). (5) The doctrine of *justification*. Paul wrote that saints "are justified freely by his grace through the redemption that came by Jesus Christ" (Rom 3:24; cf. Tit 3:7). (6) The doctrine of *regeneration*. Peter wrote concerning the heavenly Father, "In his great mercy [*eleos*] he has given us new birth" (1 Pet 1:3).

(7) The doctrine of *sanctification*. Grace delivers believers from the dominion of sin and enables them to become experientially holy. Thus Peter commanded Christians to "grow in the grace and knowledge of our Lord and Savior Jesus Christ" (2 Pet 3:18; cf. Rom 6:11-23). (8) The reality of *giftedness spiritually*. In the words of Paul, "we have different gifts [*charismata*], according to the grace given us" (Rom 12:6; cf. Eph 4:7). (9) The *victorious Christian life*. Hear Christ's words to Paul concerning his persistent illness: "My grace is sufficient for you, for my power is made perfect in weakness" (2 Cor 12:9). (10) The doctrine of *perseverance* or the *preservation of the saints*. Paul enjoined Timothy to "be strong in the grace that is in Christ Jesus" (2 Tim 2:1; cf. v. 3). Finally, (11) grace relates to the doctrine of *eternal life*. As expressed by Paul, "grace increased all the more, so that . . . grace might reign through righteousness to bring eternal life through Jesus Christ our Lord" (Rom 5:21; cf. v. 17). So pertinent is grace to each aspect of the plan of salvation that the great Spurgeon could write, "We see a golden thread of grace moving through the whole of the Christian's history, from his election before all worlds, even to his admission to the heavenly rest."[125]

IV. PRACTICAL IMPLICATIONS OF
THE DOCTRINE OF GRACE

A. *Common Grace:*
Care for the Created Order

Since "everything God created is good" (1 Tim 4:4) and represents the gift of his universal grace, believers and unbelievers alike should show respect and care for God's benevolent provisions in the natural order. God has commanded that earth's natural resources, animal life, and the environment itself should be managed wisely for the good of present and future generations (Gen 1:26, 28). Ample evidence indicates, however, that people have not done well in the stewardship of the gifts of God's grace in nature. Consider the widespread destruction of the rain forests of South America with disastrous effects on the landscape and the atmosphere. Or reflect on the widespread pollution of the soil and water table. The Rocky Mountain Arsenal, an army weapons manufacturing and storage site on the Northeast side of Denver, is said to be the most polluted piece of land on the planet. Poisoned by years of careless dumping of the effluents of chemical and nuclear weapons production, the land will take decades and hundreds of billions of dollars to clean up—if that is even possible. Twenty-five miles to the West is the Rocky Flats nuclear weapons plant, which likewise has heavily polluted the land and water table with deadly radioactive waste materials. Or consider our reckless consumption of earth's natural resources. Three or four generations will have consumed all of earth's known and accessible petroleum supplies. Moreover, in the United States 8 percent of the world's population consumes nearly 40 per cent of the world's energy production. This country uses more energy in its air conditioners than the total domestic and industrial energy consumed in the People's Republic of China with its far greater population.

Given the pollution of water, air, and soil and our reckless wastage of earth's resources, an eleventh commandment might be appended to the Decalogue: "You shall honor the created order and treat it with respect and care." Christians do not deify nor worship nature as pantheists commonly do. Neither are we rabid environmentalists with the single agenda of saving the earth. But a respectful treatment of the earth and a measured use of its resources—as gifts of God's common grace—are appropriate responses to God's lavish gifts in creation. God commands people everywhere to "subdue" the earth and not sully or spoil it, to "rule" over its creatures and not ravage or ruin them, and to have dominion over the creation and not destroy or devastate it. We do well to consider Noah who built an ark to preserve living things from being destroyed by the Flood (Gen 6:19–7:3). There is considerable truth and wisdom in the words of the Swiss theologian Emil Brunner, who said, "God's (common) grace is our task."

B. Common Grace:
Appreciate God's Gifts in Human Culture

Christians ought to recognize and celebrate the gifts of God's bounty embedded in the institutions of human society. We should give thanks for the divinely ordained institution of marriage (Gen 2:20b-24), involving the joys of spouse, children, and extended family. We ought to celebrate God's benevolent provisions in the institution of government, in the systems of education, in the provisions for health care, and in the possibilities for productive employment (Gen 1:28; 2:19-20). We should acknowledge that God's grace is reflected in all that is true and noble in the arts, and that responsible music, painting, and poetry nurture creative and emotional faculties in people. God's universal grace is further reflected in the valid discoveries of the sciences that often enhance the length and quality of our lives. God's benevolence is likewise displayed in positive systems of recreation and sport that contribute to health and well-being (1 Tim 4:8a).

Christians, of all people, should be alert for evidences of God's bounty across the entire spectrum of human life and culture. We should celebrate and announce to the world that the good, the beautiful, and the beneficial in life is not fortuitous but derives from the kindly hand of God. The doctrine of common grace should prompt us to shout from the rooftops that ours is anything but a God-forsaken world! The Creator God universally is present to the world in his kindness and beneficence, even if the world universally is not present to him. We are to look for and identify the good hand of God across the continuum of life. We should celebrate the fact that the world is under God's control, not Satan's. And Scripture informs us that the God who controls nature and history is a God of goodness and bounty.

C. Special Grace:
Experience the Reality

The believer in Jesus needs the reality of grace to prosper in the Christian life. By grace through faith one becomes a Christian, and by grace through faith one lives as a Christian. One simply cannot make it as a follower of Christ without the bounty of God's grace. That is why Paul began most of his letters with the salutation, "Grace and peace to you from God our

Father and the Lord Jesus Christ" (1 Cor 1:3; 2 Cor 1:2; Gal 1:3; etc.). Paul's words of greeting were no mere formality; they conveyed the sincere desire of his heart for his Christian readers. Thus daily there must be an opening of the believer's heart to God and a humble receiving of his favor. In the times of adversity, failure, guilt, confusion, and defeat that come upon us all, the child of God needs to grasp firmly the grace that ministers to the deepest needs of the soul. The apostle Paul knew the reality of God's grace in the severe trials that came his way. As he wrote to the Corinthians, "We are hard pressed on every side, but not crushed; perplexed, but not in despair; persecuted, but not abandoned; struck down, but not destroyed" (2 Cor 4:8-9). In the same letter Paul recorded Christ's encouragement to him as he experienced his troublesome "thorn" in the flesh: "My grace is sufficient for you, for my power is made perfect in weakness" (12:9). Only God's grace can rescue us from the dark nights of our deepest failures.

The forgiven person should not only possess a theoretical understanding of God's grace with the mind; he or she must also experience the reality of God's kindness and mercy in the heart. Intellectual assent to the doctrine of grace must be balanced by deep personal resonance with the reality of grace in the life. After being delivered by the angel of the Lord from a fearful trial (Ps 34:6-7, 17-22), David responded with the words, "Taste and see that the Lord is good; blessed is the man who takes refuge in him" (v. 8). The first verb, *ṭā'am*, means to "taste," "perceive," or "understand." It involves personal experience, discernment, and evaluation (cf. Prov 24:13-14; John 8:52; Heb 2:9; 1 Pet 2:3). The second verb, *rā'āh*, means to "see," "regard," and metaphorically, to "enjoy" (Ps 27:13). Some scholars suggest that the latter verb derives from *yr'* and so means to "be fat, sated, drink deeply." Truly what the psalmist enjoined was participation in the reality of God's goodness personally and affectively (cf. Jer 5:12; 14:13; 20:18).

The believer receives and experiences the consolation of grace by the act of dependent faith and trust. We need to remember that God's goodness comes from above as an unconditional blessing; we can not manufacture this bounty by our creaturely intellect, will, or emotions. But the saint may create an environment for the reception of grace by the regular exercise of spiritual disciplines such as Bible study and meditation, observance of the Lord's Supper, and voluntary fasting. It will also be helpful to read the biographies of great Christians and learn how they experienced the grace of God in response to their sin and guilt. We commend the life stories of great servants such as St. Augustine, whom God rescued from deep lasciviousness, and John Newton (the author of the hymn "Amazing

Grace"), who was delivered by grace from a life of drunkenness, sexual rage, and slave-trading. God customarily bestows his gifts through biblically appointed means that we recognize as the spiritual disciplines.

The Christian man or woman cannot adequately commend the grace and goodness of God to others unless he or she first experiences its healing, consoling, and revitalizing power. The Word of God promises that personal engagement with *ḥesed* or *charis* will result in a deep inner peace and contentment, compassion for others, endurance in the face of trials, and power for kingdom service. Paul, the greatest Christian apostle, recognized that his success as a godly servant of Christ was due to God's grace made real in his life. His epitaph might well read, "by the grace of God I am what I am" (1 Cor 15:10a). God's exhortation to each of his children is recorded in the letter to the Hebrews: "Let us then approach the throne of grace with confidence, so that we may receive mercy and find grace to help us in our time of need" (Heb 4:16). We do not presume on God's grace in the form of license (cf. Heb 10:26-29); rather we receive it gratefully and live and serve through its life-giving power.

D. Special Grace:
Respond Appropriately

If God has been redemptively gracious to us as Christians, we ought to respond gratefully to him. Since the word "grace" bears the fundamental sense of "thanks" or "gratitude," we who have experienced his bountiful kindness and favor in Jesus Christ should return the gift of thanks to God for blessings received. God deserves every expression of gratitude we can give, and our own hearts will be enlarged by such responses of thanksgiving and praise. A Russian peasant once complained that he had no shoes to wear on his feet. Then he saw a man crawling along the dirt path who had no feet. Grateful for his family, health, and modest possessions, the peasant gave thanks to God for his goodness.

Our gratitude toward God for grace received, furthermore, should express itself in faithful and loving service. Service to God should be performed not legalistically or out of a sense of duty. Such performance-oriented service is, in fact, no service at all. Rather, our service to God should be motivated by gratitude in response to his grace working in us. As Samuel said in his farewell speech to Israel, "be sure to fear the Lord and serve him faithfully with all your heart; consider what great things he has done for you" (1 Sam 12:24).

Since God's grace is an *attitude* of unconditional favor to the undeserving, Spirit-filled believers ought to display a gracious attitude and kindly demeanor to others about them. From the experienced superabundance of God's grace, our lives should be characterized by a winsomeness and an attractiveness that is heavenly. Christians, of all people, should exude a spirit of generosity that is not limited to the giving of seasonal gifts. Believers will joyfully discover that their generous attitude, by God's grace, will generate kindness and compassion in others. As St. Augustine on one occasion said to God, "Because you loved me, you made me lovable."

Moreover, since grace is an *action* exercised toward the unworthy, Christians ought to deal benevolently with others. Believers should treat others with liberality, generosity, and mercy, whether the latter are deserving of such favor or not. As our Lord Jesus said, "love your enemies, do good to them, and lend to them without expecting to get anything back. Then your reward will be great, and you will be sons of the Most High, because he is kind to the ungrateful and wicked" (Luke 6:35; cf. v. 27). Paul the apostle similarly added, "as we have opportunity, let us do good to all people, especially to those who belong to the family of believers" (Gal 6:10). The Anglican churchman Griffith-Thomas helpfully commented in this regard, "Grace is, first, a quality of graciousness in the Giver, and then, a quality of gratitude in the recipient, which in turn makes him gracious to those around."[126]

"JACOB I LOVED"

ROMANS 9:13

————□————

THE DOCTRINE OF ELECTION

I. INTRODUCTORY
CONCERNS

As we continue to reflect on God's grand plan of salvation, our attention in this chapter turns to the doctrine of election. Election concerns the plan or purpose of God, executed in eternity past, to save condemned sinners and restore them to fellowship with himself. Some Christians are reluctant to discuss election because of its perceived esoteric nature and the controversy it has engendered. But because Scripture considers election with some frequency and directness, faithful believers ought not dismiss the doctrine as unworthy of consideration. Rather, we should carefully search the Scriptures to determine what they teach on this difficult subject. The place within Christian theology where election is properly discussed is also significant. Election should be treated not under the doctrine of God but in the context of the doctrine of salvation as an implication of grace. The doctrine of election, in other words, is not a matter for speculation but of recalling what God has done to bless believers with salvation. Even though his own representation of the doctrine was flawed, Barth reminded us of the importance of this doctrine in the overall scheme of salvation: "The doctrine of election is the sum of the Gospel."[1]

A number of important issues associated with the doctrine require careful examination. Does election concern God's appointment of some persons to *service only*, to *salvation*, or to *both*? Moreover, is election *conditional*, based on God's foresight of a person's response to the Gospel, or is it *unconditional*, grounded entirely in God's sovereign will? This question asks whether logically divine election follows human faith or whether faith follows election. If election be unconditional, how does the doctrine differ from pagan determinism or Islamic fatalism? Is election *passive*, being God's ratification of the human decision to trust Christ, or is it *active*, being God's sovereign determination to save some? Furthermore, is election to salvation *corporate*, or *individual*, or perhaps *both*? Does God's elective decree concern the class of those who will believe, or does it pertain to specific individuals whom God has foreknown and chosen? This prompts us to ask whether election rests on God's *prescience* or his *foreknowledge*? What does Scripture mean when it affirms that God 'foreknows' the saints? Does it mean that God in his omniscience foresees the human responses of faith? Or more profoundly, is foreknowledge a biblical idiom for God graciously setting his love upon and choosing sinners to be saved? In addition, is divine election *single*, unto eternal life, or *double*, unto eternal life and eternal death? Does the doctrine of unconditional election to salvation necessitate as a corollary unconditional election to damnation (the doctrine of reprobation)? How did great saints of the past, such as Luther, Calvin, Owen, and Bunyan, justify biblically their belief in double predestination? Does the OT present a different perspective on the doctrine of election than the NT, and if so in what respects?

Furthermore, what is the role of Jesus Christ in God's elective program? What does the biblical language of election "in Christ" mean? Does the phrase signify that we are elect in our quality as believers as foreseen by God in his omniscience? Or does it specify God's purpose to bring salvation on the ground or basis of Christ's obedient life and atoning death?

How shall we respond to objections that the doctrine of unconditional election is unfair and ultimately unworthy of God? Does the doctrine of unconditional election clash with the character of God as biblically revealed? If God has sovereignly determined who will be saved, would this render preaching, persuasion, and prayer for the lost unnecessary? Does such a view of election engender complacent living and undermine the quest for a holy life, as Wesley insisted? Furthermore, what are the practical values and consolations of the doctrine of election for believers? How does Scripture set forth its positive function in the lives of the saints? This raises the question of whether the doctrine of election should be preached widely to the world, as Spurgeon urged, or whether it should be taught only to the people of God in the church.

When dealing with the subject of election we must be as honest and objective as possible, for we are dealing with a hotly debated and highly emotional issue. We must resolve to be guided by an objective under-standing of biblical teaching rather than by our human sensibilities that often prove mutable and fickle. In assessing the issue of election we must be careful not to read into Scripture our own presuppositions and biases. As Jewett reminded us, "The question of individual election has led more people to read Scripture for what they want to find (rather than to listen to Scripture for what they are afraid to hear) than virtually any other the-ological issue."[2]

II. HISTORICAL INTERPRETATIONS OF ELECTION

To gain perspective on the doctrine of election and its corollary issues iden-tified above, we will summarize the principal ways in which Christians his-torically have understood biblical teaching on this important subject.

A. Conditional Election (Classical Arminians)

Many early church Fathers, concerned to avoid pagan fatalism and Gnostic determinism, stressed the freedom of the human will and its ability to repent and exercise faith. A number of pre-Augustinian authorities thus viewed salvation synergistically, the human will freely cooperating with the Spirit to the attainment of salvation. Origen (d. 254) held that the predes-tination language of the Bible encouraged pagan fatalism. Thus he based election on divine foreknowledge of free, human actions. He wrote:

> Foreknowledge *precedes* foreordination. . . . God observed before-hand the sequence of future events, and noticed the inclination of some men towards piety which followed on this inclination; and he foreknew them, knowing the present and foreknowing the future. . . . If anyone in reply asks whether it is possible for the events which God foreknew not to happen, we shall answer, Yes, and there is no necessity determining this happening or not happening.[3]

Commenting on 2 Tim 2:20-21, Origen denied that before time *God* made persons into vessels of honor or dishonor. Rather, "he makes those into vessels of honor who purge themselves and those into vessels of dis-honor who allow themselves to remain unpurged."[4] Origen held that in the end all persons will, in fact, choose God and so be saved.

John Chrysostom of Antioch (d. 407) likewise emphasized the human initiative in salvation. "The Lord has made our nature free to choose. Nor does he impose necessity on us, but furnishes suitable remedies and allows everything to hinge on the sick man's own judgment." God elects persons on the basis of his foreknowledge of their personal worthiness. Chrysostom continued, "In order that not everything may depend on divine help, we must at the same time bring something ourselves."[5] Calvin judged that many pre-Augustinian fathers resisted the doctrine of sovereign election (1) so as to accommodate their views to influential worldly philosophers, and (2) to avoid the Christians' constant tendency to slothfulness.[6]

Fourth-century Semi-Pelagians in Southern France—notably John Cassian (d. 435), Vincent of Lérins (d. 434), Hilary of Arles (d. 449), and Faustus of Riez (d. 490)—believed that the weakened (but not lifeless) human will initiates the first movement to God. At that point divine grace assists the prior human response. The Semi-Pelagians rejected unconditional predestination, holding that it would contradict human freedom and responsibility and that it would render preaching and pastoral care unnecessary. Ultimately they regarded unconditional predestination as a fatalistic doctrine. The Semi-Pelagians explained the doctrine conditionally as the divine foreknowledge of human faith and works. Cassian, who had a high estimate of unregenerate human nature, rejected unconditional personal election. "How can we imagine without grievous blasphemy that He does not generally will *all* men, but only *some*, instead of *all* to be saved?"[7] Hilary of Arles disputed Augustine's doctrines of grace and election. He judged that God foreknew or predestined those who would believe, and to these God arranged for the Gospel to be preached. The Synod of Orange condemned the Semi-Pelagians, also known as Semi-Augustinians, in 529.

Traditional Roman Catholicism claims that although the gift of super-added righteousness was lost at the Fall, sinners retain the capacity for willing and doing the good. In the state of nature sinners long for the reception of grace (*desiderium naturale*) and possess the capacity for receiving grace (*potentia obedientais*). God responds to the human aspiration for him at baptism by bestowing sanctifying grace, which remits original sin and unites the soul to Christ. God then provides additional grace through the sacraments of penance and the Eucharist and the teachings of the church. As individuals cooperate with these means of grace, they are enabled to perform meritorious works (rosary prayers, fasting, giving, etc.) that effect moral improvement. In this way humans contribute to their salvation. Catholicism thus is Semi-Pelagian in its belief that "man really cooperates in his personal salvation from sin."[8]

Catholics generally believe that God predestines to heaven all who die in a state of grace and consigns to hell all who die in a state of sin. In the process of salvation the 'elect' are able to fall from grace, and the 'non-elect' have the power to rise to salvation on their death beds. Predestination in the Roman system thus signifies God's prevision of a person's free choices and meritorious works. "Heaven is not given to the elect by a purely arbitrary act of God's will, but it is also the reward of the personal merits of the justified."[9] Mainstream Catholicism rejects the Augustinian doctrine of sovereign election as inconsistent with divine love and Christ's death for the entire world.

The co-called 'Arminians' begin with the philosophical premise that in regard to human destiny God's sovereign choice would be incompatible with human freedom. Christ died for all, and God wills that all people be saved (1 Tim 2:4; 2 Pet 3:9). Moreover, personal obligation is limited to one's ability to perform. Since the command to trust Christ is universal, Arminians claim that all persons have the capacity to respond to the Gospel. The tradition claims that God restores to sinners universally the ability to believe through the operation of prevenient grace that mitigates inherited depravity. Arminians define election as God's general purpose to save those he foresaw would respond to prevenient grace, repent, and believe. They speak of God electing the *class* of people who exhibit a certain kind of character. "The basis for this divine choice is in the moral character which they have been enabled, through God's transforming grace, to embody and experience."[10] Salvation, then, is synergistic; both divine grace and the human will are causes of salvation. According to one authority: "There is a cooperation, or synergism, between divine grace and the human will. The Spirit of God does not work irresistibly, but through the concurrence of the free will of individuals."[11]

James Arminius (d. 1609) was a Leiden scholar who disputed the Calvinist views on predestination, limited Atonement, and the bondage of the sinner's will. In formulating his views Arminius reacted particularly against the high Calvinism (double predestination) of Beza and Gomarus, which he judged to be unjust and unworthy of God. How could God be fair, he reasoned, if he condemns persons who have no opportunity to alter their situation because not sovereignly elected? Moreover, Arminius alleged that the Calvinist denial of free will dehumanizes persons. On the contrary, pre-Christians retain free will, defined as the power of contrary choice spiritually. Even more soberly the Arminians judged that the doctrine of double predestination would make God the author of sin.

According to Arminius, God established four principal decrees concerning salvation. The first focuses on the election of Jesus Christ. God unconditionally appointed Jesus Christ to be the Savior of humankind. What is unconditionally predestined is Christ or *the way of salvation*. The second focuses on the election of the people of God. God further decreed unconditionally that the class of people who adhere to this way of salvation will be saved. "He decreed to receive into favor those who repent and believe, and, in Christ . . . to effect the salvation of such penitents and believers as persevere to the end."[12] The third relates to the provision of prevenient grace. God supplies all persons with "exciting" grace, which mitigates the effects of original sin and enables sinners to respond to the Gospel call. God confers on all people grace sufficient for salvation; it is up to the individual to believe or not believe, to be saved or not be saved. The fourth decree concerns the election of individuals on the basis of foreknowledge. God elects to life those he foresees will believe and persevere, and he punishes those who refuse to do so. "This decree has its formulation in the foreknowledge of God, by which he knew from all eternity those individuals who would, through his preventing grace, *believe*, and through his subsequent grace would *persevere*."[13] In other words, God chose those he foresaw would choose him. Hence the determining factor as to whether an individual will be saved or not is his or her own free decision.

Article I of The Five Articles of the Remonstrants (1610) affirms predestination based on divine foreknowledge of human faith and perseverance. The Remonstrants were forty-two followers of James Arminius who presented their anti-Calvinist articles to the governing body of the Netherlands at the Hague in 1610. The Synod of Dort (1618-19) judged the Five Articles contrary to Scripture and declared the Five Points of Calvinism the official position of the churches. Many Remonstrant pastors were dismissed from their pulpits and were not welcomed back to the Netherlands. Article I reads as follows:

> That God, by an eternal, unchangeable purpose in Jesus Christ his Son, before the foundation of the world, hath determined, out of the fallen, sinful race of men, to save in Christ . . . those who, through the grace of the Holy Ghost, shall believe on this his Son Jesus, and shall persevere in this faith and obedience of faith . . . even to the end; and on the other hand, to leave the incorrigible and unbelieving in sin and under wrath, and to condemn them as alienated from Christ.

John Wesley (d. 1791), the founder of Methodism, was influenced by the theology of the Eastern Fathers and by contemporary Anglicanism that had drifted from a Reformed to an Arminian stance. Moreover, the leader of the Oxford "holy club" stated, "I reject the blasphemy clearly contained in the *horrible decree* of predestination. . . . I would sooner be a Turk, a Deist, yea an atheist, than I could believe this."[14] Wesley strongly opposed Reformed views on predestination in *The Arminian Magazine*

(1778-91) and elsewhere, for several reasons. (1) He judged that unconditional election to life necessarily implied unconditional reprobation to death—which doctrine would make God the author of sin. "Election cannot stand without reprobation. Whom God passes by, those he reprobates. It is one and the same thing."[15] (2) Sovereign election renders preaching vain, for the elect then would be saved with or without preaching, and the non-elect to whom the Gospel is preached could not possibly be saved. (3) The Calvinist doctrine of unconditional election undermines biblical holiness, in that it removes the primary motivation to virtuous living, namely, the promise of rewards and the threat of punishment. "The doctrine [of election] . . . has a tendency to destroy holiness; for it wholly takes away those first motives to follow after it . . . the hope of future reward and punishment, the hope of heaven and the fear of hell."[16] (4) The doctrine allegedly destroys Christians' zeal for good works, if it be that human destinies have been settled from eternity past. And (5) unconditional election makes Christ a hypocrite for pretending love for, and inviting repentance from, persons allegedly reprobated by God.

Positively, Wesley insisted that Christ died for all and his grace is available to all. Viewed as a seamless garment, divine grace universally restrains evil, removes the guilt and penalty of original sin, convicts of sin and judgment, provides the first wish to please God, and imparts power to repent and believe. Thus, "preventing grace" heals the damaging effects of Adamic sin universally. To those who respond to prevenient grace and choose Christ, God grants justifying grace followed by sanctifying grace. Wesley saw two elections in Scripture: (1) an unconditional election of individuals to service and nations to privileges, and (2) a conditional election of persons to eternal destiny. Concerning the latter, God in eternity past elected those persons he foresaw would believe and persevere in holy living. Wesley thus understood election in the weaker sense of God's ratification of foreseen human choices. He wrote:

> I believe election commonly means one of these two things: First, a divine appointment of some particular men to do some particular work in the world. And this election I believe to be not only personal, but absolute and unconditional. Thus Cyrus was elected. . . . I believe election means . . . a divine appointment of some men to eternal happiness. But I believe this election to be conditional, as well as the reprobation opposite thereto.[17]

Wesley's view of salvation as a series of moments in which God offers people resistible grace more closely resembles the classical Roman Catholic rather than the Reformation view.

Charles G. Finney (d. 1875), the Congregationalist pastor and evangelist, held that God's government of the world divides people into two classes: the salvable and the unsalvable. The salvable are those whom God knows are capable of bringing forth saving faith. Finney defined election as the divine foresight of personal salvability. The ground of God's election is the presence of something in sinners that makes it possible and wise for God to save them. Finney believed that the elect were chosen to eternal life on the condition that God foresaw that in the perfect exercise of their freedom they could be persuaded to repent and embrace the Gospel. "Upon some God foresaw that he could wisely bestow a sufficient measure of gracious influence to secure their voluntary yielding, and upon others he could not bestow enough in fact to secure this result. . . . In all this there was nothing arbitrary or unjust. He does for all that he wisely can."[18]

B. Corporate Election
(Contemporary Arminians)

This view represents a refinement of the traditional Arminian view of conditional election. Denying the radical depravity of sinners and the unconditional election of individuals to be saved, this school affirms that God wills to save all people and that Christ died for all. Evangelical interpreters view election *passively* as God's purpose to save the *class* of people who trust Christ. In other words, election is a statement about the divine plan of salvation; it concerns God's appointment of the *believing community* to everlasting glory. Accordingly, the dynamic whereby sinners come to Christ lies not with the sovereign God but with the unregenerate themselves.

Alan Richardson, former theologian at Nottingham and dean of York Cathedral, averred that election is corporate, realized, and to service not to salvation. (1) Election is *corporate*. "The categories of predestination, foreknowledge, and so on, are valid . . . for the behavior of groups, but do not apply to this or that individual."[19] In the OT election dealt with God's choice, not of individuals, but of the nation Israel (Deut 7:6-8; Ps 135:4) and of his Anointed to be the instruments of his purposes. This OT perspective carries over to the NT. Thus in Rom 8:28-30 that which God "foreknew" and "predestined" is the church corporately. According to Richardson:

> If we read this passage as if it related to atomic individuals, we shall create difficulties which are wholly of our imagining; we will then have to ask why it was that God picked out some individuals, and not others, and 'predestined' them to salvation since the foundation of the world. Paul, of course, does not think of the Church as made

up of a collection of individuals, but as a body: it is *the body* which is foreknown, foreordained, called, justified and is to be glorified.[20]

Likewise Romans 9–11 does not concern individuals but nations or representative rulers such as Pharaoh. Richardson argues that Christ is the Elect One and those who are in the Son are the *eklektoi.* "If Christians are 'the elect,' it is because they are 'in Christ,' because they are baptized into the person of him who alone may with complete propriety be called the Elect of God."[21]

(2) Election is *realized.* Romans 9–11, moreover, says nothing about salvation or damnation in the world-to-come, but about God's purposes in history. "Election may be defined as the action of God's grace in *history*" (emphasis added).[22] That is, the election of Israel, the Messiah, and the church has respect to a present, earthly mission among the nations (Isa 45:4-6; Mark 10:45). And (3) election is exclusively to *service.* God's *euloge* has nothing to do with personal destiny in the age to come but everything to do with service for God in the world. "Election refers to God's purpose in this world. It is true that the elected ones, if they do not fall away, will be saved in the world to come, but that is not the primary meaning of election. In the NT, as in the OT, election is a matter of service, not of privilege."[23]

Richardson irresponsibly dissolves individual personhood and decisions into the corporate unit. Thus in arguing for infant baptism, Richardson avers that the faith of the family representative avails for the entire household. "The NT principle of representative faith is established. There is no place for our modern individualism in biblical thinking . . . the faith of one is available for those who are unable as yet to express their own faith."[24]

In their book *God's Strategy in Human History,*[25] the laymen Forster and Marston propose a passive corporate election. The authors argue that Scripture does not teach sovereign election to salvation; people's eternal destiny depends on their own moral responses to the universal offer of the Gospel. Jesus Christ is the chosen One, and Christians are said to be elect because through faith they are in Christ.[26] By the free responses of repentance and faith, people become part of Christ's body, the church, and thus are described as chosen. Forster and Marston write:

> The prime point is that the election of the church is a corporate rather than an individual thing. It is not that individuals are in the church because they are elect, it is rather that they are elect because they are in the church, which is the body of the elect One. . . . A Christian is not chosen to become part of Christ's body, but in

becoming part of that body [by free will, exercising faith] he partakes of Christ's election.[27]

In other words, election or predestination points to the future and describes the heavenly heritage of the people of God (Rom 8:28-30). "Predestination does not concern who should be converted; it concerns our future destiny. It is not that we are predestined *to be* Christians, it is rather that *as* Christians we receive a glorious destiny."[28] The sum of the matter is that God did not choose any individual to be saved; rather, corporately he has chosen in Christ the church to be heirs of heavenly glory.

William Klein, in *The New Chosen People*, avers that the Reformed doctrine whereby God from eternity chose some individuals to be saved and passed by others is "to most of us, a cause of bewilderment or frustration. . . . Such a claim . . . seems so arrogant, so exclusive."[29] God does not select some sinners to be saved; he wills to save *all* who believe (Matt 18:14; 1 Tim 2:4; 2 Pet 3:9). Election in Scripture, he insists, has three meanings. (1) The most common use is God's corporate choice of a people, Israel and the church, for spiritual privileges. Under the old economy God chose national Israel to be his people (Deut 7:6; 14:2); so under the new economy he chooses the people who believe in Christ (the church) to be his elect. (2) There is God's choice of individuals for service, viz., prophets, priests, kings, the seventy, and Christ's apostles. Where election focuses on individuals it is always to a task or ministry. And (3) election concerns God's unique choice of Jesus to perform his redemptive function.

Election to salvation, the immediate matter of concern, is a *corporate* reality; God has chosen to save the body of believers (the people of God) who have come to faith. The plural language of election (Rom 8:29-30; Eph 1:4-5; 2 Thess 2:13; etc.) more adequately refers to the group as a whole rather than to individuals. So the OT speaks of the chosen corporately as a "flock," a "house," and a "people," and the NT a "body," a "bride," and a "temple." Writes Klein, "God has chosen the church as a body rather than the specific individuals who populate that body."[30] Since Jesus Christ is God's Elect One (1 Pet 1:20; 2:4, 6), and those who exercise saving faith are in Christ, Klein concludes that the latter group constitutes God's chosen or "elect" people. His assumption is that since Jesus and the apostles authentically proclaimed the Gospel universally, all persons are capable of repentance and faith. In particular, the opening of Lydia's heart that enabled her to respond to the Gospel (Acts 16:14), was not caused by a special, effectual working of the Holy Spirit.[31] Klein claims that this view of election is congruent with the biblical concept of corporate solidarity, whereby God regards Israel and the church not as so many individuals but as a corporate reality.

Klein further argues that *foreknowledge* in the NT is not a synonym for predetermination, even as the OT language "to know" (Jer 1:5; Amos 3:2) and "to love" (Jer 31:3; Mal 1:2)—referred to individuals—do not mean "to choose" savingly. The divine (fore)knowledge is not selective or elective. In sum, Klein defines election as God's determination of the *benefits* that accrue to the people that believe—i.e., adoption into the family of God, conformity to Christ's image, and future glory. "Paul's concern in predestination is not *how* people become Christians nor *who* become Christians, but to describe *what* God has foreordained on behalf of those *are* (or *will be*) Christians."[32]

C. *Double Unconditional Predestination* *(High Calvinists)*

Some medieval theologians, Reformers, and high Calvinists concluded from the logic of divine sovereignty that God in eternity past chose certain persons to be elected to life and others to be damned to death. They judged the decree of reprobation to be the logical correlate of the decree of election. God's ordination of the two ends was entirely independent of foreseen human merit or demerit. Concerning reprobation, the thesis of permission was dismissed as undermining certainty of occurrence and thus the divine sovereignty and rule.

Gottschalk of Orbais (d. 869), the Franciscan follower of Augustine, was the first significant proponent of double predestination. Firmly opposed to Semi-Pelagianism, Gottschalk became entangled in the *logic* of election and reprobation. Proceeding from divine sovereignty, he argued that if God elected some to life, he necessarily must have reprobated the others to death, lest their destiny remain uncertain. His bottom line was, "There is a twofold predestination, of the elect to blessedness, and of the reprobate to death."[33] Gottschalk was condemned by the Council of Quiercy (853) for making God the author of sin. His works were burned, and he was imprisoned in a monastery where maltreatment led to his death.

Ulrich Zwingli (d. 1531), the leader of the Reformation in German-speaking Switzerland, anticipated features of Calvin's thought. Zwingli believed that the sovereign God is the cause of every occurrence, predestination being a synonym for providence. "All things are so done and disposed by the providence of God that nothing takes place without his will or command."[34] Election or predestination is God's free decision and is not based on foresight of any human work or merit. "Predestination is the free disposition of God with regard to us, and is without any respect to good or evil deeds."[35] Accordingly, the exercise of faith follows election. Zwingli regarded election and reprobation as two aspects of the sovereign will. Since God before time unconditionally elected many to life, he also fashioned many souls (Cain, Esau, Judas, Simon Magus, etc.) for reprobation to eternal death. Wrote Zwingli, "The bliss of everlasting life and the pain of everlasting death are altogether matters of free election or rejection by the divine will."[36]

Martin Luther (d. 1546) initially held to the conditional view of election advanced by the Schoolmen, but his study of the Bible and Augustine led him to affirm unconditional election. Against Christian humanists such as Erasmus, Luther insisted that because the sinner's will is in bondage to corruption, it consistently resists the truth of the Gospel. Thus a person can be saved only through God's will and working. "God has taken salvation out of my will and has put it into His own and has promised to save me, not by my own work or effort but by His grace and mercy."[37]

Luther steadfastly affirmed that God's omnipotence is the cause of all occurrences. God's hidden will, into which humans dare not pry, includes his unconditional predestination of some to be saved and his reprobation of the rest to be damned. "God rejected a number of men and elected and predestined others to everlasting life, such is the truth."[38] On one hand, God elected certain ones to be saved not on the basis of foreseen works or merits but according to his own good pleasure. On the other hand, "the will of the divine majesty purposely abandons and reprobates some to perish."[39] This decree of reprobation is seen in God's hatred of Esau (Rom 9:13), his hardening of Pharaoh's heart (Rom 9:17-18), and his energizing Judas' treachery. To say that the preceding occurred merely by divine permission, in Luther's words, is "double talk."[40] That God hardens the will of the reprobate while not sinning himself is a mystery embedded in his hidden will.

John Calvin (d. 1564) discussed predestination in his *Institutes of the Christian Religion* neither under the divine decrees nor under providence but in the context of salvation and the Christian life. Stressing the absolute sovereignty of God, Calvin attributed every occurrence to God's efficient will; he judged the thesis of permission a subterfuge that diminishes the glory of God. Hence Calvin viewed election and reprobation as parallel decrees within the single will of God. "We call predestination God's eternal decree, by which he compacted with himself what he willed to become of each man. For all are not created in equal condition; rather, eternal life is foreordained for some, eternal damnation for others. Therefore, as any man has been created to one or other of these ends, we speak of him as predestined to life or to death "[41]

Concerning the decree of election, Calvin first spoke of a general, covenantal election of ethnic Israel, which choice could be revoked by national disobedience. More fundamentally, God eternally chose particular individuals, both among Israel (the "remnant") and the Gentiles, for an irrevocable spiritual heritage in Christ. "The general election of the nation Israel does not prevent God from choosing in his most secret counsel those whom he pleases."[42] Calvin noted the following characteristics of election to life in Christ. (1) Election is according to God's sovereign will and good pleasure. It involves God's unconditional choice of a man or woman, not the latter's choice of God. (2) Election is founded on freely given mercy; God is under no obligation to save a single rebellious sinner. (3) Election is not based on foreseen faith or holiness. Although God knows all things in advance, biblical foreknowledge signifies the divine determination to save specific persons. "The foreknowledge of God . . . is not a bare prescience . . . but the adoption by which he had always distinguished his children from the reprobate."[43] (4) Election is absolutely certain as to its outcome. Since the omnipotent God infallibly accomplishes his purposes, all the elect will be saved. For Calvin election to life is a doctrine for the comfort of Christians.

Calvin went beyond Augustine to assert that God unconditionally destined the majority of humanity to everlasting destruction. "Many . . . accept election in such terms as to deny that anyone is condemned. But they do this very ignorantly and childishly since election itself could not stand except as set over against reprobation."[44] Reprobation means that God purposefully devoted to destruction whomsoever he pleased. "Since the disposition of all things is in God's hand, since the decision of salvation or of death rests in his power, he so ordains by his plan or will that among men some are born destined for certain death from the womb, who glorify his name by their own destruction."[45] God's reprobation of the non-elect occurred "for no other reason than that he wills to exclude them from the inheritance which he predestines for his own children."[46] Calvin cited as leading examples of reprobation God's rejection of Esau while yet in his mother's womb and his hardening of the heart of Pharaoh. God implements his decree by withholding from the reprobate his saving word or by depriving them of the capacity to understand it. Calvin denied that his doctrine of reprobation is fatalistic, for it derives not from the inner necessity of things (as in Stoicism) but from God's universal rule. Likewise it is not unjust, for the reason that God's will is the final standard of justice. The fact that God foreordains sin and then punishes sinners for their actions is a mystery to finite minds, hence Calvin's reluctance to preach the doctrine. The truths of God's sovereign disposition of all persons and human responsibility must be maintained, because the Bible teaches both.

Theodore Beza (d. 1605), Calvin's successor at the Geneva Academy, is commonly viewed as the "father of hyper-Calvinism." Beza went beyond Calvin by expounding predestination under the doctrine of God and creation. Beza viewed God's just and secret purpose as the efficient cause of all occurrences. "Everything happens in the manner in which God ordained it from eternity. He disposed the intermediate causes in such a powerful and effective fashion that they were necessarily brought to the appointed end to which He ordained them."[47] Beza argued that God created some persons for life and others for damnation. Thus predestination "is God's eternal and unchangeable ordinance, which came before all the causes of salvation and damnation, and by which God has determined to glorify himself—in some men by saving them through his simple grace in Christ and in other men by damning them through his rightful justice in Adam and in themselves."[48] Beza added that "The doctrine of foreseen faith and foreseen works is contrary to the doctrine that preaches and teaches the Word of God."[49] Beza asserted that the reprobate are condemned for their own sin and lack of faith. He so argued by distinguishing between God's *decree* of election and reprobation and the *execution* of that decree. Although God willed salvation and damnation, his decree was executed by the secondary means of faith and unbelief. By so reasoning, Beza sought to uphold human responsibility and to excuse God as the author of sin. Ultimately Beza referred the preceding antimonies to the mystery of the divine will.

John Bunyan (d. 1688), the English Baptist preacher and writer, is most famous for his allegories *Grace Abounding* (1666) and *The Pilgrim's Progress* (1682). According to Bunyan, the whole of salvation rests on the foundation of God's sovereign election. Wrote he, "This act of God in electing is a choosing or fore-appointing of some infallibly unto eternal life."[50] Election according to God's good pleasure is (1) *eternal*, having been executed before the foundation of the world, (2) *unconditional*, being totally independent of foreseen faith or good works, and (3) *effectual*, in that no impediment can hinder the realization of God's purposes. Finally, (4) election is "*in Christ*," since the Savior is the one in whom the elect were always considered and without whom there is neither election, grace, nor salvation.

In a lengthy section entitled "Reprobation Asserted: or the Doctrine of Eternal Election and Reprobation Promiscuously Handled," Bunyan stated that the decree of reprobation is the logical correlate of election: "if not elect, what then but reprobate?"[51] The decree of reprobation was executed not on the basis of foreseen responses of sinners, but solely on the basis of God's pre-mundane purpose. Arising out of God's *sovereignty*, reprobation excludes creatures from the sphere of divine election and publicly displays his power and wrath. Bunyan supported his doctrine of reprobation by appeal to Paul's accounts of Jacob and Esau (Rom 9:10-13), the hardening of Pharaoh's heart (vv. 17-18), and the parable of the potter and the clay (vv. 19-22). "This decree [of reprobation] is made sure by the number, measure, and bounds of election; for election and reprobation do enclose all reasonable creatures . . . election, those that are set apart for glory; and reprobation, those left out of this choice."[52] Bunyan further distinguished between the decisions of reprobation and foreordination. The latter, arising out of God's *justice*, binds the reprobate over to everlasting punishment. "Sovereignty is according to the will of God, but justice according to the sin of man."[53]

D. Universal Election in Christ (Barthians)

From his belief that sin has destroyed the *imago*, Karl Barth (d. 1968) asserted that sinners are powerless to facilitate their own salvation. Through grace alone God makes people what they cannot become by their own decisions and actions. Consistent with his rigorous Christocentrism, Barth viewed Jesus Christ and his electing activity as the grace of God. For Barth election constitutes the heart of the Gospel. His reasons for rejecting the Augustinian and Calvinist view of election in favor of a novel scheme of double predestination are as follows. (1) The Calvinist view postulates a hidden, antecedent will of God independent of Jesus Christ, who is the beginning and the sum of God's saving purposes. (2) It regards election as a static, fixed decision (*"decretum absolutum"*) rather than a dynamic history between God and persons. And (3) it suggests that God is for some persons and against others, whereas the Gospel is Good News for all.

Barth developed his mature view of election in *Church Dogmatics*, volume II, part 2 under three headings. The first heading he entitled, "The Election of Jesus Christ." The cornerstone of his doctrine is that Jesus Christ "is both the electing God and elected man in One."[54] As the eternally *electing* God, Christ is the divine freedom in action. The Son of God, in other words, is the *subject* who elects others. "Before him and without him and beside him God does not, then, elect or will anything."[55] But

Jesus Christ also is the eternally elected man. As the Son of Man (with a pre-existent humanity?) he is the *object* of God's election. Negatively, this means that Christ was elected to rejection. On the cross God said, "No" to himself as Christ bore the sentence of man's rejection. The elected man, therefore, is also the rejected or reprobated man. Positively, Christ as elected man means that God has chosen humankind for fellowship with himself. At Calvary God said, "Yes" to his Son and to humanity in him. "His election carries in it and with it the election of the rest."[56] Barth thus asserted that "Predestination is the non-rejection of man. It is so because it is the rejection of the Son of God."[57]

The second heading of Barth's development is "The Election of the Community." From his exegesis of Romans 9–11, Barth concluded that the people of God exist in the twofold form of Israel and the church. On one hand, Christ is the crucified Messiah of Israel, which signifies the judgment he has taken upon himself. On the other hand, Christ is the risen Lord of the church, which denotes the new man accepted and received by God. The believing community witnesses to the divine election of the race and the impossibility of resisting grace, and so summons the world to faith in Christ. The church boldly testifies to the reality "that this choice of the godless man is void; that he belongs eternally to Jesus Christ and therefore is not rejected, but elected by God in Jesus Christ."[58]

Barth's third heading is "The Election of the Individual." Individual election takes place in Jesus Christ and with the community (the latter taking priority over the individual). Barth reiterated that the individual, as part of the human family, is already elected in Jesus Christ, the elected man who bore his rejection. Thus each person is eternally loved and objectively justified and sanctified in God's Son. Even if an individual does not personally receive the Gospel, his or her unbelief is overcome by Christ's election. So Barth stated, "This choice of the godless man is void; he belongs eternally to Jesus Christ and therefore is not rejected, but elected by God in Jesus Christ."[59] The chief difference between explicit believers and unbelievers is that the latter do not yet know they are elected. Thus Barth often addressed general audiences as "dear brothers and sisters." Although Barth provided a theoretical basis for universal salvation, he held that to conclude every person will be saved would limit God's freedom. But since universal salvation is an affirmation of faith and hope, Barth confidently trusted that all are saved.[60] In the end, divine grace triumphs over every form of sinful opposition.

Wolfhart Pannenberg (b. 1928) rejects the classical formulation of an individualistic election from eternity. Rather he proposes "a concretely historical concept of election"[61] that affirms that through the medium of history God fulfills his purpose to bring humanity to eternal communion with himself. God has been accomplishing this salvific purpose for the race through the election and history of Israel and the Christian church. Not the sole purveyor of truth, the church functions as a sign and symbol of the destiny of humankind in the future kingdom of God. Writes Pannenberg, "The community of the church symbolizes the eschatological Kingdom of a new mankind in communion with God."[62] Consisting of people from all nations, the church witnesses to the fact that God willed through Christ's cross the reconciliation of the race. "The liberation from the power of sin and death to the enjoyment of freedom in communion with God is not meant for the Christians as the happy few. It is meant for the whole world."[63] Pannenberg believes that God's loving purpose could be none other than the salvation of the world, given men and women's creation as image-bearers and their investiture with eternal value and dignity.

E. Unconditional Single Election
(Moderately Reformed)

Some claim that the doctrine of sovereign election to life was an Augustinian invention. Most pre-Augustinian Fathers failed to articulate a clear-cut doctrine of election for at least two reasons. (1) Many early Christian authorities reacted against rigorous Stoic and Gnostic fatalism and determinism by stressing human freedom and responsibility. From Justin Martyr (d. 165) onwards many early church authorities stated that election is conditioned on foreseen free human responses to the Gospel. Salvation, according to these Fathers, was a synergistic cooperation between the sinner and God's Spirit. Thus Brunner astutely observed:

> In a world . . . dominated by the idea of Fate, it was far more important to stress the freedom and responsibility of man than the fact that he is determined. This concern led the Early Church Fathers to the other extreme of Free Will, which they developed in connexion with the Stoic idea of *autexousion* as the presupposition of moral responsibility.[64]

In addition, (2) many early Fathers succumbed to the prevailing spirit of Hellenistic naturalism. As Thomas F. Torrance noted, "The converts of the first few generations had great difficulty in apprehending the distinctive aspects of the gospel, as for example, the doctrine of grace. It was so astonishingly new to the natural man."[65] Torrance's studies identified "the urge toward self-justification in the second century fathers."[66] Under the influence of Greek humanism, many early Christian writers judged that

God gives saving grace to those who worthily strive after righteousness. These insights help us to understand why prior to Augustine the doctrines of sovereign grace and election were muted.

Nevertheless, belief in human depravity and greater commitment to the divine initiative in salvation gradually developed in the Christian community. Tertullian (d. 220) noted that, contrary to those born in a pagan home, "the children of believers were in some sense destined for holiness and salvation."[67] Athanasius (d. 373) on occasion spoke the language of unconditional divine election. Commenting on Eph 1:3-5 and 2 Tim 1:8-10, he observed that whereas the Fall was "foreseen" the salvation of some people was predestined or "prepared beforehand."[68] In the same vein Ambrose (d. 397), whose preaching greatly influenced Augustine, wrote as follows: "God calls those whom he deigns to call; he makes him pious whom he wills to make pious, for if he had willed he could have changed the impious into pious."[69]

Augustine's (d. 430) early position on election, set forth in his exposition of Romans, was synergistic: God predestined those he foreknew would exercise faith in Christ. Yet wrestling with Scripture in the course of refuting the Pelagian heresy, Augustine changed his view and described the synergism he formerly held as the "pest of the Pelagian error." According to Brunner, "Augustine was the only great teacher of the Early Church who gave reliable Biblical teaching on the subject of Sin and Grace."[70] The bishop insisted that although the unregenerate possess considerable psychological freedom, they lack the moral freedom (i.e., the power) to do the good. In particular, sinners cannot take the first step toward God unless enabled by God's Spirit. Wrote the bishop, "The human will does not attain grace through freedom, but rather freedom through grace."[71] In other words, the divine commands will be fulfilled only as God himself gives the ability to perform them. Thus his prayer to God was, "Give what you command, and command what you will."[72]

Augustine believed that by virtue of original sin all persons justly deserve judgment. But if God through unmerited mercy should choose to save some sinners and not others, none could charge him with acting unrighteously. Thus the bishop understood the Bible to teach that according to his good pleasure and apart from any human merit God in eternity past sovereignly chose out of the "mass of perdition" a certain number of sinners to be saved. "Grace came into the world that those who were predestined before the world may be chosen out of the world."[73] On this showing God gives to some more than they deserve, but no one gets less than they deserve. *Why* God chose to bless some sinners and willed to leave others in their sins has not been revealed. Yet God's elective purpose richly displays his mercy and justice. So the bishop reasoned,

> a merciful God delivers so many to the praise of the glory of his grace from deserved perdition. If He should deliver no one there-from, he would not be unrighteous. Let him who is delivered love His grace. Let him who is not delivered acknowledge his due. In remitting a debt, goodness is perceived; in requiting it, justice. Unrighteousness is never found with God.[74]

Augustine believed that predestination is sometimes signified under the name of foreknowledge. "The ordering of his future works in His fore-knowledge, which cannot be deceived and changed, is absolute, and is nothing but predestination."[75] Depraved sinners' inability morally and spiritually rules out the equation of divine foreknowledge with mere pre-science. "Had God chosen us on the ground that he foreknew that we should be good, then would he also have foreknown that we would not be the first to make choice of him."[76] Moreover, if God chose sinners because he foresaw that they would respond to Christ (a form of human merit), grace would cease to be grace. Such persons would have ground for boasting. "For it is not by grace if merit preceded: but it is of grace; and therefore that grace did not find, but effected the merit."[77] Finally, the bishop held that God did not foreordain persons to damnation in the same effectual way he foreordained to life. Rather, reprobation represents God's determination that the finally impenitent will suffer the just consequences of their sins. Whereas election to life is unconditional, reprobation to perdition is conditioned on human disobedience. Thus Augustine under-stood predestination in an infralapsarian sense.

Thomas Aquinas (d. 1274) revived Augustine's doctrines of sin, grace, and predestination. Considering predestination an aspect of divine prov-idence, Thomas noted that God achieves some of his purposes by direct "operation" and others by "precept," "prohibition," and "permission."[78] He judged that God positively decreed the salvation of some persons, whereas he permissively decreed the perdition of others. Thomas wrote, "Some men are directed by divine working to their ultimate end as aided by grace, while others who are deprived of the same help of grace fall short of their ultimate end, and since all things that are done by God are fore-seen and ordered from eternity by his wisdom . . . the aforementioned dif-ferentiation of men must be ordered by God from eternity."[79] Thomas rejected the view of certain Fathers and medieval authorities that fore-knowledge of human merit or virtue is the cause of predestination to life. "The reason for the predestination of some . . . must be sought in the good-

ness of God" and not on "the use of grace foreknown by God."[80] Thomas
likewise insisted that predestination does not destroy free will, human
effort, or prayer, for God has chosen to accomplish his purposes by these
secondary causes. "The salvation of a person is predestined by God in such
a way, that whatever helps that person towards salvation falls under the
order of predestination; whether it be one's own prayers . . . or other good
works, and suchlike, without which one would not attain to salvation."[81]
As noted, reprobation is God's *permissive* decision to allow sinners to persist in sin and to be punished for it. Thomas plainly wrote, "as predestination includes the will to confer grace and glory, so also reprobation
includes the will to permit a person to fall into sin and to impose the punishment of damnation on account of that sin."[82]

The Belgic Confession (1561) of the Reformed churches in the low countries, states that God is "merciful and just: *merciful*, since he delivers and
preserves from this perdition all whom he in his eternal and unchangeable
counsel of mere goodness has elected in Christ Jesus our Lord, without any
respect to their works; *just*, in leaving others in the fall and perdition
wherein they have involved themselves" (art. XVI). Similar is the French
Confession of Faith (1559): "From this corruption and general condemnation in which all men are plunged God, according to his eternal and
immutable council, calleth those whom he hath chosen by his goodness and
mercy alone in our Lord Jesus Christ, without consideration of their
works, to display in them the riches of his mercy; leaving the rest in this
same corruption and condemnation to show in them his justice" (art. XII).

The Thirty-Nine Articles of the Church of England (1571) likewise
opposed the conditional view of election. "Predestination to Life is the
eternal purpose of God, whereby (before the foundations of the world
were laid) he hath constantly decreed by his counsel secret to us, to deliver
from curse and damnation those whom he hath chosen in Christ out of
mankind, and to bring them by Christ to everlasting salvation, as vessels
made to honour. Wherefore, they which be endued with so excellent benefit of God, be called according to God's purpose by his Spirit working in
due season" (art. XVII). This article adds, "the godly consideration of predestination and our election in Christ is full of sweet, pleasant, and
unspeakable comfort to godly persons."

The Westminster Confession of Faith (1647) presents the mature
Reformed view on election. "Those of mankind that are predestined unto
life, God, before the foundation of the world was laid, according to his
eternal and immutable purpose, and the secret counsel and good pleasure
of his will, hath chosen in Christ, unto everlasting glory, out of his mere

free grace and love, without any foresight of faith or good works, or perseverance in either of them, or any other thing in the creature, as conditions, or causes moving him thereunto; and all to the praise of his glorious grace" (ch. 3.5).

John Gill (d. 1771), an English Baptist, believed that many Scriptures (e.g., Eph 1:4; 2 Thess 2:13; 2 Tim 1:9) plainly teach God's unconditional election to salvation. "This eternal election of particular persons to salvation is absolute, unconditional, and irrespective of faith, holiness, good works, and perseverance as the moving causes or conditions of it; all which are the fruits and effects of electing grace, but not causes or conditions of it; since these are said to be chosen, not because they were holy, but that they should be so."[83] Gill held that sovereign election is the first link in the golden chain of salvation; forgiveness of sins, redemption, justification, and perseverance all proceed therefrom as fruit from a tree. Gill defined reprobation as God (1) passing by some sinners, thus leaving them in their sins, and (2) inflicting on them just punishment for their sins.

Charles Haddon Spurgeon (d. 1892), the Baptist pastor of London's Metropolitan Tabernacle, explained the doctrine as follows. (1) Election derives from God's sovereign purpose. Salvation eventuates not because humans will it in time, but because God willed it eternally. "The whole scheme of salvation, from the first to the last, hinges and turns on the absolute will of God."[84] (2) Election is entirely of grace. Guilty sinners deserve only wrath and punishment. But from eternity past God loved the elect in consequence of his own gracious purpose, not because of any foreseen merit in them. "It is quite certain that any virtue which there may be in any man is the result of God's grace. Now if it be the result of grace it cannot be the cause of grace."[85] And (3), election is personal, not corporate. If it be unjust of God to elect a person to life, it would be far more unjust of him to elect a nation, for the latter represents an aggregate of individuals. "God chose that Jew, and that Jew, and that Jew. . . . Scripture continually speaks of God's people one by one and speaks of them as having been the special objects of election."[86]

The Baptist theologian A.H. Strong (d. 1921) held that by virtue of universal depravity God must initiate the process of salvation. The fountainhead of God's initiative is sovereign election, defined as "that eternal act of God, by which in his sovereign pleasure, and on account of no foreseen merit in them, he chooses certain out of the number of sinful men to be the recipients of the special grace of his Spirit, and so to be made voluntary partakers of Christ's salvation."[87] The divine election is not based on any activity of sinners, including faith, since depravity ensures that without special grace the unregenerate would bring forth no Godward movement. Moreover, God's foreknowledge connotes not merely to "know in advance," but more actively to "regard with favor" or "make an object of care." In key biblical texts the words "know" and "foreknow" possess the same meaning. Strong's measured conclusion is that "in spite of difficulties we must accept the doctrine of election."[88]

This position of a single, unconditional election to life is well supported not only by historical considerations but also by the biblical data, as will be explained in the section that follows.

III. Exposition of the Doctrine of Election

A. *Election to Service*

Scripture plainly attests the fact that God chose certain individuals for specific tasks or ministries. In the OT God selected Moses for leadership in Israel (Num 16:5-7), Moses' elder brother Aaron for priestly service (Ps 105:26), Eli's father to perform priestly functions (1 Sam 2:28), Saul to be king over Israel (1 Sam 10:24), David the shepherd as Israel's premier king (1 Sam 16:7-12; 2 Sam 6:21; 1 Chron 28:4), Solomon to rule as king and build the temple (1 Chron 28:4-6; 29:1), Jeremiah for prophetic ministry (Jer 1:10), and Zerubbabel for leadership in post-exilic Israel (Hag 2:23). The verb *bāḥar*, used in almost all the preceding texts, means to "choose, elect, or decide for."[89] Moreover, God chose the Levitical priesthood to minister before him on behalf of the people (Deut 18:5; 21:5; 1 Chron 15:2), and he chose kings to govern the nation (Deut. 17:15). These choices of God for service were conditional; they could be revoked by disobedience (1 Sam 2:27-36).

Scripture applies the concept of election to the Messiah, Jesus. Through Isaiah the prophet, Yahweh described his "servant" as "my chosen one [*beḥîrî*] in whom I delight" (Isa 42:1, quoted in Matt 12:18). Messiah was called of the Lord long before his birth (Isa 49:1, 5). At Jesus' Transfiguration a voice from heaven spoke the words, "This is my Son, whom I have chosen" (perfect passive participle of *eklegō*, Luke 9:35). Later the crowd hurled insinuations at Jesus as he hung on the cross: "He saved others; let him save himself if he is the Christ of God, the Chosen One" (*ho eklektos*, Luke 23:35). Peter likewise attested Christ's election in 1 Pet 2:4, 6 (*eklektos*) and 1 Pet 1:20 (*proginōskō*). Christ's election means that he was chosen (1) to stand in a unique relation to the Father, (2) to be the object of the Father's affection, and (3) to exercise the messianic office of suffering and triumph. According to Smedes, "He was elect as the concrete *individual* doing the specific task that He was chosen to do."[90] The relationship of Messiah's election to believers' election should be understood in the sense that his election is the ground and basis of our election. To say that we are chosen in Christ means that God appointed us to salvation on the basis of his merits as the obedient Servant of the Lord.

The theme of election to service extends to the NT writings. At the beginning of his ministry Jesus chose twelve apostles to preach the gospel of the kingdom and to drive out demons (Mark 3:13-15; Luke 6:13). Moreover, John, who recorded many sayings of Jesus concerning individual election to life (see below), also took note of the Lord's selection of the apostles to service: "Have I not chosen [*exelexamen*] you, the Twelve?" (John 6:70). The election of the latter included Judas; but in this regard see John 13:18 and its allusion to election to life. There Jesus said, "I am not referring to all of you; I know those I have chosen [*exelexamēn*]." Jesus likewise "appointed [*anedeixen*] seventy-two others and sent them two by two" to preach the Good News of the kingdom (Luke 10:1). Consider also Jesus' saying in John 15:16: "You did not choose [*exelexasthe*] me, but I chose you and appointed [*ethēka*] you to go and bear fruit—fruit that will last." The verbs *ethēka* ("set aside") and *hypagēte* ("go forth") suggest that Jesus primarily had in mind the mission of the disciples. As noted above, election to service does not exclude the prior event of election to salvation. The two decisions are not mutually exclusive.

B. Election Corporately of a People

God's initial purpose was to create a special people, a new humanity, for himself through the institutions of Israel and the church. Having purposed to call a people, God proceeded to choose the individuals that would form this privileged people. Thus the Lord called Abram out of Ur of the Chaldees and made a covenant with him (Gen 12:1-3; 13:14-17; 15:1-7), whereby Abram was promised a plenteous "seed" (Gen 22:17) and a mission of blessing the nations (Gen 12:3; cf. Gal 3:8). The people of the promise were constituted a nation at their deliverance from Egyptian bondage (Exod 20:2; Deut 4:20, 37-38; Ezek 20:5; Hos 11:1). Deut 7:6-8 aptly summarizes this election and formation of the nation Israel.

> The Lord your God has chosen you out of all the peoples on the face of the earth to be his people, his treasured possession. The Lord did not set his affection on you and choose you because you were more numerous than other peoples, for you were the fewest of all

> *peoples. But it was because the Lord loved you and kept the oath*
> *he swore to your forefathers that he brought you out with a mighty*
> *hand and redeemed you from the land of slavery, from the power*
> *of Pharaoh king of Egypt.*

God chose the Jewish nation to privilege and service (cf. 1 Kgs 3:8; Ps 132:13) not because of any merit (for they were a "stiff-necked people," Exod 32:9; Deut 9:6), but solely on the basis of his sovereign, purposeful love (Deut 4:37a; 10:15; Ps 47:4). By virtue of the national covenant Israel gained the status of God's "people" (Deut 7:6; 21:8; 32:9; Ps 100:3), "servant" (1 Chron 16:13; Isa 41:8-9; 43:10; 44:1-2; etc.), "inheritance" (Deut 32:9; 1 Kgs 8:51; Ps 28:9), "bride" (Isa 49:18; 61:10; Jer 2:2), "flock" (Ps 78:52; 95:7), "vine" (Jer 2:21; Ezekiel 15; Hos 10:1), and "treasured possession" (Exod 19:5; Deut 14:2; Ps 135:4).

But this election of ethnic Israel was conditional; its privileges could be forfeited by national disobedience. Thus after Aaron had made the golden calf, God threatened to destroy Israel and choose another nation, beginning with Moses (Exod 32:9-10). In the wilderness Israel refused to obey God's word, whereupon the Lord swore by an oath, "They shall never enter my rest" (Ps 95:11). One must also distinguish between the election of ethnic Israel for temporal privilege and the election of a faithful minority within the nation for salvation. Later in its history Israel broke the covenant by forsaking the Lord and worshiping foreign gods. In Elijah's day God kept a remnant of 7,000 in Israel who did not bow the knee to Baal (1 Kgs 19:18). Thus not all of *national Israel* was the *true Israel* of God. Paul concluded that both in Elijah's day and in his own "there is a remnant chosen by grace" (Rom 11:4). It is clear, however, that by choosing national Israel for present and future blessings, God exercised a certain selectivity vis-à-vis other nations. The question of 'unfairness' must be addressed at the point of Israel's corporate election for privilege and service. God's choice of Israel was a gracious selection. And since grace is never owed, it cannot be unfair of God to bestow such favor. God richly blessed Israel with his word and grace in ways that he did not bless Assyria, Babylon, or Persia. As we read in Ps 147:19-20, "He has revealed his word to Jacob, his laws and decrees to Israel. He has done this for no other nation; they do not know his laws."

Analysis of the data leads to the conclusion that the primary focus of election in the OT is corporate, the selection of a people for the praise of Yahweh. God's purpose in the OT appears to have been to differentiate the *nation* Israel—chosen, blessed, and commissioned—from her godless and pagan neighbor nations. We observe a similar phenomenon in the OT revelation of God's nature, where Yahweh's unity and uniqueness are stressed and his triune personhood muted. Thus without considering the NT the reader of the OT might adopt a Unitarian view of God as well as a doctrine of conditional election. But even as God embedded traces of Trinitarianism in the OT, he also left hints that after choosing the privileged *nation* he selected persons for salvation within that nation. Scripture does not regard the chosen nation as an *empty class* but as an aggregate of believing individuals.

The idea of the election of God's people is not absent from the NT. Jesus said to Israel's chief priests and elders, "I tell you that the kingdom of God will be taken away from you and given to a people who will produce its fruit" (Matt 21:43). The church is the "people" who inherit the promises given to the patriarchs (Gal 3:14, 29). Furthermore, Peter described the NT community in corporate language drawn from the OT: "you are a chosen people (*genos eklekton*), a royal priesthood, a holy nation (*ethnos hagion*), a people (*laos*) belonging to God" (1 Pet 2:9). Peter's addressees are "the people (*laos*) of God" (v. 10, cf. Heb 4:9; 11:25) and "God's flock" (*poimnion*, 1 Pet 5:2; cf. v. 3), "being built into a spiritual house (*oikos pneumatikos*) to be a holy priesthood" (*hierateuma hagion*, 1 Pet 2:5). As an aside, the body, which is the church, is not an empty class, for Peter addressed *individuals* within the group as "dear friends" (2:11; 4:12), "slaves" (2:18), "wives" (3:1), "husbands" (3:7), "elders" (5:1), etc..

In sum, the OT teaches the corporate election of Israel to privilege, which is not a guarantee of salvation (although many Jews thought so). On the other hand, the NT teaches the corporate election of the church (universal), and this election is to salvation. Exactly how Israel's election and place relate to the church's election is debated by covenantalists and dispensationalists, and that debate will be handled in the volumes on ecclesiology and eschatology in this series.

C. *Personal Election in the OT: A Minor Theme*

After willfully disobeying their Creator, Adam and Eve did not seek God for forgiveness; rather they hid from him out of fear and guilt (Gen 3:8-10). In vain the couple tried to cover their nakedness with leaves (v. 7), but God sought them out and provided a covering of animal skins (v. 21). This incident shows that the initiative in salvation lies with God. Gen 6:8 relates that of all the peoples on earth, "Noah found favor (*ḥēn*) in the eyes of the Lord." In grace God delivered Noah and his family from the flood that destroyed the rest of humanity. Moreover, in his sovereign freedom God blessed Shem, the head of the Semitic race, with a special relationship with himself, while rejecting his brother Ham, the progenitor of the Canaanites (Gen 9:18-26). By divine plan Japheth (the father of the Gentiles) would share in the spiritual blessings sovereignly granted to Shem.

Gen 12:1-3 (cf. 17:1-8; 18:18-19; Deut 4:37; Neh 9:7-8) records God's choice and call of Abram, made not on the basis of any foreseen virtue but solely according to God's sovereign and gracious will. Descended from a family of idol-worshipers (Josh 24:2, 14), Abram did not seek God; rather God sought out Abram, called him, and made a covenant with him. Only thereafter did Abram place faith in the Lord (Gen 15:6). Likely Abram would have persisted in his pagan milieu had God not intervened in his life. Inherent in the covenant was the promise of a posterity, a land as an inheritance, and a mission of blessing the nations (cf. 13:14-16; 15:7-21; etc.). Yet the promise clearly involved personal blessings for Abraham ("I will bless you," Gen 12:2a). Later God acknowledged that he had "chosen" Abraham for himself (Gen 18:19). The verb yāda'—to "know" or "regard with favor"—means that God set his affection on Abraham or sovereignly chose him to salvation.[91] Similarly God 'knew' or elected Moses (Exod 33:17). Consistent with our thesis above, Jewett observes that the election of Abraham and Sarah (cf. Isa 51:2) was individual and at the same time corporate in their seed.[92]

Concerning Abraham's two sons, Ishmael and Isaac, God chose the younger to be the child of promise (Gen 17:19-21; 21:12). Mention of the descendants of the two sons indicates that the author regarded Ishmael and Isaac as *individual* heads of their respective lines (Edom and Israel). God would take note of Ishmael (Gen 17:20; 25:12-18), but he chose to establish his covenant (an act of election) with Isaac Gen 17:19). Moreover, of the two unborn children of Isaac and Rebekah, God made a sovereign choice of the younger, Jacob, and his seed over Esau, the elder, and his seed. God's choice was independent of the cultural principle of primogeniture and of Jacob's character or works, for the latter schemed to obtain the birthright from Esau (Gen 25:27-34) and gained Isaac's blessing by deception (Gen 27:5-40). Thus *in spite of* his duplicitous character Jacob (and his descendants) were the objects of God's choice. This fact is confirmed by Paul's acknowledgment of the personal election of Jacob in Rom 9:10-13[93], considered in detail below. "By sovereign election, God declared that the promised line would belong to Jacob, the younger son. Jacob thus owed his supremacy not to natural order or to human will but to the divine election."[94] The rationale for such choices God revealed to Moses: "I will have mercy on whom I will have mercy, and I will have compassion on whom I will have compassion" (Exod 33:19; cf. Rom 9:16a, 18).

The Psalms frequently attest God's choice of the nation Israel, but there are hints here and there of God's choosing individuals. Consider uses of the verb *bāḥar* in the psalter. Ps 65:3-4 describes the unregenerate as overwhelmed by transgressions but chosen and brought near by forgiving grace. David wrote, "Blessed are those you choose and bring near to live in your courts!" (v. 4). The choosing clearly is soteriological ("live"), and the Piel of *qārab* (to "bring near") stresses God's gracious initiative as drawing the sinful soul to himself. Ps 78:70 and Ps 105:26 appear to embrace God's choice to salvation as well as to service. The adjective *bāḥîr* ("chosen") likewise occasionally denotes a person (Ps 89:3; 106:23) or persons (Ps 105:6, 43; 106:5; Isa 65:15, 22) chosen comprehensively to salvation and service.

Yahweh also chose Jeremiah before his birth both for salvation and for prophetic ministry: "Before I formed you in the womb I knew [*yāda'*] you, before you were born I set you apart" (Jer 1:5). That *yāda'* here means "choose" is clear from Gen 18:19 (individual) and Amos 3:2 (corporate). In the latter text Yahweh said of Israel, "You only have I chosen [*yāda'*]of all the families of the earth." Kaiser argues that "The word 'to know' in this covenantal context had nothing to do with recognition or acknowledgment of one's deeds; it had to do with God's gift of choice—an unmerited choice as Deuteronomy 7:8 *passim* had made plain."[95] Thus God's knowledge of a person is his choice, and vice versa. Election to salvation and election to service are complementary, not contradictory, concepts; the one does not exclude the other.

The teaching that God elects individuals to a task or office *supplements* but does not supplant the doctrine of election to salvation. It is important to note this point in light of the unconvincing argument of such scholars as H.H. Rowley, who affirms that God chose Israel to reveal the truth to all nations even as he chose Greece to advance civilization and culture.[96]

Individual election is implicit in Mal 1:2-3. Although Esau was Jacob's elder brother, Yahweh declared, "I have loved Jacob, but Esau have I hated." The Hebrew verb *'āhab* here means to "prefer," while the verb to "hate" signifies to "value less highly" (see Deut 22:13, 16; Prov 13:24; 14:20; cf. Gen 29:31-33; Deut 21:16-17; Matt 6:24; Luke 14:26; John 12:25).[97] The sense of a 'holy hatred' on God's part (Ps 5:5; 11:5) is not in view here. Thus God loved the younger son Jacob more intensely and the elder son Esau less so, which means that in his sovereign wisdom God elected only Jacob. "When Yahweh says, 'I have loved Jacob,' he means, 'I chose Jacob,' and when he says, 'I hated Esau,' he means, 'I did not choose Esau.'"[98] God's choice of Israel and his decision to pass by Edom commenced with the heads of their respective lines.[99] In his preaching

Jerry Falwell has stated that God loves all persons in equal measure. Scripture suggests otherwise. The point of the above texts is that salvation resides entirely with God: "Salvation comes from the Lord" (Jon 2:9).

The thesis of personal election is further supported by the OT notion of "a remnant" within Israel. Isa 10:20-22 affirms that, whereas the majority of Israel would perish in captivity, a "remnant" (*šeʾār*) would put their trust in the Lord. Yahweh designated this believing remnant "my people" (v. 24; cf. Jer 31:7). "*Šeʾār* . . . had a technical (perhaps cultic) meaning of the authentic and integral core of the people who were the genuinely elect, the genuine Israel. . . . They are the 'pious remnant,' the 'righteous remnant,' the 'faithful remnant.'"[100] The synonym *šeʾērît* ("remnant," "posterity") likewise posits the existence of a believing minority within ethnic Israel (Isa 37:32; Jer 31:7; Mic 2:12). In Isa 65:8 Yahweh described national Israel as a bunch of grapes and the believing remnant as the sweet juice thereof. The faithful within ethnic Israel Yahweh further described as his "servants" (Isa 65:9, 13-14), his "disciples" (Isa 8:16), and his "chosen ones" (Isa 65:15, 22; cf. v. 9). The *remnant*, sometimes viewed as "a tenth" of the people (Isa 6:13), are heirs of the new covenant (Jer 32:37-40; 50:4-5); they are called of the Lord (Joel 2:32); they are gathered by the Lord (Mic 2:12); and they bear spiritual fruit (Isa 37:31). In short, the remnant are the forgiven and saved (Jer 50:20). This phenomenon of the saved remnant confirms the existence of an individual election to salvation within the corporate election of ethnic Israel to temporal and earthly privileges.[101]

As noted above, the corporate election of the nation, not individual election, is the primary focus of the OT. But as we turn to the NT, that which earlier was clouded shines with clearer light. We believe that Jewett correctly assessed the situation when he wrote, "It is especially in the NT that the individual aspect of election becomes prominent, and it is largely in terms of individual election that the doctrine has been discussed by theologians."[102]

D. *Personal Election in the NT: A Major Theme*

Can we find in the teachings of Jesus and the apostles evidence of personal, unconditional election? In the parable of the workers in the vineyard (Matt 20:1-16), the Lord taught that God is not obliged to deal with everyone in the same way. To those who objected that they worked all day but received the same wage as those who worked but one hour, Jesus inferred that none get less than they deserve (justice), but some get more than they deserve (grace). It is not unjust of God to give some more than their due.

Elsewhere Jesus taught that of old God favored certain persons with his grace while passing by others. Thus there were many needy widows in Israel in Elijah's day, but the prophet was sent to minister only to the widow of Zarephath (Luke 4:25-26; cf. 1 Kgs 17:8-24). In addition, there were many lepers in Israel at that time, but only one was healed of the disease, namely, Naaman the Syrian (Luke 4:27; cf. 2 Kgs 5:1-14).

Furthermore, Jesus acknowledged the Father's sovereign right to reveal or conceal the significance of the Son's words and works as he pleases. The Lord prayed in Matt 11:25-26, "I praise you, Father, Lord of heaven and earth, because you have hidden these things from the wise and learned, and revealed them to little children. Yes, Father, for this was your good pleasure (*eudokia*)." *Eudokia*, explaining God's concealing and revealing activity, connotes the good pleasure of God's sovereign will. "*Eudokia* expresses independent volition, sovereign choice, but always with an implication of benevolence."[103] Jesus confirmed this by adding, "No one knows the Father except the Son and those to whom the Son chooses [present subjunctive of *boulomai*, to "will"] to reveal him" (Matt 11:27). Thus God sovereignly chose to extend his enlightening and saving influence to some persons, while withholding it from others (cf. Matt 13:11). Although Matt 11:28-30 likely was spoken at another time in Jesus' ministry, a universal invitation to receive Jesus (v. 28) is not inconsistent with God's purpose to reveal himself to some. This is so because (1) Christ's provision on the cross was universal (see chap. 4). And (2) all who respond positively to the invitation will be saved (John 11:26; Acts 10:43; Rom 10:11, 13); but tragically for themselves, depraved sinners are unresponsive to spiritual impulses—hence the need for a supernatural initiative (see chap. 5).

The adjective *eklektos* occurs twenty-two times in the NT, seventeen times (as a plural) in the sense of "chosen" or "elect" saints. Those envisaged are individuals within the remnant of Israel (Matt 24:22, 24, 31; Mark 13:20, 22, 27; Luke 18:7) and citizens of the church (Rom 8:33; Col 3:12; 2 Tim 2:10; Tit 1:1; 1 Pet 1:1). The elect are viewed not as an empty class, for in the preceding verses the elect cry out to God, obey Christ, are faithful to him, and reflect the fruits of the Spirit—all of which are activities of individuals, who also may be considered as a group or a class.

Although John affirmed God's love for the entire world, the Fourth Gospel, more emphatically than the Synoptics, emphasizes God's sovereign choice of certain persons to be saved. This is clear in John 5:21, where Jesus said to the Jews, "just as the Father raises the dead and gives them life, even so the Son gives life to whom he is pleased to give it." Likewise in John 13:18 Jesus said to his disciples, "I am not referring to all of you; I know those I have chosen." The Lord chose the Twelve as a group for ministry, but prior to that he chose each one, save Judas, for salvation.[104]

Speaking figuratively, Jesus in John 10 identified himself as the shepherd and his elect people as the "sheep."[105] John drew several important conclusions concerning the relation between the shepherd and the sheep, as follows: (1) *The sheep are those people whom the Father specifically has given to the Son* (v. 29). The fact that God has gifted certain persons to the Son is reiterated in John 17:2, 6, 9, 24 and 18:9, the frequency of mention suggesting that this was an important concept to John. Jesus taught more specifically in John 6:37, "All that the Father gives me will come to me" (i.e., will believe and be saved). Concerning the sheep, the Father "chose them out of the world for the possession and the service of the Son."[106] See also John 15:19, where Christ chose (*eklegomai*) the disciples out of the world both for salvation and service, a fact taught in similar language in John 17:6, 14, 16. The verb *eklegomai* (to "choose," "select") is used eight times of Jesus choosing disciples and seven times of God's choice of people for eternal life (Mark 13:20; Acts 17:13; 1 Cor 1:27 [two times], 28; Eph 1:4; Jas 2:5). Carson rightly concludes that "They are Christ's obedient sheep in his salvific purpose before they are his sheep in obedient practice."[107] (2) *The shepherd died to achieve the salvation of the sheep* (vv. 11, 15). Moreover, Jesus reveals himself redemptively to those the Father gave him out of the world (John 17:6, 8), and for these he intercedes in heaven. (3) *The shepherd "knows" his sheep and "calls" them by name* (vv. 3, 14, 27). Just as the oriental shepherd called his sheep by name, so Jesus the good Shepherd "knows" his sheep personally with a knowledge that is saving.

(4) *The sheep know the voice of the shepherd and follow him* (vv. 4, 27). Jesus said of those not his sheep, "you do not believe because you are not my sheep" (v. 26). We might have expected Jesus to say, "You are not my sheep because you do not believe," but he said precisely the opposite. A sinner, then, does not become a "sheep" by believing in Jesus; rather, he or she believes in Jesus because antecedently appointed by God as one of the "sheep." (5) Jesus' saying—"I have other sheep that are not of this sheep pen. I must bring them also" (v. 16)—refers to specific Gentiles who *de jure* belonged to Christ by divine election even though *de facto* they had not yet come to faith. In the Johannine texts cited, the "sheep" are not an empty class, for they are said to "hear," "know," "believe," "trust," "follow," and "love" the Shepherd—all of which are individual actions before being considered as actions of a group or a class.

The theme of election is not absent from the record of the explosive growth of the church in Acts. At Pisidian Antioch Paul acknowledged God's corporate election of national Israel for spiritual and temporal blessings (Acts 13:17). Yet at the conclusion of Paul's and Barnabas' ministry in that city, Luke stated that "all who were appointed to eternal life believed" (Acts 13:48). The key word is the perfect passive participle of *tassō*, to "order," "appoint," or "ordain." This verb occurs eight times in the NT, but only here in the sense of appointment to eternal life. F.F. Bruce suggested that the verb might be translated "enrolled" or "inscribed" in the Lamb's book of life (cf. Luke 10:20; Phil 4:3; Rev 13:8; 17:8).[108] Luke's words clearly indicate that God's sovereign action, be it ordaining or enrolling (or both), occurred prior to the person's believing. The Gentile hearers believed because appointed to life; they were not appointed because they believed. All of this speaks the language of God's sovereign election of certain persons for salvation.[109]

During his second missionary journey, Paul had a vision in which God encouraged him to continue preaching in Corinth notwithstanding the severe opposition he would face. Paul must persevere in sharing the Gospel, God said, "because I have many people (*laos*) in this city" (Acts 18:10). The heavenly message confirmed that God had chosen many persons in Corinth to be his own, and Paul's preaching was the divinely ordained means to bring these elect to salvation. Paul's later letters indicate that many in Corinth did come to faith and organize as Christian communities. Leon Morris comments concerning the "people" in Corinth: "They had not yet done anything about being saved; many of them had not even heard the gospel. But they were God's. Clearly it is he who would bring them to salvation in due course."[110]

In Rom 8:28-30 Paul delineated the full circle of salvation, which clinched his argument concerning Christians' hope of heavenly glory (vv. 18-27).

> *And we know that in all things God works for the good of those who love him, who have been called according to his purpose. For those God foreknew he also predestined to be conformed to the likeness of his Son, that he might be the firstborn among many brothers. And those he predestined, he also called; those he called, he also justified; those he justified, he also glorified.*

We observe, first, that the foundation of the Christian's calling to salvation is God's *prothesis*, meaning "purpose," "resolve," or "decision" (Rom 9:11; Eph 1:11; 3:11; 2 Tim 1:9). The believer's hope of future glory is grounded not in his own will but in the sovereign, pre-temporal purpose of God.

The first of the aorist verbs in the passage is the word *proginōskō*, to "foreknow," "choose beforehand."[111] With humans as subject the word means to "know beforehand" (Acts 26:5; 2 Pet 3:17). With God as subject the verb could mean either prescience or foreloving/foreordaining (Rom 8:29; 11:2; 1 Pet 1:20). The foundational verbs *yāda'* and *ginōskō* often mean to "perceive," "understand," and "know." But they also mean "to set regard upon, to know with particular interest, delight, affection, and action. (*Cf.* Gen 18:19; Exod 2:25; Ps 1:6; 144:3; Jer 1:5; Amos 3:2; Hos 13:5; Matt 7:23; 1 Cor 8:3; Gal 4:9; 2 Tim 2:19; 1 John 3:1)."[112] The verb *ginōskō* thus can convey God's intimate acquaintance with his people, specifically the fact that they are "foreloved" or "chosen." This latter sense is evident in the following Pauline sayings: "the man who loves God is known by God" (1 Cor 8:3); "but now that you know God—or rather are known by God" (Gal 4:9); and "the Lord knows those that are his" (2 Tim 2:19).

The verb *proginōskō* in Rom 8:29 and 11:2 contextually could be taken in either of the two senses, i.e., prescience or foreordination. But given the strongly relational Hebrew background to the word, the unambiguous sense of *proginōskō* in 1 Pet 1:20 (see below) and *prognōsis* in Acts 2:23 and 1 Pet 1:2 (see below), and the whole tenor of Paul's theology, the probable meaning of *proginōskō* with God as subject is to "know intimately" or "forelove."[113] F.F. Bruce concurs with this judgment. Concerning Rom 8:29, he wrote, "the words 'whom he did foreknow' have the connotation of electing grace which is frequently implied by the verb 'to know' in the Old Testament. When God takes knowledge of his people in this special way, he sets his choice upon them."[114] To the preceding considerations we add that the biblical language of foreknowledge is always used of saints, never of the unsaved. Moreover, what God "foreknows" is the saints themselves, not any decision or action of theirs. Thus divine election is according to *foreknowledge* (foreloving), not simply according to *foresight* (prescience).

Paul continues in the Romans text: "For those God foreknew he also predestined [*proōrisen*] to be conformed to the likeness of his Son . . ." (v. 29). The verb *proōrizō*, to "decide beforehand," or "predestine," occurs six times in the NT in the sense of God's predetermined plan of salvation, Christ's sufferings, or gracious election to life (Rom 8:29-30; 1 Cor 2:7; Eph 1:5, 11). Those on whom God in eternity past set his affection, he sovereignly chose for life.

Return for a moment to the larger picture of the golden chain of salvation presented in Rom 8:29-30. The verbs "foreknew," "predestined," "called," "justified," and "glorified" are in the aorist tense, which denotes

God's prior determination marking these future events with certainty. Moreover the verbs gramatically are in exact sequence; thus if the election and the calling were exclusively corporate, so also would be the justification and the glorification. But God does not justify an empty class; he justifies individuals within the class who are moved to saving faith in Christ. Similarly, it is individuals who possess the Spirit (v. 23), who "groan inwardly" awaiting the day of glorification (v. 23), who exercise "hope" (v. 24), and who display patience (v. 25). Clearly these are spiritual experiences of individual Christians who, when considered aggregately, constitute the class of believers. Thus the focus of the circle of salvation is both corporate and individual.[115]

Romans 9–11 is an important text for understanding God's saving purpose for Jews and Gentiles. Paul first recalled Israel's glorious spiritual heritage: "Theirs is the adoption as sons; theirs the divine glory, the covenants, the receiving of the law, the temple worship and the promises" (Rom 9:4; cf. v. 5). Given these lofty privileges, why are so few Jews saved? Has God's purpose for his people failed? To these questions Paul responded with a firm no! The fact is, he continued, "not all who are descended from Israel are Israel. Nor because they are his descendants are they all Abraham's children" (vv. 6-7). The existence of a believing remnant—a circle of elect ones—within ethnic Israel attests that God's purpose has not been frustrated, that his promise has not failed.

Paul further indicated God chose Isaac over Ishmael (vv. 7-9) and Jacob over Esau (vv. 10-13) before they were born or had done good or evil "in order that God's purpose [*prothesis*] in election [*eklogē*, "picking out," "election," "selection"] might stand" (v. 11). To support this argument Paul quoted from Mal 1:2-3, "Jacob I have loved, but Esau I have hated." Cranfield concludes that "loved" and "hated" here denote election and rejection respectively.[116] Paul's emphasis clearly is upon God's sovereign purpose, not man's response. God's election of Isaac and Jacob is individual unto salvation and not merely corporate (Israel and Edom) in respect of earthly privileges, since in vv. 9-13 each of the children—their birth and their deeds—is in the foreground.[117] Moreover, in v. 24 Paul stated that God chose and called not only individuals from among the Jews (such as Isaac and Jacob) but also individuals from among the Gentiles. A further factor is the flow of Paul's argument. He sought to show that in spite of the unbelief of ethnic Israel God's saving purpose has not failed, as confirmed by the election of a believing remnant exemplified by Isaac and Jacob. To say that God's purpose for Israel remains valid, notwithstanding the unbelief of ethnic Israel in general, because God chose the line of

Isaac and Jacob for temporal blessings is merely to restate the historical problem and to solve nothing.[118]

To this affirmation of God's sovereign election of a remnant within ethnic Israel, Paul's critics levied two objections. *First*, God would be *unjust* in his dealings (vv. 14-18). This objection would be of little force if the issue at hand were merely the choice of ethnic Israel for earthly privileges. But note that Paul's response to the objection was an emphatic, "Not at all!" (v. 14). Although finite beings do not comprehend God's elective purpose, God reserves the right to exercise mercy upon whom he chooses. So the apostle appealed to Yahweh's words to Moses, "I will have mercy on whom I have mercy, and I will have compassion on whom I have compassion" (v. 15; cf. v. 18).[119] God is not unjust to give a person more than he deserves while permitting the unsaved to continue in their chosen path of sin, any more than it is not unjust of an earthly governor to pardon one criminal and not another. Concerning the divine election of a remnant Paul wrote, "It does not, therefore, depend on man's desire or effort, but on God's mercy" (v. 16). The decisive factor concerning who will be saved is God's sovereign will, not human volition.

The *second* objection levied was that if God is sovereign in election and hardening, no one could be judged blameworthy (vv. 19-24). Paul responded sternly to the arrogant objector: "who are you, O man, to talk back to God?" (v. 20). Appealing to the OT imagery of the potter and the clay (Jer 18:2-6), Paul argued that as the potter has the right to mold the clay as he wills, so God has the sovereign right to bestow more grace on one of his creatures than on another (v. 21). Paul's reference to "the objects of his mercy, whom he prepared in advance for glory" (v. 23) clearly depicts his sovereign, pre-temporal election of some for heavenly destiny.[120] Pinnock has argued in the light of the potter and the clay analogy that God "has a great deal for which to answer."[121] The crucial issue is, Must the all-perfect God answer to finite and feeble-minded humans, or must we mortals bow before and answer to a sovereign, just, and all-wise God?

In the second section of our extended text, Rom 9:30–10:21, Paul argued that the fact of sovereign election, as expounded from the OT, does not eliminate the individual's responsibility for making the right choice. Quoting from Joel 2:32, Paul wrote, "Everyone who calls on the name of the Lord will be saved" (10:13). Personal response to the Gospel message is necessary if one would be saved. Paul continued that the Gospel has been published widely and to Jews first. "But not all the Israelites accepted the good news" (v. 16). Why not? Because they sought righteousness by law-keeping rather than by faith in the crucified and risen Messiah. The Lord holds unbelieving Israel morally responsible for their unbelief.

The third section, Rom 11:1-29, explains God's purpose for the future of Israel and the Gentiles. Paul again refuted the notion that God has rejected Israel: "God did not reject his people, whom he foreknew" (v. 2a). The objects of God's foreknowledge are the Jewish people, often disobedient and faithless and without praiseworthy responses on their part. Rom 11:2 thus better fits the conclusion reached above—i.e., that God's foreknowing is equivalent to his foreloving or foreordaining. The NT frequently cites the very close relationship that exists between God's loving and his choosing (Eph 1:4; Col 3:12; 1 Thess 1:4; 2 Thess 2:13). That God has not forsaken his people is evidenced by the fact that "at the present time there is a remnant chosen by grace" (v. 5). The existence of an elect remnant within the chosen nation is the outcome of God's sovereign and gracious purpose. God formed the remnant by a personal election within the corporate election to yield a spiritual seed within the institutional people. We underscore the conclusion of Jewett: "Israel was elect in a double sense: in an outward and temporal sense, the nation, as a nation, was elect; in an inward, personal, and eternal sense, a faithful remnant was elected."[122] To illustrate this choice of an elect remnant, Paul pointed to himself (v. 1b) and to 7,000 faithful souls in Elijah's day who would not bow before Baal (vv. 2b-4). The nation as a whole failed to obtain spiritual blessing (v. 7), "but the elect (*eklogē*) did [obtain it]," not by works but by grace (v. 6). We defer discussion of the salvation of many Gentiles and eventually "all Israel" (v. 26) to the volumes in this series on the church and eschatology.

The apostle, however, concluded his treatment of God's sovereign elective purpose for Jews and Gentiles with a hymn of praise (vv. 33-36). God's gracious choice of certain Jews and Gentiles to be saved lends itself more to doxology than to precise rational analysis. The salvation of the remnant is the result of the "wisdom," "knowledge," "judgments," and "mind" of the Lord.[123] God's sovereign purpose of mercy and grace to sinners is so grand and exalted that the only fitting response on the part of feeble humans is humble praise and adoration. "For from him and through him and to him are all things. To him be the glory forever!" (v. 36).

In Gal 1:15-16 Paul wrote that "God, who set me apart from birth and called me by his grace, was pleased to reveal his Son in me so that I might preach him among the Gentiles. . . ." Paul made it abundantly clear that prior to his conversion he hated the church and did his utmost to destroy it (Gal 1:13, 23; cf. Acts 9:1-2, 13-14; 22:4-5; 26:10; 1 Tim 1:13). Yet he also affirmed that God in grace took the saving initiative in his rebellious life. Thus the Father was pleased to separate him from birth—the word *aphorisas* ("separated") being related to *proōrisas* ("predestinate")—and to reveal his Son to him (cf. 2 Cor 4:6). Only then did the Lord commission Paul for Gospel ministry. The apostle thus attested God's act of separation in eternity past for salvation and in time for service. As he testified in Gal 2:20, God's saving action toward him was profoundly *personal*. Thus Paul saw himself (1) personally loved by Christ ("who loved me"), (2) personally justified ("I live by faith in the Son of God"), (3) personally regenerated ("Christ lives in me"), and (4) personally united with the Savior ("crucified with Christ"). Four times in this one verse Paul used the first-person pronoun (*egō, emou, me, emoi*). Jewett's comment again proves instructive: "The individual quality in God's electing love is reflected in the use of the singular personal pronoun in Scripture. . . . To be elect is to be aware that God has fixed his love on *me*, called *me* by name, given *me* a new name (Rev 2:17), and inscribed *my* name in the Book."[124] God had a plan for Saul/Paul and worked efficiently to bring him to faith in Christ. The same could not be said for God's relation to Judas, Pilate, or Herod.

A comprehensive Pauline text dealing with election is Eph 1:3-14, which we analyze as follows. (1) The *source* of election: "the God and Father of our Lord Jesus Christ, who has blessed us in the heavenly realms with every spiritual blessing in Christ" (v. 3). Election is a monogeristic operation of God, not a synergism (cf. 2 Tim 1:9). (2) The *fact* of election: "we were also chosen, having been predestined according to the plan of him who works out everything in conformity with the purpose of his will" (v. 11; cf. vv. 4-5, 9). Paul's election words in the preceding verses are heaped one upon the another, powerful and descriptive of what God himself accomplishes: *eklegō*, to "choose out," "select;"[125] *kleroō*, to "choose," "destine"; *proorizō*, to "foreordain," "predestine"; *protithēmi*, to "purpose," "intend"; *prothesis*, "plan," "purpose," "resolve;"[126] *boulē*, "an intention" or "deliberation" (with emphasis on the deliberative aspect of the decision;[127] *thelēma*, "will" or "intention"—i.e., "God's eternal and providential saving will,"[128] with emphasis on the volitional aspect or the will in exercise; and *eudokia*, "good pleasure," "act of the will"—a choice grounded in God's sovereign purpose.[129]

(3) The *time* of election: from eternity past, i.e., "before the creation of the world" (v. 4; cf. 2 Thess 2:13; 2 Tim 1:9). Salvation is the unfolding of God's eternal purpose. "The Scriptures say that God chose us in Christ from before the foundation of the world, not that he saw us from before the foundation of the world as choosing Christ."[130] (4) the *objects* of election: "we" (v. 7) or "us" (vv. 3-6, 8-9). Paul envisaged the elect both in

their corporate standing as the church and in their individuality. The latter is clear in Rom 16:13, where Paul wrote, "Greet Rufus, chosen (*ton eklekton*) in the Lord," and in 1 Pet 1:1, discussed below. The people of God are viewed both in their unity and in their diversity (Rom 12:4-5; 1 Cor 10:17; 12:12, 20; Eph 4:25; 5:30; Col 3:15). Berkouwer made this important observation: "We are repeatedly struck by the lack of tension between the election of the individual and the election of the church. . . . *The life of the individual does not dissolve into the community*"[131] (emphasis added). Every social unit must be defined in terms of the individuals that comprise it. The NT designates Christians as "believers," "saints," and "elect." No one doubts that it is the individual that believes and is sanctified. So ultimately it is the individual who is loved and chosen by God. Luther captured this individual dimension of salvation, often obscured by corporate advocates, when he wrote, "You must do your own believing, as you must do your own dying."[132]

(5) The *sphere* of election: "in Christ" (vv. 3-7, 9, 11; 3:11; 2 Tim 1:9). Arminians interpret "in Christ" as elect according to our quality as believers. Predestination "in Christ," however, affirms God's purpose to effect salvation through the person and work of Jesus Christ (vv. 5, 7; cf. Rom 6:23b; 2 Tim 1:9b). "Christ is the medium for the imparting of grace."[133] The phrase "in Christ" positively excludes a works-effected salvation. (6) The *motive* of election: God's freely conceived and unconditional love. So Paul wrote, "in love he predestined us" (vv. 4-5). (7) The *impartiality* of election: "in accordance with his pleasure and will" (v. 5; cf. Rom 2:11; 11:34). God's choice was not motivated by the faintest hint of favoritism. Finally, (8) the *goal* of election: that believers might "be holy and blameless in his sight" (v. 4), and that they might live "to the praise of his glorious grace" (v. 6). The outcome, not the condition, of election is righteousness of life.

To encourage Thessalonian Christians who were severely persecuted, Paul wrote that the God who had chosen them for salvation from eternity past and called them to Christ would sustain them in their present trials (2 Thess 2:13-14). Sorely tempted to renounce Christ, the believers would have found little consolation in the reminder that it was *they* who had chosen God. Rather, the supreme encouragement in a situation where their human resources were failing was that *God* had chosen them for an enduring salvation. So the apostle wrote, "we . . . thank God for you, brothers loved by the Lord, because from the beginning God chose [*eilato*] you to be saved through the sanctifying work of the Spirit and through belief in the truth." The middle voice of a verb denotes the subject acting with respect to itself. Here the aorist middle indicative of *haireomai* (to "choose," "prefer," "decide") "emphasizes . . . the relation of the person chosen to the special purpose of him who chooses. The 'chosen' are regarded . . . as they stand to the counsel of God."[134] See also 1 Thess 1:4-5, where the saints' response to the Gospel was evidence of their prior election. Election in eternity past was actualized in time by the sanctifying work of the Spirit and the Thessalonians' belief in the Gospel as preached by Paul. 2 Thess 2:13 (NRSV) indicates that God actively chose them specifically "for salvation" (*eis sōterian*). Paul also stated this truism in 1 Thess 5:9 when he wrote, "God. . . [appointed] us . . . to receive salvation" (*eis peripoiēsin sōterias*).[135] To the Christian's experiential question, Why am I a Christian?, the biblically faithful answer must be, Because God chose me.

James also stated that the initiative in salvation lies wholly with the sovereign God: "He chose [*boulētheis*] us to give us birth through the word of truth" (Jas 1:18). Jude 1 affirmed the same in its description of Christians as people "called," "loved," and "kept" by God. Observe that it is fundamentally the *individual* (and by extension the class) who is "loved" and "kept" by God; so also it is the *individual* who is "called" by God. Peter viewed the body of Christ as the new people of God (1 Pet 2:9-10); yet within this new entity he saw the election of individuals to salvation. So Peter wrote his first letter to "God's elect [*eklektois*], strangers in the world, scattered" throughout much of Asia Minor (1 Pet 1:1). Since individuals, not a class, scatter or are dispersed, Peter had in mind an aggregate of *individuals,* not an empty class. The elect ones "have been chosen according to [*kata*] the foreknowledge [*prognōsin*] of God the Father, through (*en*) the sanctifying work of the Spirit, for [*eis*] obedience to Jesus Christ and sprinkling by his blood" (v. 2). Several comments on this verse are in order. (1) The preposition *kata* indicates the *basis* of divine election—namely, the divine foreknowledge. In context, *prognōsis* denotes the divine foreloving or foreordaining, or as Selwyn stated, God's "knowing or taking note of those whom He will choose."[136] That God's foreknowledge of Christians likely indicates more than prescience is confirmed by Peter's statement that Christ "was chosen (perfect passive participle of *proginōskō*) before the creation of the world" (1 Pet 1:20; "He was destined," RSV, NRSV; cf. Acts 2:23). 1 Pet 1:2 says nothing about Christians being chosen on the basis of foreseen faith. (2) The preposition *en* signifies the means by which eternal election was effected in time—i.e., by operation of the Spirit. And (3) the preposition *eis* denotes the goal or outcome of election—i.e., obedience to Christ and the application of his atoning benefits. Peter did not state that those who obey Christ are elect, but that the elect proceed to obey Christ. See also Jas 2:5.

In 2 Pet 1:10 the disciple wrote to the dispersed believers, "Therefore, my brothers, be all the more eager to make your calling and election [eklogē] sure. For if you do these things, you will never fall." Truly it is not the undifferentiated group that falls or fails to persevere, but *individuals* who are here considered aggregately. Moreover, the brothers confirm their calling and election by cultivating the qualities listed in vv. 5-7, namely, "faith," "goodness," "knowledge," "self-control," "perseverance," "godliness," "brotherly kindness," and "love." These too are activities of individuals, not of an empty group or class. Therefore if we talk of the election of a class, it must be as the sum of elect individuals.

E. Is Predestination Double?

Some allege that the approximately ten references to God's hardening of Pharaoh's heart (Exod 4:21; 7:3; 9:12; *et al.*) support the thesis of unconditional reprobation to damnation. But prior to mentioning the divine hardening, Scripture indicates that Pharaoh freely opposed God's purposes (Exod 8:15, 19, 32; 9:7, 34, 35; *et al.*; cf. 13:15; 1 Sam 6:6). The Bible does not explain the nature of the hardening, but it appears that God's role was that of confirming Pharaoh's decisions rather than predetermining them. The most coherent explanation of the hardening is that by withdrawing his sustaining Spirit and by giving Pharaoh up to his own impulses, God permitted the Egyptian leader to actualize his hostile designs (cf. Rom 1:24, 26, 28). The hardening thus represents God's punishment of Pharaoh for rejecting God's good purposes.

A similar situation occurred in the case of Sihon, king of the Amorites, who refused to permit Israel to pass through his territory. Yet the Hebrews so attributed ultimate causality to God that Moses could say, "God had made his spirit stubborn and his heart obstinate" (Deut 2:30; cf. Num 21:23), even though God's involvement was limited to permission of the incident.[137] The language of rejection, common in the Psalms and indicated by the verbs zānaḥ (Ps 43:2; 44:9, 23; 60:1; etc.) and mā'as (Ps 53:5; 78:59, 67; 89:38), refers to a temporal forfeiture of privileges as a result of deliberate covenant-breaking. God's work among the Egyptians— "whose hearts he turned to hate [śānē'] his people" (Ps 105:25)—should be understood in the sense of his hardening of Pharaoh's heart (for human self-hardening, see Ps 95:8 and Prov 28:14). Scripture stops short of ascribing sin to God's efficient will, as indicated by repeated warnings of judgments against evil practices (Ps 81:13-15; Ecc 11:9).

Some interpreters find support for the doctrine of reprobation in certain crucial sayings of Jesus. Jesus' parable of the sheep and goats (Matt 25:31-46) differentiates between the sheep on the right hand ("blessed" by the Father) and the goats on the left ("cursed" [*katēramenoi*] by him). Jesus stated that the righteous inherit the kingdom prepared specifically for them (v. 34), whereas the accursed depart into the place of torment prepared, not for them, but for Satan and his angels (v. 41). As Brunner has noted, "The distinctive element in the biblical statement is not the 'congruity' but the 'incongruity' of the 'right hand and the left hand.'"[138] The saved are those whom God has chosen for eternal blessing; the lost are those whom God has chosen to "leave" (*aphiēmi*, Luke 17:34-35) in their self-willed state of sinful rebellion.

Paul's reference to God's hardening the human heart in Rom 9:18— "God ... hardens whom he wants to harden"—signifies not reprobation but God's ratification of the sinner's determination to steel himself or herself against the divine will of pleasure. With Shedd we can say that God hardens the hearts of the unsaved in two ways: (1) by permitting persons to exercise their sinful wills, and (2) by withdrawing his grace so that their sinful lusts go unchecked.[139] Paul's statement that God "raised up" (*exēgeira*) Pharaoh—the Hebrew of Exod 9:16 suggests that God merely sustained Pharaoh in life (see the NRSV)—communicates God's use of hard-hearted Pharaoh in the outworking of his saving plan. The Lord was not, however, the blameworthy cause of Pharaoh's actions. God does not efficiently impel sinful rebellion, but he does give sinners sufficient rope to hang themselves. According to Sproul, "It is not that God puts his hand on them to create fresh evil in their hearts; he merely removes his holy hand of restraint from them and lets them do their own will."[140]

The analogy of the potter and the clay (Rom 9:20-21), whereby the craftsman fashions out of the same lump "some pottery for noble purposes (*eis timēn*) and some for common use (*eis atimian*)" registers the point made earlier, that God purposefully sanctifies some people and leaves others in their sins. Cranfield helpfully comments, "It should be noted that *eis atimian* implies menial use, not reprobation or destruction. The potter does not make ordinary, everyday pots in order to destroy them."[141] Neither do vv. 22-23 support an unconditional predestination to destruction. They state that the saved were "prepared [*proētoimasen*] in advance for glory," whereas the lost are "prepared [*katērtismena*] for destruction." The fact that Paul here did not use the verb *prokatartizō* (cf. 2 Cor 9:5) suggests that it is not God who reprobated in eternity; rather, sinners prepare themselves for destruction by their own refusal to repent. The emphasis in these verses is not upon God's pre-mundane reprobation, but upon the temporal postponement of his wrath against unbelievers who are ripe for destruction. In sum, "there appears here no support for any dogma of predestination to damnation, while the parallel foreordination to glory is stated with no uncertainty."[142] The big idea of the potter and the clay analogy is God's absolute right to deal with his creatures as he sovereignly wills. Other texts adduced by some in support of reprobation, such as 1 Cor 9:27, Gal 4:30, 2 Tim 2:20, 3:8, likewise fall short of actually teaching what Calvin called the "horrible decree."

Israel's hardening (Rom 11:7, 25) and the Jews' subsequent spiritual insensitivity (Rom 11:8, 10) should be understood in the sense of Rom 9:18. With pleasure God willed the salvation of "a remnant" within the family of Abraham (Rom 11:5); but with displeasure he permitted the majority of Israelites to reject his offer of grace (v. 12). Thus we concur with Brunner who stated that "there is no doctrine of a double decree in the New Testament, and still less in the Old."[143]

First Pet 2:8 affirms the divinely appointed ruin of those who persistently reject the Gospel. The antecedent of the clause—"which is also what they were destined for" (*etethēsan*)—is not the verb "they disobey" (so Calvin, Beza), but "they stumble."[144] Hebrews' mention of Israel's hardness of heart in Egypt focuses on the individual as the cause of the hardening (Heb 3:8, 13, 15; 4:7). It may be that the aorist passive subjunctive, *sklērunthē* ("that none of you may be hardened," Heb 3:13) is properly "understood as a passive of permission; i.e., 'allow or permit one's self to be hardened.'"[145] Similarly, Esau was rejected by God only after he had rejected divine grace freely offered (Heb 12:17). The teaching of Scripture as a whole is that continued resistance to God's grace produces a fixed habit of opposition to God that is not easily broken.

In sum, the biblical evidence leads us to uphold 'an election within an election,' namely (1) the corporate election of the people of God for earthly privileges and eternal destiny, as well as (2) an election of individuals to the personal enjoyment of these blessings. Scripture leads us to posit first the election of the group (Israel and the church) and then the personal election of those individuals who comprise the true, spiritual people of God.

The Roman and Arminian views posit sinful men and women as the ultimate determiners of their own salvation, whereas Augustinians and Reformed identify God as the ultimate and efficient cause of eternal blessedness. According to the former traditions, the distinction between the saved and the unsaved is grounded in the choice of the creature; according to the latter, the distinction is grounded in the good pleasure and will of God, however unclear the rationale thereof may be to us mortals. The weight of biblical and historical evidence rests in favor of a single unconditional election to life. This position holds that out of the mass of fallen and responsible humanity—for reasons known to himself—God in grace chose some to be saved and to permit the others to persist in their sin. Against the symmetrical view of Romanists and Arminians (double foreknowledge) and Hyper-Calvinists and Barthians (double predestination), the biblical evidence leads us to posit an *asymmetrical* view of soteriological purpose—namely, unconditional election to life and conditional election to damnation. When we speak about damnation, we mean that God predestines persons not to sin and disobedience but to the *condemnation* that issues from sin.

Concerning this doctrine of election to life, we concur with the carefully measured conclusion of Jewett, who wrote: "In my judgment, this Augustinian approach reflects a much more impressive biblical and exegetical effort than does the Pelagian and Arminian view."[146] We do not wish to blow the importance of this debated doctrine of predestination out of proportion. But neither do we neglect what is undoubtedly a significant biblical theme. The following section will discuss the practical relevance of the doctrine of election for the life of Christian believers.

IV. PRACTICAL IMPLICATIONS OF THE DOCTRINE OF ELECTION

A. *Great Joy and Confidence in Being Chosen*

The doctrine of gracious election, as developed in the preceding pages, is not an issue for idle speculation. It is improper to pose questions such as, "Is so-and-so among the elect?" or to make statements such as, "There's no need to witness to her, for I'm sure she is not chosen to be saved." The writer has encountered new converts, especially students from other countries, who ask the following kinds of questions: "Are my unsaved father and mother in the interior of China among the elect?" "Is my unbelieving sister studying in an atheistic country in Eastern Europe predestined by God?" Scripture, however, presents the doctrine of election not as a rebuke to the world at large but as a comfort for the Lord's *saints.* The doctrine of election is to be discussed after the person has come to faith in Christ, not before. For this reason thoughtful Christians treat the biblical doctrine of election under the heading of salvation wrought by Christ, rather than under the heading of the divine nature or decrees.

Converted persons rejoice because they are assured by Scripture that before the foundation of the world God loved and chose them to be saved. Christians recall that formerly they walked in spiritual darkness and were alienated from God, burdened with sinful passions and lusts, and deserving of divine wrath. In such a hopeless state God graciously invaded the heart and brought it to faith through the Spirit's convicting ministry. As the Christian reflects on his experience of being brought to Christ—like that of Abram, Jeremiah, Saul, and Lydia in biblical times—he rejoices in the knowledge that God loved *me*, chose *me*, pursued *me*, and brought *me* savingly to Christ. In the face of such an awesome truth, the believer can only bow before the sovereign Lord in wonder and gratitude. Then when life's inevitable trials come and the child of God is tempted to throw in the towel and capitulate to the world, he remember the Father's eternal, gracious plan for *him*. Blessed with this lofty consolation the saint is encouraged and fortified to do battle with his spiritual foes, armed with the shield of faith.

Paul encouraged young Timothy with the truth of election during the severe persecutions handed out by the emperor Nero. Paul wrote, "join with me in suffering for the gospel, by the power of God, who has saved us and called us to a holy life—not because of anything we have done, but because of his own purpose and grace . . . given us in Christ Jesus before the beginning of time" (2 Tim 1:8-9). With such a truth the apostle also comforted the persecuted and wavering Christians in the church at Thessalonica: "we ought always to thank God for you, brothers loved by the Lord, because from the beginning God chose you to be saved through the sanctifying work of the Spirit and through belief in the truth" (2 Thess 2:13). Throughout history recollection of God's elective purpose has greatly consoled the hearts of believers in Christ. Consider the testimony of C. H. Spurgeon:

> I believe the doctrine of election, because I am quite certain that if God had not chosen me I should never have chosen Him; and I am sure He chose me before I was born, or else He never would have chosen me afterwards; and He must have elected me for reasons unknown to me, for I never could find any reason in myself why He should have looked upon me with special love. So I am forced to accept that doctrine.[147]

B. *Encouragement to Preaching, Evangelism, and Prayer*

Arminian friends claim that the doctrine of personal election would seriously undercut the urgency of evangelistic preaching and prayer. What need is there for pleading or prayer, the argument goes, if God has unconditionally determined each person's destiny? John Wesley judged the doctrine of election to be quite incompatible with Gospel preaching. It is true that some hyper-Calvinists have erroneously claimed that God will accomplish his sovereign purposes without human involvement. We recall the story of William Carey who shared with his Particular Baptist pastor his heart-concern for the unsaved of India and his desire to minister in that land as a missionary. Carey's hyper-Calvinist minister responded to the effect that if God wanted the people of India to be saved, he was fully able to accomplish his purpose without Carey's help!

The indisputable fact is that God has positively commanded preaching, pleading, and prayer as vehicles God uses to bring the unsaved to Christ (Isa 52:7; Matt 28:19-20; Rom 10:1, 14-15; 2 Cor 5:18-20). More to the point, God has sovereignly ordained the *goal* of salvation as well as the *means* or *instruments* (preaching, witnessing, etc.) for achieving this goal. Thus if God has sovereignly ordained certain persons to be saved, he will unfailingly enlist preachers and prayer warriors to facilitate their coming to Christ. The omnipotent God could, of course, bring people to Christ by a *miraculous* strategy, namely, by his bare power apart from any human instrumentality. But God infrequently works in this way. God ordinarily brings persons to Christ via a *providential* strategy—namely, by means of faithful human witnessing, prayer, and counsel. As an example, if a football coach devises a brilliant game plan for winning the Super Bowl, does this relieve his players of expending every effort to win the contest? Of course not. God alone knows whom he has chosen to be saved and whom he has passed by. Our task as disciples is to be faithful and serviceable instruments in God's plan and strategy for restoring sinners to himself.

In fact, the biblical doctrine of election provides the ultimate assurance that our preaching and prayer will succeed. Tempted to retreat from ministry in Corinth due to firm opposition from the Jews (Acts 18:6), Paul was encouraged to continue his mission after the Lord said to him in a vision, "Do not be afraid; keep on speaking, do not be silent . . . because I have many people in this city" (vv. 9-10). The reality is that God uses willing human instruments by his great power to accomplish his grand saving purposes. In non-Reformed schemes the final determiner of whether a sinner comes to Christ lies with the urging of the preacher and the response of the individual. At L'Abri in the 1970s an American woman chided Francis Schaeffer for devoting a few hours one Saturday afternoon to skiing a few miles up the mountain from Huemoz. She claimed that because he chose to use that time for recreation people would not hear the Gospel and thus would go to hell. In effect, she charged Dr. Schaeffer with culpability for the perdition of lost sinners. Dr. Schaeffer carefully responded that the weight of winning the world rested not on his shoulders but on

God's. Christ's primary requirement of disciples for the ingathering of the harvest is faithfulness, not hyper-activity or sleeplessness. Some of the church's most fruitful soul-winners and evangelists have held to a Reformation faith: e.g., Luther, Calvin, Whitefield, Brainerd, Edwards, Carey, Spurgeon, and Kennedy.

C. A Positive Stimulus to Holiness

Many Arminians and Wesleyans assert that a sovereign decree of election would lead to moral and spiritual indifference and thus would undermine the Christian's pursuit of holiness. But as noted in the preceding section, Scripture teaches that we are not elect because we exhibit a holy character; rather we strive to develop a holy character because of the certainty that we have been graciously chosen to life. Simply put, God elects believers not only to salvation but also to the personal holiness that leads to the heavenly goal. True Christians take very seriously their calling to reflect the holy character of the electing God (Matt 5:48; Heb 12:14; 1 Pet 1:15-16). The relationship between God's election and the Christian's practical motivation works out as follows. Reflecting on God's saving goodness to them, believers realize that they owe everything they are and will become to him. Thus in wholehearted gratitude they strive to please the Lord in thought, word, and deed throughout the course of their lives. Belief in divine election thus does not encourage antinomianism; rather it stimulates the believer's highest capacities to please and obey the Lord who has dealt with him so graciously.

Paul made clear the fact that Christlikeness is the outcome of God's sovereign election: "For those God foreknew he also predestined to be conformed to the likeness of his Son" (Rom 8:29). Furthermore, he claimed that the Father "chose us in him [Christ] before the creation of the world to be holy and blameless in his sight" (Eph 1:4). God sovereignly predestined us not only to adoption as sons (v. 5) but also to a life of moral excellence. Thus, "we are God's workmanship, created in Christ Jesus to do good works, which God prepared in advance for us to do" (Eph 2:10; cf. 5:25b-27; Col 1:22). Peter drew the same conclusion concerning the relation between God's election and the believer's pursuit of holiness. He wrote that believers are both "a chosen people" and "a holy nation" (1 Pet 2:9; cf. 1:2). The solemn message of Scripture is that those who profess to be saved without exhibiting holiness of life and Christlike character seriously deceive themselves. Such persons have no biblical basis for judging themselves Christians.

D. *Confidently Proclaim "Whosoever Will"*

The doctrine of personal, unconditional election in no way undercuts the "whosoever wills" of Scripture (Luke 12:8; John 3:15-16; 11:26; Acts 2:21). As developed in the following chapter, Christ died a death sufficient to atone for the sins of the entire world. Moreover, through the verbal call of the Gospel the Spirit invites all people indiscriminately to believe and be saved (John 6:40). The fact is that each and every person who desires to be saved must *will* to come. Yet as we have seen, rebellious sinners resist acknowledging their sin and bowing before the righteous and holy God. We recall Jesus' words to his contemporaries, "O Jerusalem, Jerusalem, you who kill the prophets and stone those sent to you, how often I have longed to gather your children together, as a hen gathers her chicks under her wings, but you were not willing" (Matt 23:37). Sinners will to come to Christ when the Spirit of God, in fulfillment of the Father's eternal purpose, softens hardened hearts and liberates stubborn wills. The preacher's "whosoever will" is God's appointed means of achieving his eternal, saving purpose.

It is helpful in this regard to recognize the biblical differentiation between "kerygmatic universality" and "didactic particularity."[148] The mandate of Scripture is that the Gospel must be proclaimed to sinners with fervent pleading *universally* (Matt 11:28; 28:19; John 7:37; Acts 17:30; Rev 22:17). All unregenerate persons need the saving Good News, and Christ's death is sufficient to atone for the sins of the world (1 Tim 4:10; 1 John 2:2). Given a universal proclamation of the Gospel, if a sinner remains lost and condemned, it is because he or she rejects God's gracious offer of life. In the divine wisdom, however, the truth of unconditional election is taught *privately* to those who have trusted Christ (John 6:37, 39; Rom 8:29-30; Eph 1:4-11; 2 Thess 2:13; 2 Tim 1:9). In other words, *kerygma* is *a priori* to the predestined human response and *didache* is *a posteriori* to the human decision for Christ. Disciples preach the Gospel of salvation to all persons, but teach the doctrine of election to reassure and comfort those who have come to faith.

E. *Does God "Will" All People to Be Saved?*

Certain biblical texts, at first blush, appear to contravene the doctrine of unconditional election by suggesting that God wills the salvation of all creatures. 1 Tim 2:3-4 reads, "This is good, and pleases God our Savior, who wants [*thelei*] all men to be saved and to come to a knowledge of the truth." The verb *thelo* means to "wish," "desire," "take pleasure in."[149] This text likely refers to one aspect of God's will, namely, his conditional will of pleasure that may be sinfully violated by the misuse of creaturely freedom. Paul's point is that the perdition of sinners brings the loving God no pleasure (cf. Ezek 18:23, 32; 33:11). The extra-biblical Wisdom of Solomon expresses this point as follows: "because God did not make death . . . he does not delight in the death of the living (1:13)." Thus God "delights in the righteousness of his judgment but is 'sad' that such righteous judgment must be carried out."[150] Consider the following analogy from the human realm. A sensitive judge takes no pleasure in sentencing a guilty criminal to death; nevertheless his office requires that he justly order the prescribed punishment.

A second text, 2 Pet 3:9, allegedly teaches a universalism that refutes the doctrine of election. "The Lord . . . is patient with you, not wanting [*me boulomenos*] anyone to perish, but everyone to come to repentance." The verb *boulomai*, to "will" or "resolve," connotes an attitude of God stronger than mere wishing or desiring. The "you" and "anyone" may refer to his elect people (cf. "dear friends," vv. 1, 8). If this be the case, the sense of the text is that the Lord delays his coming in order that the full complement of the elect may come to faith and repentance and not be lost (cf. John 6:39). In sum, the two NT texts do not contravene the substantial biblical teaching concerning personal, unconditional election to life.

II

THE PROVISION OF SALVATION

"CHRIST DIED FOR SINS ONCE FOR ALL"

I   P E T E R   3 : 1 8

———□———

THE DOCTRINE
OF THE ATONEMENT

I. INTRODUCTORY
CONCERNS

From the previously discussed saving purpose graciously conceived in eternity past, we turn in the present chapter to God's provision of salvation through the life and death of Jesus Christ. The world's major religions direct attention primarily to the teachings of their human founder or leader. While not neglecting Jesus' important teachings, Christianity uniquely focuses on the life Christ lived and the death he died on the cross as interpreted by the Scriptures. The apostle Paul upheld the focal importance of Christ's passion with his overstatement to the church at Corinth, "I resolved to know nothing while I was with you except Jesus Christ and him crucified" (1 Cor 2:2; cf. 1:18; Gal 6:14). For solid biblical reasons the cross of Christ is the central symbol of the Christian faith. Correctly the British Congregationalist P.T. Forsyth (d. 1921) spoke somewhere of the "cruciality of the cross." And the Scottish professor James Denney (d. 1917) identified the Atonement as the theme that unifies the Scriptures, both Old and New.[1] The themes of Christ's passion and death, however, appear to be muted in our day. Many mediating and liberal theologians direct attention to Christ's teaching and compassionate deeds rather than to his vicarious sufferings and death on the cross.[2]

Previous chapters of this study highlighted pre-Christians' need for grace and salvation. Here we simply state the fact that human sin is an offense to the holy and righteous God. All persons have sinned against God and his law (Rom 3:23). Thus all are guilty before the bar of divine justice (Gen 3:7; Isa 1:4; Jer 2:22), in a state of condemnation (Rom 3:19; 5:16, 18), and holistically depraved (John 3:6; Rom 8:5-8; Col 2:13). In God's justice the certain consequences of sin and depravity are physical death (Rom 5:12; 8:10; 1 John 5:16-17), spiritual death or estrangement from God (Gen 3:8-10; Isa 59:2; Eph 5:14; Col 1:21), and eternal death or everlasting punishment (Matt 25:41, 46; 2 Thess 1:9; Rev 20:13-15) at the hands of an angry God (Rom 1:18; 2:5). The fundamental issue of human existence, then, is how deeply ingrained sin can be forgiven and how the spiritual chasm between God and his creatures can be bridged. As Job posed the question millennia ago, "How can a mortal be righteous before God?" (Job 9:2).

To answer this simple but profound question we must investigate the significance of Christ's sufferings and death on the cross. Could God have atoned for sin in a way other than the death of his Son? Put in other words, was the cross of Christ absolutely necessary? What did the cross Jesus bore more than 2,000 years ago achieve for sinful and alienated people today? What did his death accomplish that we ourselves could not bring about? Did the cross achieve something objective before God? Or, was its impact only subjective in the hearts of those who receive it? If the former, how could one person assuage the guilt and penalty of people in all times and places? Moreover, what do the biblical metaphors such as ransom, redemption, passover sacrifice, and propitiation contribute to our understanding of Christ's saving work? Can we with much of Christian tradition assert that Christ took our place on the cross, bore the just wrath of God for us, and paid the penalty for our sins? Or do notions of vicarious and penal sacrifice convey a false picture of the loving God who is always ready to forgive his creatures? Of the many so-called theories of the Atonement proposed throughout the centuries, which enjoy the firm support of Scripture? In explaining the work of Christ John Calvin portrayed Christ functioning as our prophet, priest, and, king. What insights does this three-fold representation contribute to our understanding of his saving work?

As we think about Christ and Calvary, the question inevitably arises as to how forgiveness of sins and salvation were achieved in OT times before the advent of the Savior and the accomplishment of his redemptive work. Prior to Christ's life and death, on what basis were sinful people made right with God? Specifically, what role did the Jewish sacrificial system, with its repetitive meat and grain offerings, play in the mediation of salvation in pre-Christian times? What can we say about the plan of salvation in the OT and the millions of people who lived under its protocol?

In the present chapter we also address the widely debated question of whether Christ died for sinners universally or only for particular individuals known as the elect. Historically the discussion frequently focused on the extent or intent of the Savior's death. If God's purpose was to provide salvation only for the elect, what might we conclude about God's love? But if God's purpose was to provide salvation for all persons and many are not saved, what might we conclude about God's power or ability to save? It will be helpful to follow biblical guidelines and divide the question into the *provision* dimension of Christ's atonement for sinners and the *application* dimension of his work. In the present chapter we consider the provision side of the Atonement, and in parts III and IV of this book we will examine the application of Christ's work to sinners.

The issues addressed in this chapter on Christ's cross are numerous and complex. But we can concur with Emil Brunner's confident assertion that "He who understands the cross aright . . . understands the Bible, he understands Jesus Christ."[3]

II. HISTORICAL INTERPRETATIONS OF THE ATONEMENT

What the death of Jesus Christ accomplished for persons afflicted with sin and alienated from God has been variously explained in the church. We summarize the complex history of the problem by examining the following theories of the Atonement.

A. The Classic or Ransom Theory (Many Church Fathers & Aulén)

Many patristic authorities to the time of Anselm (d. 1109) and a few contemporary theologians interpret the Atonement as a cosmic victory over sin, death, and Satan. This classic, dramatic, or ransom theory, which depicts God triumphing over enslaving spiritual forces, was the dominant church view for 1,000 years. The interpretation found favor with early Christians surrounded by oppressive satanic activity in the pagan world. The theory focuses not on Christ's bearing the sinner's penalty or propitiating God's wrath but upon his act of delivering believers from enslaving powers. The theory assumes two principal forms. (1) Some interpreters, following Mark 10:45, viewed Christ's death as a ransom paid to the Devil. As a result of sin humankind had fallen under Satan's dominion. At the cross God delivered Christ over to Satan in exchange for the souls the evil one held captive. But Satan could not hold Christ permanently, and so the Son of God rose powerfully from the grave. (2) Other authorities, guided by Col 2:15, claimed that God did battle with Satan, triumphed over death and the Devil once for all, and rescued those held captive by the powers of darkness. In the ancient writers the themes of ransom, victory, and deliverance often were closely intertwined.

Irenaeus (d. 200) interpreted Christ's death as a victory over sin, death, and the Devil. By virtue of Adam's disobedience, humanity fell under the dominion of Satan. By obediently recapitulating in himself all the experiences of humankind and by rising from the dead, Christ conquered Satan, wrested believing sinners from his control, and gave them eternal life. This great victory was foreshadowed in Gen 3:15 and predicted by Christ himself in Matt 12:29. Wrote Irenaeus, "Redeeming us with his blood, Christ gave himself as a ransom for those who had been led into captivity."[4]

Origen (d. 254) maintained that as a consequence of sin, humanity was bound in the clutches of Satan and captive to hell. In exchange for the freedom of souls held under his sway, Satan demanded the blood of Christ. When the Father handed his Son over to the Devil as a ransom (*lytron*), Satan released the imprisoned souls. Origen added that Satan was deceived in the transaction in two ways: (1) Christ's humanity veiled his deity, so that when Satan swallowed the bait of Christ's flesh he was caught on the hook of his deity; and (2) Satan discovered that he could not hold Christ in hell, and on the third day the Savior rose victoriously from the grave. Origen summarized his view as follows: "The evil one reigned over us until the soul of Jesus had been given to him as a ransom—to him who deceived himself, thinking that he could be master over Jesus, not realizing that he did not suffer the agony which he applied to hold him down."[5] In this way Christ gained the victory over Satan.

Gregory of Nyssa (d. 394) similarly depicted Jesus' humanity as the bait covering the fishhook of his deity on which the Devil was snared. He envisaged sinners as bound in the prison of death by the enemy of their souls. To redeem the captives the Father gave his Son to Satan as a ransom. "In order to secure that the ransom in our behalf might be easily accepted by him who required it, the Deity was hidden under the veil of our nature, that so, as with ravenous fish, the hook of the Deity might be gulped down along with the bait of flesh."[6] Yet Satan, who deceived the race, himself was deceived as the Savior defied the grave and returned to life.

At the close of the patristic period John of Damascus (d. 749) used the same imagery, except that he identified the enemy that was snared as death rather than Satan. "God forbid that the Lord's blood should have been offered to the tyrant! Wherefore, then, death approaches, gulps down the bait of the body, and is pierced by the hook of the divinity. Then having tasted of the sinless and life-giving body, is destroyed and gives up all those whom it had swallowed down of old." In this way, "destruction is driven away at the onset of life, and life comes to all, while destruction comes to the destroyer."[7] By this victory captive sinners were liberated into the realm of life and immortality.

The Swedish theologian Gustaf Aulén (d. 1977) favored the patristic view of the Atonement erroneously (he thought) rejected by Anselm. Aulén asserted that the sometimes crude metaphors of the Fathers communicate the foundational truth that God in Christ triumphed over the law, sin, death, and the Devil. In a great cosmic drama that resulted in his demise, Christ overcame hostile spiritual powers. As a consequence of that victory, captive sinners were freed and given eternal life. The central theme of the classic view "is the idea of the Atonement as a divine conflict and victory; Christ—*Christus victor*—fights against and triumphs over the evil powers of the world, the 'tyrants' under which mankind is in bondage and suffering, and in him God reconciles the world to himself."[8] Aulén claimed that the Latin or satisfaction view, with its respect for merit and justice, looks to the OT. The *Christus victor* motif, with its focus on the deliverance wrought by grace, is faithful to the revolutionary teachings of the NT and Luther. In support of his view Aulén cited the prediction of Christ's victory in Gen 3:15, the Lord's exorcism of demons in the Gospels, and texts such as Col 2:15, Heb 2:14, and 1 John 3:8. Clearly Aulén's *Christus victor* motif emphasizes Christ's kingly rather than his priestly office.

B. *The Satisfaction or Juridical Theory (Anselm)*

This theory of the Atonement, also designated the Latin view, arose in the patristic West and achieved full expression in the Middle Ages. Influenced by the concept of a feudal overlord whose dignity was injured by his serfs or private citizens, proponents suggested that Christ's death chiefly satisfies God's wounded honor. Although reflecting the seriousness of sin and the solidarity of the race, this theory focused more on God's injured honor and less on the penal and substitutionary nature of Christ's death. Unlike the moral influence theory that follows, the focus of the juridical theory is Godward and objective.

In his essay *Cur Deus Homo?* (*Why God Become Man?*), Anselm of Canterbury (d. 1109) claimed that sin is failure to render God his due— namely, entire subjection and obedience. Through disobedience persons rob God of his honor and violate the integrity of his kingdom. God's nature is such that he requires either satisfaction or punishment for sin. But since God willed that sufficient persons should be saved to replace the number of fallen angels (an idea favored by Augustine), satisfaction for sins must be made.

The medieval mind held that the recompense must be proportional to the dignity of the offended party, in this case God. Consequently a mere human cannot make an infinite satisfaction for the offense committed against the Lord of the universe. Sinners have nothing to offer God, since they already owe him everything. "Sinful man cannot at all accomplish this justification, because a sinner cannot justify a sinner."[9] Thus adequate satisfaction must come from one who is divine, i.e., from God himself. On the other hand, satisfaction must be paid by one who genuinely represents humanity. Thus satisfaction must be made by God who became man. "If only God can make this satisfaction and only a man ought to make it: it is necessary that a God-man make it."[10] Thus God was born of a virgin, and the sinless Jesus Christ voluntarily suffered death, thereby accruing more merit than needed to pay the debt humanity owed. The just God credited Christ's reward to the sinful race and withheld his punishment against sin. <u>According to this view, Christ offered satisfaction to God's honor rather than to his wrath.</u>

Anselm's satisfaction theory appealed to later Roman Catholic thought with its theology of penance and merit. It also appealed to Protestant theology given its affirmation of the seriousness of sin and the infinite satisfaction Christ rendered to God. Yet the satisfaction theory differs from the Reformed and evangelical view of the Atonement in at least two respects: (1) Anselm made the idea of satisfaction virtually the whole of his theory; and (2) Anselm "saw *satisfactio* for our sins as the offering of compensation or damages for dishonor done." Correcting Anselm, Packer continues that "the Reformers saw it [Christ's *satisfactio*] as the undergoing of vicarious punishment (*poena*) to meet the claims on us of God's holy law and wrath (i.e., his punitive justice)."[11]

Several late medieval theologians modified Anselm's theory of satisfaction rendered to God's injured honor. Hugh of St. Victor (d. 1142) combined Anselm's judicial theory with the theory of ransom from Satan's dominion. He judged that Christ rendered satisfaction to God for the dishonor sinners caused him. But with the basis for restoration established, God is disposed to free sinners from Satan's control. Alexander of Hales (d. 1245) and the Franciscan Bonaventura (d. 1274) generally followed the Anselmic scheme, although both appeared reluctant to posit the absolute necessity of Christ's death as Anselm had done. The English reformer John Wycliffe (d. 1384) also followed the main lines of the Anselmic satisfaction logic.

C. Exemplarism or the Moral Influence Theory (Abelard and Liberals)

This subjective view of the Atonement focuses on Christ as the great teacher and example and the change of attitude his death effects in humans. Proponents claim that Christ's death accomplished nothing objective; there were no obstacles in God that needed to be overcome in order for sinners to be restored to fellowship with their Creator. No satisfaction of justice and no placation of wrath was required on God's side. The sole barrier to salvation lies in estranged persons themselves, i.e., in their ignorant minds and proud wills. This theory maintains that God's love displayed on the cross overwhelms sinners' resistance and persuades them to repent and be reconciled to God. First advanced by Peter Abelard (d. 1142) in reaction to the classic and satisfaction views, the moral influence theory finds many adherents among modern, liberal theologians.

Abelard insisted that Christ did not die to make amends for sin or to deliver captives from Satan's control. Rather, viewing sin as contempt of God, Abelard depicted Christ's death as providing compelling demonstration of God suffering with his creatures. The spectacle of Christ impaled on the cross frees people from fear of wrath, melts their stony hearts, and moves them to amend their lives. The sufferings of the innocent Christ stir sinners to love the One who demonstrated such love for them. In sum, people are saved by the power of divine love that compellingly elicits human love. "Christ died for us in order to show how great was his love to mankind and to prove that love is the essence of Christianity."[12] Abelard believed that the cross exerts the most powerful moral influence in human history.

In opposition to Reformed soteriology, the Italian Socinians modified Abelard's views with themes from Renaissance humanism. Their conception of the Atonement was rooted in (1) the Pelagian view of humanity's essential goodness; (2) the humanistic vision wherein there was no justice in God to be satisfied or wrath to be assuaged; and (3) an adoptionist view of Jesus as a human prophet chosen by God to be his Son. The Socinians claimed that Jesus in his life and death modeled the moral life that God expects of humans. The enduring example of Jesus' obedience unto death inspires persons to repent and obey God's law, thereby receiving forgiveness. Said Socinus, "Christ takes away sins because by heavenly promises he attracts and is strong to move all men to penitence, whereby sins are destroyed. . . . He draws all who have not lost hope to leave their sins and zealously to embrace righteousness and holiness."[13] Socinus believed that Christ's death was but a preliminary stage to the crucial event of his exaltation to heaven. Undertaking in the heavenly world the office of priest, Christ there offered the true sacrifice—his representation of believers before the Father. Many modern Unitarians have adopted this exemplarist theory of the Atonement.

Horace Bushnell (d. 1876), the father of American liberalism, believed that the cross displayed God suffering in love with his creatures. "It is not that the suffering appeases God, but that it expresses God—displays, in open history, the unconquerable love of God's heart."[14] Subjectively, the death of Christ releases a moral power in the world that softens hardened hearts and leads sinners to repentance. Primarily Christ's death "was designed to have a renovating power in character."[15] Seeking to retain some link with orthodoxy, Bushnell suggested that concepts such as divine anger, sacrifice, blood, and expiation ("the altar form") convey the "sentiments, states, and moral effects in the worshippers, which . . . they were unable to conceive or speak of themselves."[16] Although retaining traditional language, Bushnell viewed the Atonement as the power of love that incites persons to repent and amend their character.

The Methodist theologian L.H. DeWolf (d. 1941) also subscribed to the subjectivist view of the Atonement. He claimed that at the cross sinners see the vileness of their sin vividly represented and learn that God lovingly suffers with them in their alienation. Thus as men and women contemplate the cross upon which God acted in Christ, "they are moved to place their hope in the Father, repent with faith, and aspire to serve him in obedient love."[17]

D. *The Governmental or Rectoral Theory (Remonstrants and Arminians)*

Hugo Grotius (d. 1645), a student of Arminius and a Remonstrant jurist and theologian, was the first clear proponent of the rectoral theory of the Atonement. Grotius contemplated God as world Ruler who preserves moral government. His key Scripture text was Isa 42:21, which reads, "The Lord was pleased, for his righteousness sake, to magnify his law and make it glorious" (RSV). Grotius sought to forge a middle ground between Socinianism and the Calvinist Reformers. Against the Socinians he argued that Christ's death served the objective purpose of maintaining the moral order of the universe. And against the Reformers he insisted that Christ did not bear the full penalty of human sin, nor did he propitiate the divine wrath.

Grotius maintained that objectively Christ by his death made a token, rather than a full or equivalent, payment to God for human sins. Through the death of his Son, God upheld the moral governance of the universe while setting aside the requirement of the law that sinners must be punished. The Ruler of the universe could have relaxed his law altogether and not punished Christ, but this would not have achieved the maximum deterrence against future sins. Subjectively, the punishment inflicted on Christ is exemplary in that it communicates God's hatred of sin and motivates persons to repent of sins and reform their lives. Argued Grotius, "God, who has supreme power as to all things not unjust in themselves, and who is liable to no law, willed to use the torments and death of Christ for the setting up of a weighty example against the immense faults of us all."[18] With the moral order of the universe thus upheld, God exercises clemency and forgives sins.

The Methodist theologian John Miley (d. 1895), with other Arminians, generally accepted the outlook of Grotius in rejecting the Reformed penal satisfaction theory. Said he, "The Wesleyan soteriology . . . excludes the satisfaction theory (i.e., atonement by penal substitution) and requires the governmental as the only theory consistent with itself."[19] Arguing that sin and guilt cannot be transferred—particularly to God's Son who had no personal demerit—and that divine justice need not punish sin,[20] Miley concluded that Christ did not bear the actual punishment due to sinners. "The sufferings of Christ are not, and cannot be, an atonement by penal substitution. But while his sufferings could not take the place of penalty in the actual punishment of sin, they could, and do, take its place in its strictly rectoral end."[21] Advancing the governmental theory, Miley claimed that Christ's sufferings are atoning in the sense that they uphold law and further the interests of moral government. God dealt with sin through the death of his Son. But Christ's death fulfills justice not in the sense of a substitute who bore the punishment due to the race but insofar as it upholds the honor and authority of the divine Ruler. Christ's sufferings avail sinners in that they manifest the ugliness of sin, foreshadow the punishment of the unrepentant, and deter future sins by striking fear in human hearts. Miley flatly stated that "Penalty has no reformatory purpose respecting the subject of its infliction, no exemplary character, no office as a deterrent from sin."[22] Miley concluded that "The cross is the highest revelation of all the truths which embody the best moral forces of the divine government."[23] With rectoral justice objectively satisfied, God graciously forgives sins and restores the repentant to fellowship.

The Nazarene theologian J. Kenneth Grider claims that "The governmental theory is the one which peculiarly suits Arminianism."[24] Since Christ was perfectly sinless, he *suffered* rather than being punished, paying the penalty for sins, or making satisfaction to divine justice. Christ's suffering highlights the seriousness of sin, motivates sinners to forsake their evil ways, and upholds moral order. Christ's death thus provides a moral basis for divine clemency while maintaining God's governmental control of the universe. "According to this theory, Christ did not pay the penalty for our sins; instead, he suffered for us. Scripture never says that Christ was punished for us, or paid the penalty, as Calvinists teach. Instead. . . his death was of such a nature that a holy God could accept it as a *substitute* for penalty. Its merits as a substitute could provide a moral basis for forgiveness without compromising either God's holiness or the integrity of moral government."[25]

Turning to the issue of the extent or intent of the Atonement, Arminians consistently uphold a universal Atonement; Christ died for the purpose of providing salvation for the entire world. They appeal to texts stating that Christ died for "all" persons (2 Cor 5:14-15; 1 Tim 2:6; Tit 2:11) or for the "world" (John 1:29; 4:42; 1 John 2:2; 4:14). They note that the word "whosoever" is used more than 110 times in the NT. Since the Gospel is for all, every last person can be saved. Christ's death, however, is effectual only in those who desire it and who believe. Anticipating later developments, many patristic writers held that Christ died for the sins of the world. Athanasius (d. 373) maintained that in the divine scheme of things "death there had to be, and death for all, so that the due of all might be paid."[26] Cyril of Jerusalem (d. 386) affirmed that "Jesus truly suffered for all men."[27]

Later James Arminius (d. 1609) postulated the provisional universality of the Atonement. He said rather directly, "Christ died for all men and for every individual."[28] Desiring that none should perish in their sins, God bestows prevenient grace universally and extends salvation to all through worldwide Gospel proclamation. A year after Arminius' death a group of his followers drafted the Five Articles of the Remonstrance (1610), article two of which reads:

> Jesus Christ, the Savior of the world, died for all men and for every man, so that he has obtained for them all, by his death on the cross, redemption and the forgiveness of sins; yet that no one actually enjoys this forgiveness of sins except the believer, according to the word of the Gospel of John 3:16: "God so loved the world that he gave his only-begotten Son, that whosoever believeth in him should not perish, but have everlasting life."

Arminians such as Miley aver that an unlimited Atonement makes universal salvation theoretically possible. But since many persons fail to respond to the Gospel in faith, not everyone is actually saved. Arminians further argue that it would be duplicitous of God to offer salvation to all if, in fact, Christ did not make universal provision on the cross. Only on the basis of a universal Atonement can the Gospel be sincerely preached to all. Many Arminians envisage universal Atonement as a logical outcome of the governmental theory. Miley typically insisted that a universal Atonement maximally upholds the cause of moral government. The broader the intent of the Atonement, the greater the good that accrues. Miley thus concluded, "The atonement, as a provision of infinite love for a common race in a common ruin of sin, with its unrestricted overture of grace and requirement of saving faith in Christ, is, and must be, an atonement for all."[29]

E. Universal Reconciliation Theory (Barthians)

Opposing liberalism's subjective view of the Atonement, Karl Barth (d. 1968) affirmed that Christ in his death objectively reconciled the world to God. In its quest to be like God, humankind is godless, guilty, and condemned. To make amends, the Son of God descended into a strange land and was rejected by those he came to save. In describing the Atonement Barth freely used the language of substitution.[30] Yet his view of the Atonement diverges significantly from the orthodox formulation. Barth denied that by bearing the penalty of our sin Christ propitiated the wrath of the offended God. Rather, he held that by his incarnation and death Christ, our Representative, united humanity (*humanum*) with his divine nature: "He takes human being into unity with His own."[31] Thus in solidarity with Christ at Calvary humankind suffered and died. On the cross the punishment of God fell on him and on us. "In His person, with Him, judgment, death and end have come to us ourselves once and for all."[32] Furthermore, united with Christ in his resurrection, humanity participates in the Lord's victory over death and the Devil. Barth insisted that God pardons sinners not by means of a penal satisfaction rendered, but simply on the basis of his determination to forgive—which act of forgiveness satisfies the requirements of his righteousness. "His forgiveness makes good our repudiation and failure and thus overcomes the hurt that we do to God, and the disturbance of the relationship between Himself and us, and the disturbance of the general relationship between the Creator and the creation."[33]

The presupposition of this act of Atonement is the eternal covenant God made with the human race. Barth affirmed that God eternally elected himself in Jesus Christ for suffering and death. In this respect the cross signifies the rejection of the Son of God. In addition, God eternally predestined sinful humanity in Jesus Christ for salvation. In this latter respect the cross signifies the election of humankind in the Son. Barth maintained that ontologically Christ's death achieved a cosmic victory;

the entire world has been won back to the Father. "In the death of Christ both the destroying and the renewing have taken place for all men. . . . Unbelief has become an objective, real and ontological impossibility and faith an objective, real and ontological necessity for all men and for every man."[34] But noetically not all persons are cognizant of their redeemed status. The Spirit's task, he argued, is to awaken this realization of objective Atonement in the heart of every human being. Although Barth removed the Atonement from history to so-called meta-history, he held that Christ not only died for all but that in the triumph of grace he will savingly bring all persons to himself. Barth's position regarding the intent of the Atonement is clear: through the death of Christ God purposed to save every person in the world.

The Dutch theologian Hendrikus Berkhof (b. 1914) broadly follows Barth's line of argument. Berkhof interprets the human dilemma as estrangement and guilt due to sin (guilt being a relational, not a legal concept). Christ's death must not be interpreted in terms of the old notions of vicarious penalty or propitiation of divine wrath, which Berkhof judges as alien to the modern mind. Rather "representation" and "reconciliation" are the terms that best describe the Atonement. That is, by representing a sinful race before God, Christ identified with sinners and restores them to fellowship with their Creator. Berkhof insists that Christ made this representation not only by the cross but also through the whole of his earthly life. Berkhof sums up his view as follows: "Representation signifies that in him the relationship is restored, that is, that which *from our side* obstructed the relationship simply does not count anymore in the light of his perfect love and obedience" [italics added].[35] Berkhof concedes that the precise connection between the cross and reconciliation is not clear. "The NT asserts the 'that,' but has no answer to the 'why' and the 'how.' That is God's secret."[36]

Some modern theologians replace concepts of substitutionary sacrifice and penal satisfaction with the idea of representation and vicarious identification. Typical of this emphasis, Vincent Taylor writes, "No offer of penal suffering as a substitute for his own will meet his need, but a submission presented by his representative before God becomes the foundation of a new hope."[37]

F. Penal Substitution Theory
(Some Fathers and Most Reformed)

According to this view sin, which is primarily a violation of God's law, not his honor, results in the just penalty of death. But in love Jesus Christ, our substitute, in his *life* perfectly fulfilled the law and in *death* bore the just penalty for our sins. Expressed otherwise, on the cross Christ took our place and bore the equivalent punishment for our sins, thereby satisfying the just demands of the law and appeasing God's wrath. As repentant sinners appropriate Christ's vicarious sacrifice by faith, God forgives sins, imputes Christ's righteousness, and reconciles the estranged to himself.

Some apostolic fathers included the theme of vicarious sacrifice in their eclectic understanding of the Atonement. Clement of Rome (d. ca. 96) used the language of substitution to describe Christ's work. "Because of the love which he felt for us, Jesus Christ our Lord gave his blood for us by the will of God, his body for our bodies, and his soul for our souls."[38] Ignatius (d. ca. 107) upheld our Lord's vicarious sacrifice with the words, "All these sufferings, assuredly, he underwent for our sake, that we might be saved."[39] The *Epistle of Barnabas* (II A.D.) states that Christ offered himself as a sacrifice for our sins after the type of Isaac.[40] According to the *Epistle to Diognetus* (II A.D.) Christ's substitutionary death justifies the wicked, and his righteousness covers sins. "God gave up his own Son as a ransom for us—the holy one for the unjust, the innocent for the guilty, the righteous one for the unrighteous, the incorruptible for the corruptible, the immortal for the mortal. For what else could cover our sins except his righteousness? . . . O sweet exchange! O unfathomable work of God! The sinfulness of many is hidden in the Righteous One, while the righteousness of the One justifies the many that are sinners."[41]

In the East Cyril of Jerusalem (d. 386) described the cross in terms of penal substitution, although he grounded the sentence of death in God's veracity rather than in his justice.

> We were enemies of God through sin, and God had decreed the death of the sinner. One of two things, therefore, was necessary, either that God, in his truth, should destroy all men, or that in his loving-kindness, he should remit the sentence. But see the wisdom of God; he preserved the truth of his sentence and the exercise of his loving-kindness. Christ took our sins "in his body upon the tree; that we, having died to sin," by his death "might live to justice."[42]

Athanasius (d. 373) taught that in order to solve the problem posed by sin and condemnation God sent the divine Word into the world. In his body the Son bore the penalty and paid the debt that sinners owed to God. Thus Christ offered "the sacrifice on behalf of all, surrendering his own temple [body] to death in place of all, to settle man's account with death and free him from the primal transgression."[43] According to Athanasius, Christ's death was a penal satisfaction for the divine sentence of death. By

virtue of Christ's cross and resurrection, death is annulled and believers
are raised to immortality.

In the West Augustine (d. 430) synthesized various themes into a comprehensive view of the Atonement. Original sin brought humanity under
the sentence of condemnation and death. In love Jesus Christ yielded to
the snare of the Devil and endured the punishment that sinners justly
deserve. Thus "Christ bore for our sakes sin in the sense of death as
brought on human nature by sin. This is what hung on the tree. . . . Thus
was death condemned that its reign might cease, and accursed that it might
be destroyed."[44] In making this sacrifice to satisfy the divine justice, Christ
functioned as both priest and victim, as both offerer and offering.[45]
Christ's death achieved several significant benefits, the first being the turning away of the divine wrath. "When the Father was angry with us, he
looked upon the death of his Son for us and was propitiated towards
us."[46] Christ's penal sacrifice, furthermore, delivers saints from satanic
bondage, cleanses sins, reconciles to the Father, and offers the church an
example of humility, patience in suffering, and faith in God.[47]

The penal substitutionary view became fully developed in the
Protestant Reformers. Luther (d. 1546) taught that through his life and
death Christ bore the sin, guilt, and punishment of a condemned race. On
the cross the Savior endured the divine wrath against transgressions and
the sentence of death the law justly demanded. As a result of his propitiatory sacrifice, Christ frees trusting souls from the curse of the law,
imparts perfect righteousness, reconciles God and sinners, and conquers
sin, death, and the Devil. Luther summed up his position thusly: "putting
on your sinful person, he [Christ] bore your sin, death, and curse. He
became a sacrifice and a curse for you, in order thus to set you free from
the curse of the law."[48] Although for Luther one important outcome of
the cross is the destruction of sin and Satan, Aulén is incorrect in his claim
that the Reformer primarily represented Christ's work in terms of the classical theory of triumph over Satanic powers.[49]

John Calvin (d. 1564) held that for sinners to be freed from the penalty
of the law a fitting sacrifice must be offered. Thus the 'big idea' of Calvin's
treatment of the cross is substitutionary sacrifice. Calvin contemplated
Christ as our sacrificial victim and sin-bearer. "The Son of God, utterly
clean of all fault, nevertheless took upon himself the shame and reproach
of our iniquities."[50] By perfect obedience in life and especially in death the
Savior bore our guilt, God's wrath, and the penalty assigned to us. "Christ
abolished sin, banished the separation between us and God, and acquired
righteousness to render God favorable and kindly toward us . . . by the
whole course of his obedience."[51] By such obedience and vicarious suf-

fering Christ became the believer's righteousness. On the basis of the Savior's comprehensive work, God reckons his merits to the elect as perfect moral rectitude. Thus "We are made righteous in him . . . because we are judged in relation to Christ's righteousness."[52]

Calvin elaborated his 'big idea' of vicarious sacrifice by means of three key theological concepts. (1) *Propitiation* depicts Christ's work in its Godward aspect. By his substitutionary sacrifice, Christ satisfied the demands of a just God and appeased the divine wrath for all who believe. So Calvin asserted, "God, to whom we were hateful because of sin, was appeased by the death of his Son to become favorable to us."[53] (2) The term *redemption* represents the humanward focus of the cross. By his sacrificial death Christ liberates elect believers from sin, guilt, and the penalty of death.[54] (3) The word *reconciliation* embraces both the Godward and the humanward aspects of Christ's work. Formerly hostile to sinners by reason of their unrighteousness, God for Christ's sake is now reconciled to repentant sinners. "Christ had to become a sacrifice by dying that he might reconcile his Father to us."[55] On the other hand, the cross impacts humans and so reconciles sinners to God. Thus "God appointed Christ as a means of reconciling us to himself."[56] A significant contribution of Calvin was his development of Christ's mediatorial work in terms of the three offices of prophet, king, and priest.[57] As prophet, Christ proclaimed the grace of God and assists the church in its proclamation of the Gospel. As king, he rules over, guides, and protects the church. And as priest, he expiated sins by his sacrifice and eternally intercedes before the Father on behalf of the saints.

Question 37 of the Heidelberg Catechism (1563) enquires, "What do you understand by the word 'suffered'?" It provides the following answer:

> That during his whole life on earth, but especially at the end, Christ sustained in body and soul the anger of God against the sin of the whole human race.
>
> This he did in order that, by his suffering as the only atoning sacrifice, he might set us free, body and soul, from eternal condemnation, and gain for us God's grace, righteousness, and eternal life.

Question 40 asks, "Why did Christ have to go all the way to death?" The answer is given:

> Because God's justice and truth demand it: only the death of God's Son could pay for our sin.

B.B. Warfield (d. 1921) claimed that by the complete obedience of his life Christ fulfilled the demands of the law that Adam failed to keep, and by bearing the penalty of our sin through his sacrificial death he satisfied God's justice. "Our Lord's redeeming work is at its core a true and perfect sacrifice offered to God, of intrinsic value ample for the expiation of our guilt; and at the same time is a true and perfect righteousness offered to God in fulfillment of the demands of his law."[58] By means of his vicarious sacrifice Christ propitiated God's wrath, secured forgiveness of sins, delivers his people from satanic bondage, reconciles God to sinners and sinners to God, and liberates us from the burden of the law as a way of life.

We now turn to Reformed perspectives on the divine intent or purpose of the Atonement. We are impressed with the degree to which Calvin sought to replicate scriptural teaching on this subject. Calvin judged that, according to our finite way of viewing divine things, there are two parts to God's will. The Genevan Reformer held in tension God's purpose for humankind in general and his purpose for the elect in particular.[59] Consequently, God purposed in one respect that Christ's atonement should be universal in scope and in another respect that only some (the elect) should be saved. Thus we find in Calvin's writings a *general, conditional,* or *revealed* aspect of God's will. In this respect Calvin insisted that God loves all persons (John 3:16), Christ's death was an atonement for the sins of the entire world (John 1:29; 4:42; 1 John 2:2), God desires all to repent (1 Tim 2:4; 2 Pet 3:9), and all should be invited to the banquet table of salvation. Commenting on Gal 5:12, Calvin stated, "it is the will of God that we should seek the salvation of all men without exception, as Christ suffered for the sins of the whole world."[60] His comment on Col 1:14 reads, "by the sacrifice of his death all the sins of the world have been expiated."[61] Likewise, in his commentary on Rom 5:18 Calvin wrote, "though Christ suffered for the sins of the whole world, and is offered through God's benignity indiscriminately to all, yet all do not receive him."[62]

On the other hand, Calvin identified a *special, unconditional,* and *hidden* aspect of God's will. Thus he wrote not only about "God's other will. . . to which voluntary obedience corresponds," but also of "his secret will" that effectively leads to salvation.[63] This elective purpose to save, the outcome of "God's more special grace,"[64] is contained in the unconditional and secret aspect of God's will.[65] According to the Father's hidden purpose, Christ's death becomes savingly effective in the elect in whom the Spirit engenders faith. In them, "Christ's death has everlasting efficacy: namely, cleansing, satisfaction, atonement, and finally perfect obedience, with which all our iniquities are covered."[66] In other words, the universal benefits of Christ's death remain potential until the sheep given by the Father come to the Son by God-given faith. In this respect, Calvin commented on Eph 5:25 (cf. John 15:13) that Christ's death effectively redeemed the *church*.

Calvin brought together the two aspects of God's will in his comment on Ezek 18:23: "all men are called to repentance and the hope of salvation is promised to them when they do repent. . . . However, this will of God which he has set forth in his word does not stand in the way of his having decreed from before the creation of the world what he would do with each individual."[67]

Some moderately Reformed authorities (perhaps following Calvin) claim that Christ's saving provision includes many benefits, such as the common blessings of life, the restraint of evil, an objective provision sufficient for all, the removal of every obstacle on God's side for the forgiveness of sins, and the future resurrection of the dead.[68] On the other hand, they seek to do justice to texts that indicate a special purpose for those persons given to Christ out of the world. Many cite 1 Tim 4:10 as indicating a twofold purpose in the cross, namely, general benefits for all people and saving benefits for elect believers. In a sermon entitled "General and Yet Particular," Spurgeon maintained that Christ's death fulfilled a twofold purpose: "there is a general influence for good flowing from the mediatorial sacrifice of Christ, and yet its special design and definite object is the giving of eternal life to as many as the Father gave him."[69] Charles M. Horne wrote in a similar vein: "God's salvation is one. As applied to non-Christians, it includes their preservation in this life and the enjoyment of certain blessings which come to man by common grace. As applied to believers, however, this salvation extends into eternity. This view would seem to be the best one, because it gives the power force to the word *especially* [1 Tim. 4:10]."[70] Donald G. Bloesch arrives at a similar conclusion. He writes, "even unbelievers are affected by Christ's sacrifice which is universal in its scope and intention, and . . . even they will participate in the resurrection of the dead because of his sacrifice. . . . It must also be affirmed that even those who do not believe are benefited by the cross and resurrection of Christ, since the devil and his hosts were objectively overthrown and defeated irrespective of man's response to the cross."[71]

Other Calvinists, however, narrowed the intent of the Atonement by claiming that Christ died for the purpose of saving only the elect. Advocates generally argued that limited Atonement or particular redemption follows logically from God's sovereign, elective decree. The design of the cross was not merely to *provide* salvation but to *secure* the salvation of those persons (the "sheep") the Father in eternity past gave to the Son. On the cross Christ was a sacrifice, a ransom, and a propitiation only for the elect, although most allowed that the Gospel must be preached widely. Proponents of this position reason that Christ's death was entirely successful; the Father's eternal purpose is infallibly accomplished in the salvation of those predestined to life. This view claims that Christ died for all who were related to him, just as Adam sinned for all who were related to him.

Francis Turretin (d. 1687) was the son of a Swiss theologian of Italian ancestry. A professor at the Geneva Academy, Turretin is known for his rigid scholasticizing of the Reformed faith. He formulated his system of theology as a logical deduction from the divine decrees, in the process opposing the hypothetical universal of the Saumur Academy. Turretin's form of Calvinism greatly influenced the nineteenth-century Princeton theology. He argued that the intent of the Atonement is not universal but particular, concerning only the elect. Turretin wrote in his *Institutio* that "God willed to have mercy on only some, not all, of the human race, which had fallen into sin and death."[72] Moreover, on the cross Christ made satisfaction only for the elect who were ordained to life. Turretin insisted that the love and saving provision mentioned in John 3:16 is directed solely to the elect in the world. If God had sent Christ to the cross for the purpose of saving the entire race, he would have failed. Finally, the saving benefits of Christ's atonement are applied only to the elect. Turretin thus held that the *intent*, the *provision*, and the *application* of the Atonement, wrought by the three persons of the Trinity, have the same focus—the circle of the elect. Wrote he, "no one should be elected by the Father who would not be redeemed by the Son . . . and who would not be sanctified at the proper time by the Spirit."[73]

According to the Westminster Confession of Faith (1646), the divine decree assigning people to life or death (ch. III) precedes discussion of Christ's work (ch. VIII). Westminster's doctrine of election clearly controls its understanding of the Atonement. Thus "God did, from all eternity, decree to justify all the elect, and Christ did, in the fullness of time, die for their sins, and rise again for their justification" (ch. XI.4). The Confession states that in his death Christ secured redemption (i.e., made atonement) for the elect only. "The Lord Jesus, by his perfect obedience and sacrifice of himself . . . purchased not only reconciliation, but an everlasting inheritance in the kingdom of heaven, for all those whom the Father hath given unto him" (ch. VIII.5). Those for whom Christ purchased redemption are the very ones to whom he applies and communicates that redemption (ch. 8.8). In sum, Christ died for the purpose of effectively saving the elect given to him by the Father.

The English Puritan divine John Owen (d. 1683) held that none of God's purposes fail to eventuate. If Christ died for all and not all are saved, then Christ died ineffectively, which cannot be. If God loves all people and all are not saved, then God loves ineffectually, which also cannot be. Thus Christ did not die for all, and God does not love all people. Owen wrote, "We deny that all mankind are the object of that love of God which moved him to send his Son to die."[74] God's love is reflected in his will to save the elect—the heirs of the covenant of grace—for whose sins Christ made satisfaction on the cross. Owen concluded his defense of limited Atonement with unrelenting logic. If the death of Christ accomplishes all that the Father intended, "then died he only for those that are in the event sanctified, purged, redeemed, justified, freed from wrath and death, quickened, saved, etc.; but that all are not thus sanctified, freed, etc., is most apparent: and, therefore they cannot be said to be the proper object of the death of Christ."[75]

More recently, Arthur C. Custance asserts that Christ died for the sins of his people and to make the salvation of the elect certain. The view that claims that Christ's sacrifice was intended for all but regrettably many do not appropriate its redeeming power would "make much of that sacrifice pointless" and fatally diminish the triumph of the cross.[76] "It is hard to believe Satan has been allowed largely to defeat God's intentions."[77] Custance further reasons that if the debt of human sin has been fully paid to the satisfaction of the offended party (Rom 8:34), sinners no longer could be held accountable. Since penalty cannot legally be demanded twice (the idea of "double jeopardy," borrowed from Beza), universalism ("all will be saved") is the logical outcome of the unlimited Atonement hypothesis. Moreover, since Christian preachers cannot know beforehand who is elected, it is improper for them to declare to the unsaved, "Christ died for you." Rather, they should state that Christ died as a sacrifice for sin.[78] The elect will understand this declaration as a personal invitation to receive the sacrificial Lamb who died for them.

Many other Calvinist authorities upheld a limited Atonement, arguing that Christ died to atone for the sins of the elect. These include Theodore Beza, Johann Cocceius, William Perkins, Jonathan Edwards, John Gill, William Cunningham, Charles Hodge, A.A. Hodge, W.G.T. Shedd, L. Berkhof, Loraine Boettner, John Murray, and R.B. Kuiper. In each of these theologians the intent of the Atonement appears to be governed by the logically prior doctrine of election.[79]

Displeased by what he judged to be the harsh views of double predestination and limited Atonement held by some of Calvin's followers, Moïse Amyraut (d. 1664) developed the theory of hypothetical universalism. According to this view, the covenant of grace included a universal, conditional covenant and a particular, unconditional covenant. Against scholastic Calvinism, Amyraut averred that the Father lovingly willed the salvation of all (Ezek 18:23; John 3:16; 2 Pet 3:9) on the condition that they believe the Gospel. To realize this purpose he sent Christ into the world to make propitiation on the cross for the sins of the entire race. But since sin-debilitated persons are not able to respond in faith, the Father implemented his particular or unconditional covenant. Amyraut argued against the Arminians that God effectively creates saving faith in the elect and reprobates others. The universal provision of salvation becomes effectual when the Spirit supplies the necessary condition by engendering faith in the hearts of the elect. Amyraut's scheme incorporates Luther's emphasis upon the twofold nature of God's will—i.e., his revealed will and his hidden or secret will. Amyraut's formulation, in sum, embodies a universal design and provision in the Atonement together with a particular application of its benefits. His position was championed by later scholars such as Richard Baxter, John Bunyan, Samuel Hopkins, and Heinrich Heppe.

The penal substitutionary theory of the Atonement best accords with the considerable body of biblical data of the subject. Concerning the purpose of Christ's death, we mentioned at the beginning of this chapter that it is necessary to divide the question by considering both the *provision* Christ made on the cross and the *application* of his work to individuals. The biblical exposition of what Christ's death on the cross accomplished will be discussed in the following section.

III. EXPOSITION OF THE DOCTRINE OF THE ATONEMENT

A. *The Central Importance of Christ's Death*

Christ's death on the cross is not a peripheral issue or a secondary theme; it is the central, indeed crucial doctrine of the faith. From the Latin word for cross (*crux*) comes our English word "crucial." The cross is crucial to the Christian faith because of its absolutely critical nature. One writer plainly stated, "If the student has insufficient time to master the other important sections of Christian doctrine, let him at least have a firm grasp of this, which is the very heart and core of his faith."[80] The importance of the cross is reflected in part by the attention Scripture gives to the death of Jesus Christ. The biographer of Martin Luther King devoted only 9 percent of his work to the last week of King's life. On the other hand, Matthew devoted 33 percent of his gospel to the final week of Jesus' life, Mark 37 percent, Luke 25 percent, and John 42 percent. It has been said that in addition to the many prophetic anticipations of the Messiah's death in the OT, there are 175 direct references to his death in the NT.[81]

In the NT the cross is the place of Atonement. The theological word "Atonement" was first used in 1526, in the sense of "Reconciliation or the restoration of friendly relations between God and sinners."[82] It is not strictly a NT word, being found but once in the AV (Rom 5:11, translating the Greek word *katallage*, "being put into friendship with God") and three times in the NIV (Rom 3:25; Heb 9:5, *hilasterion*; and Heb 2:17, *hilaskomai*). The early meaning of the term as the restoration of harmony between estranged parties (suggesting "reconciliation") gradually broadened to include notions of propitiating God and expiating sins. Thereafter the word came to denote the *means* whereby reconciliation, propitiation, and expiation are achieved.

A cursory reading of the Bible reveals how the cross is woven into the warp and woof of divine revelation. At the dawn of human history, shortly after the Fall, God said to Satan, disguised as a serpent, "he [the woman's seed] will crush his head, and you will strike his heel" (Gen 3:15). This ancient prediction indicates that the Messiah's redemptive victory would be achieved at the cost of suffering. The death of Christ, moreover, was poignantly foreshadowed in the suffering and anguish of the psalmist in Israel (Ps 22; 34:20; 69; 109:25) and was anticipated in the expansive visions of her prophets (Isa 53; Dan 9:24-26; Zech 12:10; 13:1, 7).

Messiah's suffering and death, furthermore, were announced in the preaching of John the Baptist (John 1:29) and even more frequently by our Lord in his own teaching (Matt 16:21; Mark 8:31; 9:31; 10:45; John 10:11-18; 15:13). Following Calvary the first Christian missionaries boldly proclaimed Christ's death as the heart of their message (Acts 5:30; 10:39; 13:28-29; 26:23). After personally meeting the resurrected Lord, Paul expounded the theological implications of the cross in his letters (Rom 4:25; 5:8, 10; 1 Cor 15:3; Gal 3:13; Eph 5:2; Col 1:20, 22; 2:14; 1 Thess 4:14). Peter's first letter of five chapters contains a dozen striking references to the cross (1 Pet 1:2, 11, 18-19; 2:21-24; 3:18; 4:1, 13; 5:1). The death of Christ likewise was an important theme in the letter to the Hebrews (2:9, 14; 7:27; 9:14, 26, 28; 10:10, 12; 12:24; 13:12) and in John's first epistle (1 John 1:7; 3:16; 4:10; 5:6-7). Furthermore, the Apocalypse contains some twenty-two references to Jesus as the Lamb who was slain (Rev 5:6, 8, 12; 6:16; 7:10, 14, 17; etc.).

Christianity is Christ, and the crucial fact about Christ is his passion on the cross. Christ's example, teachings, and miracles must not be neglected by the inquirer into truth; but his atoning death is absolutely crucial. Scripture portrays the Savior's death as the basis of every spiritual blessing

(Rom 8:31-32), as the source of true Christian living (Rom 6:1-11; 8:3-4), and as the foundation of the church's sacraments (Rom 6:1-4; 1 Cor 11:26). John tells us that throughout eternity the inhabitants of heaven will sing the glorious praises of the Lamb who was slain (Rev 5:9-14).

B. *The Way of Atonement in the Old Testament*

How did God effect atonement in OT times before the cross? In the patriarchal history sacrifices were made for sins committed against God. Apparently taught by Adam and Eve, Cain and Abel each brought an offering (*minḥāh*) to the Lord—the former from his crops and the latter from the firstborn of his flock (Gen 4:3-4). Although each brought offerings from their respective occupations, Cain's was made in unbelief whereas Abel's was made in sincere faith (Heb 11:4). Because of the faithful attitude of the younger brother's heart, we read that "The Lord looked with favor on Abel and his offering" (Gen 4:4).

We find the first explicit mention of an altar following the Flood when Noah sacrificed burnt offerings to God for deliverance from the deluge (Gen 8:20). Later Abraham (Gen 12:8; 13:18), Isaac (26:25), and Jacob (33:20; 35:7) established altars of sacrifice to the Lord. "How clearly the patriarchs understood the meaning of their sacrifices one cannot say, but that they had a concept of vicarious atonement seems quite clear (Job 1:5)."[83] Abraham's near slaying of Isaac as a burnt offering (*'ōlāh*) in the region of Moriah (Gen 22:1-18) prefigured the substitutionary death of the Messiah two millennia later. Isaac ascended the mountain bearing the wood upon which the sacrifice would be laid. When he inquired about the lamb for the burnt offering, Abraham responded, "God himself will provide the lamb for the burnt offering, my son" (v. 8). As Abraham was about to slay his son on the altar, the angel of the Lord showed him a ram caught in a thicket. Abraham then "took the ram and sacrificed it as a burnt offering instead of his son" (v. 13). The phrase, "instead of his son [*taḥat bᵉnô*]" affirms the substitutionary nature of the animal sacrifice.

The key to Israel's sacrificial system was the Passover (*pesaḥ*) in Egypt (Exod 12:1-30). God commanded each Hebrew household to slay an unblemished yearling lamb or goat at twilight and to apply the blood of the victim to the door frame. For the Israelites who obeyed God's instructions, the sprinkled blood secured exemption from the divine judgment. But in the case of the unbelieving Egyptians who were not sheltered by the blood, the Lord struck dead all their firstborn men and animals (vv. 29-30). The Passover ritual clearly was sacrificial in nature, for v. 27 designates it as a "Passover sacrifice" (*zebaḥ-pesaḥ*). This atoning sacrifice resulted in Israel's deliverance from the land of bondage (Exod 14). We may say that the blood of the Passover sacrifice had a certain atoning power and anticipated the blood of the Lamb shed on Calvary that would remove sins and avert the divine wrath (John 1:29; Rom 3:25; Heb 2:17).

Consider also the several Levitical sacrifices. The burnt offering (*'ōlāh*, Lev 1:3-17; Judg 13:16; 1 Sam 7:9-10), fellowship or peace offering (*š͏elāmîm*, Lev 3:1-17; 7:11-21; 2 Sam 6:18), sin offering (*ḥattā't*, Lev 4:1-35; Num 6:14-16; 2 Chron 29:23-24), and guilt offering (*'āšām*, Lev 5:14-6:7; Num 6:12; 1 Sam 6:3-4) typically followed a pattern involving the following elements. (1) An unblemished animal, signifying moral perfection, was presented at the door of the sanctuary by the offerer. (2) The offerers placed their hands on the animal's head, denoting identification with the victim and the transfer of sin's penalty to the substitute. (3) The animal then was slain, signifying death as the requisite punishment for sin. (4) The priest sprinkled the blood of the victim on the altar, the blood representing the life of the victim (Lev 17:11). And (5) the offering, in part or in whole, was burned on the altar of burnt offering, its fragrance ascending to God as a pleasing aroma. Repeatedly Scripture indicates that the purpose of these sacrifices was "to make atonement" and provide forgiveness for the offerer (Lev 1:4; 4:20, 26, 31, 35; 5:13, 16; 6:7; Num 5:8; 8:12; 15:25; etc.). The verb *kāpar* ("make atonement," more than 100 times in the OT) in sacrificial contexts means to propitiate God's wrath, expiate sins, and restore fellowship between God and sinners.[84] The grain offering (*minḥāh*, Lev 2:1-16; Num 5:15, 18; Judg 13:19) was a bloodless offering of meal, oil, and incense. Part of the grain offering was burned on the altar, and part was given to the priests for food. "The idea of atonement is not specifically present in *minḥāh*, although that of propitiation certainly is."[85] Without doubt these offerings anticipated the vicarious sacrifice of Christ. "The laws in Leviticus remind us then of Christ's death and what he has done for us. . . . The worshipper might well feel very much deprived when he had paid for a choice lamb to be sacrificed. But it reminded him that the animal was a ransom, a substitute payment instead of his own life."[86]

The annual Day of Atonement (*yôm hakippurîm*, Lev 23:27; 25:9) was the most important cultic celebration in the OT. In preparation for this solemn event the high priest sacrificed a young bull as a sin-offering and a ram for a burnt-offering to atone for his own sins and those of the priesthood (Lev 16:11-14). He sprinkled the blood of the bull on the front of the golden lid of the ark designated the "atonement cover" (AV, "mercy seat"—*kappōret*, meaning "place of atonement"; cf. Exod 25:17). Then the high priest sacrificed the first male goat as a sin-offering and sprinkled its blood upon and in front of the "atonement cover" in the holy of holies, thereby expiating the uncleanness of the people (Lev 16:15-19) and making atonement (*kippurîm*; cf. Exod 29:36; 30:10; Lev 23:28). According to Lev 17:11, this act of blood-shedding represents God's ordained means of securing atonement. The helpless animals died in place of the penitent sinner. The high priest then laid his hands on the head of the second goat (the "scapegoat," AV, NIV) and confessed all the sins of the community, thus symbolically transferring guilt from the people to the victim. The second goat became a sin-bearer as it carried the sins and iniquities of the people into the wilderness. The Day of Atonement ritual dramatically depicted the holiness of God, the gravity of sin, and God's gracious provision by vicarious sacrifice.

Later in the OT David was aware of the fact that "God" his "Savior" (Ps 65:5) had atoned for the sins of the faithful. Thus he wrote, "When we were overwhelmed by sins, you forgave our transgressions" (Ps 65:3; cf. 78:38; 79:9; Prov 16:6). The Piel of *kāpar* refers to the remission of sins and the turning aside of divine judgment through the sacrificial blood shed on the altar.

In OT times atonement was wrought not on the basis of a person's best works but solely through God's free grace and mercy. OT people who practiced the prescribed sacrifices and offerings in repentance and faith toward God were saved by the yet future work of Christ prefigured by those rites (Rom 3:25). Thus the faithful OT worshiper received pardon of sins—yet a remission that was less than permanent—and they experienced genuine fellowship with God—yet a relationship that was less than perfect. Faithful OT saints, in short, experienced "a measure of atonement and remission for sins committed"[87]—yet an atonement that was incomplete and imperfect because the final sacrifice on the cross had not been made.

Scripture points up the limitations of the OT sacrificial system. (1) The *sacrifices themselves* were unable fully to atone for sin, as several OT writers attested (Ps 40:6; 51:16; Hos 6:6; Mic 6:6-8). (2) The blood of bulls and goats could not clear the consciences of the offerers (Heb 9:9-10; 10:4). They could not purify the inner defilements highlighted by our Lord in Mark 7:20-23. Only the perfect sacrifice of Christ could completely clear guilty consciences (Heb 9:14; 10:22). (3) The OT sacrifices, offered day by day and year after year (Heb 9:25; 10:11), could not permanently remove the stain of repeated sins; hence the sacrifices served as "an annual reminder of sins" (Heb 10:3). Christ's work on the cross would effect a permanent cleansing that requires no repetition (Heb 9:26; 10:10). With defilement permanently removed under the new covenant, Yahweh promises, "I . . . will remember their sins no more" (Jer 31:34b; Heb 8:12).

And (4) the OT sacrifices under the old covenant were incapable of giving "the promised eternal inheritance (Heb 9:15)"; this must await the inauguration of the new covenant mediated by Christ.

The OT sacrifices clearly were preparatory; they pointed beyond themselves to the "once for all" (Heb 10:10) and perfect sacrifice of Christ on the cross. According to Hebrews, when Christ came into the world he said, "'Sacrifices and offerings, burnt offerings and sin offerings you did not desire, nor were you pleased with them' (although the law required them to be made). Then he said, 'Here I am, I have come to do your will.' . . . And by that will, we have been made holy through the sacrifice of the body of Jesus Christ once for all" (Heb 10:8-10; cf. 9:26, 28a). The law, the priesthood, and the sacrifices were but "copies" and "shadows" of the perfect redemption to come (cf. Heb 8:5; 9:23; 10:1; Col. 2:17). Christ accomplished in reality what Aaron and his successor high priests accomplished by way of type and figure. Hence the first covenant and its sacrificial system is "obsolete" (Heb 8:13). OT saints who lived by faith did not fully realize in their lifetimes God's promises to them. But in consequence of Christ's perfect sacrifice and heavenly ministry, they have been made perfect with us (Heb 11:40).

C. The Big Idea of Atonement: Penal Substitution

Penal substitution indicates that the Messiah died in the sinner's place and took upon himself the sinner's just punishment. The idea of vicarious, penal substitution is imbedded in the warp and woof of Scripture. Israel's hymnbook contains several vivid prefigurations of Christ's penal sufferings, the most descriptive being Psalm 22. Although this song refers directly to David's personal trials, the poet's vision transcends the present to embrace the Messiah's future passion. Thus the Savior's God-forsakenness and cry of desolation are anticipated in v. 1 (cf. Matt 27:46; Mark 15:34). The words, "My God, my God, why have you forsaken me?" express "the punitive separation Christ accepted in our place, 'having become a curse for us' (Gal 3:13)."[88] Furthermore, vv. 7-8 depict the mocking insults hurled against Christ at Calvary (cf. Matt 27:39, 43; Luke 23:35), vv. 14-15 the excruciating physical suffering he experienced, v. 16 the piercing of his hands and feet (cf. Luke 24:39-40), and v. 18 the dividing of his garments (cf. Luke 23:34; John 19:23). Additional anticipations of Messiah's suffering occur in Ps 34:20, 69:4, 9, 21, and 109:25.

The prophets vividly portrayed the passion of the future "servant" and "branch." Zechariah acted out a parable to dramatize the final rejection of the Good Shepherd for a mere thirty pieces of silver (Zech 11:12-13; cf. Matt 27:3-10). Isaiah wrote that when undergoing terrible physical and emotional pain the Messiah neither resisted nor shrunk back (Isa 50:5). The prophet predicted Messiah's maltreatment by the people and his patient endurance of sufferings (Isa 53:6-7). His disfigured appearance reflected the pain he endured (Isa 52:14). Isaiah added that the Messiah "was numbered with the transgressors," anticipating Christ's crucifixion among common criminals (Isa 53:12; cf. Luke 22:37; 23:33). He was given an unfair trial, and his life was cut off by a violent death (Isa 53:8). Bewildered and guilt-stricken, the people would gaze upon the one they had pierced (Zech 12:10; cf. John 19:34, 37). Fittingly Isaiah described the Messiah as "despised and rejected by men, a man of sorrows, and familiar with suffering" (Isa 53:3).

According to Isaiah eight centuries before Christ, the one who bore the burden of sin that estranged us from God was Yahweh's "servant" (*'ebed*). Servant in Scripture is used of (1) great men of God (Isa 20:3; 37:35; 44:2), (2) the covenant people Israel (Isa 41:8-9; 42:19; 49:3), and (3) the divine Messiah. That *'ebed* cannot be limited to contemporary human personalities but designates the Christ is clear from several considerations: (1) The servant is given a mission *to* Israel (Isa 49:5-6; 52:5-6); (2) the servant's accomplishments are yet *future* to Israel (Isa 42:4; 49:6; 53:11); (3) the works the servant performs are supra-human (Isa. 42:6-7; 53:11-12); and (4) the NT specifically identifies the servant as Jesus Christ (Matt 12:17-21; Acts 8:32-35).[89]

The focus of the fourth servant song (Isa 52:13–53:12) is Messiah's substitutionary sacrifice for sins. The prophet wrote, "Surely he took up our infirmities and carried our sorrows" (Isa 53:4; cf. Matt 8:17). The verb *nāśā'* ("lift up" or "bear") and *sābal* ("carry" or "transport"), together with the juxtaposition of "he" and "our," communicate the idea of substitution. Isaiah reiterated the big idea of substitution throughout the fifty-third chapter of his prophecy. Thus in v. 6, "the Lord has laid on him (Hiphil of *pāga'*, "cause to fall on" or "assail") the iniquity of us all." Likewise, in v. 11, "he will bear [*sābal*] their iniquities," and v. 12, "he bore [*nāśā'*] the sin of many." V. 5 affirms the vicarious nature of Christ's suffering: "he was pierced for our transgressions; he was crushed for our iniquities." Similarly, v. 8: "for the transgression of my people he was stricken." V. 10 represents Christ's death as a "guilt-offering" (*'āšām*). "By calling it a guilt offering, the suffering of the Servant of the Lord is placed in the category of substitutionary satisfaction."[90] V. 5 indicates the outcome of the Messiah's substitutionary sacrifice: "the punishment that brought us peace was upon him." The divine judgment he bore provided sinners peace with God and salvation (cf. Eph 2:14-15; Col 1:20). The only coherent conclusion that can be drawn from Isa 53:4-12 is the following: "The coming servant, Messiah, lifts up and takes upon himself man's sickness and bears the weight of his worrisome sorrows. Nothing could more graphically portray the vicarious sacrificial work of Christ who bore the penalty for man's sin so that man may receive God's righteousness and stand justified before him."[91] In addition, Dan 9:24 provides a comprehensive description of the work of "the Anointed One." Some 490 years after the decree to rebuild Jerusalem the Messiah will appear "to finish transgression, to put an end to sin, to atone for wickedness [*lᵉkappēr 'āwôn*], to bring in everlasting righteousness."

Turning to the NT, the totality of Jesus' *life* as well as his death should be viewed as a sacrifice unto God. When Gal 4:4 tells us that Jesus was "born under law," it means that he was subject to the prescriptions of the Jewish law. Thus he was circumcised at eight days, kept the Passover from age twelve to the celebration in the Upper Room, and faithfully participated in the synagogue worship. In his complete obedience to the will of the Father (John 14:31; Heb 10:7-9) and in his perfect fulfillment of the law and its demands (Matt 5:17), Jesus "fulfilled all righteousness" (Matt 3:15). Theologians frequently speak of Jesus' perfect compliance with the law as his "active obedience."

Jesus spoke about his death in Mark 10:45 (cf. Matt 20:28): "the Son of man did not come to be served, but to serve, and to give his life a ransom [*lytron*] for many [*anti pollōn*]." This saying points to Jesus' vicarious suffering and death (1) because the Lord applied to himself Isaiah's description of the suffering servant (especially Isa 53:10-12), and (2) because *anti* with the genitive case is a preposition of substitution signifying "instead of" or "in the place of."[92] The noun *lytron*, "ransom price," was widely used in classical Greek to denote the payment made to free a slave or prisoner. The metaphor connotes (1) that Jesus' death possesses an atoning dimension in that it eradicates guilt and (2) it possesses a liberating dimension in that it sets spiritual captives free from sin and Satan. Jesus' saying makes no mention of the one to whom payment is made; the metaphor simply conveys the truth that it cost God dearly to free sinners from spiritual enslavement.

That Jesus' death was a substitutionary atonement is clear from the institution of the Lord's Supper. The reading of Luke 22:19, retained in the ASV, NASB, and NIV, indicates that Jesus took bread, broke it, and said, "This is my body given for you [*hyper hymōn*]." Thereafter (v. 20) the Lord took the cup of wine, gave thanks, and said, "This cup is the new covenant in my blood, which is poured out for you [*hyper hymōn*]." Mark's account

(Mark 14:24) reads, "which is poured out for many [*hyper pollōn*]." Compare Matthew's account (Matt 26:28), which uses the phrase *peri pollōn*—*peri* being equivalent in meaning to *hyper*.[93] The preposition *hyper* in these texts means "on behalf of" or "in place of" and so connotes both representation and substitution: Jesus gave his flesh and blood (i.e., his life) on behalf of sinners. Furthermore, Jesus' sayings imply that his death supplanted the Mosaic covenant sacrifices (Exod 24:6-8) and inaugurated the new covenant promised by the prophet Jeremiah (Jer 31:31-33). Under the old covenant Moses made burnt and fellowship offerings to the Lord and sprinkled the blood of animals on the altar, thereby temporarily propitiating God's anger and expiating sins. But Jesus implied that his death made an atonement for sins that was perfect and permanent.

Paul frequently represented Christ's death as a substitutionary sacrifice for sins. The apostle insisted that the message transmitted to him by the earliest Christians was a matter "of first importance." The heart of this early Christian confession is that "Christ died for [*hyper*] our sins" (1 Cor 15:3). Elsewhere Paul wrote of God "sending his own Son in the likeness of sinful man to be a sin offering" (*peri hamartias*, Rom 8:3). Furthermore, Paul established a direct relation between Christ's death and the OT Passover sacrifice when he wrote, "Christ, our Passover Lamb (*pascha*), has been sacrificed" (1 Cor 5:7). This reference to the Jewish Passover indicates that Christ's blood shed on the cross propitiates the divine wrath, delivers from the guilt of sin, and secures exemption from divine judgment. Contemplating the sin offering/suffering servant of Isaiah 53, Paul wrote, "God made him who had no sin to be sin for [*hyper*] us" (2 Cor 5:21). As our substitute, Christ suffered God's wrath against sin that we might receive God's righteousness. "God placed our sins on the sinless Jesus and as our substitute in our place God punished him with death."[94] In a similar vein Paul wrote that "Christ redeemed us from the curse of the law, by becoming a curse for [*hyper*] us" (Gal 3:13). Here the curse is the sentence of death that hung over all sinners as lawbreakers. In addition, the apostle succinctly stated that Christ "gave himself for [*hyper*] our sins" (Gal 1:4; cf. Rom 5:6, 8; 8:32; Gal 2:20; Tit 2:14; Eph 5:2).

Via several rich metaphors the Johannine writings present Jesus' death as a substitutionary sacrifice for sins. The Baptist said of Jesus, "Look, the Lamb of God, who takes away the sin of the world!" (John 1:29; cf. v. 36). Because the Passover feast was at hand when John spoke these words (John 2:13), "lamb" (*amnos*) denotes the animal for the sacrificial offering and recollects the lamb of Isa 53:7 as well as the Pascal lamb. In the Apocalypse John depicted Christ as a Lamb (*arnion*) twenty-seven times (Rev 6:16; 7:10; 12:11; 13:8; etc.). The Lamb takes his place on the throne of God, executes eschatological judgment, and is worshiped; yet he is the Lamb who was slain (Rev 5:6, 9, 12; 13:8). By portraying Christ as *arnion*, Revelation indicates that the victorious Lord is also the Christ crucified for sins. "The judge of all the earth is he who died for us, and even as sovereign Lord he still bears the marks of his passion."[95] Furthermore, John represented Jesus as "the bread of God" (John 6:33) and the "bread of life" (vv. 35, 48). In the context of the manna given to Israel in the desert (v. 31, 49), Jesus indicated that he is the spiritual food that conveys eternal life. Jesus' saying, "This bread is my flesh which I will give for [*hyper*] the life of the world" (v. 51), connotes that the eternal life offered to the Jews would be secured by the sacrifice of himself. Jesus also described his work in terms of the shepherd metaphor: "The good shepherd lays down his life for [*hyper*] the sheep" (John 10:11; cf. v. 15). Of his own accord and in full obedience to the Father, Jesus surrendered his life on behalf of others. On the cross Jesus personally demonstrated the truth of John 15:13: "Greater love has no one than this, that he lay down his life for [*hyper*] his friends."

Caiaphas uttered prophetic truth to the Sanhedrin when he said, "You do not realize that it is better for you that one man die for [*hyper*] the people than that the whole nation perish" (John 11:50). Caiaphas viewed Jesus' death as a matter of political expediency, but John interpreted this unwitting prophecy in terms of Jesus' vicarious death on behalf of Jews and Gentiles (vv. 51-52).

Employing the suffering Servant motif of Isaiah 53, Peter upheld Christ's substitutionary sacrifice by writing, "He himself bore our sins in his body on the tree" and "by his wounds you have been healed" (1 Pet 2:24). Peter added in 1 Pet 3:18 that Christ's death had reconciling power: "Christ died for sins once for all, the righteous for the unrighteous [*dikaios hyper adikon*], to bring you to God." The author of Hebrews depicted Christ as the completed sacrifice for sins (7:27; 10:5-9). As such, Christ is both priest and victim. The singular sacrifice of Christ's body on Calvary purges sins (1:3; 9:14, 26, 28), turns aside the divine wrath (*eis to hilaskesthai tas hamartias*, 2:17), consecrates to God (10:10, 14), and secures divine forgiveness (9:22; 10:18).

The notion of substitutionary sacrifice, widely attested in Scripture, means that Christ died in the place of sinners. The perfect obedience God required from his creatures, Jesus fully gave. In bearing the penalty of human sin as our substitute he made full payment to God for all our failures and misdeeds.

D. *Other Atonement Motifs*

Whereas Scripture presents no explicit theory of the Atonement, it does utilize several metaphors that illumine for finite minds the significance of Christ's death. Clustered around the big idea of penal substitution are a variety of other biblical images that describe the nature and effects of Christ's death on the cross.

(1) *Ransom*: In the OT, ransom (*kōper*) denotes the *price* paid to redeem or buy back persons from a variety of negative circumstances. Thus ransom was the price paid to free a murderer (Num 35:31-32), purchase the freedom of a relative (Lev 25:50-52), and liberate exiles (Isa 45:13). In the spiritual realm, Ps 49:7-9 states that no human is able to pay a ransom (*kōper*) powerful enough to deliver from the grave. Yet the psalmist in faith confessed that "God will redeem [Qal of *pādāh*] my soul from the grave" (v. 15). God himself pays the ransom price and redeems the trusting person from the grip of sin, death, and Satan.

Jesus spoke about his death in Mark 10:45 (cf. Matt 20:28): "the Son of man did not come to be served, but to serve, and to give his life as a ransom [*lytron*] for many." The noun *lytron*, "ransom price," was widely used in classical Greek to denote the payment made to free a slave or prisoner. Theologically, the metaphor connotes that Jesus' death possesses an atoning dimension because it wipes out guilt and a liberating dimension in that it sets spiritual captives free from sin and Satan. Jesus' saying does not state to whom the payment is made. Ransom simply conveys the truth that it cost God dearly to free sinners from spiritual enslavement.

Paul also used the figure of a ransom payment to describe the results of Christ's death. Recollecting Jesus' words in Mark 10:45, Paul wrote of "the man Christ Jesus, who gave himself as a ransom [*antilytron*] for all men" (1 Tim 2:5-6). The compound word *antilytron*, which literally means "substitute-ransom," denotes "what is given in exchange for another as the price of his redemption."[96] The figure of a "price" substantiates the ransom idea more explicitly. Thus Paul wrote, "You were bought at a price" (*timē*, 1 Cor 6:20; 7:23), indicating that Christ on Calvary paid what was needed to set spiritual prisoners free. The price handed over was Christ's own blood shed on the cross (Acts 20:28; cf. Rev. 5:9). The question, to whom was the price paid? goes beyond the main point Paul sought to make.

(2) *Redemption*: The English word "redemption" comes from the Latin *redimere*, to "repurchase" or "buy back." Redemption focuses on the *release* of persons detained in bondage. In the OT the verb *pādāh* (to "rescue," "deliver," "ransom"; Ps 31:5; 44:26; 69:18) depicts the freeing

of a female servant from the authority of a householder (Exod 21:8). Figuratively, the verb describes the deliverance God effects from the bondage of sin and Satan. Thus the psalmist wrote of the Lord, "He himself will redeem Israel from all their sins" (Ps 130:8; cf. 34:22). The noun *pᵉdût* connotes the redemption or deliverance God accomplishes through the atoning sacrifices; thus "He provided redemption [*pᵉdût*] for his people" (Ps 111:9; cf. 130:7). The verb *pādāh* alone (Mic 6:4; Zech 10:8) or in combination with *gā'al* (Jer 31:11; Hos 13:14) signifies the act of delivering or rescuing through the payment of a price.[97]

The verb *gā'al*, to "redeem," "avenge," "do the part of a kinsman," likewise emphasizes the release obtained. God redeemed by delivering Israel from Egyptian slavery (Ps 74:2; 77:15; cf. Exod 6:6; 15:13; Isa 63:9), by freeing his people from Babylonian captivity (Mic 4:10), and by rescuing persons from the consequences of sin (Ps 103:4; 107:2; Isa 44:22). Thus the Lord is known as Israel's "Redeemer" (*gô'ēl*; Job 19:25; Ps 78:35; Isa 49:7; 60:16), and the people of God are known as "the redeemed" (*gᵉ'ûlîm*; Isa 35:9; 62:12). The Messiah would liberate many who are bound by the shackles of sin and Satan. His saving mission will be "to free captives from prison and to release from the dungeon those who sit in darkness" (Isa 42:7; cf. 61:1).

Turning to the NT, Jesus' death brought about redemption (*lytrōsis*), meaning "deliverance" or "release." In Luke 1:68 (cf. 2:38) Zechariah stated that through Mary's child the Lord "has come and has redeemed his people." The deliverance Zechariah anticipated through the Christ included Israel's liberation from political bondage (v. 71) as well as release from the guilt and power of sin (vv. 77-79). The word "redemption" in Zechariah's prophecy is equivalent to the word "salvation" (*sōtēria*, "deliverance") in vv. 69, 71, 77. That Christ delivers from the bondage of sin and death is clear from the incident in the synagogue at Nazareth where Jesus read from the servant passage of Isa 61:1-2. In fulfillment of this prophecy, Jesus stated that the Lord has sent him "to proclaim freedom [*aphesis*] for the prisoners" and "to release the oppressed" (Luke 4:18). Whereas *aphesis* sometimes means "forgiveness of sins" (Matt 26:28), here in Luke it means "release from captivity."[98] Jesus' priestly ministry of self-oblation is discussed above under the categories of vicarious sacrifice, ransom, and redemption.

Paul wrote frequently of the deliverance from sin and Satan obtained through Christ's costly sacrifice: "In him we have redemption [*apolytrōsis*)]through his blood" (Eph 1:7; cf. Rom 3:24; Col 1:14; Heb 9:15). "In the Pauline writings it [*apolytrōsis*] figures largely to designate the deliverance from sin and its penalty brought about by the propitiatory death of Christ."[99] This deliverance wrought by Christ is also indicated by the verbs *lytroō* ("redeem," "liberate") in Tit 2:14 and 1 Pet 1:18; *agorazō* ("purchase, redeem") in 1 Cor 6:20; 7:23; 2 Pet 2:1; Rev 5:9; 14:3-4; *exagorazō* ("buy out of the market place," "redeem from slavery") in Gal 3:13; 4:5; *rhyomai* ("rescue," "deliver") in Col 1:13; 1 Thess 1:10; *methistēmi* ("remove from one place to another") in Col 1:13; and *exaireō* ("rescue," "deliver") in Gal 1:4. Christ's blood shed in death liberates from the divine wrath (Rom 5:9), from bondage to sin and guilt (Rom 6:6-7, 14, 20, 22; Rev 1:5), from the impossible burden of law-keeping (Rom 7:4-6; Gal 3:10, 13), and from the tyranny of death (Rom 8:2). Ransom and redemption represent God's merciful answer to the many forms of bondage that enslave men and women.

The writer of Hebrews added that Christ's sacrifice on the cross destroyed death and the Devil (2:14) and liberates sinners from the grip of satanic powers (2:15; 9:15). The print journalist Carl Rowen, in a television interview concerning youth crime, passionately stated that "learning is the great liberator." The biblical writers, on the contrary, assert that the only one who can free sinners from the shackles of sin and its consequences is Jesus Christ.

(3) *Propitiation*: The word "propitiation" derives from the Latin word *propitiare*, meaning to "render favorable." The word was widely used in the pagan world in the sense of appeasing the wrath and winning the favor of the gods. Scripture is clear that the holy and righteous God hates sin (Ps 11:5-6; Jer 44:4). Propitiation connotes the act of turning aside the wrath of the offended God by means of appropriate sacrifice. The Hebrew word *kāpar* means to "cover" or "hide," the sense being that Christ's death serves as a covering that averts the divine displeasure against sin. On the Day of Atonement, Aaron was commanded to sprinkle the blood of the slain bull and goat (Lev 16:14-15) on the "atonement cover" (*kappōret*), which is the place of Atonement. In the LXX *kappōret* is translated by *hilastērion*, which word occurs twice in the NT (Rom 3:25; Heb 9:5) and is translated "propitiation" (AV) or "sacrifice of atonement" (NIV, NRSV).

Rom 3:21-26, an important Pauline text on the Atonement, merits particular study. The focus of this passage is how God justifies or declares righteous Jews and Gentiles. The apostle began by considering (a) the *manifestation* of justification (vv. 21-23). He wrote, "But now a righteousness from God [*dikaiosynē theou*] . . . has been made known" (v. 21). The righteousness Paul contemplated (thirty-five times in Romans and twenty-four times elsewhere in the NT) is the legal status of right standing with God. Cranfield observes that *dikaiosynē* signifies "a status of righteousness before God, which is God's gift."[100] This righteousness is conferred independently of law-keeping (v. 21a), is attested by the OT (v. 21b), and is appropriated by faith in Jesus Christ (v. 22). Paul then considered (b) the *means* of justification (vv. 24-25), which is given in two word-pictures. The first is the image of redemption: both Jews and Gentiles "are justified freely by his grace through the redemption [*apolytrōsis*] that came by Christ Jesus" (v. 24). We saw above that *apolytrōsis* describes the deliverance wrought by payment of an appropriate price. The second word-picture is propitiation: "God presented him as a sacrifice of atonement [*hilastērion*], through faith in his blood" (v. 25). The meaning of *hilastērion* in this verse has been widely debated. Dodd, Von Rad, Richardson, and the RSV interpret *hilastērion* subjectively and translate it as "expiation," meaning the cleansing or neutralizing of sin. Others such as F.F. Bruce, guided by the LXX where *kappōret* is frequently rendered by *hilasterion*, translate the word as "mercy seat," i.e., the golden cover of the ark where Atonement was made. Still other authorities render *hilastērion* as "propitiatory sacrifice" and interpret it as the self-oblation of Christ that turns aside the divine wrath and purges sin from the conscience.[101]

The third interpretation satisfies the greatest amount of data with the least number of difficulties. Thus (i) in the Greek world *hilastērion* meant placating the anger of an offended person or god; (ii) the LXX employs the verb *exhilaskomai* in several places (Zech 7:2; 8:22; Mal 1:9) in the sense of appeasing God; (iii) in the OT the verb is never used with sin as its object; (iv) the *hilas-* word group often occurs in the context of the divine wrath (Rom 3:5; 5:9); and (v) in the LXX when *hilastērion* connotes mercy seat it always has the article. In sum, when Paul described the work of Christ he utilized the language of the law-court ("justified"), the slave-market ("redemption"), and the temple ("propitiatory sacrifice").[102] Finally, Paul discussed (c) the *rationale* of justification (v. 26): God "did it. . . so as to be just and the one who justifies those who have faith in Jesus." By giving Jesus as a vicarious sacrifice, God was able (i) to remain true to his holy nature that cannot overlook sin, (ii) to uphold his law which stipulates that sin be punished by death, and (iii) mercifully to acquit sinners who were deserving of death.

John explained the theological significance of Christ's death by stating that he is "the propitiation for our sins" (*hilasmos peri tōn hamartiōn hēmōn*, 1 John 2:2; 4:10, NASB). *Hilasmos*, like *hilastērion*, connotes "propitiatory sacrifice" and indicates that Christ's death appeased God's righteous anger vis-à-vis sin, allowing him to be favorably disposed to erring sinners. Thus, "By the *advocacy* of Christ (*parakletos*) God is *propitiated* (*hilasmos*) and we are *reconciled* (*katallage*)."[103] The verb *hilaskomai* occurs but twice in the NT. In the first occurrence the verb is passive; the tax collector in Jesus' parable cried out, "God, have mercy on me, a sinner" (Luke 18:13). In the second, Christ "had to be made like his brothers in every way, in order that he might become a merciful and faithful high priest in service to God, and that he might make atonement [*hilaskesthai*, "to satisfy, render well disposed, conciliate, propitiate"[104])]for the sins of the people" (Heb 2:17). Propitiation is the answer to God's righteous wrath.

(4) *Expiation*: Another important concomitant of redemption is expiation, although the word itself does not appear in the AV or NIV. Propitiation and expiation are often confused by theological liberals. We submit that the focus of propitiation is Godward—Christ's sacrifice pays the penalty of sin so as to appease God's wrath. But the focus of expiation is humanward—Christ's sacrifice removes the stain of sin and the sinner's liability to suffer sin's punishment. Expiation appears to be a clearer concept in the OT, propitiation in the NT. Thus, Yahweh declared, "I . . . am he who blots out your transgressions, for my own sake, and remembers your sins no more" (Isa 43:25). Again the Lord said, "I will cleanse them from all the sin they have committed against me and will forgive all their sins of rebellion against me" (Jer 33:8; cf. Zech 3:9; 13:1). The NT states that the blood of Jesus purifies believing lives from the pollution and punishment of sin (1 John 1:7; 9; Rev 1:5b). Divine expiation is God's answer to sinners' condemnation.

(5) *Reconciliation*: Another significant outcome of Christ's death is the reconciliation of God and sinners. The imagery here is that of the family; individuals formerly alienated and estranged (Isa 59:2) are brought into a state of harmony and peace. The verb *katallasso* literally means to "change thoroughly" and was used in classical Greek in the sense of "restoring the original understanding between people after hostility or displeasure."[105] Theologically, reconciliation connotes that enmity between God and sinners is changed to a relation of friendship and communion. Paul wrote in Rom 5:10 that before being reconciled to God by the death of his Son, "we were God's enemies." Does the enmity that hinders reconciliation reside on God's side or on ours? The answer appears to be, it lies on both. Cranfield helpfully comments as follows: "The enmity which is removed in the act of reconciliation is both sinful man's hostility to God (Rom 1:30; 8:7) and also God's hostility to sinful man (this aspect is particularly clear in 11:28), though the removal of God's hostility is not to be thought of as involving a change of purpose in God."[106] With enmity on

both sides abolished and the separation breached, Paul could write, "we also rejoice in God through our Lord Jesus Christ, through whom we have now received reconciliation" (*katallagē*, Rom 5:11). According to 2 Cor 5:18-21 it is God who initiates reconciliation (*katallagē*). Through Christ's propitiatory sacrifice God bridges the chasm between himself and wayward sinners and restores personal communion.

Moreover, reconciliation is closely associated with the non-imputation of sins (justification), for in v. 21 Paul speaks of reconciled sinners attaining the "righteousness of God," namely, that state of being righteous in relation to the law. In Eph 2:12-16 Paul elaborated on the idea of reconciliation. Through Christ's shed blood Gentiles, "who once were far away," are united to the covenant people. With the partition between Jew and Gentile dismantled, God is now creating a new humanity. In addition, through Christ God is uniting both Jew and Gentile to himself. "His purpose was . . . in this one body to reconcile both of them to God through the cross" (vv. 15-16). Paul's verb in v. 16 is *apokatallassō*, which means to "turn from hostility to friendship, to reconcile."[107] The apostle mentioned without elaboration reconciliation on a cosmic scale in Eph 1:10 and Col 1:20. While not teaching universal salvation, these texts indicate that the discord and fragmentation characteristic of the fallen universe ultimately will give way to harmony and unity as Christ sovereignly rules over the created order. Reconciliation is the answer to alienation and estrangement, both personally and cosmically.

(6) *Cosmic victory*: Paul perceived that Christ in his life and death achieved a mighty victory over evil spiritual powers. Thus through his public ministry and passion Christ has "destroyed death" (2 Tim 1:10)— the aorist participle of *katargeō* indicating that death has been rendered inoperative. Elsewhere Paul asserted that through Christ's death and resurrection God gave victory over the mortal adversaries, the law, sin, and death (1 Cor 15:55-57). Paul described the victory Christ gained at the cross over hostile spiritual forces in vivid images drawn from the ancient world: "having disarmed the powers and authorities, he made a public spectacle of them, triumphing over them by the cross" (Col 2:15). The first verb, the aorist middle of *apekdyomai*, signifies that at the cross Christ stripped the evil powers that assailed him. The imagery is that of a deposed monarch being stripped of the robes of his office. "The use of the double compound is probably to stress that it is a complete putting off and putting away, which makes a falling back into the former manner of life impossible."[108] The last verb, the aorist of *thriambeuō*, connotes that at the cross Christ roundly conquered alien powers, leading them in a triumphal procession, much as a victorious general led his captives in a pub-

lic display through the streets of the city. Thus through his life and death Christ disarmed all hostile powers that threaten citizens of the kingdom.

(7) *Moral influence/example*: Christ's death also exerted a moral and spiritual influence upon the watching world. According to Luke 23:39-43, having heard Jesus petition the Father to forgive those who had crucified him (v. 34) and having witnessed his firm faith, a criminal on a cross believed that Jesus could save him. Similarly, a Roman soldier who observed Jesus' confidence in God in the face of a humiliating death became convinced that the Nazarene's claims were true; hence he confessed, "Surely this man was the Son of God!" (Mark 15:39).

Paul also viewed the death of Christ as a powerful example of Christian conduct. Since the cross is the supreme demonstration of divine love (Rom 5:8), Paul summoned the Ephesian Christians to imitate Christ's love by living a compassionate life (Eph 5:1-2). Moreover, he enjoined the Philippians to adopt an attitude of humility and unselfish concern for others. Believers achieve this mind-set as they follow the example of Christ who, in the supreme act of self-renunciation, divested himself of the divine glory, assumed our lowly humanity, and went obediently to the cross (Phil 2:3-8). Moreover, reflection on the fact that Christ suffered and died on their behalf will compel (*synechō*, "press together," "constrain") Christians to live the rest of their lives for the good of others (2 Cor 5:14).

The apostle John likewise saw in Jesus' life and death the consummate pattern of self-sacrificing love (John 15:12; 1 John 3:16). Although the primary emphasis of Hebrews and the Petrine letters is upon the propitiatory and expiatory worth of Christ's death, both uphold the exemplary value of the cross for believers. Peter reminded persecuted Christians that "Christ suffered for you, leaving you an example, that you should follow in his steps" (1 Pet 2:21; cf. 4:1-2). And the writer of Hebrews urged his readers, "let us fix our eyes on Jesus . . . , who for the joy set before him endured the cross, scorning its shame, and sat down at the right hand of the throne of God" (Heb 12:2).

Clearly a proper outcome of Christ's death is the stimulus to moral action it affords Christians. Yet in every instance where Christ's death is presented as an example to be followed, the fundamental truth of his death as a substitutionary sacrifice for sin is also present. The power of Christ's example is the answer to human indifference and inaction.

E. *Christ as Prophet, Priest, and King*

Viewing Christ's ministry in terms of the three biblical offices of prophet, priest, and king sheds valuable light on the work he accomplished. In

Israel a prophet (*nābî*) was a servant who received messages from God and then communicated them faithfully to the people. Prophets such as Moses, Elijah, and Isaiah taught God's law, announced salvation, called people to repentance, warned of judgment, and predicted the future. Moses affirmed that after years of false prophets God would raise up another prophet like him and put God's words in his mouth. The words of the coming prophet must be heard and obeyed (Deut 18:15-19; cf. Acts 3:22). Isa 61:1-2 went beyond the son of Amoz to portray the prophetic ministry of the Messiah:

> *"The Spirit of the Sovereign Lord is on me, because the Lord has anointed me to preach the good news to the poor. He has sent me to bind up the brokenhearted, to proclaim freedom for the captives and release from darkness for the prisoners, to proclaim the year of the Lord's favor and the day of vengeance of our God, to comfort all who mourn."*

Jesus was a prophet (*prophētēs*) during his earthly life. His contemporaries viewed him as one in the line of the OT prophets (Matt 21:11, 46; John 4:19; 6:14). After Jesus raised the widow's son the people said, "A great prophet has appeared among us" and "God has come to help his people" (Luke 7:16). Jesus himself was conscious of his prophetic calling and mission (Luke 4:24; 13:33). But the Nazarene was a prophet greater than Moses (Heb 3:3) because of his unique relationship to the Father (John 1:1-2). Jesus exercised a prophetic ministry *verbally* by speaking words from the Father (John 12:49; 14:24; 17:8). He proclaimed the requirements of the law (Matt 5:17-18), preached the Good News of the kingdom (Luke 4:18-19), and infallibly predicted the future (Matt 24:2-31; Luke 19:41-44). Furthermore, he exercised a prophetic ministry *practically* by healings and other miracles. By many supernatural deeds Jesus revealed the Father's character and purpose. Moreover, Jesus continues his prophetic ministry from heaven. By the Spirit he has given the Scriptures, and from the Bible he continues to speak to the saved and the unsaved.

In Israel the *priest* (*kōhēn*), appointed from the tribe of Levi and the family of Aaron, guarded the covenant, taught God's law, and offered sacrifices (Deut 33:8-10; cf. Lev 10:11; 2 Chron 17:9). The Jewish priest served a mediatorial function between God and the covenant people. By offering sacrifices the priests represented the people before God, and by teaching the law they represented God before the people. The high priest alone entered the Most Holy Place in the tabernacle once a year to make atonement for the people (Leviticus 16). The Jewish priesthood demonstrated the need for a mediator, the more so when the priesthood became corrupted by offering blemished sacrifices and by teaching falsely (Mal 1:6–2:9).

Looking backward to the Genesis Melchizedek account and forward to the Messiah's advent, David identified Christ as the priest of a radically different order. He wrote, "The Lord has sworn and will not change his mind: 'You are a priest forever in the order of Melchizedek'" (Ps 110:4). David took notice of Melchizedek, a unique, non-Aaronic priest superior to the Jewish ministrant, neither the commencement nor the termination of whose office Scripture records. It remained for the writer of Hebrews to develop the full Christological implications of Melchizedek's royal priesthood.

Isaiah's fourth servant song (Isa 52:13–53:12), discussed above, describes Messiah's priestly work of vicarious sacrifice. Moreover, the prophet Zechariah depicts the post-exilic coronation of the high priest Joshua, son of Jehozadak. Ultimately, royal and priestly functions will be united in one called "the Branch" or Messiah. Thus Yahweh said, "It is he who will build the temple of the Lord, and he will be clothed with majesty and will sit and rule on his throne. And he will be a priest on his throne" (Zech 6:13).

The central section of Hebrews develops Christ's work under the rubric of high priest. Heb 4:14–5:10 and 7:1-28 uphold the superiority of Christ's priesthood to the Levitical order. God appointed Aaron high priest over Israel to offer gifts and sacrifices for sins (5:1-4). But Aaron's priesthood was imperfect, for he must first offer sacrifices for his own sins as well as repeat the sacrifices year after year. Consequently, by an irrevocable oath God appointed his sinless Son (Heb 4:15; 7:26) to be high priest of a radically new order typified by Melchizedek, the godly priest-king of Salem (5:5-10). This "king of righteousness" and "king of peace" exercised a priesthood that was superior to the Aaronic order (7:1-10) for several reasons: (1) Abraham, the ancestor of Levi, paid tithes to Melchizedek; (2) Melchizedek blessed the patriarch Abraham; and (3) Melchizedek "lives on" (NASB), whereas the Levitical priests all succumbed to death.

Hebrews further insists that Jesus' singular self-sacrifice was superior to the repeated offerings of the Jewish priests. As noted above, the sacrifices offered by the Aaronic high priest on the Day of Atonement wrought only ceremonial cleansing and failed to purge the inner life of the worshipers. Thus "it is impossible for the blood of bulls and goats to take away sins" (Heb. 10:4; cf. 9:9). The Day of Atonement ritual served as a "shadow" (8:5) or type of the perfect sacrifice of Christ. Faithful to the will of God, Jesus our "great high priest" (4:14) surrendered his life and shed his blood once-for-all as the truly effectual sacrifice that frees from guilt and makes holy (7:27; 9:15, 26, 28; 10:5-10, 12). Thus "we have been made holy through the sacrifice of the body of Jesus Christ once for all" (10:10). Moreover, Jesus, our high priest, faithfully petitions the heavenly Father on behalf of his people. Wherefore "he is able to save completely those who come to God through him, because he always lives to intercede for them" (7:25). On the basis of his priestly sacrifice and petition, believers boldly approach the throne of grace (4:16).

In Israel the king (*melek*) exercised executive, legislative, judicial, and military powers essential to governing the nation. When Israel clamored for a visible king, Samuel anointed Saul to that office. The serious flaws of Saul and the apostasy of later evil kings created in Israel a longing for an ideal king who would rule in truth and justice.

Jacob's blessing of his son Judah contained a prophecy that would be fulfilled in the messianic King who would rule the nations. "The scepter will not depart from Judah, nor the ruler's staff from between his feet, until he comes to whom it belongs and the obedience of the nations is his" (Gen 49:10). An oracle of Balaam likewise pointed to Israel's future messianic deliverer and ruler (Num 24:17-19). But the premier OT type of Christ as king was Solomon's son David. When the latter was appointed king, Nathan predicted that David's dynasty would endure forever through his offspring (2 Sam 7:13-16; cf. Ps 89:3-4). Ultimately Nathan's prophecy anticipated the messianic King who is both the Son of David and the Son of God (cf. Luke 1:32-33).

Several psalms reiterate this expectation of a kingly Messiah. Psalm 2 envisages the future "Anointed One" (v. 2), messianic "King" (v. 6), and "Son" (vv. 7, 12) who will subdue the nations and reign over the earth. Psalm 45, a marriage song for a Hebrew monarch, prophetically describes the splendor and righteousness of the Messiah's eternal reign. Psalm 72, a psalm that extols the glory of Solomon's reign, likewise anticipates the universal and eternal rule of the royal Messiah. According to Ps 110:1, God's vice-regent, the king, is summoned to the place of honor: "The Lord says to my Lord: 'Sit at my right hand until I make your enemies a footstool for your feet.'" In the NT Jesus (Matt 22:44), Peter (Acts 2:34-35), and Hebrews (1:13) applied this psalm-text to the glorification and world-rule of Christ from heaven.

The prophet Isaiah wrote, "the Lord is our judge, the Lord is our lawgiver; the Lord is our king, it is he who will save us" (Isa 33:22). The functions of judge (cf. 2:4; 11:4) and lawgiver (cf. 2:3; 51:4) pertain to Messiah's kingly ministry. Jeremiah beheld the "righteous Branch" and

Davidic "King" who "will reign wisely and do what is just and right in the land" (Jer 23:5). In a vision Daniel saw "one like a son of man, coming with the clouds of heaven." By the Ancient of Days he "was given authority, glory and sovereign power; all peoples, nations and men of every language worshipped him. His dominion is an everlasting dominion that will not pass away, and his kingdom is one that will never be destroyed" (Dan 7:13-14). Ezekiel portrayed the Messiah serving as a shepherd, prince, and king forever over the house of David (Ezek 34:22-24; 37:24-25). Micah similarly described the divine Messiah as "one who will be ruler over Israel" (Mic 5:2).

The Gospels, particularly Matthew, announced the arrival of Jesus, the promised messianic King. Eastern astrologers, guided by a star to Bethlehem, inquired, "Where is the one who has been born king of the Jews? We saw his star in the east and have come to worship him" (Matt 2:2). Following his baptism, Jesus preached the message of the advance-enactment of the kingdom through his person (Matt 4:17; Mark 1:15; Luke 4:43). As the the messianic King (Matt 21:5; 25:31, 34, 40) Jesus would bless his people, destroy the works of the Devil, judge his enemies, and rule over a kingdom. The phrases "kingdom of heaven" and "kingdom of God" (Matt 7:21; 13:11; Mark 12:34; Luke 17:21) interchangeably denote God's redemptive rule in Christ that defeats evil powers and liberates repentant sinners. Jesus rightly claimed total authority over people either as Savior or as judge (Matt 25:31-46). And when the Lord hung on the cross, the Roman soldiers mocked and reviled him, saying, "Hail, king of the Jews!" (Matt 27:29), and the inscription placed over his head read: "THIS IS JESUS, THE KING OF THE JEWS" (v. 37).

Messiah's kingly rule was realized invisibly and spiritually at his first advent (Matt 3:2; 12:28-29). The slain Lamb has become a conqueror, ruling from his heavenly throne (Rev 1:5; 11:15). Believers in Jesus "receive" (Heb 12:28), "enter" (John 3:5; cf. Col 1:13), and "inherit" (1 Cor 6:9-10; Gal 5:21; Jas 2:5) his kingdom by the new birth. But the kingdom will be instituted visibly and institutionally at Christ's second advent (Matt 25:31, 34, 40; Luke 1:33). Paul described Christ's exaltation to kingly rule over the universe thusly: "God exalted him to the highest place and gave him the name that is above every name, that at the name of Jesus every knee should bow, in heaven and on earth and under the earth, and every tongue confess that Jesus Christ is lord" (Phil 2:9-11). See also 1 Cor 15:24-27 and Eph 1:20-22.

In sum, Christ saves sinners by uniting in himself the offices of prophet, priest, and king. As a prophet Christ removes our sinful ignorance by his word; as a priest he purges our offending guilt by his sacrificial blood; and as a king he conquers evil and protects his people by his limitless power. Christ functioned in his threefold office during his earthly humiliation; he serves in the same manner through the Spirit in his heavenly exaltation. A person is saved when Christ becomes his or her prophet, priest, and king.

F. The Necessity of Christ's Death

The question before us is whether it was necessary that Christ should have become man and died a shameful death on the cross. Anselm (d. 1109) posed the question thusly: "For what necessity and for what reason did God, since he is omnipotent, take upon himself the humiliation and weakness of human nature in order to bring about its restoration?"[109] At first glance, the question appears to be a speculative one that evades ready solution. But on closer examination, clear thinking and biblical revelation sheds light on the problem. Consider three possible responses to the question as posed. (1) It was absolutely necessary for God to save hell-deserving sinners; therefore, the Father sent his Son into the world to suffer and die on the cross. This view of *absolute necessity* reasons from the standpoint of sheer justice to conclude that sin's penalty must be paid. But it overlooks the divine freedom whereby God might have decided not to save rebellious sinners. Moreover, since this answer borders on fatalism, it must be rejected by biblical theists.

(2) God could have decided not to save at all; or he could have decided to establish a system of moral governance that would allow him to save by the death of his Son *or* by some other means. Having purposed to save, the omnipotent God could have arranged the salvation of the fallen race in a way that is beyond our finite knowledge. Grotius (d. 1645) argued that Christ's death was the best of several means by which God could have upheld the moral order of the universe. Some Arminians follow Grotius in claiming that God could have forgiven sin without the satisfaction provided by Christ's death. On this showing, the cross is the best of several ways by which God could have chosen to uphold universal government. According to this view of *hypothetical necessity*, there is nothing inherent in the nature of God or forgiveness that requires the shed blood of God's Son. Scripture texts that indicate Jesus' death was determined by divine decree (e.g., the verb *dei* in Matt 16:21; Luke 24:7; John 3:14; etc.) could indicate what must take place in the outworking of salvation, given God's arrangement of the plan of salvation as we know it.

Alternatively, (3) God could have decided not to save at all; or he could have decided to create humans, to permit their moral fall, and to save a great multitude by the only means possible, namely, by the vicarious death of his own Son. This view, known as *consequent absolute necessity*, has been advanced by many Reformed thinkers. John Murray identified several Scripture texts judged to favor this third alternative.[110] (a) Hebrews 2:10, 17 implies that atonement can be made and sinners brought to glory only by a Savior who was fashioned like his brothers and perfected by suffering. (b) John 3:14-17 suggests that the alternative to God's decision to give his Son in death on the cross is sinners' eternal perdition. The Atonement does not elicit God's love; God's love elicits Atonement through Christ's death. (c) Heb 9:22-23 reads, "the law requires that nearly everything be cleansed with blood, and without the shedding of blood there is no forgiveness. It was necessary . . . for the copies of the heavenly things to be purified with these sacrifices, but the heavenly things themselves with better sacrifices than these." The copies of heavenly things (the earthly tabernacle, etc.) were purified by animal sacrifices. But the heavenly things themselves could be purified only by the better sacrifice of Christ. This being so, it was equally necessary that Christ should die a vicarious death for sins to be remitted (vv. 14, 22, 26). Murray concluded, "there is stated to be a necessity that can be met by nothing less than the blood of Jesus."[111]

The last response is closest to the truth, but we propose a better way of expressing it. We will avoid the terms "necessity" and "absolute necessity," for these may imply that there is a principal or power higher than God that determines occurrences. The God of the Bible is the highest explanation of all things, and he is absolutely self-determined. God always acts out of his sovereign freedom (Ps 115:3; 135:6) rather than in accord with causes external to himself. With the second and third views, we uphold the biblical principle of unmerited grace. It was not necessary for the divine Judge, after pronouncing the just sentence against sin, to move from behind the bench and take upon himself the penalty of the accused. God's decision to save was a free movement of love and grace. If the creation of the cosmos was a free act of love, how much more was Christ's provision on the cross for the re-creation of sinners an unmerited expression of sheer grace.

Having freely made the decision to save, God then acted in accord with his own intrinsic nature and perfections. He operated in harmony with his perfect wisdom (1 Cor 1:24, 30; 2:7; Eph 3:10), righteousness (Ps 51:14; 71:15-16), holiness (Exod 15:11; Isa 49:7; 1 Pet 1:15-16), mercy (Eph 2:4-5; Tit 3:5), and supremely his agapic love (John 3:16; 15:13; Rom 5:8; Eph 5:2; 1 John 4:9-10). In other words, given his own rules for how sin would be handled in his moral universe, the course of saving action God chose in light of the foreseen human situation was the wisest, most righteous, and most loving course possible. In sending his Son to be bruised and to bear our evils, God gave his highest and best. Other alleged options we might consider less optimal, out of respect of his own nature the God of perfection could not entertain. So the apostle Paul simply stated, "Thanks be to God for his indescribable gift!" (2 Cor 9:15). Augustine approved of this line of reasoning with the following comment: "this way, whereby God deigned to liberate us through the Mediator between God and men, the man Christ Jesus was both good and befitting the divine dignity . . . there was no other way more fitting, and no other needed for healing our misery."[112] God acted to save the sinful race in the *way* he did precisely because of who he is.

G. *The Purpose or Intent of Christ's Death*

Thoughtful people have addressed the question whether Christ suffered and died for the elect only or for the entire world. Older theologians enquired into the *extent* of the Atonement and debated whether it was limited or unlimited. More recently scholars have focused on the *intent* of Christ's death, with the discussion centering on whether the Atonement was particular or universal. We choose to ask the question, *For whom did Christ intend to provide atonement through his suffering and death?* Accordingly, we will divide the question in two parts. We inquire, first, into the *provision* Christ made via his death on the cross. And we explore, second, the *application* of the benefits gained by Calvary to sinners.

Concerning the *provision* side of the cross, we examine, first, general statements pertinent to the question. Isa 53:6 reads, "We all, like sheep, have gone astray, each of us has turned to his own way; and the Lord has laid on him the iniquity of us all." As sin and iniquity is universal, so also is Christ's saving provision. V. 4a adds that "he took up our infirmities and carried our sorrows"; v. 5a further states that "he was pierced for our transgressions, he was crushed for our iniquities." The objects of the Messiah's sufferings are identified in v. 6b as the people of Israel at large.

The familiar text, John 3:16-17, speaks of God's universal love, his intention to save all people on earth, and the invitation to all people everywhere to believe on Christ. Moreover, Heb 2:9 reads, "we see Jesus . . . now crowned with glory and honor because he suffered death, so that by the grace of God he might taste death for everyone." Bruce observed that "Because the Son of Man suffered, because his suffering has been crowned by His exaltation, therefore His death avails for all."[113] Vv. 14-16 adds, "he too shared in their humanity so that by his death he might destroy him who holds the power of death—that is, the devil—and free those who all their lives were held in slavery by their fear of death. For surely it is not angels he helps, but Abraham's descendants." The destruction of Satan and his work (cf. 1 John 3:8) and the ensuing spiritual liberation was accomplished on behalf of the people at large. V. 17 reiterates the point that Christ made "atonement for the sins of the people" (cf. 9:28).

Peter wrote of false prophets and teachers who "secretly introduce destructive heresies, even denying the sovereign Lord who bought them" (2 Pet 2:1). As noted, *agorazō* figuratively means to purchase from the slavemarket of sin (1 Cor 6:20; 7:23; Rev 5:9). Peter thus described prophets and teachers in the churches, bought by Christ, who made a profession of faith but who later became openly heretical. Second Pet 2:2 suggests that these denied their Master and Lord by blatant immorality. Peter's word is *aselgeia* (cf. 1 Pet 4:3; 2 Pet 2:7, 18; Jude 4), meaning "repeated habitual acts of lasciviousness."[114] Peter's statement "does not mean that the false teachers were believers. Christ's death paid the penalty for their sin, but it would not become effective for their salvation unless they trusted in Christ as Savior."[115]

Next we cite Scriptures stating that Christ died for the "world" (*kosmos*). The Baptist's words—"Look, the Lamb of God, who takes away the sin of the world!" (John 1:29)—affirm that Jesus' sacrifice would atone for the sin of all. Likewise, certain Samaritans said of Jesus, "we know that this man really is the Savior of the world" (John 4:42). Jesus, moreover, identified himself as "the bread of God . . . who comes down from heaven and gives life to the world" (John 6:33). First John 2:2 states that Jesus Christ "is the atoning sacrifice for our sins, and not only for ours but also for the sins of the whole world." As Bruce put it, "The propitiation that has availed to wipe out their [the readers'] sins is sufficient to do the same for all. Jesus is 'the general Savior of mankind' as well as the particular Savior of each believer."[116] Equally direct is the statement of 1 John 4:14: "the Father has sent his Son to be the Savior of the world." Paul stated that "God was reconciling the world to himself in Christ, not counting men's sins against them" (2 Cor 5:19a). The apostle urged believers to bring to this world the message of reconciliation (v. 19b-20). Unless we adopt the radical view (fortunately held by only a few high Calvinists) that the Gospel should be preached only to those known to be elect, "world" in the two latter texts means the totality of all living persons.

Note, in addition, Scriptures indicating that Christ died for "all men." In 1 Tim 2:6 Paul stated that Jesus is the "one mediator between God and men," and that he "gave himself as a ransom for all men." Paul's citation in v. 4 that God "wants all men to be saved" indicates that every last person is in view. In 1 Tim 4:10 the apostle presented a twofold purpose in the cross when he wrote of "the living God, who is the Savior of all men, and especially [*malista*] of those who believe."

Some interpret this text to mean that God is the Savior of all, in the general sense that he preserves humanity in existence, provides the blessings of common grace, and delays the execution of his judgment on sinners. Whereas the OT often envisages God as Savior in the sense of temporal provider and deliverer, we should be guided by Pauline usage, which is consistently soteriological (Eph 5:23; Phil 3:20; 1 Tim 1:1; 2:3; 2 Tim 1:10; Tit 1:3-4; 2:10, 13; 3:4, 6). Moreover, many NT texts upholding a universal dimension to the Atonement cannot be limited to God's general (i.e., non-soteriological) goodness to all people. Thus 1 Tim 4:10 teaches that Christ is universal Savior in that he made redemptive provision for all persons, but he is the effectual Savior of those who believe. Second Cor 5:14-15, which speaks of Christ dying "for all," may refer to every last person, in view of the statement in context that "God was reconciling the world to himself in Christ" (see above, v. 19a).

Other texts stating that Christ died for the disciples, the apostles, the sheep, the church, etc. (Luke 22:19; 1 Cor 11:24; 15:3; Gal 2:20; 3:13; Eph 5:2; 1 Thess 5:10) do not exclude other biblical teachings to the effect that the Savior atoned for the sins of the world at large. What is true for the universal set is also true of a sub-set thereof.

Paul's statement, "God our Savior . . . wants [*thelei*] all men to be saved and to come to a knowledge of the truth" (1 Tim 2:3-4), and Peter's words, "The Lord . . . is patient with you, not wanting anyone to perish, but everyone to come to repentance" (2 Pet 3:9), must be taken as genuine expressions of God's longing heart. These texts make better sense if God in Christ made objective provision on the cross for the spiritual needs of all people rather than for the elect only.

We conclude that in terms of the Atonement's *provision* Christ died not merely for the elect but for all sinners in all times and places. Christ drank the cup of suffering for the sins of the entire world. He died as a substitute, a propitiation, a ransom, etc. for the universe of sinners. The non-elect had their sins paid for on the cross, even though through unbelief they do not personally appropriate the benefits of his work. Christ, in other words, provided salvation for more people than those to whom he purposed to apply its saving benefits. The Atonement's universal provision removes every barrier between a holy God and sinners, unleashes in the world a power for good that restrains evil, guarantees the future resurrection of all people from the dead (John 5:28-29), provides an additional just basis for the condemnation of unbelievers, and offers motivation for the proclamation of the Good News to every creature. Arminians correctly emphasize the universality of the provision side of the Atonement.

We now turn to the Lord's intention with respect to the *application* of the Atonement. In Matt 1:21 an angel of the Lord informed Joseph that those who actually will be saved from their sins are "his people," i.e., the company of the chosen. According to John 10, Jesus laid down his life with positive efficacy for those whom he "calls . . . by name" (v. 3b), who hear his voice (vv. 3b, 16, 27a), who follow him (v. 27b), who receive eternal life (v. 28a), who are specially cared for (vv. 12-14), and who are preserved to the end (vv. 28b, 29b). These prove to be the "sheep" given by the Father to the Son (v. 29a). We believe that Christ accomplishes all those spiritual ends that he purposes or intends. Turning to John 17, those who believe in Jesus (v. 8b), who obey the word (v. 6b), who receive eternal life (v. 2), who are sanctified (v. 17, 19), who are protected from the evil one (vv. 11-12, 15), and who are glorified (v. 24) are those persons to whom the Son savingly reveals the Father (vv. 6a, 26a). And as indicated in Acts 20:28, those whom Christ has efficiently bought with his own blood are "all the flock," or the people of God.

In the latter part of Romans 8, Paul discussed Christ's death in relation to believers. Those to whom the Atonement's benefits are applied are specially favored (v. 32b); i.e., they experience the effectual calling (v. 30b), justification (vv. 30c, 33b), and glorification (v. 30d). Those who receive these benefits are the people of God, or the elect (vv. 29-30a, 33a). According to Eph 5:25-27 those to whom the fruits of the Atonement are applied in the form of justification, sanctification, and glorification are likewise the elect (1:4-5, 11), who constitute the church. In 1 Peter 1 those who are effectually called (v. 2b), who believe (vv. 8, 21), who are born again (vv. 3, 23), who experience salvation (v. 9), who are sanctified (vv. 15-16), who are preserved by God's power (v. 5), and who finally will be glorified (v. 9) again are "God's elect" (vv. 1-2). Paul likely had in mind the application of the saving benefits of the Atonement to believers when in Gal 1:3-4 he wrote that "the Lord Jesus Christ . . . gave himself for our sins to rescue us from the present evil age, according to the will of our God and Father."

We further observe that in his high priestly prayer Jesus prayed not for the world but for those the Father gave him out of the world (John 17:6-26). Elsewhere in Scripture, we find that Jesus (Rom 8:34; Heb 7:25; 1 John 2:1) and the Spirit (Rom 8:26-27) presently intercede for believers to whom are applied the fruits of salvation. Surely if Jesus had intended to apply salvation to all persons he would have prayed for them as he prayed for the elect. This further confirms the other Scriptures discussed above that indicate God purposed to apply the fruits of the Atonement to his sheep, his people, or the church who exercise God-given faith. The Reformed tradition correctly emphasizes the particularity of the application side of the Atonement.

In sum, regarding the question, For whom did Christ die? we find biblical warrant for dividing the question into God's purpose regarding the *provision* of the Atonement and his purpose concerning the *application* thereof. Scripture leads us to conclude that God loves all people he created and that Christ died to provide salvation for all. The *provision* side of the Atonement is part of the general will of God that must be preached to all. But beyond this, the Father loves the "sheep" with a special love,[117] and in the divine will the Spirit applies the benefits of Christ's death to the "sheep," or the elect. The *application* side of the Atonement is part of the special will of God shared with those who come to faith. This conclusion—that Christ died to make atonement for all to the end that its benefits would be applied to the elect—coheres with the perspective of Sublapsarian Calvinism. It differs from the Supralapsarian and Infralapsarian schemes, which teach that Christ died to make provision only for the sins of the elect. And it differs from the Arminian scheme of decrees, which states that God willed the application of the Atonement to all, but that the divine purpose was frustrated by human resistance. A.H. Strong reflected the biblical perspective when he wrote, "Not the *atonement* therefore is limited, but the *application* through the work of the Holy Spirit."[118]

Thomas J. Nettles designates this development a modification of the limited Atonement hypothesis.[119] Millard J. Erickson, reflecting on classical formulations of the *ordo salutis*, describes the position as a form of the unlimited or universal Atonement thesis.[120] The view presented may be neither, as it divides the question into the divine intention concerning the *provision* of the cross, which is universal, and his intention concerning the *application* thereof, which is particular. The position outlined is not Arminianism (as some allege) but a viewpoint close to that of Calvin himself—a position that was narrowed by later, scholastic Calvinism. Our perspective, moreover, offers greater specificity than the dictum frequently articulated in evangelical circles: "The Atonement is sufficient for all but efficient for the elect." Rather, it affirms that by divine *intention* Christ's suffering and death are universal in its provision and particular in its application.

IV. PRACTICAL IMPLICATIONS OF
THE DOCTRINE OF THE CROSS

A. *Realize That Christ Died for You*

The multiple purposes of Christ's death on the cross can be represented by three concentric circles. The largest circle represents the entire world for whom the Savior died as the adequate provision for sins (1 Tim 4:10; 1 John 2:2; 4:14). The middle circle delineates the sum of all believers, i.e., the church (John 10:11, 15; Acts 20:28; Rom 8:32; Gal 1:4; Eph 5:2), to whom Christ's saving provisions were actually applied. And the innermost circle represents the individual believer for whom Christ made atonement (Gal 2:20b). That Christ died for me and for you individually and personally is made clear by Paul's words in the preceding text: "the Son of God . . . loved me [*me*] and gave himself for me [*hyper emou*]." It is highly significant that in describing the true Gospel and its ministry Paul used the first-person, singular pronoun twenty-eight times in this second chapter of Galatians.

How blessed it is to realize that Christ took my place on the cross and was forsaken of God for *me*. For *my* sins he bore in his body the penalty required by a holy and just God. He appeased the divine wrath directed against *my* transgressions. By his death Christ delivered *me* from the slavery of sin and Satan, and his shed blood cleansed *my* sins. Through his cross the Savior reconciled and consecrated *me* to the waiting Father. By his death and resurrection Christ gained the victory over the spiritual foes that tormented *me*. No matter who else was loved, God in grace laid down his life for *you* and for *me*. Luther reflected on the personal focus of Christ's death: "these words, 'who loved me,' are filled with faith. . . . He who was completely God gave everything He was, gave Himself for me— for me, I say, a miserable and accursed sinner. I am revived by this 'giving' of the Son of God unto death, and I apply it to myself." Luther continued, "Therefore read these words '*me*' and '*for me*' with great emphasis, and accustom yourself to accepting this '*me*' with a sure faith and applying it to yourself. Do not doubt that you belong to the number of those who speak this '*me*.' Christ did not only love Peter and Paul and give Himself for them, but the same grace belongs and comes to us as to them; therefore we are included in this '*me*.'"[121]

Christ's suffering and death at Calvary was a very personal and individualized event. While impaled on the cross his suffering eye was on the world, but it was also lovingly directed toward *you*, the reader, and toward *me*, as his sheep. The fact that Christ loved *you* and *me* and thus was willing to suffer and die for our sins is a source of great comfort and encouragement to the wayfaring pilgrim.

B. Recognize That His Death Is Final

Some religious traditions view Christ's death on the cross as incomplete and less than final. According to Roman Catholics the Mass purports to repeat the historical sacrifice of Christ, and the faithful must continue to make satisfaction to God for post-baptismal sins. Some liberal theologians believe that through evolutionary advance a religious prophet and teacher will arise who will surpass Christ and the work he accomplished on the cross. Still others, like the Anglo-Catholic churchman Bicknell and the Scottish neoorthodox theologian D.M. Baillie, believe that the Atonement continues eternally in heaven. The latter asserted that "an eternal work of atonement, supratemporal as the life of God is . . . going on as long as sins continue to be committed and there are sinners to be reconciled."[122]

Scripture, however, unequivocally asserts that Jesus Christ's atoning work on the cross is unsurpassable and unrepeatable. Peter asserted that in his state of humiliation—in our space, time, and history—"Christ died for sins once for all, the righteous for the unrighteous, to bring you to God" (1 Pet 3:18). The most exhaustive claim, however, for the finality of the cross is found in Hebrews. This letter to Jewish converts tempted to revert to Judaism flatly asserts that Christ's sacrifice was offered once for all, as opposed to the repeated sacrifices brought by the Levitical priests (Heb 7:27; 9:25-28; 10:10-12, 14). The writer's use of *hapax* (9:7, 26-28; 10:2), *ephapax* (7:27; 9:12; 10:10), and *mia* (10:12, 14) underscore the unrepeatable sufficiency of Christ's self-oblation. Because Christ's single sacrifice has effactually cleansed and consecrated believers to God, "there is no longer any sacrifice for sin" (Heb 10:18). Christ's death definitively accomplished salvation, although its benefits continue to be applied to repentant sinners until Christ returns. Moreover, the description of Christ seated at the right hand of God figuratively asserts that the Savior's atoning work in history is complete (Heb 1:3; 8:2; 10:12). Finally, Hebrews teaches that after offering himself on the cross, Christ entered the heavenly sanctuary where he intercedes on behalf of the saints before the Father (Heb 4:14; 8:2; 9:11-12, 24). Christ exercises his heavenly petition in virtue of the full efficacy of his earthly self-sacrifice. The ongoing nature of his heavenly intercession must not obscure the once-for-all character of his earthly oblation.

Christians take great comfort in the fact that Christ's sacrifice is wholly effectual and final. His shed blood fully discharged the debt we owed to

God, and it completely covers the believer's every sin. Pilgrim saints need not search out any other religious leader, any angel, or any saint to add to the work God's Son accomplished on the cross. The uniqueness of Christ's atoning work is as invincible as the uniqueness of his divine person and his threefold office. Divine love could do no more for you and me than it did on the cross of Calvary.

C. *Allow the Cross Its Transforming Work*

If the cross be the crucial core of the Gospel, if it be the central datum of the faith, then its power must vitally affect the believer's character and conduct. A Christian truth purported to be crucial that does not change one's outlook and actions would be a sham. Consider *how* the cross transforms those who cling in faith to the crucified and risen Christ. As we noted above, *objectively* the cross liberates from the power of sin, propitiates God's wrath, washes away the guilt and stain of sin, reconciles believers to God, and achieves a cosmic victory over deadly spiritual foes. The objective effects of the cross introduce believers into a radically new situation. *Subjectively*, Christ's example of suffering on our behalf releases a new moral power that transforms our attitudes, motives, and conduct. At Calvary by faith we see the vileness of our sin and Jesus' loving purposes for our eternal welfare. This paradigm of suffering love incites believers to adopt a new set of values and to pursue a new way of living. By its objective and subjective effects, the cross leads believers into the path of righteous living vis-à-vis God and our fellows. At the practical level, consider the following ways in which the cross transforms Christians' character and conduct.

Christ's cross (1) engenders a *life of humility*. As Paul wrote to the Philippians:

> *Your attitude should be the same as that of Christ Jesus: Who, being in very nature God, did not consider equality with God something to be grasped, but made himself nothing, taking the very nature of a servant, being made in human likeness. And being found in appearance as a man, he humbled himself and became obedient to death—even death on a cross!*
>
> —Phil 2:5-8

The example of our Lord, who laid aside heaven's glory, assumed our lowly estate, and submitted himself to a shameful death, should impel Christian believers to conduct themselves with lowly humility. As Calvin wrote, "when we think upon all this, ought not all haughtiness and presumption, all pride, all harshness and all bitterness be laid aside, as we consider the way by which our Lord Jesus Christ has reconciled us to God his Father?"[123] Calvary, moreover, (2) stimulates a *life of holiness*. Paul wrote as follows: "now he [God] has reconciled you by Christ's physical body through death to present you holy in his sight, without blemish and free from accusation—if you continue in your faith, established and firm" (Col 1:22-23a; cf. 1 Cor 6:18-20; Gal 5:24). Christ's death on the cross breaks sin's mastery over the newly redeemed, freeing them to live lives consecrated to God, blameless, and beyond reproach. Calvin helpfully wrote that evil is

> so deeply rooted in our hearts that if we were told of our duty, it only half moves us. For this reason, St. Paul sets the example of God before us here. He has forgiven us in his only Son. And without delay he adds our Lord Jesus Christ, who spared not himself when it was a question of our redemption and salvation. What, then, can break down all hardness in us, what can mortify all our excessive passions, what can correct all our cruelty, bring low all our pride and loftiness and sweeten all our bitterness, is to contemplate what God has done towards us. He has so loved the world that he has given up his only Son to death for us [John 3:16].[124]

Christ's passion (3) motivates a *life of love and compassion*. Hear again Paul who wrote, "Be imitators of God, therefore, as dearly loved children and live a life of love, just as Christ loved us and gave himself up for us as a fragrant offering and sacrifice to God" (Eph 5:1-2). Attend also to John's instruction: "This is how we know what love is: Jesus Christ laid down his life for us. And we ought to lay down our lives for our brothers. . . . Dear children, let us not love with words or tongue but with actions and in truth" (1 John 3:16, 18; cf. John 15:12-13; 13:1). We imitate our Lord's loving sacrifice by renouncing personal interests and looking to the needs of others. Practically, this means giving ourselves, our time, and our material resources for the good of others, especially those in want.

Our Lord's passion (4) impels us to a *life of peace-making*. Paul wrote that "God was pleased . . . through him [Christ] to reconcile to himself all things . . . by making peace through his blood, shed on the cross" (Col 1:19-20). As Christ made peace between God and sinners, so believers should dismantle every obstacle to harmony, not only vertically with God but horizontally with other persons. Moreover, the cross (5) urges believers to *a life of patient endurance*. So Peter wrote, "if you suffer for doing good and you endure it, this is commendable before God. To this you were called, because Christ suffered for you, leaving you an example, that you should follow in his steps (1 Pet 2:20-21; cf. 4:1). Hebrews added, "Let us fix our eyes on Jesus . . . who for the joy set before him endured the cross, scorning its shame, and sat down at the right hand of the throne of God. Consider him who endured such opposition from sinful men, so that you will not grow weary and lose heart" (12:2-3). Following Christ's example, disciples will endure scorn, abuse, and unjust suffering patiently for the glory of God, as Jesus did. Such trials are God's means of promoting godly character.

Christ's death and resurrection (6) extends the promise of a *life of victory*. As John wrote, "everyone born of God overcomes the world. This is the victory that has overcome the world, even our faith. Who is it that overcomes the world? Only he who believes that Jesus is the Son of God" (1 John 5:4-5). Significantly, John used the word "overcome" three times in these two verses. The power of Christ crucified, appropriated by faith, fortifies believers to triumph over the world, the flesh, and the Devil. Finally, the cross (7) motivates saints to a *life unselfishly lived for Christ and his kingdom.* "Christ's love compels us, because we are convinced that one died for all, and therefore all died. And he died for all, that those who live should no longer live for themselves but for him who died for them and was raised again" (2 Cor 5:14-15). In response to Christ's love for us manifested in his agonizing death, Christians should invest their lives living for him and his cause on earth. Christ's death on our behalf shuts us up to this one eternally significant course of action.

D. Embrace Christ as
Your Prophet, Priest, and King

Previously in this chapter we found considerable biblical support for the Reformed insight that Christ's work can be described under the ministries of the prophet, priest, and king. These three servant ministries, though distinct from one another, beautifully unite in Jesus Christ. In an age when the work of our Savior is greatly devalued by humanists, liberals, non-Christian religionists, and cultists, we need to pay close attention to our Lord's present ministries on our behalf as prophet, priest, and king.

Christians need to understand that in his *prophetic ministry* Christ continues to make the Father known (John 1:18c). The one who is at the Father's side (John 1:18b), who personally has seen the Father (John 3:32), and whom the Father has sent (John 8:42) presently communicates the Father's words, will, and wisdom to his people. Paul wrote that in Christ "are hidden all the treasures of wisdom and knowledge" (Col 2:3). In his ministry as prophet, Christ lovingly speaks to his blood-bought people for their spiritual good. But he speaks not with the clap of thunder but with a still, small voice akin to a gentle whisper. Therefore, saints, be alert, listen carefully, and obey Christ's words, that your joy in God may be complete (John 15:10-11). Christian believers, look to no other prophet than Christ! Look only to the Lord Jesus Christ as your infallible Teacher of moral and spiritual truth.

The two poles of Christ's *priestly ministry* consist of his earthly oblation and his heavenly representation of the people of God. Through his sacrifice on the cross, Christ has washed away past sins and blotted out guilt. But the risen Christ continues his priestly ministry in the heavenly sanctuary forever (Ps 110:4; Heb 5:6; 7:17, 21). In this heavenly service Christ (1) empathizes with us in all our weaknesses (Heb 4:15). He understands and feels our deepest aspirations, needs, and hurts. Even though our Lord has left earth, we are not forgotten. Jesus Christ knows and cares for us. Moreover, (2) Christ the high priest intercedes on our behalf before the Father. His heavenly intercession includes *presentation*—his presence before the Father in the vigor of his completed sacrifice (Heb 9:24) and *representation*—his work of mediating believers' prayers and pleading their cause before the Father. And (3) through our heavenly high priest we have immediate access to the heavenly throne (Heb 4:16). Believers have no need for any earthly priest or human mediator to represent us before God (1 Tim 2:5). Confidently, then, look to Jesus Christ as your divine Advocate and Intercessor.

Moreover, the crucified and risen Christ exercises a *kingly ministry* over all persons, angels, demons, and powers in the universe (Eph 1:20-22; Phil 2:9-11). In the words of Peter, Jesus Christ "has gone into heaven and is at God's right hand—with angels, authorities and powers in submission to him" (1 Pet 3:22). Since Christ is our all-powerful King, we ought not look to human protectors, horoscopes, or psychics for safety. We look, rather, to the Lord Jesus Christ as our eternal defender and protector. We know that he will wrap his strong arms around us and keep us safe from all the evil powers we confront. We know that the Lord will never fail to meet our deepest needs. As Calvin put it, the people of God ultimately will "be victorious over the devil, the world, and every kind of harmful thing."[125] Indeed, Christ our King "arms and equips us with his power, adorns us with his beauty and magnificence, and enriches us with his wealth."[126] There are many self-styled lords in the world daily clamoring for our allegiance. But Christians give their loyalty and allegiance only to Christ, the reigning King of the universe.

III

THE APPLICATION
OF SALVATION

SUBJECTIVE
ASPECTS

"CALLED ACCORDING TO HIS PURPOSE"

ROMANS 8 : 2 8

---◻---

THE DOCTRINE
OF DIVINE CALLING

I. INTRODUCTORY
CONCERNS

We considered in Part One of this study biblical teaching on the *plan of salvation* that centers in God's gracious, pre-temporal election of some sinners to be saved. In Part Two we examined God's *provision of salvation* through the work Christ accomplished in his life, his sufferings on the cross, and his present intercession in heaven. In Parts Three and Four we focus on the several aspects of the *application of salvation,* which constitute the center of gravity of the study as a whole. The present chapter considers from a logical perspective the initial step in the temporal application of salvation at the point of the pre-Christian's conversion. It commences with discussion of the application of salvation in the subjective side—namely, as this concerns the inner nature of the person. This initial step of the application of salvation subjectively considered is designated God's calling (*vocatio*) of sinners to be saved. The theological doctrine of divine calling refers to that summons of God in time that both invites and draws the unconverted to Christ in a saving relationship.

Initially we must ask, Precisely what is the character of God's call to sinners? Is the divine call to the unconverted single, undifferentiated, and offered equally to all? Or, analogous to the distinction between common and special grace (see chap. 2), can one legitimately differentiate between a general, external call by a preacher to all persons *and* a special, internal call of the Spirit that is powerfully effectual for some? If it be true that sinners require the bestowal of a divine power to repent and believe, is the effectual calling identical to the work of regeneration, as many Reformed theologians (e.g., Strong, Bavinck, Hoekema) have asserted? Once we have defined the nature of divine *vocatio*, we must ask how God's call is extended to those who need to be saved. What means or instruments does God employ to summon the unconverted to salvation? A further important issue to be considered is whether God's call to sinners can be resisted by those who hear its invitation. Can we affirm that God's summons to salvation via the Holy Spirit is always 'irresistible'? Alternatively, might the word 'effectual' more accurately reflect the nature of the Spirit's calling? The issue we must explore is whether free human agents can finally thwart the call of the sovereign God to salvation.

Why is a divine call to salvation needed in any case? Are not pre-Christians capable of calling on the Lord freely through the power of their own resources? Or do the unconverted, in fact, disdain Christ and flee from him until God implants a genuine hunger and desire for Jesus Christ as Savior and Lord? Is it true that depraved sinners must receive a special, spiritual enabling from God that enables their coming to Christ in repentance and faith? The discussion on "The Need for Grace" in chap. 2 has considerable bearing on this important matter. Finally, we ask how a faithful understanding of the biblical doctrine of calling might impact the way Christian witnesses share the glorious Gospel with the unsaved.

II. HISTORICAL INTERPRETATIONS OF DIVINE CALLING

The issue of divine calling to salvation has been understood in several different ways by traditions within the Christian church throughout its history. The most important interpretations of the doctrine of *vocatio* are summarized below.

A. *Natural Ability to Answer God's Universal Call (Pelagians & Liberals)*

Pelagianism, the first crudely rationalistic system in the church, claimed that persons are capable of performing their moral and religious duties before God without supernatural assistance. Persons can attain righteousness and perfection merely through the universal grace of creation. Thus to become spiritual persons, men and women have no need for divine calling involving the application of an external, supernatural power.

The British monk Pelagius (d. 418) judged that the Augustinian view of spiritual inability and sovereign grace would undermine the cause of Christian morality. He argued that humanity exists in the same morally neutral condition as were Adam and Eve in the Garden of Eden. Free will (defined as the power to choose between good and evil) is a reality in all persons, he argued, since the ability to perform what God commands is essential to being human. Moreover, since the Ten Commandments are addressed to all people, everyone must be capable of perfectly keeping them. If this were not the case, personal responsibility would be a fiction. Thus Pelagius flatly stated that apart from special, divine assistance "man is able to be without sin, and he is able to keep the commandments of God."[1] According to Pelagius, the possibility of coming to God lies within nature itself, that is, within the capacity of human willing and action. There is no need for God to exert a special, internal power upon persons, for all are able to make themselves one spirit with the Lord by the energy of their own free wills. If God were to exert such a superior power, it would destroy human freedom and compromise moral responsibility.

Coelestius (d. 431), a disciple of Pelagius, claimed that persons can keep God's commandments and readily live without sin if they choose to do so. Another follower of Pelagius, Julian of Eclanum (d. 454), claimed that since all persons are in the same moral state as Adam they have no need of divine power to be saved. God gives grace, Julian argued, proportional to human merits, not in order to achieve merit. Julian's vision, in modern parlance, was, "God helps those who help themselves."

Modern liberalism—by virtue of its (1) denial of original sin and depravity, (2) affirmation of divine immanence, (3) belief in the universal Fatherhood of God, and (4) postulate of the evolution of the human spirit—dismisses the notion of a divine, special calling to salvation. Many liberal theologians describe salvation as the flowering of moral personality (at the individual level) and the creation of a community based on brotherhood and love (at the corporate level). For many liberal thinkers the doctrine of calling means that the responsibility both for the beginning and the continuation of the Christian life lies with men and women themselves.

Lyman Abbott (d. 1922), the American Congregationalist pastor and writer, denied the presence of inherent evil in persons. Thus he flatly wrote, "It has sometimes been said that there is no good in man. It would be truer to say that there is no evil in him."[2] In the absence of evil there is nothing to impede any person's free access to God. Positively, Abbott affirmed that our approach to God is facilitated by Jesus' companionship, his teaching, and the example of his life. Persons come to Jesus and follow in his steps by "a spontaneous activity of an inward spirit."[3] "Christianity means to me," Abbott concluded, "faith in a companionable God . . . with whom we can be acquainted, as a little child is acquainted with his mysterious mother."[4]

Shailer Mathews (d. 1941), a self-styled "modernist," viewed persons not as rebellious sinners but as advancing spirits whose noble ambitions are strengthened by the example and teachings of the man, Jesus of Nazareth. Salvation, according to Mathews, represents the gradual ascendancy of the spiritual personality (the higher self) over the animal nature (the lower self). From an evolutionary perspective he insisted that the "elements [of the spiritual life], or at least its potencies, are already resident in the human personality, but need to be made supreme in self-realization and self-expression."[5] By virtue of the ever-increasing revelation of God immanent in the life process and the flowering of the spiritual personality, no supernatural power, such as the Spirit's special drawing, is necessary for salvation. Mathews simply stated that "The loving God of the universe will save a man who tries to live like Jesus."[6] In sum, the Pelagian and liberal position regarding the call to salvation could be stated as, *"I came by myself."*

B. *Special Ability Provided to Hearers of the Gospel That May Be Resisted (Lutherans)*

Concerning the issue of the call to salvation, Lutherans seek a mediating position between Calvinists and Arminians. Followers of Luther stress the universality of God's grace and calling ("vocation") to salvation through the Word that is read, preached, or enacted in the sacraments. Authorities hold that the Father loves all people, that Christ provided redemption for everyone on the cross, and that the Spirit desires to convert all people everywhere. Lutherans generally dismiss the Calvinistic distinction between an external and an internal call to salvation. As one authority said of his own tradition, "Lutheran dogmaticians reject this doctrine of a double call because it jeopardizes our confidence in the universality and reliability of God's offer of salvation. If the effectual call results only from a particular election of grace then God's external call addressed to the non-elect cannot be intended seriously."[7] Lutherans insist that the (universal) call to salvation always brings a measure of illumination that reveals sinners' need of Christ and that in some measure empowers all to respond to the Gospel message. But in their self-assertion sinners may resist this grace, to the end that it fails to operate savingly in their lives. The tension between the universal and effectual nature of the call and its resistibility often is relegated to the realm of mystery hidden in the divine counsel.

According to the Lutheran Formula of Concord (1576), Christ provided salvation for the entire human race. "Through Christ the human race has truly been redeemed and reconciled with God and . . . by his innocent obedience, suffering, and death Christ has earned for us 'the righteousness which avails before God.'"[8] Moreover, against those who would limit the scope of salvation, the Formula insists that God wills that all sinners should come to Christ and receive eternal life. Thus in time through the Word and sacraments the Holy Spirit efficaciously enlightens, calls, and draws many to Christ. God's purpose is "that he would be effective and active in us by His Holy Spirit through the Word when it is preached, heard and meditated on, would convert hearts to true repentance, and would enlighten them in the true faith."[9] The Formula plainly states that "no one comes to Christ unless the Father draws him" (John 6:44).[10] Nevertheless sinners may harden their hearts and refuse the Spirit's working in their lives. "The reason for such contempt of the Word is . . . man's own perverse will, which rejects or perverts the means and instrument of the Holy Spirit which God offers to him through the call and resists the Holy Spirit who wills to be efficaciously active through the Word."[11] The tension between the Spirit's effectual working and human resistance thereto is rooted in the distinction between God's secret will and his revealed will.

The Wittenberg theologian Quenstedt (d. 1688) is typical of older Lutheranism. He defined calling as "the act of applying the grace of the Holy Spirit, by which He manifests towards the whole race of fallen man the most gracious will of God through the external preaching of the Word, in itself always sufficient and effective, and offering to all men the benefits obtained through the merit of the Redeemer, with the serious intention that all may be saved by Christ."[12] Quenstedt continues, "The form of the call consists in a serious (Matt 23:37) . . . always sufficient (Rom 8:30) and always efficacious (Rom 1:16) manifestation of the will of God and offer of the blessings procured by Christ. . . . Every call is efficacious . . . although it may be prevented from attaining its effect by *men presenting an obstacle, and thus becomes inefficacious by the fault of the wicked and perverse will of men.*"[13]

The Lutheran theologian Francis Pieper took seriously the Father's universal grace and the Spirit's universal call. He insisted that the merit of Christ's death covers the sins of everyone and that God extends the call to salvation to all, especially to those who engage the Word and the sacraments. The divine call to all who hear the Gospel is both earnest (*seria*) and effectual (*efficax*). Although earnest, God's universal call may be sinfully resisted; God's grace and call do not infallibly secure the purposes he intended in all people (Matt 23:37; Acts 7:51). Said Pieper, "Men do possess the power to thwart the operation of the divine grace whereby God intended to produce faith in them (*gratia resistibilis*)."[14] In other words, "When God deals with men through his Word and says to them, 'Come unto Me' (Matt 11:28), resistance is possible."[15] Mysteriously, however, some sinners choose not to resist the Gospel call, and in them God's grace becomes effectual and creates saving faith. "The Gospel, 'the Word of faith' (Rom 10:8), is a Word which itself creates the faith."[16] This awakening or quickening through the call of the Gospel, Pieper further designates "Illumination (*illuminatio*)."

Pieper insisted that the dual assertions of "universal grace" (*universalis gratia*) and "by grace alone" (*sola gratia*) must stand together and not be compromised by rationalistic argumentation. This paradoxical relationship, Pieper averred, mediates between the monergism of Calvinism, which denies "universal grace," and the synergism of Arminianism, which denies the Reformation tenet "by grace alone." The Lutheran view, which juxtaposes resistible grace and a resistible call with a grace and a call that is irresistible and effectual, Pieper judged to be a spiritual mystery. Analogous to the tension between God's revealed will and his hidden will, this mystery of grace will become clear only in the light of eternity.

In view of the above historical testimonies, the Lutheran position on calling to salvation could be stated as, "*God brought me to Christ and I did not resist.*"

C. Universally Restored Ability to Obey God's General Call (Arminians)

Similar to the Lutherans, Arminians claim that as there is only one kind of grace (see chap. 2), so there is but a single, general, or universal call from God to sinners to be saved. The Augustinian and Reformed notion of a resistible universal call and an irresistible (or effectual) special call to salvation was rejected by Arminius and his followers. Most affirm that God issues the call by a general working of the Spirit on the soul (John 1:9; Luke 14:16-17) and by explicit Gospel preaching (Rom 10:17). Arminians maintain that "prevenient grace," a benefit that flows from Christ's death on the cross, neutralizes human depravity and restores to pre-Christians everywhere the ability to heed God's general call to salvation. Prevenient grace and the universal call either may be accepted or rejected. Since God restores to all the ability to respond favorably to spiritual promptings, the determining factor as to whether persons heed the Gospel call is their own free decision. Those who respond positively to God's invitation to salvation are said to be "the called."

The Nazarene theologian H. Orton Wiley distinguishes between an "indirect call," immediately exerted on human consciences apart from the revealed Word (Gen 6:3; Rom 1:19; 2:15), and a "direct call," applied to hearts by the inscripturated Word of God. He argues that the call to salvation is both *universal*, being offered to all and denied to none, and *conditional*, salvation predicated upon the person's free acceptance of the invitation. The Spirit's call universally imparts *awakening*, or new understanding of the truth, and *conviction*, or persuasion of sin, guilt, and condemnation (John 16:8). Wiley observes that however it comes, "The call may be resisted; and even after having been accepted, obedience may be forfeited."[17] Scripture designates those who respond to the universal call as "the elect" and "the called." Wiley roundly rejects the Reformed understanding of the divine call. "We are not to believe that God gives a universal call to all men, and then secretly withholds the power to believe or accept the call from all those He has not especially chosen to salvation. . . . The call is not fictitious but genuine. It is not only an external offer of salvation, but is accompanied by the internal grace of the Spirit sufficient for its acceptance."[18]

The Arminian-Wesleyan authors of *Exploring Our Christian Faith* postulate the reality of a prevenient grace sufficient for salvation. By virtue of a universal, gracious bestowment, all sinners are enabled to understand the Gospel, repent, and believe on Christ for the forgiveness of sins. God's single and universal call to accept the Gospel comes through the data of creation (Rom 1:18-20), the conscience (Rom 2:14-15), and the proclaimed Word of God (Rom 10:14). The Gospel call is a genuine invitation seriously offered to all people (cf. Matt 23:37), and by virtue of prevenient grace all have the capacity to accept it. The call is an invitation, not an irresistible demand that in the nature of the case must be heeded. If the call worked compellingly in lives, then the beneficiaries thereof would cease to be responsible for their moral choices and thus would be less than authentic *persons*. The work concludes by asserting that "The Calvinistic notion that God offers an external call to the nonelect and an internal, effective call to the elect only is repugnant to the whole tenor of the Bible and to what we know about the God of John 3:16, who is no respecter of persons (Acts 10:34)."[19]

The three Nazarene authors of the volume *God, Man, and Salvation* affirm the universality of God's saving design, provision, and call to salvation. They aver that universally bestowed prevenient grace restores to sinners the freedom that makes real human choices possible. Thus the NT discloses that Jesus and his apostles preached the Gospel to all who would listen without partiality or discrimination. Reflecting on Jesus' plea to hearers in his day—"Repent, and believe in the gospel" (Mark 1:15)—the authors pose the following questions. "Could He have been guilty of double-talk, knowing that some who heard would be irresistibly caused to believe because they were intended to, while others would be left in unbelief because the call was not for them? Is the universal call inherent in the gospel proclamation authentic for some but inauthentic for others?"[20] The authors argue that the Spirit's ministry in calling to repentance and faith was neither selective nor irresistible (Acts 7:51). God ordered the Gospel proclaimed universally because of his sincere desire that all should respond positively and be saved (1 Tim 2:4-6; 2 Pet 3:9). "With the Spirit's awakening, repentance and faith are now possible but still optional."[21]

According to William Klein in *The New Chosen People*, God appeals to all people to appropriate the salvation Christ has won universally. Sinners, however, cannot come to Christ without divine enablement. From John 12:32 Klein avers that God exerts an "attracting" or "drawing" influence on all persons everywhere that provides them with sufficient power to trust Christ and be saved. In language reminiscent of the moral influence theory of the cross (see chap. 4), Klein comments that "Jesus' self-sacrifice and God's love shown through Jesus comprise the *attraction*."[22] This drawing work of God, however, is resistible and often proves ineffectual. Thus "God's 'drawing' does not override the human will. All are drawn, but not all find salvation. People are attracted by the love of God demonstrated on the Cross, but the human will may spurn God's pull."[23] Klein claims that the NT language of calling (*kaleo, klesis, kletos*) does not describe actions that God performs by his power on individuals. Rather, understood corporately, the language of calling denotes the weaker sense of God "naming" or "designating" those who have believed. Thus the doctrine of calling describes the act whereby God *names* or *labels* those who come to believe as "saints" or "holy ones." The doctrine of calling thus "specifies the divine act when God names or designates people from among Jews and Gentiles to become his own people."[24] In other words, the statement "'God called you' is a way of saying . . . 'God granted you the status (name or identity) of Christian.'"[25] The bottom line is that God subsequently calls (i.e., names) those who sincerely first call on him.

The above testimony suggests that the Arminian and Wesleyan view of calling to Christ could be stated as, "*God started the process and I cooperated.*"

D. A General Call That May Be Resisted and a Special Call Effectual for Salvation (Reformed Tradition)

Augustinian and Reformed theologians understand Scripture to teach that, by virtue of original sin and depravity, sinners for whom Christ died themselves are spiritually incapable of responding to the Gospel invitation (Rom 8:7; 1 Cor 2:14; Eph 2:1-2, 4-5; 4:18).[26] Authorities view the general call and the special call as two aspects of the one summons of God to salvation. The general call to the unsaved comes through the indiscriminate offer of the Gospel via the preached Word (Isa 45:22; John 7:37), whereas the special call is effected by the Holy Spirit's secret work on the heart (Rom 1:6-7; 1 Cor 1:9, 26; 1 Pet 2:9). The Spirit's enlightening, wooing, and subduing work vis-à-vis the elect enlightens darkened minds, frees stubborn wills, and inclines contrary affections toward Christ. In short, the Spirit's effectual call opens sinners' hearts, thereby creating a new desire and hunger to know Christ. The general call meets with a variety of responses in the unconverted, whereas the effectual call effectively draws sinners to Christ. Expressed more directly, the preacher's word in the general call is made effective by the Spirit's work in the special call.

The general call is a legitimate offer to "whosoever will," even though its efficacy depends upon the gracious power of God's Spirit. Authorities in the tradition find evidence for the two callings in Jesus' parable of the wedding banquet (Matt 22:1-14) and the account of the opening of Lydia's heart for the evocation of saving faith (Acts 16:14). Since the special call is grounded in the general call, Christ's followers diligently proclaim the Gospel to all persons everywhere. But God through the Spirit sovereignly causes chosen hearers of the preached Word to be quickened spiritually and to be drawn to Christ.

Augustine (d. 430) grounded the necessity for the Spirit's special call in the spiritual ruin of the race in Adam, its biological head. Sinners possess neither the will nor the ability to renounce self and submit to Christ; hence the need for a special enablement from God. Augustine also envisaged effectual calling as the logical outcome of God's sovereign elective purpose; those whom God in eternity past foreknew and predestined, in time he effectually calls through the Spirit. Although a general call through the preached Word goes out to multitudes, God mysteriously issues a special, effectual call to the "sheep" he has given to the Son. "There is a certain sure calling of those who are called according to God's purpose, whom he has foreknown and predestinated before to be conformed to the image of his Son."[27]

Augustine found this doctrine of special calling confirmed by many scriptural examples. Thus Lazarus who was dead and buried in the tomb illustrates the soul of the unconverted smothered by sins and hiding from God's face. Jesus' command, "Lazarus, come out" (John 11:43), signifies the spiritually dead person called by God's power and summoned to a new life.[28] The special call, Augustine averred, consists of the Spirit's secret working that makes unwilling hearts willing and incapable hearts capable of repenting and believing on Christ. As an aside, Augustine understood Scripture to represent effectual calling as both individual (Abraham, Saul of Tarsus, Lydia, etc.) and corporate (the faithful Jewish remnant, the NT churches, the body of Christ). He reasoned that if the hearts and minds of Jesus' disciples needed to be opened to spiritual truths (Luke 24:31, 45), how much more do the minds of depraved sinners require supernatural enlightening and empowering. Hence Augustine wrote, "Since . . . certainly there is no ability whatever in free will to believe, unless there be a persuasion or summons towards some one in whom to believe, it surely follows that it is God who both works in man the willing to believe, and in all things precedes us with His mercy."[29] For Augustine, "before merit the calling determines the will" (Phil 2:13).[30] In other words, the God who efficiently calls his people works in them the will and the ability to believe.

As a practical matter, when disciples preach Christ's gospel,

> some believe, some believe not; but they who believe at the voice of the preacher from without, hear of the Father from within, and learn; while they who do not believe, hear outwardly but inwardly do not hear or learn;—that is to say, to the former it is given to believe; to the latter it is not given. Because "No one," says He, "can come to me unless the Father who sent me draw him" (John 6:44).[31]

Appealing to the next verse (John 6:45)—"Everyone who listens to the Father and learns from him comes to me"—Augustine confidently concluded (1) that every person called by the Spirit infallibly comes to Christ and is saved. In this process "volition itself and the performance itself are assisted, and not merely the natural 'capacity' of willing and performing."[32] Moreover, (2) every person not called by the Spirit does not come savingly to Christ—again because of the spiritual impotence that characterizes fallen human nature. Finally, Augustine concluded by emphasizing (3) that the Johannine text does not say that everyone called by the Spirit may *possibly* come (as the Pelagians, Semi-Pelagians, and the Arminians insist). On the contrary, he argued, all those called by the Spirit will *certainly* come to saving faith in Christ.

The effectual call that leads to salvation may be illustrated by Augustine's famous crisis experience under the fig tree in the year 386. Augustine struggled vainly to find peace, and he bargained with God, hoping to come on his own terms that included continued fleshly indulgence. Thus he prayed, "Grant me chastity and continency, but not yet."[33] His soul burdened with lust and his spirit torn by moral conflict, the unconverted Augustine retired to a garden despondent and weeping over his forlorn moral and spiritual condition. Recalling this experience Augustine wrote in his *Confessions,*

> I flung myself down . . . under a certain fig-tree, giving free course to my tears, and the streams of mine eyes gushed out. . . . I sent up these sorrowful cries—"How long, how long? Tomorrow, and tomorrow? Why not now? Why is there not this hour an end to my uncleanness?

As Augustine uttered these words in the privacy of the garden, he further recalled:

> I heard the voice as of a boy or a girl, I know not which, coming from a neighboring house, chanting and oft repeating, "Take up and read; take up and read. . . ." So restraining the torrent of my tears, I rose up, interpreting it no other way than as a command to me from Heaven to open the book, and to read the first chapter I should light upon. . . . I grasped, opened, and in silence read that paragraph on which my eyes first fell—"Not in rioting and drunkenness, not in chambering and wantonness, not in strife and envying; but put ye on the Lord Jesus Christ, and make not provision for the flesh, to fulfill the lusts thereof."

Augustine concluded his account by adding,

> No further would I read, nor did I need; for instantly, as the sentence ended—by a light, as it were, of security infused into my heart—all the gloom of doubt vanished away.[34]

By striving and tears, Augustine was unable to rescue himself from his spiritual dilemma. But we may believe that the Spirit of God sovereignly led him to the place of solitude, orchestrated the voice from the house, spoke powerfully to him from Rom 13:13-14, broke the constricting chains of sin, and drew this confused and double-minded sinner savingly to Christ.

John Calvin (d. 1564) likewise argued that by virtue of spiritual blindness caused by personal depravity, the Spirit's powerful influence is needed to draw sinners to Christ (1 Cor 2:9-10, 14, 16; John 6:44). "The Word of God is like the sun, shining upon all those to whom it is proclaimed, but with no effect among the blind. Now, all of us are blind by nature in this respect. Accordingly, it [the Word] cannot penetrate into our minds unless the Spirit, as the inner teacher, through his illumination makes entry for it."[35] Appealing to the parable of the wedding banquet (Matt 22:2-14) and particularly to Jesus' words—"Many are called but few are chosen" (v. 14), Calvin judged that there are two aspects of the divine call. "There is the general call, by which God invites all equally to himself through the outward preaching of the word. . . . The other kind of call is special, which he deigns for the most part to give to the believers alone, while by the inward illumination of his Spirit he causes the preached Word to dwell in their hearts."[36] The general call is common to the wicked, but the special call is the Spirit's inner persuasion of the truth of the Gospel to the hearts of God's elect. Calvin noted that a general call goes out to all the world through the external preaching of the Word. But by a special, internal illumination the Spirit causes the preached Word to take root in those persons given by the Father to the Son. Thus Calvin wrote, "The [special] call is dependent upon election and accordingly is solely a work of grace."[37] According to Calvin, the time when the Spirit does his drawing work lies entirely in God's hands and, in fact, varies in the life of each person.

Concerning the special calling of sinners, the Westminster Confession of Faith (1647) describes the Word and Spirit "enlightening their minds, spiritually and savingly, to understand the things of God; taking away their heart of stone, and giving unto them an heart of flesh; renewing their wills, and by his almighty power determining them to that which is good, and effectually drawing them to Jesus Christ; yet so as they come most freely, being made willing by his grace" (ch. 10.1). The Shorter Catechism (Q. 30) poses the question, "How doth the Spirit apply to us the redemption purchased by Christ?" The answer follows: "The Spirit applieth to us the redemption purchased by Christ, by working faith in us, and thereby uniting us to Christ in our effectual calling." Q. 31 inquires, "What is effectual calling?" To which the answer is given, "Effectual calling is the work of God's Spirit, whereby, convincing us of our sin and misery, enlightening our minds in the knowledge of Christ, and renewing our wills, he doth persuade and enable us to embrace Jesus Christ freely offered to us in the gospel."

The British preacher C.H. Spurgeon (d. 1892) judged that Scripture teaches two kinds of calling, i.e., general and special. The general call goes out to all the world by virtue of Christ's universal mediatorship. Since he is the Mediator of all flesh, God wills that the proclamation of mercy be published universally. Although this general call is sincere, the person dead in sins and corrupted with lusts is unwilling and incapable of responding to the Gospel invitation. To such an individual sovereign grace cries out through the Word applied by the Spirit, "Come forth!" and so the person receives new spiritual life. Spurgeon acknowledged that "There is a fountain filled with blood, but there may be none who will ever wash in it unless divine purpose and power shall constrain them to come."[38] At the pastoral level, Spurgeon observed that people who sincerely desire to be saved can be certain that they are called. And if called, they can be certain that they are elected. Every seeking soul who comes to Christ shall become a finder. This is so, because behind the seeking soul is the all-powerful God who enables that person to search and to find.

The Baptist theologian A.H. Strong (d. 1921) defined calling as "that act of God by which men are invited to accept, by faith, the salvation provided by Christ."[39] Strong noted that Scripture distinguishes between the general or external call and the special or effectual call. The general call is that sincere offer of life extended to all people through the means of providence, the Word of God, and the Holy Spirit (Isa 65:12; Ezek 33:11; Matt 11:28; Rev 22:17). Strong judged that the call given to sinners to accept Christ by faith is as genuine and sincere as God's command that they love him. This general call demonstrates that on God's side no obstacle exists to preclude sinners from enjoying the blessings of the Gospel. It shows that failure to respond to God's invitation resides in the sinner's own darkened mind and evil will. Left to their sinful selves, the unconverted render this general call ineffective by their settled opposition to the things of God. To remedy the situation God graciously issues a special call to the elect (Rom 8:30; 1 Cor 1:24, 26; 1 Thess 2:12; 2 Tim 1:9) that restores moral ability, kindles spiritual affections, and leads them to trust Christ. Whereas some would describe this as an "irresistible call," Strong designates the call as *effectual* in that "it infallibly accomplishes its purpose of leading the sinner to the acceptance of salvation."[40]

According to the Anglican theologian J.I. Packer, the biblical language for calling has (1) a broader referent that focuses on all persons verbally addressed or summoned by the Word of God (Matt 22:14). It also possesses (2) a narrower and effectual focus, in the sense of "an act of summoning which effectively evokes from those addressed the response which it invites."[41] Packer continues that God's effectual calling is *creative* in that it brings into existence, and it represents the temporal execution of His eternal purposes. Packer notes that in the OT Yahweh called Abraham, the prototype of the chosen nation, into an inviolable covenant relation with himself (Isa 51:2), and he called Israel to be his elect people (Isa 43:1). The Lord also called or drew Israel from 430 years of Egyptian bondage, as Hos 11:1 beautifully testifies: "When Israel was a child, I loved him, and out of Egypt I called my son." These and other examples prove that divine calling is more than a verbal summons the outcome of which remains problematic. In the NT effectual calling is an internal, spiritual event that focuses on the individual. "The verb 'call' and the noun 'calling' (*klēsis*) now refer to the effective evocation of faith through the gospel by the secret operation of the Holy Spirit, who unites men to Christ according to God's gracious purpose in election (Rom 8:30; 1 Cor 1:9; Gal 1:15; 2 Thess 2:13-14; 2 Tim 1:9; Heb 9:15; 1 Pet 2:9; 2 Pet 1:3; etc.)."[42] Those in time effectually called to a relation with Christ are identical to the number of elect believers—i.e., those in eternity past chosen by grace (Rom 1:6-7; 8:28; Jude 1; Rev 17:14; etc.).

In sum, the Reformed position on calling to salvation could be expressed by the phrase, "*God brought me to Christ.*" The scriptural development that follows leads us to the conclusion that this latter interpretation of *vocatio* most faithfully coheres with the biblical revelation.

III. EXPOSITION OF
THE DOCTRINE OF CALLING

A. *The Language of Calling*

The verb *qārā'* and root-related words occur 689 times in the Hebrew OT. The verb means to "call (out)" and "invite," with emphasis placed on utterance of the message. Four principal senses of the word group concern us in the study of this topic. (1) The *naming of persons, places, or things*: actively as "name" or "call," and passively as "called" or "named" (Gen 1:5, 8, 10; 17:15; 25:26; Exod 15:23; Ps 147:4; Isa 7:14; Hos 1:10). (2) *Summons to a task or ministry*, as in the case of Bezalel (Exod 31:2), Cyrus (Isa 45:3-4; 46:11; 48:15), and the Servant of the Lord (Isa 42:6; 49:1). It is clear that God's call to service proceeds from his sovereign, eternal purpose. Thus,

> It is significant that in the later chapters of Isaiah, specially in the Servant Songs we have the profoundest use of *kaleō* in the sense of service and dedication, linked with an exceptionally frequent appearance of *eklegomai*, choose. It is the elect one (Isa 41:8; 43:10) whom God calls in righteousness (Isa 42:6) and by name (Isa 43:1). He is a type of all who have been called from the beginnings of humanity (Isa 41:2, 4).[43]

The divine call to service, however, is not a bare, powerless invitation. Rather, "God's call is the means by which he makes men who are entirely unqualified into instruments of his will."[44]

The verb *qārā'* and related words are used (3) of a *corporate calling to national privilege* (cf. chap. 2). God summoned Israel from harsh Egyptian bondage to privileged allegiance with himself. Thus, "When Israel was a child, I loved him, and out of Egypt I called my son" (Hos 11:1). Isaiah also spoke of God's call of Israel unto covenant blessings: "Listen to me, O Jacob, Israel, whom I have called" (Isa 48:12; cf. Isa 43:1b: "I have summoned you by name; you are mine"). (4) An *invitation to repentance and salvation* that often was neglected or disobeyed. As the Lord said to the faithless in Israel, "I called but you did not answer, I spoke but you did not listen" (Isa 65:12; cf. Isa 50:2; Jer 7:13; Hos 11:2). Finally, the word group is used (5) of God's act of *drawing people into a saving relation with himself.* Thus Yahweh called Abraham into a redemptive relationship: "When I called him he was but one, and I blessed him and made him many" (Isa 51:2). And God through his people would call pagan peoples to himself: "Surely you will summon nations you know not, and nations that do not know you will hasten to you, because of the Lord your God" (Isa 55:5). God's call to salvation is causative and effectual. In other contexts the Lord called the heavens and earth into existence (Isa 48:13), called the nation Israel into being (Isa 41:9), called forth famine (Ps 105:16), and called forth the sword (Jer 25:29). Through his powerful Word and Spirit, God efficiently causes his purposes to be realized (Isa 55:11).

As we turn to the NT, the relevant Greek words are *kaleō* (to "call," 148 times), *proskaleomai* (to "summon," thirty times), *klēsis* ("calling," "invitation," eleven times), and *klētos* ("called," "invited", eleven times). In the NT we discover a range of meanings for the word group similar to that of the OT. (1) A *naming*, as in the case of Jesus (Matt 1:21; Luke 1:32), John (Luke 1:13), Cephas (John 1:42), the temple (Mark 11:17), etc.. But when God gives persons names with specific meanings, it may be said that God "expresses, as in the OT, his control over their lives."[45] (2) A *call to a task or state of life*, for example, James and John to service (Mark 1:20), other apostles to ministry (Mark 3:13), Paul to apostleship (Rom 1:1; 1 Cor 1:1), various servants to missionary work (*proskaleomai*, Acts 13:2; 16:10), believers to a particular vocation (1 Cor 7:17, 20, 24). (3) An *invitation or command* to salvation that may be sinfully disregarded (Matt 9:13; 22:3-4, 8, 14; Mark 2:17; Luke 5:32; 14:16-17, 24). The "called" (*klētoi*) broadly are those summoned to salvation with varying outcomes, both positive and negative (Matt 22:14).

(4) God's work of *evoking or drawing into a saving relation.* In the NT Epistles and Revelation, particularly, *kaleō* and related words become technical terms for God's work of drawing sinners to Christ through his

powerful Word and Spirit. This effectual drawing that brings sinners to faith and salvation is commonplace in the NT; see Matt 22:9; Acts 2:39 (*proskaleomai*); Rom 8:30; 9:11; 1 Cor 1:9, 26; 7:20; Gal 1:6, 15; 2 Thess 2:14; 1 Tim 6:12; 2 Tim 1:9; Heb 3:1; 9:15; 1 Pet 2:9; 2 Pet 1:3; Jude 1; Rev 17:14; 19:9. In each of these texts those whom God called infallibly came to faith and salvation. The outcome is assured; the calling according to divine purpose always proves effectual.

> Paul understands calling as the process by which God calls those, whom he has already elected and appointed, out of their bondage to this world, so that he may justify and sanctify them (Rom 8:29f.), and bring them into his service. . . . God's call is mediated by the message of the Gospel (2 Thess 2:14) which comes through the witness of men. It brings the one called both into fellowship with Christ (1 Cor 1:9) and at the same time into fellowship with the other members of his body.[46]

The "called" (*klētoi*) in this final sense are the saved, the ones whom God has efficiently drawn to himself for new life by the power of the Holy Spirit (Rom 1:6-7; 8:28; 1 Cor 1:2, 24; Rev 17:14).

B. The External, Verbal Call

The single call of God to salvation may be considered from two perspectives: (1) a universal, verbal call that meets with a variety of responses; and (2) a particular, special call that infallibly leads to salvation. By the former is meant the invitation or summons to salvation conveyed through cognitive encounter with the Gospel message. The omnipotent and all-wise God could address the lost with his Word directly, if he so chooses. But the Lord has purposed to convey the verbal call through means, such as a Gospel sermon, the witness of an ordinary believer, an evangelistic Bible study, a Christian film, or personal reading of the Scriptures. Whatever the means of communication, a valid Gospel offer includes (1) a presentation of the plan of salvation, (2) an invitation to come to Christ in repentance and faith, and (3) the promise of certain forgiveness and salvation. In practice, this free offer may be met with indifference or outright rejection, and so the invitation may prove unfruitful. On the other hand, it may be met with acceptance and trust and so bear fruit unto eternal life.

We find universal invitations or general calls to turn to Yahweh and be saved given by OT prophets. For example, the Lord through Isaiah issued the summons, "Come, all you who are thirsty, come to the waters; and you who have no money, come, buy and eat! Come, buy wine and milk without money and without cost" (Isa 55:1; cf. vv. 6-7). The Lord also spoke to Israel through the same prophet, "Turn to me and be saved, all you ends of the earth; for I am God, and there is no other" (Isa 45:22). The prophetic writings attest that this general call to repentance often was not heeded by its hearers. The Lord said to Israel, "I spoke to you again and again, but you did not listen; I called you, but you did not answer" (Jer 7:13; cf. 35:15, 17; Isa 50:2; 65:12). Again the Lord said, "All day long I have held out my hands to an obstinate people" (Isa 65:2; cf. Rom 10:21). By choosing not to obey God's word, Israel forfeited the covenant blessings.

In the NT Jesus issued a general call with the words, "I have not come to call the righteous, but sinners to repentance" (Luke 5:32). Later he said, "Come to me all you who are weary and burdened, and I will give you rest" (Matt 11:28). This legitimate offer of life, however, can be spurned and rejected by those who hear it. Thus in a sad lament over the Holy City the Lord cried out, "O Jerusalem, Jerusalem, you who kill the prophets and stone those sent to you, how often I have longed to gather your children together, as a hen gathers her chicks under her wings, but you were not willing!" (Luke 13:34). The early Christian missionaries and evangelists offered a gratuitous salvation to all who would receive it (Acts 2:38-39; 4:12; 8:22; etc.). But Acts records that this universal call to life often was resisted by stubborn hearts and consequently was rendered ineffectual (Acts 7:51, 53; 13:46). The apostle John also referred to the general, external call to salvation (John 7:37; Rev 22:17) that may be sinfully resisted (John 7:41b-42; 9:40; 10:20; etc.). Likewise, the writer of Hebrews acknowledged the general call or hearing of the Word of God that may be rejected by hardened hearts (Heb 4:6-7; 12:25).

C. Why Some Hearers Are Not Saved

Inherent in every Gospel invitation is the trustworthy promise that all who accept its terms will be saved (Acts 2:21: Rom 10:13). The universal offer of the Gospel is not a sham nor a grand deception, for the reason that all who respond affirmatively *will* receive what God has promised. Deception or fraud occurs when what is promised is not given once the terms of the agreement have been properly satisfied.

Scripture teaches that the fault for a person not being saved lies not with God; it resides with the spiritual impotence and moral insolence of the person himself. In the OT many people in Israel *heard* the message with their ears but did not understand it; they saw the truth enacted with their eyes but did not perceive it; and they *encountered* the truth with their hearts but did not embrace it (Isa 6:9-10). The unsaved in Israel tragically were blind, deaf, and dumb with respect to spiritual truths sincerely presented by God's faithful messengers (Isa 29:9-10; 42:18-20; 43:8). Unregenerate Jews did not respond to the offer of life because they were spiritually incapable of doing so on their own (Jer 13:23; 17:9; 30:12). The OT occasionally describes this inability to obey God's Word by the imagery of people hardening their hearts (Exod 7:13; 8:15, 19, 32; 1 Sam 6:6). The opposite imagery of God hardening people's hearts (Exod 4:21; 7:3; 9:12; 10:20; Josh 11:20; etc.) should be understood permissively rather than efficiently, namely, of God withdrawing his striving Spirit and leaving the unregenerate to their own resources.

This truth concerning sinners' inability and unwillingness to heed the general Gospel call is even clearer in the NT. Concerning the unregenerate *intellectually,* Paul stated that "there is no one who understands" (Rom 3:11a). Moreover, "The man without the Spirit does not accept the things that come from the Spirit of God, for they are foolishness [*mōria*] to him, and he cannot understand them, because they are spiritually discerned" (1 Cor 2:14). Like a radio receiver tuned to another frequency, sin-darkened minds cannot make adequate sense of spiritual signals. "The message of the Gospel is a noise, not a communication, until God tunes the set of man's heart."[47] *Volitionally,* Paul stated that "there is . . . no one who seeks God" (Rom 3:11b). Indeed, "the sinful mind is hostile to God. It does not submit to God's law, nor can it do so" (Rom 8:7). And behaviorally, "All have turned away, they have together become worthless; there is no one who does good, not even one" (Rom 3:12). Paul summed up the problem by stating that in the spiritual realm sinners are dead in transgressions and sins (Eph 2:1-2, 4-5). As many preachers have declared, "Dead people do not kick!" For these reasons Jesus said, "No one can come to me unless the Father who sent me draws him, and I will raise him up at the last day" (John 6:44). Those drawn are not all people who happen to hear, but faithful ones whom Christ will raise from the dead. Or as Jesus plainly stated, "no one can come to me unless the Father has enabled him" (v. 65). As argued by Pink, "the affections of the natural man are alienated from God, wedded to the things of time and sense, so that he will not come to Christ."[48] In sum, the reason why some sinners do not respond to the verbal call of the Gospel is not their failure to use an alleged equal ability supplied to all by prevenient grace. Rather, the reason is that apart from the working of the Spirit in grace depraved sinners are incapable and disinclined to respond to the general offer of the Gospel. Without a superior power from above, spiritual eyes remain sightless and spiritual ears deaf to divine truth.

D. *The Internal, Effectual Call*

By the internal, effectual call we mean that act of divine power, mediated through the proclaimed Word, by which the Spirit illumines darkened minds, softens stubborn wills, and inclines contrary affections toward the living God, thus leading the unregenerate to trust Christ in a saving relation. Echoes of this special call can be found in the OT. But just as we discovered in chap. 3 that election in the OT is largely corporate, so also God's call to salvation in the OT is predominately but not exclusively corporate. Consider the following evidence.

Isa 51:2b states concerning Abraham, "When I called [*qārā'*] him he was but one, and I blessed him and made him many." Recalling Gen 12:1-3, the prophet stated that God sovereignly called a nation into existence through its individual head, Abraham. In the immediate context, note how prominently God's efficient action is set forth. (1) God prospered Abraham, multiplying his seed (v. 2c), (2) God brought forth from Abraham a multitude of believers (v. 3b), and (3) God brought salvation to the Gentile peoples of the world (vv. 4-6). We understand God's calling of Abraham and his descendants as acts of power that infallibly accomplish the divine purpose.

The language of Num 16:5 is suggestive, especially when read with Christian eyes. In this verse Moses said to Korah and his followers, "the Lord will show who belongs to him and who is holy, and he will have that person come near him. The man he chooses he will cause to come near to him." This juxtaposition of God's act of choosing and his work of causing persons to draw near to him is also seen in Ps 65:4, where David wrote, "Blessed are those you choose and bring near to live in your courts!"

In the prophetic literature, when the old covenant proved to be spiritually ineffectual, God promised that he would inaugurate a new covenant with his people. The latter would be an inward covenant that efficiently produces in its recipients a changed mind and heart and an intimate knowledge of God (Jer 31:31, 33-34). When God brings his sovereign grace to bear on hearts and so issues his effectual call, sinners respond positively to the invitation. Thus the saved remnant within Israel not only are the elect, they also are the effectually called. As the prophet Joel wrote, "on Mount Zion and in Jerusalem there will be deliverance, as the Lord has said, among the survivors whom the Lord calls" (Joel 2:32). Packer notes that "'calling' signifies a disposition of events and destinies whereby God executes his purposes. . . . God's callings express determinations which are unconditional, irreversible, and incapable of frustration (cf.

Rom 11:29). [The prophet] views God's callings as sovereign acts, the temporal execution of eternal intentions."[49]

Turning to the NT, the parable of the wedding banquet (Matt 22:1-14; cf. Luke 14:16-24) is the most explicit text in the Gospels dealing with divine calling to salvation. This parable Jesus told distinguishes between God's universal, general call and his particular, effectual call. The first group invited (Matt 22:3-4) by the king's servants (the OT prophets) were mainstream Jews offered messianic salvation. Matthew emphasized the universal call in v. 3 by the twofold use of the verb *kaleō*: the king "sent his slaves to call those who had been invited" (NRSV, *kalesai tous keklēmenous*). But consumed with worldly interests and indifferent to their spiritual needs, the invitees rejected the invitation, persecuted the messengers, and so were punished with death (v. 7). Consequently, the king sent his servants to bring to the banquet the unfit and the unworthy, an act that signifies the successful preaching of Jesus and his apostles to outcast Jews (tax-collectors and sinners) and Gentiles (Luke 14:23). The latter invitations accomplished the intended purpose, in that a crowd of people joined the king for the wedding feast.

The second and third recruiting efforts recorded in Luke involve strong language of forceful constraint and compulsion. The servants were to "bring in" the poor, the crippled, etc. (v. 21, where the verb *eisagō* means to "lead in"). Likewise, the servants were bidden to "make them come in" (v. 23), the verb *anankazō* signifying to "compel" in the sense of constrain.[50] The parable ends with Jesus' terse saying, "For many are called [*klētoi*], but few are chosen" (*eklektoi*, Matt 22:14, NRSV). The "called" represents the larger group summoned by invitation. The "chosen" were the smaller group forcefully brought to the banquet. "The calling must refer to the gospel message to which they [the first group] made a merely outward response, not being chosen by God."[51] Jesus inferred (Luke 14:24) that none who received only the general call (*tōn keklēmenōn*) "will get a taste of my banquet" (i.e., will be saved). Thus we conclude that God extends a general call externally to many via Gospel preaching (Matt 11:28-30; Luke 24:47) that may be sinfully rejected (Matt 23:37). But the special call issued inwardly by the Spirit effectually accomplishes the Father's salvific purpose (Luke 14:21-23).

Peter's comprehensive sermon on the day of Pentecost constitutes a general call to salvation (Acts 2:14-39), which tragically some of his audience failed to heed. Luke, however, identified the effectual, saving call in v. 39: "The promise [of the Holy Spirit] is for you and your children and for all who are far off—for all whom the Lord our God will call [*proskalesētai*]." The verb *proskaleomai* (to "call to oneself") here connotes God's sovereign call of his chosen people to himself. "Salvation originates with him and he grants it to all those whom he, in his sovereign grace, effectively will call."[52] No one is capable of calling on Christ (v. 21) until God through the Spirit calls him or her first (v. 39).

The conversion of Saul of Tarsus resulted from a special call by the risen Christ that was powerfully effective. Saul, who regarded the Christian movement as a blasphemous heresy, went to extraordinary lengths to terrorize the fledgling church (Acts 9:1-2; 22:4-5; 26:10-11)—indeed, as Paul himself said, "to do all that was possible to oppose the name of Jesus of Nazareth" (Acts 26:9). Outside of Damascus Christ appeared to Saul in the form of a glorious, heavenly light that, while blinding his physical eyes, opened his spiritual eyes to Jesus' true significance (Acts 9:1-9; 22:8-10). The vision and the voice of Christ conveyed the special call to salvation. Driven by a darkened mind, Saul had fought against Christ (vv. 4-5), but the Savior pursued Saul and overcame his raving, sinful heart through grace.[53] Paul later testified that Christ's summons to salvation was wholly effectual (Acts 26:19).[54] As Ananias independently said to Paul, "The God of our fathers has chosen you to know his will and to see the Righteous One" (Acts 22:14). Paul's conversion testimony in Gal 1:15-16 reaffirmed God's sovereign purpose and initiative as the basis for his radically altered life.

The effectual call to salvation is clearly seen in the spiritual experience of Lydia (Acts 16:14). During the second missionary journey, the Holy Spirit forbade Paul and Silas from preaching the Gospel in Asia (Acts 16:6-7) but supernaturally redirected the missionaries to evangelize in Macedonia (16:9-10), including the city of Philippi. In this Roman colony they proclaimed the Gospel to a group of Jewish proselyte women who had gathered by the river for prayer. The Gospel (i.e., the general call) was proclaimed to all the women, whose hearts were closed to spiritual truths. But Luke indicates that during that encounter God opened only Lydia's heart: "The Lord opened [*diēnoixen*] her heart to respond to Paul's message." Luke used the same verb *dianoigō* (to "open") to describe Jesus' illumining the minds of the disciples to recognize him (Luke 24:31) and to understand the Scriptures (Luke 24:45).

"Heart," as commonly used in Scripture, signifies the core of the person's spiritual and moral nature—namely, the understanding, will, and affections. The opening of Lydia's heart by the power of God was the efficient cause of her coming to Christ. Thus Girot faithfully wrote, "The Spirit of God penetrated the hardened heart of Lydia, warming and melting and moving it in the fires of the Spirit. . . . The Spirit of God quickened, that is, brought life to the dead heart of Lydia. All this is comprehended in these words, 'The Lord opened her heart.'"[55]

Paul's discussion of calling focused largely on God's effectual call to salvation. Consider first the key text, Rom 8:28-30. V. 28 reads as follows: "And we know that in all things God works for the good of those who love him, who have been called [*klētois*] according to his purpose." The *klētoi* here cannot mean all those who have heard the Gospel (the general call), for the *klētoi* are the ones for whom God works the good, who have come to love God, who have been effectually called—literally—"according to purpose" (*kata prothesin*). Luther wrote that the sufferers of adversity on whose behalf God works for the ultimate good "are the called, and not merely called but 'called according to purpose.' To them alone, therefore, and to no others 'he makes everything work together for good.'"[56] Luther added that "'Purpose' means here God's predestination or free election or deliberation or counsel."[57] Paul continued in the Romans text (vv. 29-30) that those whom God in eternity past "foreknew" (i.e., "foreloved") he "predestined," "called" (*ekalesen*), "justified," and "glorified." A universal, external call is not in view here, for all those called, in fact, respond positively and participate in the full sweep of salvation, including justification and glorification. According to a respected study Bible, the calling in view can only be, "Effectual calling: the call of God to which there is invariably a positive response."[58] In sum, then, Rom 8:28-30 teaches that the effectual call is rooted in God's sovereign, elective purpose and infallibly results in justification and final glorification.

Other Pauline texts deserve mention in this regard. The apostle addressed the brothers and sisters at Corinth as those whom God "has called . . . into fellowship with his Son Jesus Christ" (1 Cor 1:9). Jews and Gentiles who receive only the external call regard the Gospel as "a stumbling block" and "foolishness," respectively (1 Cor 1:23). Only when efficiently called or drawn by the Spirit do people judge the Gospel "the power of God and the wisdom of God" (v. 24); only then do they respond positively (not problematically) to the hearing of the Word. In the same chapter of 1 Corinthians, we read that the effectual call comes only to those persons whom God has chosen for himself (*eklegomai*, three times in vv. 27-28). God's effectual call to salvation, which flows from his sovereign pleasure, undercuts the human tendency to boasting (v. 29). Further linkage between calling and election occurs in Paul's second letter to Timothy. There he wrote concerning the Father "who saved us and called [*kalesantos*] us with a holy calling [*klēsis*], not according to our works but according to his own purpose [*prothesis*] and grace" (2 Tim 1:9, NRSV). Interestingly, Paul presented the sweep of salvation in reverse order from the present to eternity past: i.e., the blessing of salvation, effectual calling, the bestowal of grace, and the divine purpose.

The apostle underscored the effectual nature of God's special calling when he wrote to the Thessalonians as follows: "For we know, brothers loved by God, that he has chosen you, because our gospel came to you not simply with words, but also with power, with the Holy Spirit and with deep conviction" (1 Thess 1:4-5). The Spirit's inner calling, however, does not nullify personal responsibility to answer the external call (1 Tim 6:12b). Second Thess 2:13-14 teaches that (1) God made the Thessalonian saints the objects of his love, (2) he chose them from the beginning to be saved, and (3) he called them (*ekalesen*) to share in Christ's glory. Loving, choosing, and calling all are efficient works of the sovereign God. Observe that the outcome of effectual calling is always salvation. On the sinners' side, however, there must be belief in the truth.

Paul envisaged those enlightened in their minds, quickened in their wills, and drawn into fellowship with Christ not as an empty class, but as individuals who collectively constitute the church. The NT exegete C.E.B. Cranfield well sums up the meaning of calling as follows: "As used by God, *kalein* denotes God's effectual calling: the *klētoi* are those who have been called effectually, who have been summoned by God and have also responded to his summons."[59] This calling cannot be restricted to a summons unto service, for often the outcome is plainly stated to be salvation: e.g., "called to belong to Jesus Christ" (Rom 1:6) and "called to be free" (Gal 5:13). Likewise, the weaker sense of 'naming' or 'labeling' fails to make adequate sense in most of the above texts.

Employing the imagery of a shepherd and his sheep, Jesus in John 10 taught that he, the "good shepherd" (vv. 11, 14), "knows" (*ginōskō*) his sheep (vv. 14a, 27b). The sense is identical to that of 2 Tim 2:19, which reads, "The Lord knows those who are his." Packer comments as follows concerning the shepherd's knowledge of his sheep:

> Here God's knowledge of those who are his is associated with his whole saving purpose of saving mercy. It is a knowledge that implies personal affection, redeeming action, covenant faithfulness, and providential watchfulness towards those whom God knows. It implies, in other words, salvation now and forever.[60]

Moreover, the good shepherd "calls his own sheep by name and leads them out" (v. 3). He calls them not collectively as a flock but individually, i.e., "by name." Conversely, the sheep recognize the voice of the shepherd, infallibly come to him, and obediently follow him (vv. 3b, 4, 27). The actions of the shepherd calling and the sheep responding concern their *salvation* as well as their discipleship, for in the immediate context (v. 28)

Jesus said, "I give them eternal life, and they shall never perish." V. 26 explains that those who fail to believe and come to Jesus reject him because they are not his sheep, i.e., because they were not "given" to Jesus by the Father before time (John 6:37, 39).

Jesus, furthermore, boldly stated in John 6 that "No one can come to me unless the Father who sent me draws [*helkysē*] him, and I will raise him up at the last day" (v. 44). This important verse indisputably affirms that those who come to Christ in faith do so because the Father has efficiently drawn them. The verb *helkyō* (to "draw") is used in John 21:6, 11 in the strong sense of dragging a fishing net to shore and in Acts 16:19 of the slave owners dragging Paul and Silas into the marketplace. The following verse, v. 45, reads, "It is written in the Prophets: 'They will all be taught by God.' Everyone who listens to the Father and learns from him comes to me." By these words Jesus affirmed that only those inwardly taught by God can come to the Son. We read in John 6 that later many disciples deserted Jesus, prompting the Lord to say, "there are some of you who do not believe" (v. 64). Jesus addressed the question of why some did not believe in v. 65, where he said, "no one can come to me unless the Father has enabled him." F.F. Bruce faithfully captured the sense of these Johannine verses by commenting, "None can come to Christ in faith but those who are persuaded and enabled to do so by the Spirit; but all these will come, drawn by the irresistible grace of heavenly love."[61]

Jesus' saying in John 12:32 requires careful examination. The Lord said, "But I, when I am lifted up from the earth, will draw [*helkysō*] all men to myself." The lifting up above the earth (cf. John 3:14-15; 8:28) refers to Jesus' death on the cross (John 12:33). Jesus did not suggest by this saying that through the attraction of his cross all people would be saved. Rather, the verse builds on previous teaching in John's gospel concerning the Savior's effectual calling or drawing ministry—witness the same verb *helkyō* in 6:64, discussed above. Certain Greek Gentiles (John 12:20-21) questioned the significance of Jesus' life and mission. The Lord responded that he would draw to himself "all men," namely, both Gentiles and Jews (see John 10:16; 11:52; 12:24). Distinctions of nationality, ethnicity, or social status were irrelevant to Jesus' redemptive mission. Thus "He is speaking of a universal rather than a narrowly naturalistic religion. The death of Christ would mean the end of particularism. By virtue of that death 'all men' and not the Jews alone would be drawn."[62] Spurgeon similarly commented that "the master roll of the [called and] converted includes princes and paupers, peers and potmen."[63] In sum, John 12:32 does not mean that the Spirit applies a significant drawing power to each and every person who hears the Word of truth.

Heb 3:1 describes of the author's Jewish-Christian readers as "holy brothers, who share in the heavenly calling." The objects of the divine calling are the saints. According to Heb 9:15, God gave ethnic Israel a resistible call to earthly privileges and blessings, but he extended to some Jews an effectual call to an heavenly inheritance in Christ. This verse states that "those who are called . . . receive the promised eternal inheritance." F.F. Bruce recognizes in this text "the close connection between God's effectual calling of his people and the heritage which is theirs as His Sons and heirs, joint heirs with Christ."[64] Again, the called are identical to the saved. Likewise Peter urged Christians to "declare the praises of him who called you [*hymas kalesantos*] out of darkness into his wonderful light" (1 Pet 2:9). The language and context of God's call here exclude a general summons. Not all those addressed by the Gospel belong to God (1 Pet 2:9), not all know Christ and his power (2 Pet 1:3), and not all are "kept by Jesus Christ" (Jude 1). Neither does redefining "calling" as "naming" fit the texts; for example, try substituting "named" for "called" in 1 Pet 2:9, 20-21 and 3:9.

Other NT texts affirming God's effectual call to salvation include 1 Cor 7:18, 21, Gal 1:6, 5:13, Eph 4:4, Col 3:15, 1 Tim 6:12, and 1 Pet 5:10.

In order to safeguard the truth that holistically depraved sinners come to Christ only by the divine initiative, many Reformed theologians place regeneration before conversion in the *ordo salutis*. The preceding Scripture texts (cf. the biblical data in chap. 7) indicate that effectual calling is conceptually distinct from regeneration. The power that brings sinners to Christ inheres in the Spirit's effectual call rather than in the new birth itself. That is, the Spirit's effectual call is a movement preliminary to regeneration; it stops short of effecting in believers a radical re-creation (2 Cor 5:17), whereby the latter participate in the divine nature (2 Pet 1:4). Logically speaking, the called according to God's purpose convert, and so are regenerated. Not only is this position biblical, but we avoid the difficulty of positing, logically at least, that regeneration precedes personal belief in the Gospel, repentance from sin, and wholehearted trust in Christ.

E. *Why Other Hearers of the Gospel Are Saved*

Jesus said to religious Jews who were zealous students of the Bible, "These are the Scriptures that testify about me, yet you refuse to come to me to have life" (John 5:39-40). As we learned above, some hearers of the Gospel are *not saved* because of the debilitating effects of sin in their lives. Conversely, others *are saved* because of the Spirit's powerful working that overcomes the destructive effects of sin in their hearts. The Spirit of salvation addresses and summons sinners via the Word in its several forms. Sometimes the Spirit awakens, evokes, and draws sinners with a working that is sudden, as in the experiences of Saul and Lydia. But more often the Spirit works in ways that are imperceptibly gradual, always secret, ever gentle, and infallibly effectual. Luther described the Spirit's working, by whatever way, in the following words: "When God works in us, the will, being changed and sweetly breathed on by the Spirit of God, desires and acts not from compulsion but responsively."[65]

Further in the NT, the risen Lord commissioned Paul as follows: "I am sending you [to the Gentiles] to open their eyes and turn them from darkness to light, and from the power of Satan to God, so that they may receive forgiveness of sins" (Acts 26:17-18). Note in this text that the opening of the spiritual eyes *always* results in salvation. As Paul later wrote, "We have not received the spirit of the world but the Spirit who is from God, that we may understand what God has freely given us" (1 Cor 2:12). See also Luke 24:45 and 1 John 5:20 for further confirmation of this truth. Pre-Christians come to Christ and are saved because the Spirit powerfully quickens the Gospel message to their mind, will, and emotions and convicts their hearts of sin (1 Thess 1:5). In this way the Spirit causes the Gospel—once perceived by the unconverted as "foolishness"—to become the "power" and "wisdom of God" unto salvation (Rom 1:16; 1 Cor 1:18, 24). By virtue of the Spirit's effectual call, sinners accept Christ's death on the cross as personal food and personal drink. Pink simply but correctly stated that "No sinner ever comes to Christ until the Holy Spirit first comes to him!"[66] Spurgeon illustrated the Spirit's drawing power via the following analogy: "The moon's attractive power is drawing up the waters from the sea. Even so our glorious Christ, in ways unknown to us, draws the hearts of men by his mighty Spirit wherever he pleases."[67]

Scripture further teaches that the Spirit's effectual calling is grounded in, or flows out of, God's sovereign elective purpose. Observe in the Scriptures the close relation that exists between effectual calling and sovereign election. Paul simply wrote, "those he predestined, he also called" (Rom 8:30). Again, "from the beginning God chose you to be saved through the sanctifying work of the Spirit and through belief in the truth. He called you to this through our gospel" (2 Thess 2:13-14). The apostle further added, God "has saved us and called us to a holy life—not because of anything we have done but because of his own purpose [*prothesis*] and grace. This grace was given us in Christ Jesus before the beginning of time . . ." (2 Tim 1:9). Second Pet 1:10 also juxtaposes calling and election: "my brothers, be all the more eager to make your calling and election [*tēn klēsin kai eklogēn*] sure." The one definite article between "calling" and "election" signifies that both must be treated as a single unit. Thus "A call-ing which is of one piece with election can only be effectual calling."[68] We merely mention here what was discussed in detail above, namely, that the Spirit effectually calls or draws those persons the Father has given to the Son (John 6:37, 39; 17:2, 6, 9, 12, 24). These alone believe and receive eternal life (John 6:40); to these Christ reveals the Father (John 17:6, 26); for them he prays (John 17:9); they will be raised up in the last day (John 6:39, 44); and they—effectually called and drawn by the Spirit—will be with Jesus forever in glory (John 17:24).

Finally, as we have noted earlier, the Spirit's effectual call *always* results in salvation. As John Murray wrote, "It is very striking that in the New Testament the terms for calling, when used specifically with reference to salvation, are almost uniformly applied, not to the universal call of the gospel, but to the call that ushers men into a state of salvation and is there-fore effectual. There is scarcely an instance where the terms are used to designate the indiscriminate overture of grace in the gospel of Christ."[69] Citing verses such as Rom 1:6-7, 8:30, 1 Cor 1:9, 26 and 2 Pet 1:10, Murray concluded by saying, "With scarcely an exception the NT means by the words 'call,' 'called,' 'calling' nothing less than the call which is effi-cacious unto salvation."[70]

An insightful word from C.S. Lewis sheds light on the grace of the divine call to freedom and salvation. The late Christian literary giant wrote that "The hardness of God is kinder that the softness of men, and His compulsion is our liberation."[71] The Spirit's effectual calling through the Word gently but powerfully draws sinners into the glorious freedom of Jesus Christ. Augustine expressed this saving initiative that leads to Christ simply but powerfully from his own life experience: "Lord, You first sought me out and brought me back on Your shoulder."[72]

IV. PRACTICAL IMPLICATIONS OF THE DOCTRINE OF CALLING

A. *Realize the Purposes of Your Calling*

At some point in our lives we believers may lose a sense of our Christian identity and vocation. We may forget the miry pit from which we have been delivered, who we have become in Jesus Christ, and what our task is in life. God's effectual calling through the Word and the Spirit is highly teleological or purpose-oriented. So the apostle Paul described believers as those "who have been called according to [God's] purpose" (Rom 8:28;

cf. Eph 3:11; Heb 6:17). It is important that we adequately understand the multifaceted purpose of God's gracious calling upon our lives.

(1) Of first importance, believers must recognize that they are called to a *new identity in Christ*. In the introduction to his letter to the Romans Paul described the converts as "loved by God," "called to belong to Jesus Christ," and "called to be saints" (Rom 1:6-7). Formerly we were spiritual orphans and slaves to manifold sins; but now through the Spirit's call to faith we have become spiritual sons and daughters, cherished members of the family of God. John expressed this thought well: "How great is the love the Father has lavished on us, that we should be called children of God! And that is what we are!" (1 John 3:1; cf. vv. 2, 10). The Spirit's effectual call offers us a true identity and an authentic self-image in Christ.

(2) The chosen are called to *fellowship and a relationship with Jesus Christ*. Paul urged the Ephesian Christians to "remember that formerly you who are Gentiles by birth . . . at that time you were separate from Christ, excluded from citizenship in Israel and foreigners to the covenants of promise, without hope and without God [*atheos*] in the world" (Eph 2:12). Indeed, the unconverted are "separated from the life of God because of the ignorance that is in them" (Eph 4:18). But the good news is that "now in Christ Jesus you who once were far away have been brought near through the blood of Christ" (Eph 2:13). Saints of the Most High, lay hold of the the great Pauline truism that "God . . . has called you into fellowship with his Son Jesus Christ our Lord" (1 Cor 1:9). How lofty is our privilege to enjoy fellowship and communion with the eternal, triune God!

(3) Saints are called to *Christian freedom*. Overly scrupulous individuals may lay on new believers the yoke of the law, urging that if they only work and pray intensely enough God may become favorably disposed to them. Believers blessed by Christ's grace are not bound to keep the letter of the law as a means of pleasing God. So Paul stated in no uncertain terms, "You, my brothers, were called to be free" (Gal 5:13a). This liberty to which we are called also involves freedom from the dominion of sin (Rom 8:2, 4, 15). The call to Christian freedom means serving one another freely and unfettered in the spirit of love (Gal 5:13b-14).

(4) By grace believers have been called to *peace*. Industrialized western cultures are plagued by interpersonal conflict, anxiety, depression, and numerous other psychological disorders. The Holy Spirit, however, calls believers to live at peace with themselves and with others. Moreover, he blesses the called and the saved with the gift of peace (Gal 5:22). May we heed Paul's earnest injunction to the church at Colosse: "Let the peace of Christ rule in your hearts, since as members of one body you were called to peace" (Col 3:15; cf. John 14:27; 16:33). May we take to heart the

apostle's exhortation to the Romans: "let us . . . make every effort to do what leads to peace and to mutual edification" (Rom 14:19).

(5) Christ has called us to a *life of proclamation and praise.* Too often we Christians are content to enjoy the personal blessings salvation affords us. Christ, however, calls us not to an ego-centric but to an ex-centric life of declaring his saving Word to others, particularly to the unsaved. May we recognize the great truth Peter enunciated: "You are a chosen people, a royal priesthood, . . . that you may declare the praises of him who called you out of darkness into his wonderful light" (1 Pet 2:9). The called joyfully testify to the reality of God's saving grace.

(6) Christians are called to a *life of perseverance in suffering.* Our fleshly nature is such that we seek comfort and convenience rather than endurance through hardship and pain. But our Lord reminded his own that "'No servant is greater than his master.' If they persecuted me, they will persecute you also" (John 15:20). We do well to heed also the words of Peter, "To this you were called, because Christ suffered for you, leaving you an example, that you should follow in his steps" (1 Pet 2:21). Our mandate as called ones is well expressed in the Petrine benediction (1 Pet 5:10), "the God of all grace, who called you to his eternal glory in Christ, after you have suffered a little while, will himself restore you and make you strong, firm and steadfast."

(7) A most important biblical principle is that saints are called to a *holy life.* In our day the name of Christ is blasphemed and the cause of Christ defamed by the immoral lives of some so-called Christian leaders. Paul judged it important to write to the Ephesian saints, "I urge you to live a life worthy of the calling you have received" (Eph 4:1). The apostle added the injunction, "God did not call us to be impure, but to live a holy life" (1 Thess 4:7; cf. 1 Cor 1:2). Moreover, God "has saved us and called us to a holy life" (2 Tim 1:9). In the words of St. Peter, "just as he who called you is holy, so be holy in all you do" (1 Pet 1:15). See also 1 Thess 5:23-24. Fulfill your calling and glorify the Lord by living a holy and blameless life before a watching world.

(8) God has called us to *gain the heavenly prize.* Our divine vocation is not a life of ease and pleasure, but one of self-denial as we strive for the heavenly goal. The great apostle Paul expressed his life's goal in these words: "Forgetting what is behind and straining toward what is ahead, I press on toward the goal to win the prize for which God has called me heavenward in Christ Jesus" (Phil 3:13-14).

Finally, (9) Saints are called to *receive the kingdom of God, eternal life, and heavenly glory* (1 Thess 2:12; 1 Tim 6:12; 1 Pet 5:10). Unbelievers and sadly many believers live lives singularly lacking in a sense of personal teleology or destiny. But in this world and in the world to come the called may enter into the experience of which Paul wrote: "No eye has seen, no ear has heard, no mind has conceived what God has prepared for those who love him" (1 Cor 2:9). In whatever part of the globe or in whatever circumstances we find ourselves, believers should realize the glorious privileges that are ours from our calling in Christ Jesus.

B. Faithfully Deliver the Gospel Call

Scripture clearly teaches that it is the Holy Spirit, not you or I or the celebrated evangelist, who draws sinners convincingly to Christ. We recognize that the Spirit of God, via a miraculous strategy, is capable of drawing the unconverted to Christ by the direct operation of his limitless power. Although exemplified in the conversions of persons such as Abraham and Saul, this method of drawing sinners to salvation is not the usual way in which God works. The Spirit does not customarily accomplish his drawing work in a vacuum apart from means. Rather, by divine design he usually woos and draws sinners to the Savior through the powerful Word of the Scriptures. God ordinarily gives the internal call to salvation by means of the external call through the written or proclaimed Word.

Nearly 2,000 years ago the risen Lord Jesus said to his followers, "repentance and forgiveness of sins will be preached in his name to all nations, beginning at Jerusalem. You are witnesses of these things" (Luke 24:47-48). The Lord also said to his disciples, "you will receive power when the Holy Spirit comes upon you; and you will be my witnesses in Jerusalem, and in all Judea and Samaria, and to the ends of the earth" (Acts 1:8). While preaching Jesus as Messiah in the city of Corinth, Paul generated strong opposition from the Jewish leaders. Yet one night the Lord spoke to Paul to encourage him in his preaching ministry, saying, "Do not be afraid; keep on speaking, do not be silent. For I am with you, and no one is going to attack and harm you, because I have many people in this city" (Acts 18:9-10). God in eternity past sovereignly chose certain people in Corinth to be saved, but the Spirit would draw these to Christ only through the Word faithfully preached by his servants. This truth prompted Paul to reflect on the prophetic text of Isa 52:7 and to write these words to the Roman Christians and to the entire church.

> How, then, can they call on the one they have not believed in? And
> how can they believe in the one of whom they have not heard? And
> how can they hear without someone preaching to them? And how

can they preach unless they are sent? As it is written, "How beautiful are the feet of those who bring good news."
—Rom 10:14-15

Every last Christian today is under the same order of our heavenly Commander-in-Chief as were the disciples in Jesus' day. You and I do not know those whom God has chosen in grace to be saved and whom he will powerfully call by the inner summons of his Spirit. Therefore, we must faithfully preach the Word and trust the ministry of effectual calling to the sovereign Spirit of God. The task to which we are called is to be diligent and faithful in presenting the verbal call and to leave to the Spirit the internal call that effectively brings sinners to Christ. By thus proclaiming the incomparable Good News widely to all who are spiritually needy, we become instruments of the Spirit and agents of God's redemptive purpose. May this task of delivering the Gospel call be our constant delight and joy.

C. *Trust God to Give the Spiritual Fruit*

The doctrine of effectual calling assures Christ's servants of the ultimate success of their Gospel ministry. As Christian disciples faithfully preach the Good News in obedience to the Savior and in the power of the Spirit, we may be confident that God will bring forth the spiritual harvest that he lovingly purposes. We need not fear that our apologetic and evangelistic labors will come to naught, like some ill-conceived consumer product that fizzles in the marketplace. In our day as in the apostle Paul's day, when the Gospel is preached some will reject the message, others will postpone a decision, but some assuredly will believe and be saved (Acts 17:32, 34). After Paul had preached courageously at Pisidian Antioch, Luke informed us that "When the Gentiles heard this, they were glad and honored the word of the Lord; and all who were appointed for eternal life believed" (Acts 13:48). Scripture clearly teaches that God will call or draw to Christ those whom before time he predestined to be justified and glorified (Rom 8:30). By God's promise the wheat will grow up with the weeds (Matt 13:24-30). Assuredly, God's purposes will succeed.

We need to remind ourselves that our task is to be faithful in sharing the Word with all with whom we associate: with our unconverted family members, friends, business colleagues, and casual contacts. Ours is not to speculate whom God may or may not call to himself. As Augustine wrote, "Do not make judgments about whom God draws and whom He does not draw, unless you wish to fall into error. Accept this once and for all, and understand it: you are not yet drawn to God? Pray that you may be drawn!"[73] God's responsibility is to bring forth spiritual fruit through his Word that we share. Recall the teaching of St. Paul that human messengers sow the seed of the Word and water it, but it is God who makes the seed grow (1 Cor 3:6-7). We preach, we persuade, and we plead with sinners to repent and be reconciled to God. But ultimately we know that it is the sovereign and all-powerful God who gives spiritual fruit. It is he who draws sinners to Christ, who causes the church to multiply, who makes the Gospel prevail and break down strongholds. Thus as Christ's servants faithfully preach the Gospel we need not fear that our words will fall on deaf and unresponsive ears, for God has promised that his Word will prosper. The Lord encourages us through the prophet Isaiah:

> As the rain and the snow come down from heaven, and do not return to it without watering the earth and making it bud and flourish, so that it yields seed for the sower and bread for the eater, so is my word that goes out from my mouth: It will not return to me empty, but will accomplish what I desire and achieve the purpose for which I sent it.
>
> —55:10-11

The Spirit's ministry of effectually calling the unsaved positively guarantees that the progress of the Gospel and the advance of the kingdom is not problematic but is fully assured. God's purposes will prevail. People from every tongue, ethnic group, and nation will believe the testimony of faithful Gospel messengers. They will be saved and will become the privileged people of God. God has promised this outcome, and by his grace it shall come to pass against every form of ungodly opposition.

> I sought the Lord, and afterward I knew
> He moved my soul to seek Him, seeking me;
> It was not I that found, O Savior true,
> No, I was found of Thee.[74]

"REPENT AND BELIEVE THE GOOD NEWS!"

M A R K   1 : 1 5

———□———

THE DOCTRINE OF CONVERSION

I. INTRODUCTORY CONCERNS

In this chapter we continue discussion of the application of the Savior's atoning work to sinners. We have concluded that in eternity past God sovereignly chose out of the lot of fallen humanity some persons to be saved. Moreover, in historical time the Holy Spirit, through the Gospel message, effectually calls or draws the chosen to Christ. We now consider those events that immediately follow in the scheme of salvation—namely, the initial human response to the Spirit's working in the heart commonly known as conversion (belief, repentance, and faith). It will be seen that all the benefits of salvation—regeneration, union with Christ, justification, sanctification, and preservation/perseverance—proceed from the experience of genuine conversion.

We need to investigate the biblical concept of repentance. Can we identify common elements in every experience of true repentance, or does the nature of repentance vary from person to person? An important issue is the extent to which a person must forsake unrighteousness in order to receive God's pardon and be saved. Must a person who seeks salvation repent or turn away from *every* known sin in his life? Antinomians dispute the need for repentance, and some dispensationalists claim that in the age of grace God does not require repentance for salvation. Does insistence upon repentance involve the penitent in a form of works-righteousness?

In recent times the issue of faith has come to the forefront of theological discussion. What is the nature of the faith that saves? Is faith primarily intellectual assent to revealed truths, trust in a person, or a certain mode of existence? Are there certain elements common to every act of saving faith? Does true faith rest upon historically verifiable evidences, or is it a commitment that transcends empirical data, such as a passionate 'leap in the dark'? What or who is the true object of saving faith? Is it the Bible, a creed, one's church, or the person of Jesus Christ? Furthermore, as an increasing number of modern thinkers assert, do all persons everywhere possess a faith sufficient for salvation? Must saving faith be explicit, or can it be implicit in the sense of a vague assent to the transcendent dimension of life?

A hotly debated issue in the present, as well as an important matter of practical ministry strategy, is whether a person must confess Christ as Lord as well as Savior to be saved. Some allege that to become a Christian one merely needs to accept Jesus Christ as sin-bearer. Such people boldly state that "All the sinner needs to do is believe in Christ." Others insist that seekers of salvation must also obey Christ and acknowledge his Lordship in their lives. How can we avoid the pitfalls of an 'easy-believism' on one hand and a works-righteousness on the other? We need to assess the so-called 'Savior-Lord debate' that once again troubles the Christian community.

We investigate also the relationship between repentance and faith. Does Scripture teach that either logically or chronologically one response precedes the other? Or are both part of the sinner's one act of turning to God from idols? Moreover, do repentance and faith lie within the spiritual capability of pre-Christians, or are they in a significant sense gifts and enablements of God? By what means do unconverted people bring forth the responses of repentance and faith? If depraved sinners of themselves are incapable of repenting and exercising faith, can these responses be considered a natural duty? Classically in this regard theologians have discussed the issues of "duty-repentance" and "duty-faith." Finally, we ask whether true believers in Jesus Christ can be troubled with spiritual doubt. How do loyal followers of Christ deal constructively with the nagging problem of doubt in their lives?

II. Historical Interpretations
of Conversion

Issues of belief, repentance, and faith have been understood in various ways in the history of the church. The following discussion highlights the most important ways in which Christian authorities have understood these important matters. By attention to the issues as historically articulated, we are better enabled to arrive at a faithful understanding of these important doctrines.

A. A Humanly Contrived Work
(Pelagians and Liberals)

Positing the goodness of human nature, liberals minimize the need for radical conversion of the individual soul while stressing reformation of the collective moral life in society. Rather than a moment of decisive turning, repentance is seen as a lifelong process of growth and maturity. Liberals anchor their convictions in faith, but not in the sense of assent to timeless truths. In an evolutionary universe there are few absolutes; hence the familiar, liberal slogan, "Dogma is dead." One strand of liberalism defines faith as a person's felt sense of dependence on God. Another type assimilates faith into reason, resulting in a form of rationalism. In the latter case, faith is the mind's acceptance of the data via the usual cognitive processes. The same rational processes employed by secular fields of study must be applied to religion. Liberals generally view the goal of human existence as organizing one's life and performing God's will after the pattern of Jesus the Nazarene.

Albrecht Ritschl (d. 1889), the most influential theologian between Schleiermacher and Barth, had a great influence on later liberal thought (Hermann, Harnack, Rauschenbusch, etc.). Following Kant in rejecting theoretical (or metaphysical) knowledge of God, Ritschl emphasized the ethical (or practical) dimension of the Christian religion. The heart of his theology was value-judgments made in respect of Christ's work in the interests of our own blessedness. Faith, Ritschl insisted, is not chiefly *knowledge*, which is too abstract and impersonal to serve a religious function. He wrote that "faith means neither the acknowledgment of the correctness of traditional facts, nor the acceptance of orthodox propositions, but trust in God's grace."[1] The practical and existential focus of faith emerges in Ritschl's statement that "Faith is emotional conviction of the harmony between the divine purposes and the most intimate interests of man."[2] The "interests of man" consist "not in the discovery of truth for itself, but in the feeling of moral pleasure and in the satisfaction of our own spirit."[3] Ritschl summarized his position by stating that faith is

> the emotional trust in God, accompanied by the conviction of the value of this gift for one's blessedness, which . . . takes the place of the former mistrust which was bound up with the unrelieved feeling of guilt. Through trust in God's grace the alienation of sinners from God, which was essentially connected with the unrelieved feeling of guilt, is removed.[4]

John C. Bennett (d. 1960), a leading liberal ethicist at Union Theological Seminary, likewise focused more on the social rather than the strictly religious aspects of Christianity. He insisted that repentance is more applicable to Christians than to non-Christians. Christian people and nations are called upon to repent of their racial cruelty, economic exploitation, and militaristic adventurism that destroy human beings. "The gospel is a gospel of repentance, but repentance is very narrow and artificial if understood only in terms of our private lives."[5] Second, repentance must be directed to the open future rather than to the closed past, thereby avoiding unhealthy patterns of self-accusation and guilt. Bennett summed up:

> Repentance is a natural part of the Christian life. Often we find that the saints are the most conscious of their sins. They feel responsibility for evils of which they may have been in no degree the cause. . . . The habit of continuing repentance enables us to grow; it keeps the conscience awake; it helps to preserve us from self-righteousness. It may keep us from the socially destructive tendency to concentrate on the sins of others, particularly the sins of opponents or enemies.[6]

The literature of liberation theology makes few references to personal repentance from sin and faith in Christ as Savior. The movement defines sin in terms of unjust political, economic, and social structures and so politicizes the doctrine of conversion. Liberationists remove repentance and faith from the private sphere and reinterpret its meaning to the social and political sphere. The context of repentance and faith is not the sinful human heart but the "sinful social situation."[7] Liberation theology defines conversion as involvement in the struggle for structural liberation that inevitably involves conflict and possibly violent revolution. Gutiérrez typically claims that "To be converted is to commit oneself to the process of the liberation of the poor and oppressed, to commit oneself lucidly, realistically, and concretely. It means to commit oneself not only generously, but also with an analysis of the situation and a strategy of action."[8] Fierro states more bluntly that "'Conversion' is the Christian name for 'revolution' . . . liberating revolution in the conversion of societies."[9] Guided by the thought of Marx, Fierro insists that the NT Gospel of individual conversion was a great error. Thus he writes that "The moralism of individual conversion now appears as a great historical mistake committed by Christians."[10]

Liberation theologians, most of whom are Roman Catholics working in the developing world, deny that faith is a matter of intellectual assent to doctrinal truths or commitment to Jesus Christ as Savior. The old idea of faith as a matter of right beliefs (orthodoxy) gives way to the notion of faith as right action (orthopraxy). Faith then is the act of going outside oneself and laboring to liberate the poor and the exploited politically, economically, and socially. In the words of Boff, "faith embraces the whole order of existence, political practices included. In this sense faith concerns not only God but, indirectly, politics as well."[11] James Cone, a leading American black theologian, envisages the black Christ liberating oppressed blacks from the shackles of white racism. Thus Cone writes that "Faith is the response of the community to God's act of liberation. It means saying yes to God and no to oppressors."[12]

Process theologians define faith technically as the human *perception* of the initial aims presented by God, involving a sense of novelty, refreshment, and love. Faith is a pre-reflective phenomenon by which people engage sacred reality in the depths of their being. On this showing, faith has little to do with consciously held beliefs or formal doctrines. Cobb and Griffin typically argue that "faith is fundamentally a mode of existence."[13] In the very nature of reality, "All people necessarily believe in God at the deepest level of their being, even when they consciously affirm atheism."[14] Whiteheadians allege that all people possess varying degrees of "saving" faith.

B. Cooperation with Grace
(Arminians)

The usual arrangement of elements in the Arminian *ordo* is prevenient grace, repentance, faith, the new birth, and continued obedience. Seen primarily as *human* activities, *repentance* is defined as a voluntary separation from sin and *faith* as intellectual assent to truth and personal trust in God. The human responses of repentance and faith are made possible by universal prevenient grace, which proponents claim frees sinners spiritually to respond to the Gospel. On this showing, everyone allegedly is born in a state of grace. "This grace will shepherd one to repentance, regeneration, entire sanctification, and final perseverance if not resisted somewhere along the way."[15] Arminians deny that personal faith is the result of God's immediate work on the sinner's heart. Many affirm that the Christian faith (*fides*)—the Gospel or Jesus Christ—is God's gift to sinners. However, subjective faith (*fiducia*)—or personal belief in Jesus and the Gospel—is a human activity rather than a divine gift. "To treat subjective faith (*fiducia*) as 'a gift of God' demands the explication that God '*believed*' for you, as if your soul were nonexistent, and you were totally insignificant, over and beyond all your sinfulness."[16] Some Arminians candidly describe faith as a human, not a divine, *work*. Thus, "Faith may indeed be considered in one sense as a *work*, a good work, a right work, the rightest work which, in the case, the sinner can perform. It has in itself the same sort of *good desert*, or ethical merit, as we ascribe to every act which in its given place is morally right."[17]

John Wesley (d. 1791) held a lively doctrine of original sin and depravity. Yet depravity is only hypothetical, since the "preventing grace" that flows from the cross reverses the debilitating effects of original sin. Thus all persons from birth are blessed with free will, in the sense of the power of contrary choice. According to Wesley, prevenient grace enables the unregenerate to (1) hear the voice of God in conscience, (2) acknowledge responsibility for sins, (3) seek righteousness, and (4) trust Christ for salvation. "Preventing grace [includes] the first wish to please God, the first dawn of light concerning his will, and the first slight transient conviction of having sinned against him. All these imply some tendency toward life; some degree of salvation."[18] Pre-Christians cooperate with this prevenient grace to work out their own salvation (Phil 2:12), i.e., to repent of sin and believe in Christ. As Outler expressed Wesley's view, "faith is a human *re-action* to an antecedent action of the Holy Spirit's prevenience."[19]

Wesley posited two stages of repentance. The first, or initial, stage occurs at the point of conversion and includes the knowledge that we are guilty sinners, contrition for sin, and poverty of spirit. The second, or subsequent, stage of repentance follows conversion and involves conviction of residual sin, one's personal unworthiness, and utter helplessness. The second "change of heart (and consequently of life) from all sin to all holiness[20] focuses on the believer's need for a second blessing experience. For Wesley, *metanoia* was less sorrow for sin and more a consciousness of one's guilty condition. Justifying faith involves "not only an assent to the whole gospel of Christ, but also a full reliance on the blood of Christ, a trust in the merits of his life, death, and resurrection; . . . It is a sure confidence which a man hath in God, that through the merits of Christ *his* sins are forgiven, and *he* is reconciled to the favour of God."[21] Faith is not a free gift of God; it is a human act or work.

Charles Finney (d. 1875) viewed repentance as the sinner's change of ultimate intention, purpose, and choice and as a reformation of life extending to *all* outward sins. Repentance "is a phenomenon of the will, and consists in the turning or change of the ultimate intention from selfishness to benevolence."[22] Genuine repentance includes a sense of "shame," "self-loathing," and "self-condemnation."[23] Faith likewise is a phenomenon of the will. "It is the will's closing in with the truths of the Gospel. It is the soul's act of yielding itself up, or committing itself to the truths of the evangelical system."[24] Proceeding from a low view of sin (sin being a function of the will and not also a state of the soul), Finney averred that God commands repentance and faith. He concluded that repentance and faith lie within the natural ability of persons as free and responsible moral agents.

Three Nazarene authors of the volume *God, Man, and Salvation* see "true repentance and saving faith [as] two sides to the single act of turning."[25] Repentance is the human activity of turning from idolatry and wickedness, confessing sins to God, and amending behavior. The authors insist that repentance, no less than faith, is necessary for salvation, and that both are actions of sinners facilitated by prevenient grace. Thus, "repentance is not a state dropped irresistibly in the soul. Men who have been granted repentance by God may still elect not to repent."[26] Saving faith likewise is not something God imposes on people; sinners and saints alike—not God—voluntarily open the door of their hearts and accept his grace (Rev 3:20). Faith thus is a very personal, moral choice. Boldly the authors state that "Man voluntarily disbelieved himself away from God; it is only right that he should be required to believe his way back."[27]

C. Conversion Offered Only to the Elect (Some Hyper-Calvinists)

Certain hyper-Calvinists in the seventeenth century so stressed God's eternal decision regarding human destiny, limited Atonement, and sinners' spiritual incapacity that they denied the invitation to convert should be extended to the non-elect. Because God intended the Gospel only for the elect for whom Christ died, and because no depraved sinner is capable of producing God-honoring, spiritual responses, repentance and faith are not to be sought in the non-elect. The minister's task is to lead sinners to Christ only when the Spirit of grace is obviously at work in their lives. Preachers who used moral persuasion as a means of generating repentance in the unsaved were branded as "Pelagians." Peter Toon described the system of hyper-Calvinism in the following terms.

> It was a system of theology, or a system of the doctrines of God, man and grace, which was framed to exalt the honour and glory of God and did so at the expense of minimizing the moral and spiritual responsibility of sinners to God. . . . This led to the notion that grace must only be offered to those for whom it was intended.[28]

Article 26 of the Gospel Standard Articles illustrates the lack of moral and spiritual responsibility on the part of non-elect sinners.

> We deny duty faith and duty repentance—these terms signifying that it is every man's duty spiritually and savingly to repent and

> believe. . . . We deny also that there is any capability in man by nature to any spiritual good whatever. So that we reject the doctrine that men in a state of nature should be exhorted to believe in or turn to God.[29]

Joseph Hussey (d. 1726), an English Congregationalist minister, held that the invitation to repent and believe should not be offered to the non-elect, for whom the Gospel was not intended and for whom it would be unprofitable. Wrote he, "invitations to any supernatural acts, such as the exercise and putting forth of saving faith in the person of Christ, have no footing in the Sacred Oracles."[30] An English independent minister by the name of Lewis Wayman (d. 1764) urged preachers first to ascertain that their hearers were among the elect before exhorting them to cleave whole-heartedly to the Lord. Otherwise, there likely would be "millions in the world believing in Christ for life and salvation, to whom God hath not given eternal life in Christ, and who shall never obtain salvation by him."[31] He added that the failure of non-elect sinners to repent and believe does not heighten their guilt, for the Gospel was not intended for them in the first place. The English Particular Baptist John Brine (d. 1765), in a book entitled *A Refutation of Arminian Principles* (1743), declared that it is wrong to offer the Gospel of grace to all persons indiscriminately. Wrote he, "with respect to special faith in Christ . . . the powers of man in his perfected state were not fitted and disposed to that act."[32] Because persons cannot exercise saving faith in the unfallen state—there being no need for such—neither can faith be required of them in their fallen state.

D. Non-Cognitive Encounter with God (Kierkegaard and Existentialists)

Existentialist theologians reverse the classical order to assert that 'existence' precedes 'essence.' Humans are nothing until they freely define themselves by responsible decisions and actions. Judging the biblical cosmology to be mythological, proponents focus not on life hereafter but on concrete, human existence here and now. They insist that faith has little to do with formal beliefs and everything to do with passionate commitment. Authentic existence is realized through enhanced self-understanding mediated by the mythical *kerygma*. Through this encounter the individual exchanges the "new self" for the "old self."

Against the logical but abstract system of Hegel and the formal yet complacent orthodoxy of Danish Lutheranism, Kierkegaard (d. 1855) stressed the personal, inward, passionate, and illogical dimension of faith. Seeing few indications of vital faith in baptized Lutherans reared in the Danish church, Kierkegaard concluded that "baptism cannot be the decisive factor with respect to becoming a Christian."[33] A sinner apprehends Christ not in an atmosphere of detachment but by intense and passionate engagement. A person becomes a Christian as the human 'I' existentially engages the divine 'Thou' via a radical decision of faith. The faith Kierkegaard envisaged involves a risk or 'leap' of spiritual passion that contravenes rational arguments and historical evidences. The Dane held that if persons could grasp God and the Gospel objectively, there would be no need to believe. For Kierkegaard the proper object of faith is the rationally absurd. "Faith is the objective uncertainty due to the repulsion of the absurd held fast by the passion of inwardness, which in this instance is intensified to the utmost degree."[34] The chief example of faith, according to Kierkegaard, is Abraham's radical decision to slay his son Isaac in obedience to God's command. In this God-inspired act of subjective passion and objective uncertainty, the individual by fear and trembling decisively engages the absolute Paradox (God become a man). By so doing, the person moves from a state of non-being to being—i.e., he or she becomes a new creature.

According to Paul Tillich (d. 1965), the fundamental human problem is not disobedience or rebellion but estrangement from the ground of being, from other beings, and from oneself. This estrangement or split did not occur from a historical Fall (Tillich viewed the Edenic drama as "myth"), but is the necessary accompaniment of a created world as such. Sin, in other words, is an *existential* category rather than a moral one. The results of this universal estrangement are unbelief, *hybris* (pride), concupiscence, and psychological anxiety.

Salvation, Tillich insisted, is the conquering of anxiety and estrangement as one allows himself to be grasped by New Being—where the latter is Christ-power, *eros*-urge, or the power of creative transformation. According to Tillich, New Being may be mediated by Jesus or other charismatic personalities. Salvation—healing or personal reintegration—comes by faith, which Tillich defined as the state of "ultimate concern" or "infinite passion"[35] about matters spiritual, intellectual, aesthetic, social, or political. Faith, according to Tillich, is "ecstatic" in that it transcends the structures of the rational, conscious mind. Tillich did not specify the *object* of faith, since faith ("the state of being grasped by the Spiritual Presence"[36]) transcends the familiar subject-object relation.[37] Given the uncertainty of its object or content, faith involves risk and daring courage. According to Tillich, one has faith when he is "ultimately concerned about his state of estrangement and about the possibility of reunion with the ground and aim of his being."[38] Given his definition, every human being has faith; only the expression and degree vary according to the situation. Tillich acknowledged that "Such a description [of faith] bears little resemblance to the traditional definitions in which intellect, will or feeling is identified with the act of faith."[39]

Tillich judged that the multifaceted event designated conversion is a lengthy and unconscious *process* rather than a sudden, emotional crisis. Repentance (the rejection of existential estrangement) and faith (ultimate concern) are latent in all people everywhere. As a ministry strategy, "This means that the evangelist does not address 'lost souls,' men without God, but people in the stage of latency, to transform them into people who have received manifestation."[40]

Bultmann (d. 1976) insisted that biblical teaching concerning a historical fall in Eden, blood atonement for sins via the cross, and Jesus' bodily resurrection from the dead are mythological concepts. One must demythologize the mythical husk, he argued, to get at the existential kernel of Christian reality. God extends salvation to persons through the preached Word about the human prophet Jesus (the *kerygma*). For Bultmann salvation is not a once-for-all, divine declaration of innocence, but the transition from inauthentic to authentic existence. Inauthentic existence involves attachment to objective, historical facts and the quest for self-autonomy and worldly security. Authentic existence involves the inner realities of enhanced self-understanding, personal freedom, and openness to the future. Thus salvation is "an act of God through which man becomes capable of self-commitment, capable of faith and love, of his authentic life."[41] Faith, the instrument of this change, is not assent to propositional doctrines but a concrete decision or choice. Thus faith "is neither more nor less than the *decision . . . against the world* for God."[42] Faith as choice or decision is illustrated by Jesus' story of the rich young man (Matt 19:16-22) who must decide for and commit to Jesus' kingdom agenda. Since Bultmann demythologized even the Holy Spirit, there is no power extrinsic to oneself that enables faith. Faith depends on man's own ability to apprehend what is offered. The possibility of new life eventuates by "deliberate resolve" that emanates from persons themselves.[43]

Since salvation involves recognizing the folly of inauthentic existence, Bultmann denied the need for personal confession of sins. "It is an error to think that belief in the grace of God requires a sense of sin or a confession of sin, in the sense that a man must admit to himself how much or how often and grievously he has sinned and continually is sinning. . . . He is to consider the reason for his being, and to ask himself whence his life comes."[44]

E. Ratification of Prior Justification on the Cross (Barthians)

The earlier writings of Karl Barth (d. 1968) came close to suggesting that in the arena of salvation it is not sinful man but the Spirit within who believes.[45] In his *Church Dogmatics*, Barth softened this extremely objectivist view by conceding that subjective faith is an authentic human experience. Still Barth rejected the notion that repentance and faith are human requisites for participating in the blessings of the Gospel. He took this position because he judged that in saying yes to his Son on the cross God justified and remitted the sins of the entire race in fulfillment of his eternal covenant. Barth viewed faith as a person actualizing in his life "the victory of grace, won in Jesus Christ over human enmity against grace."[46] Conversion—i.e., turning to God, opening up the life to him, trust, and obedience—represents the human appropriation of God's prior justifying act in Jesus Christ. It is our personal entry into the peace Christ won for all on the cross. It is a subjective waking up to the fact that as part of the human race we have been objectively set right with God and our sins forgiven. Barth made clear that the one who converts and acknowledges Christ is not the person as such; it is the person *in Jesus Christ*. So he wrote:

> As the work of the Holy Spirit [faith] is man's new birth from God on the basis of which man can already live here by what he is there in Jesus Christ and therefore in truth. Faith is the temporal form of his eternal being in Jesus Christ. . . . Faith extinguishes our enmity against God by seeing that this enmity is made a lie, a lie confessed by ourselves as such, expiated and overcome by Jesus Christ, trodden underfoot and destroyed.[47]

Barth made it clear that discussion of how one appropriates salvation begins not with groping sinners and their warped notions of faith; the issue must begin with Jesus Christ as the object and foundation of our faith. Barth's approach, therefore, was Christological rather than anthropological or existential. Unless we begin entirely with Jesus Christ, "our own reality, the enemy of grace living in us all, still remains to jeopardize the whole relationship."[48] Hear Barth further on this subject:

> . . . as the one and only man ready for God, Jesus Christ has not only lived, died and risen for us once in time, so that the abounding grace of God might be an event and at the same time revelation among us, but as this same One he stands before his Father now in eternity for us, and lives for us in God himself as the Son of God he was and is and will be. Thus our appropriation of what he has won

for us has not first to be executed by us. By the fact that he is for us in eternity in God himself the man who is ready for God, it is executed in eternity in God himself, by him, in the eternal continuation of his high-priestly office. But this means . . . that Jesus Christ himself sees to it that in him and by him we are not outside but inside. He himself sees to it that his readiness is valid for us who are not identical with him, and who in ourselves are not ready for God. . . . If he is for us, this means . . . that with the eternal certainty proper to the Son of God we too are present, genuinely participating in what he is and has done.[49]

F. A Divinely Enabled Human Response (Reformed Evangelicals)

Given the fact of holistic depravity, this tradition regards repentance and faith as gifts of God's grace to the "sheep" or the elect. The spiritually dead can no more convert themselves than the physically dead can restore themselves to life. As Packer wrote, "It is God who brings men and women under the sound of the gospel, and it is God who brings them to faith in Christ."[50] Although repentance and faith are gifts from above, God commands people everywhere to exert themselves in conversion. Many hold that repentance involves knowledge of one's lost condition, sorrow for sin, and a forsaking of all known evil. Faith consists of knowledge of Christ and his saving provisions, personal assent to these truths, and commitment to Christ. Conversion may occur in an instant or as a lengthy process. Christians, of course, exercise faith and repentance throughout the whole of their lives. As noted earlier, some authorities place regeneration prior to conversion. Others (including the present writer) identify the first wish to please God as the result of the Spirit's effectual calling, and so place conversion prior to regeneration in the *ordo salutis*.

Martin Luther (d. 1546) rejected the Roman equation of repentance with penance. The repentance Luther encouraged involved renunciation of all vice and genuine sorrow for sins committed. The penance he rejected involved the effort to make satisfaction for sins by human works. Luther himself linked repentance and forgiveness of sins with faith. He wrote, "Repentance is not penitence alone but also faith, which apprehends the promise of forgiveness, lest the penitent sinners perish."[51] Luther insisted that the Spirit works repentance in the heart of the unconverted by an act of sovereign grace. He added that although prominent at the time of conversion, repentance is a lifelong process in Christians. "When our Lord and Master, Jesus Christ, said 'Repent,' He called for the entire life of believers to be one of penitence."[52]

Against Rome's intellectualist understanding of faith, Luther stressed that faith is not merely knowledge but also trust and commitment. In addition to assent to cardinal truths, faith is a clinging to God's Word, a constant looking to Christ, and an embracing of God's Son. Faith thus possesses both objective and subjective aspects. For Luther, the object of faith is not the church or its teachings but Christ mediated by the Scriptures. In short, faith is acceptance of Jesus Christ as Savior. Contrasting his view with the prevailing Roman position, Luther wrote:

> There are two ways of believing. One way is to believe *about* God, as I do when I believe that what is said of God is true; . . . This faith is knowledge or observation rather than faith. The other way is to believe *in* God, as I do when I not only believe that what is said about Him is true, but put my trust in Him, surrender myself to Him and make bold to deal with Him, believing that without doubt that He will be to me and do to me just what is said of Him.[53]

Again with an eye to Rome, Luther insisted that sinners are justified by faith alone, not by the fiction of faith formed by love and good works. He wrote that "Faith does not exist because of works, but works are done because of faith."[54] Faith and love are related as cause and effect, not vice versa. With the other Reformers, Luther held that sinners cannot initiate repentance and faith. By his Spirit, God bestows an attitude of repentance and brings forth the response of faith from the heart.

John Calvin (d. 1564) held that, because of human corruption, conversion is chiefly an activity of God's grace through the Spirit. Commenting on Phil 1:6, he wrote, "God begins his good work in us . . . by arousing love and desire and zeal for righteousness in our hearts; or, to speak more correctly, by bending, forming, and directing our hearts to righteousness."[55] Calvin defined faith as "a firm and certain knowledge of God's benevolence toward us, founded upon the truth of the freely given promise in Christ, both revealed to our minds and sealed upon our hearts through the Holy Spirit."[56] His understanding of faith, however, was hardly intellectualist: "that very assent itself . . . is more of the heart than of the brain, and more of the disposition than of the understanding."[57] Faith, for the Genevan Reformer, consisted of heart knowledge of the Gospel, persuasion of its truth, and personal trust in Christ. Calvin polemicized against the Roman view that faith is chiefly intellectual assent to church teaching and likewise against its concept of "implicit faith." Faith, according to Calvin, is the conscious human response to the divine work of regeneration. So understood, faith is God's supernatural gift implanted within the elect by the Spirit.[58] "No one, unless faith be granted to him, can believe in Christ (John 6:65)."[59]

Repentance, defined as mortification of the old nature (the flesh) and quickening of the new nature (the spirit) unto holiness, is born of faith. Wrote Calvin, "Now it ought to be a fact beyond controversy that repentance not only constantly follows faith but is also born of faith."[60] Repentance, or living in the reality of the new nature and being renewed in the divine image, is a process that continues throughout the Christian's life.[61] Calvin understood by repentance what most later divines called sanctification.

C.H. Spurgeon (d. 1892) discussed faith prior to repentance, judging that faith is the noblest virtue that contains within itself all other Christian graces. Thus, "All the fruits meet for repentance are contained in faith itself. You shall never find that a man who trusts Christ remains an enemy to God, or a lover of sin."[62] Faith involves knowledge of the Gospel, assent to its truths and promises, personal trust in Christ as sin-bearer, and obedience to the Savior. Faith, according to Spurgeon, is both credence and confidence. Faith rests upon the person of the Lord Jesus Christ; it "is not belief about a doctrine, nor an opinion, nor a formula, but belief concerning a person."[63] Spurgeon added that "A creed will not save you, but reliance upon the anointed Savior is the way of salvation."[64] Spurgeon insisted that faith is a human act, but it is also a gift and work of God. "*Faith, wherever it exists, is in every case, without exception, the gift of God and the work of the Holy Spirit. Never yet did a man believe in Jesus with the faith here intended, except the Holy Spirit led him to do so.*"[65] Indeed, wherever faith exists, one finds proof of the soul's prior regeneration. "Faith in the living God and his Son Jesus Christ is always the result of the new birth, and can never exist except in the regenerate."[66] Spurgeon added that repentance, an effect of faith, includes sorrow for transgressions and a forsaking of all known sins. Likewise a fruit of the new birth, repentance also is a gift of God's grace.

The baptist theologian A.H. Strong (d. 1921) viewed regeneration and conversion as chronologically simultaneous events, although logically the former precedes the latter. Conversion, consisting of repentance and faith, is the human act that attests the regenerating work of the Holy Spirit on the sinner's heart. According to Strong, the resuscitation of Lazarus in John 11 illustrates the relationship between the new birth and conversion. Lazarus was made alive by the power of God; in this event his soul was passive. But Lazarus came forth from the tomb; in this act his soul was active. Strong continued that conversion, the human side of regeneration, consists of repentance and faith. *Repentance* signifies the sinner's determination to turn from all known sin. It involves an intellectual element—recognition of sin, an emotional element—sorrow for sin, and a voluntary element—abandonment of sin. *Faith* connotes the sinner's determination to turn to Christ. It too involves an intellectual element—knowledge of the Gospel, an emotional element—feeling the sufficiency of Christ's grace, and a voluntary element—trusting Christ as Savior and Lord.

Millard J. Erickson's position is similar to Strong's, with the exception that conversion logically precedes regeneration. Repentance, the negative side of conversion, consists of godly sorrow for sin plus the determination to forsake iniquity. Faith, the positive aspect of conversion, consists of assent to Gospel truths together with trust in Christ's person. Temporally, conversion and regeneration occur simultaneously, but logically repentance and faith represent the condition for God's work of regeneration. Erickson attributes the enablement to repent and believe not to regeneration but to the Spirit's effectual calling.

> In the case of the elect God works intensively through a special calling so that they do respond in repentance and faith. As a result of this conversion, God regenerates them. The special calling . . . is not the complete transformation which constitutes regeneration, but it does render the conversion of the individual both possible and certain. Thus the logical order of the initial aspects of salvation is special calling—conversion—regeneration.[67]

The biblical exposition to follow will show that the last hypothesis, which explains conversion as a divinely enabled human response, best accords with the data of revelation as well as personal experience.

III. EXPOSITION OF THE DOCTRINE OF CONVERSION

A. What Is Biblical Conversion?

By spiritual conversion we mean a person's decisive turning from sin, self, and Satan unto God through Jesus Christ and the power of the Spirit. The Greek verb *epistrephō* ("turn back," "return") translates the Hebrew verb *šûb*. It literally means a change of direction, but the verb occurs several times in the NT in the sense of a spiritual turning from sin to God. The emphasis is upon the change in the person's manner of life. Speaking of John the Baptist, the angel said to Zechariah, "Many of the people of

Israel will he bring back to the Lord their God. And he will go on before the Lord in the spirit and power of Elijah, to turn the hearts of the fathers to their children and the disobedient to the wisdom of the righteous—to make ready a people prepared for the Lord" (Luke 1:16-17; cf. Matt 13:15; Mark 4:12). These verses suggest that sinners require a superior power beyond themselves to bring about their conversion. The noun *epistrophē* ("conversion") occurs only once in the NT. We read that while passing through Phoenicia and Samaria, Paul and Barnabas "reported the conversion of the Gentiles" (Acts 15:3, NRSV).

There is no one archetypical model of conversion, for God works spiritual reformation in different ways in people's lives. A prime example of biblical conversion is the parable of the lost son (Luke 15:11-32). The younger son's journey into a far country with his share of the family wealth denotes humankind's rebellious departure from God in pursuit of self-gratification (vv. 13-16). The steps in religious conversion in Luke's story are (1) awareness of one's lost condition and destructive behavior (v. 17), (2) honest confession of personal sins and guilt (vv. 18, 21), (3) acknowledgment of one's utter unworthiness before a righteous God (v. 19), and (4) the determination to return to the Father's home (vv. 18-20a). The Father anticipated the wayward son's return and responded with undeserved mercy and forgiveness (vv. 20b-24).

The account of Saul's conversion (Acts 9:1-18) offers an instructive case study of a dramatic spiritual turnaround. Saul was a zealous Jew who outwardly lived an exemplary moral and religious life (Acts 26:4-5; Gal 1:14; Phil 3:4-6). He was also a keen persecutor of the early Christian movement (Acts 9:1-2; 26:9; 1 Tim 1:13). As Saul approached Damascus on a mission of terrorism against Christians there, Christ revealed himself to the raging Pharisee with such brilliance as to render him blind (vv. 3, 8-9). Cast to the ground by the light of Christ's glory, Saul was stripped of all self-sufficiency. Jesus' words to him from heaven—"Saul, Saul, why do you persecute me?" (v. 4)—aroused his awareness of sin and alienation. Overcome by Christ's power and grace, Saul experienced conversion at this time. After Ananias laid hands on him, Saul was filled with the Holy Spirit (v. 17) and was baptized (v. 18). Shortly thereafter, as a servant of the risen Lord, he preached Christ in the synagogues (v. 20) and upheld the Christian way against the Jews (v. 22).

The book of Acts records numerous dramatic conversions of Jews and pagans to Christ. The risen Jesus said to Paul on the road to Damascus, "I will rescue you from your own people and from the Gentiles. I am sending you to them to open their eyes and turn them from darkness to light, and from the power of Satan to God, so that they may receive forgiveness of sins and a place among those who are sanctified by faith in me" (Acts 26:17-18). Luke's history of the early church records the conversion of Aeneas (Acts 9:34-35), Cornelius (Acts 10:44-48), Lydia (16:14-15), and many other people (11:21; 15:19).

Paul viewed spiritual conversion as a radical turning from idols to the Lord. He wrote that the Thessalonian Christians "turned [aorist of *epistrephō*] to God from idols to serve the living and true God" (1 Thess 1:9). Christian conversion thus is a turning from an evil lifestyle (2 Cor. 12:21) unto the Lord (2 Cor 3:16) in total submission and obedience. The verb *epistrephō*, in the sense of religious conversion, also occurs in Jas 5:20 and 1 Pet 2:25. One's conversion experience may be so dramatic that the time of its occurrence may be recalled (so Paul and the Philippian jailer). On other occasions it may be sufficiently gradual as not to be readily identifiable (Timothy). The former is more common among those who have no prior knowledge of the Gospel; the latter is frequent among youth nurtured in a Christian home.

Conversion to God or to Jesus Christ involves the two closely related but distinguishable aspects of repentance and faith. We now reflect on where we have been (repentance) followed by where we are going (faith).

B. The Language of Repentance

The common Hebrew word for conversion or repentance (the terms are elastic and overlap) is the verb *šûb*, which occurs more than 1,050 times in the OT. Fundamentally, it means to "turn in an opposite direction" or "return" in a physical sense (Gen 18:33; Lev 22:13). From this derives the primary theological meaning, which is to turn penitently from sin to God. *Šûb* bears the latter meaning some 130 times in the Qal form (Deut 4:30; 30:2; Isa 19:22) and eleven times in the Hiphil stem (Neh 9:26; Ezek 14:6; 18:32). In its theological sense, *šûb* "includes repudiation of all sin and affirmation of God's total will for one's life."[68] The Septuagint version of the OT (the LXX) translates *šûb* by the Greek verb *epistrephō*. The Hebrew verb *nāḥam* in the Niphal means to "be sorry, have pity, repent." It is used of God being grieved and relenting (Gen 6:6-7; Exod 32:12-14; 1 Sam 15:11; Ps 106:45; Jer 18:8; Joel 2:14) more often than of humans repenting. Yet Job exclaimed, "I despise myself and repent in dust and ashes" (Job 42:6; cf. Jer 8:6; 31:19). The LXX translates the Hebrew verb *niḥam* by *metanoeō*. The OT verbs for repentance denote, negatively, a turning from old sinful ways (1 Kgs 8:35; Neh 9:35; Isa 59:20; Ezek 3:19) and, positively, a turning to the Lord (Ps 51:13; Jer 4:1; Hos 14:1; Mal 3:7).

In Mark's Gospel, John the Baptist went about "preaching a baptism of repentance (*metanoia*) for the forgiveness of sins" (Mark 1:4; cf. Luke 3:3). According to Matthew, the essence of John's message was, "Repent (present imperative of *metanoeō*), for the kingdom of heaven is near" (Matt 3:2). *Metanoia* occurs twenty-three times in the NT and literally means a "change of mind" (Matt 21:29) and, by extension, "repentance." *Metanoia*, however, is "not just a change of inward disposition but a complete turn-about of one's life, with all that such a re-direction implies of the need for God's help on the one side and of ethical conduct on man's side."[69] The Baptist's message (Mark 1:4; Luke 3:3) suggests that his baptism was linked with impending judgment and the need for forgiveness of sins. John's additional saying recorded in Matt 3:11—"I baptize you with water for repentance [*en hydati eis metanoian*]"—is instructive. The preposition *eis* is causal and should be translated "because of."[70] Thus John's baptism was a sign of prior repentance and a transformed life. The rite of baptism itself was not the efficient cause of the recipient's repentance or salvation.

C. The Nature of Repentance

Repentance is a change of mind, ultimate loyalty, and behavior whereby pre-Christians turn from sin unto God. In the Pentateuch Yahweh issued frequent warnings to Israel against profaning the sacred covenant. Yet the loving God also specified the path of return from violations thereof. After willfully sinning, Israel must acknowledge their "treachery" and "hostility" (Lev 26:40b), confess it to the Lord (v. 40a), and humbly repent of all known offenses (v. 41b). After Israel turned to the Lord, he would renew the covenant and bless them (v. 42). Moses commended the need for repentance and consecration by the metaphorical command to "circumcise" (*mûl*) the heart (v. 41; cf. Deut 10:16; 30:6; Jer 4:4). Figurative circumcision is commanded (Deut 10:16; Jer 4:4, 14) and performed by God (Deut 30:6). Repentance, moreover, is taught in Deuteronomy 30. Moses commanded Israel to "return (Kal of *šûb*) to the Lord your God and obey him with all your heart and with all your soul" (v. 2). According to v. 6, circumcision of the heart is a work of God himself. "God will transform the wills of his repentant people, bringing them once again in line with the covenant ideals."[71]

The OT historical books tell the story of Israel's repeated spiritual defection from Yahweh and consequent chastisement. Faithfully the Lord raised up leaders to call the covenant people to repentance. Toward the end of his life Joshua led Israel in a renewal of the sacred covenant. Central to this event was the summons, "throw away the foreign gods that are among you and yield your hearts to the Lord, the God of Israel" (Josh

24:23). Later, amidst widespread idolatry, Samuel called Israel to a similar act of repentance. "If you are returning [Kal of *šûb*] to the Lord with all your hearts, then rid yourselves of the foreign gods and the Ashtoreths and commit yourselves to the Lord and serve him only" (1 Sam 7:3). Inherent in their repentance were the responses of mourning, fasting, and prayer (v. 6). Solomon's prayer of temple dedication anticipated Israel's idolatry and prescribed the path of repentance. The penitent soul must "have a change of heart" (1 Kgs 8:47a), confess wrongdoing (v. 47b), pray and make supplication (v. 33), turn from known wickedness (v. 35), and return to the Lord with one's entire being (v. 48). Only then would Yahweh hear from heaven and forgive their sins (vv. 49-50). The verb *šûb* ("turn") occurs six times in this prayer of Solomon. Second Chron 7:14 also captures the essence of repentance: "if my people, who are called by my name, will humble themselves and pray and seek my face and turn (*šûb*) from their wicked ways, then will I hear from heaven and will forgive their sin and will heal their land."

Psalm 51, a penitential psalm David composed after his sin with Bathsheba, outlines God's pattern of repentance. (1) David expressed *awareness of sins* (vv. 1-3). David faced up to his sins when the prophet Nathan's charge convicted his conscience. (2) David offered heartfelt *confession of sins* (vv. 4-5). He acknowledged to the Lord not only the specific sins of which he was guilty (vv. 3-4) but also his inherently sinful character (v. 5). (3) David evidenced a true *attitude of contrition*, reflected by his acknowledgment of "a broken spirit" and "a broken and contrite heart" (v. 17). (4) He uttered a *prayer for pardon of sins* (vv. 7-9), beseeching God to "cleanse" and "wash" him and to "blot out" all his iniquities. (5) David sought an experience of profound *inner renewal* (vv. 10-12). So he prayed, "Create in me a pure heart, O God, and renew a steadfast spirit within me" (v. 10). The verb *bārā'* ("create") suggests that the radical change of heart is God's doing (cf. Ezek 11:19; 36:26). Finally, (6) David experienced the *joy* that comes from deliverance from sin and its consequences (v. 12).

Repentance, expressed by the verb *šûb*, is one of the dominant themes in the prophets (e.g., Isa 31:6; 44:22; 55:7; Ezek 18:30, 32; 33:11; Hos 3:5; Zech 1:3), and especially in Jeremiah (e.g., Jer 3:14; 18:11; 25:5; 26:3; 35:15; 36:3). Yahweh declared to his people through Isaiah, "In repentance [*šûbāh*, "returning"] and rest is your salvation, in quietness and trust [*biṭḥāh*, "confidence," "hope"] is your strength" (Isa 30:15). Similarly, the Lord through Ezekiel said to the house of Israel, "I will judge you, each one according to his ways, declares the Sovereign Lord. Repent! Turn away from your offenses; then sin will not be your downfall" (Ezek

18:30). The results of sincere repentance will be forgiveness of sins, healing of the land, and answered prayer (2 Chron 7:14; cf. Isa 55:7).

The prophets repudiated perfunctory, ritual forms of repentance (Isa 1:11; 29:13; 58:5; Jer 14:12; Hos 7:14). True repentance consists of acknowledgment of personal guilt (Jer 3:13), remorse for sins (Jer 31:19; Ezek 36:31; Jon 3:8a), forsaking evil thoughts and deeds (Isa 55:7; Jer 18:11; Ezek 14:6; Jon 3:8b), turning to the Lord with one's entire being (Isa 55:6; Joel 2:12), and bringing forth fruits indicative of a changed heart (Hos 12:6; 14:2). In response to genuine repentance, the Lord would withhold punishment (Jer 26:3), forgive sins (Isa 55:7), and grant life (Ezek 33:15-16). Those who fail to repent genuinely can expect divine judgment and death (Ezek 33:8-11, 14).

True repentance possesses three essential aspects. (1) An *intellectual* element. The repentant soul must understand God's holiness, righteousness, and displeasure against sin (Deut 25:16; 1 Kgs 14:22; Luke 16:15); must be aware of personal sin and guilt (Isa 6:5; Luke 18:13; Rom 3:20); and must be persuaded of God's readiness to forgive (Matt 6:14; Eph 4:32). (2) An *emotional* element, in which the penitent abhors sin (Ps 119:104; Ezek 20:43) and experiences godly sorrow and remorse, not for the pain it has caused himself, but for the grief it has caused God and others (Joel 2:12-13; Ps 51:4; 2 Cor 7:10). This aspect of repentance appears in the verb *nāḥam*, to "be sorry," "regret," "repent"—where the root idea means to breathe deeply. After gaining a fuller knowledge of God and a clearer perspective on himself, Job exclaimed, "I despise myself and repent (Niphal of *nāḥam*) in dust and ashes" (Job 42:6; cf. Jer. 31:19). (3) A *volitional* element, which involves determination to forsake sins and amend one's life. This aspect of repentance is emphasized by the verb *šûb*. Eliphaz replied to Job, "If you return [Kal of *šûb*] to the Almighty, you will be restored" (Job 22:23; cf. 36:10). According to Prov 28:13 (cf. Ps 32:3-5), repentance begins with confession of known sins followed by a forsaking of them: "He who conceals his sins does not prosper, but whoever confesses and renounces them finds mercy."

Significantly, the NT begins and ends with a call to repentance (Matt 3:2; Rev 3:19). Jesus began his ministry in Galilee with a summons to repentance identical to that of the Baptist (Matt 4:17). He also said, "I have not come to call the righteous, but sinners to repentance" (Luke 5:32). Repentance, as taught in the parable of the two sons (Matt 21:28-32), involves confession of sins and obedient action. Peter's response following his denial of Jesus points up the emotional aspect of true repentance: "he went outside and wept bitterly" (Matt 26:75). Christ gave an object lesson on repentance by placing a little child in the midst of his disciples and saying, "Unless you change [aorist subjunctive of *strephō*] and become like little children, you will never enter the kingdom of heaven" (Matt 18:3). Jesus contrasted the trust and humility of a child with the pride and self-seeking of many older people. The Lord plainly stated that failure to repent would result in judgment and death (Matt 3:10; 11:20-24; Luke 13:3, 5).

Paul taught that true repentance involves the emotional element of sorrow for misdeeds. Thus his "painful" letter to the Corinthians stimulated a "godly sorrow" that led to repentance unto salvation (2 Cor 7:9-11). Paul distinguished "godly sorrow" (*lypē kata theon*) from "worldly sorrow" (*lypē tou kosmou*)—the latter characterized not by remorse for offending God (the root of repentance), but by self-pity and self-anger (the root of depression). We note that God commands sinners to repent (Acts 3:19; 17:30; 26:20; Rev 3:3). Repentance thus is an action of the human will in ways that regeneration and justification are not.

The principal focus of repentance is that initial act by which sinners enter into the Christian life. But in addition, repentance is an ongoing response in the lives of the saints. In this sense Calvin wrote of Christians' need to "give attention to continual repentance."[72] Scripture speaks often of this neglected aspect of *metanoia* (Ps 51:7, 9-10, 12; Luke 22:31-32; Eph 4:22-23; Rev 2:5, 16, 22; 3:3, 19).

D. Repentance as a Divine Gift

Scripture suggests that the initiative in conversion and repentance lies with God himself. Thus the psalmist uttered the petition, "Restore [Kal of *šûb*] us again, O God our Savior" (Ps 85:4; cf. Ps 80:3, 7). And in Ps 85:6 he inquired of the Lord, "Will you not revive us again, that your people may rejoice in you?" The psalmist's desire was that God's people would turn to him rather than "return to folly" (Ps 85:8).

The prophets concurred that repentance is a divine enablement; the unsaved cannot turn from sins to the Lord by their own strength. Ephraim petitioned God, "Restore me, and I will return, because you are the Lord my God" (Jer 31:18). This text contains a play on words, for it literally reads, "Turn me back [Hiphil of *šûb*], and I will be turned" (Kal of *šûb*). A similar play on words occurs in Lam 5:21, "Restore us to yourself, O Lord, that we may return; renew our days as of old . . ." Jeremiah added that since sin is so ingrained, unbelievers (apart from special grace) cannot repent, any more than an Ethiopian can change his dark skin or a leopard his spotted coat (Jer 13:23).[73] With an eye to Israel's pervasive sinfulness, Yahweh said, "Their deeds do not permit them to return to their God" (Hos 5:4). Thus God must grant a spirit of prayerful repentance, as Zech 12:10 plainly teaches: "I will pour out on the house of David and the inhabitants of Jerusalem a spirit of grace and supplication." See also Lam 1:13.

Jesus himself suggested that apart from grace the unsaved cannot bring forth the positive spiritual responses necessary for salvation (Matt 7:17-18). The Lord's words, "Apart from me you can do nothing" (John 15:5) include the human act of repentance from sin. Peter and the apostles declared that "God exalted [Jesus] to his own right hand as Prince and Savior that he might give repentance and forgiveness of sins to Israel" (Acts 5:31). The Jewish-Christian leaders at Jerusalem, reflecting on the conversion of Cornelius' household, acknowledged that "God has even granted the Gentiles repentance unto life" (Acts 11:18). Paul agreed that repentance is a gift and enablement of God (Rom 2:4; 2 Tim 2:25). The gift of repentance cannot be understood as the general fruit of prevenient grace, for God's gift in the preceding Scriptures is not the *possibility* of repenting but the actual *enabled act*.[74] Repentance thus is a divinely enabled human response. God sovereignly arranges the circumstances and grants sinners the power to repent.

For sins to be forgiven God requires a repentant heart and life (Luke 24:47; Acts 2:38; 3:19). Depraved and darkened sinners, however, lack the spiritual will and power to turn from sin to God. Luther frequently stated that "Human nature utterly lacks the ability to obey God."[75] Under such circumstances God bestows on unworthy sinners the spirit of repentance as a gracious gift. The objection is frequently levied that God would not command what sinful humans are not capable of performing. However, as Custance observes, "God's command, *not man's ability*, is the measure of man's duty."[76] For example, God's command to love him is a valid requirement (Luke 10:25-28), even though self-centered sinners lack the ability to do so. Likewise, God commands sinners to keep his precepts and statutes so as to live (Lev 18:5; Rom 10:5), although he knows this to be an impossibility. God commands repentance at least for the reason that sinners never could say, "I did not know God expected this of me!"

E. The Language of Faith

Gen 15:6 presents the first biblical use of the verb to "believe." The Qal form of 'āman means to "stay," "nourish," or "support," whereas the Niphal connotes "be firm," "be established," hence metaphorically, "be faithful" (2 Sam 7:16; 1 Chron 17:23). The Hiphil of the verb means to "trust" or "believe in" (Exod 14:31; Num 14:11; Deut 9:23; Ps 78:22;

106:12; etc.). The LXX translates the Hiphil of *'āman* by the Greek verb *pisteuō*. The Hiphil of *'āman* followed by *kî* ("that") signifies belief in certain facts (Exod 4:5; Job 9:16), whereas with the preposition *be* ("in") it connotes belief or trust in a person or promise (Gen 15:6; Exod 14:31; 2 Chron 20:20; Jon 3:5). The noun "faith" is rare in the OT. The primary meaning of *'emûnāh* is "faithfulness" or "loyalty." Yet according to Rom 1:17 and Gal 3:11, Paul understood *'emûnāh* in Hab 2:4 as the "faith" that justifies and saves (ASV, RSV, NIV).

Righteous persons in OT times placed faith in Yahweh. 2 Kgs 18:5 states that "Hezekiah trusted in the Lord, the God of Israel." The verb *bāṭaḥ* occurs nine times in 2 Kings 18–19 alone. Frequently used with *be* ("in") or *'al* ("upon"), *bāṭaḥ* signifies to "confide in," "lean upon," or "trust" (Ps 13:5; 25:2; 84:12; Prov 16:20; Isa 26:3-4). The verb denotes not mere intellectual assent but confident reliance upon God and the well-being that attends such trust. See also 1 Chron 5:20. The verb *bāṭaḥ* occurs fifty times in Israel's hymnbook. Thus David said to the Lord, "I trust in your unfailing love; my heart rejoices in your salvation" (Ps 13:5; cf. 22:4; 26:1; 33:21). And Solomon wrote, "Trust [Kal of *bāṭaḥ*] in the Lord with all your heart and lean not on your own understanding" (Prov 3:5; cf. 16:20; 28:25; 29:25).

On the basis of the preceding Scriptures we must disagree with theologians such as the liberal Knudson, who asserted that only with the coming of Jesus Christ did the inner life become in any significant way a life of faith. Knudson insisted that "In the Old Testament comparatively little was said about faith."[77] The OT data clearly repudiate such a judgment.

The NT writers used the noun *pistis* and the verb *pisteuō* some 240 times. *Pistis* ("faith," "trust," "belief"), used in a soteriological sense with respect to God, Christ, or the Gospel, occurs in various combinations: (1) *Pistis* is used with the objective genitive, literally in the sense of faith "in," "toward," or "concerning" (Mark 11:22; Acts 3:16; Rom 3:22; Gal 2:20; Phil 3:9; etc.). In various prepositional phrases, it is used with (2) *pros* plus the accusative, in the sense of faith "directed toward" (1 Thess 1:8; Phile 5; 1 Pet 1:21); (3) with *eis* plus the accusative, in the literal sense of "in" or "into" (Acts 20:21; 24:24; 26:18); (4) with *epi* plus the dative, in the sense of "on" or "upon" (Rom 9:33); (5) with *epi* plus the accusative, in the sense of "toward" (Heb 6:1); and (6) with *en* plus the dative, in the sense of "in" or "on" (Rom 3:25; Gal 3:26; Eph 1:15; 1 Tim 3:13; 2 Tim 3:15).

The verb *pisteuō* ("believe [in]," "have faith [in]," "entrust") is used in a soteriological sense (1) alone (Mark 15:32; John 4:42, 53; 9:38; Rom 3:22; 10:4; 2 Cor 4:13; 2 Thess 1:10), (2) with a dative noun, chiefly in the sense of believing assent (some forty-five times in the NT: e.g., Matt 21:25;

27:42; John 2:22; 4:50; 5:3, 46; Rom 4:3; 2 Thess 2:12), and (3) with *hoti* plus a noun clause (Rom 10:9; Jas 2:19). John used the latter construction fourteen times to denote revealed truths to which one must give assent (e.g., John 6:69; 8:24; 16:27, 30; 20:31; 1 John 5:1, 5). The verb is also used with various pronouns in the more religiously profound sense of trust or reliance, such as (4) *epi* plus the accusative (Matt 27:42; Acts 9:42; 16:31; Rom 4:5, 24); (5) *epi* plus the dative (Rom 9:33; 10:11; 1 Tim 1:16; 1 Pet 2:6); (6) *eis* plus the accusative (Matt 18:6; Phil 1:29; Col 2:5; and some forty times in John: 1:12; 2:11; 3:15, 16, 18; etc.); and (7) *en* plus the dative (Mark 1:15; John 3:15; Eph 1:13). John had a strong preference for the verb *pisteuō* (ninety-eight times in the Gospel, ten times in 1 John), while using *pistis* sparingly (only in 1 John 5:4; Rev 2:13, 19; 13:10; 14:12).

F. The Nature of Saving Faith

Faith is the means by which we receive justification and salvation. Faith's reality is seen in an incident early in OT history. Concerning the offspring of Adam and Eve, Gen 4:4-5 states that "The Lord looked with favor on Abel and his offering, but on Cain and his offering he did not look with favor." Outwardly, both brothers presented to the Lord offerings from the firstfruits of their respective occupations. Yet God was pleased with Abel's offering but not with Cain's because the former, unlike the latter, brought his gift with trust in God. Hence the inspired writer of Hebrews commented, "By faith Abel offered God a better sacrifice than Cain did. By faith he was commended as a righteous man, when God spoke well of his offerings" (Heb 11:4).

Consider also the example of Abram the Chaldean, the chief example of faith in the OT. In Gen 12:1-3 the Lord called Abram and promised him a posterity and a land (cf. Gen 13:14-17; 15:4-5; etc.). Persuaded that God would do what he had promised, Abram obediently moved from Haran to Canaan, built an altar, and called on the name of the Lord. Later God renewed the covenant and promised Abram and Sarah a son in their old age (Gen 15:4). Concerning Abram's response to God's promise, it is written, "Abram believed [Hiphil of *'āman*] the Lord and he credited it to him as righteousness" (Gen 15:6). The patriarch's faith was both cognitive and personal; he believed God's word of promise (cf. Heb 11:8-12, 17-19), and he committed his soul to the God who had revealed himself. The NT extols Abraham as a paradigm of saving faith (Rom 4:16-22; Gal 3:7). We learn from Gen 15:6 and 17:10-14 that the patriarch was justified fourteen years before he was circumcised. The order of events in Abraham's life likely was faith, justification, followed by circumcision (cf. Rom 4:9-

11). Later Judaism inverted this divine order of internal reality followed by external ritual.

The OT incident of the brazen serpent further illustrates the character of saving faith. God commanded Moses to place a bronze snake on a pole so that "when anyone was bitten by a snake and looked at the bronze snake, he lived" (Num 21:9). The serpent fixed to the pole anticipated Christ who took the form of a man and who was cursed for us. For the healing to occur, no religious work was involved; a person simply looked in faith and lived (cf. John 3:14-15).

With a play on words the prophet Isaiah (7:9) exhorted wavering Ahaz, "If you do not stand firm in your faith [Hiphil of 'āman], you will not stand at all" [Hiphal of 'āman]. Compare the RSV, "If you will not believe, surely you shall not be established." According to Isa 28:16, "the one who trusts [Hiphil of 'āman] will never be dismayed." The same verse identifies the *object* of that trust as "a tested stone, a precious cornerstone for a sure foundation"—which the NT identifies as Christ (cf. Rom 9:33; 1 Pet 2:6). Emphasizing the idea of confident reliance, Jeremiah wrote, "blessed is the man who trusts [bāṭaḥ] in the Lord, whose confidence [mibṭāḥ] is in him" (Jer 17:7). Essential to genuine conversion is the personal response of faith. As a result of Jonah's preaching, "The Ninevites believed [Hiphil of 'āman] God [bē'lōhîm]. They declared a fast, and all of them, from the greatest to the least, put on sackcloth" (Jon 3:5). Note how closely faith and repentance are related in this text.

Foundational to saving faith is *knowledge* of Christ's person and saving work. John envisaged faith as having a solid intellectual basis; hence he commended belief in Jesus' preexistent deity (John 8:24), ontological unity with the Father (John 14:11), identity as the Son of God (John 11:27; 1 John 4:15) and promised Messiah (John 6:69; 1 John 5:1), incarnation at the Father's initiative (John 11:42; 17:8, 21), and full humanity (1 John 4:2). In the Acts the object of faith most often was the person of Jesus Christ (Acts 11:17; 14:23; 16:31; 19:4; etc.); but it was also the preached word (Acts 4:4; 17:11) and the body of saving doctrine revealed by God (Acts 6:7; 13:8; 14:22; 16:5). In the sense of assenting to crucial truths about Jesus Christ, Christians were designated "the believers" (*hoi pisteusantes*, Acts 2:44; 4:32).

Similarly, in Paul's letters saving faith meant correct beliefs about Christ's person and work: for example, "saved . . . through belief in the truth" (2 Thess 2:13; cf. Tit 1:1). There can be no saving faith without hearing and understanding the Gospel (Rom 10:14, 17; 1 Cor 15:1-8, 11). In this sense Paul wrote of "the faith" (*hē pistis*), namely, the body of Christian doctrine one must believe in order to be saved (Gal 1:23; Eph

4:5; Phil 1:27; often in the Pastorals: 1 Tim 3:9; 4:1, 6; 6:10, 21; 2 Tim 4:7; Tit 1:13). The object of faith determines its character and saving efficacy; a vague and unspecified faith (e.g., "I believe") avails for naught. Scripture allows for degrees of faith (Rom 14:1). But the minimum beliefs one must assent to for salvation include Christ's coming in human flesh, his atoning death, and his resurrection from the grave. Against those of existentialist persuasion, faith is not a blind leap in the dark. Knowledge of who Christ is and what he has done is indispensable to saving faith.

To intellectual knowledge of essential doctrines must be added emotional *assent* of the heart to the realities they signify. Jesus said to his disciples, "How foolish you are, and how slow of heart to believe all that the prophets have spoken! Did not the Christ have to suffer these things and then enter his glory?" (Luke 24:25). The personal assent dimension of faith is reflected in John's use of *pisteuein* with the dative (John 2:22; 4:50; 5:47) and with *hoti*. Saving faith meant believing assent to OT teachings or to the words of Jesus himself. John stated the purpose of his Gospel: "that you may believe that [*hoti*] Jesus is the Christ, the Son of God" (John 20:31).

For Paul, to become a Christian one must assent from the heart to the realities of Jesus' atoning death (1 Cor 15:3; 1 Thess 4:14), resurrection (Rom 10:9; 1 Cor 15:4, 17; 1 Thess 4:14), and divine lordship (Rom 10:9). Intellectual knowledge of God's saving plan, while absolutely necessary, is not sufficient for salvation. Correct beliefs must be followed by assent to their personal relevance. Another way of putting this is to say that knowledge of the mind must be followed by knowledge of the heart (Col 1:9-10).

Saving faith, finally, must include wholehearted *trust* and *commitment* to Christ, evidenced by obedience and good works. This aspect of faith involves cleaving to Christ and appropriating his benefits. While occasionally expressing this reality by *pisteuein en* (John 3:15), John's favorite expression was *pisteuein eis*, "to believe on" Christ (John 1:12; 2:11; 3:16, 18, 36; 4:39; 6:29, 35, 40, 47; 8:30; 9:35-36; 10:42; 11:25-26; etc.). This element of volitional trust or appropriation of the Savior is evident in John 1:12, which reads, "to all who received [*elabon*] him, to those who believed in [*pisteuousin eis*] his name, he gave the right to become children of God." The aorist of *lambanō* connotes the personal act of receiving Christ into one's life, whereas the present participle of *pisteuō* with *eis* implies the continuous exercise of faith in the Savior. The appropriational element of faith is strikingly clear in John 6:53-56, where the dramatic imagery of eating Christ's flesh and drinking his blood signifies making the benefits of Christ's atoning death a profound part of one's deepest being.

Paul also affirmed that saving faith involves trust in and commitment to Christ (Acts 16:31; Col 2:5) or God (Rom 4:24; 1 Thess 1:8). For the apostle, faith involves intellectual understanding and emotional assent to cardinal truths (see above); but it also means volitional surrender to Christ, evidenced by love (1 Cor 13:2; Gal 5:6), obedience (Rom 1:5; 16:26), and good works (1 Thess 1:3; Tit. 2:14; 3:8). Biblically speaking, a great gulf exists between knowing *about* a person and *knowing* the person in a relationship of trust and commitment. The former is theoretical and formal, the latter is experiential and personal. One may be a brilliant philosopher or theologian, be able to discourse eloquently about God, but fail to know Christ the Lord in a trusting relationship. Such a person has a form of knowledge but not the knowledge of faith. Calvin insightfully defined this third aspect of faith as our "warm embrace of Christ, by which he dwells in us, and we are filled with the Divine Spirit."[78] We noted that true faith results in obedience—disobedience reflecting absence of faith (Eph 2:2; 5:6). In this respect Paul agreed with James's definition of faith mentioned below (Jas 2:14-26). As in our discussion of repentance, faith is not only the initial response by which one is saved; it is also a mode of living before God that should grow extensively and intensively (2 Cor 10:15; 2 Thess 1:3). From the above considerations, Scripture knows much about "explicit faith," but little about so-called "implicit faith."

James opposed the view, held by certain Christians, that assent to truths can stand alone, i.e., without being validated by good works. The NIV translation of Jas 2:14 highlights the issue with the rhetorical question, "Can *such* faith save him?" (italics added). James responded that correct beliefs if not followed by loving deeds are not merely unfruitful, they are useless and dead (v. 17). James added that like his opponents, the demons believe in the unity and uniqueness of God (v. 19). But such a faith, though composed of right beliefs, lacks saving power. At first blush it appears that Paul and James clashed on their views of faith. But whereas the former appealed to Abraham's faith in God's promise given before Isaac was born, the latter pointed to the evidence of Abraham's faith manifested by his willingness to sacrifice his beloved son (vv. 21-23). James wrote, "You see that a person is justified by what he does and not by faith alone" (v. 24). Paul and James thus held complementary, rather than contradictory, views of justification. The former used the verb *dikaioō* in the sense of a secret vindication by God, the latter in the sense of a public vindication by others. "For both Paul and James 'justify' means to *declare righteous*. In the case of Paul, it is God who declares the believer righteous. In the case of James, it is a man's works which declare him righteous by showing that he is a man of faith."[79]

Hebrews presents a distinctive portrait of faith. The author, who used *pisteuō* twice but the noun *pistis* thirty-one times, viewed faith as patient endurance and hope in the face of persecution. Writing to believers tempted to revert to the security of Judaism, Hebrews depicts faith as the confidence that God will fulfill his promises and uphold his people (3:6; 10:23; 11:11). Similar to hope (cf. 1 Pet 1:21), faith enables Christian converts to go beyond present trials to apprehend future and invisible realities promised by God. Thus Heb 11:1 (NRSV) states, "Now faith is the assurance [*hypostasis*, "reality"] of things hoped for, the conviction [*elenchos*, "proof" or "conviction"] of things not seen." Heb 11:4-40 catalogues many examples of this kind of faith among Israel's heroes. The writer invited wavering saints to "believe that [*pisteuein hoti*] he [i.e., God] exists and that he rewards those who earnestly seek him" (Heb 11:6).

G. *Faith as a Divine Gift*

Just as we found repentance to be a gift and an enablement of God, so also is faith. Although in his ministry Jesus repeatedly called for faith, he seemed to suggest that faith is inspired and sustained by God the Holy Spirit. For example, people who witnessed Jesus feed the 5,000 asked him, "What must we do to do the works God requires?" (John 6:28). There by the Sea of Galilee, Jesus shifted the focus from themselves to God; so he responded to the crowd, "The work [*ergon*] of God is this: to believe in the one he has sent" (v. 29).

Paul likewise envisaged saving faith as a free gift of God. It is likely that in Eph 2:8, "it is by grace you have been saved, through faith—and this not from yourselves, it is the gift of God," the antecedent of "this" (*touto*, neuter) is salvation in its totality, of which faith is one important element. Elsewhere the apostle explicitly attributed the rise of faith to God. Thus, "no one can say, 'Jesus is Lord,' except by the Holy Spirit" (1 Cor 12:3). Furthermore, "it has been granted [*echaristhē*] to you on behalf of Christ not only to believe on him, but also to suffer for him" (Phil 1:29).[80] As Paul recalled his conversion experience he wrote, "The grace of our Lord was poured out on me abundantly, along with [*meta*] the faith and love that are in Christ Jesus" (1 Tim 1:14). The preposition *meta* connects grace with faith and love as divine bestowments. See also 1 Cor 3:6, Eph 6:23, and 2 Thess 2:13.[81]

Heb 12:2 describes Jesus as "the author and perfecter of our faith." By this the writer meant that Christ not only begins the work of faith in believers, but also that he will bring faith to a triumphant conclusion. Peter likewise regarded faith as a divine endowment when he addressed those "who through the righteousness of our God and Savior Jesus Christ have received a faith as precious as ours" (2 Pet 1:1).

The preceding texts show that neither oratorical excellence, nor heavy-handed persuasion, nor clever evangelistic methods can elicit true faith. Only the power of God through the Spirit can produce living faith in spiritually dead sinners (1 Cor 2:1-5; cf. 1:17). Calvin simply but profoundly stated that "faith is the principal work of the Holy Spirit."[82] More boldly, Karl Barth added, "in himself and from his own resources man has not an atom either of willingness or even of capacity for faith."[83] Faith is not the human *condition* for receiving new life; it is the divinely given *instrument* by which God saves lost souls.

How God justly could require faith in those who are spiritually incapable of believing follows the lines of our discussion of repentance above. God requires faith as man's proper duty based on his saving work in Christ, and thus he extends to all a legitimate invitation to believe (John 3:15; 20:31; 1 John 5:4). However, sinners rendered spiritually impotent by sinful necessity are incapable of bringing forth saving faith. Whereupon God the Holy Spirit engenders the required faith in dead sinners as authentic human responses—although not universally. Hence Christ's disciples preach the Gospel to all people, not knowing to whom God will graciously grant saving faith. Sin-caused inability does not absolve one's duty to believe. For example, persons intoxicated by alcohol or drugs are not released from the obligation to drive their automobiles in accordance with the law even though, in their impaired condition, they are incapable of doing so. Kevan helpfully sums up the matter, as follows:

> God's call exhibits, not man's power, but God's claim; not what man is able to do, but what he ought to do. Man must be told that although he cannot come to Christ, he must come. It is in this strange antinomy of experience that the sinner flings himself into the arms of God's mercy, being enabled so to do by sovereign grace, yet in so doing discovering that it is God and God alone who has saved him and brought him to Himself.[84]

H. *Reflection on Ordering Relations*

Arminians commonly assert that in conversion the act of repentance precedes faith. Wiley wrote that "Repentance leads immediately to saving faith, which is at once the condition and the instrument of justification."[85] Most high Calvinists, on the other hand, reverse the order. Calvin held that repentance is produced by faith as fruit from a tree. He wrote, "it ought to be a fact beyond controversy that repentance not only constantly follows faith, but is also born of faith."[86] Conversion, however, is a single act that has two distinct but inseparable aspects. *Repentance*, the forsaking of sin and the cultivating of a new hope, and *faith*, turning to Christ in belief and trust, are related to one another as two sides of a coin. The two are *interdependent* responses, each incomplete without the other. Thus conversion involves both a believing repentance and a penitent faith. True repentance requires belief, and full-orbed faith requires a repentant spirit. It is psychologically impossible to believe in the biblical sense without a broken, penitent spirit that renounces sin. Likewise, it is equally impossible to repent properly without assent to the imperatives of God's word. As stated by Murray, "It is impossible to disentangle faith and repentance. Saving faith is permeated with repentance and repentance is permeated with faith."[87] We may isolate the two for purposes of discussion. For example, we may say that repentance is chiefly conversion in its backward glance (turning from sin), whereas faith is primarily conversion in its forward glance (turning to God). In reality, however, repentance and faith are two aspects of the unified experience of conversion. Thus it is unwise to assert the priority of one over the other chronologically or logically.

It appears inconsistent with the biblical data to view repentance as an effect or fruit of faith. In *Christians*, ongoing repentance undoubtedly is a fruit of faith. But with regard to *unbelievers*, the many direct calls to repentance by Jesus (Matt 4:17; Luke 5:32; 13:3, 5) and the apostles (Mark 6:12; Acts 2:38; 17:30; 26:20a) forbid us from regarding repentance as a discrete response subsequent to faith. Add to this the instances in which the summons to repentance precedes that of faith in the ministry of Jesus (Matt 21:32; Mark 1:15), the preaching of Paul (Acts 20:21), and the letter to the Hebrews (6:1). Conversion is an effect of sovereign election and effectual calling; and growing obedience (1 John 3:23-24) and good works (Matt 3:8; Acts 26:20b; Jas 2:20-22) are fruits of conversion. The same relation, however, does not hold with respect to faith and repentance. The Reformational distinctive of *sola fides* does not exclude the godly sorrow for sin and the turning therefrom that constitutes biblical repentance.

Furthermore, faith does not appear to be an effect or fruit of regeneration, as many Calvinists maintain. Rather, clear biblical texts suggest that the act of faith logically precedes regeneration. John 1:12-13 indicates that receiving Christ in faith results in the new birth and inclusion in the family of God. According to John 7:37-39, faith precedes the gift of the Spirit in regenerating and sanctifying power. First John 5:1, however, states that faith and love are signs that persons have been born of God. Most Scriptures represent saving faith as a condition of God's regenerating work. The notion that God regenerates prior to the sinner's response of penitent faith (chronologically or logically) appears to be biblically unwarranted. The spiritual dynamic that prompts and empowers sinners to convert resides not in regeneration but in the power of the Spirit's effectual calling (see chap. 5). Special calling stops short of effecting the complete transformation of life commonly represented by the term regeneration (see chap. 7).

I. The 'Lordship Salvation' Debate

The issue at hand is whether, in addition to belief in the Gospel, repentance from sin, obedience to God, and submission to Christ's lordship are necessary for sinners to be saved. Is the addition of a requirement other than belief consistent with the Reformation principle of *sola fides* (salvation by faith alone)? Ryrie rejects the need for sinners to commit their lives to Christ as Lord to be saved. Submission to Christ's lordship, he argues, cannot be a condition of salvation in the same way that faith is. States Ryrie, "The message of faith only and the message of faith plus commitment of life cannot both be the gospel; therefore, one of them is a false gospel and comes under the curse of perverting the gospel or preaching another gospel (Gal 1:6-9)."[88] The NT call to receive Jesus Christ as Lord (Acts 2:36; 16:31; Rom 10:9) is a summons to acknowledge his *deity* rather than his sovereignty. Ryrie observes that all the world's religious and cult leaders demand mastery over their followers; hence, there is nothing unique about Christ being a sinner's master. Neither, he adds, is repentance—defined as sorrow for sin—required for salvation: "being sorry for sins or even changing one's mind and thus his life will not of *itself* bring salvation."[89] Ryrie claims that the Christ's lordship is strictly a matter of Christian discipleship, i.e., of instruction and growth. One can become a Christian without being Christ's disciple. "To make the conditions for the life of discipleship requirements for becoming a disciple is to confuse the gospel utterly by muddying the clear waters of [the] grace of God with the works of man."[90]

Zane Hodges also argues that faith alone, apart from repentance or submission to Christ's lordship, is necessary for salvation. Hodges rejects the Reformational view of faith as *notitia, assensus,* and *fiducia.* Rather, faith is simply believing saving facts about Jesus or taking God at his Word. Thus faith is "the *inward conviction* that what God says to us in the Gospel is true. That—and that alone—is saving faith."[91] Hodges focuses on Jesus' conversation with the Samaritan woman at the well and notes that the Lord required her to *receive* the water of life, not to surrender her life to him.

> It must be emphasized that there is no call here for surrender, sub-
> mission, acknowledgment of Christ's Lordship, or anything else of
> this kind. A gift is being offered to one totally unworthy of God's
> favor. And to get it, the woman is required to make no spiritual
> commitment whatsoever. She is merely invited to ask. It is precisely
> this impressive fact that distinguishes the true Gospel from all its
> counterfeits.[92]

Repentance, Hodges avers, is a response that properly occurs later on
in the Christian life. It has to do with the believer's communion with God
and discipleship, not with the gift of eternal life. He writes that "the call
to faith represents the call to eternal salvation. The call to repentance is
the call to enter into harmonious relations with God."[93] To make repentance a requisite for salvation, he argues, corrupts the doctrine of justification by faith, confounds the simplicity of salvation, and turns the
Gospel of free grace into a system of works. Hodges concludes that "The
doctrine of lordship salvation destroys the very foundation on which true
holiness must be built. By returning to the principles of the law, it has forfeited the spiritual power of grace."[94]

On the other side of the debate, A.W. Tozer (d. 1963) frequently claimed
that saving faith includes submission to Christ's lordship. He wrote that the
increasingly popular, evangelical view that says, "There is no need to
repent, surrender and obey Christ; just come to him and believe on him as
Savior" is flatly heretical. Tozer insisted that the Nazarene is the *Lord Jesus
Christ*! Accordingly, sinners must believe on, surrender to, and obey the
One who is Savior and Lord. Tozer wrote, "We take Him for what He is—
the anointed Savior and Lord who is King of kings and Lord of lords! He
would not be who He is if He saved us and called us and chose us without
the understanding that He can also guide and control our lives."[95]

John Stott likewise argues that saving faith must submit to the lordship
of Christ, on the basis of three considerations. Saving faith (1) presupposes
repentance (renunciation of sin), (2) includes obedience (total commitment
to Christ), and (3) issues in newness of life (holiness). Writes Stott, "it is as
unbiblical as it is unrealistic to divorce the Lordship from the Saviorhood
of Jesus Christ. He is 'our Lord and Savior Jesus Christ,' and saving faith
is commitment to Him who is both Son of God and Savior of men."[96]

J.I. Packer also opposes forms of evangelism that cheapen and trivial-
ize Christ's demands. He asks rhetorically whether presentations of the
Gospel that require only mental assent will "leave [sinners] supposing that
all they have to do is to trust Christ as a sin-bearer, not realizing that they
must also deny themselves and enthrone Him as their Lord (the error
which we might call only-believism)?"[97] James Boice rejects as "cheap

grace" the notion that Christ can be received as Savior without being received as Lord. He writes, "there is only one Savior, the *Lord* Jesus Christ, and . . . anyone who believes in a Savior who is not the Lord is not believing the true Christ and is not regenerate. We call for commitment to Christ, the true Christ."[98]

John MacArthur also repudiates the easy-believism of present-day evangelicalism that asks sinners to invite Jesus into their hearts with no evident commitment to his lordship. MacArthur makes at least four points relative to the Savior-Lord issue. (1) *The call to salvation is a call to discipleship.* The notion that one may decide to become a disciple subsequent to profession of faith is a perversion of the Gospel. "The gospel Jesus preached was a call to discipleship, a call to follow him in submissive obedience, not just a plea to make a decision or pray a prayer."[99] (2) *Repentance is a critical element in saving faith.* MacArthur observes that Jesus called sinners to repentance (Matt 4:17; Luke 5:32), as did his apostles in their preaching (Acts 3:19; 20:21; 26:20). Repentance involves three essential elements: "a turning to God; a turning from evil; and the intent to serve God. No change of mind can be called true repentance without including all three elements."[100] MacArthur adds that "No evangelism that omits the message of repentance can properly be called the gospel, for sinners cannot come to Jesus Christ apart from a radical change of heart, mind, and will."[101] (3) *Faith is inseparable from obedience.* The idea that faith is merely knowledge of (*notitia*) and assent to (*assensus*) truths about Christ is false and dangerous. To these two must be added personal commitment to Jesus Christ (*fiducia*). "Mere knowing and affirming facts apart from obedience to the truth is not believing in the biblical sense."[102] In sum, (4) *one must confess Christ's lordship to be saved.* MacArthur believes that Christ's lordship and his saviorhood are inseparable. "Lord" signifies not only Jesus' deity but also his sovereign prerogative over human lives. From Scriptures such as Acts 2:21, 2:36, 16:31, and Rom 10:9, he concludes, "it is clear that people who come to Christ for salvation must do so in obedience to Him, that is, with a willingness to surrender to him as Lord."[103] Thus the lordship of Christ (involving ideas of authority, sovereignty, and the right to govern) is an essential part of the Gospel one must believe for salvation.

What light does Scripture shed on this debated issue? Consider (1) the meaning and relations of repentance. Sometimes the Bible enjoins repentance alone (Matt 4:17; Luke 13:3, 5; Acts 2:38; 3:19; 17:30; 26:20; etc.), other times faith alone (Luke 8:12; Acts 16:31; frequently in John: 1:12; 2:23; 3:18; 5:24; 6:29; etc.), and still other times both repentance and faith (Matt 21:32; Mark 1:15; Acts 20:21; Heb 6:1). Such variations were prompted by the needs of the original hearers and the writer's audience. Moreover, faith is implicit in repentance, and repentance in faith within the unity of the act of conversion. Hence it is impossible to sever repentance from the faith that saves. Calvin correctly observed that "repentance and faith are so linked together that they can not be separated."[104] Repentance involves turning from the old way of life and renouncing every known sin. It involves the decision to relinquish all our idols, false loves, and splendid vices in order to come to Christ. For conversion to be genuine the penitent must, *as far as he or she can determine*, turn from all ungodly loyalties. There is no such thing as a partial repentance; it is psychologically impossible to turn away from sin and to cling to sin simultaneously. As Finney noted, "To talk of partial repentance as a possible thing is to talk nonsense. It is to overlook the very nature of repentance."[105] The prodigal son had to leave behind the swine and the prostitutes in the far country before returning to the waiting father. Spurgeon correctly claimed "That there is a repentance that needs to be repented of"—i.e., a pseudo-repentance that lacks complete abhorrence and renunciation of sin.[106] Finally, we have seen that repentance (like faith) is a gift of God. Thus, the sinner's act of repentance involves not the slightest hint of legalism or works-righteousness.

Moreover, (2) saving faith is an act of commitment to Christ and in some sense an act of grateful obedience. The latter is inherent in what theologians denominate as *fiducia*. Observe how often Scripture juxtaposes faith and obedience. John wrote, "Whoever believes [*pisteuōn*] in the Son has eternal life; whoever disobeys [*apeithōn*] the Son will not see life, but must endure God's wrath" (John 3:36, NRSV). In Scripture disobedience clearly is failure to believe (Rom 11:30; Eph 2:2; Tit 3:3; Heb 4:6). Conversely, believing is an act of obedience. Luke observed that in Jerusalem "the word of God spread . . . and a large number of priests became obedient to the faith" (Acts 6:7). Paul wrote that "not all the Israelites accepted [*hypēkousan*] the good news. For Isaiah says, 'Lord, who has believed [*episteusen*] our message?'" (Rom 10:16). In the Romans doxology the apostle longed that the Gospel, now proclaimed to Gentiles, might "bring about the obedience of faith" (*eis hypakoēn pisteōs*, Rom 16:26; cf. 1:5). Obedience to God, therefore, is virtually a synonym for saving faith, as many texts indicate (Matt 19:17; Acts 5:32; Rom 15:18; 2 Thess 1:8; 1 Pet 1:2; 4:17). Spurgeon subscribed to the thesis of this paragraph with great passion. "The only trust that saves is that practical trust which obeys Jesus Christ. Faith that does not obey is dead faith,—nominal faith. It is the outside of faith, the bark of faith, but it is not the vital core of faith."[107] Girod helpfully summed up the nature of the faith that saves: "Faith is knowledge;

faith is conviction; faith is surrender. These three. Blessed is the man who adds to knowledge, conviction, and to conviction, surrender. To him belongs the kingdom of God."[108]

Eugene Peterson's contemporary translation of the NT (*The Message*) is refreshing and enlightening. Hear his translation of John 1:12: "whoever did want him [Jesus], who believed he was who he claimed *and would do what he said* (italics added), he made to be . . . their child-of-God selves."[109] Consider also his rendering of John 5:24: "Anyone here who believes what I am saying right now and aligns himself with the Father, *who has in fact put me in charge*, has at this very moment the real, lasting life and is no longer condemned to be an outsider" (italics added).[110] Obedience to Christ's lordship is an intrinsic aspect of saving faith.

Consider (3) the title "Lord" ascribed to Jesus in the NT. *Kyrios* applied to Jesus is used as a polite form of address akin to "Rabbi" (Matt 8:8; Luke 9:59). Nevertheless, "This form of address also implies recognition of Jesus as a leader, and willingness to obey him (Matt 7:21; 21:29ff.; Luke 6:46)."[111] *Kyrios* also denotes Christ's deity (Luke 2:11; Rom 10:9; 1 Cor 12:3; Phil 2:11). But inherent in Christ's deity is the fact of his sovereignty over all. As the risen, ascended, and seated Lord, Christ exercises dominion over the entire universe (Eph 1:20-23; Phil 2:9-11), including those who would be saved. That the title "Lord" includes the sense of "sovereign" is clear from the following texts. (a) John 13:13-14, where Jesus said to his disciples, "You call me 'Teacher' and 'Lord,' and rightly so, for that is what I am. Now that I, your Lord and Teacher, have washed your feet, you also should wash one another's feet." (b) John 20:28, where believing Thomas addressed Jesus as "My Lord and my God!" (c) Rom 14:9, where Paul wrote that "Christ died and returned to life so that he might be the Lord of both the dead and the living." (d) 1 Cor 8:5-6, where Paul noted that unbelievers worship "many 'gods' and many 'lords'" (i.e., masters), but for Christians "there is but one God, the Father . . . ; and there is but one Lord, Jesus Christ, through whom all things came and through whom we live." (e) Eph 4:5-6, where the apostle stated that there is "one Lord, one faith, one baptism; one God and Father of all, who is over all and through all and in all." (f) Col 2:6, "just as you received Christ Jesus as Lord, continue to live in him, rooted and built up in him . . ." (cf. v. 10). And (g) Jude 4 describes the godless unsaved as those who deface the grace of God and "deny Jesus Christ our only Sovereign (*despotēs*) and Lord" (cf. 2 Pet 2:1).

In addition, (4) seekers of salvation cannot partition Christ's work any more than his person. The Lord Jesus Christ exercised the redemptive ministries of prophet, priest, and king. We saw in chap. 4 that Christ as prophet faithfully communicates God's Word; as priest he shed his blood as atonement for sins and he intercedes for his people in heaven; and as king he conquers evil and protects and defends his people forever. Sinners who come to Christ must embrace the Savior whom God appointed prophet, priest, and king. We cannot accept the prophet who speaks the saving Word and the priest who laid down his life on the cross while rejecting the king who rules over his subjects. A truncated ministry betrays a truncated Christ who would be no Savior at all. God, who is wiser than we, has wisely ordained that sinners embrace his Son as prophet (herald), priest (sacrifice), and king (sovereign over life).

We conclude that for conversion to be authentic and transforming, pre-Christians must make the Lord Jesus Christ the object of their exclusive loyalty. This means that *to the best of their knowledge* penitents will forsake all known vice and cling to the Savior as their only hope of salvation. Genuine conversion thus will involve sincere repentance, total commitment to Christ, and submission to the Lord's sovereign rule. We are not saying that faith *plus* works saves; we simply invite an honest assessment of what biblical conversion involves. We tremble at the fact that it is possible for a person to believe in Christ without being united to him savingly. As James wrote, the "demons believe—and shudder" (Jas 2:19, NRSV). We must avoid a cheap and easy-believism that fails to repent and commit the whole of life to the Lord Jesus Christ, our prophet, priest, and king.

IV. PRACTICAL IMPLICATIONS OF THE DOCTRINE OF CONVERSION

A. *Live a Life of Repentance and Faith*

Since believers are not perfected in this life and the flesh relentlessly assaults the Spirit (see chap. 10), there is need for continual repentance subsequent to conversion. In the first of his ninety-five theses Luther wrote that "Our Lord and Master Jesus Christ . . . willed that the whole life of believers should be repentance." Calvin likewise observed that in our slow and painful advance toward holiness, Christians need to practice repentance until the day of their death. "We must strive toward repentance itself, devote ourselves to it throughout life, and pursue it to the very end if we would abide in Christ."[112] Ongoing repentance in the Christian life involves sorrow for sin, a deliberate turning from sin, honest confession of known sins (1 John 1:8-9; Jas 5:16), making restitution wherever possible (Acts 26:20), mortifying the old nature (Col 2:11; 3:5, 8-9), and putting on the new self (Col 3:10). Repentance thus is an important constituent in the believer's life of sanctification and perseverance until finally perfected in glory.

Likewise, the Christian life involves continual exercise of faith—namely, daily looking to the Lord, trusting him, and committing ourselves to his care. The initial act of believing on Jesus is only the opening refrain in the larger symphony of faith. After hearing Jesus' teaching and sensing their inability to please him, the disciples implored the Lord, "Increase our faith!" (Luke 17:5). Paul's rule of the Christian life was, "We live by faith, not by sight" (2 Cor 5:7). Faith occupied a prominent place in Paul's citations of Christian virtues (1 Tim 6:11; 2 Tim 2:22; 3:10; Tit 2:2). The apostle plainly stated that "The only thing that counts is faith expressing itself through love" (Gal 5:6). Paul further wrote that "everything that does not come from faith is sin" (Rom 14:23). The writer of Hebrews stated the profound truth that "without faith it is impossible to please God" (Heb 11:6). The letter gives many examples of OT saints who bore fruit and triumphed by the exercise of faith: Enoch (Heb 11:5), Noah (11:7), Abraham (11:17-19), Moses (11:24-27), etc.

Scripture thus calls men and women not only to an initial conversion to Christ that enrolls them among the justified, but to a continual conversion that makes them more like Jesus Christ in word and deed. Progressive conversion validates the reality of initial conversion. It provides public proof that the seed of the Word has fallen on good soil (Matt 13:23). Only by the exercise of daily repentance and daily faith can the saints become more Christlike, more fruitful, and more glorifying to God.

B. Call for Commitment to Christ as Savior and Lord

Surrender to Christ's sovereign rule is inherent in the act of true repentance. As we have seen, repentance is a radical turning from all known sin, from all lesser gods and lords, and from all inferior loyalties to the living God. Men and women *will* be mastered by someone or something. Jesus himself said that "No one can serve two masters. Either he will hate the one and love the other, or he will be devoted to the one and despise the other" (Matt 6:24). The real question is by *whom* people will be mastered—by sin and Satan or by Jesus Christ the Lord?

Commitment to Christ's Lordship is an intrinsic part of saving faith. Faith is not only mental assent to truths about Christ; it is also trust in and commitment to his person and kingdom values. Many people who hear the Gospel assent to its truths without being genuinely converted. Faith requires submission and commitment to Christ and his sovereign author-ity. We must commit to Christ before he will commit to us (Ps 31:5; John 2:24). Os Guinness put it bluntly: "For the person who becomes a Christian the moment of comprehension leads to one conclusion only—commitment. At that point the cost has been counted, a shoulder has been put to the yoke, a hand to the plough, and a contract for discipleship has been signed. The decision is irreversible. It is not faith going a second mile; it is faith making its first full step and there is no going back."[113] The only appropriate response to the One who gave his life for us is to give our all to him. Anything less than full surrender fails to express the gratitude we owe.

Early Christian preachers called sinners to own Christ as Savior from sin (Acts 2:38; 10:43; 13:38). But equally earnestly they pled with pre-Christians to acknowledge Christ as Lord of their lives (Acts 2:21, 36; 10:36; 16:31; Rom. 10:9-10, 12). To claim Christ as *kyrios* means to own him as Sovereign, Ruler, and Master. As MacArthur points out, Christ is designated *kyrios* 747 times in the NT and ninety-two times in Acts alone; but he is called *sōtēr* only twice in Acts (5:31; 13:23). In the early church a decision for Christ was a serious and costly matter, not lightly entered into. Often it was tantamount to signing one's death warrant. Today preachers make it much too easy to become a Christian.[114] Dietrich Bonhoeffer explained how this situation came about. "As Christianity spread, and the Church became more secularized, the realization of the costliness of grace gradually faded. The world was christianized, and grace became its common property. It was to be had at low cost."[115] We have made it too easy to believe by divorcing faith from commitment and obe-dience, and in so doing we have cheapened grace. Bonhoeffer powerfully delineated the difference between cheap and costly grace in his day:

> Cheap grace means grace as a doctrine, a principle, a system . . . no contrition is required, still less any real desire to be delivered from sin. . . . Cheap grace is the preaching of forgiveness without requir-ing repentance, baptism without church discipline, Communion without confession, absolution without personal confession. Cheap grace is grace without discipleship, grace without the cross, grace without Jesus Christ, living and incarnate.[116]

On the other hand, Bonhoeffer defined the grace that is costly:

> Costly grace is the treasure hidden in the field; for the sake of it a man will gladly go and sell all that he has. . . . Such grace is *costly* . . . because it costs a man his life, and it is grace because it gives a

man the only true life. . . . Grace is costly because it compels a man
to submit to the yoke of Christ and follow him. . . . The only man
who has the right to say that he is justified by grace alone is the man
who has left all to follow Christ. . . . The word of cheap grace has
been the ruin of more Christians than any commandment of
works.[117]

In this day of cheap grace and easy-believism, contemporary evangelists and disciple-makers must summon sinners to believe, repent, trust,
commit, obey, and faithfully follow Jesus Christ. We must call pre-
Christians to embrace Christ as definitive Teacher, as unique Savior, and
as absolute Lord. Nothing less will fulfill the command of our Lord to "go
and make disciples of all nations, baptizing them . . . and teaching them
to obey everything I have commanded you" (Matt 28:19-20).

C. Deal Constructively with Doubt

The person who comes to Christ in repentance and faith finds in this new
relationship a life of peace, joy, and purpose. But somewhere along the pilgrim path doubts creep in to cast a shadow over the new life in Christ. The
psalmist David doubted God's ways when he uttered the lament, "How
long, O Lord? Will you forget me forever? How long will you hide your
face from me? How long must I wrestle with my thoughts and every day
have sorrow in my heart?" (Ps 13:1-2). When Peter walked to Jesus on the
water and then began to sink, the Lord responded by saying, "You of little faith, why did you doubt?" (Matt 14:31). Later when the disciples
gathered at a mountain in Galilee to meet the risen Lord they all saw and
worshiped him, "but some doubted" (Matt 28:17). Doubt is an attitude
of questioning God and his ways, a state of inner conflict that oscillates
between faith and unbelief. Doubt is not firm unbelief, which connotes a
conscious decision to distrust God. McGrath observes that in the physical realm life is a constant struggle to ward off disease. Likewise, in the
spiritual realm "the life of faith [is] a permanent battle against doubt."[118]
Doubt is endemic in the lives of Christian people, but it is not always sinful. Consider three principal causes for doubt and constructive ways to
deal with this problem.

(1) Doubt may be *intellectual* in nature ("cognitive doubt"). By virtue
of finitude and residual sinfulness, some believers struggle with intellectual problems vis-à-vis spiritual realities. According to the verificational
method of doing theology,[119] faith rests on probabilities rather than on
absolute certainties. Thus as we develop our Christian worldview from the

Scriptures legitimate areas of doubt will arise. "There will always be an element of doubt in any statement that goes beyond the world of logic and self-evident propositions."[120] Seminary students and layfolk struggle with doubt relative to the doctrine of the Trinity, the problem of evil, the relation between sovereign election and human responsibility, or the case of a child born with Down's Syndrome. Such doubt is normal unless it involves prolonged uncertainty over cardinal Christian doctrines. The process of honestly struggling with doubts of this nature can result in more settled convictions and deeper spiritual commitment. Augustine cited the positive outcome of intellectual doubt by stating that to recognize that one doubts is the beginning of truth. He wrote:

> Everyone who knows that he has doubts knows with certainty something that is true, namely, that he doubts. He is certain therefore about *a* truth. Therefore everyone who doubts whether there be such a thing as *the* truth has at least a truth to set a limit to his doubt; and nothing can be true except truth be in it. Accordingly, no one ought to have doubts about the existence of the truth, even if doubts arise for him from every possible quarter.[121]

When struggling with intellectual doubts, several steps may prove helpful. Delve deeply into the teachings of Scripture in the area of your uncertainty. Furthermore, reflect on the writings of great Christian thinkers throughout history, especially those who have struggled with problems of doubt. Read their theological writings, biographies, and apologetic works (such as C.S. Lewis, *The Screwtape Letters*). It will also be helpful to discuss your intellectual problem with a knowledgeable pastor or seminary teacher.

(2) Doubt may result from past *emotional scars* ("affective doubt"). A young Christian's soul may be injured by serious misconduct by professing Christian leaders. Only heaven knows how many impressionable Christians have come to doubt God and his ways by the sinful follies of contemporary televangelists. The church in which I was reared had a pastor of vindictive spirit who was highly suspicious of others. He ruthlessly charged faithful, longstanding church members with "heresy" and expelled them from the church they loved and served. Such pathological behavior left scars of doubt on many in the congregation, especially the young and naive. Augustine wrote centuries ago, "It is often the case that a man who had experience of a bad doctor is afraid to trust himself even to a good one."[122] Doubting saints afflicted in this way should recall that God is absolutely kind, good, faithful, and true. They should meditate on the fact that "God is light; in him there is no darkness at all" (1 John 1:5).

To heal deep emotional scars of doubt, it is important to talk out your hurtful memories with the Lord and possibly with a skilled Christian counselor.

(3) Some doubt is *spiritual* in nature ("spiritual doubt"). This kind of doubt is less constructive and even sinful in nature. Christians whose spiritual growth is stunted, who neglect the exercise of faith, who are half-hearted in their commitment, and who are cold and backslidden are prime targets for doubts of this sort. Sarah appears to have doubted God's promise because she was deficient in faith (Gen 18:12-15). The same appears true of Jesus' disciples (Matt 17:19-20), particularly Peter (Matt 14:29-31). This kind of doubt caused by sin can be overcome by the application of spiritual resources and the exercise of spiritual discipline. Spiritual doubt dissipates as the struggler spends time alone with the Lord, speaks to the Lord in prayer about his indecision, applies the Word of God to his situation, and finds encouragement from supportive brothers and sisters.

The Lord knows and cares deeply about our doubts. We may be assured that as we honestly bring to him our doubts he will dispel our personal darkness. In the words of an anonymous author:

> *Whoso draws nigh to God one step*
> *Through doubtings dim,*
> *God will advance a mile*
> *In blazing light to him.*

SEVEN

"Unless a Man is Born Again"

JOHN 3 : 3

———□———

THE DOCTRINE OF REGENERATION

I. Introductory
Concerns

In the present chapter we continue our study of the application of Christ's atoning work on the cross. Our attention turns to another crucial aspect of salvation, namely, the new birth or the creation of new life in those who repent and trust Christ. In his book *Mere Christianity* C.S. Lewis observed that every person born into the world possesses *bios*, or biological life, that is sustained by oxygen, water, and food. But only those who are born again by God's Spirit move beyond natural existence to possess *zoe*, new spiritual life that endures forever. In the natural realm there can be no life without physical birth; likewise, in the spiritual realm there can be no spiritual life without a supernatural rebirth.

Initially, we inquire into the need for new birth. Given man's breathtaking technological achievements, why need we call for the transformation of human life? Have humans not proven that they can control their environment and their future? A further important issue is the nature of the new birth. Is the focus of regeneration the individual or, as many political theologians aver, society as a whole? If the former, what does it mean to say that the one who repents and believes is born again? With Nicodemus of old we ask, "How can a man be born when he is old? . . . Surely he cannot enter a second time into his mother's womb to be born!" (John 3:4). Some may respond to this question as did that Pharisee, who in bewilderment said to Jesus, "How can this be?" (John 3:9). What actually happens to the person when God transforms him or her from spiritual death to spiritual life? It will be instructive to consider the manifold results of the Holy Spirit's regeneration in a life. When a person is regenerated, is the fallen, sinful nature replaced by a new, metaphysical nature? What do we mean by the 'old nature' and the 'new nature'?

In addition, we ask whether regeneration is a work of God alone (monergism), or whether the individual cooperates in the new birth (synergism). What role, if any, does the human will play in regeneration? Can pre-Christians via their human resources contribute anything to their spiritual renovation? Can the modern conviction that psychotherapy and personal improvement schemes bring about new life and dispositions be sustained? A further matter for consideration is whether regeneration in OT times was a promise or a reality. Were OT saints such as Adam, Abraham, and David truly reborn by the Spirit of God? Or must regeneration in some sense have awaited the full flowering of salvation under the new covenant inaugurated by Jesus?

In addition, we explore whether God works regeneration through human instrumentalities such as the sacrament of baptism, membership in a church, or birth to Christian parents in a godly family. What role, if any, does water baptism play in the new birth? How shall we understand biblical texts such as John 3:5, Acts 22:16, and Tit 3:5 that link regeneration to water and washing? In Scripture is water baptism identical to or concurrent with Spirit baptism? Can the claims of baptismal regeneration, historically made by Roman Catholics and other sacramentalists, be sustained? As a matter of practical, pastoral concern, are children who die in infancy assured a place in God's heaven? What answer will we give to grieving parents at the grave site of a deceased infant? These are some of the issues we will consider in the remainder of this chapter.

II. Historical Interpretations of Regeneration

Several important interpretations of regeneration, or the new birth, have been proposed in the broad history of the Christian church. In order to clarify our own understanding of this important doctrine, we summarize five major views on the subject of the new birth.

A. Self-Actualized Regeneration (Pelagians and Liberals)

We saw in an earlier chapter that Pelagians and liberals repudiate original sin and depravity; hence they envisage little need for radical, spiritual rebirth in all persons. Liberal authorities maintain that each person born into the world is a child of God and thus is indwelt by the divine principle. Pelagians and liberals broadly envisage regeneration as the process of ethical development stimulated by the ideals of Jesus. Liberal preachers and theologians in the early decades of the twentieth century focused on social regeneration—i.e., the collective renewal of humanity in the kingdom of God. Liberals both old and new identify regeneration as a process of self-improvement realized by self-effort and the example of Christ. Some believe that regeneration is brought about by the inexorable forces of spiritual evolution.

Pelagius (d. 419) claimed that every person is born into the world free from the taint of inherited sin. Consequently, Pelagius vigorously opposed the early church practice of infant baptism for the remission of sins. Many persons sin when, following the example of Adam, they willfully violate God's law. According to Pelagius, salvation occurs as people forsake sins and obey the divine law. The stimulus for such action comes from the illuminatory power of the truth upon human minds and from the example of Jesus. Pelagius' soteriological agenda, then, was not supernatural regeneration but personal, moral reformation. Because of his high view of human capabilities, Pelagius "made God only a spectator in the drama of human redemption."[1]

Walter Rauschenbusch (d. 1918) rejected original sin and depravity and claimed that by natural birth all people are children of God. Since sin is a social force (chiefly the denial of human fraternity), so also is salvation. Rauschenbusch optimistically envisaged "the salvation of the collective life of humanity, the fulfillment of the theocratic hope."[2] He defined regeneration as the gradual transformation of the social order—specifically, as "the spread of the spirit of Christ in the political, industrial, social, scientific, and artistic life of humanity."[3]

Lyman Abbott (d. 1922) claimed that regeneration describes the awakening of the virtue latent in all people as God's children. The rekindling of life in the human heart through the force of spiritual evolution as the Eternal Energy, concentrated in Jesus, continually enters into human consciousness. Abbott wrote that "Christ comes, not merely to show divinity to us, but to evolve the latent divinity which he has implanted in us."[4] Abbott explained his understanding of regeneration as the progress of spiritual evolution in the following words:

> Regeneration does not mean to me a new faculty miraculously given to man by some magic formula, as baptism, or by some supernatural experience for which man must wait. In every normal man is

the capacity for goodness and truth, for love and service, for hope and joy. But this sleeping capacity is naught unless it is awakened into life. It is a seed, but a lifeless seed until it is given life by a divine power above itself.[5]

According to Abbott, history attests the spiritual evolution of men and women at two separate levels: the evolution of the *individual* into divinity and the evolution of *humanity* corporately into the kingdom of God.

While there exists no official liberation theology, the movement embraces a theology not of discourse but of concrete action in specific social contexts. The literature of liberation theology contains few references to the spiritual regeneration or salvation of persons. Proponents allege that people as social groups are corrupted by political, economic, racial, and sexual oppression born of the capitalist system. Thus salvation, or the recovery of human wholeness, occurs when dehumanizing injustices are swept away by revolutionary action (sometimes violent). Liberationists generally explain regeneration as people remaking themselves by dismantling oppressive structures and creating a more humane and humanizing society. In other words, regeneration is man's self-creation of a new social order that embodies the hopes and dreams of the marginalized and the oppressed. It involves the creation of a "little utopia" in anticipation of the "absolute utopia" in the kingdom of God. Liberationists follow Hegelian philosophers in viewing history as the process whereby humans free the divinity within them and progress to the union of the finite with the infinite.

Gustavo Gutiérrez, the Peruvian father of liberation theology, argues as follows: "By working, transforming the world, breaking out of servitude, building a just society, and assuming his destiny, man forges himself."[6] The Brazilian priests Leonardo and Clodovis Boff aver that regeneration is "the struggle for the transformation of the world into one more worthy of the human being and more like the new world of the kingdom of God."[7] According to the American black theologian James Cone, new life involves the black Christ liberating oppressed blacks from the shackles of white racism. Writes Cone, "Faith is the response of the community to God's act of liberation. It means saying yes to God and no to oppressors."[8]

Within the framework of a panentheistic worldview (whereby God is a part of the world and the world a part of God), process theology asserts that the divine Eros presents to all persons the lure or initial aim that provides for their maximum fulfillment. Lewis Ford asserts, "Everywhere God's creative urging toward the establishment of increased levels of intensity is present, but only with intelligent life can there be any awareness of this."[9] The presentation of novel initial aims may come through Jesus, Plato, the Buddha, or other prophets and philosophers. According to process thinkers, personal re-creation results from positive human response to the novel initial aims God presents at every moment to his intelligent creatures. Reflecting on John 3:3, Ford makes the following observation about the new birth: "In terms of the perishing occasions of our temporal life, we are being born anew and from above as we receive novel initial aims from God originating our subjectivity from moment to moment."[10] According to Norman Pittenger, positive human response to the divine lure "ennobles and enriches, vitalizes and makes new."[11] Since the novel initial aims offered by the cosmic Lover are persuasive and not coercive, salvation or regeneration is self-salvation. So Pittenger asserted that as persons respond to the divine lure constantly presented to them, we "make ourselves."[12]

B. Baptismal Regeneration
(Roman Catholics, Lutherans, and Anglo-Catholics)

Citing Scriptures such as John 3:5 and Tit 3:5, these traditions claim that God gives regenerating grace via the sacrament of baptism. Although differing in some details, the sacramental traditions agree that baptism confers cleansing of sin, the infusion of regenerating grace, and union with Christ. In children, baptismal regeneration generally turns on the faith of the sponsor, whereas in adults the good disposition of the recipient (faith, repentance, and in some cases good works) is required. Richard P. McBrien, a prominent Roman Catholic theologian, asserts that "The Church has always taught that Baptism is necessary for salvation."[13]

Some early church authorities drifted toward ceremonialism by linking regeneration with baptism. According to Hermas (d. 140), "Your life was saved and shall be saved through water."[14] Justin Martyr (d. 165) referred to baptism as "the washing that is for the remission of sins and unto regeneration."[15] Irenaeus (d. 200) claimed that God gave the OT story of Naaman the leper washing in the Jordan river (2 Kings 5) as a type of baptism. "We are made clean by means of the sacred water and the invocation of the Lord from our old transgressions, being spiritually regenerated as newborn babes."[16] Cyril of Jerusalem (d. 386) spoke rapturously of baptism as "a ransom to captives, a remission of offenses, a death to sin, a new spiritual birth, a chariot to heaven, the delight of paradise, a passport to the kingdom."[17] Cyril judged that only martyrs can be regenerated and saved apart from baptism.

Augustine (d. 430), the great theologian of the western church, held that God's unmerited gift of grace regenerates, creates faith, and effects repentance. Baptism, however, is an outward, visible sign of the Gospel of grace. Those who receive baptism properly consecrated receive the Gospel. At the baptismal font ("the saving laver of regeneration"[18]) the elect receive both the external sign (the water of baptism) and the spiritual reality (regeneration and union with Christ); the non-elect, however, receive only the physical sign. For these reasons Augustine insisted that "the sacrament of baptism is undoubtedly the sacrament of regeneration."[19] By the fourth or fifth century infant baptism had become customary practice in the church. Augustine held that at baptism infants die to original sin and adults to original sin and sins personally committed. He held that God via baptism "cleanses even the tiny infant, although itself unable as yet with the heart to believe unto righteousness and to make confession with the mouth unto salvation."[20] Unbaptized infants, however, remain under the control of the Devil. In the case of elect infants, Augustine claimed that personal conversion will inevitably follow baptismal regeneration. In the case of adults, like Augustine himself, the new convert gladly receives (i.e., does not resist) the water of baptism. For Augustine, then, salvation consisted of baptismal regeneration, conversion, and growth in grace. In baptism we die to sin and "live through being reborn at the baptismal font."[21]

In the scholastic era it became settled that the sign of the sacrament accomplishes what it signifies. According to Thomas Aquinas, baptism effects spiritual generation, confirmation spiritual growth, Eucharist spiritual nourishment, and penance and extreme unction spiritual healing.[22] Assuming that the recipient imposes no obstacle, baptism efficiently regenerates when administered on church authority (the *ex opere operato* concept). Thus Thomas claimed that the visible sign of water imparts to the baptized infant invisible, regenerating grace. "Through baptism, which is a spiritual generation, not only are sins taken away . . . but also every guilt of sin. For this reason, baptism not only washes away the fault, but also absolves from all guilt."[23] In short, "Baptism opens the gates of the heavenly kingdom to the baptized."[24] Where the sacrament was not available or where a person died before being baptized, Thomas upheld the so-called "baptism of desire." Thus he wrote, "Such a man can obtain salvation without actually being baptized, on account of his desire for Baptism . . . whereby God . . . sanctifies man inwardly."[25] For simple folk who have not developed a faith that is explicit, Thomas held that implicit faith suffices for salvation.[26]

Regeneration, which Catholicism confused with justification and sanctification, came to be viewed as a process whose outcome was not established until the end. The Council of Trent (1545-63) stated that regeneration commences with the sacrament of baptism. "If anyone . . . denies that the said merit of Jesus Christ is applied, both to adults and to infants, by the sacrament of baptism rightly administered in the form of the Church, let him be anathema" (Sess. V.3). "Even infants, who could not as yet commit any sin of themselves, are for this cause truly baptized for the remission of sins, that in them that may be cleansed away by regeneration, which they have contracted by generation" (Sess. V.4). In the Tridentine scheme, infants are baptized in the faith of the church. In the case of adults, penitence for sins and faith augmented by hope and love should precede baptism (Sess. VI.6). "For faith, unless hope and charity be added thereto, neither unites man perfectly with Christ, nor makes him a living member of his body" (Sess. VI.7).

The Second Vatican Council (1963-65) insisted that for Roman Catholics faith and baptism are necessary for salvation. But given its bent toward a panentheistic worldview—where humankind is oriented to the life of God—post-conciliar Catholicism claims that all people are saved by the "baptism of desire." The baptism of desire is equivalent to the non-specific implicit faith all human beings possess. Thus the Council affirmed:

> Those who, through no fault of their own, do not know the Gospel of Christ or his Church, but who nevertheless seek God with a sincere heart, and, moved by grace, try in their actions to do his will as they know it through the dictates of their conscience—those too may achieve eternal salvation. Nor shall divine providence deny the assistance necessary for salvation to those who, without any fault of theirs have not yet arrived at an explicit knowledge of God, and who, not without grace, strive to lead a good life.[27]

In a similar vein Gregory Baum commented, "One may seriously wonder whether baptism of desire is not the way of salvation for the great majority of men in this world, chosen to be saved."[28] Likewise the Notre Dame theologian McBrien writes, "Everybody does not strictly 'need' baptism to become a child of God and an heir of heaven. Every person, by reason of birth and God's universal offer of grace, is already called to be a child of God and an heir of heaven."[29] Do the sacraments, then, retain any saving relevance? McBrien responds, "The sacraments signify, celebrate, and effect what God is, in a sense, doing everywhere and for all."[30]

While rejecting the Roman synergism of sacramental grace and meritorious works, Luther nevertheless upheld the doctrine of baptismal regeneration. For the Reformer, God's usual way of regenerating a life is at the baptismal font. Baptism effects justification and the forgiveness of sins, imparts the gift of the Spirit, and re-creates in the divine image. Wrote

Luther, God "himself calls it [baptism] a new birth by which we are . . . loosed from sin, death, and hell, and because children of life, heirs of all the gifts of God, God's own children, and brethren of Christ."[31] In the customary infant baptism, regeneration occurs at the moment when the invoked Word of God unites with the sign (water) and as the infant responds to the Gospel with rudimentary faith. Baptism does not regenerate simply because performed (the Roman *ex opere operato* concept); Luther judged that baptism without faith is useless. Rather, the infant believes in a simple way the word of the Gospel presented in the sacrament. "In baptism children themselves believe and have faith of their own. God works this within them through the intercession of the sponsors who bring the child to the font in the faith of the Christian Church."[32] At the age of maturity children must ratify their new birth by repentance, mature faith, and obedience. In the rarer cases of adult baptism, the individual is made new by the word received in faith (*regeneratio prima*) and by the strengthening of the new life through baptism (*regeneratio secunda* or *renovatio*).

In *The Small Catechism* (1529) Luther wrote the following: "Baptism is not merely water, but it is water used according to God's command and connected with God's Word" (IV). To the question, "How can water produce such great effects?" Luther responded, "It is not the water that produces these effects, but the Word of God connected with the water, and our faith which relies on the Word of God connected with the water. . . . When connected with the Word of God [the water] is a Baptism, that is, a gracious water of life and a washing of regeneration in the Holy Spirit" (IV). Melanchthon advanced a similar view in *The Augsburg Confession*, art. IX.

Post-Reformation Lutheranism upheld Luther's view of baptismal regeneration. The Lutheran theologian David Hollaz (d. 1713) typically argued that the Spirit works regeneration through the word of God at the baptismal font. Thus, "the intellect of infants in regeneration is imbued with a saving knowledge of God by the Holy Spirit in Baptism, and their will is endowed with confidence in Christ."[33] Hollaz added, "In infants, as there is not an earnest and obstinate resistance, the grace of the Holy Spirit accompanying Baptism breaks and restrains their natural resistance that it may not impede regeneration; wherefore their regeneration takes place instantaneously."[34] In our century the German martyr Dietrich Bonhoeffer (d. 1945) insisted that baptism incorporates the infant or adult into the body of Christ. "In baptism man becomes Christ's own possession. . . . From that moment he belongs to Jesus Christ. He is wrestled from the dominion of the world, and passes into the ownership of Christ."[35] The Missouri Synod Lutheran theologian Francis Pieper similarly wrote that baptism "is a means to awaken and strengthen faith and therefore also a washing of regeneration and renewing of the Holy Ghost (Tit 3:5). . . . Observe also that even as the remission of sin and regeneration are bestowed through Baptism as a means . . . so also the implantation into the body of Christ . . . is wrought, and not merely portrayed, by the Holy Ghost through Baptism."[36]

The Church of England officially teaches the regeneration of infants via baptism. Thus *The Thirty-Nine Articles* (American revision, 1801) states, "Baptism is . . . a sign of Regeneration or New-Birth, whereby, as by an instrument, they that receive Baptism rightly are grafted into the Church; the promises of the forgiveness of sin, and of our adoption to be the sons of God by the Holy Ghost, are visibly signed and sealed" (art. XXVII). As prescribed by *The Book of Common Prayer*, the priest prior to baptism prays that God would "Give thy Holy Spirit to this child, that he may be born again, and be made an heir of everlasting salvation." Following baptism, the priest gives thanks that God was pleased "to regenerate this infant with thy Holy Spirit, to receive him for thy own child, and to incorporate him into thy holy Church."[37]

C. Presumptive and Promissory Regeneration (Covenant Reformed)

This view, although rejecting the high sacramentalism of Roman Catholicism and Lutheranism, often posits a close relation between baptism and regeneration. Covenant theologians, with other evangelicals, define regeneration as that radical change of nature from spiritual death to spiritual life wrought in us by Christ through the power of the Spirit. The new birth is the impartation by the triune God of a new heart. In this supernatural work the elect are entirely passive. Regeneration is not a *cooperative* work between God and sinners (synergism); rather, salvation is God's work from beginning to end (monergism). Hence most theologians in the tradition place regeneration before conversion in the scheme of salvation (*ordo salutis*).

Some covenant theologians subscribe to *presumptive regeneration*, which asserts that infants of believing parents are baptized not to become regenerated but because in some important sense they already possess the seeds of faith and regeneration. The sacrament of baptism is a sign or promise of the covenantal grace God is working in the elect, including infants born within the Christian community. According to this view, the unconscious, divine work of regeneration precedes the conscious, human responses of faith and repentance. The more common view, however, is *promissory regeneration*, according to which baptism is judged a visible sign of God's covenant promise of new life to believing adults and their children. Proponents insist that baptism does not effect regeneration; rather, it portrays as a sign and confirms as a seal the blessing of redemption. Thus understood, baptism introduces the baptized into the visible church and promises future regeneration. In the case of both hypotheses, divine regeneration logically precedes the human responses of faith and repentance.[38] Conversion, justification, sanctification, and perseverance all presuppose the existence of new spiritual life.

John Calvin (d. 1564), a precursor of the covenant view, defined regeneration broadly as the whole process of spiritual vivification, inclusive of the new birth, conversion, and sanctification. Begun in baptism, regeneration "does not take place in one moment or one day or one year." Rather it is accomplished "through continual and sometimes even slow advances."[39] Calvin painted a rudimentary picture of presumptive regeneration. He argued that the Spirit's work of regeneration often commences at the very beginning of life in the womb, as illustrated by the yet-unborn John the Baptist who was filled with the Spirit in Elizabeth's womb (Luke 1:15). Whether in the womb or in earliest infancy, God can give regenerating grace to his elect by the Spirit's inner illumination apart from the preached Word.[40] According to Calvin, OT circumcision and NT baptism are related. Although differing in external details, both circumcision and baptism signify spiritual regeneration. In the case of infants of believing parents, the sacrament connotes forgiveness of sins, union with Christ, and Spirit regeneration. Calvin insisted that infants are not capable of faith and repentance, but as members of the covenant family they are able to receive the seed of regeneration and sanctification.[41] In response to the question, What does baptism signify? Calvin responded: "It has two parts. For there is remission of sins; and then spiritual regeneration is symbolized by it (Eph 5:26; Rom 6:4)."[42] The purpose of infant baptism is "to testify that they are heirs of the blessing promised to the seed of the faithful, and that, after they are grown up, they may acknowledge the fact of their Baptism, and receive and produce its fruit."[43] For Calvin, baptism "is like a sealed document to confirm to us that all our sins are so abolished, remitted, and effaced that they can never come to his sight, be recalled, or charged against us."[44]

The Scots Confession (1560), the first Reformed standard in the English language, presents the elements of presumptive regeneration. It asserts that as the old covenant under the law had the two sacraments of circumcision and Passover, so the new covenant instituted by Christ possesses the sacraments of baptism and Eucharist. Baptism is a seal or sign that God's saving action has begun to operate in the souls of the elect, including infants of Christian parents. "We assuredly believe that by Baptism we are engrafted into Christ Jesus, to be made partakers of his righteousness, by which our sins are covered and remitted" (art. 21).

The Westminster Confession (1647) favors the perspective of promissory regeneration. Thus baptism is "a sign and seal of the covenant of grace, of his ingrafting into Christ, of regeneration, of remission of sins, and of his giving up unto God, through Jesus Christ, to walk in newness of life" (chap. 28.1). Not only may adult believers receive baptism, "but also the infants of one or both believing parents are to be baptized" (chap. 28.4). In chap. 28.5 the Confession states that it is possible to be regenerated without being baptized and that not all those baptized (i.e., faithless covenant breakers) are regenerated.

W.G.T. Shedd (d. 1894) insisted that infant regeneration is taught *scripturally* in Luke 1:15, 18:15-16, Acts 2:39, and 1 Cor 7:14 and *symbolically* via OT circumcision and NT infant baptism. In adults, "Regeneration immediately exhibits its fruit in the converting acts of faith and repentance. In the case of infant regeneration, there is an interval of time between regeneration and conversion."[45] Added Shedd, "The regenerate infant believes and repents when his faculties will admit of the exercise and manifestation of faith and repentance. In this . . . instance, regeneration is *potential* or *latent* faith and repentance."[46]

Virtually all Reformed, covenant theologians uphold the logical priority of regeneration to conversion (faith and repentance). Shedd insisted that regeneration—the origination of spiritual life—precedes conversion—the effect of spiritual life. Persons are not regenerated because they first believe and repent; rather, they believe and repent because first regenerated. Shedd wrote that "The Holy Ghost is not given as a converting and a sanctifying Spirit, until he has been given as a regenerating Spirit" (Matt 12:33; John 3:3).[47] John Murray spoke for many covenant theologians when he asserted, "Without regeneration it is morally and spiritually impossible for a person to believe in Christ, but when a person is regenerated it is morally and spiritually impossible for that person not to believe."[48] Louis Berkhof flatly added that "A conversion that is not rooted in regeneration is no true conversion."[49]

D. Synergistic Regeneration (Arminian Theologians)

The usual order of elements in Arminian soteriology is prevenient grace, repentance, faith, the new birth, and continued obedience. Regeneration—

viewed by some Arminians as a change of moral purpose but by many as a change of nature from sin to holiness—occurs through the synergism of human willing and divine working. God regenerates when the pre-Christian believes by a free act of the will, which involves ceasing to resist the moral influence of the truth presented to all persons everywhere. This action is said to be possible by means of prevenient grace, which works in sinners universally to remove intellectual blindness and volitional hardness. On this showing, every person allegedly is born in a state of grace. Since this divine grace can be resisted, ultimately it is the will of the pre-Christian that determines whether or not the person will be reborn. The saved are those who choose to cooperate with God's (resistible) prevenient grace; the unsaved are those who fail to cooperate. "This grace will shepherd one to repentance, regeneration, entire sanctification, and final perseverance if not resisted somewhere along the way."[50] Some Arminians view regeneration as inclusive of everything from conversion to sanctification, or what the Wesleyan-holiness tradition calls the first and second works of grace. Many Arminians deny assurance of final destiny in heaven, since regenerating grace may be lost by willful sin.

John Wesley (d. 1791) held that the unregenerate are corrupted by sin and lack knowledge of God and love for him. Yet he also held that "preventing grace," which allegedly flows from Christ's cross, reverses the debilitating effects of original sin. Thus Wesley argued that the unregenerate, since blessed by prevenient grace, are able (1) to hear the voice of God in conscience, (2) acknowledge responsibility for sins, (3) seek righteousness, and (4) trust Christ for salvation. "Preventing grace [includes] the first wish to please God, the first dawn of light concerning his will, and the first slight transient conviction of having sinned against him. All these imply some tendency toward life; some degree of salvation."[51] Pre-Christians cooperate with this prevenient grace to work out their own salvation (Phil 2:12), namely, to repent of sin and believe in Christ. Thus for Wesley the enlightened human will is one of the causes of the new life breathed into the soul at regeneration. Whereas justification changes the sinner's outward relation to God, regeneration changes the inward nature so that believers are initially made holy. Wesley added that renewal in the image of God, or the new birth, can be lost due to deliberate sin. Hence assurance of forgiveness of sins extends no further than the present moment.

John William Fletcher (d. 1785), a contemporary of Wesley and a leading Wesleyan spokesman, set forth the essential theology of early Methodism. In his major work *Checks to Antinomianism* (1771-75), Fletcher argued that the gift of universal, prevenient grace (John 1:9; Tit

2:11) frees the human will to cooperate with God in the work of salvation. Human free will and divine grace work together to produce the new birth, or regeneration, which consists of justification and sanctification.

In the following century, Charles Finney (d. 1875) rejected the Reformed belief that regeneration is totally a work of God in which the human subject is passive. Positing a bold synergism, Finney insisted that both God and sinners are active in regeneration. The Spirit presents the truth of God to the soul, and sinners change the disposition of their hearts and then turn themselves to God. Tending toward Pelagianism, Finney defined regeneration as a change in the attitude of the will, a change of moral character, or the inauguration of a new spiritual direction. "Regeneration consists in the sinner changing his ultimate choice, intention, preference; or in changing from selfishness to love or benevolence."[52] Finney's view of pre-Christians actively engaged in regeneration in obedience to God rests on his rejection of human depravity. Non-Christians possess a natural ability to choose God, alter their fundamental affections, and obey all God's commands. Given his unique view of regeneration, Finney made the following observation concerning the duty of preachers: "Ministers should . . . aim at, and expect the regeneration of sinners, upon the spot, and before they leave the house of God."[53]

E. Regeneration a Work of God in Response to Faith (Reformed Evangelicals)

Evangelicals in the Reformation tradition maintain that sinners, afflicted with holistic depravity, must receive a new spiritual nature in order to gain eternal life. They view regeneration as an instantaneous work of God, not a humanly generated process. Advocates claim that the Spirit regenerates not on the basis of the faith of godly sponsors, church membership, or performance of the sacraments. Rather, God grants new spiritual life by virtue of the individual's conscious decision to repent of sins and appropriate the provisions of Christ's atonement. Some note that in the early church bornagain believers subsequently were baptized, and the public rite that attested this conversion came to be called (by the figure known as metonymy) a "regeneration."[54] The sacrament of baptism, however, is not the efficient cause of regeneration. Furthermore, proponents of this view uphold the monergism of regeneration: the new birth is entirely the work of the sovereign God. As we have seen, some authorities view regeneration as logically prior to conversion. Others identify the first wish to please God as the result of effectual calling, and so place conversion prior to regeneration in the *ordo salutis*.

George Whitefield (d. 1770), the Calvinistic Methodist, protested the nominal Christianity of his day that trusted in church membership or baptism for salvation. His sermon "The Nature and Necessity of our New Birth in Christ Jesus" played a crucial role in the evangelical awakening in England. Whitefield stated in this sermon, "it [is] too plain, beyond all contradiction, that comparatively but few of those who are 'born of water' are 'born of the Spirit' likewise; or, to use another scriptural way of speaking, many are baptized with water which were never, effectually at least, baptized with the Holy Ghost."[55] For Whitefield, regeneration is that instantaneous creation wrought on the soul by the Holy Spirit producing new inclinations, new desires, and new habits. As the Spirit quickens people dead in trespasses and sins, they become partakers of the divine nature, thereby being renewed in the divine image. Whitefield added, in the new birth "our souls, though still the same as to essence, yet are so purged, purified and cleansed from their natural dross, filth and leprosy, by the blessed influence of the Holy Spirit that they may properly be said to be made anew."[56]

The great British preacher C.H. Spurgeon (d. 1892) likewise inveighed against the view that baptism regenerates. He stated in his sermon "Baptismal Regeneration," "Facts all show that whatever good there may be in baptism, it certainly does not make a man 'a member of Christ, the child of God, and an inheritor of the kingdom of heaven,' or else many thieves, whoremongers, drunkards, fornicators, and murderers are members of Christ."[57] Moreover, Spurgeon opposed the view that birth in a Christian family guarantees regeneration. "There can be no such thing as sponsorship in receiving Christ or in faith. If you are an unbeliever, your father and your mother may be the most eminent saints, but this faith does not overlap and cover your unbelief. You must believe for yourself."[58] Spurgeon was firmly persuaded that each person individually must be born again by God's Spirit through faith. Regeneration involves the spiritual renovation of one's entire being, the implantation of the divine life, and mystical union with Christ.[59] The new birth is "a change of the entire nature from top to bottom in all senses and respects."[60]

The baptist theologian A.H. Strong (d. 1921) viewed regeneration and conversion as chronologically simultaneous events, although logically the former precedes the latter. "Regeneration, or the new birth, is the divine side of that change of heart which, viewed from the human side, we call conversion. It is God turning the soul to himself,—conversion being the soul's turning itself to God, of which God's turning it is both the accompaniment and cause."[61] Conversion, consisting of repentance and faith, is the human act that attests the regenerating work of the Spirit on the sinner's heart. According to Strong, the resuscitation of Lazarus in John 11 illustrates the relationship between the new birth and conversion. Lazarus was made alive by the power of God; in this event his soul was passive. But Lazarus came forth from the tomb; in this his soul was active.

Millard J. Erickson's position is similar to Strong's, with the exception that conversion logically precedes regeneration. Temporally conversion and regeneration occur simultaneously, but logically repentance and faith represent the condition for God's work of regeneration and come first. Erickson attributes the enablement to repent and believe not to regeneration but (as we saw in chap. 5) to the Spirit's effectual calling.

> In the case of the elect God works intensively through a special calling so that they do respond in repentance and faith. As a result of this conversion, God regenerates them. The special calling . . . is not the complete transformation which constitutes regeneration, but it does render the conversion of the individual both possible and certain. Thus the logical order of the initial aspects of salvation is special calling—conversion—regeneration.[62]

Against competing hypotheses, Erickson insists that regeneration is not a process, but an instantaneous work wrought in the soul by the Spirit as God applies salvation to elect believers.

The following study of the biblical data will show that this final view of regeneration most thoroughly comports with the evidence given by divine revelation.

III. EXPOSITION OF THE DOCTRINE OF REGENERATION

A. *The Need for Regeneration*

In his book *The Varieties of Religious Experience*, the American psychologist and philosopher William James (d. 1910) claimed that there are some healthy-minded and well-adjusted people who have no need of conversion or new birth.[63] James said that this is particularly true of congenitally happy people who harbor no ill-will toward God or others and who have no consciousness of sin. Still other persons are of such a temperament as to be incapable of undergoing a regenerative change. For many people, being "once-born" is an adequate basis for a rich and satisfying life. At bottom James judged that "Protestantism has been too pessimistic as regards the natural man."[64]

With candid realism Scripture paints a very different picture of the human condition. God's Word states that (1) the unregenerate are morally evil (Gen 8:21; Matt 7:11; 12:34; John 3:19) and need to be made pure and clean. As Jesus said, "every good tree bears good fruit, but a bad tree bears bad fruit" (Matt 7:17). Moreover, (2) the unsaved are spiritually sick and need to be made spiritually healthy (Matt 9:12). Major spiritual surgery is required to bring about spiritual wholeness. In addition, (3) pre-Christians live in spiritual darkness (Matt 4:16; John 3:19; Eph 5:8a) and need to be made light in the Lord (2 Cor 4:6; Eph 5:8b). Unbelievers, furthermore, (4) are slaves to sin (John 8:34; Rom 6:6, 16-20; 2 Tim 2:26) and must be liberated to become free men and women (John 8:32, 36; Rom 6:18; Heb 2:15). Finally, the unsaved (5) are under the sentence of physical (Rom 5:12; 8:10), spiritual (Eph 5:14), and eternal (Rom 6:23a; 2 Thess 1:9) death and need to receive eternal life (John 3:15-16, 36; Rom 6:23b).

Furthermore, due to hereditary depravity the minds of the unsaved are blinded (Rom 3:11a; 1 Cor 2:14), their wills are predisposed to sinful choices and actions (John 6:44a; 2 Pet 2:19), their emotions are disordered (Isa 57:21; Tit 3:3; 1 Pet 2:11), and their relationships with God (Gen 3:8-10; Jas 4:4) and others (Jas 4:1-2) are broken or strained. From the biblical perspective, 'once-born' persons cannot see God (Matt 5:8; Heb 12:14), and they cannot enter the kingdom of heaven. As Jesus said, "I tell you the truth, no one can see the kingdom of God unless he is born again" (John 3:3; cf. v. 5). The unconverted need to be made entirely new in order to know, love, and serve the Creator and their fellow human beings. Psychotherapy and human potential movements may make the unsaved temporarily feel better and perhaps function more adequately, but they fail radically to transform fallen natures. Neither can education or higher learning apart from knowledge of Christ fundamentally change depraved hearts. The same verdict applies to so-called cultural evolution. Apart from regenerating grace, sinners are incapable of changing their hearts and dispositions (Jer 13:23). We can no more will spiritual birth by a volitional act than we can cause our physical birth. As Jesus said, "Flesh [i.e., fallen human nature] gives birth to flesh" (John 3:6).

These considerations indicate that the spiritual condition of pre-Christians is grave; superficial remedies cannot redress such a cluster of problems. The only hope lies in a radical, spiritual solution. What 'once-born' people need is supernatural transformation of their lives by the power of God. This transformation the Bible calls regeneration or the new birth.

B. The Language and Meaning of Regeneration

Regeneration is that work of the Spirit at conversion that renews the heart and life (the inner self), thus restoring the person's intellectual, volitional, moral, emotional, and relational capacities to know, love, and serve God. The noun *palingenesia* ("rebirth," "regeneration") occurs only twice in the NT. Jesus used the term in Matt 19:28 eschatologically concerning the renewal of the world at his second advent. The implication of this usage is that the new heavens and new earth belong to an entirely new order of things. Relevant to the topic at hand, Paul used the noun in a soteriological sense in Tit 3:5, where he wrote that God "saved us, not because of righteous things we had done, but because of his mercy. He saved us through the washing of rebirth [*palingenesia*] and renewal by the Holy Spirit, whom he poured out on us generously through Jesus Christ our Savior." The NT describes regeneration via several descriptive figures and word pictures that employ other instructive nouns and verbs.

Paul represented the new birth (1) as a *re-creation*, a radical inner change wrought by God's power, whereby one becomes a new spiritual being. In the key text on the subject, the apostle wrote to the Corinthians, "if anyone is in Christ, he is a new creation [*kainē ktisis*]; the old has gone, the new has come!" (2 Cor. 5:17). In Gal 6:15 he said to the Galatian believers, "Neither circumcision nor uncircumcision means anything; what counts is a new creation" (*kainē ktisis*). See also Eph 2:10. (2) A *spiritual revivication and resurrection* from death to life by identification with the risen Christ. "When you were dead in your sins and in the uncircumcision of your sinful nature, God made you alive [aorist of *syzōopoieō*] with Christ" (Col 2:13). Paul also wrote, "because of his great love for us, God, who is rich in mercy, made us alive [aorist of *syzōopoieō*] with Christ even when we were dead in transgressions. . . . And God raised us up [aorist of *synegeirō*] with Christ and seated us with him in the heavenly realms in Christ Jesus" (Eph 2:4-6; cf. 1 Pet 1:3). Regeneration is not the addition of a new element to human nature; it is the making alive of what was dead. (3) A *circumcision of the heart* or an inner spiritual transformation born out of penitent faith, not a mere cutting of the flesh. "In him you were also circumcised, in the putting off of the sinful nature . . . with the circumcision done by Christ" (Col 2:11). (4) A *washing*, signifying the cleansing of former sins. "But you were washed [aorist of *apolouomai*], you were sanctified, you were justified in the name of the Lord Jesus Christ and by the Spirit of our God" (1 Cor 6:11; cf. Eph 5:26).

Another image of regeneration, favored by John, is (5) a *new spiritual birth*. John wrote of "children born not of natural descent, nor of human decision or a husband's will, but born of God" (John 1:13). The aorist passive of *gennaō*, "be born," denotes that instantaneous event whereby believers receive the new nature—an event qualitatively different from ordinary physical birth. Later in dialogue with Nicodemus, an orthodox Jew, Jesus explained the meaning of the new birth (John 3:3-8). The Lord began the conversation by astutely shifting the discussion from the inquirer's materialistic understanding of the kingdom to his need for a radical, spiritual transformation. "I tell you the truth, no one can see the kingdom of God unless he is born again" (John 3:3). Does the phrase *gennaō anōthen* mean "born again" or "born from above"? *Anō*, an antonym for *katō*, means "up" or "above" (John 8:23; 11:41; Acts 2:19; Col 3:1). Elsewhere in John *anōthen* clearly bears the spatial meaning "above" (John 3:31; 19:11; cf. *anōthen* in John 19:23). In addition, John envisaged believers as born of God (John 1:13; 1 John 3:9; 4:7; 5:1, 4, 18). As Ladd noted, the Fourth Gospel reflects "the tension between the above and the below, heaven and earth, the sphere of God and the world" (John 3:12-13, 31; 6:33, 62; 8:23).[65] Thus Jesus probably meant that Nicodemus must be "born from above," which includes the idea of a rebirth.

Jesus explained the nature of this new birth from above to Nicodemus, who had difficulty understanding the teaching. "No one can enter the kingdom of God unless he is born of water and the Spirit [*ex hydatos kai pneumatos*]" (John 3:5). The Greek construction closely links the agencies of the water and the Holy Spirit. Historically several interpretations of the "water" have been proposed: (a) water as a symbol of purification (Lightfoot, Murray, Bruce, Carson); (b) the water of John's baptism (Bengel, Godet); (c) the water of Christian baptism (Luther, Cullmann, Barrett, Guthrie); (d) water as a synonym for the Spirit (Calvin); (e) water as a symbol for the Word of God (Ironside, Pink, Boice); and (f) the water that accompanies physical birth (a popular view). The first interpretation is preferred, for the following reasons: As a studious Jew, Nicodemus was familiar with the OT use of water as a symbol for purification from the defilement of sin (Lev 14:8-9; 2 Kgs 5:10; Ps 51:2-3; Zech 13:1). Moreover, the purifying function of water and the renovating power of the Spirit are juxtaposed in the prophecy of the new covenant in Ezek 36:25-27. Hence by "water and the Spirit" Jesus likely meant that in order to enter God's kingdom Nicodemus must be purified from sin and be spiritually renewed. Note that John's baptism also involved water and the Spirit; the Baptist applied the water, and the coming Messiah would baptize with the Spirit (John 1:33). Jesus' further statement—"Flesh gives birth to flesh, but the Spirit gives birth to spirit" (John 3:6)—pointed up the radical difference between a natural, human birth and supernatural rebirth by the Holy Spirit. Jesus insisted that not only Nicodemus but all Jews "must be born again" (v. 7).

Other biblical texts describe regeneration in terms of a new birth. Jas 1:18 depicts the new birth by the verb *apokyeō*, to "give birth" or "bear," whereas 1 Pet 1:3, 23 employ the verb *anagennaō* (only here in the NT), in the sense of "cause to be born again." According to these verses, the instrument by which the new birth is effected is the Word of God or the truth of the Gospel.

It should be clear that regeneration differs from conversion in several important respects. (1) Conversion involves a synergism of divine and human working, whereas regeneration is strictly a *monergistic operation.* Independently of any human agency, God re-creates, imparts new life, circumcises the heart, and washes away sins. (2) Whereas conversion is a sinner's conscious act of turning to God in penitent faith, regeneration is an *unconscious* transformation wrought by the Holy Spirit. Like a variable wind, "you cannot tell where it comes from or where it is going" (John 3:8). (3) Conversion generally occurs over a period of time, whereas regeneration is an *instantaneous* work. (4) If we consider a secondary use of the term, the conversion of believers from sin may be repeated again and again, but regeneration is a uniquely *unrepeatable event* in a life.

C. Does Water Baptism Regenerate?

Does the NT support the regeneration of sinful people, either children or adults, via the ceremony of baptism, as Roman Catholics, Lutherans, and some Episcopalians claim? Does Scripture represent baptism as the necessary means by which the Spirit effects the new birth?

Some proponents of this position appeal to Mark 16:16, which says, "Whoever believes and is baptized will be saved, but whoever does not believe will be condemned." We respond that Mark 16:9-20 is not found in the most important early Greek manuscripts. Thus it is likely that this portion of the Gospel, including v. 16, is not an authentic part of Mark's inspired writing. Lacking divine inspiration, Mark 16:9-20 at most reflects the conviction of a segment of the apostolic church. In addition, the presence of the verb *pisteuō* ("believe") and *apisteuō* ("disbelieve"; see also vv. 11, 13) in v. 16 indicates that the emphasis lies on the act of believing and not upon the rite of water baptism. The latter is secondary to the primary emphasis of belief in the Gospel (v. 15).

The account of the conversion of Cornelius and his relatives begins with hearing and believing the Gospel message (Acts 10:33, 36, 42-44; 11:14). Then occurred the outpouring and reception of the Holy Spirit (10:44-45,

47b), followed by water baptism (10:47a, 48a). The record of Lydia's conversion states that the woman heard Paul's message (Acts 16:14), responded to it in faith (vv. 14-15), and with members of her household was baptized (v. 15). Consider also the account of the Philippian jailor's conversion in Acts 16. When in *extremis* the jailer asked Paul and Silas, "What must I do to be saved?" the missionaries responded, "Believe in the Lord Jesus, and you will be saved—you and your household" (vv. 30-31). The jailer and his family were instructed in the faith, thereafter were baptized, and experienced great joy in believing (vv. 32-34). Note that the jailer was told he must must believe in Christ to be saved, not that he must be baptized in order to be saved. Acts 18:8 states that "Crispus, the synagogue ruler, and his entire household believed in the Lord; and many of the Corinthians who heard him [Paul] believed and were baptized."[66] These four accounts endorse salvation (or new birth) by faith, not by the sacrament of baptism.

A superficial reading of Acts 22:16 might suggest that baptism effects regeneration. Ananias said to Saul, who had just met the risen Christ and undoubtedly had been born anew, "What are you waiting for? Get up, be baptized and wash your sins away, calling on his name." The first two aorist verbs literally may be translated: "Permit yourself to be baptized and have your sins washed away." In the NT the symbol (baptism) and the reality it symbolizes (new birth and cleansing of sins) are closely connected (Acts 2:38; Tit 3:5; 1 Pet 3:21). In this text Ananias urged baptism as a visible sign of the invisible cleansing of sins through the blood of Christ. The final verb in Acts 22:16 is the aorist middle participle of *epikaleō*, to "call upon"—the tense signifying that Saul's act of calling on the Lord temporally preceded the two previous verbs. Saul should permit himself to be baptized and have his sins forgiven *by first* calling on the Lord in faith.[67]

Does the focal text Tit 3:5 (where alone the word *palingenesia* appears) teach the doctrine of baptismal regeneration? Paul wrote that Christ in mercy "saved us through the washing of rebirth and renewal by the Holy Spirit." Consider first the phrase, "through the washing of rebirth" (*dia loutrou palingenesias*). The converts Titus served had "trusted in God" (v. 8). The phrase in question, analogous to the cleansing action of water specified in 1 Cor 6:11 and Eph 5:26, likely signifies the cleansing of sins effected at the new birth by the Word of God. In a secondary sense, given the close connection between the reality (new birth) and the symbol (baptism), Paul may have thought of water baptism as the outward sign of this inward cleansing. The second phrase, "through . . . renewal (*anakainōsis*) by the Holy Spirit," does not describe the subsequent process of sanctification. Rather, it is an amplifying description of the new birth in terms of a making new (cf. 2 Cor 5:17 and Gal 6:15, which use *kainē*). Jesus similarly linked water and the Spirit in his teaching on regeneration in John 3:5. In that text we concluded that John cited "water" as a symbol for purification of sins. Thus neither John 3:5 nor Tit 3:5 offer adequate support for the hypothesis that baptism effects the regeneration of the person baptized.

Neither do other texts that link water and salvation teach that the rite of baptism regenerates. The intricate argument of 1 Pet 3:18-22 affirms that the Flood, by cleansing the world of wickedness and delivering the faithful in the ark, is a picture of salvation, a salvation symbolized by the rite of baptism. What saves sinners is not the external rite of baptism, but the completed work and resurrection of Christ (vv. 21b-22) appropriated by faith.

The preponderance of evidence leads us to conclude that the order of events in the NT appears to be conversion and regeneration followed by water baptism (see Acts 2:38, 41; 10:47). Acts 2:38 records Peter's words, "Repent and be baptized . . . in the name of Jesus Christ for (*eis*) the forgiveness of your sins." The preposition *eis* may mean "because of."[68] The apostolic order followed the practice of John the Baptist, who baptized those who heeded his message and repented of their sins (Mark 1:4-5). So F.F. Bruce concluded, "baptism in water continued to be the external sign by which individuals who believed the gospel message, repented of their sins, and acknowledged Jesus as Lord, were publicly incorporated into the Spirit-baptized fellowship of the new people of God." He added, "It is against the whole genius of Biblical religion to suppose that the outward rite had any value except in so far as it was accompanied by true repentance within."[69] In sum, no ceremony—even an important Christian rite such as baptism—is able to regenerate fallen human nature and remit sins. What changes hearts is the powerful, inner work of the Spirit, not a humanly administered ceremony or even the Spirit *and* the religious ceremony.

D. *The Holistic Results of Regeneration*

What are the effects of Holy Spirit regeneration on repentant sinners? In brief, regeneration breaks the paralyzing bonds of holistic depravity and radically renews the sinner's heart, mind, and soul into the image of Christ. As in the case of sinful depravity, the transformation wrought by the new birth is *holistic*; not merely some, but all of the sinner's capacities are significantly renewed and enabled. The new spiritual life, being supernatural in origin, manifests itself in renewed abilities and righteous actions. In some people the visible evidences come to light soon after regeneration; in other lives time is required for their manifestation. Whether sooner or later, Jesus' promise holds true: "every good tree bears good fruit. . . . A good tree cannot bear bad fruit" (Matt 7:17-18).

Consider the following results of Holy Spirit regeneration. (1) *Intellectually*, regeneration enables minds of sinners once blind and ignorant of spiritual truths to comprehend the things of God (1 Cor 2:12, 14-16; 2 Cor 4:4, 6; Col 3:10). The new birth effects renewal of the human capacity to know, love, and affirm God's purposes. Holy Spirit transformation results in spiritual discernment formerly incapacitated by sin. (2) *Volitionally*, the new birth liberates believers' wills from moral bondage, enabling them to affirm and pursue kingdom values (Rom 6:13; Phil 2:13; 2 Thess 3:5). Lesser loyalties give way to supreme loyalty to God and his purposes. In the twice-born, enmity toward God is replaced by a new passion to glorify the King of kings and Lord of lords. (3) *Emotionally*, regeneration initiates the reintegration of disordered affections and feelings (Rom 8:15). As Paul wrote, "God did not give us a spirit of timidity, but a spirit of power, of love and of self-discipline" (2 Tim 1:7). Twice-born persons are far more capable of manifesting love, empathy, compassion, etc., than once-born persons. (4) *Morally and ethically*, regenerate believers are freed from depraved and enslaving passions. Indeed, the saved progressively become like Christ in thought, word, and deed. Spirit-transformed people exchange the sordid works of the flesh (Gal 5:19-21) for the attractive fruits of the Spirit: i.e., "love, joy, peace, patience, kindness, goodness, faithfulness, gentleness and self-control" (vv. 22-23). And (5) *relationally*, the new birth establishes genuine fellowship with the triune God (1 Cor 1:9; Eph 2:22; 1 John 1:3) and meaningful relationships with other believers (Rom 12:5; Eph 2:14-15, 19-20). The twice-born come to know experientially that God created them to enjoy community. Spirit regeneration motivates newborn children of God to move from lonely isolation to rejuvenating fellowship. In sum, the new birth effects a significant transformation and renewal of the capacities inherent in man and woman as *imago Dei*.

E. Regeneration and the 'New Nature'

Thinking of Spirit regeneration, Peter made the bold statement that God "has given us his very great and precious promises, so that through them you may participate in the divine nature [*theia physis*] and escape the corruption in the world caused by evil desires" (2 Pet 1:4). Prior to the new birth we possessed only an "earthly nature" (Col 3:5), a "sinful nature" (*sarx*, Rom 7:5, 18; 8:3-5, 8-9, 12-13; Gal 5:13, 16-17; etc.) or an "old self" (Rom 6:6; Eph 4:22). These phrases describe the unregenerate state:

the self arraigned against God, oriented toward the base elements of the world, consumed by sinful cravings, and driven to evil deeds. In this regard the NIV translates Paul's phrase *kata sarka peripatountas* (2 Cor. 10:2) as, "live by the standards of this world." The biblical terms "earthly nature," "sinful nature," etc., describe the unconverted person turned in on himself and energized by Satan to corrupt works. By the antithetic phrase "divine nature," Peter borrowed from current hellenistic language to describe new spiritual life with Christ that imparts to the soul transformed capacities and godly virtues. As a result of the Spirit's regenerating work, the believer receives a new disposition, a new set of affections, new moral qualities, and new aspirations. The NT describes the result of this transformation as the "new self" (Eph 4:24; Col 3:10), which is the glorified Christ living his life in the believer (Gal 2:20). This new being expresses itself in an entirely new manner of life and conduct (Rom 6:4; 7:6). Aquinas claimed that at baptism God injects into the soul a new nature ("created grace" or "habitual grace"), viewed almost as a new substance. But the new birth creates no new, metaphysical entity. Rather, it effects the transformation and revitalization of intellectual, volitional, moral, emotional, and relational capacities inherent in the person as *imago Dei*, as indicated in the previous section. For example, the new birth energizes and redirects *love* from preoccupation with self to a new focus on God and others. As Strong commented, "Regeneration does not add to, or subtract from, the number of man's intellectual, emotional or voluntary faculties. But regeneration is the giving of a new direction or tendency to powers of affection which man possessed before."[70]

Significantly, Peter stated that the twice-born "participate in the divine nature" (*physis*) rather than in the divine being (*ousia*). He meant that by Spirit regeneration believers become partakers of God's grace, mercy, holiness, etc., *not* of God's essence. Participation "in the divine nature" is Peter's way of describing the reality Paul set forth in Rom 8:9—"You . . . are controlled not by the sinful nature but by the Spirit, if the Spirit of God lives in you." It is Peter's way of describing what the anonymous writer conveyed in Heb 3:14—"share in Christ," in Heb 6:4—"shared in the Holy Spirit," and in Heb 12:10—"share in his holiness." No NT writer suggested that the new birth alters the sinner's essential constitution. Regeneration does not change the sinner's substance by forming a new metaphysical entity, such as a 'spirit.' Evidence is lacking to support the view that by the new birth dichotomous sinners become trichotomous saints. Neither did Peter imply that Christians in any sense become divine. God's own divine nature and our renewed human nature are not commingled in the new man or woman. The human and divine personalities remain forever distinct. And certainly Peter never envisaged any pantheistic notion of the Christian's absorption into the whole.

Calvin's insightful comment on 2 Pet 1:4 highlights the figurative sense in which Peter used the phrase "divine nature."

> Let us then mark that the end of the gospel is to render us conformable to God, and if we may so speak, to deify us. . . . The word *nature* is not here essence but quality. Only fanatics imagine that we thus pass over into the nature of God. . . . The image of God in holiness and righteousness is restored to us for this end, that we may at length be partakers of eternal life and glory.[71]

The formation of the "new self" or new nature via Spirit regeneration does not totally efface the old nature. The born-again believer struggles with the old self and unfortunately often ratifies it, as Paul testified from painful, personal experience in Romans 7. Our discussion in chap. 10 of the doctrine of sanctification treats in detail how the Spirit works in Christians to diminish the power of the old nature and to strengthen the graces of the new nature.

F. Were Old Testament Believers Regenerated?

An interesting but perhaps not a crucial issue is whether faithful souls in OT times were regenerated by the Spirit and given a new nature. The OT refers to the phenomenon of spiritual circumcision. Often God is the one who circumcises (Deut 30:6). In other instances the people were to circumcise (*mûl*) their own hearts (Deut 10:16; Jer 4:4). Both a divine work and a human response, spiritual circumcision is a figure signifying the deepest spiritual reality of the Hebrew religion, namely, the opening of the heart to God (Col 2:11).[72] This event undoubtedly includes repentance and communion with God, but we submit that it falls short of regeneration in the full Christian sense.

First Sam 10:9 speaks of a work of the Spirit on the heart of Saul: "God changed (*hāpak*, to "turn" or "bend") Saul's heart" (cf. v. 6). The NRSV translates this, "God gave him another heart." The language likely speaks of God reshaping Saul's heart in preparation for leadership and battle. That is, God gave Saul a new heart in the sense of a new attitude and new courage for the task to which he was called. The record shows that Saul turned way from the Lord (1 Sam 15:11) and flouted his law (13:12-13; 15:20-23). Hence God rejected Saul as king (15:26-28) and removed his Spirit from him (16:14). Tormented by an evil spirit (16:15-16, 23; 18:10; 19:9), Saul experienced fits of jealousy, depression, and paranoia. He

sought to kill David (1 Samuel 19) and committed atrocities against innocent Gibeonites (2 Sam 21:1). Unable to defeat the Philistine army, Saul
sought help from a medium (1 Samuel 28). What kind of a man was Saul?

> King Saul . . . was basically carnal, willfully disobedient, insanely
> jealous, and bloodthirsty in the later years of his reign. The purpose
> of Saul's reign was to prepare Israel to appreciate all the more the
> reign of a true man of God, David, son of Jesse, who came from the
> tribe of Judah, and who was determined to serve as a faithful theo-
> cratic ruler and an obedient servant of Yahweh.[73]

God used Saul for a time to deliver Israel from heathen oppressors, even
as Satan used the man for his own purposes. It is quite unlikely that Saul
experienced Spirit regeneration as described in the NT.

The OT prophets vividly expressed the hope of future spiritual rebirth.
Yahweh promised his people that he would create in them a new heart: "I
will give them a heart to know me, that I am the Lord" (Jer 24:7). In Jer
31:31-34 the Lord stated that in coming days he would make a "new
covenant" (v. 31) with his people that would be far superior to the old
covenant. The latter, instituted at Sinai, was (1) a national covenant (made
with "the house of Israel and with the house of Judah," v. 31); (2) an external covenant, inscribed on stone or parchments; and (3) a conditional
covenant that Israel repeatedly broke (v. 32). Sealed by circumcision, the
old covenant could not give life (Gal 3:21). In this prophecy God promised
that the new covenant (inaugurated by Jesus, Matt 26:28; Mark 14:24)
would transform the human heart as the old covenant could not. "I will
put my law in their minds and write it on their hearts. I will be their God,
and they will be my people" (v. 33). This internalization of the law on the
heart would be realized through regeneration and union with Christ in the
new age of the Spirit. "The entire transformation implies the new birth set
forth in the gospel."[74] Jeremiah added that as a result of the Spirit's regenerating work Yahweh "will forgive their wickedness and will remember
their sins no more" (under the old covenant sins were remembered). In
sum, the law inscribed within by the Spirit "gives intimate knowledge of
and fellowship with God, forgiveness of sins, and peace of heart."[75] These
promises came to fruition in the age of the Spirit through Christ's cross,
resurrection, and ascension to heaven.

Ezek 36:25-27 extends a further promise of future, spiritual transformation. Consistent with the comprehensive nature of biblical prophecy,
Yahweh's promise to restore Israel to the land also anticipated a qualitatively new work of the Spirit on the heart. The text promises (1) complete
purification of sins: "I will sprinkle clean water on you . . . ; I will cleanse

you from all your impurities and from all your idols" (v. 25; cf. Jer 31:34). There follows the promise (2) of a radically new nature: "I will give you a new heart and put a new spirit in you; I will remove from you your heart of stone and give you a heart of flesh" (v. 26; cf. Ezek 11:19; 18:31). In the future God will replace the old heart with a spiritually transformed heart. The Lord promised (3) a permanent bestowal of the Spirit in the Gospel era. Said Yahweh, "I will put my Spirit in you and move you to follow my decrees and be careful to keep my laws" (v. 27; cf. Ezek 37:14; 39:29; Joel 2:28-29). A distinctive feature of existence under the new covenant would be the permanent, indwelling ministry of the life-giving Spirit (cf. 2 Cor 3:6). Finally, the outcome of the Spirit's ministry is (4) instinctive obedience to the law in a God-honoring life (v. 27b; Jer 31:33). In OT times God was *with* his people. But the glorious promise is given that in the future God would dwell *in* his people by virtue of the Spirit's transforming work. The reader is impressed by the number of times in Ezekiel 36 that the phrase "I will" occurs with God as the subject—a dozen times in vv. 24-30 alone. This, of course, indicates that the divine activity is the efficient cause of spiritual regeneration.

The vision of Ezek 37:1-14 anticipated, proximately, Israel's restoration to the land and, ultimately, the Spirit's regenerating work under the new covenant (cf. Jer 31:31-34; Ezek 11:19). God gave Ezekiel a vision of a valley filled with dry bones. Like the host of bones in the vision, Israel in Babylon was spiritually dead. Yet at God's first word through Ezekiel the bones came together (vv. 7-8), signifying immediately Israel's national restoration (vv. 12-14). At God's second word "the breath [*hārûaḥ*] came into them" (v. 10, NRSV), and the lifeless forms came alive and stood on their feet. The latter aspect of the vision likely anticipates the spiritual renewal of believers in the Gospel era and perhaps the end-time conversion of multitudes of Jews (Rom 11:25-32). Again it is God who breathes the dry bones into life and wholeness (vv. 5, 10).

Turning to the NT, Jesus explained to Nicodemus the necessity of new birth by water and the Spirit (John 3:3-8). Judaism acknowledged the coming of the messianic kingdom (Dan 2:44; 7:14, 27), which they defined as a new creation or "regeneration" (*palingenesia*, Matt 19:28) in the future age. But of a personal, spiritual regeneration in the present the learned Nicodemus was totally ignorant, as his bewildered reply confirms (vv. 4, 9). This argument from silence may suggest that Spirit regeneration was not a conscious feature of Jewish spiritual life under the old covenant. Tenney agrees with this judgment, in the following words: "In Old Testament teaching, the Spirit came upon the prophets or other specially chosen men for unusual reasons, but nowhere in Judaism was taught the coming of the Spirit upon all men for their personal regeneration."[76]

Jesus made a distinction between the Spirit's occasional ministry prior to Pentecost and his permanent, transformational ministry thereafter. In John 14:17 Jesus instructed his disciples about the ministry of the "Counselor" or "the Spirit of truth," saying, "you know him, for he lives with you and will be in you" (*hymeis ginōskete auto, hoti par hymin menei kai en hymin estin*). Prior to Pentecost the Spirit was "with" or "beside" (*para*) the disciples and OT saints as a variable influence.[77] But after this eschatological event the Spirit would be "in" (*en*) them permanently as a transforming and indwelling presence. Jesus added, "On that day you will realize that I am in my Father, and you are in me, and I am in you" (v. 20; cf. Rom 8:9). While Jesus was with his disciples, they did not fully possess the Spirit, as John 14:26 and 16:7, 13 make clear. But after Jesus was glorified, the life-transforming ministry of the Spirit would take place (John 7:38-39). Following Easter and Pentecost, Christ would take up his abode in believers and they in him in a manner analogous to the mutual indwelling of the Father and the Son.

Although it is best not to be dogmatic on this issue, we propose the following conclusion as befitting the biblical data. God set believing men and women in OT times in a right relationship with himself. Their sins were forgiven (Ps 32:1-2; 85:2), they communed with the Lord, and they anticipated the blessings of heaven (Heb 11:13-16, 39). But before the completion of Christ's work and the Pentecostal outpouring, OT believers did not possess the Spirit as a permanent endowment (Ps 51:11), and they were not completely transformed thereby. A principal benefit of the new covenant is the qualitatively different ministry of the Holy Spirit—including a radical, spiritual transformation that the NT identifies as the new birth. Expressed in other words, it seems unlikely that NT texts such as 2 Cor 5:17 and 2 Pet 1:4 could be applied to OT believers. We recognize that there are not two ways of salvation. The saving of the soul in both the pre-Christian and the Christian eras is achieved by faith in God's faithful word of promise. But salvation under the new covenant is a fuller, richer reality than that experienced under the old. Otherwise, it would have been unnecessary for Christ to enter this hellish scene, suffer, die a cruel death, and rise victoriously from the grave.

G. Are Children Who Die in Infancy Saved?

A variety of answers have been given to this difficult question of the spiritual condition of infants who succumb to death. (1) For most liberal theologians the question is moot, in that they believe infants are born into the world free from sin and en route to salvation. Modernists claim that the loving God accepts into heaven all people, who are all his children by birth. (2) Traditional Roman Catholics, on the other hand, maintain that infants inherit from their parents the contagion of sin. The sacrament of baptism administered to children is said to remove the guilt and penalty of original sin. Thus children who receive a legitimate baptism are united with Christ and inherit heaven's glory. Infants who are not baptized will endure a just penalty in the netherworld. (3) Many Arminians accept the reality of original sin, depravity, and punishment. But through the benefit of prevenient grace, guilt and punishment are said to be removed, such that no infant is condemned eternally. Blessed by universal grace, those who die in infancy are freely welcomed into God's heaven. (4) Covenant Reformed, or high Calvinists, likewise view infants as defiled by Adamic sin. But God is said secretly to work regeneration in those infants who are elect. Many, such as John Owen, identify infants born into a Christian family and so blessed by the covenant of grace as among God's elect. At death these are said to inherit heaven's glory, whereas non-elect infants are justly damned. The Westminster Confession of Faith (chap. X.3) states that "Elect infants, dying in infancy, are regenerated and saved by Christ through the Spirit, who worketh when, and where, and how he pleaseth." (5) Moderately Reformed Christians acknowledge that infants are born with the affliction of original sin. Many, such as Charles Hodge, A.A. Hodge, and A.H. Strong, recall that infants have not deliberately flaunted God's will for their lives. Thus by virtue of the absence of premeditation, naiveté, and trustfulness in children prior to the "age of moral accountability," God applies to them the benefits of Christ's saving work at their death. Thus all little ones who die in infancy, as well as adults who are mentally incompetent, are regenerated and saved by Christ. Arminians and moderately Reformed thus arrive at the same conclusion, albeit by different lines of reasoning.

The Baptist and broadly Reformed theologian A.H. Strong argued that since infants prior to the age of moral accountability have not personally and volitionally transgressed God's law, they are characterized by "a relative innocence" and "trustfulness."[78] If children should die in the state of infancy, they become the objects of special, divine compassion and receive a secret application of the Atonement. Thus, "those who die in infancy receive salvation through Christ as certainly as they inherit sin from Adam."[79] Strong surmised that this transaction occurs at the infant soul's first view of Christ in the heavenly world. Strong further theorized that the reason for Scripture's silence on this issue may be that if Scripture had spoken more directly to this issue, some Christian parents might have killed their infant children to guarantee their entry into the kingdom.

We affirm straightaway that Scripture provides no explicit answer to this debated matter of great practical concern. Implicit biblical statements, however, lead us to the probable conclusion that the proposal of Strong and others may be the most viable. Consider the following. When God consigned most of the people of Israel to death in the wilderness, the children who had not come to a state of personal accountability were exempted from execution of the penalty. Thus the Lord said to the people of Israel through Moses, "your children who do not yet know good from bad—they will enter the land. I will give it to them and they will take possession of it" (Deut 1:39). In one text the age of responsibility is given as twenty years (Num 14:29). Later, after David had committed adultery with Bathsheba, God caused the child of that illicit union to become ill and to die (2 Sam 12:15-19). David then said to his servants, "Can I bring him back again? I will go to him, but he will not return to me" (v. 23). At the child's death David was encouraged in his spirit, likely at the prospect of seeing his child in heaven one day.

Our Lord's attitude toward little children is also instructive. During his final ministry in Galilee, Jesus placed a little child among his disciples and said to them, "I tell you the truth, unless you change and become like little children, you will never enter the kingdom of heaven. Therefore whoever humbles himself like this child is the greatest in the kingdom of heaven. And whoever welcomes a little child like this in my name welcomes me. But if anyone causes one of these little ones who believe in me to sin, it would be better for him to have a large millstone hung around his neck and to be drowned in the depths of the sea" (Matt 18:3-6). Jesus added, "your Father in heaven is not willing that any of these little ones should be lost" (v. 14). Later in Judea, when the disciples rebuked those who brought little children to Jesus for blessing and prayer, Jesus said, "Let the little children come to me, and do not hinder them, for the kingdom of heaven belongs to such as these" (Matt 19:14). Jesus accorded special worth and status in the kingdom to children by virtue of their dependence, humility, and lack of pretension.

The most cogent explanation of this problem is that children incapable of committing willful and responsible violations of God's law may receive a special application of Christ's universal atonement and so be welcomed into heaven's glory. In other words, children who die in infancy prior to becoming responsible moral agents prove to be among God's elect. If true, this judgment is a source of great comfort and consolation to godly parents who grieve over the premature death of an infant child.

IV. PRACTICAL IMPLICATIONS OF
THE DOCTRINE OF REGENERATION

A. Don't Trust Christian Parentage or
Baptism for New Life

Contrary to Roman Catholic, Lutheran, and high Anglican views, the water of baptism applied to infants and adults does not of itself regenerate and unite souls with Christ. We noted above that the sign of the sacrament (i.e., water) and the reality symbolized (i.e., washing of sins and new birth) are closely related. Yet the sign of the sacrament does not of itself accomplish what it signifies. For example, a wedding ceremony does not create love or commitment; it celebrates and seals existing love and commitment between a man and a woman. Likewise, a Christian funeral does not promote the deceased saint to glory; it celebrates God's great work of glorifying his departed son or daughter. Biblical Christians thus will avoid all forms of ritualistic religion that claim that baptismal water, applied on ecclesiastical authority, works spiritual regeneration. Although some churches teach the *ex opere operato* concept (i.e., that the mere performance of baptism regenerates the soul), Scripture stops well short of such a claim. Water baptism under the aegis of a church or birth into a Christian family cannot produce a new creation, quicken a dead soul, circumcise a proud heart, or cleanse deeply ingrained sin. This is to say that water baptism is not the indispensable condition by which God regenerates sinful souls. External ceremonies, however rich in religious symbolism, are impotent to bring new spiritual life to depraved hearts. The evangelist should not cite the requirement of water baptism in the invitation to receive Christ and spiritual life.

B. Rely on the Holy Spirit to Make
Sinners New Creations

We have seen that regeneration is not a matter of personal re-education, nor is it a self-wrought process of moral reformation and character enhancement. Neither is regeneration achieved by birth in a Christian family, by baptism, by psychotherapy, or by a host of modern self-improvement schemes. If regeneration is not achieved by humans alone, neither is it a synergistic affair, i.e., of a person's cooperation with God to accomplish the desired end. The Bible is absolutely clear on this; no carnal means can effect supernatural regeneration from above. Flesh cannot give birth to spirit; sinners cannot alter their depraved dispositions. God's Spirit alone must effect the radically new creation of which the NT speaks (2 Cor 5:17; Gal 6:15).

The responsibility of Christians in all this is to *proclaim* to sinners that they must be born again (John 3:7). We must *explain* clearly the Gospel offer of new birth and life from above (Acts 5:20). Disciples also must *plead* with sinners to trust Christ and become God's forgiven children (2 Cor 5:20). We must do the work of an evangelist in the power of the Spirit of life (1 Cor. 12:3-11), for even Jesus, the Son of God, needed the Spirit's power in his ministry (Matt 3:16-17; Luke 3:21-22), as did his immediate disciples (Luke 24:48-49; John 20:22; Acts 1:8). Our task as Jesus' followers is to proclaim the Gospel clearly and persuasively (Acts 2:38; 16:30-32; Rom 10:14), trusting the Spirit of God to bring forth new life as it pleases him. Faithful disciples will know that the *basis* of regeneration is Christ's death and resurrection (1 Cor 6:11; 1 Pet 1:3); the *means* of regeneration is the Word of God (Eph 5:26; Jas 1:18); the *providential instrument* is the preacher or herald of God's truth (Rom 10:13-15); and the *agent* of regeneration is the Spirit of God (John 3:5; Tit 3:5).

African believers help us western Christians understand the full scope of preaching and witness. By "preaching" they mean everything from sharing one's personal testimony with a needy soul, to telling the story of Jesus under a tree in the market, to delivering a sermon in a crowded church. In disagreement with Finney and certain other revivalists, we do not dictate to the Spirit of God when he must regenerate a soul. We dare not command God to regenerate sinners before the close of a given evangelistic service, for example. The creation of new spiritual life is God's gracious work done in God's good time. Our task is to be faithful witnesses and fervent prayer-warriors and to leave the results to the sovereign, wise, and loving God.

C. Personal Regeneration Followed by Social Transformation

Viewing sin primarily as deprivation caused by institutionalized injustice, social gospel proponents and liberationists call for the transformation or regeneration of society. Those of liberal theological persuasion allege that the replacement of corrupt social, political, and economic structures with just ones will humanize society and in time inaugurate the kingdom of God. These social idealists identify the instruments of social transformation as better housing, law enforcement, health care, job training, and the like.

Historic Christians will insist on the primacy of personal conversion and regeneration as the only sound basis for social transformation.

Institutional change alone cannot solve the intractable problems caused by human sinfulness. Absent personal regeneration that changes individuals' motives, passions, and behavior, society's institutions will go from bad to worse. History amply attests that social improvement without personal regeneration is a romantic dream and a forlorn hope. Society will continue to be deranged, despotic, and demonic unless founded on sound biblical principles and shaped by twice-born people. Eighteenth-century England was characterized by illiteracy, poverty, rampant crime, mob violence, wild orgies, brutal treatment of offenders, and general debauchery.

> It was the England of the slave-trader, the kidnapper, the smuggler; the England of gin-shops, sodden ignorance and incredible child neglect; the England of bestial sports, mad gambling and parading wantonness. It was the England of corrupt politics and soulless religion: the England of "materialism," "dim ideals" and "expiring hopes."[80]

Yet the spiritual revival God's Spirit wrought through John Wesley and others radically changed the whole of English society. The power of the Gospel brought about genuine reform of the economy, the educational system, land ownership, medical care, the penal system, and the nation's moral climate, to name a few areas of change. Wesley's revival of Christian faith "made the selfish man self-denying, the discontented happy, the worlding spiritually minded, the drunkard sober, the sensual chaste, the liar truthful, the thief honest, the proud humble, the godless godly, the thriftless thrifty."[81] Wesley's class meetings and Sunday schools created the middle class in a society that knew only a privileged aristocracy and an impoverished, laboring underclass. The Wesleyan revival was the primary impetus for the abolition of the slave trade in early nineteenth-century Britain. Many historians judge that Wesley's spiritual revival saved England from the social chaos of the French Revolution (1789-1799). A further example of social transformation via personal regeneration is the Welsh revivals (1904-1905), where 100,000 conversions to Christ reduced drunkenness by 60 percent and the jail population by 40 percent and fortified Britain for the trauma of World War I.

Even the World Council of Churches, anticipating its Fourth Assembly at Uppsala in 1968 under the theme of "Behold, I make all things new," stated that "neither the renewal of the world nor of the church can be adequately understood without the reorientation of people as persons."[82] This is a significant admission from an international religious organization noted for its commitment to transformation via social and political action. Latin American evangelicals remind us that when radical liberation movements have swept away unjust institutions, the replacement structures often are more corrupt and oppressive than the originals. It appears true that the decency and compassion of a society is directly proportional to the number of its twice-born people. Reflecting on history, Francis Schaeffer concluded, as a rule of thumb, that no society manifests decency, compassion, and stability unless at least 10 percent of its populace are born-again followers of Christ. Evangelical Christians thus regard personal regeneration as the non-negotiable basis for constructive social change. To adopt any other solution is to build on a foundation of shifting sand that cannot withstand the destructive forces of a fallen world (Matt 7:24-27). Social action grounded in personal, spiritual transformation under God's good hand will lead to success. Programs that attempt to renew society without changing the hearts of the people are doomed to disappoint and frustrate.

IV

THE APPLICATION
OF SALVATION

OBJECTIVE
ASPECTS

"Christ Lives in Me"

G A L A T I A N S   2 : 2 0

———□———

THE DOCTRINE OF
UNION WITH CHRIST

I. Introductory
Concerns

In this chapter we examine yet another doctrine in the application of salvation, which is union with Christ, otherwise known as identification with Christ or incorporation into Christ. It commences discussion of the objective aspects of the application of salvation—namely, those aspects that concern the relationship between the individual and God. In the history of Christian thought this reality has been described as "mystical union," stimulated in part by the language of Eph 5:30-32. The concept of union with Christ arises from familiar NT imagery that depicts Christ in the believer (John 15:5; Gal 2:20; Col 1:27) and the believer in Christ (John 15:5; 1 Cor 15:22; 2 Cor 5:17). Yet outside the broadly Reformed tradition[1] the idea of union with Christ has been undervalued. The outcome of this deficiency is that "the majority of Christians much more frequently think of Christ as a Savior outside of them, than as a Savior who dwells within."[2] Yet the biblical writers, especially Paul and John, were anything but reluctant to expound the imagery of the believer's union with Jesus Christ. Indeed, expressions such as *en Christō, en kyriō, en Christō Iēsou, en autō*, etc. occur 216 times in the Pauline corpus and twenty-six times in the Johannine writings. Amply attested in the NT, union with Christ proves to be a central verity, indeed a touchstone reality of the Christian life and experience. The statement of James S. Stewart is hardly exaggerated: "The heart of Paul's religion is union with Christ.

This, more than any other conception . . . is the key which unlocks the secrets of his soul."[3]

A number of issues surrounding this concept beg for answers. Precisely what is the nature of this union between Christ and the Christian? How can one person reside in or be united to another person? Indeed, how can one who is *God* abide in a human who is finite and sinful? In terms of the actualization of this union, is the Christian's selfhood merged into or absorbed by the Deity as a drop of water is absorbed in a vast ocean? How does the NT depict and explain incorporation into Christ? Should we regard the union primarily as a legal or an experiential reality? Moreover, is mystical union something that occurred in eternity past, or is it initiated in the present? Furthermore, is incorporation into Christ an individual reality, a corporate reality, or perhaps both? What are the potential social implications of this doctrine for the church?

By what means does incorporation into Christ occur? Is it initiated, as some authorities suggest, by the sacraments of baptism and the Eucharist? Practically, what are the spiritual outcomes of union with Christ in the life and experience of believers? How does this reality affect the living of the Christian life in terms of empowerment, sanctification, and service? Also we inquire whether OT saints, prior to the advent of Christ and the out-pouring of the Holy Spirit, experienced this kind of union. The previous chapter explored the same question with regard to the new birth.

Finally, is union with Christ a discrete event in the scheme of salvation (*ordo salutis*), or, is it a more comprehensive reality embracing the whole of redemption? If the former, what is the relation of union with Christ with other elements in the application of the salvation wrought by Christ?

II. HISTORICAL INTERPRETATIONS OF UNION WITH CHRIST

Union with Christ is a somewhat enigmatic concept, and as such has been interpreted in quite different ways in the broad history of the church. The following section outlines the principal ways in which the notion of the Christian's union with Christ has been understood.

A. An Ontological Union
(Neoplatonists and Mystical Theologians)

Church authorities that subscribed to this view described the soul's union with Christ in language that suggests absorption into the divine life.

Mystical union with Christ was said to involve experiences of ecstasy and rapture, suspension of human faculties, and "deification"—the latter explained as "an entrance upon a new order of life so high and so harmonious with reality that it can only be called divine."[4] Notwithstanding the fact that some leading mystics were devout Christians, their emphasis on the divine immanence threatened to collapse the Christian world-and-life view into pantheism. Their quest for immediate and exalted consciousness of God tended to give way to personal deification, where the self is absorbed in the ocean of Divine Love. Advocates found justification for this viewpoint in the words of the apostle Paul, who wrote, "I have been crucified with Christ and I no longer live, but Christ lives in me" (Gal 2:20).

A strong mystical strand occurred in the spirituality of the Eastern church arising from the synthesis of Christianity and Neoplatonism. Alexandrian Neoplatonists insisted that the souls of the truly spiritual become lost in God or even fused with God. According to the authority known as Pseudo-Dionysius (c. 500), the threefold mystical way involves (1) purification, (2) illumination, and (3) union with God (*henōsis*). The goal of the spiritual life was to lose oneself completely in the Absolute or the Abyss. This outcome, achieved only by highly disciplined practitioners of imageless (apophatic) prayer, involved abandonment into the darkness of unknowing, sharing in the divine nature, and deification. This unknown Syrian monk challenged true spiritual seekers as follows: "in the earnest exercise of mystical contemplation, abandon all sensation and all intellectual activities . . . thus you will unknowingly be elevated, as far as possible, to the unity of that beyond being and knowledge."[5]

The western mystics Eckhart, Tauler, and Suso were members of the informal society known as the Friends of God. Meister Eckhart (d. 1327), a German Dominican monk and Neoplatonist theologian, postulated that all things have flowed from God and all will return to their ineffable Source. Sin caused man's fall from the One, whereas Christ's work restores the broken unity. Eckhart described the soul's becoming one with God in perfect union succinctly: "the soul is completely dissolved in God and God in it."[6] He further wrote, "He who is one with God, is 'one spirit' with God, *the same existence.*"[7] Eckhart used several analogies to illustrate this union of the soul with God. The first was the transformation of the sacramental bread into the body of Christ. Analogously, "I am so changed into him that he produces his being in me as one, not just similar."[8] Others include fire invading wood until it changes the wood into itself, and a drop of water mixed in a cask of wine (cf. Eutychianism). Eckhart judged that union with God is achieved by imageless contemplation, detachment from all created things, and suffering for Christ. A papal bull issued by John

XXII declared twenty-eight of Eckhart's propositions pantheistic, seventeen heretical, and eleven dangerous.

John Tauler (d. 1361), a German Dominican preacher, taught that before emanating from God the person was one in essence with God: "man was everlasting in God, before his creation in time. When he was in Him, he was God in God."[9] The goal of the mystical way is to reestablish this pre-temporal union by return into God. The latter involves "the transition into a divinized life, into a union of our created spirit with God's uncreated spirit." Tauler elaborated upon this idea as follows: God "raises man from a human to a divine mode of being . . . in which man becomes so divinized that everything which he is and does, God is and does in him. Such a person is raised so far above any natural mode that he truly becomes by grace what God is essentially by nature. In this state, man feels himself lost in God. He neither knows nor feels nor experiences his former self; he knows only God's simple essence."[10] Tauler echoed Eckhart's thought when he illustrated the nature of the union: "Man's spirit is as it were sunk and lost in the Abyss of the Deity, and loses the consciousness of all creature-distinctions. All things are gathered together in one with the divine sweetness, and the man's being is so penetrated with the divine substance that he loses himself therein, as a drop of water is lost in a cask of strong wine. And thus the man's spirit is so sunk in God in divine union, that he loses all sense of distinction."[11]

Henry Suso (d. 1365), the Dominican disciple of Eckhart, wrote the following about the earthly goal of the Christian mystic: "he forgets himself, he is no longer conscious of his selfhood; he disappears and loses himself in God, and becomes one spirit with him, as a drop of water which is drowned in a great quantity of wine. . . . All human desires are taken from them in an indescribable manner, they are rapt from themselves, and are immersed in the Divine Will."[12]

The anonymous fourteenth-century English work *The Cloud of Unknowing* reflects the mystical theology of Dionysius. The subtitle of the book reveals the author's guiding presupposition: "in the which [cloud] a soul is oned with God." In the practice of imageless contemplation the Christian suspends all mental and bodily activities and enters the cloud where the self becomes lost in the reality of God. More radically still, "the stark awareness of your own existence . . . must go, before you experience contemplation in perfection."[13] *The Cloud* does not shrink from employing the daring language of deification: "it is only by his wholly undeserved mercy that you are made a god by grace, inseparably united to him in spirit, here and hereafter in the bliss of heaven, world without end."[14]

B. A Sacramental Union
(Roman Catholics, Lutherans, Anglo-Catholics)

Proponents of this view claim that persons are united with or incorporated into Christ in a *substantial* sense by partaking of the sacraments, particularly baptism and the Eucharist. Roman Catholicism traditionally claims that the church, headed by the pope, is an extension or continuation of the Incarnation. Through the church, or the mystical body of Christ, the divine-human life of Jesus is channeled to the world. Thus, "The Church is a 'sacrament,' that is a sign and instrument both of a very close knit union with God and of the unity with the whole human race."[15] Specifically, Rome claims that through the sacraments of baptism and the Mass the faithful are united to the glorified Lord and partake of the divine nature.

Baptism, Rome claims, unites participants to Christ and to his body, the church, through the grace of regeneration. Thus the term "christening," applied to infant baptism, denotes being made one with Christ. As one Catholic authority typically expressed it, "It is through baptism in faith (Col 2:11-12; Rom 6:3-14; 1 Cor 12:13; Eph 5:26) that the sinner . . . is attached to Christ and to the work wrought by Christ in His own Body, and is made one Body with Christ living now as 'spiritual body' and 'life-giving Spirit' (1 Cor 15:44-45)."[16]

Moreover, the Eucharist unites participants most intimately with Christ and with other members of his body, the church. Based on the real presence of Christ in the Supper ("this is my body," "this is my blood," Matt 26:26-28) and the notion of eating Jesus' flesh and drinking his blood (John 6:50-57), Rome claims that Christians take Christ into themselves via a literal feeding in the Mass. The claim is made that as food is ingested into the body thereby nourishing it, so Christ is taken into the soul and graciously enriches it each time the Mass is offered (*ex opere operato*).

Karl Adam (d. 1966) wrote that the sacraments instituted by Christ "are the truest expression and result of that original and central Christian belief that the Christian should be inseparably united with Christ and should live in Christ."[17] Baptism and the Eucharist, particularly, suggest the fundamental idea of permanent union or incorporation of the faithful in Christ. Concerning the first he wrote, "In the sacrament of Baptism . . . the sacrificial blood of Christ flows into the soul, purifies it from all the infirmity of original sin and permeates it with its own sacred strength."[18] And with respect to the second he added, "We eat His flesh and drink His blood. So greatly does Jesus love His community, that . . . He enters into a real union of flesh and blood with it, and binds it to His being even as the branch is bound to the vine."[19]

Anthony Wilhelm also views the church's sacraments as effectual operations of the Spirit whereby union with Christ is accomplished and
strengthened. By the sacrament of baptism participants are united with
Christ and his body, the church. So Wilhelm writes that by baptism "we
are raised to the very level of God, transformed more and more into
him."[20] And by the Eucharist, as Christ's sacrifice is mysteriously renewed,
the Lord comes to participants as sacred food and sacred drink. Through
celebration of the Mass the participant is perfectly united with God.
Writes Wilhelm, "If our eyes could see what is really happening at any
Mass . . . we would see ourselves being drawn into an indescribable union
with divinity."[21]

Andreas Osiander (d. 1552), a Lutheran pastor at Nuremberg and later
professor at Königsberg, promoted certain of his pre-conversion Catholic
beliefs. The Logos or divine Christ, Osiander averred, unites with the elements in the Lord's Supper in a kind of hypostatic union. As one partakes
of the Eucharist, the substance of Christ according to his divine nature is
infused within the person, resulting in a union of essence. That is, at the
table Christ indwells the Christian essentially (2 Pet 1:4), not merely spiritually. As interpreted by Steinmetz, "There is a sense, then, in which
Christians by receiving the indwelling word and participating in the divine
nature become themselves Jesus Christs. Having been restored to the image
of God through him and in constant dependence on him, they are like him
in every important respect. He is the original, and they are the carbon
copies."[22] This essential union of the Christian with Christ, effected by the
sacrament, results in the infusion of an "essential righteousness." Osiander
thus upheld a real or imparted, rather than a legal or imputed, righteousness. Osiander's views were extensively refuted by John Calvin and
opposed by the Lutheran Formula of Concord (1576/84).[23]

The Oxford Anglo-Catholic theologian E. L. Mascall (b. 1905) wrote
that "The Christian is a man to whom something has *happened.*"[24] The
reintegration of humanity by God occurs in three stages. The *first* stage,
the Incarnation, involved Christ's assumption of generic human nature,
whereby manhood was taken up into the life of God. The *second* stage,
the Passion of the universal man, involved payment of the debt owed to
God and the conquest of spiritual foes. Mascall viewed Calvary as a further act of re-creation, not merely an antecedent condition thereof. And
the *third* stage, Incorporation into Christ, represents the outworking of the
fruits of the aforementioned in individual lives.

Mascall viewed Incorporation into Christ as the union of the person
with Christ's human nature, which is hypostatically united with the Being
of God. Wrote he, "because the Christ is both God and man, the Christian,

by his incorporation into Christ, has received a share in the life of God himself. He has been made a partaker of the divine nature, the nature of God who is Trinity."[25] In other words, union with Christ involves "a real supernaturalization of the soul in its ontological depths."[26] Notwithstanding this union, the person remains a creature just as Jesus did. "In the order of supernature he is identified with the Saviour in everything except his indestructible and inconvertible personal individuality."[27] Thus united with Christ, individuals are united with one another in Christ's Body, the extension of the Incarnation, which is the Church.

Mascall averred that the means of incorporation into Christ in the new ontological order is baptism, the sacrament of regeneration. "By baptism, without loss of personal identity, we are incorporated into Christ, that is to say, established *in corpore Christi*, given an ontological union with, and participation in, his glorified human nature, so that all that he possesses in it becomes ours."[28] And whereas one enters this union through baptism, by the Eucharist the Christian is maintained and strengthened in union with Christ, and so the body—the church—is progressively knit together. Wrote Mascall, in the Eucharist "the Christian receives Christ, he is received into Christ, he is received into the glorified Body by partaking of the Sacramental Body and so is built up into the Mystical Body. And for this very reason, in the Eucharist the Mystical Body is itself receiving and being received into its exalted Head."[29] Wherefore Mascall concluded, "in the last resort the sacraments do not exist to remind us of anything, but to make and preserve and extend the Body of Christ, the holy people of God."[30]

C. *A Covenantal Union*
   (Reformed Covenant Theologians)

Reformed theologians who adhere to the system of covenant theology generally interpret union with Christ not as a discrete step in the *ordo salutis* but as a comprehensive concept that embraces the whole scope of salvation from eternity past to eternity future. Covenant theologians hold that all people are united with Adam in the old humanity by virtue of his federal headship under the covenant of works. Analogously, the elect are united with Christ, the second Adam, by virtue of his federal headship under the covenant of grace. This latter union of the saints with Christ comprehends every aspect of salvation from their election to their glorification. Advocates thus aver that Scripture describes the saints as predestined in Christ (Eph 1:4-5), called in Christ (2 Tim 1:9), regenerated in Christ (Eph 2:10), justified in Christ (Rom 8:1), sanctified in Christ (1 Cor 1:4-5), and glorified in Christ (Rom 8:17). Proponents designate the "in

Christ" relation a "mystical" union because it transcends all earthly analogies and all human understanding. They claim that (1) *formally* the federal union of Christ and the elect was established in eternity past in the Covenant of Redemption (Eph 1:4). (2) *Objectively* it was brought about by the Incarnation and atoning work of Christ. And (3) *subjectively* believers experience identification with Christ personally by operation of the Holy Spirit. Kevan expressed the comprehensive scope of union with Christ thusly: "It begins in the eternal thoughts of God and comes to subjective realization in human experience by the power of the Holy Spirit. It is the very beginning of salvation to a sinner, and it is the guarantee of its final consummation."[31] As to its nature, union with Christ is *legal* or *forensic*, in that it determines the believer's standing with God, together with all the privileges associated therewith. In the words of Kuiper, union "is both the fountain and guarantee of every Christian virtue and of every Christian exercise."[32] The union is also *experiential*, involving Christ's indwelling the life through his Spirit, transforming personal character and relationships. Berkhof (d. 1957) addressed this latter aspect when he wrote that union with Christ is "that intimate, vital, and spiritual union between Christ and his people, in virtue of which He is the source of their life and strength, of their blessedness and salvation."[33]

John Murray (d. 1975) viewed union with Christ as the central truth of the doctrine of salvation. It is a broad category that brings together every aspect of the plan of salvation, past, present, and future. Wrote Murray, "Union with Christ is a very inclusive subject. It embraces the wide span of salvation from the ultimate source in the eternal election of God to its final fruition in the glorification of the elect."[34] With regard to (1) the *inception* of salvation, union with Christ involves the election of all believers in Christ (Eph 1:3-4). "There was no election of the Father in eternity apart from Christ. And that means that those who will be saved were not even contemplated by the Father in the ultimate counsel of his predestinating love apart from union with Christ—they were *chosen* in Christ."[35] Concerning (2) the *continuation* of salvation, union involves establishment of fellowship with the risen Christ. By an actual partaking of Christ, the saving grace, life, and power of the Savior become operative in the believer (Rom 6:4, 11). This present aspect of union involves effectual calling, regeneration, conversion, justification, adoption, sanctification, and perseverance. Finally, with respect to (3) the *consummation* of salvation, union involves the believer's bodily resurrection (1 Cor 15:22-23) and glorification (Rom 8:17b) with Christ.

Anthony A. Hoekema (d. 1988) agreed with Murray that union with Christ is not merely one phase of the temporal application of redemption;

rather it is a comprehensive concept that undergirds the whole of redemption from eternity past to eternity future. Without explicitly relating the concept to the system of covenant theology, he argued that union with Christ has its *roots* in divine election, its *basis* in Christ's redemptive work, its *establishment* with believers in time, and its *consummation* in heaven.

Expanding on this summary, Hoekema affirmed that (1) union with Christ began with God's elective decision, made before the creation of the world, to save his people in and through Jesus Christ (Eph 1:3-4). Thus, "Union with Christ is not something 'tacked on' to our salvation; it is there from the outset, even in the plan of God."[36] (2) Union with Christ is grounded in the Savior's redemptive work on the cross in history. Christ performed his saving work, Hoekema insisted, not on behalf of the world as a whole but for a distinct group of people, i.e., those in union with him (Eph 5:25; Tit 2:14). (3) Union with Christ is actually established with the elect after they are born and throughout the course of their lives. Hoekema added that the elect (a) are initially united with Christ in regeneration (Eph 2:4-5, 10), (b) live out this union by faith (Gal 2:20; Eph 3:16-17), (c) attain righteousness or justification through this union (2 Cor 5:21), (d) experience sanctification of life through union with Christ (John 15:4-5; Rom 6:4, 11), and (e) persevere to the end in union with him (Rom 8:38-39). Finally, (4) union with Christ is consummated following death in the life to come. Thus at the *Parousia* believers (a) will be raised with Christ (1 Cor 15:22-23; 1 Thess 4:16) and (b) will be glorified with him forever (1 Thess 4:17). In sum, "Union with Christ was planned from eternity, and is destined to continue eternally."[37]

D. A Moral or Filial Union
(Socinians, Rationalists, Liberals)

Naturalistically inclined theologians compromise the supernatural, mysterious, and indissoluble character of Christ's union with his people in favor of weaker definitions. They variously explain the union of Christ and the Christian morally and relationally in terms of (1) the alliance of friendship and trust that existed between the man Jesus and the Father (John 17:21-26), (2) the brotherly fellowship that exists between believers (Acts 4:32), (3) the sentimental union that exists between friend and friend (1 Sam 18:1), and (4) even God's natural presence in all human spirits (cf. Acts 17:27-28).

Lyman Abbott (d. 1922), a Congregationalist minister with a Puritan upbringing, viewed himself as a "Christian evolutionist." He held that all persons are children of the Father, made in his image, and redeemed by his love. Humanity, however, has wandered from God and needs to be brought back to their spiritual home. Union with God (John 17:21) means that people are restored to companionship with God and then work with Jesus to build a new social order. Concerning the nature of this union, God and man are united in Christ "not as the river is united with the sea, losing its personality therein, but as the child is united with the father or the wife with the husband, the personality and individuality of man strengthened and increased by the union."[38] This restorative union of man with God, Abbott insisted, occurs through the forces of moral and spiritual evolution. Thus, the immanent God, who indwelt the man Jesus, now enters into human consciousness, filling lives with himself. Abbott wrote, "whether we look at the individual, the church, or society, we see the process of that spiritual evolution by which, through Jesus Christ, men are coming first to know God, and then to dwell with him. Under the inspirational power of the divine spirit their spiritual nature is growing stronger and their animal and earthly nature more subjugated."[39] Furthermore, "The Bible, . . . revealing in the person of Jesus Christ an incarnate God dwelling in a perfect man, emphasizes the fundamental truth that in their essential natures God and man are the same, and points forward to the time when man, redeemed from the earthly and animal debris which still clings to him, shall be presented faultless, because filled with the divine indwelling."[40]

Adolf von Harnack (d. 1930), the Protestant church historian and disciple of A. Ritschl, drew a distinction between (1) the simple religion of Jesus and the early church and (2) the Hellenized dogma of the later Christian movement. For the primitive community, "religion was *an actual experience*, and involved the consciousness of a living union with God."[41] The early Christian church enjoyed a union of personal relation involving a Spirit-energized "immediacy of religious life and feeling."[42] This brotherly union of the disciples with one another illustrates believers' union of devotion and reverence for Jesus. In the second century, Harnack averred, this simple life relation was transformed into a formal dogma as part of the "acute Hellenization" of the faith. In this fashion, Greek philosophy altered the simple ethical relation into the formula of a mysterious and supernatural union of Christians with the Christ of the Trinity.

Shailer Mathews (d. 1941), Dean of the University of Chicago Divinity School and a self-styled "modernist," viewed God as immanent in the historical process, in persons, and especially in the man Jesus. "The Modernist . . . believes that God is active and mysteriously present in the ordered course of nature and social evolution."[43] Mathews posited a renewing and vitalizing union with God that occurs in those who follow the ideals of Jesus. Elaborating on the nature of this union, he insisted that it is life ordered in accord with God's perfect plan; it is an alignment of the person with the mind, will, and values of Jesus. In short, union describes a life lived in fellowship with God. Thus, Mathews wrote of "voluntary personal union with God and the consequent all-sufficient reinforcement of [man's] spiritual life by God."[44] The outcomes of union with God are chiefly psychological, namely, the transformation and ennoblement of human personality. Mathews interpreted union with God both individually and socially. "Modernism . . . seeks to bring men both individually and socially into intelligent, helpful relations with God."[45]

E. An Experiential Union
(Many Evangelicals)

This interpretation views union with Christ as a discrete stage in the *ordo salutis*. It regards the born-again believer's union with Christ as a profound relation of personal identification and fellowship with the Savior. Inherent is the notion that the believer has died with Christ and is raised to a new life with him (Rom 6:3-11). Accordingly the NT portrays the believer in Christ (John 14:20; Rom 8:1; 2 Cor 5:17; Eph 2:13; 1 John 2:6; 4:13), Christ in the believer (John 14:20; Rom 8:10; Gal 2:20; Col 1:27), Jesus and the Father in the believer (John 14:23), and the Christian as a partaker of the divine nature (2 Pet 1:4). Concerning the *en Christō* motif, *en* has a local sense; it describes the believer's new situation, sphere, or environment as transferred from the domain of sin to the realm of new, spiritual life. Union with Christ thus marks the end of the old existence and the beginning of the new.

Advocates of this interpretation describe the new reality as (1) a *supernatural* union effected not by human initiative but by the Spirit of God himself (1 Cor 12:13; 1 John 3:24). The relation between the believer and Christ is not grounded in the nature of things, as is the relation between Adam and the human race (Rom 5:12-21). It is further (2) a *vital* union. In the new relationship with Christ, spiritual life and fruitfulness are imparted experientially to believers (John 15:2-7; cf. Rom 6:11; 12:2; 2 Cor 4:16). Proponents deny that union with Christ involves a unity of essence between man and God, as proposed by Christian mystics and pantheists. Rather, the human soul retains its creatureliness and individuality while being graciously energized by the Spirit. It is, moreover, (3) a *mysterious* union, in the sense that Scripture does not unfold the precise nature of the relation. Paul described the relation between Christ and the church as "a profound mystery" (Eph 5:32; cf. Col 1:27). Scripture assists our comprehension by illustrating the union by means of analogies from the world of experience (see the section to follow). In addition, it is (4) an *eternal and indissoluble* union (John 10:28; Rom 8:38-39). Once formed, the union between Christ and the believer is never broken. Finally, (5) the spiritual union between Christ and his people is both *individual and corporate*. It is a relation ensuing from the Spirit's operation in the believing soul (2 Cor 5:17; Phil 3:8-11). By extension ("to [all] the saints in Christ Jesus," Eph 1:1; Phil 1:1; cf. Col 1:2) the union can be conceived as between Christ and the entire church (1 Thess 1:1; 2 Thess 1:1). As Shedd comments, the union "results from regeneration, not from creation. Consequently it is not universal but particular."[46]

Proponents of this experiential interpretation further state that union with Christ was *planned* in eternity past in the sovereign counsel of God (Eph 1:4; cf. John 17:2), was *objectively factualized* via Christ's death and resurrection (Rom 6:5), and is *subjectively realized* by the baptizing ministry of the Spirit in individual lives (1 Cor 12:13). Incorporation into Christ first occurs as an actual experience the moment a believing sinner is made alive in Christ (Eph 2:5). Thus the logical order of the application of salvation on the *subjective* side is calling, conversion, and regeneration and on the *objective* side is union with Christ, justification, and adoption. Logically, Christ's righteousness can only be applied to a person in union with the Savior. As Shedd commented, "The impartation of Christ's righteousness presupposes a union with him."[47]

John Calvin (d. 1564) interpreted the union as an experiential appropriation or clothing of the believer with Christ (Gal 3:27). The "mystical union" involves no merging of Christ's essence with ours; rather, it connotes the spiritual indwelling of Christ and his gifts in believing hearts. Calvin stressed that the union describes our participation in Jesus' humanity and in the benefits he achieved via his obedient life and substitutionary death. He wrote, "the flesh of Christ is like a rich and inexhaustible fountain that pours into us the life springing forth from the Godhead into itself."[48] Calvin's point is that we cannot share Christ's saving benefits without possessing him. Thus, "As long as Christ remains outside of us, and we are separated from him, all that he has suffered and done for the salvation of the human race remains useless and of no value to us."[49] This experience of mystical union involves fellowship with Christ, participation in his risen life, and a sharing in his redemptive blessings. In Calvin's words, union describes the experience "when man is received into grace by God to enjoy communion with him and be made one with him."[50] Union logically follows election, effectual calling, and conversion and is effected by the Spirit's grace and power at baptism (Gal 3:26-27).

The old Southern Presbyterian theologian Robert L. Dabney (d. 1898) broadly followed Calvin and the Westminster Confession of Faith. Union with Christ, according to Dabney, assumes three forms: (1) *legal* as the imputation of Christ's righteousness (i.e., justification), (2) *spiritual* or *mystical* as participation in the graces or qualities of Christ our Head (i.e., sanctification), and (3) *social* as the communion of the saints. Biblical analogies include the union of a vine and its branches, the head and members of the body, a husband and wife within the bond of marriage, and the foundation and cornerstone of a building. Dabney noted that Scripture also compares the union of Christ and his people to the bond between the Father and the Son. Yet this analogy does not infer the deification of believers. "The resemblance must be in the community of graces, of affections, and of volitions; and not in the identity of substance and nature."[51] Dabney continued that the bond of the union is the indwelling Spirit, who cements together Christ and his people (1 Cor 6:17; 12:13; 1 John 4:13). Moreover, the instrumental bond of the union is faith; obedient trust initiates and maintains the new relationship (John 14:23; Gal 3:26-28). The result of union with Christ is the application of full redemption to the sinner's soul: "justification, spiritual strength, life, resurrection of the body, good works, prayer and praise, sanctification, perseverance, etc.."[52]

The baptist theologian A.H. Strong (d. 1921) likewise interpreted the NT imagery of the believer "in Christ" and Christ in the believer as a profound relation of fellowship and life. Union with Christ constitutes "a union of life, in which the human spirit, while then most truly possessing its own individuality and personal distinctness, is interpenetrated and energized by the Spirit of Christ, is made inscrutably but indissolubly one with him, and so becomes a member and partaker of that regenerated, believing, and justified humanity of which he is the head."[53] Strong further explained this relation as (1) an "organic union," in which believers become members of Jesus Christ, (2) a "vital union," in which Christ's life becomes the believer's life-principle, (3) a "spiritual union," where the relation is effected and maintained by the Spirit of God, (4) an "indissoluble union," which by God's grace can never be severed, and (5) an "inscrutable union," which transcends the limits of human knowledge and experience. According to Strong, the believer's union with Christ represents the first step in the application of Christ's redemption. Union follows sovereign election and calling. And although the moment of union is also the moment of regeneration, conversion, and justification, union logically precedes these latter movements. In Strong's own words, "union with Christ . . . is begun in regeneration, completed in conversion, declared in justification, and proved in sanctification and perseverance."[54] We concluded in chap. 5, however, that the divine power that enables conversion is the Spirit's calling rather than regenerating work.

The view of an experiential union most faithfully coheres with the biblical point of view, as the discussion in the following section will confirm.

III. EXPOSITION OF THE DOCTRINE
OF UNION WITH CHRIST

A. Variety of Biblical Uses of "In Christ"

The *en Christō* and related expressions found in the Pauline writings do not embody a single idea but are elastic phrases that embrace a wide range of meanings.[55] Paul used *"en Christō," "en Kyriō,"* etc. (1) as a synonym for one who is a Christian (Rom 16:7; 2 Cor 12:2; cf. Phile 16); (2) as a dative of instrument or agency, in the sense of "by" or "through Christ" (Rom 3:24; 5:10b; 1 Cor 1:2; 2 Cor 3:14; 5:19 (cf. v. 18); Gal 2:17; 3:8, 14); (3) as a dative denoting locale (Rom 8:39; Phil 2:5); (4) to connote authoritative basis, i.e., "on the authority of Christ" (1 Thess 4:1); (5) in the sense of "on behalf of Christ" (Phil 1:13); (6) as a dative signifying sphere of reference (Rom 16:8-12; 1 Cor 7:39; 15:31, 58; Eph 1:9; 3:11; Phil 3:3; 1 Thess 4:1). Here the objective sense of the phrase is in view; it denotes the new historical order, the new situation that prevails for those who trust in Christ's death and resurrection. An important aspect of the "in Christ" theme, this usage should not be overlooked.[56] Finally (7) *en Christō* and related expressions are used in the sense that concerns us in the present chapter, namely, of incorporative union or identification with Christ.[57]

The last usage of *en Christō, en Kyriō,* etc. had its genesis in the Johannine idea of the mutual indwelling of believers in Jesus and in the Father. So John recorded Jesus' saying, "On that day you will realize that I am in my Father, and you are in me and I am in you" (John 14:20; cf. 17:21). The reciprocal indwelling of Jesus and believers is also presented in 1 John 4:13: "We know that we live in him and he in us, because he has given us of his Spirit." The indwelling of believers in Jesus alone is attested in 1 John 2:6 and 5:20 and in Jesus and the Father in 1 John 2:24. On the other hand, the indwelling of the Son in believers is indicated in John 17:23 and 1 John 5:20. John alternatively expressed this union of fellowship by the concept of 'abiding.' Thus Jesus said to his disciples, "If you remain in me [*meinēte en emoi*] and my words remain in you, ask whatever you wish" (John 15:7; cf. vv. 9-10). According to 1 John 4:15, believers abide in God and he in them. First John 2:24 states that believers abide in both the Son and the Father. So close is the believer's state of abiding in Jesus that John spoke quite naturally of Jesus' indwelling the believer.

The mutual indwelling cited in John 14:20 (cf. v. 21, 23-24) and John 15:7 (cf. vv. 12-13) involves multiple believers. The abiding cited in 1 John 2:5-6 and 4:15 is explicitly individual. John apparently envisaged no contradiction between believers indwelling Jesus individually and also collectively (see 1 John 4:13, 15; 5:18-20).

John's notions of indwelling and abiding stimulated the distinctive Pauline concept of the believer "in Christ" and Christ in the believer. By means of the phrase *en Christō* and variants (*en Kyriō, en Christō Iēsou, en autō, en hō*) the apostle described the personal union of the believer or believers with Jesus Christ. In certain texts Paul envisaged the intimate relationship of the individual Christian with Christ (2 Cor 5:17; Phil 3:9). In other texts he wrote of the union of multiple believers with Christ, viewed as an aggregate of individuals. In the following Scriptures Paul juxtaposed the many and the one who are in union with Christ (Rom 8:1, cf. v. 2; 1 Cor 1:30, cf. vv. 29, 31; Eph 1:3-4, cf. v. 13; Phil 1:1, 14; 2:1, cf. v. 4; Col. 1:27, cf. v. 28). In still other texts the union envisaged is corporate (1 Cor 15:22; Gal 3:28; Eph 2:13, cf. v. 15). Sometimes Paul contemplated entire churches as being in Christ (and the Father) (Gal 1:22; 1 Thess 1:1; 2:14; 2 Thess 1:1). Guthrie made the important point (true also of the corporate vs. individual election issue) that "What is true of the individual is also true of the community. Indeed, it is questionable whether Paul separated the two concepts in his own mind."[58]

On the other hand, so thorough and intimate is the identification of the believer with Christ that Paul could write of Christ being in the believer. This he did by means of the expressions *en emoi* and *en hymin*. Thus Christ indwells the believer individually (Gal 2:20), collectively as an aggregate of individuals (Rom 8:10, cf. vv. 6-7; 2 Cor 13:5, cf. v. 12; Col 1:27, cf. v. 28), and corporately without differentiation (1 Cor 15:22a). As noted above, so intimate is the union between Christ and the believer (or believers) that the apostle regarded Christ in the believer and the believer in Christ as virtually equivalent expressions.

B. *Illustrations of the Union Between Believers and Christ*

Scripture presents several analogies drawn from the spectrum of human experience that illumine the nature of the union between the Christian and Christ. (1) John illustrated the coincidence of Christ and his people by the imagery of a vine and its branches (John 15:1-17). Significantly, the combination *menō en*—the prototype of Paul's *en Christō* theme—occurs ten times in vv. 1-10 to describe the reciprocal union between Christ and his disciples. As branches live and bear fruit only in union with the vine, so disciples derive their life and productivity from intimate union with Christ and in fellowship with his Word (v. 4).

(2) John compared Jesus' union with believers with the union the divine Son shared with the Father. Thus, "I am in my Father, and you are in me, and I am in you" (John 14:20; cf. 17:21-23). Jesus never said that the latter union is a metaphysical union, as the former is. See the discussion on 2 Pet 1:4 (participation in "the divine nature") in the previous chapter on regeneration. The stated similarity is that Jesus' union with the Father and his union with believers are both unions of life and love (John 14:23) in the bond of the Spirit. In John's language, the union between the Son and the Father is one of 'being' (John 10:38), whereas the union between the Son and believers is one of 'abiding.' John 14:20 and 17:21-23 in no wise endorse an ontological union between Christ and his people.

(3) Paul employed the symbolism of a building to explain the union of the Christian with Christ and with other believers (Eph 2:19-22). The cornerstone (Jesus Christ), the foundation (the apostles and prophets), and individual stones (Jewish and Gentile believers) together constitute a single building (*oikodomē*) or temple (*naos*) in which God lives by his Spirit. Paul further represented the Christian community as "God's temple" (*naos theou*), which constitutes a holy abode for the Spirit (1 Cor 3:16-17). Compare the apostle's words in 1 Cor 3:9: "You are . . . God's building (*oikodomē*)." Similar is the description in 1 Pet 2:4-8. Christ is the "cornerstone," and believers are "living stones" that together form a "spiritual house" (*oikos pneumatikos*)—namely, a building formed and indwelt by the Spirit of God.

(4) Paul further illustrated the union of believers with Christ corporately via the union of the human race in Adam. Thus, "as in Adam all die, so in Christ all will be made alive" (1 Cor 15:22a; cf. Rom 5:12, 15-19). All persons by birth possess natural solidarity with Adam, the biological head of the race. Seminally the human race is one in Adam in a union of death. Analogously, by faith Christians enjoy a spiritual solidarity with Christ, the head of the new race. Spiritually, the people of God are one in Christ in a solidarity of life. "The unity of persons 'in Christ' is analogous to their unity 'in Adam' because both Christ and Adam began an order of life by their decision and actions."[59]

(5) Another picture Paul used to describe union with Christ is that of the parts of the human body that constitute the whole. Paul reasoned that many members or parts (e.g., eye, ear, arm) make up the human body in

its unity as an organism. Correspondingly, Christian believers, though many in number, by Spirit baptism are united with Christ and one another as part of his body, the church (Rom 12:4-5; 1 Cor 12:12-27; Eph 1:22-23; 4:4, 12, 15-16; 5:23, 30). The "body" image is corporate, describing the church universal, and yet the individual believer is not lost sight of in the community of saints. As Parsons observes, "The words ['the body of Christ'] themselves imply two things: personal union with Christ and incorporation in the collective Christian fellowship. This is expressed in Rom 12:5, 'so in Christ we who are many form one body, and each member belongs to all the others.'"[60] Moreover, the union symbolized by the 'body'" language is experiential and not merely formal, for Paul compared it to the body-spirit union with a prostitute (1 Cor 6:15-17). Note that the word "joined" (*kollōmenos*) in vv. 16-17 signifies "join together," "cling to," or "enter into a close relationship with." Finally, as the head of the physical body provides life and direction to the organism, so Christ mediates vitality and growth to the spiritual body of which he is the head.

(6) A final illustration of union with Christ is the lifelong physical, spiritual, emotional, and legal union between a husband and wife in Christian marriage (Eph 5:23-32; cf. Rom 7:2-4). Formerly two unrelated individuals, a man and woman in marriage become an interdependent unity; indeed, "the two . . . become one flesh" (Eph 5:31). In like manner, saints are united with the Savior in the body of Christ, which is the church. The preceding relational images suggest that "in Christ" should be understood in a subjective or experiential sense; the data does not allow us to limit the "in Christ" motif strictly to the formal or objective meaning of the believer's new situation in the state of salvation.

C. The Basis of Union with Christ

Scripture uniformly testifies that the basis or ground of union with Christ is the Savior's atoning death and resurrection. The apostle Paul stated that identification with Christ in his death ("I have been crucified with Christ") and participation in his supernatural life ("Christ lives in me") is made possible by "the Son of God, who loved me and gave himself for me" (Gal 2:20). Elsewhere Paul indicated that Christ's death and resurrection is the prerequisite for the impartation of new life to those who, in identification with him, have died to sin and self (Rom 6:8-10; 2 Cor 5:14-15, 17). "Christ is the 'last Adam,' whose life-giving death has given birth to the new creation as truly as the death-dealing disobedience of the first Adam has doomed the old creation."[61]

Through the agency of Christ crucified and risen, believers are under new ownership. As Paul put it, "So, my brothers, you also died to the law through the body of Christ, that you might belong to another, to him who was raised from the dead, in order that we might bear fruit to God" (Rom 7:4). The Savior's vicarious death served to redeem and sanctify a people for his own possession. Paul again wrote, "Jesus Christ . . . gave himself for us to redeem us from all wickedness and to purify for himself a people that are his very own, eager to do what is good" (Tit 2:13-14). As stated by the writer to the Hebrews, Christ through his death disarmed the Devil and brought us into solidarity with himself in the family of his holy people (Heb 2:9-11, 13-15). Verse 11 reads, "Both the one who makes men holy and those who are made holy are of the same family. So Jesus is not ashamed to call them brothers." Incorporation into the family of God and restoration to fellowship with him are likewise accomplished through Christ's sacrificial death on the cross (Eph 2:13; Col 1:20-22).

D. The Nature of Union with Christ

We have come to the point of describing the nature of identification or union with Christ insofar as this is given in the biblical revelation. Scripture (1) represents this as a *supernatural* union rather than a natural union as commonly represented by liberal theologians. Thus Jesus said concerning the Father and himself, "we will come to him and make our home (*monē*) with him" (John 14:23). The Lord's saying is rooted in the OT idea of God's special dwelling with his people in the tabernacle (Exod 25:8; 29:45; Lev 26:11-12) and in Solomon's temple (1 Kgs 8:10-13; 2 Kgs 21:7; 2 Chron 5:13-14; 7:1-3, 16), and it will find its consummation in the eternal sanctuary in heaven (Ezek 37:26-28; 40–47; Rev 21:3). The revolutionary concept Jesus introduced is that the divine Father and Son dwell in the believer here and now, since he and the Father are one (John 10:30). We note that the indwelling Jesus spoke about in John 14:23 is personal and individual.

(2) The relation is further a *spiritual* union, in the sense that the Christ indwells believers (or the community) by the Holy Spirit. Jesus said, "the Father . . . will give you another Counselor to be with you (*meth hymōn*) forever—the Spirit of truth. . . . But you know him, for he lives with you [*par' hymin menei*] and will be in you [*en hymin*]" (John 14:16-17; cf. 15:26; 16:7-15). These texts speak of the Spirit's abode with individual believers viewed aggregately. Using the illustration of sexual union, Paul noted that a man who is joined to a prostitute "is one with her in body." Analogously, "he who unites himself with the Lord is one with him in spirit" (1 Cor 6:16–17). The latter text means that the union between the individual Christian and Christ is a spiritual, not a carnal, union since it

is effected by the Holy Spirit (cf. v. 19). Employing the figure of the temple sanctuary in which God's glory dwelt, Paul wrote with respect to the individual believer, "your body is a temple (*naos*) of the Holy Spirit, who is in you, whom you have received from God" (1 Cor 6:19). With a collective focus he wrote to the church at Corinth: "Don't you know that you yourselves are God's temple (*naos*) and that God's Spirit lives in you (*en hymin*)? . . . God's temple (*naos*) is sacred, and you are that temple" (1 Cor 3:16-17). Corporately, the church is the special dwelling-place of God's Spirit (Eph 2:21-22). Again we see that the NT moves comfortably from the idea of the Spirit indwelling individual believers to the Spirit abiding with the church collectively.

Paul indicated that the believer's union with Christ is wrought by Holy Spirit baptism. "For we were all baptized by one Spirit into one body (*sōma*) . . . and we were all given the one Spirit to drink" (1 Cor 12:13; cf. Rom 6:3-4). Spirit baptism, coincident with personal regeneration, is the point of entry into the body of Christ, the church. So Paul wrote, "all of you who were baptized into Christ have clothed yourselves with Christ" (Gal 3:27). Thus baptized—i.e., regenerated, indwelt, and energized—by the Holy Spirit, believers are marked with the seal of the same Spirit (Eph 1:13). This figure of sealing by the Spirit openly identifies the disciples as irrevocably belonging to the Lord (2 Cor 1:22; cf. Eph 4:30; 2 Tim 2:19). Whereas Paul frequently wrote of the Spirit of God indwelling the believer (Rom 8:9, 11; 1 Cor 3:16; 6:19; 2 Tim 1:14), he also stated that believers live in the Spirit (Rom 9:1; 14:17).

The apostle comfortably moved between the concept of Christ indwelling the believer (Rom 8:10) and the Spirit indwelling the believer (Rom 8:9, 11 [twice]). We note in Romans 8 that the Spirit (vv. 5-6, 9a, 11b), the Spirit of God (v. 9b, 11a), the Spirit of Christ (v. 9c), and Christ (v. 9d, 10) are all used interchangeably. We do not account for this equivalence by recourse to a modalistic theology. Rather, in the economy of the Godhead the Father and the Son live within us and apply their benefits to us via the Spirit (Rom 5:5; 1 Cor 3:16; Eph 2:22; 3:16-17; 1 Pet 1:12; 1 John 3:24; 4:13). From a biblical perspective, the Holy Spirit is the Spirit of God (Rom 8:14; 1 Cor 2:11, 14; 12:3) and the Spirit of Christ (Acts 16:7; Phil 1:19; 1 Pet 1:11). "The apostle never makes any significant distinction between the function of Christ and of the Spirit within the believer. The indwelling Christ is possible only through the indwelling Spirit."[62]

(3) The union of which we speak, furthermore, is an *organic* union, which means that it has an organization similar in complexity to that of living things. The NT represents the organic nature of the union figuratively by the "body of Christ" (*sōma Christou*) motif. Christ, the

Christian, and all other Christians are united under the metaphor of the human body. Romans (12:5) and 1 Corinthians (6:15; 12:12-27) stress the unity and mutual interdependence of the different members of the body: "so in Christ we who are many form one body, and each member belongs to all the others" (Rom 12:5). Ephesians (1:22-23; 4:12-16; 5:23, 30-32) and Colossians (2:19) emphasize the supremacy of Christ as Head of the multi-membered body and source of its unified life. Thus, "we will in all things grow up into him who is the Head, that is, Christ. From him the whole body, joined and held together by every supporting ligament, grows and builds itself up in love, as each part does its work" (Eph 4:15-16).

(4) The union, moreover, is a *vital* union, or a union involving a new quality of life. Since Christ himself is the source and repository of life (John 1:4; 5:26; 11:25; 14:6; 1 John 5:20), those who are related to him by faith participate experientially in his supernatural life. Jesus affirmed, "Because I live, you also will live" (John 14:19; cf. 20:31). John testified that "God has given us eternal life, and this life is in his Son [*en tō huiō autou*]. He who has the Son has life" (1 John 5:11-12a). Those identified with Christ by faith possess eternal life, the dynamic of which the faithful enter here and now (John 3:15-16, 36; 1 John 5:13). Following in the steps of the suffering Savior, Paul expected "that the life of Jesus may also be revealed in our body" (2 Cor 4:10; cf. v. 16). The apostle understood that Christ lives his supernatural life at the center of the Christian's new existence when he wrote, "Christ lives in me" (Gal. 2:20b; cf. Phil. 1:21). The Galatians text confirms that the vital union is not ontological, for there is no obliteration of the human personality, no fusion of being with the Son of God. Identification with Christ involves putting off the old self ("I no longer live") and putting on the new self defined in Christ, for in this same text Paul twice affirmed, "I live." Phil 3:7-14 confirms this judgment, for in his mature state of spirituality Paul staunchly asserted his own personal identity: namely, "I" (vv. 7, 8 [four times], 10, 12 [twice], 13 [twice], 14), "me" (v. 14), and "my" (vv. 8, 9).

(5) The relation, moreover, is a *comprehensive* union. The Christian's entire life and actions are exercised in relation to Christ—his life, values, power, and rule. The believer's speech is in Christ (Rom 9:1), his labors are in Christ (1 Cor 15:58; cf. Rom 16:3, 9, 12), his proclamation of the truth is in Christ (2 Cor 2:17), and his exercise of spiritual authority is in Christ (Phile 8). Paul testified that he was meek or gentle in Christ (2 Cor 13:4) and even that his imprisonment was in Christ (Phil 1:13). All this means that the entire Christian life is Christ-centered. "The whole of life, from its funda-mental being, to its discrete actions, is surrounded by the reality of Christ."[63]

(6) The NT additionally describes the mutual interpenetration of Christ and the believer as a *mysterious* union. The union of Christ and his Bride, the church, transcends complete human understanding. This side of eternity, where profound spiritual mysteries are anything but clear, we do not fully comprehend how Christ is united to his believing people. The images given by revelation, discussed above, offer at most helpful insights into the truth of this relation. Paul's bottom-line assessment of the matter is: "This is a profound mystery—but I am talking about Christ and the church" (Eph 5:32; cf. Col 1:26-27).

(7) Union with Christ is *not* initiated sacramentally through baptism, when the baptized allegedly are regenerated and incorporated into the body of Christ. Our study of the new birth showed that baptism does not regenerate or impart new life in Christ. Neither does partaking of the Eucharist incorporate into Christ, as many sacramentalists allege from John 6:51-58. In John 6 Jesus claimed to be the "bread of God" (v. 33), the "bread of life" (vv. 35, 48), and "the living bread that came down from heaven" (v. 51a). He further said, "If anyone eats of this bread, he will live forever" (v. 51b); also "Whoever eats my flesh and drinks my blood remains in me [*en emoi menei*], and I in him [*en autō*]" (v. 56). The imagery of 'eating' Christ's flesh (vv. 50-53, 55-56) and 'drinking' his blood (vv. 54-56) signifies faith appropriation (vv. 35, 40, 47, 51) of Christ's vicarious sacrifice on the cross (v. 51c)—"This bread is my flesh, which I will give for the life of the world." Jesus thus taught the mutual coinherence of himself and the believer by an act of *faith*, not by a sacramental ritual. Augustine expressed the meaning of the text when he said that Jesus' command to eat his flesh and drink his blood "is a figure, enjoining that we should have a share in the sufferings of our Lord, and that we should retain a sweet and profitable memory of the fact that his flesh was wounded and crucified for us."[64] Succinctly, he stated, "Believe, and thou hast eaten."[65] Note, in addition, that the union Jesus envisaged is singular, for the individual ([*pas*] *ho*) exercises faith (vv. 35, 37, 40, 45, 47) and the individual (*ho*) is united with Jesus (v. 56).

E. Results of Union with Christ

According to the NT, the results to the believer of identification with the Savior are several and significant. Paul expounded these spiritual outcomes by reference to major historical events in the experience of Jesus and by the phrase "with" (*syn*) Christ, which occurs a dozen times in the Pauline letters (Rom 6:8; 8:32; 2 Cor 4:14; 13:4; Phil 1:23; Col 2:13, 20; 3:3-4; 1 Thess 4:14, 17; 5:10).

By virtue of this union, the Christian (1) has been *crucified* and has *died* with Christ. In writing that "our old self was crucified with him" (aorist passive of *systauroō*, Rom 6:6), Paul referred to the moment of identification with Christ when born anew by the Spirit. So also his words in Gal 2:20a: "I have been crucified with Christ" (perfect passive of *systauroō*). Christ was crucified in history on the cross, and believers are regarded as having been crucified with him. The bold imagery of crucifixion emphasizes that the old order of existence, with its anti-God bias and sinful passions, has been rendered powerless (cf. Gal 5:24; 6:14). Union with Christ thus is a profoundly ethical relation.

Of this union Paul further wrote that believers "have been united with him [*symphytoi*] like this in his death" (Rom 6:5). The adjective *symphytos* ("grown together" or "engrafted") signifies a union that is exceedingly close; it "denotes the organic union in virtue of which one being shares the life, growth, and phases of existence belonging to another."[66] The line from the early Christian hymn (2 Tim 2:11b) cryptically states, "we died with him" (aorist indicative of *synapothnēskō*, to "die together"). So also Col 3:3: "For you died, and your life is now hidden with Christ in God." Regarded as having died with Christ, the believer does not respond to the world and its ways (Col 2:20). Paul made the same point via the imagery of spiritual circumcision: "In him (*en hō*) you were also circumcised, in the putting off of the sinful nature, not with a circumcision done by the hands of men but with the circumcision done by Christ" (Col 2:11). In identification with Christ, the old sinful nature *de jure* has been excised, and a radical change of life has occurred. Faith identification with the crucified Christ and the consequent destruction of sin's dominion is richly symbolized by the rite of Christian baptism. Paul wrote that "all of us who were baptized into Christ Jesus [*eis Christon Iēsoun*] were baptized into his death" (Rom 6:3). Again, "for all of you who were baptized into Christ [*eis Christon*] have clothed yourselves with Christ" (Gal 3:27; cf. Col 2:12a). Union with Christ once again is seen to have profound ethical consequences (Rom 6:1-2).

(2) In identification with Christ the believer is further regarded as having been *buried* with him: "We were therefore buried with him [aorist passive of *synthaptō*, to "bury together"] through baptism into death" (Rom 6:4). The significance of the burial imagery is personal death to sin's domination and a complete breach with the old way of life. Paul also linked the figure of burial with Christian baptism in Col. 2:12a ("having been buried with him in baptism"). Descending into the waters of baptism graphically depicts the burial aspect of incorporation into Christ (Rom 6:4a, 5a; Col 2:12a).

(3) A further result of the union is that the believer is *made alive* with Christ. "God, who is rich in mercy, made us alive with Christ [*synezōopoiēsen tō Christō*] even when we were dead in transgressions" (Eph 2:4b-5). Moreover, "When you were dead in your sins and in the uncircumcision of your sinful nature, God made you alive with Christ" (*synezōopoiēsen syn autō*, Col 2:13). The prefix *syn* in the twice used verb indicates that new life occurs in union with Christ. Rom 8:10 makes the same point: "if Christ is in you, your body is dead because of sin, yet your spirit is alive because of righteousness." Rom 6:23 and 2 Tim 2:11b contemplate eternal life as the great outcome of union with Christ. In all these texts Paul asserted that in association with Christ at conversion believers move from a condition of spiritual death to a state of unending, spiritual life.

(4) The believer, moreover, is *raised* with Christ. Paul wrote, "having been . . . raised with him [aorist passive of *synegeirō*, to "be co-resurrected"] through your faith in the power of God, who raised him from the dead" (Col 2:12). Again, "Since, then, you have been raised with Christ . . ." (aorist passive of *synegeirō*, Col 3:1; cf. Eph 2:6a). The verbs in the past tense denote an accomplished event—namely, the putting on of "the new self" (Col 3:10) and entry into the new quality of life by virtue of Christ's resurrection (Rom 6:4b). The ethical implications of being raised with Christ are prominent (Rom 6:11-14, 18, 22). Note also that the dying and the rising are both individual and corporate events. Paul's further affirmation, "God . . . seated us with him [aorist active indicative of *synkathizō*, to "cause to sit down with another"] in the heavenly realms in Christ Jesus" (Eph 2:6b) figuratively signifies present nearness to God and enjoyment of his presence. The event of ascending from the waters of baptism symbolizes the resurrection aspect of incorporation into Christ (Rom. 6:4b, 5b, 8; Col 2:12b).

(5) A final outcome of union with Christ is that believers will be *glorified* with him. Paul wrote, "When Christ, who is your life appears, then you also will appear with him [*syn autō*] in glory" (Col 3:4; cf. Col 1:27b). Glorification includes the future resurrection of the Christian's physical body (Rom 6:5b; 8:11; 1 Cor 15:22b; 1 Thess 4:16), the enjoyment of everlasting life in heaven (1 Thess 4:17b), and participation in Christ's heavenly rule (Rom 8:17). The early Christian hymn celebrated this latter event: "if we endure we will also reign with him" (future indicative of *symbasileuō*, to "rule together," 2 Tim 2:12). The goal and outcome of the spiritual journey with Christ is participation in his glory and reign in the eternal kingdom.

The NT identifies many specific benefits that accrue through union with Christ. These include freedom in Christ from the yoke of the law (Gal 2:4), comfort and encouragement in Christ (Phil 2:1), peace or inner tranquility in Christ (John 14:27; Phil 4:7), strengthening in Christ (2 Cor 12:9; Phil 4:13), being wise in Christ (1 Cor 4:10), rejoicing in Christ (Phil 4:4, 10), being spiritually enriched in Christ (1 Cor. 1:5), spiritual victory in Christ (2 Cor 2:14), acquiring hope in Christ (1 Cor 15:19; Eph 1:12), and being safe in Christ (Rom 16:20). It is eminently true that all of God's goodness is mediated to believers in union with Christ. As Paul wrote, the Father "has blessed us in the heavenly realms with every spiritual blessing in Christ" (*en Christō*, Eph 1:3; cf. Phil 4:19). Indeed, the Christian believer possesses an ideal completeness in Christ. Since the fullness of the Godhead indwelt Christ, and since believers are in the exalted Lord, Paul could affirm, "you have been given fullness in Christ, who is the head over every power and authority" (Col 2:10; cf. John 1:16). Luther heartily endorsed this perspective.

> Through faith you are so closely united with Christ . . . that you can say with confidence: . . . Christ's righteousness, victory, life, etc., are mine; and Christ, in turn, says: I am this sinner, that is, his sins, death, etc., are Mine because he clings to Me and I to him; for through faith we have been joined together into one flesh and bone.[67]

F. The Relations of Union with Christ

Union with Christ in scriptural teaching is profoundly related to other doctrines of salvation, as the following demonstrate. (1) The relation to *grace*. It is by the sheer grace of God that believers are incorporated into Christ. So Paul celebrated "the praise of his [God's] glorious grace, which he has freely given us in the One he loves" (Eph 1:6). He also wrote, "I always thank God for you because of his grace given you in Christ Jesus" (1 Cor 1:4). Westcott noted that "the working of God's grace gift by incorporating the believer in Christ makes him capable and meet for the presence of God."[68]

(2) The relation to *sovereign election*. God planned the union of Christ and his people in eternity past by his own free decision. Paul wrote, "For he [God] chose us in him [*en autō*] before the creation of the world to be holy and blameless in his sight" (Eph 1:4). Again, "In him [*en hō*] we were also chosen, having been predestined according to the plan of him who works out everything in conformity with the purpose of his will" (Eph 1:11). See also 2 Tim 1:9.

(3) The relation to *faith*. Union with Christ is appropriated and sus-

tained by faith centered in the Son of God. Paul wrote, "you also were included in Christ (*en hō*) when you heard the word of truth, the gospel of your salvation. Having believed, you were marked in him [*en hō*] with a seal, the promised Holy Spirit" (Eph 1:13). Similarly, Gal 3:26 could be translated from the Greek as, "by faith in Christ Jesus [*en Christō Iēsou*] you are all children of God." Gal 2:20c makes the same point.

(4) The relation to *regeneration*. Union with Christ is established in the believing life by the grace of regeneration: "we are God's workmanship, created [*ktisthentes*] in Christ Jesus [*en Christō Iēsou*] to do good works, which God prepared in advance for us to do" (Eph 2:10; cf. v. 5). The aorist tense of the verb *ktizō* points to God creating new life at the moment of regeneration. The person in Christ has experienced a new birth and shares the life of the age-to-come provided by his Lord (2 Cor 5:17).

(5) The relation to *justification*. Scripture presents legal justification as an important outcome of personal identification with Christ. So Paul wrote, "there is now no condemnation for those who are in Christ Jesus" (*en Christō Iēsou*, Rom 8:1). The abolition of condemnation is the essence of legal justification, which issues from the believer's new situation in Christ. Moreover, "God made him who had no sin to be sin for us, so that in him [*en autō*] we might become the righteousness of God" (2 Cor 5:21). Since righteousness is inherent in God's justifying verdict, it is clear that justification ensues from union with Christ. See also 1 Cor 1:30 and Phil 3:9. As Shedd wrote, "Because they [Christ's people] are spiritually, vitally, eternally, and mystically one with him, his merit is imputable to them, and their demerit is imputable to him. The imputation of Christ's righteousness supposes a union with him."[69] Personal reconciliation, an adjunct to legal justification, is likewise presented as an outcome of union with Christ. Paul wrote, "But now in Christ Jesus [*en Christō Iēsou*] you who were far away have been brought near through the blood of Christ" (Eph 2:13). Thus reconciled to God, believers are reconciled to other saints in Christ (Gal 3:28; Col 3:11).

(6) The relation to *forgiveness of sins*. "In him [*en hō*] we have redemption through his blood, the forgiveness of sins" (Eph 1:7; cf. 4:32; Col 1:14). Incorporated into Christ and made members of his body, believers are emancipated from the realm of darkness and enjoy remission of sins. Eadie noted that redemption and forgiveness of sins is bestowed "in Christ the Beloved, in loving, confiding union with Him as the one sphere—a thought pervading the paragraph (Eph 1:3-14) and the entire epistle."[70] The "we" refers to the aggregate of individuals, for forgiveness is applied to sinners not corporately but one by one.

(7) The relation to *adoption*. Paul wrote that the Father "predestined

us to be adopted as his sins through Jesus Christ, in accordance with his pleasure and will" (Eph 1:5). Legal membership in the family of God results from identification or union with Jesus Christ.

(8) The relation to *sanctification*. Paul wrote, "To the church of God in Corinth, to those sanctified in Christ Jesus [*en Christō Iēsou*] and called to be holy" (1 Cor 1:2). By virtue of union with Christ, believers are positionally set apart for God and consecrated to a holy purpose. Experiential sanctification also follows from union or identification with Christ. Paul wrote, "Those who belong to Christ Jesus have crucified the sinful nature with its passions and desires" (Gal 5:24). Only in union with Christ is crucifixion of the works of the flesh (vv. 19-21) and cultivation of the fruits of the Spirit (vv. 22-23) possible. The connection between union and experiential sanctification is made in 1 Cor 6:17-20: "But he who unites himself with the Lord is one with him in spirit. Flee from sexual immorality." United with Christ, believers are being transformed into his image by the Spirit's ministry (2 Cor 3:18). The apostle John also recognized the same connection: "This is how we know we are in him [*en autō*]: Whoever claims to live in him [*en autō*] must walk as Jesus did" (1 John 2:5b-6). Note also 1 John 3:6: "No one who lives in him [*en autō*] keeps on sinning. No one who continues to sin has either seen him or known him" (cf. 1:6; 3:24a).

(9) The relation to divine *preservation* or *perseverance*. Referring to the "sheep" given to him by the Father, Jesus said, "no one can snatch them out of my hand" (John 10:28) and "no one can snatch them out of my Father's hand" (v. 29). Although this issue will be discussed in chap. 11, the biblical evidence suggests that once formed the union is irrevocable; the Father and the Son relentlessly guard the relationship. The truism thus stands firm: once "in Christ," always "in Christ." See also Rom 8:35-39 and 1 Thess 4:14.

G. Were Old Testament Believers Incorporated into Christ?

The biblical evidence suggests that only NT believers are united with or incorporated into Jesus Christ by the Holy Spirit. Consider the following lines of evidence. (1) Many Christian authorities have noted that incorporation into Christ involves participation in our Lord's humanity (John 6:48-56). With an eye to this Johannine text, Calvin wrote, "By these words he [Christ] teaches . . . that by coming down he poured that power upon the flesh which he took in order that from it participation in life might flow unto us."[71] There could be no such incorporation until Christ's assumption of human flesh at the Incarnation. (2) Scripture plainly asserts that the basis of union with Christ is the Savior's atoning death and resurrection. The NT writers linked incorporation and the resultant new quality of life to Calvary in Gal 2:20 and to Easter in John 14:19 and Rom 7:4. Union with Christ necessarily must await the Lord's death and resurrection from the grave.

(3) The Holy Spirit is the bond by which believers are united to Christ. The indwelling Christ and the indwelling Spirit are a coincident reality. But Jesus promised his disciples that he would return to them in a dynamic way through the Counselor after he was glorified (John 15:26; 16:7). Not in OT times but only following Pentecost would the Counselor "live with you and be in you" (John 14:17). Unlike the OT, the NT says much about the Holy Spirit indwelling believers individually and corporately (Rom 8:9, 11; 1 Cor 3:16; 6:19; 2 Tim 1:14) and, conversely, believers living in the Spirit (Rom 9:1; 14:17). Moreover, (4) the NT links union with Christ with distinctive *ministries* of the Spirit. The first such ministry is the Spirit's work of baptizing believers into Christ (Gal 3:27) and his body, the church (1 Cor 12:13). The second is the Spirit's work of sealing believers in this new relation (2 Cor 1:21-22; Eph 1:13; 4:30) unto the day of redemption. The OT does not speak this language of the Spirit's baptizing, indwelling, and sealing ministries, as does the NT with such richness and variety.

We conclude, strictly speaking, that OT believers did not receive the new nature via Holy Spirit regeneration and they were not united to Jesus Christ in an indissoluble relation by the ministry of the same Spirit. As we have seen, there is ample evidence to suggest that believers under the old covenant received a measure of atonement. They were justified by faith, they experienced removal of the defilement of sins (albeit via repeated sacrifices), they enjoyed fellowship with God, and they possessed the hope of eternal life. But the fullness and perfecting of salvation as incorporation into Christ had to await the once-for-all sacrifice of the Messiah.

IV. PRACTICAL IMPLICATIONS OF THE DOCTRINE OF UNION WITH CHRIST

A. *Seek Vital Communion in Union*

Although no one has even seen God with physical eyes (John 5:37; 1 John 4:12), believers can and ought to see the Lord with the eye of the heart. Union with Christ should be expressed in a deeply enriching 'I-Thou' communion between the believer and her Savior. The equivalent realities of Christ in the believer, the believer in Christ, the Spirit in the believer, and the believer in the Spirit involve a number of spiritual outcomes. These include (1) an awareness of the divine presence in the heart, (2) a heightened sense of dependence on the Savior, (3) experiential knowledge of the Father's love, the Son's grace, and the Spirit's consolations, (4) fellowship with the Father and the Son through the Spirit, and (5) a quickening of the believer's spiritual faculties. The Pauline benediction succinctly expresses the communion to which we refer: "May the grace of the Lord Jesus Christ, and the love of God, and the fellowship [koinōnia] of the Holy Spirit be with you all" (2 Cor 13:14). This truth is also represented by the figurative words of the risen Lord to the church at Laodicea: "I stand at the door and knock. If anyone hears my voice and opens the door, I will go in and eat with him, and he with me" (Rev 3:20).

Saints of God experienced deep communion with the Lord from the beginning of history. For 300 years Enoch "walked with God" (Gen 5:22, 24)—a metaphor indicating profound, personal communion with his Redeemer. Noah likewise walked with the Lord (Gen 6:9) and conversed with him heart to heart (Gen 6:13-21; 7:1-4; 8:15-17). Abraham also engaged Yahweh in intimate personal communication and worship (Gen 17:1-22, passim). In a theophany, Moses at the burning bush saw the Lord, conversed with him, and experienced godly fear and a profound sense of his presence (Exod 3:1–4:17). Saul saw the risen Christ on the road to Damascus (Acts 26:13; 1 Cor 9:1) and while in a trance in Jerusalem (Acts 22:17-18). He spoke with Christ (Acts 22:10, 18-21; 26:15-18) and communed with him during his extended sojourn in the Arabian desert (Gal 1:17-18). John, "the beloved disciple," experienced deep, spiritual communion with Jesus during the Last Supper (John 13:23-26; 21:20). He lovingly beheld Jesus during his crucifixion (John 19:26-27), was present at the grave (John 20:2-8), and engaged Jesus at the Sea of Galilee (John 21).

These biblical examples suggest that Christians in union with Christ practice a true mysticism. Skeptics quip that "mysticism is something that begins in mist and ends in schism." But union with Christ is mystical, first, in the sense that it is a mystery not fully explicable in human language and concepts (Eph 5:32; Col 1:27). And union, second, involves the finite person's gracious experience of the infinite God in Jesus Christ through the Spirit. The biblical data suggest that Christian mysticism has at least three dimensions. We can safely affirm (1) a *relational* mysticism, whereby believers enter into the holy of holies to engage and commune with the Father and the Son through the Spirit (John 15:9-10; 2 Cor 6:16b; Phil

2:1); (2) a *moral* mysticism, wherein corruption in the believer gives way to holiness of life and ethical conduct in union with Christ (John 12:46; 2 Cor 3:18; Phil 3:10; 1 John 2:10; 3:24); and (3) an *epistemological* mysticism, where the worshiper gains knowledge of God and his truth in fellowship with Christ (1 Cor 13:12b; 2 Cor 4:6; 12:2-4; Phil 3:8; 1 John 5:20; 2 John 2). In the words of the Calvinist scholar John Murray, "there is an intelligent mysticism in the life of faith."[72] Every authentic believer, to some degree, should be a mystic in the Johannine and Pauline sense. Biblical Christians, however, never posit a *metaphysical* mysticism, where the individual allegedly melts into the Divine as a drop of water is absorbed into the ocean. While allowing for an 'I-Thou' *meeting*, we find no basis in Scripture for an 'I-Thou' *merging*. In authentic Christian mysticism there may be peak experiences of communion and communication, but never absorption into the Divine, loss of personal identity, or deification of the worshipper. The German language is more exact than the English at this point, expressing the legitimate mysticism of which we speak by the word *Mystik*, the illegitimate form by the word *Mysticismus*.

B. Seek Fruitfulness in Union

God's purpose for believers is that they should bring forth spiritual fruit of lasting quality (John 15:16). According to Isaiah 5, God looked to Israel, the vine of his planting, to produce good fruit (i.e., justice and righteousness); but instead his covenant people brought forth bad fruit (i.e., bloodshed, drunkenness, and bribery). They rejected God's law (v. 24); hence the righteous God reluctantly would reject them. Jesus stated that the only way a person may bring forth good fruit is if the core of the life is alive and well. The Lord said, "make a tree good and its fruit will be good, or make a tree bad and its fruit will be bad" (Matt 12:33; cf. 7:17-18). Jesus laid down the conditions for fruit-bearing in the allegory of the vine and branches (John 15:1-16). Fruitfulness in prayer (v. 7) and other matters (v. 8) is possible only as disciples abide in him and his love and obey his commands (vv. 4-7, 10, 12). Fruit-bearing is not a natural outworking of unaided, human nature. Rather, it is enabled by the infusion of supernatural life brought about by spiritual union with Christ, the source of new life. Jesus added that the Father lovingly "prunes" the disciples that they might bring forth even more fruit (v. 2). Believers should expect the loving God to bring discipline into their lives for the purpose of increasing fruitfulness (Heb 12:7-10).

Paul added that the works of the sinful nature will always be evil and displeasing to God (Gal 5:19-21). Healthy and God-honoring fruit-bearing, in other words, is foreign to the natural or fallen person. Good fruit is produced solely by the working of God's Spirit in the core of the life (vv. 22-23; cf. Eph 5:9). Wholesome fruit of lasting quality will come forth only as we "live by the Spirit" and "keep in step with the Spirit" (v. 25). Elsewhere, Paul wrote that only believers in Christ controlled and energized by the Spirit "bear fruit to God" (Rom 7:4). The uniform testimony of the NT, then, is that "the peaceable fruit of righteousness" (Heb 12:11, AV) is produced only by a supernatural dynamic—namely, as we live in intimate, loving, and obedient union with Jesus Christ. This is the Christian's lofty goal and lifelong challenge.

C. Seek Togetherness in Union

In the twentieth century, the worldwide ecumenical movement has indulged a peculiar fascination with the goal of visible Christian unity. The unity envisaged and in part realized, however, has focused largely on structural and institutional oneness rather than on spiritual commonality. Among world ecumenists, serious lack of agreement exists relative to the biblical and spiritual components of Christian unity.

The NT, however, affirms that all true believers *are* spiritually one in Christ. This is clear from Paul's imagery of the "body" (*soma*); he wrote, "Just as each of us has one body with many members, and these members do not all have the same function, so in Christ we who are many form one body, and each member belongs to all the others" (Rom 12:4-5). Baptized into Christ's body by the Spirit, all true believers are united with the Lord and with one another (1 Cor 6:15-17; 12:12-27; Eph 4:4, 15-16; 5:23, 30; Col 1:18). This reality of spiritual unity is confirmed by the NT image of a "building." Peter likened believers to "living stones, [who] are being built into a spiritual house to be a holy priesthood, offering spiritual sacrifices acceptable to God through Jesus Christ" (1 Pet 2:5). And Paul in Eph 2:21-22 wrote, "In him [Christ] the whole building is joined together [*synarmologeō*, "fit together"] and rises to become a holy temple in the Lord. And in him you too are being built together [*synoikodomeō*] to become a dwelling in which God lives by his Spirit." The essential point is that in spite of their various differences, all true believers are united by the Spirit to Christ and to one another. Clearly, then, the unity of genuine Christians presently exists as a spiritual reality. This *de facto* spiritual unity of true believers past, present, and future can neither be controverted nor ignored.

The people of God must, however, give practical and tangible *expression* to the unity that exists within the body of Christ. In his high-priestly prayer, Jesus petitioned the Father as follows: "that all of them may be one, Father, just as you are in me and I am in you. May they also be in us so that the world may believe that you have sent me. I have given them the glory that you gave me, that they may be one as we are one: I in them and you in me. May they be brought to complete unity to let the world know that you sent me and have loved them even as you have loved me" (John 17:21-23). Jesus longed that believers' spiritual unity would be demonstrated in a practical unity of heart, mind, and will, thereby enabling the world to discern God's loving purpose.

The book of Acts depicts the early church living, worshiping, and serving in practical, unified action. Luke's use of the word *homothymadon* ("together," "by common assent") conveys this tangible demonstration of unity. We read that the believers were "all together in one place" on the day of Pentecost (2:1); they were united "together" in prayer (1:14; 4:24); they met "together" for worship (5:12) and table fellowship (2:46); they were of "one accord" in making church decisions (15:25, AV); and they were "together" in glorifying God (Rom 15:6, NRSV). The notion of living a solo brand of Christianity was thoroughly alien to the primitive church.

Paul likewise urged believers to live out their spiritual unity in Christ: "May the God who gives endurance and encouragement give you a spirit of unity [*to auto phronein*, "the same mind"] among yourselves as you follow Christ Jesus, so that with one heart and mouth you may glorify the God and Father of our Lord Jesus Christ" (Rom 15:5, 6). To the Ephesians he wrote, "Make every effort to keep the unity of the Spirit through the bond of peace" (Eph 4:3), adding as the rationale for his command, "There is one body and one Spirit" (v. 4). Paul also prayed that the body might be built up, "until we all reach unity in the faith and in the knowledge of the Son of God and become mature, attaining to the whole measure of the fullness of Christ" (v. 13).

Christian believers need to *become* outwardly and practically what they *are* inwardly and spiritually. We need to give loving, tangible expression to the spiritual unity that exists among us in the body of Christ. It is encouraging to recall that a Roman Catholic wrote the hymn "Lead Kindly Light"; a Plymouth Brethren, "Jesus, Thy Name I Love"; a Congregationalist, "Jesus Thou Joy of Loving Hearts"; an Episcopalian, "There Is a Fountain Filled With Blood"; a Methodist, "Love Divine, All Love Excelling"; a Baptist, "He Leadeth Me"; and a ten year-old Presbyterian lad, "Jesus and Shall It Ever Be a Mortal Man Ashamed of Thee."[73] Believing Christians—be they Baptists, Presbyterians, Pentecostals, Episcopalians, Eastern Orthodox, or Roman Catholic—should express the spiritual unity that God has given them by concrete acts of fellowship, united worship, and cooperative mission. How can any professing Christian hold at arm's length a fellow believer whom Jesus Christ has eternally accepted? A symphony orchestra consisting of only one or two kinds of instruments would be quite impoverished. But an orchestra with a full range of instruments—strings, brass, wind, and percussion—playing together in harmony produces music of great richness and beauty. As true Christians give outward, tangible expression to their inward, spiritual unity, the world will come to know that "we are Christians by our love."

NINE

"THE LORD OUR RIGHTEOUSNESS"

J E R E M I A H   2 3 : 6

―――□―――

THE DOCTRINE OF JUSTIFICATION

I. INTRODUCTORY
CONCERNS

Ages ago in a speech before Job, Bildad posed the crucial question of human destiny: "How then can a man be righteous before God? How can one born of woman be pure" (Job 25:4). The biblical doctrine of justification deals with the fundamental issue of how guilty sinners can be acquitted and restored to favor with an infinitely righteous and just God. As absolutely righteous, God is the perfect standard of what is right. As absolutely just, God consistently rewards moral good and punishes moral evil. Because he is "the righteous Judge" (2 Tim 4:8), the Lord cannot by simple fiat absolve the guilty (Exod 23:7), either by altering his inviolable word or by overlooking appalling sin. Thus the question arises, how can a perfectly righteous, just, and holy God acquit guilty and condemned sinners? On what basis can God reckon as righteous those who are wholly unrighteous? Furthermore, how does God accomplish this great justifying work? By what means does God absolve the sin and guilt of rebels against the divine Lawgiver and Judge of the universe?

Justification is related to other important theological concepts such as forgiveness of sins, restoration to fellowship, adoption into the family of God, and the gift of eternal life. Reformation Protestantism regards the doctrine of justification by faith as a crucial article of the Christian religion, upon which the Gospel absolutely stands or falls. One leading authority correctly describes the doctrine of justification as "the chief doctrine of Christianity and the chief point of difference separating Protestantism and Roman Catholicism."[1] Not a few modern theologians, however, regard justification as a doctrine encrusted with hoary Jewish legalism and thus of little bearing for modern people. For example, the late Southern Baptist theologian Dale Moody drew attention to the Reformation doctrine of forensic justification and described it as "this Latin legalism."[2] Is the doctrine of justification by faith an indispensable part of the Good News about Christ, or is it a dispensable relic from a previous age?

The doctrine of justification by faith proves to be the focal point of other salvific doctrines. The *backdrop* against which justification is set is humanity in its fallen condition—guilty, condemned, and alienated from God. The *ground* of justification is the death of Christ on the cross as he took the sinner's place, bore his guilt, and suffered the just penalty for sins. The *implementation* of justification focuses on the application of Christ's atoning provisions to chosen and specially loved sinners. The *outcome* of justification is the sanctification and final preservation of those God has made right with himself. And the *completion* of justification will occur when the just of all ages are raised in transformed bodies to experience heaven's eternal joys.

A number of problems cluster around the biblical doctrine of justification. Fundamentally, is justification an instantaneous event that happens to sinners, or is it an ongoing process in the lives of professing Christians? If the latter, is justification merely another name for sanctification or moral improvement? If the former, is justification a matter of restoring a person to fellowship with God without regard to legal categories? A crucial issue is whether justification is the event by which God objectively *declares* a person righteous or by which he subjectively *makes* a person righteous. If the former view be true, does God reckon a person righteous simply on the basis of personal acceptance of Christ's work on the cross or on the ground of the imputation of Christ's righteousness received by faith? If this last view be accepted as biblically certified, is the notion that God pronounces a sinner to be what he actually is not—i.e., perfectly righteous—a legal fiction? Does the legal or forensic view of justification encourage a life of moral laxity or license (antinomianism)? Furthermore, what is the meaning of the phrase, so essential to a correct understanding of justification, "the righteousness of God" (Rom 3:21-22, AV)? Is it a description of how God acts in saving sinners, or is it a quality in God that may be attributed to sinners?

In addition, can a person contribute to their own justification, as Roman Catholics traditionally affirm? What about the so-called surplus of merits allegedly possessed by Mary and exceptional saints? Can an alleged overflow of merit be shared with those who are less holy in order to facilitate their salvation? Moreover, what are the far-ranging benefits that justification imparts to believing sinners? Concerning the subject of personal reconciliation, who is reconciled to whom? Do the obstacles to reconciliation reside on God's side, on the human side, or both? A further issue concerns assurance of present and future justification. Can believers in Christ be confident of permanent forgiveness of sins and reconciliation with God? These and other important issues will occupy our attention in the sections that follow.

II. HISTORICAL INTERPRETATIONS OF JUSTIFICATION

Several divergent views of justification and reconciliation appear in the history of the church's theological reflection. We now turn to consider the most important of these interpretations.[3]

A. *The Process of Moral Improvement (Pelagians and Liberals)*

This religious tradition displays a naive, theological optimism. It alleges that God is a God of love, not wrath, and that the souls of non-Christians are inherently upright. Moreover, God's relation to people is not that of stern lawgiver and judge who exacts the demands of penal law, but of a loving father who seeks the rehabilitation of his prodigal children. The tradition denies as impossible or absurd the legal imputation of Christ's alien righteousness to sinners. It is said that God regards as just and worthy of fellowship those who, inspired by Jesus' example, improve themselves morally. The liberal tradition thus replaces the Reformation doctrine of justification by grace through faith with an agenda of justification by personal virtue.

The British monk Pelagius (d. 419) regarded men and women as morally free agents unimpaired by Adam's fall. Grace, defined as enlightenment afforded by the law of Moses and Christ's teachings and example, enables people to discern God's will and empowers them to perform it. People could live morally and please God without grace, only with greater difficulty. Baptism in adults signifies a break with the past and actually remits past sins. Thereafter, assisted by grace, people attain righteousness and merit eternal life by doing worthy moral deeds. Justification, according to Pelagius, involves persons overcoming sinful habits, pursuing noble ethical goals, and fulfilling God's law. Pelagius claimed that people are capable of realizing their own justification, and many, in fact, do so.

The sixteenth-century Socinians, forerunners of modern Unitarianism, held a view of justification similar to that of Pelagius. The Socinians strenuously denied that Christ's death was a satisfaction rendered to the divine justice. "That Christ by his death has *merited* salvation for us and has *made satisfaction* freely for our sins . . . is fallacious and erroneous and wholly pernicious."[4] The Socinians appealed to the following arguments in pressing their case against the satisfaction theory. (1) Righteousness is not a quality in God; it is a description of how God acts. (2) Since wrath is antithetic to goodness, there is no anger in God that needs to be appeased. (3) Moral qualities such as guilt and righteousness are non-transferrable; hence each person must make amends for himself. And (4) since humans can forgive wrongdoing by a simple determination, so also can God. The Socinians viewed justification as the human process of moral self-improvement. God forgives and raises to immortality all who repent, who follow the precepts and example of Christ (a human prophet whose death was the supreme display of obedience), and who strive to live virtuously.

Albrecht Ritschl (d. 1889), the German father of modern liberal theology, in a major work on the subject, regarded justification and reconciliation as the fundamental datum of Christianity. The context for justification is not God's holiness or wrath but his love. "The conception of love is the only adequate conception of God."[5] God as loving Father stands ready to forgive all persons unconditionally and to restore them to fellowship with himself. But people in a state of sin (defined as ignorance and weakness) construct a false picture of God as unapproachable holiness and wrath and form a false attitude toward God involving fear and mistrust. To correct these erroneous conceptions, God made himself known in Jesus Christ. As human founder of the kingdom of God, Jesus experienced loving fellowship with God, revealed God as a gracious Father eager to forgive, and through word and deed inspired persons to return to God. Ritschl described as "altogether false"[6] the view that justification is the judicial act whereby God imputes Christ's righteousness to sinners. Interpreted morally, justification involves forgiveness of sins, eradication of *consciousness* of guilt, and removal of mistrust of God. In spite of residual sin and guilt, reconciliation effects the restoration of a harmonious relation with the Father and adoption into his family. Ritschl concluded that persons who experience justification and reconciliation will replicate the ethical life of Jesus and so collectively will hasten the coming of God's kingdom.

The Congregationalist pastor Lyman Abbott (d. 1922) insisted that all people by birth are God's children. The crucial question is, how can men and women who have wandered from the Father return to him? Abbott claimed that justification means not remission of some penalty charged to us, but forgiveness of sin and renovation of character through the wooing of the Divine Lover. Justification thus is not a declaration of God with respect to us, but a change that comes about in us. Abbott wrote:

> Justification by faith no longer means to me that Christ has suffered the penalties of my sins and therefore if I accept his sacrifice God will treat me as though I were innocent although I am guilty; it means that Jesus Christ offers himself to me as my divine companion and if I accept his companionship I can be made virtuous although I have been guilty.[7]

Shailer Mathews (d. 1941) rejected the imputational view of justification because he alleged it appeals to ancient analogies rather than to contemporary images. Modern man's

> fundamental conception of the universe makes it difficult for him to respond to the forensic conception of God as a monarch who establishes days of trial and passes individual sentences upon millions of lives. His idea of law makes it hard for him to think of a remitted penalty in a moral world, where relations are genetic and only figuratively to be conceived of in terms of the law court and a king.[8]

Mathews reasoned that the loving God who conceived the plan of salvation has no need to be placated or appeased. Salvation represents the triumph, via social evolution, of the higher spirit of Jesus over lower, vestigial, animal impulses. As humans emulate the ideals of Jesus (the revealer of God's purposes and character), they attain a higher level of moral and spiritual development, are reconciled to God and to one another, and forge a true human brotherhood in a renewed social order. Mathews concluded, "To be saved is to be so transformed by new relations with spiritual forces both human and divine that past mistakes and sins have their effects offset by new life."[9]

Process theology judges that the Reformational doctrine of justification by faith is irrelevant to the modern, scientific vision of reality. According to Pittenger, the classical formulation of justification "seems to make little or no sense to our contemporaries."[10] We cannot accept as literally true Paul's teaching of a forensic imputation of Christ's righteousness. According to the Canadian theologian, the seed-bed of justification is not the offended justice of the heavenly Lawgiver and Judge but the spurning of divine love. Pittenger assimilates justification into sanctification and redefines it consistent with the Whiteheadian conceptuality. Thus justification is the divine approval of positive human responses to the divine lure—optimally displayed in Jesus—that leads to the vanquishing of love-lessness, the overcoming of estrangement, and personal transformation.[11]

B. The Infusion of Righteousness
   ## (Roman Catholics)

Viewing justification as a process, Catholicism speaks both of the inception and the increase of justification. Concerning the inception of justification, God through Christ's merits and via the sacrament of baptism remits past sins and infuses into the soul new habits of grace. Although this first stage of justification makes persons inherently righteous via the impartation of the divine nature (2 Pet 1:4), "concupiscence" (desire that is the seed-bed of sin but not itself sin) remains in Christians. Catholic authorities judge it inconceivable that the holy God would accept into his family those who remain contaminated by sin. Moreover, they insist that imputed righteousness would seriously undermine moral effort. Concerning the increase of justification, the baptized work for eternal life by means of love-inspired virtues that are the fruit of the grace infused into the soul. Rome upholds the "merit of worthiness" (*meritum de condigno*)—i.e., the merit wrought by free moral acts performed in this state of grace. Justification is not a once-for-all event; righteousness increases or decreases proportional to the person's faith and works. Traditional Roman Catholics, in other words, trust in God's infusion of a new nature and plead the worth of their God-enabled works. Justification in Catholic theology is a comprehensive term that includes, among other things, what Protestants understand by regeneration and sanctification. For Rome, justification is not divine-wise an objective *pronouncement* of righteousness but is human-wise a lifelong *process* of becoming righteous.

The church traditionally has taught that surplus merits earned by Christ and exceptional saints can be transferred to ordinary wayfarers. Mary, in particular, contributes to the justification of the faithful in several ways. (1) By her holy life and good works on earth, Mary earned excess merit that can be credited to others. (2) Mary shared in the pain and sufferings of her Son on the cross, and so possesses additional merit that can bless those with a deficit. And (3) Mary, as "Mother of God," effectively pleads with the Father in heaven. According to one Catholic source, Mary contributes "her share to the justification of the human race, beginning with herself and extending to everyone ever justified."[12] Catholics believe that assurance of final justification normally is not possible. Justifying grace, defined as the infusion of righteousness to the soul, can be forfeited by mortal sin but may be restored by the sacrament of penance (involving confession, satisfaction, and absolution). If the process of justification (i.e., the attainment of righteousness or transformation) is not completed in this life, the individual must endure the purifying sufferings of purgatory. According to Rome, the duration of the soul's stay in purgatory can be shortened by prayers, masses, and the superabundant merits of the saints.

Augustine (d. 430), the first post-biblical theologian to explore in depth the concept of justification, helped to shape the Roman view. Augustine stressed that God infuses the principle of righteousness into the soul at baptism. Thus at the baptismal font "We are justified, but righteousness itself grows as we go forward."[13] Not well versed in the Greek, the bishop interpreted *dikaioo* as to "make righteous," rather than to "pronounce righteous." "What else does the phrase 'being justified' signify than 'being made righteous.'"[14] Justification for Augustine is that gracious work whereby God makes baptized Christians righteous by renewing their inner beings and infusing their hearts with love for him (*amor Dei*). Justification progresses as the Spirit gradually supplants the concupiscence (or evil desire) that remains in the baptized with love. As a result of this infusion of divine grace and love, believers can avoid sinning, work righteousness, and fulfill the law.[15] The bishop added that God views the righteous deeds of Christians as meritorious. Yet he insisted (against Pelagius) that since the inspiration for the good will and work comes from God, the merit derives entirely from grace.[16] Augustine concluded that if Christian love is perfected in this life, the believer will go directly to heaven. If not, then justification will be completed after death by the purifying sufferings of purgatory (1 Cor 3:13-15).[17]

Augustine subsumed under justification what Protestants understand by regeneration and sanctification.[18] Since Augustine concisely represented the *ordo salutis* as predestination, calling, justification, and glorification,[19] he viewed justification broadly as the entire movement of salvation from regeneration through sanctification. This is supported by the fact that he employed as synonyms for justification the Latin terms *regeneratio, vivificatio, renovatio,* and *sanctificatio.* When describing salvation, Augustine regularly used these terms rather than the word justification. In sum, whereas Protestants have followed Augustine in his doctrines of sin and grace, Roman Catholic theology expanded upon his notion that justification is the process that actually makes a person righteous. The Augustinian view of justification dominated Roman thought through the medieval era, the Council of Trent (1545-63), and beyond.

The canons and decrees of the Council of Trent represent the authoritative statement of the Counter-Reformation. Session six of the Council

(1546-47) stated that justification occurs in three stages. (1) The *preparation* for justification. Blessed by prevenient grace and addressed by the call of God, the individual "is able by his own free will . . . to move himself to justice in His sight" (chap. 5). In adults this preparation includes faith, repentance, and the intention to accept baptism. (2) The *beginning* of justification. Through the Spirit's regenerating work, God infuses grace, hope, and love into the soul at baptism, thereby remitting past sins and making the person righteous. Thus justification "is not only a remission of sins but also the sanctification and renewal of the inward man through the voluntary reception of the grace and gifts whereby an unjust man becomes just" (chap. 7). (3) The *increase* of justification. Because Trent defined justification as the process of becoming righteous, justification must be augmented if the *viator* would attain heavenly glory. Thus, "through the observance of the commandments of God and the church, faith cooperating with good works," believers "increase in that justice received through the grace of Christ and are further justified" (chap. 10). Justification can be forfeited by mortal sin, but also can be recovered by the sacrament of penance (chap. 14). Since justification can be lost, the pilgrim possesses no certainty of present and future pardon. "No one can know with the certitude of faith, which cannot admit of any error, that he has obtained God's grace" (chap. 9). The realistic attitude of the pious person is hope mixed with "fear and apprehension" (chap. 9). Agreeable with tradition, Trent maintained that God regards the good works individuals perform (Matt 10:42; 16:27; Heb 6:10) as meritorious. Such God-enabled human efforts increase righteousness and facilitate the attainment of eternal life (chap. 16).

In the Canons that follow, Trent repudiated the Reformation tenet of justification by faith alone. "If anyone says that the sinner is justified by faith alone, meaning that nothing else is required to cooperate in order to obtain the grace of justification . . . let him be anathema" (canon 9). The Council, moreover, placed the ban on Protestant Reformers who insisted that justification is not increased by good works. "If anyone says that the justice received is not preserved and also not increased before God through good works, but that those works are merely the fruits and signs of justification obtained, but not the cause of its increase, let him be anathema" (canon 24). Canon 32 added an anathema against the Reformers who denied that a person's good works merit eternal life. In sum, according to Trent, justification is more a matter of spiritual and moral renewal than the judicial absolution of guilt and the forgiveness of sins.

From a panentheistic perspective, some post-Vatican II Catholic theology affirms the universality of justifying or divinizing grace. Richard P.

McBrien, for example, denies that Christ died to bear sins and expiate offenses against the divine majesty. The notion of Christ as "a curse," he argues, is strictly metaphorical. Christ's blood shed on the cross was not a literal payment for sins; rather it was a peace offering that unites God and sinners. "It was not that God was so enraged by the world's sin that a price was to be exacted (the prevalent idea of God among the pagans), but that God 'so loved the world that he gave his only Son.'"[20] McBrien acknowledges the traditional Catholic definition of justification as "The event by which God, acting in Jesus Christ, makes us holy (just) in the divine sight."[21] The "event" McBrien envisages actually is a continuous process. By virtue of the universality of revelation and grace (as argued also by K. Rahner and H. Küng), justification (or divinization) extends to all people everywhere. Thus, "Every human person, by reason of birth and of God's universal offer of grace, is already called to be a child of God and an heir of heaven."[22]

C. Restoration of the Moral Order of the Universe (Remonstrants and Many Arminians)

Consistent with the governmental theory of the Atonement, the seventeenth-century Remonstrants and many Arminians explained justification as forgiveness of sins that enhances God's wise governance of the universe. Many Arminian authorities deny that justification involves the imputation of Christ's righteousness to believers. Thus the Calvinist view, whereby God reckons the obedience of Christ to believers and accepts said obedience as if it were their own, "is fictional."[23] The claim that God regards persons as holy when they are not empirically so encourages antinomianism and careless living. More conservative Arminians, such as John Wesley (d. 1791), held that justification signifies (1) God's acceptance of believers as free from sin and guilt and (2) the renovation of their moral character. The practically-minded Wesley could not resist assimilating justification into sanctification—the latter being his preeminent and enduring interest. The Lutheran notion that the believer is "*simul justus et peccator*" (at once both righteous and a sinner) Wesley firmly rejected.[24] Many Arminians further assert that faith is not merely the *instrument* of justification but the *ground* on which justification rests. Thus Wesley wrote that "any righteousness created by the act of justification is real because of the ethical or moral dimension of faith."[25] Arminians generally believe that obstacles to reconciliation reside on the side of sinners rather than on the side of God. The latter always is disposed to restore fellowship with sinners. Most

Arminian authorities, furthermore, hold that justification can be forfeited by willful sin; thus certainty of final justification is impossible.

Richard Watson (d. 1833), the first Wesleyan systematic theologian, defined justification as the sentence of pardon and the exemption from sin's penalty. He denied as "fictitious" both the imputation of Adam's sin to his posterity and the imputation of Christ's righteousness to those who believe. "For this notion, that the righteousness of Christ is so imputed as to be accounted as our own, there is no warrant in the Word of God."[26] Watson perceived in the Reformational view great danger of antinomianism; that is, belief in the imputation of Christ's perfect righteousness would discourage believers from pursuing holiness in daily life. The only imputation Watson allowed is God's act of reckoning the human act of faith as righteousness. In the final analysis, Watson followed the Remonstrant jurist, Grotius, in setting justification within the context of God's moral governance of the universe. "The fruit of the death and intercession of Christ," he argued, "renders it consistent with a righteous government [for God] to forgive sin."[27]

Charles Finney (d. 1875) also viewed justification (i.e., pardon of sins and acceptance by God) from a governmental rather than a judicial perspective. To uphold the moral order of the universe, God substituted Christ's death for the punishment required by the law. "The Godhead desired to save sinners, but could not safely do so without danger to the universe, unless something was done to satisfy public, not retributive justice."[28] Denying (1) the imputation of Adam's sin to the race, (2) the imputation of the sins of the elect to Christ, and (3) perpetual justification by imputation of the righteousness of Christ to believers,[29] Finney argued that God pardons and accepts into favor sinners who reform their lives in accordance with the moral order of the universe. Since Jesus, like any other man, owed full obedience to the law, he possessed no surplus of obedience that could be applied to others. Thus, "For sinners to be forensically pronounced just, is impossible or absurd."[30] Finney held that the one *ground* or *procuring cause* of justification is the benevolence of the Godhead in the interests of moral government. The several *conditions* of justification he identified as Christ's sacrifice, personal repentance, faith in Christ, present sanctification (or entire consecration to God), and perseverance to the end (manifested in complete obedience to the moral law). In other words, Finney believed that God declares righteous persons who actually *are so*. He continued that justification can be forfeited by forsaking "full-hearted consecration" and perfect obedience to the law. When this occurs, the wayward soul becomes condemned and must seek a fresh experience of God's justifying work. Clearly Finney predicated justification on sanctification and perseverance, not the reverse.[31]

D. Political and Social Emancipation
(Liberation Theologians)

In the main, liberation theology views salvation (1) corporately rather than individually, (2) structurally rather than spiritually, and (3) this-worldly (horizontally) rather than other-worldly (vertically). The tradition makes political and social liberation in history the focus of salvation and spiritual and eternal concerns subservient thereto. Liberationists generally define faith as practical commitment to the revolutionary struggle, and justification as the implementation of justice across the social arena via political action, confrontation, and struggle. Liberation theologians often link the doctrines of justification and sanctification under the rubric of "discipleship."

Against what he perceives to be Trent's individualistic, ontological, and a-historical view of justification, Leonardo Boff insists that we must define justification of the sinner in concrete, process-oriented terms. The theological term *justification* is equivalent to the praxeological term *liberation*. Thus for Boff justification or liberation is the work of God who helps "human beings to make the liberating transition from their situation as enemies of God, offenders against their fellows, and alienated beings in the world."[32] The outcome of justification, which is realized only at the end of the historical process, is the attainment of a "utopia" marked by fraternal love and social justice. Inherent in the utopia is "the divine filiation of humanity,"[33] whereby people become sharers in the divine nature. Boff makes clear that although God motivates the aforementioned human efforts, justification nevertheless is a human activity freely effected by human beings who are offended by social, political, and economic injustices.

Clodovis Boff rejects the classical *extra ecclesiam nulla salus* doctrine of the Catholic church. The Brazilian priest posits a salvation antecedent to and outside the traditional, sectarian values of revelation, explicit faith, church membership, sacraments, theology, etc.. From a panentheistic perspective, Boff boldly states that "every human being enjoys a de facto relationship to Jesus Christ."[34] But salvation is anterior to the personal consciousness thereof. Boff writes that "it is in and by concrete, definitive practice, unified in a basic project, that salvation . . . comes to the human being, and to every human being."[35] Salvation is consciously realized in personal experience through the exercise of love in the social contexts in which people live. The doctrine of justification by faith, he argues, amounts to an interpretation by religious people of what actually happens through the social, political, and economic liberation of oppressed men and women via agapic practice. In this regard, good works are not an expression of grace; "Rather it is the works themselves that concretely constitute this essence: grace."[36]

From the perspective of black liberation theology, James Cone, of New York's Union Theological Seminary, agonizes over the fact that persons are oppressed simply because they are black. Cone calls for a theological revolution that prescribes courses of action to liberate the oppressed black community from their bondage. Cone argues that traditional theological talk must be restated for the present realities of the black experience. Thus he views sin as denial of God's liberating activity in Jesus Christ that expresses itself in the oppression and exploitation of non-white people. Moreover, he perceives salvation as a this-worldly, social reality that fulfills black hopes and aspirations. Cone judges that "God's act of reconciliation is not mystical communion with the divine; nor is it a pietistic state of inwardness bestowed upon the believer."[37] On the contrary, justification is God's righteous deliverance of the oppressed from socio-political bondage.[38] Moreover, justification involves the participation of the liberated in the human struggle for social and political justice. Cone argues that the Reformation view of justification by faith misses the mark by virtue of Luther and Calvin's view of the state as the servant of God, even while the state was torturing the oppressed.

E. God's Eternal Verdict on Mankind (Neoorthodox Theologians)

Karl Barth's (d. 1968) objectivist view of justification is rooted in God's eternal election of humanity in Christ. This gracious election is identical to God's eternal covenant with the race. Mankind, however, broke the covenant through sin. But God has bound himself to his image-bearers as Creator and Lord and hence cannot countenance disruption of the covenant. God must be just (Rom 3:26); he must act consistently with his nature and will to overcome the impediment to fellowship caused by sin. Therefore, "He does not renounce the grace of election and the covenant."[39] For Barth, justification represents God's "affirmation and consummation of the institution of the covenant between Himself and man which took place in and with the creation."[40] Justification is that decision of God regarding humankind made before the world but given historical expression through the experience of Jesus Christ. In order to reveal God's eternal, justifying decision and restore the covenant relation broken by sin, Christ became a man, died on the cross, and rose from the grave. Through Christ's death God said No! to himself, and through Christ's resurrection God said Yes! to humanity—thereby putting an end to sin and condemnation. For Barth, justification is not a subjective reality that can be experienced (as in Schleiermacher and most liberals), but God's eternal verdict enacted in time by Christ that forgives sins, accepts sinners into sonship, and grants eternal life. Barth clearly insisted that persons are justified in Christ before they exercise faith. Küng, in his definitive study of Barth, affirms that for the latter "justification [is] the accomplishment and revelation of God's verdict upon man."[41]

Since God's covenant with humankind is universal in scope (cf. the covenant with Noah), Christ, our representative, became a man, died, and was resurrected for the justification of all. "Jesus Christ died totally for the reconciliation of every man as such."[42] God's eternal verdict objectively (*de jure*) has justified the entire human family. It is impossible for humankind not to be elected, restored to the covenant, and justified. Even stubborn, human unbelief cannot thwart God's gracious covenant purpose. Barth boldly stated, "there has to be a reconciling of the world, and this has already taken place."[43] Subjectively (*de facto*), however, many people have not yet personally experienced justification by faith and reception of the Spirit.

In explaining the doctrine of justification, Barth focused on Christ repairing the broken relation between God and humans rather than on God imputing Christ's righteousness to believers. The core of Barth's doctrine of justification is the loving God achieving his sovereign right as Creator by reestablishing the broken covenant relation with humans. Moreover, in Barth's scheme persons do not respond to the Gospel in order to be justified. Rather, having been justified by the divine verdict in eternity past, individuals respond to the Good News in time, thereby making justification for them an existential reality.

Gustaf Aulén (d. 1977), the Swedish, Lutheran neoorthodox, minimized wrath and retributive justice in God in deference to the divine *agape*. God's attitude toward persons is not governed by legal categories. According to Aulén, Christ did not bear sinners' punishment, and God does not impute Christ's righteousness to those who believe. "The Christian conception of atonement is obscured if it is interpreted . . . as a compensation to divine righteousness rendered by Christ as Man."[44] Aulén added that the hostile powers of sin, death, the Devil, and the tyrannical powers of the law and divine wrath have created a separation between God and humankind. But on the cross divine love triumphed over the enslaving forces of evil that held sinners in alienation from God (the 'classic' theory of the Atonement). "The sole purpose of God's loving will is to realize the dominion of love."[45] Justification, which is grounded entirely in the divine *agape*, involves forgiveness of sin, the reestablishment of fellowship between God and sinners, and the gift of eternal life. Aulén observed that justification is not only an event that marks the beginning of the Christian life, it is also a process that continues throughout the entire journey of faith. Thus, "forgiveness [or justification] is both the essential foundation of the Christian life and its continually active power."[46] Aulén was uncertain whether all or only some persons are justified, although he repeatedly referred to the reconciliation God effects between himself and the world.[47]

F. God's Legal Declaration of Righteousness (Reformers and Many Evangelicals)

The early church fathers, occupied with pressing Christological and Trinitarian controversies, failed to explore in depth the doctrine of justification by faith. Their discussions of salvation focused on forgiveness of sins and the gift of eternal life. The first serious engagement with justification was undertaken by Augustine in his fourth-century dispute with the Pelagians. Not until the personal discovery of Martin Luther was the forensic interpretation of justification developed in detail.

Claiming to recapture the NT emphasis, the Reformation interpreted justification as God's judicial declaration whereby, for the sake of Christ, he freely pardons sins and reckons believers as righteous and worthy of eternal life. Justification, distinct from sanctification, involves a change in the believer's *standing* before God rather than a change of *nature*. Justification, moreover, is an instantaneous event rather than a lifelong process of moral and spiritual renewal. According to Reformation theology, the *ground* of justification is Christ's righteousness imputed to the believer. The *means* or *instrument* of justification is God-given faith in the Redeemer. Most authorities held that obstacles to reconciliation exist on the side of God and sinners. With respect to God, righteous enmity against sin must be assuaged. And with respect to sinners, fear of God's just judgment must be overcome. Moreover, persons who trust in Christ's finished work can be assured that they have passed from a state of condemnation to life and favor.

Martin Luther (d. 1546) was a pious Augustinian monk who sought peace with God through good works and monastic disciplines. In spite of earnest striving, his troubled soul found no repose. In pursuit of the question, "How can I find a gracious God?" Luther turned to the letters of St. Paul. Formerly he had understood the phrase "the righteousness of

God" in Rom 1:17. AV actively as that quality in God that punishes unrighteous sinners (i.e., punitive justice). After considerable prayer and reflection, Luther understood "the righteousness of God" passively as the great gift God imputes to sinners through faith in the crucified Christ. It "is the righteousness with which God clothes us when he justifies us."[48] As a mother hen covers her chicks with her wings, so God covers sinners with the perfect righteousness of the Savior. The noble intentions and 'good works' of sinners are of no value in God's eyes. A figure derived from the law courts, justification means to "*declare* righteous or blameless." It connotes that God imputes Christ's alien righteousness to those who trust in the Savior's atoning death. Indeed, justification is that imputation, whereby for the sake of Christ "God reckons imperfect righteousness as perfect righteousness and sin as not sin, even though it really is sin."[49] Christ's righteousness imputed to believers is "alien" because it comes from another and because no sinners could possibly merit it. Justified by faith, believers receive forgiveness of sins, union with Christ, and eternal life.

Essential to Luther's forensic view is his contention that the justified believer is "righteous and a sinner at the same time (*simul iustus et peccator*")[50] In principle believers are righteous, but in practice they are sinful—although the remnants of sin are not charged to their account. "The righteous are not wholly perfect in themselves, but God accounts them righteous and forgives them because of their faith in his Son Jesus Christ."[51] Against Rome Luther held that, notwithstanding spiritual struggles, believers possess assurance of their new standing in Christ. "We must by all means believe for a certainty . . . that we are pleasing to God for the sake of Christ."[52] Although good works contribute nothing to justification, they serve as a litmus test as to whether people truly have been justified by faith. "True faith is not idle. We can, therefore, ascertain and recognize those who have true faith from the effect or from what follows."[53] Luther differentiated between the "inward righteousness" before God that is born of justification and the "outward righteousness" before others that takes form through faith and love.

Philip Melanchthon (d. 1560), the systematizer of the Lutheran wing of the Reformation, challenged the prevailing Roman view by claiming that justification is not a making righteous but a legal declaration of righteousness: "All of our righteousness is a gracious imputation of God."[54] Justification signifies that God clothes believers with the alien righteousness of Christ so that sins are forgiven, we are made pleasing to God, and his wrath is averted. Although God views believers as righteous in Christ, the passions of the sinful nature remain a force to be reckoned with. Thus

Melanchthon endorsed Luther's formula that the believer is *simul iustus et peccator.* The *ground* of justification is the righteousness of Christ, acquired by his total obedience in life and death. The *means* of justification is the believer's faith. Following Luther, Melanchthon distinguished between the instantaneous event of justification and the ensuing process of sanctification. Melanchthon summed up his understanding of justification as follows: "the Mediator's entire obedience, from his incarnation until the resurrection, is the true justification which is pleasing to God, and is the merit for us. God forgives us our sins, and accepts us, in that he imputes righteousness to us for the sake of the Son, although we are still weak and fearful. We must, however, accept this imputed righteousness with faith."[55]

John Calvin (d. 1564) regarded justification as "the principle of the whole doctrine of salvation and the foundation of all religion."[56] Against Rome's infusion view of justification, he developed at length a forensic interpretation: God justifies guilty sinners by freely imputing to them the righteousness of Christ. The *material* cause of justification is the entire obedience of Christ in his life and death, whereas the *instrumental* cause is faith apart from all works or personal merit. "Justified by faith is he who, excluded from the righteousness of works, grasps the righteousness of Christ through faith, and clothed in it, appears in God's sight not as a sinner but as a righteous man."[57] As God imputes or reckons Christ's righteousness, believers receive forgiveness of sins past, present, and future, removal of guilt and condemnation, reconciliation with God, and the gift of eternal life. For Calvin, the obstacles to reconciliation chiefly reside on God's side. Sin turns "God's face away from the sinner; and . . . it is foreign to his righteousness to have any dealings with sin. For this reason . . . man is God's enemy until he is restored to grace through Christ."[58]

Countering Roman doctrine, Calvin held that believers should possess a basic assurance of present and future salvation. This is so *objectively*, as faith lays hold of the biblical promises concerning the Father's elective purpose and the Son's atoning work. And it is true *subjectively* through the Spirit's ministry in the inner life. Assurance, like faith, admits of degrees. Thus believers may not always sense *full* assurance of final salvation. Calvin wrote, "Surely, while we teach that faith ought to be certain and assured, we cannot imagine any certainty that is not tinged with doubt, or any assurance that is not assailed by some anxiety. On the other hand. . . we deny that, that in whatever way they are afflicted, believers fall away and depart from the certain assurance received from God's mercy."[59] Those who lack significant assurance of salvation, according to Calvin, are not true believers.

More carefully than Luther, Calvin distinguished between the initial, external event of justification and the subsequent, internal process of sanctification. "To be justified means something different from being made righteous."[60] Yet sensitive to the Roman charge that the Reformation view of justification denigrated good works, Calvin held together the operations of justification and sanctification. The latter is related to the former as rays of light to the sun. From 1 Cor 1:30—Jesus Christ is "our righteousness, holiness and redemption"—Calvin reasoned that "you cannot possess Christ without being made partaker in his sanctification." In the same section he observed that "in our sharing in Christ, which justifies us, sanctification is just as much included as righteousness."[61] Worthy of mention is what some Calvin scholars call his doctrine of "double justification." God justifies the sinner; but he also justifies the works of the justified. Because Christians remain sinners by nature, their works are defiled. God, however, adorns Christians' works with Christ's righteousness, covering any unrighteousness in them, so that both they *and* their works are pleasing and acceptable to him. "As we ourselves, when we have been engrafted in Christ, are righteous in God's sight because our iniquities are covered by Christ's sinlessness, so our works are righteous and are thus regarded because whatever fault is otherwise in them is buried in Christ's purity, and is not charged to our account."[62] This insight of Calvin undergirds his understanding of the place of works in the Christian life. No sinner is justified by works; but God justifies believers' works—which works demonstrate obedience to God and accumulate rewards in heaven.

The Heidelberg Catechism (1563) posed the question, "How are you right with God?" (Lord's Day 23, Q. 60). The answer follows that in spite of gross sin and disobedience "without my deserving it at all, out of sheer grace, God grants and credits to me the perfect satisfaction, righteousness, and holiness of Christ, as if I had never sinned nor been a sinner, as if I had been as perfectly obedient as Christ was obedient for me. All I need to do is to accept this gift of God with a believing heart." The Westminster Shorter Catechism (1647) in response to Q. 33, "What is Justification?" replied: "Justification is an act of God's free grace, wherein he pardoneth all our sins, and accepteth us as righteous in his sight, only for the righteousness of Christ, imputed to us, and received by faith alone." The Westminster Confession of Faith (1646) states that God freely justifies "not by infusing righteousness into them [i.e., the effectually called], but by pardoning their sins, and by accounting and accepting their persons as righteous: not for any thing wrought in them, or done by them, but for Christ's sake alone . . . but by imputing the obedience and satisfaction of Christ unto them, they receiving and resting on him and his righteousness by faith" (Chapter 11.1). The Confession added that although assurance of justification can be dulled by sin, believers in Christ "may in this life be certainly assured that they are in a state of grace, and may rejoice in the hope of the glory of God, which hope shall never make them ashamed" (Chapter 18.1).

J.I. Packer offers a concise summary of the Reformation-evangelical view of justification. The Hebrew (*ṣādēq*) and Greek (*dikaioō*) verbs bear the forensic meaning to "pronounce," "accept," or "treat as righteous." God's act of justification means, negatively, that sinners are freed from the penalty of the law and, positively, that they are reinstated into divine favor and privilege. The former involves remission of all sins, removal of guilt, and the end of divine enmity and wrath. The latter includes bestowal of a righteous status, fellowship with God, and the gift of eternal life. The problem posed by justification is how the immutably just Lawgiver and Judge can remain righteous in himself and acquit sinners (Rom 3:21-26). The Gospel communicates that "the claims of God's law upon them have been fully satisfied. The law has not been abated, or suspended, or flouted for their justification, but fulfilled—by Jesus Christ, acting in their name."[63] On behalf of sinners, Christ in his life perfectly obeyed the law and in his death bore its just penalty. Thus on the ground of Christ's perfect satisfaction of the law, God does not impute sin; rather, he imputes righteousness to all who believe. God "reckons righteousness to them [i.e., sinners], not because he accounts them to have kept his law personally (which would be a false judgment), but because he accounts them to be united to the one who kept it representatively (and that is a true judgment)."[64] Faith is the instrumental means whereby Christ and his righteousness are appropriated; it is "the outstretched empty hand which receives righteousness by receiving Christ."[65]

This last interpretation of justification by faith best accords with the manifold biblical evidence on the subject, as the following section will demonstrate.

III. EXPOSITION OF THE DOCTRINE OF JUSTIFICATION

A. The Problem Defined

We now seek to answer the question posed in the introduction to this chapter, concerning how fallen and alienated persons can be made right with God. The obstacles to God acquitting and restoring guilty rebels to a harmonious relationship with himself chiefly are three in number. The first is *humanity's sinful condition.* We examined in chap. 2 humanity's sinfulness in relation to the need for grace. It will suffice here to reaffirm that pre-Christians possess a radically sinful nature inherited from Adam (Rom 8:4-5; Gal 5:13, 16-17, 19, 24). As such, the unsaved are holistically depraved (Rom 1:28-29; 2 Tim 3:8; 2 Pet 2:19), hostile to God (Rom 5:10; 8:7; Col 1:21) as children of the Devil (John 8:44), alienated from Christ (Eph 2:12-13, 19), and guilty and condemned before the just Judge of the universe (Rom 3:8; 5:16, 18). Locked in a vicious cycle of sin and guilt, pre-Christians cannot justify themselves, however diligently they attempt to do so (Luke 16:14-15; Rom 10:3).

The second obstacle is the *holy and righteous character of God.* Scripture depicts God as perfectly *holy,* in the sense that he is separated from all evil and he abhors all sin and uncleanness (Hab 1:12-13). Moreover, God is absolutely *righteous,* in that he embodies the perfect standard of the true, the good, and the right (Isa 45:21). Furthermore, he is wholly *just,* in the sense that he gives persons what they deserve. The upright God faithfully rewards the righteous, and he unerringly punishes the perverse (Ps 62:12; Rom 2:6-8). Finally, God is *unchanging* in that he consistently acts in accordance with his being, character, and promises (Ps 119:89; Mal 3:6; Jas 1:17). God will not deviate from who he is, what he is like, and what he has said in his word. The divine perfections ensure that "If we disown him, he will also disown us" (2 Tim 2:12b).

The third obstacle is the *intransigent moral law,* written on the human heart (Rom 2:14-15) and contained in the Scriptures (Acts 7:53; Rom 2:12). The immutable God cannot bend nor rescind the moral law to suit our sinful condition. Jesus fulfilled the law of ceremonies and sacrifices by his perfect life and obedient death (Heb 10:9-14); but under the new covenant he firmly upheld the moral law (Heb 8:10; 10:16). As "spiritual" (Rom 7:14), the moral law has its origin in God. As "holy, righteous and good" (*agathē,* Rom. 7:12), the law is the revelation of God's perfect character. As "good" (*kalos,* Rom 7:16), the law is a system characterized by moral beauty and perfection. Given all these qualities, God's moral law is the inviolable standard against which all human conduct is measured (Rom 3:31; 13:8-10). Believers order their lives by the Spirit's enablement according to the law's righteous requirements (Rom 8:4). Sinners, however, find little consolation in the durability of God's moral law against which all of their actions are measured.

In sum, humanity's sinful condition, God's perfectly righteous character, and the law's inviolable demands pose powerful obstacles to the justification of sinners. Luther sensed the gravity of the situation when he said on one occasion, "Here is a problem which needs God to solve it."

B. The Doctrinal Seed-Bed of Justification

Two major OT texts present the skeleton of the doctrine of justification. The first, Gen 15:6, taken from the life of Israel's great patriarch, states that "Abram believed the Lord, and he credited it to him as righteousness." The NT quotes or paraphrases Gen 15:6 five times—Rom 4:3, 9, 22; Gal 3:6; and Jas 2:23—as the foundation of its doctrine of justification by faith. The Hiphil form of the verb 'āman ("believed") in the Genesis text means to "hold fast," "believe firmly," or "trust" (cf. Gen 45:26; Exod 4:8; Ps 116:10). The verb ḥāšab ("credited") here means to "count" or "impute" (Lev 7:18; 17:4; Num 18:27, 30; Ps 32:2). The latter verb occurs in Ps 106:31, where it is recorded that Phinehas' priestly zeal for the Lord "was credited to him as righteousness for endless generations to come."[66] The noun ṣᵉdāqāh ("righteousness") implies conformity to the nature and will of God (Deut 6:25; Ps 5:8; Isa 32:17).[67] Gen 15:6 thus states that Abram gave God firm confidence in the covenant promise (Gen 15:4-5), whereupon God credited to Abram righteousness or right standing with himself. God justified Abram in the sense that he accepted Abram's faith in the covenant promise as righteousness, even though the latter was experientially sinful.

The second text is Ps 32:1-2, which Paul expounded in Rom 4:6-8. Three thousand years ago King David committed adultery with Bathsheba and suffered the agonizing consequences of this sin. After being forgiven, David composed Psalm 32 to teach us how God justifies repentant sinners. We focus on David's words, "Blessed is he whose transgressions are forgiven, whose sins are covered. Blessed is the man whose sin the Lord does not count against him" (Ps 32:1-2). Justification, according to David, involves three movements on God's part. Sinners are afflicted with transgression (pešaʿ), which signifies rebellion against the authority and laws of God (cf. 2 Kgs 3:7; 8:20). Such spiritual rebellion against the Law-giver of the universe God (1) forgives—the verb nāśāʾ denoting to "lift up," "bear," or "carry away" (cf. Lev 16:22; Isa 53:4). Justification means that in response to sincere faith God forgives, i.e., bears and carries the crushing burden of our sinful rebellion against him. Moreover, the unrighteous are laden with sin (ḥaṭṭāʾh), which connotes a missing of the mark (cf. Judg 20:16) or a failure to measure up to the standards of the holy and righteous God. Such falling short God (2) covers or conceals—the verb kāsāh connoting that God blankets our failures such that they are never seen again (Neh 4:5; Ps 32:5). In addition, the sinner is afflicted with iniquity (ʿāwôn), a comprehensive term indicating perverse behavior (Gen 15:16), the resultant guilt or blameworthiness (1 Sam 25:24; Ps 51:2), and the inevitable divine punishment (Jer 51:6). This iniquity God (3) "does not count against him" (*lō'-ḥāšab*)—the same verb encountered in Gen 15:6 and Ps 106:31. Justification means that through God's gracious action the debt of iniquity is no longer reckoned to the sinner's account. Rather, in the act of justification God lays the guilt and punishment of the world on his Son, and so pronounces believers innocent and righteous in his sight. This gracious justifying work of God is contingent upon sinners honestly acknowledging and confessing their sins (Ps 32:5).

C. The Language and Meaning of Justification

Here we examine more closely the biblical language used to describe God's justifying activity. In the OT the Qal form of the verb *ṣādaq* means to "be just" or "be righteous" (Gen 38:26; Job 9:15; Ezek 16:52). The Hiphil form of the verb in legal contexts means to "vindicate," "acquit," or "declare to be in the right." This sense prevails in Exod 23:7, where in a judicial setting involving both a guilty and an innocent party Yahweh said, "I will not acquit ['aṣdîq] the guilty." Similar is Deut 25:1, which reads, "When men have a dispute, they are to take it to court and the judges will decide the case, acquitting the innocent and condemning the guilty." In this verse the Hiphil of *ṣādaq* is parallel to the Hiphil of *rāša'* (to "condemn," "declare guilty"), thus establishing the legal sense of the primary OT verb to "justify" (so also Prov 17:15). Moreover, in Isa 50:8 the Servant of the Lord declared, "He who vindicates [Hiphil participle of *ṣādaq*] me is near. Who then will bring charges against me? Let us face each other! Who is my accuser? Let him confront me!" Similarly, Isaiah in a legal context pronounced a woe on judges "who acquit [Hiphil participle of *ṣādaq*] the guilty for a bribe, but deny justice to the innocent" (Isa 5:23). The verb *ṣādaq* has the same forensic meaning of "declare innocent" or "acquit" in 1 Kgs 8:32 and Job 32:2. It is clear that in justification God does not *make* a sinner righteous, any more than a judge in a court of law makes a defendant innocent or guilty. By his own actions the defendant is innocent or guilty; and on the weight of the evidence the judge declares him or her to be so. Note that although acquitted by God, the devout Hebrew was conscious of sin in his or her disposition and thought-life and was conscious of deeds of omission and commission (Job 31:33; Ps 51:1-9; 130:3; Prov 20:9).

The Greek verb corresponding to the Hebrew *ṣādaq* is the word *dikaioō*, to "acquit," "declare righteous," or "justify." *Dikaioō* occurs forty times in the NT, whereas the adjective *dikaios* ("upright," "righteous," "in a right relationship with God") occurs eighty times, and the nouns *dikaiosynē* ("righteousness," "uprightness," "[God's] putting [man] in a right relationship [with himself]"), *dikaiōma* ("righteous deed," "acquittal"), and *dikaiōsis* ("putting in a right relationship [with God]," "acquittal") occur ninety, ten, and two times respectively.

A precursor to Paul's doctrine of justification by faith occurs in the parable of the Pharisee and the tax-collector (Luke 18:9-14). The Pharisee boasted of his own righteousness, sought by punctilious observance of the law (vv. 11-12). All his religious endeavors, however, failed to make him acceptable to God. The tax-collector, in striking contrast, acknowledged his inability to make himself right with God with the honest plea, "God, have mercy on me, a sinner" (v. 13). The aorist verb *hilaskomai* ("be merciful") suggests that the idea of propitiation lies in the background of justification. Jesus concluded the story by saying, "I tell you that this man, rather than the other, went home justified [*dedikaiōmenos*] before God" (v. 14). The perfect passive participle of *dikaioō* is an intensive perfect, indicating the existing state of being declared in the right. The tax-collector pled no works of his own but cried out to Jesus for salvation. By virtue of his honest and humble trust, God forgave the man's sins and set him in a right relationship with himself.

Several non-theological uses of *dikaioō* in the Gospels confirm the forensic and declarative sense of the verb, the meaning of which is to "declare righteous, to recognize as righteous, proved to be in the right and accepted by God."[68] Jesus' saying that "wisdom is proved right [aorist passive of *dikaioō*] by her actions" (Matt 11:19) means that God's wise and saving purpose was vindicated by Jesus' miracles. Luke's report that "all the people and the tax-collectors justified [aorist of *dikaioō*] God" (Luke 7:29, RSV), signifies that they acknowledged God to be in the right. Luke's observation that the lawyer "wanted to justify [aorist infinitive of *dikaioō*] himself, so he asked Jesus, 'And who is my neighbor?'" (Luke 10:29) indicates that *dikaioō* here means to "acquit." Jesus' words to the Pharisees, "You are the ones who justify [present participle of *dikaioō*] yourselves in the eyes of men" (Luke 16:15a) likewise confirm that the verb means to "acquit" or "vindicate." Finally, Jesus' saying to the Pharisees—"by your words you will be acquitted, and by your words you will be condemned" (Matt 12:37)— demonstrates that *dikaioō* (used in parallel with "condemn") bears a legal or forensic meaning.

Paul understood justification to mean God's sovereign act of declaring a sinner to be in the right. This theological sense appears in Rom 2:13: "it is not those who hear the law who are righteous [*dikaioi*] in God's sight, but it is those who obey the law who will be declared righteous" (*dikaiōthēsontai*, future indicative passive of *dikaioō*). In the context of a judicial trial and verdict, Rom 3:20 reads, "no one will be declared right-eous [*dikaiōthēsetai*] in his sight by observing the law." In Rom 8:33-34a "justify" and "condemn" are parallel verbs representing two opposite legal verdicts: "Who will bring any charge against those whom God has chosen? It is God who justifies [*ho dikaiōn*]. Who is he that condemns? [*ho katakrinōn*]."

Other uses of *dikaioō* in Paul further support the declarative sense of the word. Of the incarnate Christ Paul wrote in an early Christian hymn, "he . . . was vindicated [*edikaiōthē*] by the Spirit" (1 Tim 3:16). The mean-ing may be that the Holy Spirit vindicated the scorned and rejected Christ by means of his resurrection from the dead. Whatever the precise mean-ing of the line, all the main interpretations assert that the aorist passive of *dikaioō* means to "declare righteous." In addition, we read in Rom 3:4, "Although everyone is a liar, let God be proved true, as it is written, 'So that you may be justified [*dikaiōthēs*] in your words, and prevail in your judging'" (NRSV). God cannot be made just; but his punishment of the sin of unbelief publicly declares and demonstrates his just character.

In the light of the biblical language and its use in context, we define jus-tification as God's gracious, legal verdict in respect of those who believe in Christ, forgiving their sins and declaring them righteous through the imputation of Christ's righteousness. Leon Morris some years ago estab-lished from his major study of *dikaioō* and related words that "the verb is essentially a forensic one in its biblical usage, and it denotes basically a sentence of acquittal."[69] This interpretation does not, as some allege, involve a legal fiction. Surely the Judge of the universe on appropriate grounds has the right and the ability to forgive sins, cancel all charges against sinners, declare believers to be in the right, and clothe them with righteousness. This divine verdict of pardon occurs at the moment of con-version but logically follows the person's conscious decision to believe the Gospel, turn from sin, and trust Christ as Savior and Lord.

The preceding study leads to the conclusion that justification is a once-for-all, completed decision and not an ongoing process in believers' lives. Contrary to traditional Roman theology, justification does not describe God's act of infusing righteousness in Christians. Neither, against some Arminians, does it signify being made experientially holy, in the sense of progressive freedom from indwelling sin. Indeed, Scripture depicts great saints of God as beset with weakness and uncleanness. Thus Noah became drunk, Abraham lied, Moses killed a man, David committed adultery, Jonah disobeyed God's call, and Peter disowned Jesus. The judicial under-standing of justification we have reaffirmed does not deny that God works to make disciples experientially holy. The latter, subjective process in the

Reformation tradition rightly describe as the believer's sanctification. In truth, an organic connection exists between justification and sanctification. God legally declares sinners to be in the right to the end that they may become holy in lived experience. Although progressive sanctification follows upon and is continually rooted in justification, the two are not identical, nor ought one be subsumed under the other.

D. The Ground and Means of Justification

On what basis, or through what provision, does God see fit to acquit guilty sinners and pronounce them righteous? Consider the following evidence drawn from relevant Scripture passages.

NOT ON THE BASIS OF PERSONAL WORTH OR WORKS. Scripture is quite clear (1) that God does not justify pre-Christians on the basis of personal *character or worth*. As the psalmist wrote, "no one living is righteous before you" (Ps 143:2; cf. Rom 3:10). Again, "All have turned aside, they have together become corrupt; there is no one who does good, not even one" (Ps 14:3). Consequently, "if you, O Lord, kept a record of sins, O Lord, who could stand?" (Ps 130:3). Moreover, (2) no sinner could possibly merit favor with God on the basis of personal *pedigree or privileges*. Paul, reflecting on his pre-Christian life in Judaism, wrote, "If anyone else thinks he has reasons to put confidence in the flesh, I have more: circumcised on the eighth day, of the people of Israel, of the tribe of Benjamin, a Hebrew of Hebrews" (Phil 3:4b-5). This highly credentialed Jew soberly judged that his personal qualifications were worthless as the basis for acceptance with God. And (3) God does not justify on the basis of *works of the law*. The former rabbi noted that only perfect compliance with God's law warrants the attribution of righteousness: "it is not those who hear the law who are righteous [*dikaioi*] in God's sight, but it is those who obey the law who will be declared righteous" (*dikaiōthēsontai*, Rom 2:13; cf. 10:5; Gal 3:12). Since no one keeps the law in its entirety (Rom 10:5, 10-18), no human can be justified on the basis of works required by the law. Paul learned the hard way by personal experience that "no one will be declared righteous in his sight by observing the law; rather through the law we become conscious of sin" (Rom 3:20; cf. Rom 3:28; Gal 2:16; 3:11). The apostle's bottom line was that "All who rely on observing the law are under a curse" (*katara*, Gal 3:10).

BUT ON THE BASIS OF CHRIST'S MERITS. Paul affirmed that sinners are justified on the basis of the satisfaction rendered to God's moral law through Jesus Christ. The biblical ground of justification is thoroughly Christological rather than anthropological. Peter simply stated that "the good news of peace [comes through] Jesus Christ" (Acts 10:36; cf. 1 Cor 6:11). The basis of right standing with God is not the sinner's character, privileges, works, or even faith; it is all on account of Jesus Christ. The ground of justification, in the first place, is Christ's *virtuous life*. The Lord Jesus perfectly fulfilled God's will, thereby satisfying the Father's righteous and holy demands (Matt 3:15). Prophets of old predicted the perfect righteousness of the coming Messiah (Isa 11:5; 53:11; Jer 23:5; 33:15), who in word and in deed would satisfy God's law (Isa 53:9b). John pointed to Christ's perfect righteousness, when he wrote that the Son always strove to please the Father (John 5:30), sought to do the Father's will and work (John 4:34; 6:38; 17:4), and was entirely obedient to the Father's commands (John 14:31; 15:10). Because of his complete fulfillment of God's law and wholehearted dedication to his service, Jesus is "the Holy and Righteous One" (Acts 3:14; cf. 7:52; 22:14; 1 John 2:1; 3:7). Heb 5:7-9 speaks of Jesus' "reverent submission," his perfect obedience at every stage of his life (cf. Heb 10:7), and his "being made perfect" (aorist passive participle of *teleioō*, to "perfect," "complete"). Consequently, the anonymous writer described Jesus as "one who is holy, blameless, pure, set apart from sinners" (Heb 7:26). As Jesus said to his disciples concerning himself, the Son of Man, "On him God the Father has placed his seal of approval" (John 6:27).

The biblical ground of justification, in the second place, is Christ's *obedient death* on the cross. In 2 Cor 5:21 Paul linked the imputation of righteousness to sinners with Christ's substitutionary sacrifice on Calvary. As the apostle stated in Rom 5:9, "we have now been justified by his blood." Paul reaffirmed this point in Rom 5:18-19: "just as the result of one trespass was condemnation for all men, so also the result of one act of righteousness was justification that brings life for all men. For just as through the disobedience of the one man the many were made sinners, so also through the obedience of the one man the many will be made righteous." The "one act of righteousness" (v. 18, cf. "the obedience of the one man," v. 19) identifies the ground of justification as Christ's obedient submission to death that crowned his entire life of fidelity to the Father. Moreover, 1 John 2:2 states that on the basis of Christ's atoning sacrifice God is propitiated and those who believe are reconciled to him. Peter affirmed that Christ's death makes believers acceptable to God and establishes a right relationship between the Creator and the creature. "Christ died for sins once for all, the righteous [*dikaios*] for the unrighteous, to bring you to God" (1 Pet 3:18). The preceding Scriptures assert that the Messiah, who had no need to offer any sacrifice for himself (Heb 7:27), could and did die once for the sins of the people. The exclusive ground for acceptance with the holy God is the atoning sacrifice of the sinless Christ.

"THE RIGHTEOUSNESS OF GOD." This and the following section will show that what God reckons to believing sinners is "the righteousness of God." Many mediating scholars (Dodd, Käsemann, etc.) interpret "the righteousness of God" in terms of a subjective genitive, namely, as an attribute of God by which he acts to save his people. Admittedly, OT texts such as Isa 45:8, 46:13, 51:5-8, 56:1, and 62:1 juxtapose "righteousness" with "salvation." But the OT does not restrict ṣedek and ṣᵉdāqāh to the narrow meaning of salvation or victory. Rather, God manifested his righteousness in salvation in the sense that those without any righteousness of their own become clothed with his righteousness. This great truth is hinted at by the phrase "the Lord our righteousness" (Jer 23:6; 33:16). Moreover, the prophet Isaiah exclaimed, "I delight greatly in the Lord; my soul rejoices in my God. For he has clothed me with garments of salvation and arrayed me in a robe of righteousness" (ṣᵉdāqāh, Isa 61:10). Hear Isaiah again: "in the Lord all the descendants of Israel will be found righteous and will exult" (Isa 45:25; cf. Job 27:6; Ps 132:9). E.J. Young argued that one should not interpret "righteousness" as a synonym for God's conquering action on behalf of his people. "Quite possibly the prophet anticipates Paul, and the righteousness of which he speaks originates with God and comes to man from Him, and in it man may stand before him."[70]

This concept shines with clearer light in the NT. Amidst universal human unrighteousness and guilt, Paul in Rom 1:17, 3:21-22, and 10:3 advanced the notion of a righteousness that comes from God, the revelation of which constitutes the Gospel. "For in the gospel a righteousness from God [dikaiosynē theou] is revealed, a righteousness that is by faith from first to last, just as it is written: 'The righteous will live by faith'" (Rom 1:17). The righteousness of which Paul spoke has its origin in God, satisfies the demand of divine justice, and accomplishes the justification of the unrighteous. Elsewhere, with an eye to the Savior's work, Paul wrote that Christ "has become for us wisdom from God—that is, our righteousness [dikaiosynē], holiness and redemption" (1 Cor 1:30). Moreover, Paul expressed the longing that he might "be found in him [i.e., Christ], not having a righteousness of my own that comes from the law, but that which is through faith in Christ—the righteousness that comes from God and is by faith" (Phil 3:9). Through the obedience of his life and death Christ acquired righteousness that the Father would credit to sinners who believe in him. Thus the righteousness believers possess is not their own accomplishment. It is the right standing of another—even Jesus Christ—that is credited to their account as a free gift.

THE LEGAL RECKONING OF CHRIST. Here we develop more fully God's act of imputing the righteousness earned by Christ, mentioned above. Yahweh said to the rebellious nation of Israel, "Though your sins are like scarlet, they shall be as white as snow; though they are red as crimson, they shall be like wool" (Isa 1:18). The penitent (v. 19) come to God with a sin-stained soul but depart pure and blameless in his sight. Young believed that "The doctrine of a forensic justification is found in these words."[71] Consider also the imagery in Zech 3:1-5, where Joshua the high priest, as representative of the people, stood before the judging angel of the Lord. The "filthy clothes" Joshua wore (v. 3) symbolize the iniquity of the people. The command of the angel to remove the defiled garments connotes the pardoning of iniquity (cf. v. 9; 13:1), whereas the order to put on white, festive garments suggests the clothing of sinners with divine righteousness. The ground of Joshua's and the people's acceptance clearly was no righteousness of their own, but the perfect righteousness of another attributed to them. Isaiah upheld imputed justification in Isa 53:11, which reads, "by his knowledge my righteous servant will justify [Hiphil of *ṣādaq*] many, and he will bear their iniquities." Young observed that "If the verb is not taken as forensic and if it is held that it refers to *iustitia infusa*, it would follow that the servant, in bearing the iniquities of the many, is himself infused with these iniquities and himself becomes sinful."[72] This, of course, cannot be.

In Romans 4 Paul expounded the meaning of justification by appealing to the examples of Abraham (vv. 1-3, 9-24) and David (vv. 6-8). The apostle used the verb *logizomai* (a word meaning to enter into a ledger, hence to "reckon to one's account," "credit") eleven times in this chapter (vv. 3-6, 8-11, 22-24). Paul's purpose was to show that believers are justified not by works but as God credits righteousness to their account. By appeal to Gen 15:6 (vv. 3, 9, 22), Paul again (cf. Gal 3:6) argued that God reckoned Abraham's faith in the divine promise as righteousness (*dikaiosynē*). "The words, 'it was credited to him' were written not for him alone, but also for us, to whom God will credit righteousness—for us who believe in him who raised Jesus our Lord from the dead" (vv. 23-24). Likewise, from the history of David, Paul concluded that justification involves, negatively, the non-imputation of sin and guilt: "Blessed is the man whose sin the Lord will never count against him" (*ou mē logisētai*, v. 8). And, positively, justification involves the imputation to the believer of divine righteousness: "David . . . speaks of the blessedness of the man to whom God credits righteousness [*theos logizetai dikaiosynēn*] apart from works" (v. 6). On the other side of Calvary, faithful believers legally were set in right relation to God.

Rom 5:19, cited above, also attests the imputational sense of justification. "For just as through the disobedience of one man the many were made [aorist passive of *kathistēmi*] sinners, so also through the obedience of the one man many will be made [future passive of *kathistēmi*] righteous." The verb *kathistemi* means to "constitute" or "establish." Thus just as God imputed the first sin of Adam to the human race, and just as he imputed the guilt of the race to the Lamb on the cross, so he imputes Christ's righteousness to all who believe. On the ground of Christ's virtues, God places believers in the category of righteous persons. The foregoing simply means that God has the right to bestow unearned and unmerited grace to whom he will. With justice satisfied and the penalty paid through Christ's sacrifice, God is free graciously to pardon and attribute innocence to unworthy sinners.

THE MEANS OF JUSTIFICATION: FAITH. Whereas the ground or basis of justification is Christ's virtuous life and obedient death, the means of appropriating righteousness is faith enabled by the Spirit. We read in Hab 2:4, "the righteous will live by their faith" (*'emûnāh*, NRSV, cf. AV). Other versions translate *'emûnāh* as "faithfulness," the sense being that the righteous will live by the faithfulness or steadfastness that springs from faith. Paul (Rom 1:17; Gal 3:11) and the author of Hebrews (Heb 10:38) linked justification with the individual's faith. It appears that both Habakkuk and the NT writers understood that persons are judged righteous and live in the spiritual realm by means of their faith relationship with the Lord. F.F. Bruce commented that *'emûnāh* (LXX, *pistis*) "means 'steadfastness' or 'fidelity' based on a firm belief in God and his Word, and it is this firm belief that Paul understands by the term."[73]

In the final moments of his life the repentant thief on the cross was justified before God (Luke 23:40-43). A true sense of his own sinfulness and Jesus' ability to save led to his cry of faith: "Jesus, remember me when you come into your kingdom" (v. 42). The Lord's reply—"today you will be with me in paradise" (v. 43)—indicates that at that very moment the criminal was reckoned right with God and restored to fellowship with the Father in heaven. In John 6:29 Jesus said to his disciples, "The work [*to ergon*] of God is this: to believe in the one he has sent." The disciples undoubtedly thought of many works of the law they must do to please God (v. 28). But Jesus stated in no uncertain terms that there is but one work, or one moral act, they must perform—namely, to exercise faith in himself as the one sent by the Father.

The apostle Paul, rehearsing his conversion and call to ministry before King Agrippa, testified that Christ commanded him to preach the Gospel to the Gentiles so that they "may receive forgiveness of sins and a place among those who are sanctified by faith in me" (Acts 26:18). The perfect passive participle of *hagiazō*, to "sanctify," connotes the state or condition of being positionally sanctified or justified (cf. 1 Cor 6:11). The means of achieving this status clearly is faith in Christ. In his sermon at Pisidian Antioch (Acts 13:39), Paul proclaimed the doctrine of justification by faith alone. "Through him everyone who believes is justified [*dikaioutai*] from everything you could not be justified [*dikaiōthēnai*] from by the law of Moses." The apostle insisted that people are justified solely by faith and not by the futile efforts of law-keeping.

Paul reaffirmed in his letters that the means of appropriating righteousness from God is faith. He frequently wrote that justification is mediated "by" or "through faith:" viz., *pistei* (instrumental dative; Rom 3:28), *ek pisteōs* (Rom 3:30; 5:1; 10:6; Gal 2:16; 3:24), *dia pisteōs* (Rom 3:30; Gal 2:16; Phil 3:9), and *epi tē pistei* (Phil 3:9). In his discussion of God's act of crediting righteousness to Abraham and David (Rom 4:1-25), Paul used the noun "faith" (*pistis*) ten times and the verb "believe" (*pisteuō*) six times. Abraham and David trusted God and believed the promises, whereupon God gave them righteous standing with himself. Paul also wrote these words to the church at Philippi: "that I may gain Christ and be found in him, not having a righteousness of my own that comes from the law, but that which is through faith in Christ—the righteousness that comes from God and is by faith" (Phil 3:8b-9). Paul conceded that he never could generate sufficient righteousness on his own to please God. Instead, by an act of faith in Christ he freely received righteousness from God as a gift.

Heb 11:7 links righteousness with faith in a manner reminiscent of Paul, when it says of Noah, "By his faith [*pistei*] he . . . became heir of the righteousness [*dikaiosynē*] that comes by faith [*kata pistin*]." Faith is the means by which righteousness came to obedient Noah. The cumulative biblical data confirm that pre-Christians are justified through the instrumentality of faith. On the basis of Christ's work and through the sinner's desperate cry for forgiveness, God faithfully justifies or bestows perfect standing with himself.

A KEY TEXT ON JUSTIFICATION. An important Pauline text, Rom 3:21-26, recapitulates the main points established thus far. In vv. 5-18 (cf. v. 23) of Romans 3 Paul demonstrated that both Jews and Gentiles are unrighteous and guilty before God. In vv. 21-26 Paul expounded God's gracious solution to this fatal, human problem, as follows. (1) The *announcement* of justification through the Gospel disclosed a way, other than the futile venture of law-keeping, whereby sinners are made acceptable to God. The key to the problem of the justification of sinners is found in the phrase "the righteousness from God." *Dikaiosynē theou*, as in Rom 1:17, signifies a righteousness from God that provides right-standing with him.[74] (2) The *instrument* by which God justifies sinners is faith directed toward Jesus Christ. "This righteousness from God comes through faith [*dia pisteōs*] in Jesus Christ to all who believe" (v. 22). To make this point absolutely clear, Paul reiterated in vv. 25b-28, 30 the instrumental function of faith in justification. The preposition *dia* with the genitive often signifies means or instrument—not only in vv. 22, 25, 27 of the present text, but also in Scriptures such as 2 Cor 5:10, Gal 3:19, and 2 Pet 1:3.[75] Note that Paul never stated that justification is *dia pistin* ("on account of faith"; cf. Rom 8:11; Rev 12:11)—which construction would posit faith as the basis or ground of justification. Indeed, (3) the *ground* of God's gracious acts of justification is the propitiatory sacrifice (*hilastērion*) of Christ, who bore the just punishment for our sins and so averted the divine wrath. We "are justified freely by his grace through the redemption that came by Christ Jesus. God presented him as a sacrifice of atonement through faith in his blood" (vv. 24-25a). Finally, (4) Paul referred to the *demonstration* of justification in vv. 25c-26. By virtue of Christ's penal sacrifice, God vindicated his own character not only by remaining *dikaios* in punishing his Son, but also by finding a just way to acquit guilty sinners and set them in right relation with himself.

E. The Results of Justification

God's justifying act imparts several, significant spiritual outcomes, beginning with (1) the *forgiveness of all sins*. At Pisidian Antioch, Paul spoke of God's justifying work (Acts 13:39) and announced to his hearers that "through Jesus the forgiveness of sins is proclaimed to you" (Acts 13:38; cf. 2:38; 10:43). Rehearsing his conversion and call to ministry before Agrippa, Paul testified that Christ commanded him to preach the Gospel so that his hearers "may receive forgiveness of sins and a place among those who are sanctified by faith in me [Christ]" (Acts 26:18). The perfect passive participle of *hagiazō* affirms the state or condition of being positionally sanctified or justified (cf. 1 Cor 6:11). Comparing the superiority of Christ's shed blood to the blood of animals, Hebrews states, "How much more, then, will the blood of Christ . . . cleanse our consciences from acts that lead to death" (Heb 9:14). This first outcome means that God no longer counts sins against justified believers (2 Cor 5:19) but regards them as clothed with the perfect righteousness of his Son (1 Cor. 1:30; Phil 3:9).

We have shown that under the old covenant God graciously forgave sins (Exod 34:6-7; Num 14:18; Ps 32:1-2, 5; 51:1-2). But with the completion of Christ's atoning work the new covenant brings full and final forgiveness of sin and guilt, even the complete obliteration of iniquities. In addition to Heb 9:14, quoted above, v. 26 is relevant: "Then Christ would have had to suffer many times since the creation of the world. But now he has appeared once for all at the end of the ages to do away with sin by the sacrifice of himself" (Heb 9:26).[76] Under the new covenant inaugurated by Christ's blood, no further action need be taken against sin. No necessity exists for temple, priests, or blood sacrifices. Sin is so obliterated in the justified that God remembers it no more, as Jeremiah (31:34), Isaiah (43:25), and Micah (7:19), anticipating Messiah's work, confidently proclaimed.

Because pardoned of all sins, (2) the *sentence of condemnation is annulled*. This is true of saints under both covenants. Jesus said, "Whoever hears my word and believes him who has sent me . . . will not be condemned" (John 5:24; cf. 3:18). Paul similarly wrote, "there is now no condemnation [*katakrima*] for those who are in Christ Jesus" (Rom 8:1). By virtue of the divine sentence of acquittal, all legal charges of guiltworthiness past, present, and future have been dropped by the Judge of the universe (v. 33). No one can bring any condemning judgment against God's elect (v. 34). Justified saints, in other words, possess perfect, legal standing in Christ.

A further outcome of justification is (3) the *gift of eternal life*. Jesus' saying to the repentant thief on the cross—"today you will be with me in paradise" (Luke 23:43)—attests the immediate gift of eternal life to the justified criminal prior to Jesus' death. Subsequent to Christ's death, Paul encouraged Titus by writing, "having been justified by his grace, we might become heirs having the hope of eternal life" (Tit 3:7). Paul likewise described eternal life as the outcome of justification in Rom 5:18 and 21.

Furthermore, God's justifying action results in (4) *spiritual peace*, or the cessation of hostilities between God and repentant sinners. Addressing Gentiles at the house of Cornelius, Peter proclaimed "the good news of peace through Jesus Christ, who is Lord of all" (Acts 10:36). Paul wrote that "since we have been justified through faith, we have peace with God through our Lord Jesus Christ" (Rom 5:1). Because of the atoning work of Christ, the peacemaker, the justified are no longer at war with the Father; on the contrary, they draw close to him in a new relation of peace (cf. Luke 2:14). Once we were his enemies; but now as believers we are his beloved friends.

Justification amounts to (5) *positional sanctification*. As Paul wrote, "you were washed, you were sanctified, you were justified in the name of the Lord Jesus Christ and by the Spirit of our God" (1 Cor 6:11). The justified are positionally sanctified in that their standing before God is perfect as a result of Christ's imputed righteousness. But at justification the old, corrupt nature is not eliminated; this must await our glorification, when we see Christ. When God sets us in right relation with himself, we are not freed from sin's influence in our lives or its corrupting power on our beings. Our life-experience as believers thus does not match our legal position. Positional sanctification, however, means that we who are united with Christ and set in a right relation with him are rid of sin's dominion over our natures. Justified saints are delivered from the slavery and bondage to sin that characterized the unconverted state. As Paul wrote in Rom 6:14, "sin shall not be your master, because you are not under law, but under grace" (cf. v. 16). In other words, the positionally sanctified need not allow sin to reign over their mortal bodies (v. 12). The justified need not necessarily sin, although they regretfully do commit sins.

F. Legal Adoption

A significant concomitant of justification is legal adoption into God's family. In a court of law a person may be acquitted by the judge of all charges against him; but this acquittal does not make the person a member of the judge's family! Adoption is that act of grace, logically following conversion and justification, by which God confers on forgiven sinners the status of sonship. Adoption thus is a soteriological decision not to be confused with mankind's natural sonship given by creation. The NT word for adoption is *huiothesia*, which literally means "placing as a son." The word occurs five times in the NT, once in the corporate sense of Israel's adoption as the chosen people (Rom 9:4), once in the sense of the redemption of the believer's body at the *Parousia* (Rom 8:23), and three times in the sense of God's declaration of sonship. So Paul stated that the Father "predestined us to be adopted as his sons through Jesus Christ" (Eph 1:5). Moreover, God sent his Son into the world "to redeem those who were under the law, so that we might receive adoption as children" (Gal 4:5, NRSV; cf. v. 7). Paul further wrote in Rom 8:15 (NRSV), "you did not receive a spirit of slavery to fall back into fear, but you have received a spirit of adoption" (cf. v. 17).

Employing the language of sonship, Scripture explains several outcomes of legal adoption for believers. By virtue of adoption into God's family, (1) we now bear a new name and a new identity as "children of God" (1 John 3:1). As adopted children (2) we experience the intimate indwelling of God's Spirit. "Because you are sons, God sent the Spirit of his Son into our hearts, the Spirit who calls out, '*Abba*, Father'" (Gal 4:6; cf. Rom 8:14). Adoption into the family of God (3) assures us that we are the objects of his special love (1 John 4:9-11). As beloved children (4) believers receive special care and provision from the heavenly Father (Luke 11:11-13). As members of God's family (5) we have the right and privilege of bold access into the father's presence (Heb 4:14-16; cf. 2:10-13). This new, adopted status means (6) that God lovingly disciplines and chastens believers as a human father would his own children (Heb 12:7-8). Finally, adoption into the family of God means (7) that we are heirs of the Father's eternal kingdom and glory (Rom 8:17).

G. Personal Reconciliation

Scripture indicates that prior to legal acquittal pre-Christians are alienated and estranged from the Lord of the universe. Like Adam and Eve in the Garden, sinners compulsively hide from their loving Creator. Paul wrote that in the unconverted state we were "separate from Christ" (Eph 2:12; cf. v. 13), "foreigners and aliens" (Eph 2:19), "hostile to God" (Rom 8:7), and "God's enemies" (Rom 5:10; cf. Col 1:21). Indeed, sinners are "separated from the life of God because of the ignorance that is in them due to the hardening of their hearts" (Eph 4:18). Psychologically and spiritually a seemingly intractable breach of enmity exists between God and rebellious sinners.

As long as the verdict of condemnation prevails, sinners lack loving fellowship with the triune God. But since on the ground of Christ's perfect sacrifice believers are declared free from sin and guilt, enmity is abolished and restoration to communion with the God of love becomes a new reality. The reconciliation in view involves both the initial restoration of relationship and its continued maintenance. Jesus' parable of the lost son (Luke 15:11-24) teaches this grand truth. The younger son who took his inheritance and left home to engage in riotous living in a distant country (vv. 12-13) symbolizes the alienation and estrangement of the unconverted. The son's return to his father's embrace and joyous celebration (vv. 20-24) signifies reconciliation with God and restoration to favor. The wayward son petitioned his father to treat him as a hired hand (v. 19), but the father in grace dealt with him as a beloved son.

Paul indicated that the initiative in healing the breach between the Creator and the creature comes from God himself. He wrote, "For if, when we were God's enemies, we were reconciled to him through the death of his Son, how much more, having been reconciled, shall we be saved through his life! Not only is this so, but we also rejoice in God through our Lord Jesus Christ, through whom we have now received reconciliation" (Rom 5:10-11; cf. 2 Cor 5:18-19; Col 1:20, 22). Paul established the logical relation between legal justification and personal reconciliation in the following pairs of Scripture texts: "justified by his blood" (Rom 5:9) and "reconciled to him [God]" (v. 10); "not counting men's sins against them" (2 Cor 5:19b) and "God was reconciling the world to himself in Christ" (v. 19a; cf. v. 18); "the blood of Christ" (Eph 2:13b) and "you who once were far away have been brought near" (v. 13a); and lastly, "making peace through his blood" (Col 1:20b) and "to reconcile to himself all things" (v. 20a). Peter also wrote, "Christ died for sins once for all, the righteous for the unrighteous, to bring you to God" (1 Pet 3:18). By virtue of a person's faith response to Christ's sufficient work and the Father's verdict of acquittal, enmity is transformed into friendship (Rom 5:10), hostility into peace (Rom 5:1; Eph 2:17), and estrangement into fellowship (Col 1:21-22).

On which side, God or humans, does the obstacle to personal reconciliation reside? The biblical perspective seems to be, on *both* the divine and the human sides. God can have no fellowship with guilty sinners, and sinners are distrustful of God. So Ralph Martin astutely observes, "To Paul estrangement which the Christian reconciliation has to overcome is indubitably two-sided; there is something in God as well as something in man which has to be dealt with before there can be peace. . . . It is God's earnest dealing with the obstacle on His own side to peace which prevails on man to believe in the seriousness of His love, and to lay aside distrust. It is God's earnest dealing with the obstacle on His own side which constitutes the reconciliation."[77]

IV. Practical Implications of the Doctrine of Justification

The implications of the doctrine of justification by grace through faith for Christian citizenship and living are manifold. Some of these outcomes are addressed in the discussion that follows.

A. Possess Assurance of Justification

Believers in Christ should possess reasonable assurance of their acceptance by God and new standing in the family of the redeemed. In the words of the apostle John, "I write these things to you who believe in the name of the Son of God so that you may know that you have eternal life" (1 John

5:13). Assurance of justification and salvation is possible at several levels. (1) *Doctrinally*, believers can be assured of justification and eternal life on the basis of Christ's deity, atoning death, and victorious resurrection from the dead as attested by the Scriptures (John 4:14; 5:24). Paul, for example, wrote that Christ "was raised to life for our justification" (*dikaiosis*, Rom 4:25). Because of who Christ is and what he has done, believers may know that they belong to him forever. John makes this crystal-clear by his eightfold use of "we know" in 1 John 5. (2) *Morally*, Christians gain assurance of being united with Christ in a saving relationship forever as they obey God's commands (1 John 2:3, 5; 3:24). (3) *Relationally*, the saints gain assurance as they spontaneously perform loving deeds toward others. John wrote, "Dear children, let us not love with words or tongue but with actions and in truth. This then is how we know that we belong to the truth, and how we set our hearts at rest in his presence" (1 John 3:18-19; cf. 4:7). And (4) *experientially*, believers gain assurance of salvation through the presence and power of the Spirit in the heart. In the words of Paul, "The Spirit himself testifies with our spirit that we are God's children" (Rom 8:16; cf. v. 15; Gal 4:6). Hear John's plain affirmation, "We know that we live in him and he in us, because he has given us of his Spirit" (1 John 4:13). Add to the foregoing the subjective experience of the peace and hope God grants to justified believers (Rom 5:1-2) and assurance can be a glorious, experiential reality.

It appears clear, then, that the normal Christian experience in an age of spiritual confusion is assurance of final salvation. To this end the author of Hebrews wrote, "We want each one of you to show the same diligence so as to realize the full assurance of hope to the very end" (Heb 6:11, NRSV; cf. 1 Pet 1:3-4). Unlike justification and adoption, assurance of salvation admits of degrees and thus may fluctuate in strength and intensity. Since much of the evidence (moral, relational, and experiential) is subjective, assurance can be expected to vacillate with our circumstances and feelings. Believers ought not be shaken by the presence of honest doubts in their lives. They should be encouraged, however, that assurance of justification and salvation can be strong and vital, as the writer of Hebrews suggested to sorely harassed Jewish-Christians: "Let us draw near to God with a sincere heart in full assurance of faith" (Heb 10:22). Assured of acceptance with God forever, Christians can live and serve courageously with hearts filled with peace and confidence.

B. Be Delivered from Feelings of Guilt

Guilt is associated with actual violations of God's law (objective guilt) and with "the emotion that follows judging oneself in violation of a standard" (subjective guilt).[78] Many Christians labor to varying degrees under the burden of guilt feelings and accusing consciences. The causes of guilt feelings in genuine Christians appear to be several.

(1) Believers may be *inordinately severe on themselves*. Some Christians live in the legacy of a stern and legalistic upbringing, in the home or in the church, that has imposed on them a stringent code of ethics with accompanying taboos. Unfortunately, certain Christian churches have been legalistic, more negative than positive, stressing personal wretchedness rather than God's grace in Christ. Other believers may have had imposed upon them the unrealistic burden of sinless perfection, which insists that God accepts them only on the condition that they be perfect. The solution to this unreasonable sense of guilt is to recall that the omniscient Lawgiver and Judge declares believers "not guilty!" and, indeed, clothes them with the righteousness of Christ. Christians need to remind themselves that they are God's forgiven, justified, and adopted children. The righteous God has pardoned, cleansed, and freed true believers from the burden of sin and guilt. Overly scrupulous Christians need to celebrate this glorious reality.

(2) Other subjective guilt may be explained as a *heightened sense of unworthiness due to an unusually close relationship with God*. Isaiah was one of the most godly men of Israel in his day. While in the temple seeking the Lord during a time of national crisis, the prophet saw in a vision the Holy One of Israel high and exalted and adored by heavenly seraphim. The response of the man of God to this awesome vision was the self-abasing retort, "Woe to me! . . . I am ruined! For I am a man of unclean lips, and I live among a people of unclean lips, and my eyes have seen the King, the Lord Almighty" (Isa 6:5). The closer a Spirit-filled Christian draws to the heart of the holy God, the more unworthy he or she may feel. A well-known Christian leader lamented to the church his sense of personal unworthiness before the Lord. A perceptive brother replied that, far from being worthless, the leader lived so close to the Lord that he sensed his spiritual needs more acutely than the rest of us. Paul Tournier acknowledged the validity of this phenomenon: "The nearer we get to God the more we experience His grace, and the more we experience His grace, the more too we discover faults in ourselves which we did not discern before, and the more we suffer from them."[79]

(3) Feelings of guilt may arise from *unconfessed sins of omission or commission* in the believer's life. S. B. Narramore has argued that believers ought not experience guilt in a punitive sense but as constructive sorrow for sins.[80] Consider Peter's sorrow following his threefold denial of the Lord. We read that following his denial Peter "went outside and wept

bitterly" (Matt 26:75). This third type is objective guilt, which "appears as guilt towards God, a breakdown in the order of man's dependency towards God."[81] Christ's atoning provisions provide the basis for the Christian's continued forgiveness, but this forgiveness must be repeatedly sought and received from God. Christians with unconfessed sin in their lives must not engage in the inauthentic responses of rationalization, self-justification, or repression of conscience. Rather, believers must be honest before their heavenly Father by faithfully acknowledging sins, truthfully confessing them to God, and accepting his forgiveness and peace. John's exhortation leads us to the path of freedom and joy: "If we confess our sins, he is faithful and just and will forgive us our sins and purify us from all unrighteousness" (1 John 1:9). If the Christian deals with sins in this constructive manner, guilt will serve as a positive, internal alarm system to our behavior in relation to God's righteous law.

The final form of guilt (4) is *neurotic guilt* or a "guilt complex," where the individual is consumed with a deep sense of having committed some mortal sacrilege, such as the unpardonable sin (Mark 3:29). Here the subject accuses and often flagellates himself as punishment for perceived sins. This inauthentic response only results in humiliation, shame, and depression. The attempt to comfort such a one by suggesting that he suffers from "false guilt" produces little relief. Neurotic guilt warrants intervention by a wise and sensitive Christian counselor.

C. Cast Off the Burden of Perfectionism

Psychologists inform us that perfectionism (the attitude and behavior pattern that seeks complete attainment of the ideal) is perhaps the most common emotional problem among evangelical Christians.[82] God in his wisdom has endowed human image-bearers with an internalized concept of the ideal or the perfect. However, this is an *ideal*, not an *achievable reality* in this life for finite human beings. Even great saints of God such as Abraham and David—lauded in Scripture as examples of those justified by faith (Romans 4)—were fallible and sinful. Because of residual sin within, we *will* to do the good, but we often fail to *realize* our moral and spiritual aspirations (Rom 7:15-20). Consequently, those who expect perfection of other people and institutions more often than not end up discouraged and disillusioned. And those who expect perfection of themselves wind up despairing and depressed.

The fact is that moral and religious perfectionism is not a precondition for pardon and reconciliation with God. Neither is perfectionism a precondition for an ongoing relationship of intimacy with God. We have seen that no works and no virtue that we can manufacture merit acceptance with God. St. Paul's rigorous polemic against the works of the law applies to those who seek right standing with God as well as those who seek the maintenance of that relation. We begin the new life and we continue the new life by faith in Christ, not by any effort of our own. We should understand, however, that regeneration, justification, and reconciliation inaugurate the process of Christian maturity, holiness, and sanctification (see chap. 10). The attainable goal of the new life is *growth* into Christian perfection, not the unattainable standard of *perfectionism*. Christians strive for the goal of Christlike maturity, knowing that we will never attain the ideal this side of glory.

For Christians, the antidote to perfectionism lies in the following considerations. (1) God regards the imperfect character and works of true believers as perfectly acceptable to him in Christ. Although in their *character* believers fall short of God's absolute standard, the Lord has clothed them with the righteousness of his Son so that they are now pleasing to him. Calvin simply stated, "the lives of believers, framed to holiness and righteousness, are pleasing to him."[83] The good news is that in Christ the Father now regards believers as perfect when measured against the ideal. Moreover, (2) believers' *works and service* in practice fall short of God's standard of perfection. Nevertheless, God views the deeds of his blood-bought people framed in the perfection of his Son. Peter recognized this when he wrote that the saints "[offer] spiritual sacrifices acceptable to God through Jesus Christ" (1 Pet 2:5). In this regard, Calvin commented as follows:

> [A]s we ourselves, when we have been engrafted in Christ, are righteous in God's sight because our iniquities are covered by Christ's sinlessness, so our works are righteousness and are thus regarded because whatever fault is otherwise in them is buried in Christ's purity, and is not charged to our account. Accordingly, we can deservedly say that by faith alone not only we ourselves but our works as well are justified.[84]

Scholars designate the preceding as Calvin's doctrine of "double justification." The point is that Christians should not engage in the impossible pursuit of perfectionism, because God views both our persons and our labors as pleasing and acceptable to him through the merits of his Son.

Perfectionist believers give every labor, every service their very "best shot." But realistically they understand that their *de facto* progress toward Christlikeness will not be completed in this life. In the present the saints are, as Luther insisted, "both righteous and a sinner." Perfect conformity to Christ will be realized at the resurrection and in the life to come (1 Cor 13:10).

V

THE PROGRESS

OF SALVATION

"TRANSFORMED INTO HIS LIKENESS"
2 CORINTHIANS 3:18

———□———

THE DOCTRINE OF SANCTIFICATION

I. INTRODUCTORY CONCERNS

The God revealed in Scripture is infinitely righteous and holy in character. Such a God can have no fellowship, no concourse, with unrighteousness in any form. Hence those who would relate to God and be his special people must be holy in character. The present chapter considers how the Spirit makes those who are holy in *principle* (i.e., positionally sanctified by grace) holy and godly in *practice* (i.e., experientially sanctified in word and deed). The doctrine of experiential sanctification follows closely upon the doctrines of faith, regeneration, and justification. Christians are saved *de jure* by faith acceptance of Christ's work on the cross; but they are saved *de facto* by faith repudiation of the old nature and cultivation of the new. The close relation between justification and sanctification means that God not only declares repentant sinners righteous but that through the Spirit's graces he actually makes them so. The God who re-creates sinners via the new birth (1 Pet 1:3, 23) faithfully renews them into the image of his Son.[1] Sanctification, then, is God's means of actualizing in forgiven sinners his original creative purpose. The doctrine of sanctification involves a number of important theological and practical concerns, as follows.

Of first importance, what is meant by sanctification, holiness of life, or moral perfection? Is sanctification entirely a work of God, primarily a work of the human will, or a joint effort involving both parties? If both God and the Christian are involved in sanctification, what is the relation between the Spirit's working and the human will? An important concern is whether the believer achieves sanctification instantaneously or through a lengthy process. Does the born-again Christian attain a state of sanctification by a single act of faith and surrender—the so-called "second blessing" experience? With Holiness advocates, can we equate this decisive, post-conversion experience of sanctification with the baptism in the Holy Spirit? Or, contrariwise, is the attainment of holiness more of a process, involving life-long surrender, effort, and spiritual discipline? If this be the case, does the maturing Christian life involve a conscious and sometimes painful struggle between the old and new natures? Need the growing Christian be discouraged by the presence of residual sin in his heart and life?

Another important issue to be considered is whether sanctification can be brought to completion in this life. Can the child of God this side of eternity attain to the condition known as "entire sanctification," "Christian perfection," or "perfect love"? Were great saints of God in biblical times entirely free from the presence and the power of sin in their lives? Should the mature Christian expect to be delivered in the present life from all sinful thoughts, impulses, and even the consciousness of indwelling sin? Moreover, can we legitimately differentiate, as some allege, between the "carnal Christian," who fails to live a victorious life, and the "spiritual Christian," who through the Spirit's power experiences victory over sin and attains a state of spiritual rest?

Finally, what is the positive function of God's law in the growing life of the Christian? Did Christ terminate the OT law insofar as Christians are concerned? Or are the precepts of the law of unchanging validity and relevance for God's people today? How can growing Christians steer a responsible course between the extremes of legalism and antinomianism?

II. Historical Interpretations
of Sanctification

The means by which Christians attain spiritual maturity and progress toward the image of Jesus Christ has been widely interpreted by authorities within the church. Such proposals will significantly influence how the Christian life should be lived. In the following section we examine the principal interpretations of the doctrine of sanctification.

A. The Process of Personal Reformation
(Pelagians and Liberals)

Theological liberals posit a low view of sin and a high view of human nature and its accomplishments in the moral realm. The older liberal tradition held that the inexorable, upward ascent of the human spirit is hindered by the weight of man's animal nature. Contemporary liberal thought tends to identify the obstacles to personal fulfillment as unjust political, social, and economic structures. The liberal school of thought generally interprets sanctification as personal reformation and self-improvement facilitated by the ideals of Jesus. Accordingly, the traditional Protestant distinction between justification and sanctification weakens and ultimately vanishes altogether.

The British monk Pelagius (d. 419) denied the tenet of inherited sin and claimed that infants are born in the same moral condition as Adam prior to the Fall. Most people sin by imitating the negative example of Adam's disobedience. But since all people have the power of free will and self-determination, God expects them to use such to effect moral improvement. Jesus demonstrated how persons must overcome fleshly passions and negative habits and advance toward moral perfection. By drawing on their human powers and by following the precepts and example of Jesus, converts can fulfill God's moral requirements and live sinless lives (perfectionism). Pelagius denied that the convert requires a special, inner enablement from the Spirit to advance in holiness.

During the century following the Reformation, the rationalistic Socinians in Italy also denied original sin and upheld human freedom and ethical ability. Even when persons sin, they experience no diminution of moral power. Like Adam and Eve in the Garden, all persons are capable of obeying God's commands. Endowed with sufficient natural ability, sinners require only enlightenment in the form of additional knowledge to please God and advance in righteousness. Christ met this human need in his role as a human prophet revealing God's will. Christ incites persons to holiness by extending promises and threats and by serving as an example of obedience to God. Christians progress in holiness and receive justification as the outcome by obeying God's commandments and by imitating Christ. The leading Socinian doctrinal standard states the following: "What is the imitation of Christ? It is the composure of our life according to the rule of his life. Wherein doth it consist? In the exercise of those virtues which the Lord Jesus proposed to us in himself, as a living pattern."[2]

From the perspective of the social gospel, the American Baptist Walter Rauschenbusch (d. 1918) argued that sanctification is communal rather than individualistic, anthropocentric rather than theocentric, and the result of human striving rather than the inner working of God's Spirit. He understood sanctification to be the cultivation of the spiritual life of religious people through productive acts of charity and service in solidarity with others. Compared with the traditional 'mystical' or 'spiritual' approach, Rauschenbusch judged that "The way of holiness through human fellowship and service is slower and lowlier, but its results are more essentially Christian."[3] Rauschenbusch concluded that people attain moral perfection only in the life beyond the grave.

The American Ritschlian theologian W.A. Brown (d. 1943) viewed sanctification as the renewal of personality and the transformation of character through the experiences of filial trust and brotherly love as exemplified by Christ. Sanctification represents the exchange of self-gratification for the service of one's fellows, or the adoption of the outgoing life in lieu of the self-centered life. Since Brown, in concert with other liberals, viewed the future life as a direct continuation of present existence, he held that the gradual growth of all persons toward perfection (i.e., maturity and wholeness) will continue and be completed beyond the grave.[4]

B. The Sacramental Process of Making Righteous (Roman Catholics)

As seen in the previous chapter, Roman Catholicism classically interprets the increase of justification as sanctification.[5] Via the sacrament of baptism, God infuses into the soul justifying grace that remits original sin and imparts the habit of righteousness. This initial justification (or sanctification) then is augmented by the grace of Christ mediated through other sacraments (i.e., confirmation, Eucharist, penance, last anointing), love-inspired works, and the so-called surplus merits acquired by Mary and the saints. Since baptism remits all sin (leaving only concupiscence, which is not sin), the good works Christians perform are perfect. Hence Christians can perfectly fulfill the law and thereby earn or merit eternal life. Some faithful, however, are said to perform more good than the law requires. In the medieval era, for example, Rome distinguished between "precepts" (or "commandments") and "councils" (or "advices"). The former connote specific injunctions of the law that bind the conscience and issue in rewards or punishments. The latter signify virtues not specifically imposed by God that warrant excess merit. Specific counsels include poverty (Matt 19:21), celibacy (Matt 19:12), and monastic obedience (Luke 14:26). The alleged excess merit of persons in religious orders (i.e., priests, nuns, monks) who perform such counsels can be transferred to those who lack. Thus there arose a hierarchy of holiness and spirituality in the Catholic church—the clergy and the "religious" elevated to a higher plane than the laity.

If the process of transformation (making righteous) is not completed in this life, the faithful must endure the purifying sufferings of purgatory. Catholics find support for purgatory in the early Christian practice of prayers for the dead and in texts such as 2 Macc 12:46, Matt 5:26, 12:32, and 1 Cor 3:11-15. The duration of one's stay in purgatory depends upon the number and intensity of sins committed. Following the purifying work of purgation, sanctification (and justification) is said to be complete.

The sixth session of the Council of Trent (Jan. 13, 1547) treated sanctification under the heading of justification. The infusion of justifying grace remits sins and effects spiritual transformation. The baptized "through the observance of the commandments of God and of the Church, faith co-operating with good works, increase in that justice which they have received through the grace of Christ, and are still further justified."[6] Trent claimed that baptized persons progress in sanctification unto eternal life not by faith alone but also by good works and perseverance to the end. Thus, "the good works which he performs through the grace of God and the merits of Jesus Christ . . . doth merit increase of grace, eternal life, and the attainment of that eternal life."[7] For Trent, progress in sanctification (justification) requires complete fulfillment of the commandments. Catholics pray, "Give unto us, O Lord, increase of faith, hope, and charity."[8] Trent reaffirmed that Catholics not perfected in this life must endure the sufferings of purgatory. There they are assisted by "the sacrifices of masses, prayers, alms, and other works of piety . . . performed by the faithful for other faithful departed."[9]

The Dutch theologian F.G.L. Van Der Meer explained the sacramental functions of sanctification as follows. (1) Sanctification begins with *baptism*, which purifies original and actual sin and imparts new life. Baptized persons actually *are* holy. In the early church catechumens were clothed with white garments, signifying that they were perfectly sanctified. (2) *Confirmation*, which involves anointing with oil, connotes the gift of the Holy Spirit as the enabler for growth into spiritual maturity. (3) The *Eucharist*, or sacrament of the altar, is the rite of spiritual nourishment. The church claims that as Christians partake of Christ's body and blood in the Mass, they feed on Christ himself. Van Der Meer says of the Eucharist, "the state of grace is maintained by it, preserved from ruin, strengthened and augmented."[10] The preceding three sacraments (baptism, confirmation, and Eucharist) constitute an abiding gift known as the state of "sanctifying grace." In this state Christians cooperate with grace by observing God's commandments—which works convey actual merit. Thus, "The Church has declared emphatically that we can earn an increase of grace and glory."[11] Following Trent, Van Der Meer affirmed three things about the state of grace enjoyed by the baptized. (a) It is *unequal*. "Some are more intimately united with God than others, and grace is increased in some more abundantly than in others."[12] (b) It can be *forfeited*. Grace "can be lost, since divine life does not perish only through unbelief but through every mortal sin."[13] And (c) it is *insecure*. "No one knows for certain that he has received the grace of God [and] it is impossible to know whom God has chosen, except by means of a special revelation."[14]

(4) The sacrament of *penance*, or "second pardon," restores baptismal righteousness when forfeited by mortal sin. As fallen Christians repent, receive absolution, and perform works of satisfaction, the benefits of Christ's death are reapplied; the repentant experience anew the mystery of justification. Van Der Meer held that one Christian can do penance for another and that the treasury of merits accumulated by saints can be applied to those in want. (5) The *last anointing*, or extreme unction, is the sacrament that equips the *viator* for the final conflict with death itself. Van Der Meer upheld the common view that the souls of the righteous are purged of venial sins through the sufferings of purgatory. "The decisive element in these punishments is the temporary privation of the vision of God."[15] A soul's experience in purgatory may be ameliorated by the prayers, alms, and offerings of living believers.

C. Entire Sanctification Via a "Second Blessing" Experience (Wesleyans and the Holiness Tradition)

Wesleyans—together with the broader Holiness tradition embracing Free Methodists, Nazarenes, the Christian and Missionary Alliance, the Pilgrim Holiness Church, and the Salvation Army—opposed the Lutheran and Reformed conviction that holiness is imperfectly realized through lifelong process and struggle. Rather, sanctification begins at justification and the new birth ("initial sanctification"), but is perfected by an instantaneous, transforming work of the Holy Spirit called the "second work of grace" or the "second blessing." Holiness advocates claim that following the "second blessing" experience Christians enter the sphere of "entire sanctification," "Christian perfection," "perfect love," or "fullness of the blessing." The "second blessing" experience, which most modern Wesleyans equate with the baptism of the Holy Spirit, in this life removes inherited sin, eradicates the carnal nature, enables Christians to live without willful sin, and fills the heart with perfect love for God and man. A key text for many Holiness people is Rom 6:6 (AV): "Knowing this, that our old man is crucified with him, that the body of sin might be destroyed, that henceforth we should not serve sin." Holiness advocates argue that the Lutheran and Reformed position, which regards the presence of residual sin as a normal state of affairs, breeds moral laxity and antinomianism.

Wesleyan Methodism arose in reaction to sterile rationalism and deism within the eighteenth-century Church of England. John Wesley (d. 1791) was influenced by strands of Catholic mysticism that stressed themes of pure love and perfect conformity to Christ and by the older Arminianism. The doctrine of sanctification was the centerpiece of Wesley's theology. Appealing to Heb 12:14, Wesley held that entire sanctification is a prerequisite for final justification at the last judgment. Thus Christians should fervently seek moral perfection that God graciously gives by faith via an instantaneous crisis experience known as the "second work of grace" or "second blessing." Wesley posited two great moments in the Christian life: (1) *justification*, which includes forgiveness of sins, regeneration, and initial sanctification; and (2) *"entire sanctification,"* the "second work of grace," which Wesley also called "Christian perfection," "perfect love," or "full salvation." Wesley, who did not flaunt the term "sinless perfection," nevertheless wrote, "By perfection . . . I do not contend for the term *sinless*, though I do not object against it."[16] Wesley held that some believers are entirely sanctified shortly after conversion, others later in life, and still others at death when the soul leaves the body. Wesley explained that the crisis of entire sanctification, negatively, eliminates all sinful desires from the heart (e.g., pride, envy, jealousy, anger, lust), destroys inbred moral depravity, and delivers from outward transgressions of the law. Positively, entire sanctification effects complete purity of intentions, tempers, and actions, stimulates perfect love of God and neighbor, and restores the moral *imago* in the soul. Wesley boldly stated that "A Christian is so far perfect, as not to commit sin."[17] Again, "So long as he believes in God through Jesus Christ and loves Him and is pouring out his heart before Him, he cannot voluntarily transgress any command of God, either by speaking or acting what he knows God has forbidden."[18] Since governed by pure love, the wholly sanctified saint is freed from "pride, self-will, anger [and] unbelief."[19] The Christian whose heart has thus been spiritually circumcised is "so 'renewed in the image of our mind,' as to be 'perfect as our Father in heaven is perfect.'"[20] Wesley insisted that entire sanctification, or Christian perfection, is the goal and norm for every Spirit-born child of God.

Wesley elaborated that the perfection of the Christian believer is not the absolute perfection of God himself, but is a relative perfection consisting of freedom from willful transgression of a known divine law (which is the essence of sin).[21] Wesley's definition of sin allowed him to say that perfected Christians, while not voluntarily transgressing any known command of God, do remain subject to ignorance, mistakes, infirmities, temptations, and involuntary transgressions.[22] The wholly sanctified Christian thus is not faultless, but is sinless. Saints who have experienced entire sanctification "feel all faith and love; no pride, no self-will, or anger; and . . . have continual fellowship with God."[23]

Wesley held the seemingly contradictory statement that Christian perfection admits of degrees and is capable of increase or decrease. He believed that the typical Christian life follows the pattern of *process-crisis-process*; hence the suggestion of some that Wesley advocated a "perfecting perfection."[24] Following justification and the new birth, the Christian dies to self and grows in grace. Then the crisis of entire sanctification occurs, followed by continued growth in holiness.[25] The event of entire sanctification is not accompanied by tongues-speaking, for Wesley held that the "extraordinary gifts" of the Spirit (i.e., healings, prophesying, and tongues) died out by the time of Constantine. Said Wesley, "I utterly disclaim the 'extraordinary gifts of the Spirit' and all those other 'influences and operations of the Holy Ghost' than those that are common to all real Christians."[26]

Charles Finney (d. 1875) adopted the Wesleyan doctrine of entire sanctification. Finney argued that as the gratification of the lower nature (i.e., sin) involves an action of the will, so holiness resides in the right exercise of the will. "Entire sanctification"—otherwise known as "Christian perfection" and "entire consecration"—consists of the following four elements: (1) total, volitional consecration of the person to God; (2) uninterrupted communion with the Father; (3) unswerving love of God and neighbor; and (4) perfect and continued obedience to the requirements of God's law—adjusted, Finney argued, to human knowledge and ability. In essence, "Entire sanctification implies the complete annihilation of selfishness in all its forms."[27] Finney followed Wesley in claiming that believers achieve entire sanctification instantaneously by an act of faith. Because God calls Christians to complete and permanent sanctification, it must be attainable in this life by human powers assisted by grace.

Finney noted that entire sanctification was *promised* in the old dispensation (Jer 31:31-34; Ezek 36:25-27) and became a *possibility* in the new (2 Cor 7:1; 1 Thess 5:23-24; Jude 24). The apostle Paul, Finney continued, repeatedly acknowledged his own entire sanctification (Acts 24:16; 2 Cor 6:3-7; 1 Thess 2:10). In particular, Gal 2:20 "strongly implies that he [Paul] lived without sin and also that he regarded himself as dead to sin in the sense of being permanently sanctified."[28] Furthermore, Rom 7:14-25 describes pre-Christians who live in sin under the law, whereas Romans 8 depicts Christians in a state of entire sanctification through the Gospel. Finney wrote concerning Paul, "He nowhere confesses sin after he became an apostle."[29] With Wesley, Finney believed that continued growth in grace ought to follow upon the experience of entire sanctification.

J. Kenneth Grider follows Wesley by viewing salvation under the rubric of two instantaneous works of grace. "The first work of grace" at conversion consists of justification, regeneration, initial sanctification, reconciliation, and justification. The outcome of this first work is forgiveness of actual sins. "The second work of grace," which may occur anytime between conversion and death, effects the believer's entire sanctification. This second, crisis experience also bears the name "second blessing," "Christian perfection," "Christian holiness," "heart purity," or "perfect love." Scripture describes the latter, crisis experience in terms of Spirit-baptism (Acts 1:5-8; 2:2-4; 8:4-25; etc.), sealing (2 Cor 1:22; Eph 1:13; 4:30), and circumcision (Col 2:11). (As an aside, Wesley did not equate the crisis of entire sanctification with the Pentecostal experience recorded in the book of Acts.) According to Grider, entire sanctification radically cleanses Adamic sin, eradicates depravity, removes the inherited racial inclination to sinful deeds, inspires wholehearted love of God and neighbor, and empowers for service. Grider boldly states, "Entire sanctification is a sanctification, a cleansing that is entire. No carnality, or original sin, remains to deprave our faculties, to incline us to acts of sin."[30] As a result of this experience of "entire sanctification" the carnal mind is expelled.[31] The crisis of entire sanctification, however, does not preclude growth in grace and continued cleansing of the heart. Grider added that the first work of grace is necessary for salvation, whereas the second work is important but not strictly necessary. However, Christians who willfully refuse to follow God's leading toward entire sanctification will lose their justification (i.e., salvation).

D. Through Holy Spirit Baptism
(Pentecostals)

Pentecostalism divides into two main branches. The earlier, minority wing influenced by the Wesleyans is known as the Holiness Pentecostal movement. The later, majority wing includes the Assemblies of God, the Church of the Foursquare Gospel, and the Elim Pentecostal Church. In recent years a third movement known as neo-Pentecostalism has flourished in many mainline Protestant denominations and in the Roman Catholic church.

Holiness Pentecostals, represented by the Church of God (Cleveland, Tennessee), the Pentecostal Holiness Church, the Church of God in Christ, and the Pillar of Fire Church, trace their roots to the nineteenth-century Wesleyan-Holiness revival. They identify three instantaneous works of grace, as follows. (1) The *regenerating* work of grace includes justification and the new birth. Here God forgives sins and imputes to believers

Christ's righteousness. (2) A post-conversion, *sanctifying* work of grace eradicates the Adamic nature and completely purifies the Christian's heart and mind. Following Wesley, the believer's state following this second blessing is known as "entire sanctification," "Christian perfection," or "perfect love." This second work of grace renders believers purified vessels fit for the Spirit's filling. The Pentecostal Holiness Church affirms, "We believe that entire sanctification is an instantaneous, definite second work of grace, obtainable by faith on the part of the fully justified believer."[32] (3) The *empowering* work of grace represents the Pentecostal experience of baptism in the Spirit. Here the Holy Spirit takes full possession of perfected believers. Tongues-speaking represents the initial *sign* that this Spirit-baptism has occurred. The Church of God (Cleveland, Tennessee) sums up the sequence as follows: "we believe . . . in sanctification subsequent to the new birth . . . and in the baptism of the Holy Ghost subsequent to a clean heart."[33] The Holiness Pentecostals thus are a hybrid tradition, combining elements of Holiness and Pentecostal theology (see below).

Other Pentecostal groups arose independently of Wesleyanism. The Assemblies of God and related groups deny the experience of entire sanctification that destroys inbred sin. They hold to the following sequence of events. (1) *Positional sanctification.* At justification and the new birth God imputes righteousness to believers. Positionally, although not experientially, believers are sanctified through Christ's work on the cross. Every Christian believer thus is a saint. (2) *Baptism in the Holy Spirit.* Through this second work of grace Christians by faith are totally immersed in the Spirit (Mark 1:8; Acts 2:1-4; 8:15-17; 11:15-17). This crisis experience allows for subsequent fillings of the Spirit. Spirit-baptism does not completely purify, for the old nature and its passions remain in Christians. The principal function of Spirit-baptism is empowerment for witness; hence every believer should seek and expect this "second blessing" experience. The Assemblies of God declare that Spirit-baptism endows Christians with "an overflowing fullness of the Spirit, a deepened reverence for God, an intensified consecration to God and dedication to his work, and a more active love for Christ, for his Word, and for the lost."[34] Speaking in other tongues is the initial *sign* that a person has been baptized in the Spirit (Acts 2:4; 10:45-46; 19:6). Another sign or evidence of Spirit-baptism is the exercise of spiritual gifts (1 Cor 12:8-10, 28-30; Rom 12:6-8; Eph 4:11), all of which (including prophecy, healing, glossolalia, and interpretation of tongues) are applicable to the present age. Some have suggested that the majority stream of Pentecostalism places greater importance upon spiritual gifts (*charismata*) than on purity of heart (*sanctification*). In the words of one Pentecostal authority, "The baptism in the Holy Spirit . . . leads to a life of service marked by gifts of the Spirit that bring power and wisdom for the spread of the gospel and the growth of the church."[35]

(3) *Progressive sanctification.* This third stage involves the gradual process of making holiness a reality in daily life. Christians grow in holiness by identification with the crucified and risen Christ, by separation from the sinful world, and by consecration to God's service. Final perfection is not attainable in this life, since the old sin nature remains in believers. Horton sums up this view as follows: "The Scriptural pattern is first new life by the Spirit, then the empowering experience of the baptism in the Holy Spirit, then a life of spiritual growth that makes progress in both sanctification and service."[36] (4) *Entire sanctification.* Provided they do not fall away, Christians attain moral perfection in the glorified state by being fully conformed to the image of Christ. Entire sanctification awaits the final transformation at the resurrection.

Ernest S. Williams, an Assemblies of God theologian, posits a sanctification that is both *positional* and *progressive.* Of the former he writes, "Each believer in Christ is sanctified positionally when he accepts Christ."[37] Williams finds in Acts a definite crisis experience of Spirit-baptism subsequent to conversion that is normative for all believers. The principal evidences of immersion in the Spirit are endowment with power for witness, speaking in other tongues, and the exercise of spiritual gifts (including miracle-working, healing, prophecy, glossolalia, and interpretation of tongues). Glossolalia enhances private worship of God. "Those who have spoken in tongues in private worship can testify to the enriching, spiritual rest, and refreshing to the soul that results from such communion with God."[38] And when interpreted, tongues-speaking edifies the church in its corporate worship. Williams claims that progressive sanctification does not eradicate the old, Adamic nature in this life. Sanctification is a gradually unfolding reality that involves mortification of the deeds of the flesh and appropriation of Christ's grace, thereby producing the fruits of righteousness.

Neo-Pentecostalism represents the extension of the Pentecostal spirit in the mainline denominations. Championed by people like David du Plessis, John Sanford, Larry Christenson, Michael Harper, and J. Rodman Williams, neo-Pentecostalism holds that the Acts 2 Pentecost experience is breaking out in churches today. It identifies "baptism in the Spirit" as an experience distinct from and subsequent to conversion. "There are two distinct moments: conversion and baptism with the Spirit. They may be separated from each other by years, although both belong to the full life of the Christian."[39] The release or outpouring of the Spirit via this second blessing provides spiritual revitalization, empowerment for service, and renewal of the church. An important fruit of Spirit-baptism is the bestowal of the spiritual gifts, of which prophecy, healing, and glossolalia are the most important. The Roman Catholic renewal movement regards baptism in the Spirit as the conscious actualization of spiritual benefits received at water baptism. This event deepens a person's relationship with Christ and offers a new sense of the presence of the Spirit and his gifts. Many Catholic charismatics do not consider tongues as a necessary sign of the Spirit's baptism but as a "prayer gift" that enhances personal devotion to God.

E. Through a Decisive Act of Surrender to Christ (Keswick and Victorious Life Advocates)

Stimulated by Holiness teaching, the Keswick movement began meetings in England in 1875 as a "Convention for the Promotion of Practical Holiness." The North American counterpart of Keswick is the Victorious Life movement. The broad tradition features names such as W.E. Boardman, Robert Pearsall Smith, his wife Hannah Pearsall Smith, F.B. Meyer, Charles G. Trumbull, H.C.G. Moule, Andrew Murray, J. Robertson McQuilkin, and W. Graham Scroggie. Keswick teaching is similar to Holiness doctrine, although it rejects the tenet of "sinless perfection" or "perfect love." According to Keswick theology, sanctification occurs in three stages. (1) *Positional sanctification*, or accepting Christ as Savior, is gained through the experiences of forgiveness of sin, justification, and regeneration. (2) *Experiential sanctification*, commencing with a post-conversion, decisive surrender to Christ as Lord, effects victory over indwelling sin and the attainment of a higher level of Christian living. This second step, which produces a truly spiritual Christian, involves both an initial crisis and a subsequent process. And (3) *complete or final sanctification* occurs when the Christian is transformed into the likeness of Christ at the *Parousia*.

Fundamental to Keswick thought is the distinction made in the *Scofield Reference Bible* (1909/1917) and the *New Scofield Reference Bible* (1967) between two types of believers—namely, the "carnal (*sarkikos*) Christian" and the "spiritual (*pneumatikos*) Christian." The same distinction has been made by Campus Crusade for Christ in their representation of the "spiritual man" (the Christian in whose life Christ is enthroned) and the "carnal man" (the Christian in whose life Christ is not enthroned).[40] J. Robertson McQuilkin writes, "Scripture recognizes a basic difference among Christians. It distinguishes between carnal ('of the flesh') Christians, who behave like unconverted people, and spiritual Christians, whose life is dominated by the Spirit of God (1 Cor 3:1-3)."[41] The "carnal" or *average* Christian fails to abide in the Spirit's power and so lives a defeated life in the flesh. Some Keswick advocates depict the carnal believer as "only partially Christian."[42] The "spiritual" or *normal* Christian, however, lives a life of unbroken victory in the power of the Spirit. Keswick authorities aver that one becomes a "spiritual Christian" by a post-conversion, crisis experience of unconditional surrender or complete abandonment to Christ. The Christian receives the fullness of the Spirit not by protracted spiritual effort and struggle, but simply by a decision of the will to dethrone self and enthrone Christ—hence the slogan, "Let go and let God!" That is, God works sanctification in the believer to the extent that the latter ceases to strive and permits the Lord to do it all. The point is made that just as by a simple act of faith one was regenerated, so by a similar act of faith one is sanctified. "Faith throws the switch, releasing the current of divine power."[43]

As a result of this crisis experience, negatively, inbred sin is overwhelmed and rendered powerless by the greater power of the indwelling Spirit. Thus in relation to sin, Wesleyanism is "eradicationist," whereas Keswick theology could be called "counteractionist." Surrendered and Spirit-filled Christians are freed from the desire for sin, from the power of sin, and even from the consciousness of sin. Those who have experienced this second blessing enjoy complete victory over known sin and a life of spiritual rest on the highest plane. "Keswick does not teach the perfectibility of human beings prior to the eternal state, but it does teach the possibility of consistent success in resisting the temptation to violate deliberately the known will of God."[44] Or as Barabas expressed the Keswick view, "We believe the Word of God teaches that the *normal* Christian life is one of uniform sustained victory over known sin."[45] Since Keswick advocates define sin at the level of intentionality, when the struggle with conscious sin ceases, believers experience the victorious life. Keswick authorities add that growth in holiness normally follows this post-conversion, crisis experience. The act of total consecration represents "a decision which initiates . . . sanctification in real earnest."[46] According to many victorious life authorities, Rom 7:7-25 describes the frustration of "carnal Christians" who struggle to overcome sin by their own strength. Romans 8, in contrast, describes the victory experienced by "spiritual Christians" through the volitional act of total surrender to Christ.

Charles G. Trumbull (d. 1941), a British Victorious Life advocate, claimed that salvation is a twofold gift. Jesus offers to set us free from the *penalty* and also from the *power* of sin. Many people who find Jesus as their

Savior do not find him as their life and victory. This explains why so many born-again Christians fail miserably in their spiritual lives—why their fellowship with God fluctuates so and why they struggle with besetting sins. In a chapter entitled "Victory Without Trying," Trumbull argued that the secret to the victorious life is for the Christian to make an unconditioned and absolute surrender to God in faith. One must not strive for spiritual victory; rather one must simply "Let go, and let God!" "Any victory that you have to get by trying for it is counterfeit. If you have to work for your victory, it is not the real thing; it is not the thing that God offers you."[47]

Trumbull inveighed against the view that represents sanctification as a gradual process. He wrote, "A victory gained . . . by a gradual conquest over evil, getting one sin after another out of your life, is *counterfeit* victory. The Lord Jesus does not give us any such gradual victory over the sins of our life."[48] As a result of the decisive, post-conversion act of surrender, Christ now becomes the Christian's life and victory. It enables saved individuals to live habitually on a higher plane of close fellowship with God. And in this new life of victory "there need be no fighting against sin, but complete freedom from the power and even the desire of sin."[49]

F. An Objective, Accomplished Fact
(Neoorthodox)

In his *Church Dogmatics*, Barth (d. 1968) retreated from his earlier position that sanctification is identical to justification. Nevertheless, he did not view justification and sanctification as two successive steps in a supposed *ordo salutis*. For the Swiss theologian, the two doctrines are not temporally sequential; they represent two inseparable "moments" or "movements" in the *one* act of God's reconciliation in Jesus Christ. According to Barth, justification and sanctification are as inseparable as the two natures of Christ. "The *simul* of the one redemptive act of God in Jesus Christ cannot be split up into a temporal sequence, and in this way psychologized."[50] To eliminate all human merit and pride, Barth insisted that sanctification is God's doing and God's work: "His (i.e., God's) action is man's sanctification."[51]

Consistent with his rigorous Christocentrism, Barth related the sanctification of the Christian to Jesus Christ, who is both the holy God and the sanctified man. Christ needed to be sanctified because he entered the world with a sinful human nature. Christ's sanctification consisted in the fact that he committed no sinful act and that his humanity was raised by divine power to a new level of existence. Christians, Barth argued, are sanctified as they participate in the sanctification of the Son of Man (1

Cor 1:30). Christ was sanctified in a way that was authoritative for the whole world. "We are saints and sanctified because we are already sanctified, already saints, in this One. Already in Him we are summoned to this action."[52]

By virtue of the divine decision, Barth insisted that *objectively* all persons are reconciled to God, justified, and sanctified. The entire world in principle has died in Christ, renounced its sin, and turned to God, which is what sanctification means.[53] All persons are sanctified or converted through Christ's victory. "The sanctification of man . . . is actually accomplished in the one Jesus Christ in a way which is effective and authoritative for all, and therefore for each and every man, and not merely for the people of God, the saints."[54] Barth continued that *subjectively*, however, not all persons are properly sanctified, since only some of the elect have appropriated and confessed their sanctification. So he wrote, "The sanctification of man, his conversion to God, is, like his justification, a transformation, a new determination, which has taken place *de jure* for the world and therefore for all men. *De facto*, however, it is not known by all men, just as justification has not *de facto* been grasped and acknowledged and known and confessed by all men, but only by those who are awakened to faith."[55]

What, in Barth's view, is the practical difference between the two classes of sanctified Christians? Those who subjectively acknowledge justification and sanctification are sinners who have been disturbed out of their spiritual slumber by the Spirit's power.[56] Those who are sanctified objectively but not subjectively remain undisturbed in their sleep. The latter are reconciled and sanctified, but they live unaware of this great fact. On the individual level, disturbed sinners enter a new form of existence as *faithful* covenant partners of God. While muting the quest for perfection in holiness, Barth insisted that awakened sinners should live a life of love, good works, cross-bearing, and praise to God. On the corporate level, the church is the provisional, *de facto* representation of the *de jure* sanctification of all humanity in Jesus Christ. The church's task is to serve as "the revelation of the sanctification of all humanity and human life as it has already taken place *de jure* in Jesus Christ."[57]

Reinhold Niebuhr (d. 1971), a leader in the American school of dialectical theology, emphasized with Barth the objective dimension of sanctification. At the individual level, Niebuhr claimed that sin is overcome and persons are sanctified in principle rather than in fact. Like Barth, Niebuhr minimized the goal of moral perfection, emphasizing rather Christians' existential predicament in their lifelong conflict with sin. Justified believers, Niebuhr averred, struggle to the grave with the contradictions of freedom and finitude, of being justified *de jure* but not *de facto*, of being holy but full of sin. Such is the paradoxical relation between justification and sanctification. Claims of personal sanctity, in any case, would breed spiritual pride and arrogance. "The conquest of sin in the heart of man and the merciful power of God over the sin . . . is never entirely overcome in any human heart."[58] For Niebuhr, forgiveness of sin does not effect internal or ontic change in the life of the professing Christian. The goal of the Christian conflict is the rule of *agape* in human relationships, which (given the Christian's existential predicament) Niebuhr called an "impossible possibility." *Agape* (although never perfectly attainable in this life) manifests itself in deeds of forgiveness, reconciliation, and justice individually, but more importantly in the social sphere.

G. Solidarity with the Poor and Oppressed (Liberation Theologians)

Consistent with their definition of theology as praxis, liberation theologians typically interpret sanctification as love-generated transformation wrought by action on behalf of the marginalized and oppressed. The tradition adopts as a presupposition the conviction that "Action imbued with correct understanding transforms reality."[59] Thus those who engage the poor in history engage Christ, and those who love the poor love Christ (Matt 25:35-45). The liberator who freely gives his or her life for the other experiences the fulness of God's life. In other words, liberative action on behalf of the poor and oppressed is said to be transforming and sanctifying. Theologians in the tradition argue that a person cannot be mature and compassionate oneself when half the human race remains dehumanized and oppressed. They claim that as Christians engage in the struggle for justice, a transformation of self-consciousness occurs that traditional theology calls sanctification.

In this spirit the Argentinian Bonino claims that sanctification occurs as we become active partners in the cause of the disenfranchised. "Our sanctification must not be measured by some idealistically conceived norm of perfection or by some equally unreal purity of motivation, but by the concrete demand of the present kairos. There is an action, a project, an achievement that is required of us now; there is an action that embodies the service of love today; . . . It is *perfection*—the mature, ripe form of obedience."[60] Christians are radically *transformed* and *humanized* as they struggle against injustice wherever it occurs and as they forge a better future for the oppressed. Liberationists claim that human deeds of love on behalf of the powerless possess redeeming and sanctifying virtue. The

Peruvian theologian Gustavo Gutiérrez explains this concept in terms of "the sacrament of our neighbor." By going outside of one's self in love for the neighbor, the disciple draws closer to God, grows in wholeness, and so is morally and spiritually transformed. "The encounter with Christ in the poor man constitutes an authentic spiritual experience. It is a living in the Spirit, the bond of love between Father and Son, God and man, man and man. Christians . . . find the love of Christ in their encounter with the poor and in solidarity with them."[61] Freedom and wholeness, in other words, develop through openness to God and others and through concrete action on behalf of the downtrodden and oppressed.

The black theologian James Cone likewise envisages sanctification as resulting from identification and involvement with the poor in the concrete tasks of social justice. Wrote he, "Sanctification in black religion cannot be correctly understood apart from black people's struggle for historical liberation. Liberation is not simply a consequence of the experience of sanctification—sanctification *is* liberation—that is, to be politically engaged in the historical struggle for freedom." Cone added, "When sanctification is defined in that manner, it is possible to connect it with socialism and Marxism—the reconstruction of society on the basis of freedom and justice for all."[62]

H. The Gradual Process of Becoming Holy (Reformed Evangelicals)

The broad, Reformational tradition posits a clear distinction between justification and sanctification while affirming that they are inextricably related. As for differences, (1) justification is the legal declaration of right standing before God (imputed righteousness), whereas sanctification is the Spirit's work of making believers holy (imparted righteousness). (2) Justification is an instantaneous event, whereas sanctification is a lifelong process. And (3) justification allows for no degrees, whereas sanctification admits of degrees. In terms of their inner unity, justification issues in sanctification, thereby eliminating the error of cheap grace. And sanctification is grounded in justification, thereby avoiding the heresy of works-righteousness.

Reformed authorities insist that sanctification is not man's autonomous work; rather, it is a divine-human operation initiated and continued by God the Holy Spirit (Phil 2:12-13; Heb 13:20-21) and appropriated by faith (Acts 26:18; 1 John 5:4). At every moment of the pilgrim life, God enables believers to renounce sin and Satan and respond to the Spirit's promptings toward Christlikeness. Moreover, there is but one Spirit-baptism, but there are many Spirit fillings. The divine work of Spirit-baptism occurs simultaneously with the believer's regeneration and union with Christ, not later. Filling with the Spirit occurs continuously as believers yield to God's will moment by moment. Christians are positionally holy by virtue of being in Christ (1 Cor 1:2; 6:11; Heb 10:10), although experientially they remain tainted with sin. Advocates of this view are not embarrassed to state that Christians are forgiven sinners.

The Reformed tradition generally identifies two natures in the believer. The old nature ("the flesh") represents the believer's capacity to serve self, sin, and Satan; the new nature ("the spirit") signifies the capacity to serve others, righteousness, and God. Given these two opposing inclinations, Christians advance in Christlikeness by *effort* (1 Cor 9:24; 1 Tim 4:10; Heb 12:1), *struggle* (Rom 7:15-23; Gal 5:17), *warfare* (Eph 6:10-18; 1 Tim 6:12), *suffering* (Rom 5:3; Heb 10:32-34), and *divine chastening* (Ps 119:71; Heb 12:5-11). Via Holy Spirit sanctification, believers are freed from the power and dominion of sin, although not from the presence thereof. By daily yielding to God's will in faith, Christians cooperate with the Spirit's initiative to mortify sinful impulses and deeds and to bring forth holy dispositions and good works. Thus sanctification "is nothing less than the progressive uprooting of sin within him by the conquering energy of the Spirit of God."[63] Motivated by love rather than fear, believers honor God by keeping the moral provisions of the law as expressions of God's character and will. Christians may attain to a relative perfection in this life (Phil 3:15), but not to absolute perfection (Phil 3:12). "Entire sanctification" will be realized in the life-to-come, when the saints behold Christ (1 John 3:2-3) and exchange mortality for immortality (1 Cor 15:45; Phil 3:21).

Augustine (d. 430) maintained that sovereign grace instantaneously transforms human hearts (regeneration) and then progressively conforms believers to the image of Christ (sanctification). Sanctification involves both God's provision and the Christian's participation. God initiates sanctification as grace breaks the dominion of sin and heals the will so that it may freely love the Lord and neighbor and fulfill the law. Although the initiative in sanctification is with God, necessary also are the believer's willing and working. "It is he who makes us will what is good; . . . it is he who makes us act by supplying efficacious power to our will."[64] Augustine believed that the regenerate Christian possesses two natures. The old nature or "flesh" (not eradicated by the new birth) represents the will or inclination to sin, whereas the new nature or "spirit" constitutes the inclination to glorify God. The two natures contend with each other throughout the Christian's earthly life. Although the Spirit urges the believer toward spiritual perfection, indwelling sin ensures that no one actually attains the goal this side of heaven. Wrote Augustine, "There is not a man living in the present life who is absolutely free from sin."[65] Yet as believers, cooperating with grace, resist temptations and cultivate the fruits of the Spirit, they progressively become like Christ. The Christian, then, advances in sanctification "insofar as he does not yield to evil concupiscence," but overcomes it by his "desire to live according to the Law."[66]

John Calvin (d. 1564), appropriately designated "the theologian of sanctification,"[67] held justification and sanctification in close relation, analogous to the light and the heat of the sun. "Christ justified no one whom he does not at the same time sanctify."[68] Calvin stressed the importance of personal sanctification by insisting that "No one can be an heir of heaven who has not first been conformed to the only begotten Son of God."[69] Sanctification consists of mortification of the old nature and vivification of the new nature. Via mortification God breaks the dominion of sin, subdues the flesh, and weakens carnal desires. Through vivification the Spirit enables Christians to put on the "new man," to be renewed in the image of Christ, and to perform works pleasing to God. Calvin insisted that sanctification is gradual and progressive. "This restoration does not take place in one moment or one day or one year; but through continual and sometimes even slow advances God wipes out in his elect the corruptions of the flesh, cleanses them of guilt, consecrates them to himself as temples renewing all their minds to true purity that they may practice repentance throughout their lives and know that this warfare will end only at death."[70] The goal of sanctification, toward which all Christians must strive, is perfect conformity to God's will in thought and deed. Saints perfectly attain this goal, however, only on the other side of the grave.

Concerning the relevance of the law, Calvin favored the continuity view between the OT law and NT believers. He wrote, "I understand by the word 'law' not only the Ten Commandments, which set forth a godly and righteous rule of living, but the form of religion handed down by God through Moses."[71] As part of the covenant of grace, the law performs three main functions. (1) It upholds divine righteousness and discloses human sinfulness for what it is (Rom 3:20; 5:20a). (2) The law restrains malefactors' evil deeds (1 Tim 1:9-10). "By the dread of divine vengeance they are restrained at least from outward wantonness."[72] And (3) it instructs believers and encourages them in well-doing (Ps 19:7-8; 119:105). This third and principal function of the law has two parts. First, through the law the saints "learn more thoroughly each day the nature of the Lord's will to which they aspire;"[73] second, "by frequent meditation upon it [they are] aroused to obedience, strengthened in it, and drawn back from the slippery path of transgression."[74] In sum, the law serves the positive purpose of directing believers to live righteous lives.

In what sense has the law been abrogated for Christians? By virtue of Christ's death, believers are free from the curse of the law (Rom 7:6; 10:4). The law "may no longer condemn and destroy their consciences by frightening and confounding them."[75] Moreover, Christians are not required to observe the OT ceremonies and sacrifices, which served as types and shadows of the Christ to come. Nor are they constrained to keep the many judicial laws that regulated Israel's civil life. Although under the new covenant the ceremonial and judicial law have been superseded, the moral law remains in force, since "it is the true and eternal rule of righteousness, prescribed for men of all nations and times, who wish to conform their lives to God's will."[76] Christians do not perform in order to be accepted; rather, freely accepted in Christ, they delight to honor the spirit of the law, which is the rule of love (Deut 6:5; Mark 12:30-31). Christ walked in the way of the law, and Christians must follow in his steps.

Others, holding to Reformed views on soteriology, posit greater discontinuity between the OT law and NT believers. Moo, for example, observes that "Christ is the end [*telos*] of the law" (Rom 10:4), since in his life and teachings he fulfilled the law of Moses (Matt 5:17). Consequently, NT believers are not obliged to keep its ordinances as a code of conduct. The new rule applicable to Christians is "the law of Christ" (Gal 6:2). In love and by the power of the Spirit, NT believers fulfill "Christ's law" (1 Cor 9:21). "While the Mosaic Law does not stand as an undifferentiated authority for the Christian, some of its individual commandments remain authoritative as integrated into the law of Christ."[77]

Calvin concluded that through the process of sanctification, Christ is the believer's example of holiness. The Reformer emphasized that however earnestly Christians strive for moral perfection, they never attain the ideal of perfect conformity to God's moral law. "We accordingly teach that in the saints, until they are divested of mortal bodies, there is always sin; for in their flesh there resides that depravity of inordinate desiring which contends against righteousness."[78] The lofty ideal of sinless perfection is not achievable this side of glory. Thus Calvin wrote, "I do not so strictly demand evangelical perfection that I would not acknowledge as a Christian one who has not yet attained it. For thus all would be excluded from the church, since no one is found who is not far removed from it."[79]

Leading Protestant confessional statements reiterate this view. The Heidelberg Catechism (1563) states, "To be washed with Christ's Spirit means . . . that more and more I become dead to sin and increasingly live a holy and blameless life" (Lord's Day 26, Q. 70). The Christian life involves a struggle with the "sinful nature" (Lord's Day 21, Q. 56); hence perfection is not possible in this life. The Catechism refers to "the sins we do" and "the evil that constantly clings to us" (Lord's Day 51, Q. 126). Indeed, "the longer we live the more . . . we come to know our sinfulness and the more eagerly look to Christ for forgiveness of sins and righteousness" (Lord's Day 44, Q. 115). The Westminster Shorter Catechism (1647) offers the following answer to Q. 35, "What is Sanctification?": "Sanctification is the work of God's free grace, whereby we are renewed in the whole man after the image of God, and are enabled more and more to die unto sin, and live unto righteousness" (cf. The Westminster Confession of Faith, ch. 13.1-3). The answer to Q. 36, concerning the benefits that flow from justification, adoption, and sanctification, reads, "assurance of God's love, peace of conscience, joy in the Holy Ghost, increase of grace, and perseverance therein to the end."

Louis Berkhof (d. 1957) defined sanctification as "the gracious and continuous operation of the Holy Spirit, by which He delivers the justified sinner from the pollution of sin, renews his whole nature in the image of God, and enables him to perform good works."[80] The two parts of sanctification are mortification of the "old man" (human nature controlled by sin) and quickening of the "new man" (human nature renewed by the Spirit). Although the strengthening of holy dispositions is a divine work, believers must cooperate with grace by the proper use of spiritual means. Facilitators of grace include the Word of God, the sacraments, prayer, the constant exercise of faith, confession of sins, and providential discipline. Berkhof insisted that in Christians the flesh and the Spirit struggle against one another and that the process of sanctification never reaches perfection in this life. "Believers must contend with sin as long as they live."[81] Concerning the Mosaic law, Berkhof wrote: "the law as the system of penalty and as a method of salvation . . . is abolished in the death of Christ. The law as the standard of our moral life is a transcript of the holiness of God and is therefore of permanent validity also for the believer."[82]

Sanctification as a work of God's Spirit progressively realized in believers best accords with the biblical data, as the exposition that follows will make clear.

II. EXPOSITION OF
THE DOCTRINE OF SANCTIFICATION

A. *The Language of Sanctification*

The concept of holiness lies at the heart of the biblical doctrine of sanctification. In the OT the verb *qādaš* ("be consecrated," "be holy"), the noun *qōdeš* ("apartness," "holiness"), and the adjective *qādôš* ("holy," "pure") derive from the Hebrew root *qad* meaning to "cut" or "separate." The principal OT idea of holiness, then, is cultic and ceremonial. Persons, places, or objects are holy because separated from what is profane and set apart and devoted to God. In this sense *persons* are declared holy, such as angels (Deut 33:2; Ps 89:7), the Jewish priests (Lev 21:7-8), prophets (2 Kgs 4:9; Jer 1:5), and collectively the people of Israel (Exod 19:6; Deut 7:6; Isa 62:12). Moreover, *places* are designated holy, such as Mt. Sinai (Exod 3:5), Mt. Zion (Ps 15:1; Zeph 3:11), and Israel's territory (Ps 78:54; Zech 2:12). Furthermore, *objects* are holy, including the tabernacle (Exod 40:9), the altar (Exod 29:37; 40:10), the sacrifices (Lev 27:9; Num 18:17; Ezek 44:13), the temple (Ps 11:4; 138:2; Isa 64:11), a field (Lev 27:21), and the produce thereof (Lev 19:24). Finally, *institutions* are holy, such as the covenant (Dan 11:28, 30) and the sabbath day (Gen 2:3; Exod 20:11; Deut 5:12). In support of the judgment that the root meaning of holiness is devotedness is the fact that the Hebrew word for a prostitute (*qādēš/qᵉdēšāh*) derives from the same *qad* root—a prostitute being one who is dedicated to that particular activity (Gen 38:21-22; Deut 23:18; 2 Kgs 23:7).

The OT reflects as a minor theme the moral aspect of holiness—namely, the condition of persons who are inwardly separated from evil and who conduct themselves uprightly. In this sense God himself is said to be holy (Lev 20:26; Ps 99:5; Isa 5:16), as are his people. Thus the Lord said to Israel through Moses, "Be holy, because I, the Lord your God, am holy" (Lev 19:2; cf. 11:44-45). Holiness of life is urged in Ps 24:3-4: "Who may ascend the hill of the Lord? Who may stand in his holy place? He who has clean hands and a pure heart, who does not lift up his soul to an idol or swear by what is false." This ethical sense is also present in 2 Sam 22:21, Ps 51:10, 73:1, and Ezek 18:15-17.

The NT language for holiness is more diverse. The noun *hosiotēs* ("holiness") and the adjectives *hieros* ("sacred," "holy," "pertaining to the temple") and *hosios* ("piety," "devoutness") occur two, two, and eight times respectively. The nouns *hagiasmos* ("consecration," "sanctification," "holiness") and *hagiosynē* ("consecration," "holiness") occur ten and three times respectively. The related verb *hagiazō* ("consecrate," "purify," "make holy") occurs twenty-eight times and the adjective *hagios* ("consecrated," "holy," "upright") some 225 times.

In the NT the ceremonial aspect of holiness greatly diminishes. Nevertheless, the covenant (Luke 1:72), the law (Rom 7:12), the prophets (Luke 1:70), the temple (Matt 24:15; Acts 6:13), Jerusalem (Matt 4:5), the Scriptures (Rom 1:2; 2 Tim 3:15), and angels (Mark 8:38; Acts 10:22; Rev 14:10) are stated to be holy, in the OT sense of being devoted to God and his service. The predominant force of the holiness language in the NT, however, is moral and ethical. In everyday living, holiness involves inner freedom from evil thoughts and attitudes (Eph 5:27; Heb 3:1), abstinence from immoral acts (1 Thess 4:3-4; 1 Pet 1:15), and a positive commitment to good and the neighbor (Col 3:12-14; Tit 1:8). Following Pentecost, holiness manifests itself as the fruit of the Spirit in redeemed lives. Holiness, in a word, is Christlikeness daily manifested in the midst of a godless world.

B. *Positional Sanctification*

By positional or objective sanctification—which we may call the indicative of sanctification—we mean the believer's being set aside for God's possession and declared holy by faith in Christ's justifying work. A common designation of Christians in Paul and the book of Revelation is "saints" (literally, "holy ones," *hagioi*: e.g., Rom 8:27; 1 Cor 6:2; Eph 1:18; Rev 11:18; 16:6). In his salutation to local churches, Paul commonly designated his readers as "saints in Christ Jesus" (*hagioi*, Eph 1:1; Phil 1:1; Col 1:2), thus emphasizing that their holy status is rooted squarely in the Savior's work. Believers in Christ are "saints" since they are inwardly separated from sin and set apart for the worship and service of God. Paul applied the designation "saints" even to erring believers at Corinth who were empirically quite sinful. He addressed the wayward Corinthian believers as "those sanctified [*hēgiasmenois*] in Christ Jesus and called to be holy" (*hagiois*, 1 Cor 1:2). Paul spoke approvingly to the Christians at Corinth not because of their deepening spirituality (progressive sanctification), but because of their justified standing in Christ (positional sanctification). This view of positional sanctification in no way denies that the calling to practical holiness is an inherent element in the title "saints."

Formerly the Corinthians lived according to the ethos of the sinful world—their lives characterized by idolatry, adultery, prostitution, homosexuality, thievery, drunkenness, and slander (1 Cor 6:9-10). Notwithstanding their immoral lives, Paul, led of the Spirit, wrote, "And that is what some of you were. But you were washed, you were sanctified, you were justified in the name of the Lord Jesus Christ and by the Spirit of our God" (v. 11). The aorist passive of *hagiazō* denotes not the process of moral and spiritual growth, but the fact that God claimed the erring believers as his justified people. The apostle likewise stated that he ministered the Gospel beyond Judaism "so that the Gentiles might become an offering acceptable to God, sanctified [*hēgiasmenē*] by the Spirit" (Rom 15:16). Regarded by Jews as unclean, believing Gentiles were graciously accepted by God and declared to be positionally holy. The writer to the Hebrews also acknowledged positional sanctification. Referring to Christ's determination to do the Father's will, he wrote, "by that will we have been made holy [*hēgiasmenoi*] through the sacrifice of the body of Jesus Christ once for all" (Heb 10:10; cf. v. 29). Similarly, "Jesus also suffered outside the city gate to make the people holy [*hagiasē*] through his own blood" (Heb 13:12).

C. Progressive Sanctification

The God who declares believers righteous demands that they make strides in practical holiness of life. As Thomas Watson stated, "It is absurd to imagine that God should justify a people and not sanctify them, that He should justify a people whom He could not glorify."[83] Progressive or subjective sanctification—which we call the imperative of sanctification—denotes the justified believer's advance toward spiritual maturity (Heb 6:1; Jas 1:4). In the OT God announced that Israel must mirror his holy character: "I am the Lord your God; consecrate yourselves and be holy, because I am holy" (Lev 11:44; cf. 19:2; 20:7-8, 26). Although formally holy because set apart to be God's peculiar people, Israel must become morally and spiritually holy. They were to do this, negatively, by avoiding the sinful practices of their pagan neighbors (Deut 18:9-14) and, positively, by wholly obeying God's commands (Deut 28:9, 14). In their quest for uprightness of life, Israel must know that the Lord is the sanctifier who makes his people holy (Exod 31:13; Lev 21:8, 15; 22:32).

Turning to the NT, an important outcome of God's call is that by the pursuit of holiness believers should elevate their moral condition to the level of their legal status conferred by justification. As Paul wrote to persecuted Thessalonian believers, "It is God's will that you should be sanctified: that you should avoid sexual immorality; that each of you should learn to control his own body in a way that is holy and honorable. . . . For God did not call us to be impure, but to live a holy life" (1 Thess 4:3, 4, 7). Scripture indicates that the Spirit's work of producing Christlikeness in believers is gradual and progressive rather than sudden or instantaneous. Peter commanded the dispersed Christians to "grow [*auxanete*, present, active imperative] in the grace and knowledge of our Lord and Savior Jesus Christ" (2 Pet 3:18; cf. 1 Pet 2:2). And Paul wrote, "Inwardly we are being renewed [present passive of *anakainoō*] day by day" (2 Cor 4:16). Again, "let us purify ourselves from everything that contaminates body and spirit, perfecting holiness out of reverence for God" (2 Cor 7:1). The present tense of the verb *epiteleō*, to "complete" or "finish," stresses the Christian's gradual advance in holiness. Paul also taught the reality of progressive sanctification in Phil 3:13b-14 and 2 Thess 1:3. Heb 10:14 beautifully juxtaposes positional sanctification with progressive sanctification: "by one sacrifice [Christ] has made perfect [*teteleiōken*] forever those who are being made holy" (*hagiazomenous*).

The apostle Paul made the connection between progressive sanctification and Christlikeness in several places. He wrote that "those God foreknew he also predestined to be conformed to the likeness of his Son" (Rom 8:29). In addition, "we, who with unveiled faces all reflect the Lord's glory, are being transformed [present passive of *metamorpheō*] into his likeness with ever-increasing glory" (2 Cor 3:18). Moreover, "speaking the truth in love, we will in all things grow up into him who is the Head, that is, Christ" (Eph 4:15). Paul shared his spiritual aspiration for the Galatians with the words, "I am again in the pains of childbirth until Christ is formed in you" (Gal 4:19). See Eph 4:13 for the same linkage.

Whereas in Romans 5 Paul discussed believers' justification, in Romans 6 he expounded the nature of their sanctification. Antinomians in Paul's day argued that since Christians have been made right with God, why not sin boldly that grace may abound (Rom 6:1)? Paul opposed this line of reasoning with a firm, "By no means!" (v. 2) and argued his case using the symbol of water baptism. Sanctification *negatively* signifies the mortification of the old nature. At conversion believers were united with Christ in his death and burial (vv. 4a, 5a). This means that Christians died to the old life of sin (vv. 6-8a; cf. Gal 5:24) and so experientially must allow sin no place in their lives (vv. 12-14). *Positively* sanctification implies the vivification of the new nature. At conversion believers were united with Christ in his resurrection (vv. 4b-5) and thus have come alive in Christ (v. 8b). Hence experientially they must reckon themselves alive to God (v. 11b) and become servants of God and righteousness, which leads to holiness (vv. 13b, 18b, 19b, 22).

Eph 4:22-24 makes the same point employing the concept of the two selves. Sanctification *negatively* involves the decision to put off the "old self" (*palaios anthrōpos*) and *positively*, through the continual process of the mind's renewal, to put on the "new self" (*kainos anthrōpos*). The verb in v. 23 specifying renewal (*ananeousthai*, "be made new") is a present tense, denoting the continual process of making new. In Col 3:5-10 Paul described sanctification as the progressive discarding of the "earthly nature" or "old self" and the putting on of "the new self, which is being renewed [*anakainoumenon*] in knowledge in the image of its Creator" (v. 10). The old nature is the capacity to serve Satan, sin, and self acquired through Adam, whereas the new nature is the capacity to serve God and righteousness acquired through the new birth.

Against most "victorious life" emphases, Paul affirmed that Christian growth involves struggle—sometimes intense—against the remnants of indwelling sin. Thus within true believers the "sinful nature" (*sarx*) and the "Spirit" (*pneuma*) do battle, hindering the other's operations. Paul wrote, "For the sinful nature desires what is contrary to the Spirit, and the Spirit what is contrary to the sinful nature. They are in conflict with each other, so that you do not do what you want" (Gal 5:17). Peter likewise attested that by virtue of fleshly lusts that war against the soul (1 Pet 2:11) the Christian life requires godly effort (2 Pet 1:5-7) and struggle (Heb 12:14a). J.C. Ryle faithfully observed that "A true Christian is one who has not only peace of conscience, but war within. He may be known by his warfare as well as his peace."[84] Believers who struggle against sin should not feel that their lives are a failure and displeasing to God.

The nature of this struggle is spelled out in Romans 7. Paul stated in vv. 1-6 that Christians are free from the law in the sense of its power to condemn. Does this mean, then, that the law is sin? Not at all, Paul responded, for the problem rests not with the law but with the human propensity to sin. The apostle elaborated in vv. 7-25. It is probable that vv. 7-13 describe Paul's pre-conversion experience and vv. 14-25 his post-conversion experience, for the following reasons. (1) The first section employs past tenses, whereas the second uses the present tense throughout. (2) The first section shows absence of inner tension—the subject being at ease with sin. The second section reflects a powerful inner tension between good and evil (vv. 15, 18b, 20a). And (3) in the second section the subject wills the good (vv. 15a, 18b, 19a, 21a), delights in the law of God (vv. 22, 25b), and hates evil (vv. 15b, 16a)—all of which are responses of a regenerate person. Thus the mature apostle boldly confessed, "I am unspiritual [*sarkinos*], sold as a slave to sin" (v. 14; cf. v. 18a). The presence of residual, sinful impulses means that "There is something in man— even regenerate man—which objects to God and seeks to be independent of him."[85] Indwelling sin (v. 20b) hindered Paul from fulfilling the law and, indeed, urged him to do what the law forbids. This tension between the law of the mind and the law of sin (v. 23) lingers with growing Christians as long as they live. Bloesch notes that because the Christian is both justified and a sinner, "The victorious life is a striving towards victory rather than a matured possession of victory. The life of faith is a life of conflict and struggle."[86] Horne similarly observed, "Sanctification does not mean the abolition of sin in regenerate and sanctified persons. Though the saints do not live in sin, it still lives in them, and sometimes it becomes very active and powerful."[87] The point is that on the journey toward Christian maturity, faithful saints will taste and feel the spiritual struggle in their lives.

Since sanctification is a process not completed in this life, the goal of perfect likeness to Christ will be achieved only at the *Parousia* and resurrection. As Paul wrote, "May the Lord . . . strengthen your hearts so that you will be blameless and holy in the presence of our God and Father when our Lord Jesus comes with all his holy ones" (1 Thess 3:12-13; cf. 5:23). Similarly, John wrote, "we know that when he appears, we shall be like him, for we shall see him as he is" (1 John 3:2). Only at the sight of Christ will believers achieve perfect moral purity (v. 3), absence of sins (v. 5), and actual righteousness (v. 7). Meanwhile, Christians advance in sanctification by abiding in Christ (John 15:4, 7), walking in the light of God's presence (1 John 1:7), holding fast to their Christian profession (Rev 2:25; 3:11), purifying themselves from sin (1 John 3:3), continuing in Christ's teaching (John 14:23; 15:7), and submitting to providential discipline (John 15:2).

D. Sanctification Via a "Second Blessing" Experience?

As indicated in the summary of views section, some Christian life writers claim that believers advance to a higher spiritual plane by a sudden, post-conversion experience known as the "second blessing." Do the Scriptures actually support such an experience for which Christians must travail? Concerning Jesus' coming ministry, John the Baptist predicted that "He will baptize you with the Holy Spirit and with fire" (Matt 3:11; cf. Mark 1:8; Luke 3:16; John 1:33). The resurrected Christ gave the following promise to the eleven disciples, "John baptized with water, but in a few days you will be baptized with the Holy Spirit" (Acts 1:5). The baptism of which John and Jesus spoke is a metaphor that describes the outpouring of the Spirit upon believers at Pentecost. The fact that the eleven disciples trusted Jesus for some time before being baptized or indwelt by the Spirit must be attributed to the unique, pre-Pentecost situation. The Spirit promised in OT prophecy (Ezek 36:27; 39:29; Joel 2:28) would be poured out only after Jesus had risen from the dead and ascended to heaven (Acts 1:2; John 7:39).

Holiness and Pentecostal claims that Jesus' act of breathing into his disciples the Spirit (John 20:22) constitutes the "second blessing" experience of "entire sanctification" and/or empowerment is exegetically and theologically weak. What occurred in the Upper Room was a unique and non-repeatable event. John noted that "the Spirit had not been given, since Jesus had not yet been glorified" (John 7:39b). But after his death and resurrection and before returning to the Father, Christ dispatched his disciples into the world as his representatives (John 20:21) and equipped them with the Spirit's power for ministry (v. 22). Jesus' breathing was a symbolic act denoting the impartation of the Spirit's power in the new age on the basis of Christ's exaltation. This act was not a prefiguration of Pentecost. As Bruce commented, "What John records is no mere anticipation of Pentecost but a real impartation of the Spirit for the purpose specified. The Pentecostal outpouring of the Spirit was more public, and involved the birth of the Spirit-indwelt community, the church of the new age."[88] Neither was Jesus' act of breathing on his disciples a paradigm of an alleged post-conversion "second blessing" experience all believers must experience.

Holiness advocates and Pentecostals claim that Jesus' promise of a post-conversion Spirit-baptism came to pass in Acts 2, 8, 10, and 19, which validate a "second blessing" experience of sanctification and empowerment normative for believers today. Let us examine these four accounts of the Spirit's outpouring to determine what they teach. (1) On the day of Pentecost (Acts 2:1-13) the disciples witnessed extraordinary manifestations of wind and fire, symbols of the Spirit's purifying and judging ministry. We read that suddenly "all of them were filled with the Holy Spirit and began to speak in other tongues as the Spirit enabled them" (v. 4). The Spirit's activity is variously described as a baptism (Acts 1:5; 11:16), a filling (Acts 2:4), and a pouring out (Acts 2:17). The "other tongues" (*glōssa* meaning "tongue," "language," "utterance") that the disciples spontaneously spoke represent xenolalia, or foreign languages not previously learned (vv. 6, 8, 11). In v. 11 Luke used the word *glōssa*; but in vv. 6 and 8 he used *dialektos*, which in Acts 1:19 refers to the Aramaic language. The Spirit's outpouring at Pentecost, accompanied by wind, fire, and tongues, constitutes the definitive sign of the dawning of the messianic age (Joel 2:28-32). The disciples, like OT saints, were justified believers in Jesus prior to Pentecost, but the promised effusion of the Spirit occurred only on that day. Concerning the disciples at Pentecost, Packer correctly comments that "Their two-state experience must be judged unique and not a norm for us."[89]

(2) According to Acts 8:12-17, certain Samaritans believed the message Philip preached and were baptized in the name of the Lord Jesus. Hearing of this development, the Jerusalem apostles dispatched Peter and John, who laid hands on the Samaritans and prayed that they receive the Holy

Spirit. Forthwith the Spirit descended upon the new believers in Samaria. The text does not explicitly mention tongues-speaking; the excited response of Simon the sorcerer (vv. 18-19) may be due to his observing Philip's miracles (v. 13). Should the time interval between the Samaritans' act of believing and their Spirit-baptism be explained as a subsequent "second blessing" experience? Probably not. The granting of the Spirit after some delay publicly certified that the Samaritan believers were true Christians and full-fledged members of the church.[90] We view this scenario in Acts 8 not as a normative pattern for all believers but as a special situation in the life of the early church.

(3) Acts 10:44-48 records the outpouring of the Spirit on representative Gentiles in Caesarea. Although the Roman centurion Cornelius and his family were God-fearers who attended the Jewish synagogue (vv. 1-2), they were not converted and thus had not been baptized by the Spirit into the body of Christ. Led by the Spirit, Peter proclaimed Christ to the household of Cornelius, who then believed (glōssai, cf. Acts 10:43), were endued with the Spirit (10:44), spoke in tongues (10:46), and were baptized (10:48). Concerning this 'Gentile Pentecost,' there was no time interval between their believing in Christ and receiving the Spirit. Since all who believed Peter's message spoke in tongues, the latter is not the grace gift discussed in 1 Corinthians 12–14. What happened to these Gentiles was similar to the disciples' experience at Pentecost (Acts 10:47; 11:15, 17; 15:8-9). Thus the phenomenon of tongues-speaking at Caesarea is best understood as a supernatural sign certifying to the Jerusalem church that believing Gentiles were not second-class citizens but spiritual equals with believing Jews in the body of Christ.

(4) Acts 19:1-7 recounts the Spirit's outpouring on disciples of John at Ephesus. The recipients were OT-type believers who knew only John's baptism of repentance (Acts 18:25; 19:3) and who were ignorant of Pentecost (Acts 19:2). After being instructed by Paul, John's followers believed in Jesus, were baptized in his name, received the Spirit, and then spoke in tongues (glōssai) and prophesied (vv. 4-6). The experience of John's disciples, like that of believing Samaritans in Acts 8 and believing Gentiles in Acts 10, represents a unique historical occurrence. "Somehow knowledge of Jesus separate from the Christian message about his resurrection and outpouring of the Spirit seems to have spread to Ephesus and probably elsewhere."[91] Concerning the tongues phenomenon, Marshall adds, "in the present case some unusual gift was perhaps needed to convince this group of 'semi-Christians' that they were now fully members of Christ's church."[92] Since all of John's disciples spoke in tongues, the phenomenon likely was not Pauline charismata. There is no indication in any of the post-Pentecost

events of tongues-speaking that they spoke recognizable languages. The prophesying likely describes speaking under the influence of the Holy Spirit. In sum, the tongues-speaking recorded in Acts is linked to the centrifugal movement of the Gospel geographically (to Jerusalem, Samaria, Caesarea, Ephesus) and ethnically (to Jews, Samaritans, and Gentiles).

Concerning the claim that Acts 2, 8, 10, and 19 represent a "second blessing" experience attested by tongues and normative for Christians of all ages, observe the following: (1) Luke clearly stated that new converts received the gift of the Spirit the moment they exercised faith in Christ and were regenerated (Acts 2:38; 5:32; 19:2, 5-6). Thus all believers experience their own 'Pentecost' (short of tongues-speaking) at the time of their conversion to Christ. (2) Acts records numerous instances where persons who came to Christ apparently did not speak in tongues (Acts 3:7-8; 4:4; 5:14; 6:7; 8:36; etc). (3) Luke cited many cases where persons were filled with or were full of the Holy Spirit with no mention of tongues (Acts 4:8, 31; 6:3, 5; 7:55; 9:17; 11:24; etc.). And (4) those who spoke in tongues did not seek the experience (Acts 2:1-4; 10:44-46; 19:2-6). In many cases tongues-speaking and other "miraculous signs and wonders" (Acts 5:12; 14:3) served an evidential purpose in the early church. According to Packer, "Luke seems to have understood his four cases of 'Pentecostal manifestations' as God's testimony to having accepted on equal footing in the new society four classes of folk whose coequality might hereto otherwise have been doubted—Jews, Samaritans, Gentiles, and disciples of John."[93] We conclude that the outpouring of the Spirit in Acts 2, 8, 10, and 19 does not legitimize a post-conversion "second blessing" experience of sanctification normative for all believers.

Paul explicitly taught that at the *commencement* of the Christian life (i.e., simultaneous with regeneration and union with Christ) the believer is baptized by the Spirit into Christ's mystical body. He wrote, "For we were all baptized by one Spirit into one body . . . and we were all given the one Spirit to drink" (1 Cor 12:13). Paul's repetition of the word "all" indicates that at the new birth *every* Christian—including the carnal Corinthians—received Spirit-baptism as an immediate and once-for-all event. We note, against traditional Pentecostalism, that not all the Corinthians spoke in tongues, nor were they expected to do so (1 Cor 12:30). Paul made clear in two other texts that Spirit-baptism is a figure for union with Christ at the commencement of a believer's new life. (1) Rom 6:3-4: "don't you know that all of us who were baptized into Christ Jesus were baptized into his death? We were therefore buried with him through baptism into death in order that, just as Christ was raised from the dead through the glory of the Father, we too may live a new life." And

(2) Gal 3:27: "all of you who were baptized into Christ have clothed your-selves [aorist middle indicative of *enduomai*, to "put on"] with Christ." This event of being baptized into or clothed with Christ marks the believer's entry into Christian salvation at the new birth and is not an event later in the Christian life. Whereas Paul allowed but one Spirit-*baptism* at conversion, he taught that believers experience many subsequent *fillings* of the same Spirit (Eph 5:18).

E. Does Scripture Recognize Two Classes of Christians?

Our task now is to investigate whether the NT supports the distinction sometimes made between a "spiritual Christian" and a "carnal Christian." Victorious life advocates and proponents of the "second blessing" expe-rience often allege that believers belong to one of these two classes. For example, Chafer claims that

> there are two classes of Christians: those who "abide in Christ" and those who "abide not," those who are "walking in the light" and those who "walk in darkness," those who "walk by the Spirit" and those who "walk as men," those who have the Spirit *in* and *upon* them, those who are "spiritual" and those who are "carnal," those who are "filed with the Spirit" and those who are not.[94]

The key Scripture text on this subject is 1 Cor 2:14–3:3, where Paul gave four descriptive words or phrases that represent persons in various spiritual conditions. The apostle cited (1) "the man without the Spirit" (*psychikos anthrōpos*, 1 Cor. 2:14), which all agree describes the purely natural person lacking the life of the Spirit. There follows (2) "the spiri-tual man" (*ho pneumatikos*, 2:15; cf. 3:1), which depicts the person who has been regenerated by and who possesses God's Spirit. This clearly refers to the saved man or woman, the person "in Christ." Paul further refers to (3) "brothers" who are "worldly" (*sarkinoi*, 3:1). The vocative "broth-ers" addresses the entire church; hence the descriptive "worldly" pertains in a broad sense to the body of believers at Corinth. The suffix *-inos* denotes "mode of being" (cf. 2 Cor 3:3) and stresses the physical side of their existence as "fleshly" or "made of flesh." The Corinthians were "mere infants in Christ" (3:1); they were childlike in their thinking and not yet mature in the faith of Christ (3:2). (4) Paul again described the "brothers" as "worldly," this time (3:3) using the adjective *sarkikos*. The *-ikos* suffix signifies "characterized by" (2 Cor. 1:12) and conveys strong ethical overtones. Though believers in Christ, the "worldly" Corinthians were living like those who made no profession of the Savior. Their jealousy, quarreling, and partisan spirit showed that they conducted themselves like unbelievers. Paul's concern was not to identify distinct classes of Christians or a hierarchy of spirituality, but to motivate the immature saints to think and live maturely as the people in Christ they really were.

No sharp dividing line exists to separate an alleged "carnal Christian" from a "spiritual Christian." All true believers in Christ have been "washed," "sanctified," and "justified in the name of the Lord Jesus Christ and by the Spirit of our God" (1 Cor 6:11). Every Christian is characterized by a measure of holiness and truth on one hand, and by a dose of carnality and worldliness on the other. The Christian is a pilgrim who progresses along the spectrum toward holiness and maturity in Christ. The believer does not arise one morning as a "carnal Christian" and settle in that night as a "spiritual Christian." One can imagine the discouragement a believer might feel in being branded a "carnal Christian." One might conceive of the false confidence a "spiritual Christian" might possess in viewing himself as beyond temptation. What would a church be like where its members were designated either "carnal" or "spiritual"? The terms "spiritual" and "carnal" apply to every Christian, although not in equal measure or in the same respects. Each of us struggles with carnality in different ways and with varying intensity as we press toward the goal of our high calling in Christ. The task before each of us is to "become mature, attaining to the whole measure of the fullness of Christ" (Eph 4:13).

F. Is Sinless Perfection a
Present Possibility?

Consider first the spiritual experiences of great OT saints. Within a covenant context God called Abraham to holiness of life: "walk before me and be blameless [tāmîm]" (Gen 17:1). Before entering the land Moses urged Israel to "be blameless [tāmîm] before the Lord your God" (Deut 18:13). Whereas the AV translates tāmîm as "perfect" and the LXX renders it by teleios (thus giving rise to perfectionist notions), the Hebrew word group denotes the idea of completeness, soundness, and integrity.[95] A person described as tāmîm spiritually is "wholehearted in commitment to the person and requirements of God,"[96] without being entirely free from sin. Gen 6:9 states that "Noah was a righteous man, blameless [tāmîm] among the people of his time, and he walked with God." Relatively speaking, Noah was "blameless" in that he obeyed God's commands and offered sacrifices. Yet Noah was not experientially free from sin, as his drunkenness and sexual misconduct clearly indicate (Gen 9:21).

Moreover, the saintly Abraham did not fully believe God's promise to bless him with offspring. Hence he and Sarah sinfully attempted to fulfill God's promise by having a family through the Egyptian Hagar (Gen 16:1-4). Isaac, a man of faith (Heb 11:20) and prayer (Gen 25:21) but motivated by fear, lied to Abimelech that Rebekah was his sister (Gen 26:7). Jacob deceived his father Isaac so he would inherit the blessing (Gen 27:18-29). Moses' disobedient act of striking the rock twice at Meribah displayed his inner rebellion against God (Num 20:24), his sinful anger against the people (v. 10), and his lack of trust in God's word (v. 12). Moses failed to do what he was commanded and did what he was not commanded (cf. Rom 7:15, 19). For this he and Aaron were excluded from entering the promised land (v. 12). How candidly the OT records the sins of the Lord's mature servants!

To the question, "Lord, who may dwell in your sanctuary? Who may live on your holy hill?" (Ps 15:1), the psalmist responded, those whose lives are characterized by righteous character (v. 2), righteous speech (v. 3a), righteous relations (v. 3b), and righteous dealings with others (v. 5). The word "blameless" (tāmîm) in verse 2 (cf. Ps 37:37; 119:1) indicates, as we have seen, not sinless perfection but moral soundness, uprightness, and integrity. Ps 24:3 poses the further questions, "Who may ascend the hill of the Lord? Who may stand in his holy place?" Persons worship God truly whose thoughts, motives, and deeds are pure and noble (v. 4). The OT depicts the life of the godly as a progressive moral and spiritual development. So Prov 4:18 likens the devout life to the path of the sun. As the sun progresses from the dim glow of first light to the full brilliance of its midday zenith, so the believer advances in knowledge of God and spiritual virtue. "It is not necessary that every thing should be perfect at once. There may be an occasional cloud, or even (as in the case of David and Peter) a temporary eclipse. . . . Religion must be a shining and progressive light."[97]

Scripture describes Job as "blameless (tām) and upright (yāšār)" (Job 1:1, 8; 2:3) and as "righteous [ṣaddîq] and blameless [tāmîm]" (Job 12:4). Like tāmîm, tām connotes one who is "complete, innocent, having integrity."[98] Moreover, yāšār (cf. Ps 33:1; Prov 14:9) signifies one who is "straightforward, just, upright."[99] The Lord said of Job, "There is no one on earth like him; . . . a man who fears God and shuns evil" (Job 2:3). Yet these testimonies do not imply sinless perfection, as the following considerations indicate. Job himself acknowledged personal sins (Job 9:20; 13:26; 14:16-17); he admitted that he was not innocent but guilty (9:28-29); he needed God's mercy and forgiveness (7:20-21; 9:15); and at the end of the book he repented wholeheartedly for his imperfections (42:6).

Similarly, Scripture represents David as "righteous and upright in heart" (1 Kgs 3:6). David described his heart's intention to live a "blame-

less [*tāmîm*] life" and to possess a "blameless [*tām*] heart" (Ps 101:2). Yet
David acknowledged not only overt and heinous sins, including adultery
(Ps 32:1-2, 5; 51:1-5, 7-9), but also the seemingly trivial sins of ignorance
or inadvertence buried in the depths of his heart. Thus he cried out to God,
"Who can discern his errors? Forgive my hidden faults" (Ps 19:12). David
knew fully well that not even the most devout believer measures up to
God's holy law (Ps 130:3; 143:2). Solomon likewise admitted that no mortal in this life is free from sin. "Who can say, 'I have kept my heart pure;
I am clean and without sin'?" (Prov 20:9). Even godly saints commit sins
of omission and commission: "There is not a righteous man on earth who
does what is right and never sins" (Ecc 7:20).[100]

Isaiah, a faithful believer and a devout servant of the Lord, had a vision
of God's awesome glory and holiness. As a result of this extraordinary
encounter, the man of God cried out: "Woe to me! . . . I am ruined! For I
am a man of unclean lips" (Isa 6:5). Having seen God's glory, Isaiah knew
that he was unclean and his heart must be purified if he would worship
and serve the Lord (cf. Isa 64:6). Isaiah's experience suggests that the
closer believers come to God, the more conscious they are of ingrained sinfulness. Daniel, another devoted servant of God, confessed in a moving
prayer his wickedness and guilt and that of the people (Dan 9:4-16).
Daniel's spiritual greatness, in part, lay in his keen sensitivity to the sinful
impulses that lurked in the heart.

Turning to the NT, the Holiness tradition appeals to Jesus' beatitude
"Blessed are the pure in heart, for they will see God" (Matt 5:8) as support for the doctrine of sinless perfection. But seeing God figuratively
denotes the experience of engaging God spiritually in worship (cf. Heb
12:14). This privilege extends to the *katharoi* in heart—i.e., those whose
lives, while not holy in an absolute sense, nevertheless are free from deceit
and falsehood and marked by sincerity of purpose. The Holiness tradition
also appeals to Jesus' exhortation to his disciples, "Be perfect, therefore,
as your heavenly Father is perfect" (Matt 5:48). The adjective *teleios* (cf.
Matt 19:21) conveys the sense of spiritual maturity. It "does not mean 'sinless,' 'incapable of sinning,' but 'fulfilling its appointed end, complete,
mature.'"[101] That the meaning is spiritual maturity rather than absolute
moral perfection is clear from the use of *teleios* in 1 Cor 2:6, Eph 4:13,
Phil 3:15, Col 4:12, and Jas 1:4. The context of Matt 5:48 (i.e., vv. 43, 44,
46) suggests that God's purpose for Christian disciples is maturity in love.
Jesus' command to the Pharisees and Sadducees—"Love the Lord your
God with all your heart and with all your soul and with all your mind"
(Matt 22:37; cf. Deut 6:5)—indicates that love for God must be whole-

hearted and undivided. The righteous should love the Lord with all their intellectual, volitional, ethical, emotional, and spiritual powers.

Jesus urged Peter and the other disciples to prayer and watchfulness so as not to yield to temptation. The Lord added, "The spirit is willing, but the body [*sarx*] is weak" (Matt 26:41). Here *sarx* connotes human nature, which, afflicted by remnants of original sin, is morally and spiritually weak. The thoughts, desires, and passions that arise from the old nature resist obedience to God's will. Similarly, Jesus taught his disciples to pray, "Forgive us our debts [*opheilēma*], as we also have forgiven our debtors" (Matt 6:12). *Opheilēma* here signifies a moral debt that is owed to God; hence the parallel text in Luke 11:4, "Forgive us our sins [*hamartia*]." Jesus recognized that even committed disciples commit sins that require divine forgiveness.

John realistically understood that Christians commit sins. He recorded Jesus' saying to his disciples, "A person who has had a bath needs only to wash his feet; his whole body is clean. And you are clean" (John 13:10). The disciples were "clean" in the sense that original sin and guilt had been canceled; hence they had no need to be entirely bathed (*louō*, v. 10). On the other hand, their feet needed to be washed (*niptō*, vv. 5-6, 8, 10), signifying the purifying of daily sins. Moreover, 1 John 1:8 states that those who deny sin (*hamartia*) in their lives deceive themselves. V. 10 adds that those who claim that they have not committed sinful acts make God out to be a liar. In old age John acknowledged the presence of personal sins that require divine forgiveness (1 John 1:7, 9). Yet John explained that the believer who abides in Christ does not practice habitual sin (1 John 3:6). He reasoned that "No one who is born of God will continue to sin, because God's seed (*sperma*) remains in him; he cannot go on sinning, because he has been born of God" (v. 9). Since the new nature has been implanted in believers through regeneration, sin does not *rule* their lives.

Significantly, Paul stated that he had not yet "been made perfect" (Phil 3:12; perfect passive indicative of *teleioō*, "to be perfect"). The great apostle indicated that even *he* had not yet attained to moral and spiritual perfection. In the following verse he admitted to failure in the spiritual life: "Brothers, I do not consider myself yet to have taken hold of it." Although Paul had not achieved moral and spiritual perfection, he included himself among the *teleioi*, the spiritually "mature" (v. 15). The *teleioi* are not those who are perfect but "Those who have made reasonable progress in spiritual growth and stability"[102] (cf. 1 Cor 14:20; Eph 4:13). In none of his writings did Paul indicate that that goal of perfection for which he longed and which he pursued, he actually attained.

James denied that believers attain sinless perfection in this life: "we all stumble in many ways" (Jas 3:2). The present iterative of *ptaiō* (to "stumble," "go wrong," "sin") signifies that the Christian errs from time to time morally and spiritually. Yet the goal of the Christian life, according to Jas 1:4, is that the saints might "be mature [*teleioi*] and complete [*holoklēroi*, "sound," "whole"], not lacking anything."

A favorite text of sinless perfectionists is Heb 12:14: "Make every effort to live in peace with all men and to be holy; without holiness [*hagiosmos*] no one will see [*opsetai*] the Lord." The writer likely had in mind Jesus' Beatitude, "Blessed are the pure in heart, for they will see [*opsontai*] God" (Matt 5:8). Both Jesus and Hebrews affirmed that only those whose lives are characterized by moral purity and practical holiness will "see" God. This vision of God must not be limited to the future eschatological vision (1 John 3:2-3). To "see" the Lord is a common biblical figure meaning to encounter, experience, and enjoy God and his salvation in this life (Job 42:5; Ps 34:8; Isa 52:10; 62:2; Luke 3:6). Hebrews had in mind the holiness of life, short of perfection, that is required to engage the Lord in worship. As the Psalmist said, "I have *seen* you in the sanctuary and *beheld* your power and your glory" (Ps 63:2; cf. Ps 48:8; Isa 6:1, 5). Heb 12:14 thus teaches that the defiled person will never experience and enjoy the Lord, particularly in times of worship. "To see the Lord is to behold his face in peace, to receive his smile and enjoy his favor and fellowship."[103] Thus this text does not deal with the issue of sinless perfection.

Luther made an insightful observation regarding the debated issue of sinless perfection. Concerning believers in Christ and their quest for perfection, he wrote, "You will most certainly never attain sinless perfection here on earth; otherwise you would have no further need of faith and Christ."[104]

G. The Law of God and Sanctification

As noted in chap. 2, the law (*tôrāh*, *nomos*) is a term with flexible meanings that broadened with time. Law in Scripture denotes (1) the first five books of the OT (1 Chron 22:12-13), (2) the Mosaic code with its civil, ceremonial, and moral statutes (Deut 4:5, 8), and (3) more broadly all the provisions and precepts enjoined by God in the OT (Ps 1:2; 19:7-9; John 10:34). As the transcript of God's holiness, the law applies to believers and unbelievers alike. But in this section we focus on the role of the law in the sanctification of NT believers. We have noted that Christians are freed from the law's power to condemn. Does this release mean that the law has no bearing on the lives of Christian believers? What role, if any, does the OT law play in the progressive sanctification of NT saints?

Scholars have answered these questions in quite different ways. On one end of the spectrum are those who emphasize the radical discontinuity between the OT law and NT believers. Ryrie, for example, argues that because the Mosaic code was given to Israel in the dispensation of law, it is irrelevant for Gentiles in the dispensation of grace. He writes that "Every time we pray in the name of Christ we are affirming that the Mosaic law is done away."[105] Moreover, the primary function of the law was to show people their sin, not to save or to sanctify. Ryrie's bottom line is that "our Lord . . . terminated the Law and provided a new and living way to God."[106] In a more popular vein, appealing to Scriptures such as Rom 6:14, 7:1-6, 10:4, Gal 2:19, 5:18, Larry Richards claims that "the law is not for good people (1 Tim 1:9),"[107] adding that "Christians are not to relate to the law as a moral guide."[108]

On the other end of the spectrum are authorities who posit substantial continuity between the OT law and NT believers. Robert Dabney, for example, denied that Christ made any changes or significant additions to the OT law.[109] Christian Reconstructionists claim that much or all the Mosaic law remains binding today for Christians and non-Christians alike. Bahnsen, for example, argues that Christ did not abolish any part of the law; hence, the entire Mosaic law is normative for today. In particular, the moral law remains in full force. Specific case applications retain the general principles contained therein. Civil and political laws apply directly, and the ceremonial laws' manner of observance will differ in today's world.[110] The Theonomy movement believes that as the OT law is imposed on society, the kingdom of God will be inaugurated in the present age.

We propose the following solution to this important issue. Scripture fails to specify a clear-cut distinction between ceremonial, civil, and moral sections of the law given to Israel. Rather, Jesus Christ and his certified apostles represent the filter or grid through which the law in its unity transmits to Christians under the new covenant. Christ is the fulfillment of the law (Rom 10:4; Gal 3:24) and its definitive and final interpreter (Matt 5:17), as Calvin clearly showed.[111] Moreover, Jesus' apostles continued the inspired work of reinterpreting the law that the Lord began.

Thus (1) *many provisions of the law given to Israel fail to pass through this grid of Christ and apostolic teaching* (Heb 9:9-10). Noteworthy are the various OT animal and grain sacrifices (Heb 9:11-14, 19-28), the mandatory circumcision of all male infants, and the whole complex of civil laws regarding taxation, military drafts, and judicial penalties for adultery, homosexuality, cursing, etc.. The church of Christ, for example, does not require stoning as punishment for adultery, as did Israel (Lev 20:10; Deut

22:22; cf. John 8:5). Further examples include the commands not to cook a young goat in its mother's milk (Exod 34:26), not to weave cloth made of two kinds of material (Lev 19:19), not to eat a rabbit or a pig (Lev 11:6-8), and the requirement to construct a parapet around the roof of a new house (Deut 22:8). The civil laws for the structuring of the nation and the ceremonial laws regulating its worship were temporary, terminating with Christ and the church. This does not deny that such OT prescriptions and practices did not embody general principles from which Christians can profit.

(2) Other requirements of the law *pass through the Christological and apostolic grid unchanged*. Paul wrote not only that "the law is holy, and the commandment is holy, righteous and good" (Rom 7:12), but also that "the law is spiritual" (v. 14), and "in my inner being I delight in God's law (Rom 7:22). See also Rom 3:31; 7:13, 16; 13:8-10; 1 Tim 1:8. Paul revered the law because it discloses God's righteous character and will, and it establishes our basic obligations to God (Lev 19:1-2). Since God's moral character and human needs have not changed, neither have the moral provisions of the law. We further note that Christ and his apostles endorsed without change nine of the Ten Commandments given by Yahweh through Moses (see discussion of the sabbath command, below). Other stipulations that endure unchanged include the obligation to "Love the Lord your God with all your heart and with all your soul and with all your strength" (Deut 6:5; cf. Luke 10:27a), "Love your neighbor as yourself" (Lev 19:18; cf. Luke 10:27b), and God's command to "be holy, because I am holy" (Lev 11:44-45; 19:2; 20:7; cf. 1 Pet 1:15-16).

(3) Still other commands *were reinterpreted or enlarged by Jesus and his apostles*. Such elaborations are consistent with John's observation that "the law was given through Moses; grace and truth came through Jesus Christ" (John 1:17; cf. Luke 16:16). Examples include the law concerning adultery (Exod 20:14), which Jesus modified to get at the heart of the issue (Matt 5:27-28; Mark 10:11-12; Luke 16:18). Likewise, the Mosaic law concerning divorce (Deut 24:1-4), which Jesus and the apostles expanded (Matt 5:31-32; 19:3-9; 1 Cor 7:10-16). Moreover, Jesus "broke" the Mosaic Sabbath regulation (Luke 6:1-9; 13:10-16; 14:1-5), and the apostles later changed its observance from the seventh day of the week to the first (John 20:19; Acts 20:7; 1 Cor 16:2). The Saturday Jewish Sabbath of rest under the new covenant became the Sunday Lord's day devoted to worship and service.

The law of God as enlarged by Christ and his apostles exerts a legitimate authority over believers. The law enables Christians to recognize sins of commission and omission as sin. Paul wrote, "through the law we become conscious of sin" (Rom 3:20), and "Indeed I would not have known what sin was except through the law" (Rom 7:7). The law serves a constructive purpose by revealing what is inherently right, what is wrong, and what is morally neutral (*adiophora*). Through the law's light we understand what is permitted and what is forbidden. The law also serves as a rule of conduct, reminding us of our duties to God and others. It regulates our thoughts, desires, and actions for the glory of God. Everything the Scriptures condemn, Christians seek to avoid. Everything they command, believers strive to perform. With respect to those things on which the Scriptures make no pronouncements, saints enjoy liberty while being careful not to offend the consciences of weaker brothers and sisters (1 Cor 8:9-13). As interpreted by Christ and his apostles, the law provides believers with a powerful guide for Christlike growth (Jas 2:8).

In the age of the Spirit, the enduring features of the law and the new formulations thereof by Christ and his apostles constitute not an external code but an internal principle inscribed on hearts (2 Cor 3:3). Christians instinctively order their lives by God's law and please him in a spirit of gratitude for mercies received. By the Spirit's enablement, Christians seek to do God's will not mechanically, but from the heart in love (Rom 14:15; Gal 5:14). As Paul wrote, "The commandments 'Do not commit adultery,' 'Do not murder,' 'Do not steal,' 'Do not covet,' and whatever commandments there may be, are summed up in this one rule: 'Love your neighbor as yourself'" (Rom 13:9). Indeed, "love is the fulfillment of the law" (v. 10). Compliance with God's law thus is a matter of inward delight spontaneously embraced. It is in this sense that Christians live not under the law of Moses but according to "the law of Christ" (Gal 6:2; cf. 1 Cor 9:21).

It should be evident that Christians' serious regard for God's law does not constitute *legalism*. The plague of legalism seeks mechanical compliance with the letter of the law while violating its inner spirit. Legalism strives to obey in order to acquire merit. Christian believers have been set free in Jesus Christ from compulsive legalism. They fulfill the law of Christ by the power of the Spirit out of heart gratitude to God. Likewise, respect for God's law as interpreted by Jesus and his apostles avoids the error of *antinomianism*. The latter claims that Christ released Christians from the task of ordering their lives according to God's law. In mind and action, Christians owe grateful loyalty to God and his law revealed for our highest good. Saints avoid the twin pitfalls of legalism and antinomianism by imitating Jesus Christ (1 Cor 11:1; Phil 2:5; 1 Pet 2:21), the interpreter *par excellence* of God's law.

IV. Practical Implications of
the Doctrine of Sanctification

To believers at Thessalonica Paul wrote, "It is God's will that you should be sanctified: that you should avoid sexual immorality. . . . For God did not call us to be impure, but to live a holy life" (1 Thess 4:3, 7). How do Christians overcome sin and grow in likeness to Jesus Christ, God's holy Son (Rom 8:29)? How do pilgrim saints allow Christ to be formed spiritually in them (Gal 4:19) and to "share in his holiness" (Heb 12:10)? The following guidelines will assist us to attain that level of personal sanctity "without [which] . . . no one will see the Lord" (Heb 12:14).

A. Identify God's Part and Your Part
in Sanctification

Scripture clearly depicts sanctification as a work of God. Paul wrote, "May God himself, the God of peace, sanctify you through and through" (1 Thess 5:23). We recall the Shorter Catechism (A. 35), stating that sanctification is "the work of God's free grace." Contrary to agendas of self-reformation, humans labor in vain to establish holiness on their own. Holiness is God's gift and work in his people (Jas 1:17). No one less than God is able to purge sins (Eph 5:26; Rev 1:5b), purify defiled consciences (Heb 9:14), and infuse into us new aspirations and powers. According to Hebrews, "Jesus . . . suffered outside the city gate to make the people holy through his own blood" (13:12). The prospect and possibility of holiness is due to God's gracious implantation of new life in the believing heart (1 John 3:9; 5:4).

In the sanctification process, believers must also expend purposeful effort. As Yahweh said to erring Israel, "wash and make yourselves clean. Take your evil deeds out of my sight! Stop doing wrong, learn to do right! Seek justice, encourage the oppressed. Defend the cause of the fatherless, plead the case of the widow" (Isa 1:16-17). Against victorious life advocates who urge passivity ("let go and let God!") and some high Calvinists who attribute sanctification almost entirely to God's sovereign working, Scripture urges Christians to faithful action and obedience. As Paul wrote to the Corinthians, "let us purify ourselves from everything that contaminates body and spirit, perfecting holiness out of reverence for God" (2 Cor 7:1; cf. 1 John 3:3). The author of Hebrews similarly wrote, "let us throw off everything that hinders and the sin that so easily entangles, and let us run with perseverance the race marked out for us" (12:1). He then tersely added, "Make every effort . . . to be holy" (v. 14). Growing Christians must do battle with Satan and his hosts (Eph 6:10-18). Bunyan's *Pilgrim's Progress* commends personal discipline and effort in pursuit of the heavenly city. In his classic work on holiness, Bishop Ryle wrote, "A holy violence, a conflict, a warfare, a fight, a soldier's life, a wrestling, are spoken of as characteristics of the true Christian."[112]

Sanctification is a cooperative venture; the Spirit blesses believers with sanctifying grace, but the latter must faithfully cooperate therewith. Faith alone justifies; but faith joined with our concerted efforts sanctifies. Scripture urges believers seeking sanctification to focus on Jesus and heavenly realities (Col 3:1-2; Heb 12:2), draw upon the Spirit's power (Gal 5:25), resist Satan's devices (Jas 4:7), renounce evil desires and deeds (Rom 8:13; Eph 4:22; Col 3:5-10), and pursue the path of godliness (Eph 4:23-24; Col 3:12-14). The biblical pattern is not that God does some of the sanctifying and we do the rest. Rather, believers strive for holiness in every area of life through the enabling Spirit. Paul upheld this divine-human interaction with the programmatic statement, "continue to work out your salvation with fear and trembling, for it is God who works in you to will and to act according to his good pleasure" (Phil 2:12-13). Recall that Paul wrote, "I am toiling strenuously with all the energy and power of Christ at work in me" (Col 1:29, NEB). Peter stated that God's "power has given us everything we need for life and godliness through our knowledge of him who called us by his own glory and goodness" (2 Pet 1:3). But he immediately urged believers to "make every effort to add to your faith goodness; and to goodness, knowledge; and to knowledge, self-control; and to self-control, perseverance; and to perseverance, godliness; and to godliness, brotherly kindness; and to brotherly kindness, love. For if you possess these qualities in increasing measure, they will keep you from being ineffective and unproductive in your knowledge of our Lord Jesus Christ" (vv. 5-8).

Augustine somewhere said of this divine-human interaction, "Without God we cannot; without us God will not." In the words of another writer, "Human effort by itself is futile; inspired and enabled by the Spirit, it is fruitful."[113] Sanctification, then, results from the initiative and grace of God to which is joined the diligence of believing people. According to the biblical order, our actions are a response to the prior, sanctifying action of God in us. Our task is to be fit *channels* through whom God pours his grace and willing *agents* who practice biblical precepts and mortify fleshly passions.

B. Be Filled with the Spirit

'Filling with the Spirit' is a figure of speech that describes the release of the Holy Spirit in the Christian's life. Baptism in the Spirit is an instantaneous work at conversion not admitting of degrees; filling with the Spirit occurs throughout the Christian life and admits of degrees. God's Spirit came upon OT believers intermittently and with temporary effect. But subsequent to Jesus' glorification (John 7:39b) and the Pentecostal outpouring (Luke 24:49; Acts 1:5, 8; 2:4), Christians receive the Holy Spirit fully at conversion. Texts such as John 7:38-39a, Acts 2:38, Rom 5:5, and Eph 1:13-14 confirm that one receives the Spirit completely at the new birth. Acts records that in their life and ministry Peter (Acts 4:8), the seven (6:3), Stephen (7:55), Barnabas (11:24), and the new disciples at Antioch (13:52) were "full of" or "filled with" the Holy Spirit.

Unfortunately, Christians do not consistently allow the Spirit unhindered freedom to promote his work of holiness. Too often we "grieve the Holy Spirit" (Eph 4:30) and even "put out the Spirit's fire" (1 Thess 5:19). To the extent that we are preoccupied with self and sin, the Spirit's purifying and empowering work is snuffed out, much as water extinguishes fire. Conversely, to the extent that we yield our wills to Christ and obey him, the Spirit has liberty to do his sanctifying work. For this reason, Paul commanded Ephesian believers to "be filled (*plērousthē*) with the Spirit" (Eph 5:18b). The present imperative of the verb *pleroō* denotes a habitual action, and the passive voice indicates that believers should allow themselves to be filled by the Spirit who longs to accomplish that work in them. The context of this verse teaches that the Spirit's filling is associated with avoidance of evil (v. 15a), discernment of God's will (v. 17), self-control (v. 18a), joyous worship of God (vv. 19-20), and healthy relationships in the family and the community (vv. 21-33).

Believers, therefore, must offer the third person of the Trinity a wideopen door to their hearts. We must permit the Spirit to infuse every part of our intellectual, volitional, moral, emotional, and relational being. By trust, yieldedness, and obedience, we allow the Spirit of God to do his work of transformation and sanctification in our hearts. As one writer put it, "When the Holy Spirit has the *entire* monopoly of my being, then I know in maximum continuance His infilling and renovating of all my inner life."[114] When the Spirit has permission to control our lives, the results will be glorious. The Spirit then will teach us spiritual things (John 14:26; 1 Cor 2:13), lead us in God's way (Rom 8:14), empower us spiritually (Eph 3:16), cause us to bear good fruit (Gal 5:22-23), promote fellowship with other believers (Phil 2:1), and seal us unto the day of redemption (Eph 4:30).

C. Cultivate the Fruit of the Spirit

Paul prayed on behalf of the Philippian believers that they might be "filled with the fruit of righteousness that comes through Jesus Christ—to the glory and praise of God" (Phil 1:11). The apostle elaborated on the nature of this Spirit-produced fruit in Gal 5:22-26. Whereas "the acts [*ta erga*] of the sinful nature" are given in the plural (vv. 19-21), "the fruit [*ho karpos*] of the Spirit" is single, like a beautiful diamond with many facets. Both spiritual gifts and spiritual fruit are needful for believers in the church at all times. Not all Christians possess all of the spiritual gifts (*charismata*, 1 Cor 12:29-30), but all are expected to manifest spiritual fruit (*karpos*, Matt 7:17). This is so because spiritual gifts pertain to service, whereas spiritual fruit pertains to Christian character. The quality of Christians' lives is foundational to the service of their hands. Spiritual gifts apart from godly Christian character are useless or even harmful.

Spiritual fruit denotes the virtues or graces the Spirit produces in the lives of Christ-honoring believers. Since the fruits of the Spirit are qualities of Jesus Christ, we cultivate these graces in a growing life by becoming like the Savior. Ancient Greece identified four cardinal virtues: wisdom, courage, justice, and temperance (or moderation). The apostle Paul identified nine noble qualities that the Spirit produces in the lives of believers (Gal 5:22-23). The mere thought of fruit in the Bible (figs, grapes, pomegranates, etc.) stimulates pleasurable thoughts and sensations, even causing the mouth to salivate! So the graces of the Spirit should evoke pleasurable prospects in our lives.

The first triad of graces involves basic dispositions. Heading the list as the foundational Spirit-produced virtue is "love." Paul wrote elsewhere that "Love is the golden chain of all the virtues" (Col 3:14, *Phillips*). The love Paul envisaged is not *eros* (passionate love), *storgē* (parental love), or *philia* (fraternal love), but *agapē*—the love of God in Christ, the love that is self-giving, sacrificial, and supernatural (John 15:13). In season and out of season, God enjoins Christians to "follow the way of love" (1 Cor 14:1; cf. Eph 5:2), which involves *agapē* to God and others. The second manifestation of the Spirit's fruit is "joy" (*chara*, a word from the same root as *charis*, "grace"). More than happiness, joy is buoyancy of spirit born of unshakable hope in God in the midst the circumstances of everyday life (Acts 13:52; Rom 14:17). It may be said of believers in whose hearts the Spirit is working, "the joy of the Lord is your strength" (Neh 8:10). The third grace Paul cited is "peace" (*eirēnē*, cf. the Hebrew *šālôm*). This fruit denotes not only peace with God but the state of integrity or wholeness that includes inner quietude and freedom from anxiety (John 14:27; Rom 14:17; Phil 4:7).

The second triad of graces concern relationship to others. The fourth virtue we should cultivate is "patience" (*makrothymia*), signifying "long-suffering" (AV) or endurance. The Spirit produces patience in the face of vexing situations or troublesome people (2 Cor 6:6; Eph 4:2; Col 3:12). Patience involves the capacity to bear with annoyances and to endure delays to our timetable. The fifth virtue cultivated by the Spirit is "kindness" (*chrēstotēs*), meaning a charitable or generous disposition toward others (Rom 11:22; Col 3:12). The Spirit leads us to deeds of kindness in the great and small matters of life. The next grace is "goodness" (*agathōsynē*), which connotes not sinlessness but integrity and uprightness of heart (Rom 15:14; Eph 5:9) manifested in kindly deeds (Matt 5:16; Gal 6:10).

The final triad of graces focuses on the individual himself. The seventh grace is "faithfulness" (*pistis*), signifying steadfastness or reliability (Rev 2:10). The faithful Christian is one who keeps his or her word and who may be depended upon. The eighth virtue is "gentleness" (*prautēs*), meaning "meekness" (AV), "humility" (GNB) or a gentle considerateness (Num 12:3; 2 Cor 10:1; 1 Thess 2:7). The gentle Christian does not insist on his own way but defers to the feelings of others. The final grace Paul cites is "self-control" (*enkrateia*), meaning self-discipline, self-restraint, or temperance (Acts 24:25; 2 Pet 1:6). Contemporary culture indulges in unrestrained self-gratification. But the Spirit enables Christians to master their appetites (food, drink, sex) and emotions (anger, jealousy, fear) rather than be mastered by them in the form of evil habits and addictions.

How are these supernatural graces produced in Christians? How do we realize Jesus' promise to his followers, "I chose you and appointed you to go and bear fruit—fruit that will last" (John 15:16)? Their designation as "*fruit* of the Spirit" suggests that the graces are wrought by the divine power that changes us from the inside out. But since Christians are not robots, *we* have a part to play in this process. Scripture teaches that we bear fruit pleasing to God by abiding in Christ (John 15:4b-5), by loving Christ (v. 9), by obeying Christ and his word (vv. 7, 10, 14), by giving ourselves to others (v. 17), by allowing ourselves to be controlled by Christ (2 Cor. 5:14-15), and by keeping pace with the Spirit's movements in our life (Gal 5:25). Manifesting the fruit of God's Spirit requires time and patience, even as the production of an orange or a grapefruit does. But cultivating and displaying the fruit of the Spirit is an integral part of growing into Christlikeness.

D. *Imitate Jesus Christ*

In simplest form, holiness is moral likeness to the living God (Lev 19:2; 1 Pet 1:14-16). But the invisible God is known and seen in Jesus Christ—God clothed in our humanity (John 14:9). Therefore, to become holy one must become like the Lord Jesus Christ. We become like Christ as we imitate him—his values, goals, words, and deeds. Jesus Christ is the Christian's example, model, and guide. Jesus' command to his followers rings down the corridors of time: "Follow me." Peter informed saints in the *diaspora* that Christ has "left you an example; it is for you to follow in his steps" (1 Pet 2:21, NEB). Other Scriptures that explicitly or implicitly urge the imitation of Christ are 1 Cor 11:1 and Heb 12:2-3 (cf. Eph 5:1).

Our lives will grow in holistic holiness as we imitate Jesus' qualities of reverence for God (Luke 2:46-49), gentleness (2 Cor 10:1), courage (Luke 4:1-12), generosity (Matt 20:1-15), a forgiving spirit (Luke 23:34; Col 3:13), compassion for the needy (Matt 9:36; Luke 7:13), and perseverance (2 Thess 3:5). We become enlarged spiritually as we follow Jesus' example of self-denial (Matt 10:38; 16:24), warfare against the powers of darkness (Matt 16:23; Mark 1:13), submission to the will of God (Mark 14:36; John 4:34; Luke 23:46), and a lifestyle of suffering (Matt 20:22-23; Phil 3:10; 1 Pet 2:21-23) and service to others (Mark 10:43-45; John 13:14-15). We will advance in sanctification as we emulate Jesus' life of practical love (John 13:34-35) and self-sacrifice (John 15:12-13; Eph 5:2), his life of prayer (Matt 6:9-13; John 17; Heb 5:7), and his contemplation of the cross (Matt 26:39, 42, 44). Jesus' life was perfectly normal, thoroughly practical, but intensely spiritual. We will grow in holy maturity as we imitate him who was "sinless in essence, stainless in conduct, guileless in motive, and quenchless in love."[115] In his classic work, *The Imitation of Christ*, Thomas à Kempis (d. 1471) wrote these powerful lines about courageous pursuit of the Master.

> Jesus has many lovers of His heavenly kingdom, but few actually carry His cross. He has many who like consolation; few desire tribulation. Many wish to feast with Him; few want to fast with Him. All want to rejoice with Him; few will endure for Him. Many follow Jesus to break bread; few follow to drink His cup of sorrow. Many respond to His miracles; few share the disgrace of His cross. Many love Jesus with this proviso: no adversities.[116]

The Holy Spirit will fortify Jesus' disciples to follow their Master wholeheartedly and to grow thereby. May our prayer be that of Thomas, the spiritual master:

> O Lord Jesus, you took the narrow way; the world despised You. Give me the grace to model my life after Your life, the life the world hated; for the servant cannot be greater than his lord, nor can the disciple be above his master. Instruct me in Your life, for there lies my salvation, there lies my true holiness.[117]

"PROTECTED BY THE POWER OF GOD"

I PETER 1 : 5

———□———

THE DOCTRINE OF
PRESERVATION AND PERSEVERANCE

I. INTRODUCTORY
CONCERNS

In this chapter we discuss a second aspect of salvation that occurs subsequent to conversion during the course of the Christian life. The progress of salvation involves not only Spirit sanctification but also divine preservation and human perseverance in the faith. The doctrines of preservation and perseverance form a transition to the perfecting of salvation, in that they deal with the issue of whether believers endure to *the end*. We inquire in this study whether effectually called, regenerated, Spirit-sealed, and justified believers can irrevocably fall from the state of grace and be condemned to eternal punishment. Does Scripture credibly teach the doctrine of the perseverance of the saints, or is it a logical deduction from the premise of sovereign election? Historically the doctrine of the perseverance of the saints has been highly controversial, rivaling the debate over the doctrine of election.

In terms of the divine and human dimensions of the issue, we ask whether perseverance is primarily a matter of continued faith and obedience, or whether God's saving purpose and limitless power ensure the endurance of the elect to the end. Alternatively, do believers persevere in the Christian way by their own efforts, or are they preserved by divine power? Where is the ultimate source of Christians' security found? What roles do the three persons of the Trinity play in the saints' perseverance?

On the other hand, what must believers do to persevere in the faith? Is it true, as some allege, that the doctrine of eternal security would lull professing Christians into a state of indolence and moral laxity? Would the doctrine of eternal security afford Christians license to live as they please? Accordingly, is the doctrine of divine preservation a hindrance to the Christian's growth in holiness? Or contrariwise, does the doctrine prove to be a source of great spiritual confidence and hope for struggling saints on their earthly pilgrimage?

Furthermore, we inquire what it means for a person to commit apostasy (cf. 1 Tim 4:1). Can genuine Christians be guilty of this crime, or merely those who make a false profession of the faith? How does the so-called "unpardonable sin" (Matt. 12:31-32; Mark 3:28-30) relate to the discussion at hand? Are there specific sins that non-Christians or even Christians commit that place them beyond the reach of divine forgiveness and restoration? What are we to think of biblical examples of professing believers who fell badly (e.g., Solomon, David, Peter) or who made shipwreck of their faith (e.g., Judas)? How are we to understand Scriptures that warn of the danger of falling from grace and forfeiting Christ and salvation (John 15:6; Heb 4:4-6)? What are we to think of professing Christians who exuded great enthusiasm in their faith, but who subsequently turned back and ceased to walk in the path of righteousness? Furthermore, what does backsliding involve, and how is it distinguished from spiritual apostasy?

II. HISTORICAL INTERPRETATIONS OF PRESERVATION AND PERSEVERANCE

To determine how these questions have been answered, we turn to the principal interpretations of the doctrines of divine preservation and human perseverance as proposed by Christian authorities through centuries of reflection on the subject.

A. Saving Grace Forfeited by Mortal Sin (Roman Catholics)

Catholics claim that baptism remits sins, imparts new life, and unites the soul with Christ and his church. Yet in actual experience Christians commit venial and mortal sins. The former represent lesser sins or greater sins committed ignorantly. The latter constitute grave sins committed with willful intent. Perpetration of a mortal sin by a Christian results in the forfeiture of baptismal righteousness. The faithful who have committed venial sins suffer the pains of purgatory, but those who have perpetrated mortal sins are liable to eternal punishment. "After his initiation a person can still sin and thus lose the life that he won, squander his riches, and even throw away the happiness that was promised to him."[1] The guilt of mortal sins may be removed and saving grace restored by the sacrament of penance (involving contrition, confession, absolution, and works of satisfaction). Since perseverance is dependent on the baptized cooperating with divine grace and performing good works, certainty of final salvation normally is not possible. In sum, "It is the defined teaching of the Church that actual perseverance to the end is impossible without a special grace; it remains uncertain whether this latter will be granted."[2]

The sixth session of the Council of Trent (Jan., 1547) set forth the mature Catholic view of perseverance under the heading of justification. Christians require assistance from God ("the gift of perseverance," chap. 13) to remain established in the justice received at baptism. "If anyone says that the justified . . . is able to persevere, without the special help of God, in the justice received . . . let him be anathema" (canon 22). No one, however, can know that he has received this gift of perseverance to the end except by special revelation (canon 16). For their part the baptized must work out their salvation by keeping the commandments of God and the church, by meritorious works, and by pious exercises. Such works performed "merit increase of grace, everlasting life, and, provided that a man dies in the state of grace, the attainment of that life everlasting and an increase of glory" (canon 32). The baptized, however, can lose justifying grace by apostasy, infidelity, or other mortal sin (1 Cor 6:9-10). Justifying grace may be restored by the sacrament of penance (John 20:23; Rev 2:5). The Council noted that in special cases (e.g., the virgin Mary) God gives special grace whereby sins (both venial and mortal) and a fall from grace can be avoided (canon 23).

According to the *New Catholic Encyclopedia*, the church distinguishes between "potential perseverance" and "final perseverance." The former is the grace or assistance God extends to the baptized to fortify them for the practice of spiritual virtues. It involves the divine illumination of the intellect and the inspiration of the will. The grace of perseverance and human virtue cooperate in the process of salvation. Many recipients of this grace do not actually persevere to the end of their lives. "The gifts of God's grace are not so secure that they cannot be lost."[3] By committing grave or mortal sin—such as willful denial of the church's teachings, namely, apostasy or heresy—the baptized forfeit salvation. "The result of mortal sin is the loss of sanctifying grace, the loss of the gifts of the Holy Spirit, remorse, and the punitive effect of eternal separation from God."[4] Hence the need for the gift of final perseverance that enables the just to persevere in the good life. It is said that "The Bible contains no explicit teaching on the grace of final perseverance."[5] The church teaches that the just may obtain this special grace of final perseverance by fervently seeking it in prayer. The church also teaches the related doctrine of "confirmation in grace"—i.e., that special grace that enables certain individuals to persevere in friendship with God to the very end. Most Catholics have not received this benefit, for "It is conferred as a rare gift on chosen persons of outstanding holiness—the Blessed Virgin and the Apostles—who exercise some special office or function with reference to Christ or the Church."[6]

The Dutch theologian F.G.L. Van Der Meer likewise held that saving grace can be forfeited. "It can be lost, since divine life does not perish only through unbelief but through every mortal sin."[7] Persons who deliberately cut themselves off from the church fall away and become lost. "This those do who repudiate their baptism and belief. If the break with Christian faith is complete, they are apostates or renegades."[8] Christ empowered his bishops to excommunicate such ones and to exclude them from the life of the church. It follows that the Christian life is insecure, since all but the few who receive a special revelation have no knowledge of their final outcome.

Catholic theology clearly is synergistic in nature: God and humans cooperate in the work of salvation. God will not fail the faithful; but if the latter commit grievous or mortal sins, they fail God and forfeit salvation. Berkouwer observed that the heart of Rome's opposition to the Reformational doctrinal of perseverance "lies in the synergistic interpretation of the correlation of faith and grace, along with the doctrine of the meritoriousness of good works and penance."[9]

B. Saving Grace Lost by Walking After the Flesh (Many Arminians)

Rejecting the doctrines of unconditional election and effectual grace and affirming unqualified free agency, Arminians posit conditional perseverance or the possibility of final apostasy in believers. Authorities insist that the danger of a final fall from grace must not be taken lightly. Biblical warnings have meaning only if the threat is real, not hypothetical. Advocates hold that maintenance in grace is dependent on the believer's continued faith, obedience, and perseverance ("conditional salvation"). By sins of omission or commission Christians may make shipwreck of their spiritual lives and fall away from Christ totally and finally. For heaven to become a hope again, fresh justification must be sought. Final perseverance in the faith thus rests with believers and is dependent on their willing and actions. This view lays a burden on struggling saints to produce the character and works acceptable to the holy and righteous God.

James Arminius (d. 1609) initially was guarded on the issue of true Christians lapsing into perdition. Yet he settled on the view that believers retain freedom of will to resist grace and defect from the Way. He allowed that true Christians may yield to temptation, abandon faith, and forfeit salvation. Arminius held that all the elect ultimately will be saved; but the elect are those whom God foresees will *believe* and *persevere* to the end. He reasoned that Christians who cease to trust God no longer are believers, and that those who fail to endure do not persevere. Thus those who cease to believe and persevere are not among the elect and will suffer final perdition. "It is certain that the regenerate sometimes lose the grace of the Holy Spirit, because they sin with full consent of the will, when they sin against conscience."[10] Citing a specific example, Arminius wrote that "If David had died in the very moment in which he had sinned against Uriah by adultery and murder, he would have been condemned to death itself."[11]

John Wesley (d. 1791) held that through neglect believers can forfeit grace and by willful sin can lose their salvation and be damned. Those who today are regenerated and justified children of the Father tomorrow may become children of the Devil. Wesley held that God's grace is not invincible; its efficacy depends on Christians continuing in faith, love, and obedience to God's law. Believers possess freedom of will, namely, the power to choose good *and* evil and deliberately to depart from grace. There is no spiritual state (even "entire sanctification") from which one cannot fall and be lost. Wesley claimed that the doctrine of eternal security would lull Christians into a sense of false security. The believer who takes eternal security for granted "grows a little and a little slacker till ere long he falls again into the sin from which he was clean escaped. . . . So he sins on, and sleeps on till he awakes in hell."[12]

Wesley found no biblical support for the idea that God preserves Christians from falling from grace and losing the first experience of justification. He advanced his position in a series of statements with biblical citations, the most important of which follow in his own words. (1) "One who is holy or righteous in the judgment of God himself may nevertheless so fall from God as to perish everlastingly (Ezek 18:24)." (2) "One who is endued with the faith that purifies the heart, that produces a good conscience, may nevertheless so fall from God as to perish everlastingly (1 Tim 1:18-19)." (3) "Those who are grafted into the good olive tree, the spiritual, invisible Church, may nevertheless so fall from God as to perish everlastingly (Rom 11:17, 20-22)." (5) "Those who so effectively know Christ, as by that knowledge to have escaped the pollutions of the world, may yet fall back into those pollutions, and perish everlastingly (2 Pet 2:20-21)." (6) "Those who have seen the light of the glory of God in the face of Jesus Christ, and who have been made partakers of the Holy Ghost, of the witness and fruits of the Spirit, may nevertheless so fall from God as to perish everlastingly (Heb 6:4, 6)." (8) "Those who are sanctified by the blood of the covenant may so fall from God as to perish everlastingly (Heb 10:26-29)."[13] Wesley claimed that the justifying grace that is lost may be recovered by a fresh act of repentance and faith.

The Nazarene theologian J. Kenneth Grider claims that saved Christians through deliberate sin may lose their salvation. "If a justified person willfully refuses light on holiness, and deliberately refuses to seek entire sanctification when he knows God wants him to, he would lose his justification by disobedience to God—and would go into perdition if he were to die in that state."[14] Although entire sanctification expels original sin and destroys Adamic depravity ("establishing grace"), it is possible even for recipients of the second grace to sin deliberately and be eternally lost. "The Christian who has been sanctified wholly can fall completely from saving grace. But just as surely, such a person is wonderfully enabled *not* to fall from grace."[15] Grider avers that if the life of the entirely sanctified is insecure—depravity allegedly having been eradicated—the life of the once-sanctified is even more tenuous.

The late Southern Baptist theologian Dale Moody (d. 1992) claimed that Christians may break the chain of salvation (Rom 8:29-30) by their own godless choices and actions. Scripture is replete with warnings of the danger that true disciples (e.g., Judas) may turn back to the wilderness and become reprobates. Hebrews, in particular, holds out the possibility of the saints' apostasy (Heb 2:1-4; 3:12-14; 6:4-6; 10:26-31). New converts who do not press on to maturity may fall away from faith as the Devil did (1 Tim 3:6-7). Moody argued that God preserves those who abide in Christ, but a Christian may choose not to abide in him. The apostle Paul acknowledged that after preaching to others he himself might become a castaway and lose personal salvation (1 Cor 9:27). Moody asserted that the preservation of the justified is not unconditional but conditional (Col 1:23). He concluded that "Eternal life is the life of those who continue to follow Jesus. No one can retain eternal life who turns away from Jesus."[16]

Pentecostals likewise insist that believers can lose their salvation by walking after the flesh. Horton comments as follows: "We recognize that all [Christians] have carnal moments, but we would say that Christians who continue to sin are in danger of losing their salvation."[17] The

Assemblies of God theologian Ernest S. Williams observed that God has made ample provision for Christians' perseverance unto the end. Yet the scriptural exhortations to persevere (Heb 3:6, 14; 2 Pet 1:10) and the warnings against apostasy (Heb 3:12; 6:4-6) suggest that believers are capable of willfully forfeiting salvation. God has called believers into the fellowship of his Son, and he has the power to keep them from falling (Jude 24); but his children may abandon faith and become lost. "When a person leaves holiness and begins to walk after the flesh, he has lost his sanctification."[18]

Synergism is at the bottom of the Arminian perspectives just cited. Authorities allege that God and humans cooperate in the work of salvation. But if the latter fail to perform in a way sufficiently pleasing to God, salvation is forfeited. Kevan calls this synergistic view of perseverance "a form of quasi-evangelical doctrine which leaves the issue in an . . . uncertain position." He continued by saying, "It would be wrong to call this view completely unevangelical, but it seems not unfair to say that it is not evangelical enough. There is not sufficient 'good news' in it."[19]

C. *Elect Believers Persevere, Non-Elect Believers Fall Away (Many Lutherans)*

Lutherans and Calvinists were of one mind on the doctrine of justification by faith, but they differed on the doctrine of the saints' perseverance. Lutherans traditionally rejected the *a priori* approach that stressed the "gift of perseverance" as the logical outcome of sovereign election; they favored instead the *a posteriori* way concerned with the life of faith, continuance in holiness, and biblical warnings against spiritual defection. Lutherans built on Martin Luther's distinction between God's *hidden will*, into which one dare not pry, and his *revealed will*, which one is obliged to obey. Focusing on God's revealed will, they argued that in actual practice believers may sin grievously against the Holy Spirit. Through serious (mortal) sins they may resist God's grace, lose faith, and forfeit sonship and salvation. God's preservation of believers, in other words, is properly contingent on their perseverance in faith and obedience. Lutherans generally hold that not all those regenerated are elected by God. The elect may fall into sin *totally* but not *finally*; but the regenerated who are non-elect may fall from grace *both* totally and finally. Those who fall from grace into sin need a new experience of conversion and justification. The Lutheran view differs from the Roman Catholic and Arminian positions in that the elect persevere as a consequence of God's sovereign decree (admittedly *a priori* and hidden in the mind of

God). It differs from the Reformed view by allowing that the non-elect regenerate can fall totally from the state of grace.

Martin Luther (d. 1546) was somewhat equivocal on the issue of perseverance, by virtue of the tension he perceived between law and grace. But in the end the Reformer judged it possible for believers to fall entirely from grace and faith (Isa 1:2; Luke 8:13; 1 Cor 10:12). Luther cited biblical examples of saved individuals who allegedly lost faith and the Holy Ghost. By committing adultery and murder, *David*, a man after God's own heart, lost grace and justification and became the object of God's wrath. By denying Christ, *Peter* lost faith, grace, and the Holy Spirit. Christ prayed for Peter that he might not fall into final perdition. Moreover, "God permitted the apostasy and damnation of *Judas*, one of the most important apostles, and of *Saul*, one of the greatest of the kings."[20] These and other examples were recorded in Scripture for our consolation "lest we be frightened by great offenses."[21] Luther concluded from Scripture and experience that "when a Christian turns apostate, there will be no more bitter enemy of the church and of piety than he is."[22] Saints persevere because they are the elect, the object of God's choosing. The difference between Judas and Peter was that Jesus chose the latter and preserved him from falling unto final perdition. Christians, however, must not presume on grace and the Holy Spirit. They must keep faith active lest it be lost. Saints are obliged to remain faithful to the Gospel and cling to Christ. For those who have fallen, repentance and renewal are possible (2 Cor 12:21).

Melanchthon, in the Augsburg Confession (1530), confirmed Luther's belief in the possibility of saints capitulating from grace and faith. The Confession simply reads, "Rejected here are those who teach that persons who have once become godly cannot fall again" (art. XII).

J.T. Mueller (d. 1967), a Missouri Synod theologian, judged that Christ's earnest admonitions to stand firm (Matt 10:22; 24:13) imply that many Christians fail to endure in faith to the end and, consequently, become lost. He noted that those who fall from faith, like Peter of old, do so through their own fault—i.e., via unbelief, sinful neglect of the means of grace, or reliance on the law. Apostasy occurs by "man's willful rejection of God's Word and his malicious opposition to the operation of the Holy Spirit in the divine Word."[23] Believers who endure in faith do so as a result of God's omnipotent grace and power, or what Mueller called the "divine monergism" of "the believer's preservation unto salvation (Phil 1:6; 1 Pet 1:5; John 10:28-30)."[24] The reason some believers, such as David and Peter, repented and were rescued and others, such as Saul, perished in unbelief is hidden in the mystery of divine election (Matt 20:16; 22:14).

D. *God Preserves the Converted in Perseverance to the End (Reformed)*

Reformed authorities assert that regenerated and justified believers may lapse in their faith, resist God, and sin for a season. But their unbelief and resistance is temporary rather than incorrigible and final. This is so because God through the Spirit secures the final salvation of all true believers by bringing about their free perseverance to the end. God's eternal *purpose* to save (John 6:39-40), his *perfections* of grace, immutability, power, and faithfulness (1 Pet 1:5; 2 Pet 1:3), his *promises* to keep his own people secure to the end (John 6:37; 10:28-29; 1 Cor 1:8; Phil 1:6), and Christ's *prayers* for his own (John 17:9, 11, 15; Rom 8:34; Heb 7:25) guarantee true believers' perseverance. The final outcome of the saints rests not on their own resources but in God himself. "The greatness of the Father, not of the flock, is the ground of the safety of the flock."[25] Nevertheless, believers are anything but idle in this process. For their part, Christians who rely on the Spirit continue in faith (Col 1:23; Heb 3:14), renounce sin (Gal 5:24), pursue holiness (Heb 12:14), endure hardships (Heb 12:7), and pray without ceasing (1 Thess 5:17). When genuine Christians lapse in faith, God deals with them graciously and patiently. The safety of true believers rests on their God-enabled perseverance. Grace and faith work together to ensure a positive outcome. As Bloesch remarks:

> The Christian knows that in the last analysis it is the Holy Spirit who wins the victory for us, sometimes even against our own efforts. We are called on to press on towards the goal, but from God's perspective we are carried towards this goal by His Spirit. . . . The Spirit of God completes and crowns our broken efforts and indeed makes these efforts possible.[26]

Augustine (d. 430) held that every aspect of salvation, from initial conversion to final perseverance, is the gift of God's grace. In particular, by a secret inspiration God gives his chosen ones the unmerited gift of perseverance. Augustine taught that some who hear the Gospel, receive baptism, and become church members are changed for the better; they do good and appear to be Christians. Although recipients of a certain grace, such persons (being "called" but not "chosen") are not granted the gift of perseverance, and so they fall away and are eternally condemned. John wrote about such people: "They went out from us, but they did not really belong to us. For if they had belonged to us, they would have remained with us; but their going showed that none of them belonged to us" (1 John 2:19). Said Augustine, "Since they did not have perseverance, they were not truly children of God, just as they were not truly disciples of Christ, even when they seemed to be such, and were called such."[27]

But to the children of the covenant, or the elect, God in sovereign pleasure bestows both the gift of saving faith and the gift of perseverance in holiness. "See how foreign it is from the truth to deny that perseverance even to the end of this life is the gift of God. . . . He makes the man to persevere even unto the end."[28] This latter benefit means that God endues the elect with the will and the strength to repudiate evil and to persevere unto eternal life. The gift of perseverance works effectually in the chosen and called according to God's purpose (John 6:39). It enables them to avoid wickedness, purpose righteously, cling to the good, and persevere with unconquerable faith. God strengthens the will of the elect to act in concert with his will and so to arrive at the heavenly goal. Augustine observed that persevering grace in the redeemed works more powerfully than the first grace given to Adam. The former "is more powerful, because it affects the will itself, a strong will, a burning charity, so that by a contrary will the spirit overcomes the conflicting will of the flesh."[29] To foster godly fear and eliminate pride, the faithful should not presume themselves to be among the predestined and the preserved.[30] Rather, they should cling to Christ with faithfulness and fortitude; only by persevering does one know himself to be among the divinely preserved. If the child of the covenant should deviate from the path of righteousness, God will either restore him through admonition and chastening or take him home by a swift death.[31] Augustine added that the reason God gives this grace of perseverance to some and not to others is hidden from mortal beings.

Contrary to some critics, John Calvin (d. 1564) did not develop the doctrine of perseverance in a rigorously *a priori* manner. He took seriously the need for perseverance in the life experience of struggling believers. Calvin's bottom line was that God brings the whole of his saving work to completion by confirming saints in perseverance. By his free gift and work, God endows the justified with the inclination and the power to persevere. From the *divine* side, believers persevere to the end by virtue of the Father's elective purpose, the Son's intercession, and the Spirit's sealing and empowering ministries. The indelible seed of faith and the Holy Spirit remain in genuine Christians even when they sin. From the *human* side, perseverance requires believers' active appropriation of grace by looking to Christ in faith and depending on him alone. "Does not the Spirit of God, everywhere self-consistent, nourish the very inclination to obedience that he first engendered, and strengthen its constancy to perseverance?"[32] Commenting on Phil 2:13, Calvin added, "Paul . . . teaches that God acts in us in such a manner, that he, at the same time, does not allow us to be inactive, but exercises us diligently, after having stirred us up by a secret influence."[33]

In true Christians the light of faith occasionally flickers, but it will never be extinguished. Although believers occasionally fall into sin, Calvin insisted that God allows none of his elect to lose faith and finally perish. Believers' sins are "venial," not "mortal," for there is no condemnation for those who are in Christ (Rom 8:1). Scripture certifies that Christ safely preserves to the end all those whom the Father has entrusted to his care and protection (John 6:37, 39; 17:12). Ultimately, the stability of the Christian life depends on God, not on the resources of finite mortals. The faithfulness of God inerrantly sustains the faith that perseveres. Concerning Heb 6:4-6, Calvin maintained that the "enlightened, who have tasted the heavenly gift, [and] who have shared in the Holy Spirit" (v. 4) are not believers who subsequently fell away. Rather, they are "reprobates" and "apostates" who gained some knowledge of the Gospel and some taste of God's grace, but who profaned Christ's blood and refused to repent.[34]

The Westminster Shorter Catechism (1647), in the answer to Q. 36, cites the benefits that flow from justification, adoption, and sanctification: "assurance of God's love, peace of conscience, joy in the Holy Ghost, increase of grace, and perseverance therein to the end." The Westminster Confession of Faith (1646) represents salvation as a package deal, from election in eternity past to glorification in eternity future (ch. 3.6; 12). The perseverance of the saints means:

> They whom God hath accepted in his Beloved, effectually called and sanctified by his Spirit, can neither totally nor finally fall away from the state of grace; but shall certainly persevere therein to the end, and be eternally saved (ch. 17.1).

Concerning the basis of this blessed reality, the Confession continues:

> This perseverance of the saints depends, not upon their own free-will, but upon the immutability of the decree of election, flowing from the free and unchangeable love of God the Father; upon the efficacy of the merit and intercession of Jesus Christ; the abiding of the Spirit and the seed of God within them; and the nature of the covenant of grace.

The Confession adds that true believers may backslide for a season, but they will never be eternally lost (ch. 17.2).

> They may, through the temptations of Satan and of the world, the prevalency of corruption remaining in them, and the neglect of the

means of their preservation, fall into grievous sins; and for a time continue therein; whereby they incur God's displeasure, and grieve his Holy Spirit; come to be deprived of some measure of their graces and comforts; have their hearts hardened, and their consciences wounded; hurt and scandalize others, and bring temporal judgments upon themselves (ch. 17.3).

C.H. Spurgeon (d. 1892) observed that there is a kind of faith that appears lively but that does not personally commit to Christ and obey the Gospel. Professors of Christ who finally fall away never were converted in the first place. On the other hand, the Lord so establishes his saints in righteousness that not one shall perish. Spurgeon buttressed his conviction by arguing, on the *divine* side, (1) from the inviolability of the everlasting covenant (Jer 32:40), by which God in Jesus Christ has pledged himself to his people and they have pledged themselves to him. "If any one child of God should perish, where were Christ's covenant engagements? What is he worth as a mediator of the covenant and the surety of it, if he hath not made the promises sure to all the seed? . . . Where is the efficacy of the precious blood, if it does not effectually redeem? If it only redeemeth for a time and then suffereth us to perish, where is its value?"[35] Moreover, (2) the Lord has united true believers to himself in the body of Christ. Thus the Father cannot reject his true people any more than he could reject his own Son. "Firmly believe that until the Lord rejects Christ he cannot reject his people; until he repudiates the atonement and the resurrection, he cannot cast away any of those with whom he has entered into covenant in the Lord Jesus Christ."[36] (3) The perseverance of true saints is further assured from the nature of the new life God bestows. He has put the seed of divine life within believers' hearts (1 John 3:9), and this seed cannot perish (1 Pet 1:23). "The new life which is planted in us when we are born again is not like the fruit of our first birth, for that is subject to mortality, but it is a divine principle which cannot die nor be corrupt; and, if it be so, then he who possesses it must live for ever."[37] This new life is eternal (John 3:36; 6:47; etc.); hence the blessedness of true believers in Christ is everlasting. And (4) the doctrine of final perseverance flows from all the other doctrines of grace.

> We believe that God has an elect people whom He has chosen unto eternal life, and that truth necessarily involves the perseverance in grace. We believe in special redemption, and this secures the salvation and consequent perseverance of the redeemed. We believe in effectual calling, which is bound up with justification, a justification which ensures glorification. The doctrines of grace are like a chain—

> if you believe in one of them you must believe the next, for each one
> involves the rest; therefore I say that you who accept any of the doc-
> trines of grace must receive this also, as involved in them.[38]

From the *human* side, Spurgeon insisted that God preserves regenerated
believers by appointed *means*. The biblical warnings against apostasizing
are important means God uses to keep his covenant people from falling
away. Other human means include believers' daily prayer, watchfulness,
reliance on the Holy Spirit, obedience to God, struggle against sin, and
avoidance of evil company. Spurgeon's bottom line was that "he who truly
receives the Holy Ghost, so that he believes in the Lord Jesus Christ, shall
not go back, but persevere in the way of faith."[39]

On the issue of the perseverance of the saints, the neo-Reformational
theologian Karl Barth (d. 1968) modified somewhat the Reformers' view
(Calvin's in particular) with his Christomonist emphasis. For Barth the
basis of election and perseverance is not the "absolute decree" but the person, promises, and performance of Jesus Christ himself. In spite of sin,
death, and the Devil, God preserves those who are in Jesus Christ totally
and finally. Sin may lead them to a fall, but not to a total falling away. "If
the faith of the elect lives with Jesus Christ as its basis and with Jesus
Christ as its goal, it is impossible to see how it [faith] can be absolutely
lost."[40] Barth further wrote that

> the election of the elected man and the grace bound up with it are
> preserved to him under all circumstances, even the most contradic-
> tory. This is the assertion of the *perseverantia* (the perseverance,
> constancy, divine preservation) *sanctorum*. Weighty scriptural pas-
> sages such as Luke 22:32, John 10:28f., Rom 8:28-39, 1 Cor 1:8,
> Phil 1:6, 1 John 3:9, 24, 5:18 and the ideas of divine patience and
> faithfulness and Christian endurance all point undeniably in this
> direction.[41]

Barth insisted that although Christians stumble and even draw back for
a season, God will sustain them spiritually to the end. He gloried in Paul's
words that no earthly or heavenly force "will be able to separate us from
the love of God that is in Christ Jesus our Lord" (Rom 8:39). The eternal
covenant, the sacrifice of Christ, and the ministry of the Holy Spirit "ensure
the continuity of the Christian life, the perseverance of the saints."[42]

Anthony Hoekema (d. 1988) asserted that those whom God has eternally chosen in Christ, regenerated, and sanctified by the Spirit cannot
finally fall from the state of grace. The predestined, the called, and the justified *will* be glorified (Rom 8:29-30). True believers may wander from

God for a season, but the Lord will not permit them finally to be lost. Considered from the divine side, God *preserves* to the end those chosen for salvation. From the human side, elect believers *persevere* in faith and love. God preserves by his limitless power, but believers must persevere in the faith as a lifelong activity. Hoekema averred that the divine preservation makes possible and certain the saints' perseverance. He wrote, "The spiritual security of believers . . . depends primarily not on their hold on God but on God's hold of them."[43] The popular saying, "Once saved, always saved" is misleading, for it may suggest that believers will be saved irrespective of how they live. True believers evidence the genuineness of their faith by continuing in the path of holiness and obedience. We know we are in the faith only as we stand firm in Christ to the very end.

Our study of the biblical material in the following section will show that this last view offers the most viable interpretation of the interrelationship between divine preservation and human perseverance.

III. Exposition of
the Doctrine of Preservation

A. *God's Initiative in Preservation*

OT saints were confident that the Lord would ensure their continuance in the path of righteousness. The Psalms reflect confidence in the faithful God who preserves trusting believers to the end. Psalm 37 teaches God's guardianship of the believer in these words: "though he stumble, he will not fall, for the Lord upholds him with his hand" (v. 24; cf. Ps 55:22). Moreover, "the Lord . . . will not forsake his faithful ones. They will be protected forever" (Ps 37:28). Ps 73:23-24 records the confidence of Asaph: "you hold me by my right hand. You guide me with your counsel, and afterward you will take me into glory." Other texts such as Job 17:9, Ps 66:9, and Prov 18:10 also teach the believer's security in God amidst life's struggles and trials. OT prophets related the believer's security to new-covenant promises. In Jer 32:40 the Lord spoke the following powerful words that never would be broken: "I will make an everlasting covenant with them: I will never stop doing good to them, and I will inspire them to fear me, so that they will never turn away from me."

Under the new covenant, Jesus taught that believers in the Son immediately possess eternal life (John 3:15-16, 36; 4:14; 5:24; 6:40, 47; 1 John 5:11-13). The life Jesus bestows is eternal (*aionios*) both qualitatively (a radically new kind of life) and quantitatively (life without end). A new life that could be forfeited or terminated would not be *eternal*. So Jesus made the unconditional promise, "He who believes in me will live, even though he dies; and whoever lives and believes in me will never die" (John 11:25-26; cf. 6:51). Jesus furthermore taught that true believers never will come into judgment (John 3:18): "whoever hears my word and believes him who sent me has eternal life and will not be condemned; he has crossed over from death to life" (John 5:24). The perfect of *metabainō* ("pass from one place to another") indicates the believer's accomplished transition from the state of death to the state of life (cf. 1 John 3:14). Eternal life is a present possession; there is no reverting to one's pre-regenerate condition; judgment is forever behind the believer in Jesus. "The action picture [of John 5:24] is final and irrevocable, like that of a person who has burned his bridges behind him."[44]

Jesus said that he knows his sheep individually and calls them by name; hence they listen to his voice and follow him (John 10:27). The Lord continued, "I give them eternal life, and they shall never perish [*ou mē apolōntai eis ton aiōna*]" (v. 28a). The Greek contains the strongest possible negation and affirms that the sheep assuredly will not be forever lost. Jesus then added, "no one can snatch them out of my hand" (v. 28b) and "no one can snatch them out of my Father's hand" (v. 29). These sayings place the security of the sheep squarely in the power of the Father and the Son within the unity of the Godhead (v. 30).

Earlier Jesus said in John 6:39-40, "this is the will of him who sent me, that I shall lose [aorist subjunctive of *apollymi*, to "destroy," "lose"] none of all that he has given me, but raise them up at the last day. For my Father's will is that everyone who looks to the Son and believes in him shall have eternal life, and I will raise him up at the last day" (cf. vv. 44, 54). All those given by the Father to the Son will be kept by the Father's purpose and the Son's power and will be raised to heavenly glory. The inviolable order here is *believe*, *acquire eternal life*, and *be raised* on the last day. Bruce comments that "In this perfect unity of will and purpose the Father and the Son stand engaged for the salvation of all believers."[45] God secures the final salvation of every true believer by effecting his free perseverance in faith and obedience (cf. Rev 12:11).

Jesus' effectual prayers to the Father enable true believers to endure in faith. According to John 17:6-19, Jesus interceded for his disciples (those given by the Father to the Son, vv. 6-7, 9), petitioning the Father to protect them from the evil one (vv. 11, 15) and to set them apart from worldly to holy purposes (vv. 17, 19). In vv. 20-26 Jesus enlarged the scope of his prayers, asking the Father that believers of all times might be spiritually one (vv. 21-23), that they might know the Father's love for the Son (v. 26), and that they might be with Christ in heavenly glory (v. 24). In Luke 22:32 Jesus prayed for Peter that his faith might not fail completely (aorist subjunctive of *ekleipō*, to "leave off," "fail utterly"). Jesus knew that Peter would lapse and become unfaithful, but also that he would not be completely destroyed. God's power would restore Simon and enable him to strengthen other disciples.

Rom 8:34—"Christ Jesus . . . is at the right hand of God and is also interceding for us"—is set in the context of the absolute security and final salvation of God's elect (vv. 31-39). Hebrews states that "because Jesus lives forever, he has a permanent priesthood. Therefore he is able to save completely those who come to God through him because he always lives to intercede for them" (Heb 7:24-25). The phrase *eis to panteles* may imply that Jesus saves both "completely" and "for all time." First John 2:1 teaches that God's provision for post-conversion sins is the advocacy of the "Righteous One," who presents the believer's case before the Father in heaven and secures from the latter forgiveness and cleansing. By virtue of the Son's perfect obedience in life and death, his prayers to the Father are fully effectual. As Jesus said, "I knew that you always hear me" (John 11:42). The Father faithfully honors the Son's prayers for the preservation of his chosen people.

Paul's portrait of the unbreakable circle of salvation in Rom 8:29-30 sheds light on the issue of whether true Christians can forfeit salvation. The text contains a series of aorist verbs signifying past action—i.e., "foreknew," "predestined," "called," "justified," and "glorified." The final verb ("glorified") is a proleptic aorist, the action (the final perfecting of the saints) being so certain of occurrence that it is viewed as past. Salvation is a package deal embracing the whole of God's action from election in eternity past to glorification in eternity future. The following verses (vv. 31-34) ground the believer's eternal security in the Father's justifying verdict (cf. Rom 5:1-2; Tit 3:7) and in the Son's atoning death, resurrection, and heavenly intercession. Paul thus asserted in strong language that no force in heaven or on earth can separate true believers from Christ's active love (vv. 35-39). It is valid to say both with respect to national Israel and Christians, "God never goes back on his gifts and call" (Rom 11:29, *Moffatt*).

In 1 Cor 3:11-15 Paul wrote that on the day of judgment the servant's good work will survive the test of fire and will receive its joyous reward. On the other hand, unworthy work will be burned up and "he will suffer loss" (i.e., lose his reward, v. 15a). Paul then added, "he himself will be saved, but only as one escaping through the flames" (v. 15b). The image is that of a worldly Christian dashing safely through the flames with the

smell of fire upon him. Paul further wrote that the saints can be "confident of this, that he who began a good work in you will carry it on to completion (*epitelesai*) until the day of Christ Jesus" (Phil 1:6). The verb
(*epiteleō*) connotes the idea of bringing to the intended goal. In the same
letter the apostle asserted that "the peace of God, which transcends all
understanding, will guard your hearts and your minds in Christ Jesus"
(4:7). The freedom from care that characterizes those whose sins are forgiven garrisons the saints for their earthly pilgrimage. We also recall that
toward the end of his life Paul confidently asserted, "The Lord will rescue
me from every evil attack and will bring me safely to his heavenly kingdom" (2 Tim 4:18). The spiritual work God began through Christ he will
assuredly bring to completion.

Paul further grounded the Christian's perseverance in the multifaceted
character of God. In a statement that applies to believers of all ages, Paul
wrote, "it is God who makes both us and you stand firm [*ho bebaiōn*] in
Christ" (2 Cor 1:21). The verb *bebaioō* ("make firm," "confirm") appears
also in 1 Cor 1:8: "He will keep you strong [*bebaiōsei*] to the end, so that
you will be blameless on the day of our Lord Jesus Christ." The noun
form, *bebaiōsis*, was a legal term denoting a guarantee clause in a com-
mercial transaction. Thus Paul insisted that *God*, in the fullness of his
character, will preserve believers safely to the end. Saints in Christ are preserved by God's perfect knowledge (2 Tim 2:19a), unflinching constancy
(Jer 32:40; Mal 3:6), unswerving faithfulness (Hos 2:19-20; 1 Cor 1:9;
10:13; 2 Thess 3:3; 2 Tim 2:13), righteousness and justice (Hos 2:19), limitless power (Ps 138:7; 1 Cor 1:8; Eph 3:20; Col 1:11; 1 Thess 3:13; 2 Tim
1:12; 1 Pet 1:5), and unflagging covenant love (Ps 138:8; Hos 11:8; John
13:1). At the heart of the saints' preservation is the Lord's faithfulness to
his covenant promises and his power to keep his people secure.

Paul further grounded believers' final salvation in the Spirit's diverse
ministries. (1) *Indwelt* by the Spirit (Rom 8:9, 11, 15), believers focus all
their Spirit-energized faculties on his values and goals (Rom 8:5b). (2) *Led*
by the Spirit as God's children (Rom 8:14), believers follow his promptings and do his will. (3) *Controlled* by the Spirit rather than by the flesh
(Rom 8:6, 9), believers submit to God's law. Importantly, (4) *sealed* by the
Spirit (Eph 1:13; 4:30; cf. 2 Tim 2:19), believers are stamped with the
mark of divine ownership and maintained in this bond to the end. (5)
Interceded for by the Spirit (Rom 8:26-27), saints are preserved by the lis-
tening Father. Finally, (6) believers possess "the firstfruits [*aparchē*] of the
Spirit" (Rom 8:23). *Aparchē* signifies the first portion of the harvest that,
as a down payment, served as the guarantee of the eschatological redemption. The Spirit's presence serves also as a "deposit [*arrabōn*], guarantee-

ing what is to come" (2 Cor 1:22; cf. 5:5; Eph. 1:14). *Arrabōn* denotes a "pledge, earnest, downpayment . . . which is in itself a guarantee that the full amount will be paid."[46] The Spirit works in a multitude of ways to keep true believers in the path of faith, godliness, and security. For Paul all three persons of the Godhead work efficiently to preserve Christians in the way of salvation.

The apostle John taught the certainty of the believer's final salvation in 1 John 5:18: "We know that anyone born of God (perfect passive participle of *gennaō*, to "bear") does not continue to sin; the one who was born of God (aorist passive participle of *gennaō*) keeps him safe, and the evil one cannot harm him." John stated that believers do not persist in a life of sin, for the uniquely begotten Son keeps them safe from the deadly attacks of Satan (cf. John 10:28-29; 17:12, 15). The Evil One is not able to "take hold of" (present middle indicative of *haptō*) Christians in the sense of inflicting deadly, spiritual harm on them.

As to whether salvation can be forfeited, the lot of those who trust Christ is said to be an "eternal salvation" (Heb 5:9), an "eternal redemption" (Heb. 9:12), an "eternal inheritance" (Heb 9:15), and an "eternal glory" (1 Pet 5:10). God gives true believers "an inheritance that can never perish, spoil or fade" (1 Pet 1:4). From the divine side, believers are "kept by Jesus Christ" (Jude 1) and "shielded by God's power" (1 Pet 1:5). Jude wrote in the doxology to his small letter: "To him who is able to keep you from falling and to present you before his glorious presence without fault and with great joy . . ." (Jude 24). The abundant evidence presented in this section confirms the priority of the grace of divine preservation. As Augustine prayed in the *Confessions*, "Lord, those who are bowed down with burdens You lift up, and they do not fall because You are their support."[47]

B. *The Believer's Response in Perseverance*

From the human side, believers must apply spiritual resources to maintain their relationship with Christ. Christians have an indispensable role to play in their perseverance unto final salvation. As the letter to the Hebrews said to tempted saints, "You need to persevere so that when you have done the will of God, you will receive what he has promised" (10:36). In the words of Jesus, "he who stands firm to the end will be saved" (Matt 10:22). For their part, disciples (1) must continue in faith (Eph 6:16; Col 1:23a; 2 Pet 1:5). Paul wrote that "it is by faith you stand firm" (2 Cor 1:24). Faith "recognizes that it is preserved in God's hand and holds fast to this preservation."[48] Christians (2) must hold fast to Christ's teachings (John 8:31; 15:7; 2 Thess 2:15; 2 John 9) and obey his commands (John

14:15, 21, 23). Saints (3) must be constant in prayer (Rom 12:12c; Eph 6:18; Col 4:2; 1 Thess 5:17; Heb 4:16) and (4) pursue holiness of life, an important mandate in the NT (2 Cor 7:1; 1 Tim 5:22; 2 Tim 2:19b; Heb 12:14; 1 John 3:3). Moreover, they (5) must be alert and vigilant (Luke 21:36; 1 Pet 5:8; 2 Pet 3:17), (6) maintain steadfastness (Heb 3:6b; 4:14b; 10:23a; 1 Pet 5:9, 12), and (7) practice endurance (1 Cor 16:13; Col 1:23a; Rev 2:25; 3:11; 13:10b; 14:12). Believers, moreover, (8) must be patient in affliction (Rom 12:12; Heb 10:32), (9) do battle against sin (Eph 6:11-15; Heb 12:4), and (10) resist the Devil (Eph 4:27; 6:11; Jas 4:7; 1 Pet 5:8-9). They must (11) diligently press on toward the heavenly goal (Phil 3:12-14). As Paul wrote, "I have fought the good fight, I have finished the race, I have kept the faith" (2 Tim 4:7). While striving to do all the above, believers (12) focus on the person of Jesus (Heb 12:2) and seek to be faithful to him (Rev 14:12b).

In Col 1:22-23 Paul informed believers wavering under the force of heretical teaching that their new status as God's reconciled friends requires that they continue steadfastly in the Gospel. Persistence in the way of Christ is evidence of the genuineness of their faith.

> Continuance is the test of reality. If it is true that the saints *will* persevere to the end, then it is equally true that the saints *must* persevere to the end. And one of the means which the apostle uses to ensure that his readers within the various congregations of his apostolic mission do not fall into a state of false security is to stir them up with warnings such as this.[49]

The early Christian hymn preserved in 2 Tim 2:12-13 ("if we endure . . . if we disown . . . if we are faithless") serves the same purpose. Paul urged saints to steadfastness in afflictions, to confession of their Lord in the hour of trial, and to faithfulness of life. But since even the best saints sometimes are faithless, God will remain faithful to his people and bring them to final salvation. Similarly, the "if" texts in Heb 3:6b and 3:14 encourage wavering Jewish Christians to hold fast to their profession of Christ to the very end. The writer offered the example of Israel's rebellion and punishment in the wilderness (vv. 7-11; cf. Ps 95:7-11) as a further inducement to fidelity.

God issued more direct admonitions and warnings to stimulate believers to persevere to the end. Paul wrote, "if you think you are standing firm, be careful that you don't fall!" (1 Cor 10:12). The apostle warned the Corinthians against the danger of thinking that their security resided in themselves rather than in God. Since the end is near, believers at Philadelphia must hold fast to Christ in faith, love, and obedience lest anyone take their crown (Rev 3:11; cf. v. 8). The God who issued stern warnings against defection also gave blessed promises that preserve us from the world's corruption (2 Pet 1:4). Jesus' promise to the church at Smyrna applies to believers today: "Be faithful, even to the point of death, and I will give you the crown of life" (Rev 2:10b). God will make good his promises to his people: "Let us hold unswervingly to the hope we profess, for he who promised is faithful" (Heb 10:23).

The biblical representation of the believer's role in perseverance allows no room whatsoever for passivity, moral carelessness, easy-believism, or antinomianism. The Christian strives for godliness as if everything depended on him or her, while confident that the outcome ultimately rests with God. Concerning 2 Pet 3:18—"But grow in the grace and knowledge of our Lord and Savior Jesus Christ"—Calvin commented that Peter "exhorts us to make progress; for it is the only way of persevering, to make continual advances and not to stand still in the middle of our journey; as though he had said, that they only would be safe who labored to make progress daily."[50]

Paul united the two strands of divine preservation and the believer's perseverance in Phil 2:12-13, where he urged his readers to "continue to work out your salvation with fear and trembling." The context together with the present imperative of *katergazomai* suggests the meaning, "keep on working." But Paul recognized that believers' faithful working is enabled by God's prior working in them. So he added the words, "for it is God who works in you to will and to act according to his good purpose." The conjunction *gar* ("for," "since") indicates that "because God works and has worked, therefore men must and can work."[51] The same relation occurs in 2 Pet 1:3: "his divine power has given us everything we need for life and godliness through our knowledge of him who called us by his own glory and goodness." Likewise Jude 21 and 24: "Keep yourselves in God's love. . . . To him who is able to keep you from falling and to present you before his glorious presence without fault and with great joy." See also 2 Pet 1:4-5. God's preservation and the believer's perseverance represent two sides of the same coin. For purposes of analysis they may be considered separately, but in truth and in life they are one. God faithfully and powerfully preserves genuine believers; but the latter must persevere with the strength that God provides. In short, Christians *persevere* by virtue of God's effectual *preservation*.

C. The Redeemed May Backslide for a Season

The OT prophets repeatedly chronicled Israel's spiritual defection. *Mᵉšûbāh* ("backsliding") occurs twelve times in the OT, nine times in

Jeremiah alone. Thus the Lord said of Judah, "their rebellion is great and their backslidings many" (Jer 5:6; cf. 2:19; 3:22; 14:7; Hos 14:4). Isaiah said of God's people, Israel, "they rebelled and grieved his Holy Spirit. So he turned and became their enemy" (Isa 63:10; cf. Ps 78:40). Isaiah indicted the people of his day sternly: "They have forsaken the Lord; they have spurned the Holy One of Israel and turned their backs on him" (Isa 1:4). The covenant people refused to listen to the Lord's instruction (Isa 30:9), exchanged the glory of Yahweh for worthless idols (Jer 2:11), and engaged in ritual prostitution (Hos 4:10-11, 14). In every instance save one (Prov 1:32), *mᵉšûbāh* refers to national backsliding; the people collectively have turned from the Lord and violated the covenant. But in spite of their faithlessness, Yahweh would not abandon his people. The faithful Lord said, "How can I give you up, Ephraim? How can I hand you over, Israel?" (Hos 11:8). "I will heal their waywardness and love them freely" (Hos 14:4). True to his promise, Yahweh would restore Israel and Judah and join them to himself "in an everlasting covenant that will not be forgotten" (Jer 50:5). God himself will ensure the perpetuity of his covenant with his elect (Isa 55:3; Jer 31:31-33; Ezek 16:60).

Solomon is an example of a backsliding believer. After Solomon ascended the throne, "the Lord his God was with him and made him exceedingly great" (2 Chron 1:1). Moreover, "Solomon showed his love for the Lord by walking according to the statutes of his father David" (1 Kgs 3:3). At Gibeon Solomon chose wisdom over riches, honor, and long life (2 Chron 1:10-12). He built a great temple in which God would dwell (2 Chron 6:2). His prayer at the dedication of the temple shows great spiritual sensitivity and understanding (1 Kgs 8:22-53; 2 Chron 6:14-42). During his life Solomon wrote major portions of the Wisdom literature: Psalm 72, Psalm 127, most of the book of Proverbs, Ecclesiastes, and the Song of Songs. Yet in later years Solomon's spiritual fervor diminished. He took 700 wives and 300 concubines, in violation of God's prohibition against marrying foreign women. He built high places and worshiped the gods (Ashtoreth, Molech, Chemosh) of his foreign wives (Neh 13:26). Scripture records that "As Solomon grew old, his wives turned his heart after other gods, and his heart was not fully devoted to the Lord his God, as the heart of David his father had been" (1 Kgs 11:4). Indeed, "his heart had turned away from the Lord, the God of Israel" (v. 9). Yet significantly our Lord compared himself with Solomon, saying that "one greater than Solomon is here" (Luke 11:31).

Consider also the experience of David. Samuel anointed David as the future king of Israel, "and from that day on the Spirit of the Lord came upon David in power" (1 Sam 16:13). When David volunteered to fight

Goliath he affirmed his faith and utter confidence in God (1 Sam 17:37). After David was appointed king, God gave the Davidic covenant with its great promises (2 Sam 7:13b-16). Said the Lord, "I will establish the throne of his kingdom forever. I will be his father, and he will be my son . . . my love will never be taken away from him" (vv. 13-15). A few months later, however, David committed adultery with Bathsheba. He caused Bathsheba's husband to become drunk and schemed to get Uriah to have intercourse with his wife. When the attempt failed, David ordered Uriah to the front line where he was killed in battle. When the prophet Nathan confronted David with his sin, David immediately repented (2 Sam 12:13a) and received God's forgiveness (v. 13b) and discipline (v. 20). David wrote about his experience of God's forgiving grace in Psalm 51. What David received in return for his sincere repentance was not his salvation, but the renewed experience of the *joy* thereof (v. 12). Later David wrote many psalms in praise and adoration of God. In a speech toward the end of his life, David said, "Is not my house right with God? Has he not made with me an everlasting covenant, arranged and secured in every part? Will he not bring to fruition my salvation and grant me my every desire?" (2 Sam 23:5). The NT gives a positive assessment of David, stating that he was a man after God's own heart (Acts 13:22; cf. 1 Sam 13:14). David was a man of God who stumbled, but who was restored to fellowship by God's grace.

Peter is a further example of a believer who lapsed spiritually for a season. Peter held a position of leadership among the Twelve and was one of the three apostles closest to Jesus (Matt 17:1-4; 26:37; Mark 5:37). The high point of Peter's early life was his bold confession of Jesus as "the Christ, the Son of the living God" (Matt 16:16; cf. John 6:69). Jesus blessed Peter for this confession and assigned him a foundational role in the building of the church (Matt 16:17-19). The Gospels reveal, however, that Peter's faith was not as strong as his name (*petros*) implied (Matt 14:28-31; 16:22-23). Peter was overly confident of himself (Matt 26:35; Mark 14:31), impulsive (John 18:10-11), and occasionally profane of speech (Matt 26:74; Mark 14:71). Peter's denial of the Lord (Matt 26:69-75; Mark 14:66-72; Luke 22:54-62; John 18:25-27) represents the low point of his life. After Jesus' arrest three people claimed that they recognized Peter as a follower of Jesus. Three times Peter denied that he knew the Lord or was his disciple. Peter recalled the Lord's prediction of his denial (v. 34), was overcome with godly sorrow for his failure to confess Christ, and "went outside and wept bitterly" (v. 62). Stricken with genuine sorrow for his lapse, Peter repented of his sin. His turning back to Christ was due largely to Christ's prayer that his faith might "not fail" (v.

32). The risen Lord later fully restored Peter to fellowship and thrice commissioned him to care for his people (John 21:15-17). Acts records Peter's bold preaching of Christ beginning at Pentecost, the miracles he wrought by God's power, and the thousands that he won to the Savior even in distant places of Asia Minor (1 Pet 1:1).

Demas may have been a Christian who experienced painful backsliding rather than the loss of salvation. Demas was one of Paul's close associates (Col 4:14) and a fellow-worker (Phile 24) who assisted the apostle during his Roman imprisonment. Paul later wrote to Timothy that "Demas, because he loved this world, has deserted me and has gone to Thessalonica" (2 Tim 4:10). Perhaps fearful of being identified with a man marked out for martyrdom, Demas set his heart on the world and returned to Thessalonica. Several commentators (Bernard, Spicq, Guthrie, etc.) favor the judgment that 2 Tim 4:10 means only that "Demas grew discouraged and returned home, not that he turned apostate."[52]

Interpreters are divided as to whether Jas 5:19-20 refers to a backslidden Christian or to an unregenerate apostate. "My brothers, if one of you should wander from the truth and someone should bring him back, remember this: Whoever turns a sinner from the error of his way will save him from death and cover over a multitude of sins." On balance, the text likely refers to a Christian who backslides, for the following reasons. The word "brother" appears fifteen times in James and designates a true believer in Christ (Jas 1:2, 9, 16, 19; 2:1, 5, 14, 15; etc.). James wrote that if one of the "brothers" should be deceived (cf. 1:16), wander from the truth (cf. 1:14-15), and fall into Satan's snare (cf. 3:15; 4:7), the faithful should minister to him and restore him to the Way. "Death" refers in a general sense to the peril from which the brother is recovered, and the covering of a "multitude of sins" signifies God's forgiveness of errors committed by the backslider (cf. Ps 32:1; 1 Pet 4:8). The text clearly focuses on the responsibility believers have for one another's spiritual welfare in the community.

There is no mistaking that God will chasten backslidden believers who persist in sin and fail to repent. In extreme situations the wayward will be judged and even taken home to be with the Lord through death. We recall that God cut short the lives of Ananias and Sapphira (Acts 5) rather than allow them to corrupt the church in its early, formative period. Likewise, God afflicted disobedient and unrepentant saints in the Corinthian church with physical sickness and even death (1 Cor 11:30).

Certain Pauline texts that appear to teach loss of salvation actually teach the loss of heavenly rewards. Concerning the Christian's works in the day of judgment, Paul wrote, "If what he has built survives, he will receive his reward. If it is burned up, he will suffer loss; he himself will be saved, but only as one escaping through the flames" (1 Cor 3:14-15). Having built on the proper foundation, which is Jesus Christ (v. 11), believers will inherit eternal life, even if their works are of inferior quality (v. 13). Paul also wrote, "I beat my body and make it my slave so that after I have preached to others, I myself will not be disqualified for the prize" (1 Cor 9:27). The "prize" in view is reward for service, not Paul's salvation. The apostle buffeted his body, thereby restraining sinful impulses, so that when the fruit of his service is examined in the judgment he might not be *adokimos*, or unapproved (for the opposite sense of "approved," see Rom 14:18; 16:10; 2 Tim 2:15).

It is clear that genuine believers may stumble morally, relapse spiritually, and dishonor their Lord by grievous sins. But such lapses are temporary and not final or absolute. The judgment of Scripture is that true believers will not *persist* in a life of disobedience and debauchery (1 John 3:9-10; 5:18a). God will not abandon erring believers to sin, such that they permanently fall under its dominion. Nowhere does Scripture categorically state that the truly converted actually fall from grace into everlasting perdition. As the Lord said through the prophet, "I will make an everlasting covenant with them: I will never stop doing good to them, and I will inspire them to fear me, so that they will never turn away from me" (Jer 32:40). And as Job testified, "the righteous will hold to their ways, and those with clean hands will grow stronger" (Job 17:9).

D. Some Apostatize Because Unconverted

Apostasy is an authentic, biblical concept that we do well to understand. The noun *apostasia* ("apostasy," "rebellion") occurs twice in the NT (Acts 21:21; 2 Thess 2:3). The first usage deals with Gentiles who turned away from Moses' teaching, and the second the final opposition to God and his truth that will precipitate the appearance of the Antichrist. The verb *aphistēmi* ("leave," "desert," "commit apostasy") several times refers to a physical departure, but at least three times describes some form of spiritual declension (Luke 8:13; 1 Tim 4:1; Heb 3:12). As a theological term, apostasy connotes "the serious situation of becoming separated from the living God after a previous turning towards him, by falling away from the faith."[53] It remains to be determined whether those who fell away were genuine or merely professing Christians.

Some hold that "the blasphemy against the Spirit" (Matt 12:31-32; Mark 3:28-30) describes a sin by which salvation is lost. In the patristic and medieval church the blasphemy was identified as murder, adultery, or renunciation of the church. In response to Jesus' healing of a demon-possessed man, the Pharisees alleged that he performed the miracle by the power of Beelzebub, the prince of demons (Matt 12:24). By attributing the healing power of God's Spirit to Satan, the Pharisees demonstrated their resolute hostility to God's purposes. Such deliberate resistance to divine grace, Jesus taught, renders impossible the genuine repentance and trust in God necessary for salvation. Such self-chosen "blasphemy against the Spirit" places the individual beyond the reach of forgiveness and in this specific sense is unpardonable. Hence, this incident focuses on Christ-rejecters who were not believers rather than on any sin of genuine believers.[54]

Some suggest that Judas Iscariot was a believer whose gross sins precipitated his fall from grace. Judas heard Jesus' teaching, witnessed his miracles, and enjoyed the company of the Twelve. Judas objected to Mary's act of anointing Jesus with expensive oil because, as keeper of the purse, he was stealing money belonging to the disciples (John 12:1-6). Later, having come under Satan's control (Luke 22:3; cf. John 13:2, 27), Judas negotiated with the high priests to hand Jesus over for thirty silver coins (Matt 26:14-16). In the upper room (John 17:12) Jesus prayed to the Father, "None has been lost except the one doomed to destruction [*ho huios tēs apōleias*]"—a phrase used of the man of sin in 2 Thess 2:3. Matthew wrote that with deep sorrow Jesus pronounced Judas' doom: "Woe to that man who betrays the Son of Man! It would be better for him if he had not been born" (Matt 26:24; cf. v. 25). After handing Jesus over to the crowd (Matt 26:47-49), the following morning Judas "was seized with remorse" and returned the pieces of silver to the chief priests and elders (Matt 27:3-4). Judas experienced agonizing pain due to his sin, but he showed no repentance, confession of sin, or change of behavior.[55] Consumed with despair, Judas left the temple and hung himself (v. 5; cf. Luke's account of Judas' death in Acts 1:18).

It is clear that Judas never possessed saving knowledge of Christ. With Judas in mind, Jesus said to his disciples, "there are some of you who do not believe" (John 6:64). Referring to the Twelve, John wrote, "'And you are clean, though not every one of you'. For he knew who was going to betray him, and that was why he said not every one was clean" (John 13:10-11). All the disciples save Judas were "clean" in the sense that their sin and guilt had been removed (cf. 1 John 1:7, 9). Jesus, moreover, pronounced Judas "a devil" (*diabolos*, John 6:70), a word used of Satan in John 8:44, 13:2, and 1 John 3:8, 10. Judas was chosen to be an apostle (John 6:70-71) but not to salvation (John 13:18). We can only postulate why Jesus included Judas among the Twelve, knowing he would be a traitor (cf. Ps 41:9; Zech 11:12-13). Luke referred to the "apostolic ministry, which Judas left to go where he belongs" (Acts 1:25). Judas turned aside from following Christ to depart to the place that was uniquely his own— i.e., hell. John MacArthur offers the following observation:

> Judas is a prime example of a professing believer who fell into absolute apostasy. For three years he followed the Lord with the other disciples. He appeared to be one of them. . . . Yet, while the others were growing into apostles, Judas was quietly becoming a vile, calculating tool of Satan. Whatever his character seemed to be at the beginning, his faith was not real (John 13:10-11). He was unregenerate, and his heart gradually hardened so that he became the treacherous man who sold the Savior for a fistful of coins. In the end, he was so prepared to do Satan's bidding that the devil himself possessed Judas (John 13:27).[56]

As to whether true believers can forfeit salvation, consider Jesus' allegory of the vine and the branches (John 15:1-8). Jesus said, "my Father . . . cuts off every branch in me that bears no fruit, while every branch that does bear fruit he prunes so that it will be even more fruitful" (vv. 1-2). The dry and fruitless branches cut off signify professed believers whom Christ rejects because their relation to him was not genuine. The Lord referred to the perdition of unregenerate professors such as Judas in v. 6: "If anyone does not remain in me, he is like a branch that is thrown away and withers; such branches are picked up, thrown into the fire and burned." "The absence of fruit in the branch of the vine casts grave doubt upon its real union with the central stem, however attractive it may appear. Such useless members must be cut off."[57]

Did Paul teach that Christians can forfeit salvation when he wrote to the Galatians, "you have fallen away from grace" (Gal 5:4)? The apostle clarified the meaning of this statement by the words that precede: "You who are trying to be justified by law have been alienated from Christ." Paul's readers were immature believers who, influenced by Jewish legalists, lapsed in their understanding of God's plan of salvation by grace through faith. What the erring Galatians did was to defect from a *theology* of justification by grace to a theology of justification by law-keeping. They were running the race well until the Judaizers caused them to turn aside. Paul expressed confidence that the erring saints would soon return to the truth (v. 10). Thus this text does not uphold the apostasy of genuine Christians.

Other texts teach the *apostasy* of individuals who professed Christianity but who were never converted. "By rejecting conscience, certain persons have suffered shipwreck in the faith; among them are Hymenaeus and

Alexander, whom I have turned over to Satan, so that they may learn not to blaspheme" (1 Tim 1:19-20, NRSV). The two persons cited willfully rejected *tēn pistin*, the essentials of the Christian faith. Paul later wrote (2 Tim 2:17-18, NRSV) that Hymenaeus and Philetus "have swerved from the truth [*tēn alētheina*] by claiming that the resurrection of the dead has already taken place. They are upsetting the faith of some." Hymenaeus was an unconverted false teacher whose teaching was "godless" and "ungodly" (v. 16). Paul added that Alexander "did me a great deal of harm" (2 Tim 4:14)—perhaps by testifying against him in Rome—and that "he strongly opposed our message" (v. 15). Because Hymenaeus and Alexander showed their true character by blaspheming the truth (cf. Rev 13:6; 17:3), Paul removed them from the church. Hymenaeus, Alexander, and Philetus made ingenuous professions of faith, and in due course they publicly fell away. The apostle, moreover, was acutely aware of demonically inspired false teachers in the churches who would lead many professing Christians astray. "In later times some will abandon [*apostēsontai*] the faith and follow deceiving spirits and things taught by demons" (1 Tim. 4:1). "The faith" must be taken objectively as the body of Christian truth and not subjectively as the act of believing. The verb *aphistēmi* is a strong verb meaning to "fall away" or "become apostate."

John plainly taught that those who withdrew from the believing community never were saved in the first place. "They went out from us, but they did not really belong to us. For if they had belonged to us, they would have remained with us; but their going showed that none of them belonged to us" (1 John 2:19). It is not always possible to distinguish between the saved and the unsaved. But God grants the saved grace that enables them to endure; those who fail to endure do so because they never possessed regenerating and preserving grace. In writing "Anyone who runs ahead and does not continue in the teaching of Christ does not have God" (2 John 9a), John described Gnostic/Docetic teachers who claimed to have advanced beyond apostolic teaching about Christ but who failed to continue therein.

Second Pet 2:1 describes "false prophets" who "secretly introduce destructive heresies, even denying the Sovereign Lord who bought them." These persons professed to be Christians and were influential teachers of the church. Peter's elaboration of them as "brute beasts, creatures of instinct, born only to be caught and destroyed" (v. 12), "springs without water and mists driven by a storm" (v. 17), and "slaves of depravity" (v. 19) shows that the subjects were unregenerate professors of the faith. The end of their apostasy is described as "swift destruction" (cf. v. 12b, 17b). Vv. 18b-19 turns to professing converts who were deceived by the false teachers. The subjects of vv. 20-22 have been interpreted either as the false teachers (Alford, Mayor, Cranfield, Mounce, Green, Kistemaker) or as the new converts entrapped by the false teachers (Bengel, Bigg, Kelly, Moffatt). Peter wrote that these (either the false teachers or the deceived converts) gained some (speculative) knowledge of Christ and the Gospel, broke with the world, and entered the church. To a certain extent their lives were externally reformed. But later they turned their backs on Christ and returned to their true place in the world. Their actions reminded Peter of two proverbs: "a dog returns to its vomit," and "a sow . . . goes back to her wallowing in the mud" (v. 22). V. 22, together with absence of any mention of repentance and faith, suggest that the subjects were unsaved professors of Christianity who repudiated the Gospel. Thus we conclude that 2 Peter 2 describes the apostasy (i.e., the deliberate rejection of the Gospel by professing but unconverted persons) of false teachers and possibly of new converts deceived by them.[58] Jude described similar (proto-Gnostic?) apostate teachers in Jude 4, 8, 10-13, 16-19.

In sum, several NT writers assert that some who profess Christ renounce their profession and actively oppose the faith. They do so because they possessed no more than a superficial belief. These did not fall from grace, because they never *were* in a state of grace. Apostasy from Christ and the Gospel is a certain sign that the people involved never belonged to Christ. Genuine faith is characterized by longevity; by God's grace it perseveres to the end, notwithstanding the obstacles.

E. The Hebrews Warning Passages

Of the several warning texts in Hebrews, the most widely debated is Heb 6:4-6. The Jewish-Christian addressees (perhaps converted priests, Acts 6:7) lacked assurance of their heritage in Christ (Heb 6:11) and so had become spiritually sluggish (Heb 6:12; cf. 5:11). In this immature condition (Heb 5:12-13) and under the pressures of persecution (Heb 10:32-34), they were tempted to revert to the security of Judaism. Those whom the writer warned are described by four aorist participles. (1) They "have been enlightened" (*phōtisthentas*, v. 4), which suggests the spiritual illumination they received at their new birth (cf. Heb 10:32; 2 Cor 4:6; Eph 1:18). (2) They "have tasted the heavenly gift" (*geusamenous*, v. 4), where tasting metaphorically connotes genuine appropriation and personal spiritual experience (Ps 34:8; 1 Pet 2:3). This phrase suggests that the readers had firsthand knowledge of God's grace in Jesus Christ (cf. Eph 3:7). "*Tasted the heavenly gift* . . . refers to those who, through repentance and faith, have had a definite spiritual experience of Jesus Christ."[59] (3) They "have shared in the Holy Spirit" (*metochous genēthentas*, v. 4), where the noun *metochos* ("one who shares in," cf. Heb 3:1, 14, 12:8) signifies a genuine participation in the Spirit who is the seal of the new birth. And (4) They "have tasted the goodness of the Word of God and the powers of the coming age" (*geusamenos*, v. 5). This additional tasting denotes personal experience of God's Word (*rhēma*) and mighty works (*dynameis*). The "once" (*hapax*, v. 4; cf. 9:26-28; 10:2; 12:26-27) points to a completed experience. Thus the addressees likely were true (Jewish) believers in Christ. So the writer addressed them warmly as "(holy) brothers" (3:1, 12; 10:19; 13:1, 22).

The author continued that "It is impossible" for these "if they fall away, to be brought back to repentance" (vv. 4, 6). *Adynaton* signifies an actual impossibility (cf. 6:18; 10:4; 11:6). The writer never asserted there is no remedy or possible restoration for professing Christians who defect from the faith. Rather, he argued that if the wavering Jewish believers forsake Christ for Judaism they forfeit all possibility of repentance unto life, since they abandon the only basis for salvation, which is Jesus Christ, the effectual high priest. The fact that the writer shifted from the first person (vv. 1, 3) to the third person ("those," "they," vv. 4, 6) and his statement "in your case" (v. 9) indicate his confidence that the defection of the "*agapētoi*" would not occur.[60] Their good works, love, and service to the saints (v. 10) confirm their perseverance. This stern warning issued to wavering Jewish Christians (cf. 2:1-3; 3:7-13; 12:25) represents an important strategy God uses for achieving believers' perseverance. This text focuses on the side of *human* responsibility in the preservation-perseverance relation. Other readers who do, in fact, apostasize were not Christians in the first place (cf. 1 John 2:19).[61]

In Heb 10:26-31 the author again warned "some" (v. 25) of his Jewish-Christian, believer friends against spurning Christ, the covenant, and the Christian assembly. These (1) had "received the knowledge of the truth" (*epignosis tes aletheias*, v. 26; cf. 6:4), (2) had been sanctified by the blood of the covenant (v. 29; cf. 1 Cor. 6:11), and (3) had "received the light" (v. 32; cf. 6:4)—all of which suggest that they were born-again persons. Abandonment of God's truth and reversion to Judaism amounts to contemptuous rejection of Christ, a profane regard for his sacrifice, and an insolent spurning of the Spirit of grace (v. 29). The penalty for forsaking the only effectual sacrifice for sins (v. 26b) is the judgment of divine discipline (vv. 27-31). Guthrie noted that in this second text "the sin is again mentioned in a hypothetical way and no information is given whether anyone had committed it."[62] Heb 10:26-31 should be understood in the same sense as 6:4-6—namely, as a stern warning to Jewish Christians against forsaking Christ and reverting to the ineffectual religion of Judaism. In both texts the author is confident that his readers will *not* abandon Christ but will continue in faith unto final salvation (v. 39; cf. 6:9). To encourage his wavering friends, the author presented a catalogue of ancient heroes whose faith remained steadfast in various trials (Hebrews 11).

Berkouwer concluded that Hebrews 6 (and the other warning texts) "is an admonition, whose purpose is to lead [the readers] to a more secure walk in the way of salvation." The writer of Hebrews "does not offer a view concerning the apostasy of the saints, but he comes with his earnest admonition to the endangered Church and calls her to keep the faith and to avoid all toying in her thoughts with possibilities to the right or to the left."[63]

IV. Practical Implications of the Doctrine of Preservation

A. Be Comforted: God Will Never Abandon Us

The primary outcome of the doctrine of divine preservation is spiritual comfort and consolation. Christian believers find great encouragement in the fact that God has taken the initiative in perfecting the salvation of his blood-bought children. It is by God's grace that persons come to Christ, and it is by his grace that believers remain wedded to Christ. Our comfort and hope derives from the certainty that the *Father* in all his perfections will not permit his children to be lost, that the *Son* will not allow his sheep to be snatched from his hands, and that the *Holy Spirit* infallibly seals the saints unto the day of consummated redemption. In the final analysis, the hope of true believers resides not in our feeble hold of God but in his powerful grasp of us. The stability and constancy of our spiritual lives rests not in our human powers but in God's eternal purpose and infinite resources. The preservation of the saints is the great gift of God's unfathomable grace, and this well attested fact of Scripture engenders incomparable solace in the hearts of the saved.

Were the final salvation of believers ultimately dependent on their own native powers, consolation would be fleeting and illusory. This is so because the earthly life of most believers is beset with frailty, faults, and failures. In our present state of imperfection we have no assurance that our faith will not fail, that our strength will not give way, that our courage will not falter. We have no promise that Satan or his hosts, with their vastly superior power, will not overwhelm us and cause us to fall irrevocably. In the course of his painful trials, Job knew that his resources were insufficient; consequently, the man of God cried out, "What strength do I have that I should still hope? What prospects, that I should be patient? Do I have the strength of stone? Is my flesh bronze? Do I have any power to help myself, now that success has been driven from me?" (Job 6:11-13). At a practical level, the possibility of the saints' apostasy would engender uncertainty, anxiety, and the forfeiture of hope.

Christians who are honest find no sufficiency in themselves. Any comfort and hope they possess derives solely from One who is God. Spiritual consolation flows from God's promises, God's powers, God's provisions, and God's protection. Frail and fallible believers are comforted by David's word of assurance: "The Lord will fulfill his purpose for me; your love, O Lord, endures forever—do not abandon the works of your hands" (Ps 138:8; cf. 57:2). Pilgrim saints resonate with Paul's word of comfort to the Thessalonian Christians: "the Lord is faithful, and he will strengthen and protect you from the evil one" (2 Thess 3:3). How reassuring it is that the Lord will never leave or forsake us, that God's faithfulness does not depend on our faithfulness, that his performance is not predicated on our performance, that his love is not contingent on our love. John looked to Jesus and took great hope in the Savior; he wrote, "having loved his own who were in the world, he loved them to the end" (John 13:1, RSV). It is blessedly true that "The doctrine of the perseverance of true believers is one of the most comforting teachings of Scripture."[64]

B. *Be Diligent: Utilize God's Appointed Means of Grace*

Scripture is clear in teaching that the triune God—Father, Son, and Holy Spirit—holds true Christians secure to the end. Nevertheless, saints must respond to the divine initiative with faithfulness and diligence. The doctrine under consideration is not one-sided; it is two-sided. God preserves his redeemed children, but they must diligently persevere. For their part, believers must desire to be preserved, and they must actively respond to God's prevenient grace, faithfulness, and power. As outlined in the exposition section, the regenerate must ask God for his gift of preserving grace through prayer. They must then exercise faith, self-examination, patient endurance, and reliance on God's Word. To progress in the Christian life believers must mortify the flesh, contend against Satan, and grow in spiritual graces. Those who wish to gain the crown must earnestly contend for it. Contemplating his heavenly reward, Paul wrote, "I do not run like a man running aimlessly; I do not fight like a man beating the air. No, I beat my body and make it my slave so that after I have preached to others, I myself will not be disqualified for the prize" (1 Cor 9:26-27).

The truly regenerate in whose hearts God's Spirit is at work will eschew sin, seek holiness, and pursue God's will. Hence, this doctrine is both a comfort and a challenge to God's children. We know that God keeps us, but we must zealously strive to keep ourselves in his favor. Assured of the victory, we wholeheartedly give ourselves to the spiritual battle. In the mystery of grace, our constructive efforts prove to be enablements of God's grace. God's working empowers his children to work for the persevering of their souls. We know that we are secure in Christ precisely as we continue in faith and holiness to the end of our lives on this planet. Christians cannot claim the grace of divine preservation while living lives that are lukewarm, self-serving, and indifferent to sin. Those who do not contend against evil and do not pursue holiness likely are not born-again. As John Gill rhetorically asked, "Can a man believe he shall persevere to the end and yet indulge himself in sin, as if he was resolved not to persevere?"[65]

C. Be Steadfast in Trials and Persecutions

Scripture plainly teaches that true Christians will suffer trials and persecutions unjustly from the Devil, lesser evil powers, and the world (Matt 5:11; 10:17-18; 2 Tim 2:8-9; Heb 10:32-34; 1 Pet 1:6; 4:14, 16). Let us bear in mind Jesus' words to his followers: "I have chosen you out of the world. That is why the world hates you. . . . If they persecuted me, they will persecute you also" (John 15:19-20). According to Paul, they are true Christians who believe on and suffer for Christ: "it has been granted to you on behalf of Christ not only to believe on him, but also to suffer for him" (Phil 1:29). The point is that the Christian's steadfast endurance of the inevitable trials and sufferings (2 Thess 1:4) demonstrates the genuineness of one's profession. Those who stand fast in the face of opposition openly display the reality of their faith and their standing in Christ (Rom 8:17). But those who seek to avoid hardship and persecution by denying the faith demonstrate that their Christian profession is hollow and inauthentic.

The faithful Word exhorts believers to be steadfast and true to Christ when the inevitable trials and persecutions come. "Resist him [the Devil], standing firm in the faith, because you know that your brothers throughout the world are undergoing the same kind of sufferings" (1 Pet 5:9). John described himself as a "brother and companion in the suffering and kingdom and patient endurance that are ours in Jesus" (Rev 1:9). In our spiritual battle against the world, the flesh, and the Devil, we must equip ourselves with the full armor of God—with the "breastplate of right-eousness," the "shield of faith," the "helmet of salvation," and "the sword of the Spirit" (Eph 6:10-17). Only then will we be spiritually fortified to stand our ground. James wrote to Jewish Christians scattered abroad, "Consider it pure joy, my brothers, whenever you face trials of many kinds, because you know that the testing of your faith develops persever-ance" (Jas 1:2-3).

God calls Christian disciples to stand faithful to Christ whatever the cost. The fidelity to Christ that accompanies salvation may cost the disci-ple his or her life (Acts 22:20; Rev 6:9; 12:17). Indeed, the Greek word for witness (*martys*) forms the basis for the English word "martyr." Unflinching commitment to the will of God cost our Lord Jesus Christ, "the faithful witness [*martys*]," his earthly life (Rev 1:5). The encourage-ment Hebrews offered Jewish believers wavering under severe persecution applies equally to us today: "In your struggle against sin, you have not yet resisted to the point of shedding your blood" (Heb 12:4). If we are called upon to suffer patiently for Jesus Christ, we can be assured that God will count us worthy of his eternal kingdom and glory (2 Thess 1:5).

Therefore, may we resolve to heed the sound instruction of St. Augustine, who said:

> Your first task is to be dissatisfied with yourself, to fight sin, and to transform yourself into something better. Your second task is to put up with the trials and temptations of this world that will be brought on by the change in your life and to persevere to the very end in the midst of these things.[66]

VI

THE PERFECTING
OF SALVATION

"THOSE HE JUSTIFIED, HE ALSO GLORIFIED"

R O M A N S   8 : 3 0

———□———

T H E   D O C T R I N E   O F   G L O R I F I C A T I O N

I. THE HOPE
OF GLORIFICATION

The indescribable bliss of future glory is the hope of the Christian. The Hebrew word *kabod* ("heaviness," "weight") by extension means "splendor," "brilliance," and "beauty." The Greek word *doxa*, which translates *kabod* in the LXX, similarly means "honor," "radiance," and "glory." By "glory" we mean the outshining of the essence of the triune God (Isa 6:3; Heb 1:3; 2 Pet 1:17). Scripture makes the grand claim that true believers in Christ one day beyond history will share fully in the divine glory that humans lost after the Fall. So to encourage Colossian believers who had believed the Gospel, Paul wrote of "the hope that is stored up for you in heaven" (Col 1:5).

True believers in Christ and followers of the Lamb have entered into the initial good of salvation; but this side of the *Parousia* they have not received the blessing in full. As noted in the previous chapter, Paul described believers' present experience of salvation as the "firstfruits of the Spirit" (Rom 8:23). Moreover, the ministry of the Spirit in the heart is "a deposit [*arrabon*], guaranteeing what is to come" (2 Cor 1:22; 5:5; cf. Eph 1:14). The final stage of the redemption secured by Christ, the consummation of our "great salvation" (Heb 2:3), lies in the future. With great expectation saints await the full realization of God's saving promises (Heb 11:13, 39).

By virtue of their decision for Christ believers spiritually have been raised with Christ (Eph 2:6; Col 3:1), but they await the completion of that process with the resurrection of their bodies in the last day. Children of God have been born anew by the Spirit, but they anticipate the future rebirth of all things (Rev 21:5). Pilgrims have been called out of darkness into Christ's marvelous light (Acts 26:18; 1 Pet 2:9), but they have not reached the city above whose light is the glory of God (Rev 21:23-24). Christians presently are being sanctified by the Spirit, but they will realize perfection personally (1 John 3:2-3) and the perfecting of all things cosmically (Acts 3:21) in the world to come. True believers in Christ have been saved, are being saved, and will be saved—which is to affirm the "already" but "not yet" character of the Christian salvation. Christ inaugurated the new aeon, but it has not yet arrived in fullness. The redemptive process that began before the worlds were formed will be brought to perfection in the new world of heavenly glory. As Prior expressed it well, "God's work is never an unfinished symphony."[1]

Many Scripture texts teach the believer's hope of future glory. The psalmist expressed to the Lord his heartfelt confidence: "You guide me with your counsel, and afterward you will take me into glory" (Ps 73:24). To the Romans Paul wrote that by grace "we rejoice in the hope of the glory of God" (Rom 5:2). To the Thessalonians Paul wrote that God "called you to this through our gospel, that you might share in the glory of our Lord Jesus Christ" (2 Thess 2:14). Peter stated that "when the Chief Shepherd appears, you will receive the crown of glory that will never fade away" (1 Pet 5:4). The crown of glory is a symbol for the final perfecting in Christ. Further teaching on the glorification of the saints occurs in Rom 8:17; Col 1:27, 1 Thess 2:12, 2 Tim 2:10, and Heb 2:10.

Glorification thus concerns the final event in the salvation of true believers that began in eternity past with God's elective decision. It is the fitting conclusion to our spiritual journey in which God's glory is becoming progressively revealed. Our spiritual struggles will not go on for ever. Our pilgrimage will issue in a marvelous consummation in which the vestiges of the old self are eradicated and the new self is perfectly realized. Glorification is the bringing to a triumphant conclusion our redemption in Christ. It is the final realization of our unfolding salvation in Christ (Rom 13:11; 1 Pet 1:5).

The NT describes the glorification of the saints via several richly descriptive images. Glorification means (1) entering into "the riches of his glorious inheritance" (Eph 1:18; cf. Col 3:24; Heb 9:15; 1 Pet 1:4), even the full realization of "our citizenship . . . in heaven" (Phil 3:20), which we presently possess as a sure hope. Glorification is symbolized by (2) the promised "crown of life" (Jas 1:12; Rev 2:10) or the "crown of glory" (1

Pet 5:4)—the crown being a symbol of triumph and perfection (1 Cor 9:25; Rev 3:11). Moreover, glorification (3) is a rich welcoming into Christ's "eternal kingdom" (2 Pet 1:11; cf. 2 Tim 4:18) and the attainment of God's "eternal glory" (1 Pet 5:10; cf. 2 Pet 1:17). Hebrews pictorially described glorification (4) as entry into "the city with foundations, whose architect and builder is God" (Heb 11:10) and as the attainment of "a better country—a heavenly one" (v. 16). Prospectively, glorification means that "you have come to Mount Zion, to the heavenly Jerusalem, the city of the living God. You have come to thousands upon thousands of angels in joyful assembly" (Heb 12:22). In sum, glorification signifies the full inheritance of the kingdom of God (Matt 25:34; Jas 2:5), complete attainment of everlasting life (Dan 12:2; Matt 25:46; Rom 2:7; Tit 3:7), and perfect conformity to the image of Jesus Christ. "To those who . . . seek glory, honor and immortality, he will give eternal life" (Rom 2:7). Eternal life begins with one's decision for Christ in this life; but it will be fully manifested in the age-to-come at the glorious return of Christ to consummate all things.

II. THE SEVERAL PHASES
OF GLORIFICATION

In the broadest sense the glorification of the saints will occur in four phases or stages. The *first* phase will occur at the believer's death when the immaterial soul/spirit departs this sin-cursed body to enter Christ's immediate presence in glory. In this so-called "intermediate state" the saints are guided bodiless to heaven by angels (Luke 16:22). At this transformation personal identity will continue (Matt 17:3), and the saints as spirits will enjoy conscious fellowship with Christ and God's people of all times. Here disembodied believers will know that they are "at home with the Lord" (2 Cor 5:8). This intermediate condition, however, is not perfect, for the saints as spirits long for reunion with their bodies. Nevertheless, the term "heaven" may properly be used of this preliminary, bodiless state of glory.

Several Scriptures testify to this initial phase of glorification. Jesus said to the repentant thief hanging next to him on the cross, "today you will be with me in paradise" (Luke 23:43). Although the thief's physical body hung on the cross and then was buried, the Lord received his soul/spirit into heavenly glory. Luke relates that as Stephen was being stoned to death, he cried out, "Lord Jesus, receive my spirit" (Acts 7:59). Paul referred to this initial stage of glorification in 2 Cor 5:8: "We . . . would prefer to be away from the body and at home with the Lord." Heb 12:23

also describes the blessed condition of deceased saints in the intermediate state: "You have come . . . to the spirits [*pneumata*] of righteous men made perfect." The "spirits" are not angels, for the latter were mentioned in the previous verse. Alford observed that the saints "are not sleeping, they are not unconscious, they are not absent from us: they are perfected, lacking nothing . . . but waiting only for bodily perfection."[2] The death of a Christian is not the end but the beginning of a far better existence in the world to come. The Shorter Catechism (1647) states in response to Q. 37 ("What benefits do believers receive from Christ at death?"), "The souls of believers are at death made perfect in holiness, and do immediately pass into glory: and their bodies, being still united to Christ, do rest in their graves till the resurrection."

Glorification proper occurs in a *second* stage. This involves the resurrection of the saints' transformed bodies in reunion with their spirits. This great event will occur at Christ's second coming in glory (Tit 2:13). "It is the complete and final glorification of the whole person when in the integrity of body and spirit the people of God will be conformed to the image of risen, exalted, and glorified Redeemer, when the very body of their humiliation will be conformed to the body of Christ's glory (cf. Phil 3:21)."[3] This great event is a corporate experience that the saints of all ages will experience together. Christ was glorified in that he received a glorious body and returned to heaven (Luke 24:26). Scripture teaches that the saints will share in Christ's glory (John 17:24; 2 Thess 2:14), and this will occur at their elevation to heaven at the second advent (John 14:3). Paul wrote of this experience of glorification proper: "we eagerly await a Savior from [heaven], the Lord Jesus Christ, who . . . will transform our lowly bodies so that they will be like his glorious body" (Phil 3:20-21). Likewise, to the Romans he wrote, "we ourselves, who have the firstfruits of the Spirit, groan inwardly as we wait eagerly for our adoption as sons, the redemption of our bodies" (8:23; cf. v. 11). This glorious event will occur "when the perishable has been clothed with the imperishable, and the mortal with immortality" (1 Cor 15:54). In the Millennium and the eternal state the saints will experience "heaven" in physical bodies with vastly renewed powers. Thus in the midst of chronic illness or terminal disease that cause the wasting away of this fleshly body, believers find encouragement in Paul's words, "I consider that our present sufferings are not worth comparing with the glory that will be revealed in us" (Rom 8:18). Again he wrote, "we do not lose heart. Though outwardly we are wasting away, yet inwardly we are being renewed day by day. For our light and momentary troubles are achieving for us an eternal glory that far outweighs them all" (2 Cor 4:16-18a).

In the *third* phase of glorification believers finally will be vindicated before the judgment seat of Christ. We learned in our study of justification that God clothes sinners who trust in Christ with the righteousness of his Son and declares them free from guilt and shame. The penalty for sins will not be exacted a second time. At the evaluation before Christ's judgment seat (*bema*), the character of believers' works will be examined as evidence of their faith, gratitude, and love (Rom 14:10-12; 1 Cor 3:12-15; 2 Cor 5:10). The criteria for judgment concern the heart motives that drive the Christian's life and service. Paul wrote, "judge nothing before the appointed time; wait till the Lord comes. He will bring to light what is hidden in darkness and will expose the motives of men's hearts" (1 Cor 4:5a). That the final judgment of Christians is a glorification is evident from the words that follow in v. 5b: "At that time each will receive his praise from God." Glory will flood the believer's soul when she hears the Lord Jesus Christ say, "Well done, good and faithful servant! You have been faithful with a few things; I will put you in charge of many things. Come and share your master's happiness!" (Matt 25:21). In one way or another Christ will reward the faithful service of the justified for loving labors performed in the body (1 Cor 9:25; 1 Thess 2:19; 2 Tim 4:8; Jas 1:12; 1 Pet 5:4). Jesus' words, "Be faithful, even to the point of death, and I will give you the crown of life" (Rev 2:10) concern the eschatological reward meted out to faithful saints. Blomberg argues that Christians' rewards will be recognized at the final judgment but not throughout the eternal state.[4] On the other hand, future rewards may concern the saints' ability to enjoy God and the nobility of their service in heaven.

The *fourth* phase of glorification involves the believer's entry, as embodied spirits, into heaven—the place of perfect holiness for perfected people. Rev 21:1–22:5 is a highly symbolic description of the eternal state. The first event described here is the replacement of the present universe, cursed for man's sin (Gen 3:17-19; Rom 8:20), with a new cosmos, even "a new heaven and a new earth" (21:1; cf. Isa 65:17). The saints' glorification is linked to the renewal of the entire creation (Rom 8:21; 2 Pet 3:13). The new heaven and new earth become the setting for "the Holy City, the new Jerusalem," that will come down "out of heaven from God" (21:2) and that will shine "with the glory of God" (21:11). Jerusalem, the site of the temple, was the special dwelling-place of God (Ps 48:2; 132:13; Joel 3:17). Scripture promises that the city will be a place of great righteousness (Isa 1:26; 60:17; 2 Pet 3:13), peace (Ps 122:6-8; Isa 66:12), and glory (Isa 62:2; Ezek 43:1-2). John relates that after the new Jerusalem has descended to the renewed earth, "the dwelling (*skene*) of God is with men, and he will live with them" (21:3), suggesting that the new Jerusalem symbolizes the saints' eternal home in heaven. In this glorified state the sorrows of the old order will be gone forever; with sin abolished, death, mourning, crying, and pain will be no more (21:4). Ramm commented, "The new Jerusalem is the eternal home of the redeemed, in which city the Triune God lives in unbroken communion with the redeemed. The entire description of it is one of glory. Glorified saints live in a glorious city in glorious existence surrounded by the new cosmos." He continued that the city is "the eternal home of man and the eternal tabernacle of God. It is the glorified environment and glorified society which corresponds to the glorified soul and glorified body of the redeemed."[5] Humanity's first habitat was a richly adorned garden; redeemed humanity's final dwelling will be a city of incomparable glory.

In this city there will be no need for a temple, "because the Lord God Almighty and the Lamb are its temple" (21:22). The temple (*naos*) here symbolizes the saints' eternal worship of God in the eternal state. Moreover, the city needs neither sun nor moon for illumination, "for the glory of God gives it light, and the Lamb is its lamp" (21:23). In the city there will be an idyllic garden (Rev 22:1-5), recalling the garden of Eden in Genesis 3. The garden symbolizes the unsurpassed vitality and beauty of the eternal state after death forever is abolished. "The river of the water of life" that flowed perpetually "from the throne of God and of the Lamb" (22:1) signifies the endless life-giving stream that blesses the glorified saints. Planted beside the river is the "tree of life," bearing abundant fruit (22:2; cf. 2:7; 22:14). The tree denotes believers' immortality, when the perishable becomes imperishable and death itself dies (cf. 1 Cor 15:52-54). In this glorious condition in the eternal state "his servants will serve him. They will see his face, and his name will be on their foreheads" (22:3-4). However we understand the rich imagery of the last two chapters of the Apocalypse, the new Jerusalem locates glorified believers in a restored Eden with a totally perfected environment. There the sanctification, perfection, and glorification of God's people will be complete.

III. THE NATURE
OF GLORIFICATION

God's goal for his people involves the perfecting of the redemption begun in those who believe (Heb 11:40; 12:23). We saw in chap. 10 that Christians in the present age attain various degrees of spiritual maturity, but not absolute moral and spiritual perfection (Eph 4:13; Phil 3:15; Col 1:28). The claims of some relative to attaining a high state of perfection in this life reflect a low view of sin. But in the age-to-come the varying degrees of maturity Christians now possess will give way to the fullness of perfection in Christ. Consider now what glorification in the age-to-come will mean for God's children spiritually, bodily, and socially.

A. The Perfecting of the Soul

Christians in the intermediate state will enjoy extraordinary blessings only dimly perceived in the present vale of sorrow. (1) Then glorified saints will see Christ directly, face-to-face. Immediately following the death of the body, the saints will awake in Christ's presence, beholding his glorious countenance. The psalmist wrote, "in righteousness I will see your face; when I awake, I will be satisfied with seeing your likeness (Ps 17:15). Anticipating being with Christ in heaven, Paul confidently wrote, "then we shall see face to face . . . .then I shall know fully, even as I am fully known" (1 Cor 13:12). This sight of Christ will provide the most perfect knowledge of the Lord and other realities available to finite beings. Our fragmentary and imperfect knowledge will give way to a knowledge that is complete and perfect. John highlighted the tension between the "already" and the "not yet" in 1 John 3:2: "now we are children of God, and what we will be has not yet been made known. But we know that when he appears, we shall be like him, for we shall see him as he is." We can only wonder what glory will be ours when we see Christ face to face.

(2) Glorified saints in the intermediate state will experience the moral perfecting of their souls/spirits. The NT writers expressed this perfecting via several instructive Greek words. (a) *Amemptos*, from the verb *memphomai* ("to find fault or blame"), means to be "blameless" or "faultless." Paul wrote, "May [the Lord] strengthen your hearts so that you will be blameless [*amemptos*] and holy [*hagiosynē*] in the presence of our God and Father when our Lord Jesus comes with all his holy ones" (1 Thess 3:13; cf. 5:23). (b) *Amōmos*, the negation of *mōmos* ("blemish," "fault," or "occasion for blame"), connotes "without blemish" or "blameless." So Jude wrote, "To him who is able to keep you from falling and to present you before his glorious presence without fault and with great joy . . ." (Jude 24; cf. Eph 1:4; Col 1:22). (c) *Anenklētos*, from the verb *enkoleō* (to "bring a charge against someone," Acts 23:28; 26:2, 7), means to be "without fault" or "beyond reproach." Thus Paul wrote that God "will keep you strong to the end, so that you will be blameless on the day of our Lord Jesus Christ" (1 Cor 1:8; cf. Col 1:22). (d) *Aproskopos*, a word that means "blameless," "faultless," "without offense." Paul prayed that the Philippian saints "may be pure [*eilikrinēs*] and blameless [*aproskopos*] until the day of Christ" (Phil 1:10). (e) *Eilikrinēs*, connoting the idea of being tested by the sun, means "pure"

and "sincere" (Phil 1:10, quoted in [d] above). (f) *Hagios*, implying separation from everything unclean, means "holy," "morally pure," "upright" (many times in the NT). God's holy heaven will be occupied by holy people; impure sinners will be excluded from the Holy City (Rev 21:27; 22:15). (g) In Eph 5:27 Paul wrote concerning God's corporate people that Christ would "present her to himself as a radiant [*endoxos*, "glorious"] church, without stain [*spilos*, "blemish"] or wrinkle [*rhytis*] or any other blemish, but holy (*hagios*) and blameless [*amōmos*]." (h) Finally, John gave a description of the church under the imagery of a bride clothed in dazzling wedding garments, which depict her moral and spiritual purity. "His bride has made herself ready. Fine linen, bright [*lampros*, "shining," "clear"] and clean [*katharos*], was given her to wear" (Rev 19:7-8).

(3) Glorified saints will experience freedom from the vestiges of sin. Although in the present regenerated, justified, and being sanctified, believers here and now experience only partial freedom from indwelling sin (2 Cor 3:17; Gal 5:1, 13). Sin lodged in the old nature remains a stubborn enemy, crippled by Christ's work but not obliterated. But when the saint beholds Christ in the world to come, the old nature will be completely abolished. Then saints will be freed from the *deception*, the *power*, and the very *presence* of sin. With the eradication of the remnants of sin, believers finally will be free only to do the good. In glory they will share in the freedom of God, and they will actualize themselves in accord with his will. In the language of classical theology, glorified saints will realize their God-intended destiny by being *non posse peccare* ("not able to sin").

(4) Glorified believers will be thoroughly transformed into the likeness of Jesus Christ everlastingly. Presently believers are being gradually transformed by the Spirit into the Savior's likeness (2 Cor 3:18). Through the Spirit's ministry Christians are becoming more like Jesus Christ (Phil 3:10). But this transformation into the image of Christ will be completed only at the Lord's second advent. Perfection will occur in the future consummation. Paul anticipated this change in Rom 8:29, where he wrote that God "predestined [us] to be conformed to the likeness (*eikōn*) of his Son." The apostle John gave us the definitive word concerning this future transformation: "Dear friends, . . . what we will be has not yet been made known. But we know that when he appears, we shall be like (*homoioi*) him, for we shall see him as he is" (1 John 3:2).

B. The Perfecting of the Body

(1) God will raise, transform, and glorify the bodies of Christians at Christ's second coming. In the future age life with Christ will be commu-

nion in a glorified body. The God who fashioned the human body from dust (Gen 2:7) highly values the human frame. The biblical view is not that of Plato and the ancient Greeks who devalued the body as the prison-house of the soul. Nor is it the view of the Sadducees who denied a bod-ily resurrection (Matt 22:23; Acts 23:8). Neither is the biblical view that of modern liberals (e.g., Clarke, Fosdick, Brown) who reject bodily res-urrection in favor of the survival of the individual personality at death. Biblically speaking, God created man and woman not as a soul wedded to a body but as an ensouled body, a complex unity that breaks down at death due to sin. God's high regard for the body is attested by Christ's assumption of the body of our flesh (John 1:14), the surrender of his body on the cross, and the Spirit's indwelling the believer's body as its temple (1 Cor 6:19).

The OT anticipated the resurrection of the body in the last day (Job 19:26-27; Isa 26:19; Dan 12:2). But the NT offers unmistakable testimony to the resurrection and transformation of believers' bodies at the end of the age. Jesus said to the Jews, "a time is coming when all who are in their graves will hear his voice and come out—those who have done good will rise to live, and those who have done evil will rise to be condemned" (John 5:28-29). Paul wrote in Rom 11:23, we "who have the firstfruits of the Spirit, groan inwardly as we wait eagerly for our adoption as sons, the redemption of our bodies." In 1 Cor 15:35-50 Paul argued for the resur-rection and transformation of believers' bodies as a consequence of Christ's exaltation. Contemplating persons in Christ, Paul wrote that "we will all be changed" (v. 51). In 2 Cor 5:1-5 the apostle contrasted our "earthly tent" (the mortal body) with the "building from God, an eternal house in heaven" (the glorified, immortal body). Finally, we cited above the very clear statement of Phil 3:20-21, where Paul wrote that "we eagerly await a Savior from [heaven], the Lord Jesus Christ, who . . . will transform our lowly bodies so that they will be like his glorious body."

We briefly mention the nature of the believer's resurrection body, as it will be discussed in detail in another volume in this series. Paul described the believer's resurrection body via three suggestive images. (a) He asserted that God will raise the believer's "natural body" (*sōma psychikon*) in the form of a "spiritual body" (*sōma pneumatikon*, 1 Cor 15:44). The phrase "spiritual body" suggests not incorporeality but a body transformed and animated by the life-giving Spirit. (b) The present "earthly" body will be transformed into a heavenly body. Paul wrote, "just as we have borne the likeness of the earthly man, so shall we bear the likeness of the man from heaven" (1 Cor 15:49). And (c) the believer's resurrection body "will be like [*symmorphos*] his [i.e., Christ's] glorious body" (Phil 3:21; cf. Rom

8:29; 1 John 3:2). Persons spiritually joined to Christ "will enter into the glory of Christ's risen body and share this glory in their own bodies."[6] At Christ's return to earth, the believer's body will be thoroughly transformed into a qualitatively different kind of body suited for existence in the heavenly world. Precisely what the nature of this body is, Paul does not indicate. He does state that the new body is related to the old as a full grown head of grain is related to the tiny seed (1 Cor 15:35-41). But with this continuity exists discontinuity; our present mortal body will be radically changed into a "spiritual body" like Christ's "glorious body," and "so shall we bear the likeness of the man from heaven."

(2) Clothed with the resurrected body, saints will be free from torment, pain, and death. Rom 8:35 teaches that saints presently experience "trouble," "hardship," "persecution," "famine," "nakedness," "danger," and "sword." According to vv. 17-18, present sufferings (*pathēma*) borne in the name of Christ will give way to indescribable glory. In 2 Cor 4:16-17 he said that at the resurrection all our troubles and pain will appear as "light and momentary." The reward that awaits faithful saints is "an eternal glory that far outweighs them all." John told us that when the saints reach their eternal home, suffering, pain, and heartache will be left behind. God finally "will wipe every tear from their eyes. There will be no more death or mourning or crying or pain, for the old order of things has passed away" (Rev 21:4). The glory of heaven will dry up eyes teared by the sorrows of the fallen world.

Several OT prophecies wonderfully anticipated death's final demise. Isaiah wrote that God "will swallow up death forever. The Sovereign Lord will wipe away the tears from all faces" (Isa 25:8, quoted in part in 1 Cor 15:54; cf. Isa 26:19). Hosea cited a similar promise of the Lord: "I will ransom them from the power of the grave; I will redeem them from death. Where, O death, are your plagues? Where, O grave, is your destruction?" (Hos 13:14, quoted in 1 Cor 15:55). Paul in 1 Cor 15:25-26 asserted that at Christ's second advent death will be destroyed in the lake of fire. Christ "must reign until he has put all his enemies under his feet. The last enemy to be destroyed is death." In vv. 52-56 of this same chapter Paul insisted that because of Christ's resurrection death no longer holds believers under its sway.

Paul further wrote of "our Savior, Christ Jesus, who has destroyed death and has brought life [*zoē*] and immortality [*aphtharsia*] to light through the gospel" (2 Tim 1:10). The aorist of the verb *katargeō* means to "render inoperative" or "annul" (cf. Rom 3:3; 1 Cor 1:28). John wrote that following the Great White Throne judgment, death will be destroyed forever (Rev 20:14). In the new Jerusalem God "will wipe every tear from their eyes. There will be no more death or mourning or crying or pain, for the old order of things has passed away" (Rev 21:4). In the eternal city Christians will enjoy deathless existence in resurrection bodies. The physical, mental, and emotional decline we presently experience will end when we receive new and imperishable capacities in our final triumph over death.

(3) At glorification believers will retain, as distinct and recognizable persons, gender and ethnic characteristics. Jesus did not say we would cease to be male or female when he taught that resurrected people in the life to come would not marry or be given in marriage (Luke 20:35-36). Gender is an intrinsic part of who we are as persons. Male characteristics helped Peter, James, and John identify Moses and Elijah at the Transfiguration (Matt 17:3). Jesus' form and voice in his resurrection appearances were recognizably male. Since female and male souls and bodies are created in God's image, they will be renewed at the re-creation into his image. Our maleness or femaleness will be necessary to our recognition of one another in heaven. As for ethnic qualities, witnesses recognized the resurrected Jesus as the same Jewish person. And non-Jewish people from the East and West will relax for a feast with Abraham, Isaac, and Jacob (Matt 8:11). The God who loves variety in rocks, flowers, and animals will not reduce the saints to an unrecognizable mass. Racial characteristics will be recognizable features of our identities, but our fleshly pride in them will vanish. In heaven we will experience the joy of loving our ethnically different neighbors as ourselves and the bliss of endlessly, multiplying friendships with all our brothers and sisters in Christ.

C. Full Participation
in the Life to Come

(1) The glorification of the saints will mean fully realized citizenship in the heavenly City. Believers presently enjoy a form of dual citizenship. They have a passport issued by Jesus Christ stamped "heaven" (cf. Phil 3:20). But they are also citizens of an earthly domain, with a passport appropriately stamped: in Paul's case Rome (Acts 22:25-29), in our case Canada, India, the U.S., or Nigeria. The saints' glorification means that the earthly pilgrimage, full of dubious loyalties, pitfalls, and perils, finally will come to an end. Abraham was "like a stranger in a foreign country" (Heb 11:9). In Hebrews we further read, "here we do not have an enduring city" (13:14). At our graduation to the heavenly city, we will no longer be "aliens and strangers on earth" (Heb 11:13). Glorification means that the tension between citizenship in the imperfect, temporal world and in the perfect, heavenly world will be permanently resolved in favor of the lat-

ter. It means that we will have graduated to "the city with foundations" (Heb 11:10), even to the heavenly city God has prepared for his faithful ones (v. 16).

Jesus told his followers that he was returning to heaven to usher his people into the Father's house—situated not on earth (John 2:16) but in heaven—to be with him forever (John 14:2-3). In the Apocalypse Jesus said to the church at Philadelphia, "Him who overcomes I will make a pillar in the temple of my God. Never again will he leave it" (Rev 3:12). Jesus added in the same verse that he would write upon the overcomer the name of the Father, the Son, and the new Jerusalem, indicating ownership (contrast the mark of the beast in Rev 13:16). The name of the heavenly city marked upon them connotes irrevocable citizenship in the eternal kingdom. Similarly, in John's description of the new Jerusalem the saints "will see his face, and his name will be on their foreheads" (Rev 22:4). The symbolism suggests that nothing can challenge the saints' safe haven in the city of the great King.

(2) Commencing with the intermediate state, glorified saints will enjoy blessed fellowship with Christ in heaven. Believers experience fellowship with the Savior here and now (John 14:23; 1 John 3:1; Rev 3:20), but due to spiritual sluggishness this fellowship is variable and imperfect. At salvation's consummation our quest for unmediated experience and fellowship with God will be satisfied. Paul testified that he "would prefer to be away from the body and at home with the Lord" (2 Cor 5:8), which presumes a state of glorious fellowship with the Savior. In the Apocalypse John recorded the heavenly voice that said, "Now the dwelling of God is with men, and he will live with them. They will be his people, and God himself will be with them and be their God" (Rev 21:3). The tabernacle of God residing with humans describes God's glorious presence in fellowship with his people. This experience in the new Jerusalem will involve direct and unspoiled communion with Christ through the endless ages of eternity.

(3) Glorified saints will engage in perfected and perpetual worship of God and the Lamb. Israel worshiped in the tabernacle and later in the Jerusalem temple. In his vision of glorified existence in the new Jerusalem, John wrote, "I did not see a temple in the city, because the Lord God Almighty and the Lamb are its temple" (Rev 21:22). In the heavenly city there will be no temple (cf. Ezekiel 40–48), no building for worship, and no priestly ministrations. In the new Jerusalem the saints' approach to God will be direct, their worship immediate, and their communion unbroken. John added that "The throne of God and of the Lamb will be in the city, and his servants will serve him" (Rev 22:3). In glory the redeemed, including the twenty-four elders (4:10-11; 5:8-10; 11:16-18) and those

who conquered the beast (15:2-4), will join "angels" (5:11-12, 14; 7:11-12) and the "four living creatures" (4:6-9; 5:8-10, 14; 7:11-12) in endless worship of the Lord God and the Lamb. "All that the human tongue has not been able to say or sing in *this* life shall be gloriously overcome in *that* life and we shall praise him as he ought to be praised."[7]

(4) Glorification will also mean sharing in Messiah's royal reign and serving his kingdom purposes. In the future believers will face the glorious prospect of reigning with Christ and serving him in the millennial kingdom. This appears to be the sense of Matt 19:28 (cf. Luke 22:30), where Jesus said to his disciples, "at the renewal [*palingennesia*] of all things, when the Son of Man sits on his glorious throne, you who have followed me will also sit on twelve thrones, judging [*krinontes*] the twelve tribes of Israel." Likewise, Paul's words in 1 Cor 6:2: "Do you not know that the saints will judge [*krinousin*] the world?" More glorious still will be the saints' everlasting reign and service to Christ in the eternal state. In a great vision of the end John wrote of saints who came through the great tribulation: "they are before the throne of God and serve him day and night in his temple" (Rev 7:15). This temple service of adoration and praise will not be restricted to the tribe of Levi, but will be shared by all the faithful in heaven. Finally, in the closing snapshot of the new Jerusalem we read that "The throne of God and of the Lamb will be in the city, and his servants will serve him" (Rev 22:3). Two verses later John added the final words, "And they will reign for ever and ever" (v. 5).

Finally, (5) Glorified saints will experience the great joy of fellowship with ethnically diverse believers of all centuries. Jesus' words, "In my Father's house are many *rooms*" (John 14:2) stimulates the imagination to think of a Christian resort where the guests enjoy sweet fellowship with one another. In Jesus' teaching, however, the holiday will never end; the saints' dwelling in the Father's house will be permanent. NT teaching about the heavenly feast and the wedding supper of the Lamb (Matt 8:11; 22:1-14; Luke 22:30; Rev 19:9) portray the joys of the coming kingdom. The shared meal at table implies celebration and fellowship between the people of God of all ages. Heb 12:22-23 points to the perfected fellowship of saints in glory. Verse 22 describes myriads of angels in community in heaven. And verses 22b-23a read, "you have come . . . to the church of the firstborn [*prōtotokoi*], whose names are written in heaven." Those in view are believers in community reigning with Christ in heaven. In glory we will enjoy the presence of departed loved ones, great biblical heroes such as Abraham, Moses, and Paul, and spiritual giants of the church such as Augustine, Luther, and Wesley. Our beatific vision of God in heaven will not exclude the blessed communion of the saints.

IV. Practical Implications
of Glorification

The reality of the glorious future of God's children offers practical motivation for the living of the Christian life. (1) The reality of heavenly glory should motivate all persons to be certain of their relationship to Jesus Christ. Those who do not know Christ must understand that their eternal destiny is based on decisions made in this life. In the parable of the ten virgins Jesus taught that upon his return to glorify his saints, the door to heaven will be permanently shut (Matt 25:10-12). We should emulate the five wise virgins who were prepared and watching for the Lord's coming, not the five foolish maidens who were unprepared and thus excluded from the wedding banquet. C.S. Lewis reminded us that "There are only two kinds of people in the end: those who say to God, 'Thy will be done,' and those to whom God says, in the end, '*thy* will be done.'"[8] If you are unsure of your relationship to Christ, search your heart and resolve to trust Christ for eternal life.

(2) The prospect of future glorification should stimulate Christians to live holy lives. Peter presented the ethical implications of the future day of the Lord as a challenge to his readers: "the day of the Lord will come like a thief. The heavens will disappear with a roar; the elements will be destroyed by fire, and the earth and everything in it will be laid bare. Since everything will be destroyed in this way, what kind of people ought you to be? You ought to live holy and godly lives as you look forward to the day of God and speed its coming" (2 Pet 3:10-12a). Peter continued, "So then, dear friends, since you are looking forward to this, make every effort to be found spotless, blameless and at peace with him" (v. 14). In 2 Cor 6:16b, 17b, 18 Paul cited several promises of God, adding, "Since we have these promises, dear friends, let us purify ourselves from everything that contaminates body and spirit, perfecting holiness out of reverence for God" (2 Cor 7:1). Pilgrim saints must cleanse themselves from sins of the body (e.g., drunkenness, fornication) and sins of the spirit (e.g., pride, envy, malice). John identified the Christian's hope as Jesus' future appearing and our being made like him (1 John 2:28; 3:2). He then added, "Everyone who has this hope in him purifies himself, just as he is pure" (3:3). Christians who anticipate the coming glory must renounce everything that defiles body and spirit. As we anticipate the future glory, we recall the words of Jesus who said, "Blessed are the pure in heart, for they will see God" (Matt 5:8).

(3) The hope of future glory should fortify believers to face the end of all things with confidence. Even though people are living longer lives today,

the end is not far off, either by reason of death or the Lord's coming. Christians facing the end of all things need not despair as do the masses who have no hope. Believers face the future with glowing confidence by virtue of their Lord's victory as he faced his personal end. The human body may die physically, but it need not die spiritually. Even physical death will not have the last word, for like Christ we will rise from death's cold grip at the *Parousia* (1 Cor 15:42-44; Rev 20:4). Saints of God enjoy the good of eternal life here and now (John 3:16; 10:28; Rom 6:23; 8:1).

Disciples take courage in the fact that they will face God not as a stern judge but as a loving Father who has forgiven them. Those who have trusted Christ will never face the curse of condemnation (Rom 8:1, 34), either in this life or in the life to come. We recall Paul's words to Timothy: "God's solid foundation stands firm, sealed with this inscription: 'The Lord knows those who are his'" (2 Tim 2:19). Strengthen assurance and fortify hope by recalling that your names are written in the heavenly book of life (Luke 10:20; Rev 21:27). And in the case of sins committed as a Christian, we should judge them, repent of them, and make appropriate restitution. As Paul wrote, "if we judged ourselves, we would not come under judgment" (1 Cor 11:31). In this way our consciences will remain clear and our hope of future glory bright.

Christians are further encouraged by the realization that their departure from this world either by death or by rapture represents a portal into the presence of Christ (Acts 7:59; Phil 1:21-23; 1 Thess 5:10). Heaven is the Christian's home, and our highest and noblest fulfillment will occur there. Believers should enjoy pleasant moments now, anticipating the joys of their heavenly home. Such anticipation of eternal glory will greatly fortify Christian hope in a bleak world. In a moment of lofty contemplation Paul rehearsed the great OT prophetic hope: "No eye has seen, no ear has heard, no mind has conceived what God has prepared for those who love him" (1 Cor 2:9). Amen!

C H A P T E R   I

1. I. Howard Marshall, "Salvation," , *NDT* p. 610.
2. Blaise Pascal, *Pensees* (New York: Penguin, 1966), no. 131, p. 64.
3. Joseph Alleine, quoted in *The Golden Treasury of Puritan Quotations*, comp. I.D.E. Thomas (Chicago: Moody, 1975), p. 266.
4. Dietrich Bonhoeffer, *Ethics* (New York: Macmillan, 1965), p. 110.
5. As observed by Thomas Brooks, cited in *Puritan Quotations*, p. 137.
6. Thomas Watson, in *Puritan Quotations*, p. 137.
7. James Denney, in *Studies in Theology* (London: Hodder and Stoughton, 1904), p. 255, cited Jesus' teaching in Matt 25:30, 41, 46 concerning "the broad way which leads to destruction," "the outer darkness," "the worm that dies not," "the fire that is not quenched," and "the everlasting punishment." Denney added, "The ideas which seem to me to comprehend all that is of faith on the subject are those of separation and finality. There is such a thing as being excluded from fellowship with God and with good spirits; there is such a thing as final exclusion."
8. David F. Wells, *The Search for Salvation* (Downers Grove, Ill.: InterVarsity, 1978), p. 14.
9. M.M. Thomas, "The Meaning of Salvation Today," *International Review of Missions*, LXII, 246 (April 1973): 162. See also his book, *Salvation and Humanization* (Bangalore: CISRS, 1971).
10. Donald Bloesch, *Christian Life and Salvation* (Grand Rapids: Eerdmans, 1967), p. 148, n. 19, observes that "In Barth's thinking salvation takes place not in man but in Christ who represents man. What takes place in man is the effect of salvation."
11. John Murray, *Redemption Accomplished and Applied* (Grand Rapids: Eerdmans, 1955), p. 80.
12. F.G.L. Van Der Meer, *The Faith of the Church* (London: Darton, Longman & Todd, 1966), p. 367.
13. Ibid., p. 391.
14. Ibid., p. 434.
15. For example, Anthony A. Hoekema, *Saved by Grace* (Grand Rapids: Eerdmans, 1989), p. 17-19.
16. D.M. Lloyd-Jones, *God's Ultimate Purpose: An Exposition of Eph 1:1-23* (Grand Rapids: Baker, 1978), p. 53.

C H A P T E R   2

1. Pelagius, cited by Augustine, *Retractations*, 22.1.
2. Pelagius, cited by Augustine in *The Grace of Christ*, 33.
3. Pelagius, "Defense of the Freedom of the Will," I, cited by Augustine, *The Grace of Christ*, 29.
4. George B. Foster, "The Contribution of Critical Scholarship to Ministerial Efficiency," in George B. Smith, ed., *A Guide to the Study of the Christian Religion* (Chicago: University of Chicago Press, 1916), p. 736.
5. Norman Pittenger, *Becoming and Belonging* (Wilton, Conn: Morehouse, 1989), p. 38. Pittenger urges that we must not speak pessimistically of humans as "lost souls."
6. Norman Pittenger, *Freed to Love: A Process Interpretation of Redemption* (Wilton, Conn.: Morehouse-Barlow, 1987), p. 83.
7. Norman Pittenger, *Process Thought and the Christian Faith* (New York: Macmillan, 1968), p. 47. Pittenger adds, *Abounding Grace* (London & Oxford: Mowbray, 1981), p. 23: "He does his work . . . by eliciting from them their own free response, as they answer to the lures, persuasions, invitations, and solicitations which press in upon them; and he asks them to decide for the right things in the right way."
8. Hilary of Potiers, cited in W.T. Whitley, ed., *The Doctrine of Grace* (New York: Macmillan, 1931), p. 111.

9. Augustine, *Predestination of the Saints*, 8, 38. Augustine strove to correct the views of the Semi-Pelagians in his essays "The Predestination of the Saints" and "The Gift of Perseverance."

10. John Cassian, *Conferences*, 13.8 (*NPNF*, 11:426). Cf. ibid., 13.7 (*NPNF*, 11:425): "when His goodness sees in us even the very smallest spark of good will shining forth . . . He fans and fosters it and nurses it with His breath." Cf. ibid., 13.11 (*NPNF*, 11:428).

11. John Cassian, *Institutes*, 12.14 (*NPNF*, 11:283).

12. John Cassian, *Conferences*, 21.6 (*NPNF*, 11:505).

13. Duns Scotus, cited by Luther, *Works*, 26:128.

14. Council of Trent, Session VI, chap. 1; cf. Session VI, canon 5.

15. Council of Trent, Session VI, chap. 5.

16. Council of Trent, Session VI, canon 24.

17. Council of Trent, Session VI, chap. 16. Cf. Trent, Session VI, chap. 10 and canon 32.

18. See William G. MacDonald, ". . . The Spirit of Grace," in Clark H. Pinnock, ed., *Grace Unlimited* (Minneapolis: Bethany Fellowship, 1975), pp. 77-80.

19. Harold B. Kuhn, "Wesleyanism," *BDT*, p. 546.

20. R.W.A. Letham, "Arminianism," *NDT*, p. 46.

21. James Arminius, "Declaration of Sentiments," *The Works of James Arminius*, trans. James and William Nichols, 3 vols. (Grand Rapids: Baker, reprint, 1986), 1:659.

22. Arminius, *Works*, 2:700.

23. Arminius added, *Works*, 1:664: "I believe that many persons resist the Holy Spirit and reject the grace that is offered."

24. John Wesley, "Working Out Your Own Salvation," *Works*, 6:509 [1872 edn.].

25. Wesley, "On Conscience," *Works*, 7:187. [1872 edn.]. Cf. "Sermon 43," *Works: Sermons*, 2:156 [new edn.].

26 Wesley, "Working Out Our Salvation," *Works*, 6:513 [1872 edn.].

27. Ibid., 6:509 [1872 edn.].

28. John Wesley, "What Is an Arminian?" *Works*, 10:360 [1872 edn.].

29. John Wesley, "Free Grace," *Works*, 7:373 [1872 edn.].

30. Wesley, *Letters*, 2:118. Cf. 6:214; 7:168 [new edn.].

31. Richard Watson, *Theological Institutes*, 2 vols. (New York: Lane & Scott, 1851), 2:447.

32. Ibid., 2:377.

33. Ibid., 2:445.

34. Karl Barth, *CD*, vol. II/1, p. 152.

35. Karl Barth, *God, Grace and the Gospel*, trans. James S. McNab (Edinburgh and London: Oliver and Boyd, 1959), p. 6. Cf. ibid., pp. 7-8, 24-25.

36. Barth, *CD*, vol. II/2, p. 94.

37. Ibid., vol. IV/1, p. 80.

38. Ibid., vol. III/1, p. 44.

39. Karl Barth, *The Knowledge of God and the Service of God*, trans. J.L.M. Haire and Ian Henderson (New York: Charles Scribner's Sons, 1939), p. 75. Cf. Karl Barth, "No!" in Emil Brunner, *Natural Theology* (London: Geoffrey Bles, 1946), pp. 75, 83, 85.

40. Barth, *CD*, vol. IV/1, p. 743.

41. Ibid., vol. II/2, p. 19.

42. Ibid., vol. II/2, p. 11.

43. Ibid.

44. Ibid., vol. II/1, p. 355.

45. Barth, *KD*, vol. II/2, p. 555. It is this sense that G.C. Berkouwer, *The Triumph of Grace in the Theology of Karl Barth* (Grand Rapids, Mich.: Eerdmans, 1956), described the triumph of divine grace in Barth's theology.

46. Barth, *CD*, vol. I/2, p. 314.

47. Ibid., vol. I/2, pp. 299-300.

48. Ibid., vol. I/2, p. 302.

49. Ibid., vol. I/2, p. 280; cf. ibid., p. 345.

50. Karl Rahner, "Controversial Theology on Justification," *TI*, 4:216-18.

51. Rahner, "Ideology and Christianity," *TI*, 6:51. Cf. TI, 9:36; 16:40.

52. Rahner, "The Works of Mercy and Their Reward," *TI*, 7:273.

53. Rahner, "History of the World and Salvation-History," *TI*, 5:98-99.

54. Rahner, "On Truthfulness," *TI*, 7:254.
55. Rahner, "Nature and Grace," *TI*, 4:183.
56. Rahner, "The Universality of Salvation," *TI*, 16:206.
57. Rahner, "Church, Churches and Religions," *TI*, 10:36.
58. Rahner, "Philosophy and Theology," *TI*, 6:79.
59. Karl Rahner, *Foundations of the Christian Faith* (New York: Seabury, 1978), p. 143.
60. Leonardo Boff, *Liberating Grace* (Maryknoll, N.Y.: Orbis, 1979), p. 4; cf. p. 116.
61. Ibid., p. 89.
62. Ibid., p. 120; cf. p. 119.
63. *Pastoral Constitution on the Church in the Modern World*, I.17. [in Austin P. Flannery, ed., *Documents of Vatican II* (Grand Rapids, Mich.: Eerdmans, 1975), p. 917].
64. *Declaration on the Relation of the Church to Non-Christian Religions*, 2 [in Flannery, p. 739].
65. *Dogmatic Constitution on the Church*, II.16 [in Flannery, pp. 367-368]. Cf. *Decree on the Church's Missionary Activity*, 1.7 [in Flannery, p. 821].
66. *Dogmatic Constitution on the Church*, II.13 [in Flannery, p. 365]. Cf. *Decree on the Church's Missionary Activity*, I.7 [in Flannery, p. 821].
67. Augustine, *City of God*, 21.4; 22.24.
68. Augustine, *Admonition and Grace*, 11.
69. Ibid., 8. Cf. Augustine, *The Spirit and the Letter*, 52: "grace breaks the will whereby righteousness may be freely loved."
70. Augustine, *Admonition and Grace*, 3.
71. Augustine, *Retractations*, 68.
72. Augustine, *The Grace of Christ*, 25.
73. Augustine, *Against Two Letters of the Pelagians*, 15.
74. Augustine, *Confessions*, 10.29.
75. Augustine, *Grace and Free Will*, 43.
76. Ibid. Cf. Augustine, *Letter*, 215; *Admonition and Grace*, 45.
77. Augustine, *Grace and Free Will*, 44.
78. Augustine, *Nature and Grace*, 35.
79. Augustine, *Grace and Free Will*, 33.
80. Martin Luther, *What Luther Says*, in Ewald M. Plass, ed. (St. Louis: Concordia, 1959), p. 613.
81. *What Luther Says*, p. 1444. Cf. "in a man devoid of the Spirit there is nothing left that man can turn toward the good, but only toward evil." *The Bondage of the Will*, in Timothy F. Lull, ed., *Martin Luther's Basic Theological Writings* (Minneapolis: Fortress, 1989), p. 224.
82. *What Luther Says*, p. 603. Cf. "Against Latomus," *Works*, 32:227: "I take grace in the proper sense of the favor of God—not a quality of the soul."
83. *What Luther Says*, pp. 611-612.
84. Martin Luther, *Disputation Against Scholastic Theology*, 29, in Lull, *Basic Theological Writings*, p. 15.
85. Martin Luther, *Bondage of the Will*, in Lull, *Basic Theological Writings*, pp. 207-208.
86. Luther, "Lectures on Galatians," *Works*, 26:126.
87. Martin Luther, *Heidelberg Disputation*, 26.
88. *What Luther Says*, p. 604.
89. Martin Luther, *Bondage of the Will*, in Lull, *Basic Theological Writings*, pp. 212-13.
90. John Calvin, *Institutes of the Christian Religion*, II.2.18.
91. Ibid., II.2.17; II.4.1.
92. Ibid., II.2.16.
93. Ibid., III.14.2.
94. Ibid., III.14.5.
95. Ibid., II.3.6.
96. John Calvin, *CR*, 50, 22. Cf. *Institutes*, II.17.1.
97. Charles Haddon Spurgeon, "Sin and Grace," *SEE*, 8:208.
98. Spurgeon, "The Exceeding Riches of Grace," *SEE*, 8:281.
99. Ibid., 8:282.
100. Spurgeon, "Grace for Grace," *Metropolitan Tabernacle Pulpit*, 35:291.

101. H.-H. Esser, "Grace, Spiritual Gifts," *NIDNTT*, 2:116.
102. Ibid., 2:117.
103. W. Zimmerli, "charis," *TDNTAbr*, p. 1302.
104. Esser, *NIDNTT*, 2:115.
105. William Manson, "Grace in the New Testament," in William T. Whitley, ed., *The Doctrine of Grace* (New York: Macmillan, 1932), p. 33, wrote: "In classical Greek, *charis* meant personal charm, a kindness, gratitude, but had no religious connection."
106. Esser, *NIDNTT*, 2:115.
107. Calvin, *Institutes*, II.1.5.
108. Luther, *LW*, 1:66.
109. Augustine, *The Spirit and the Letter*, 5.
110. See Frank Vandenberg, *Abraham Kuyper* (Grand Rapids, Mich.: Eerdmans, 1960), p. 207. Cf. Charles Hodge, *Systematic Theology*, 3 vols. (Grand Rapids, Mich.: Eerdmans, reprint, 1973), 2:667.
111. Esser, *NIDNTT*, 2:119.
112. Elmer A. Martens, *God's Design: A Focus on Old Testament Theology* (Grand Rapids, Mich.: Baker, 1981), p. 222.
113. *NIV Study Bible*, p. 1621. Cf. F.F. Bruce, *The Gospel of John* (Grand Rapids, Mich.: Eerdmans, 1983), pp. 267-68.
114. According to F. Büchsel, "*Elencho*," *TDNT*, 2:473-474, *elencho* means "to show people their sins and summon them to repentance." Cf. Alfred Plummer, *The Gospel According to St. John* (Grand Rapids, Mich.: Baker, reprint), p. 292.
115. Ernest F. Kevan, *Salvation* (Grand Rapids, Mich.: Baker, 1963), p. 72.
116. Donald G. Bloesch, *Essentials of Evangelical Theology*, 2 vols. (New York: Harper & Row, 1978-79), 1:205.
117. James A. Carpenter, *Nature and Grace* (New York: Crossroad, 1988), p. 171. Norman Pittenger, *Abounding Grace* (London & Oxford: Mobray, 1981), p. 35, adds: "God's graciousness is so 'abounding,' that it can bring within its range all of his children, even (and perhaps especially) those whom in our sin and self-centeredness we might wish to reject or condemn."
118. Tite Tienou, "Eternity in Their Hearts?" in *Through No Fault of Their Own?*, eds. William V. Crocket and James G. Sigountos (Grand Rapids, Mich.: Baker, 1991), p. 212.
119. Gordon Lewis and Bruce Demarest, *Integrative Theology*, 3 vols. (Grand Rapids, Mich.: Zondervan, 1987-94), 1:72-76.
120. J.I. Packer, "Are Non-Christian Faiths Ways of Salvation?" *BibSac* 130/518 (Apr.-June 1973):115-16. Cf. Aida Besaçnon Spencer, "Romans 1: Finding God in Creation," in *Through No Fault of Their Own*, pp. 131-35.
121. Carl F.H. Henry, "Is It Fair?" in *Through No Fault of Their Own?*, p. 248. Cf. Gleason L. Archer, *Encyclopedia of Bible Difficulties* (Grand Rapids, Mich.: Zondervan, 1982), pp. 386-87.
122. Karl Rahner, "Christianity and the Non-Christian Religions," *TI*, 5:123.
123. Karl Rahner, "Observations on the Problem of the 'Anonymous Christian,'" *TI*, 14:283.
124. Clark Pinnock, "The Finality of Jesus Christ in a World of Religions," in M. Noll and D. Wells, eds., *Christian Faith and Practice in the Modern World* (Grand Rapids, Mich.: Eerdmans, 1988), p. 161. Cf. Pinnock, "Toward an Evangelical Theology of Religions," *JETS* 33.3 (Sept. 1990):364, 366.
125. Spurgeon, "Salvation All of Grace," *SEE*, 8:265.
126. W.H. Griffith-Thomas, *The Principles of Theology* (London: Church Book Room Press, 1945), p. 181.

CHAPTER 3

1. Karl Barth, *CD*, vol. II/2, p. 3.
2. Paul K. Jewett, *Election and Predestination* (Grand Rapids, Mich.: Eerdmans, 1985), p. 67.
3. Origen, *Commentary on the Epistle to the Romans*, 1.
4. Origen, *On First Principles*, III.1.20.
5. Chrysostom, cited by John Calvin, *Institutes of the Christian Religion*, II.2.4.
6. John Calvin, *Institutes*, II.2.4.

7. John Cassian, *The Conferences*, 13.7 (*NPNF*, 11:425).
8. A. J. Maas, "Salvation," *The Catholic Encyclopedia*, 16 vols. (New York: Encyclopedia Press, 1913), 13:408.
9. J. Pohle, "Predestination." ibid., 12:380.
10. Ross E. Price, "Elect, Election," *BDT*, p. 182.
11. R. Larry Shelton, "Initial Salvation," in Charles W. Carter, ed., *A Contemporary Wesleyan Theology*, 2 vols. (Grand Rapids, Mich.: Zondervan/Francis Asbury, 1983), 1:485.
12. *The Works of James Arminius*; 3 vols. (Auburn and Buffalo: Derby, Miller and Orton, 1853), 1:247.
13. Ibid., 1:248.
14. Cited by V.H.H. Green, *John Wesley* (London: Thomas Nelson, 1964), pp. 114, 116.
15. John Wesley, "Predestination Calmly Considered," *The Works of John Wesley*, 14 vols. (Grand Rapids, Mich.: Zondervan, reprint, 1958), 10:207.
16. Wesley, "Free Grace," *Works*, 7:376.
17. Wesley, "Predestination Calmly Considered," *Works*, 10:209-10.
18. Charles G. Finney, *Lectures on Systematic Theology* (Whittier, Calif.: Colporter Kemp, 1944), p. 494. In *Finney's Systematic Theology* (Minneapolis: Bethany Fellowship, 1976), p. 429, Finney explained election in terms of "those chosen by God who have fulfilled the requirements of salvation and are now in a right relationship with God and fellowman. (It is not an unconditional predestined choosing by God for salvation.)"
19. Alan Richardson, *An Introduction to the Theology of the New Testament* (New York: Harper & Row, 1958), p. 277.
20. Ibid., p. 279.
21. Ibid.
22. Ibid., p. 272.
23. Ibid., p. 275.
24. Ibid., p. 358. Richardson, ibid., adds: "When the head of the family, or the parents of the children, are baptized, something happens to the children; they are no longer pagans, outside the fellowship of the Spirit."
25. Roger T. Forster and V. Paul Marston, *God's Strategy in Human History* (Wheaton, Ill.: Tyndale House, 1974).
26. Ibid., p. 145.
27. Ibid., p. 136.
28. Ibid., p. 131.
29. William W. Klein, *The New People of God: A Corporate View of Election* (Grand Rapids, Mich.: Zondervan, Academie, 1990), p. 19. Klein, ibid., p. 122, concedes that his explanation of election is more like the Arminian than the Reformed view.
30. Ibid., p. 259.
31. Ibid., p. 123.
32. Ibid., p. 185.
33. Quoted by Arthur C. Custance, *The Sovereignty of Grace* (Phillipsburg, N.J.: Presbyterian & Reformed, 1979), p. 37.
34. Ulrich Zwingli, *Commentary on True and False Religion*, Samual M. Jackson, ed. (Durham, N.C.: Labyrinth Press, 1981), p. 272.
35. Ulrich Zwingli, *On Providence and Other Essays* (Durham, N.C.: Labyrinth Press, 1983), p. 185. Cf. ibid., p. 200: election "is so absolutely free that no account is taken in it of our works or merits."
36. Quoted by W.P. Stephens, *The Theology of Huldreich Zwingli* (Oxford: Clarendon, 1986), p. 99.
37. Martin Luther, *What Luther Says*, in Ewald M. Plass, ed. (St. Louis: Concordia, 1959), p. 456.
38. Quoted by Harry Buis, *Historic Protestantism and Predestination* (Philadelphia: Presbyterian & Reformed, 1985), p. 47.
39. Martin Luther, "The Bondage of the Will," *LW*, 33:146.
40. Luther, "Romans," *LW*, 25:83.
41. Calvin, *Institutes*, III.21.5.
42. John Calvin, *Commentaries on the Epistle of Paul to the Romans*, p. 345.
43. Ibid., p. 317. Cf. Calvin, *Institutes*, III.22.1-9.

44. Calvin, *Institutes*, III.23.1.
45. Ibid., III.23.6. Cf. III.24.12: the reprobate God "created for dishonor in life and destruction in death, to become the instruments of his wrath and examples of his severity."
46. Ibid., III.23.1.
47. Theodore Beza, *Quaestiones et responsiones* (Geneva, 1570), p. 107; cited by John S. Bray, *Theodore Beza's Doctrine of Predestination* (Nieuwkoop: De Graf, 1975), p. 88.
48. Beza, *Quaestiones*, p. 107; cited in Bray, p. 88
49. Theodore Beza, *Novum Testamentum*, on 2 Tim 1:9; cited by Bray, 88.
50. John Bunyan, *The Works of John Bunyan*, 3 vols. (Glasgow, Edinburgh & London: Blackie, 1862), 2:337.
51. Ibid., 2:336.
52. Ibid., 2:341.
53. Ibid., 2:342.
54. Karl Barth, *CD*, vol. II/ 2, p. 3. Cf. ibid., p. 103: "In its simplest and most comprehensive form the dogma of predestination consists, then, in the assertion that the divine predestination is the election of Jesus Christ. . . . Jesus Christ is the electing God, and . . . also elected man."
55. Ibid., p. 94; cf. ibid., p. 54.
56. Ibid., p. 117; cf. ibid., p. 167.
57. Ibid., p. 167. Cf. ibid., p. 117: "God has ascribed to man . . . election, salvation, and life; and to Himself He has ascribed reprobation, perdition, and death."
58. Ibid., p. 306.
59. Ibid., Cf. ibid., p. 322: "in Jesus Christ his rejection, too, is rejected, and his election is consummated."
60. Barth's Swiss compatriot Emil Brunner, *Christian Doctrine of God: Dogmatics: Vol. I*, trans. Olive Wyon (Philadelphia: Westminster, 1950), p. 348, commented that Barth went much further than Origen and his followers in positing universalism. "None of them ever dared to maintain that through Jesus Christ, all, believers and unbelievers, are saved from the wrath of God and participate in redemption through Jesus Christ. But that is what Karl Barth teaches. . . . Not only for those who are 'in Him' through faith, but for all men, Hell has been blotted out, condemnation and judgment eliminated."
61. Wolfhart Pannenberg, *Human Nature, Election, and History* (Philadelphia: Westminster, 1977), p. 59.
62. Ibid., p. 31; cf. ibid., p. 99.
63. Ibid., p. 25.
64. Brunner, *Christian Doctrine of God*, p. 340. Concurring in this judgment is the evangelical scholar Alister E. McGrath, *Iustitia Dei: A History of the Christian Doctrine of Justification*, 2 vols. (Cambridge: CUP, 1986), 1:128: The primary concern of the early Christian writers "appears to have been the defense of what they understood to be an authentically Christian understanding of free will in the face of astral fatalisms, such as Gnosticism. The confusion between the concepts of predestination and fatalism or determinism unquestionably served to lessen patristic interest in the idea of divine predestination, with the inevitable result that the early patristic period is characterized by a theological optimism quite out of character with the Pauline corpus of the New Testament."
65. Thomas F. Torrance, *The Doctrine of Grace in the Apostolic Fathers* (Grand Rapids, Mich.: Eerdmans, 1959), p. 136.
66. Ibid.
67. Tertullian, *On the Soul*, 39.4.
68. Athanasius, *Discourse Against the Arians*, 2.75-76.
69. Ambrose, *Exposition of the Gospel of Luke*, 7.27.
70. Brunner, *Christian Doctrine of God*, p. 325.
71. Augustine, *Admonition and Grace*, 8.17. Cf. *The Spirit and the Letter*, 52: "grace breaks the will whereby righteousness may be freely loved."
72. Augustine, *Confessions*, 10.29.40.
73. Augustine, *Against Julian*, 6.2.5. Cf. *Predestination of the Saints*, 37: "God chose us in Christ before the foundation of the world, predestinating us to adoption of children, not because we were going to be of ourselves holy and immaculate, but he chose and predestined us that we might be so." The bishop speculated that God predestined to salvation persons equal in

number to the fallen angels, thus ensuring that the inhabitants of the heavenly city would be at least as great as in the beginning.

74. Augustine, *On the Gift of Perseverance*, 16. Cf. ibid., 28: "By giving to some what they do not deserve, He has willed that his grace should be gratuitous, and thus genuine grace. By not giving to all, He has shown what all deserve."
75. Augustine, *On the Gift of Perseverance*, 41.
76. Augustine, *On the Gospel of St. John*, 86.2.
77. Ibid.
78. Thomas Aquinas, *ST*, I-I, q. 19, art. 12.
79. Thomas Aquinas, *SCG*, III/2.163.1.
80. Aquinas, *ST*, I-I, q. 23, art. 5.
81. Ibid., I-I, q. 23, art. 8.
82. Ibid., I-I, q. 23, art. 3.
83. John Gill, *The Cause of God and Truth* (Grand Rapids, Mich.: Baker, reprint, 1980), p. 85.
84. Charles Haddon Spurgeon, "God's Will and Man's Will," *The Metropolitan Tabernacle Pulpit*, 63 vols. (Pasadena, Tex.: Pilgrim Publications, 1969-80), 8:183. Cf. ibid., 8:189: "every blessing we receive hangs upon the absolute will and counsel of God, who gives these mercies even as he gives the gifts of the Spirit according as he wills."
85. Spurgeon, "Grace Abounding," ibid., 10:172.
86. Spurgeon, "Election," ibid., 1:319.
87. Augustus H. Strong, *Systematic Theology* (Valley Forge, Penn.: Judson, 1907), p. 779.
88. Ibid., p. 785.
89. John N. Oswalt, "*bāḥar*," *TWOT*, 1:100.
90. Lewis Smedes, *Union with Christ* (Grand Rapids, Mich.: Eerdmans, 1983), p. 87.
91. Payne, *Theology of the Older Testament*, p. 179, observed: "To 'know' carries the idea of electing grace and is equivalent to saying 'choose' (cf. Exod 1:8; 33:12; Hos 13:5; Amos 3:2; Rom 8:29)." E. D. Schmitz, "Knowledge," *NIDNTT*, 2:400, concluded that *yāda'* in this sense signifies "God's loving, electing knowledge of men." The latter, ibid., p. 385, added: "When God knows a person (Jer 1:5) or a people (Amos 3:2) he chooses or elects him. This knowledge, understood as election, is gracious and loving, but it demands a personal response." D. A. Carson, *Divine Sovereignty and Human Responsibility* (Atlanta: John Knox, 1981), p. 4, concurs that *yāda'* here speaks the language of election.
92. Paul K. Jewett, *Election and Predestination* (Grand Rapids, Mich.: Eerdmans, 1985), p. 118.
93. See *The NIV Study Bible*, Kenneth Barker, ed. (Grand Rapids, Mich.: Zondervan, 1985), p. 1719, note on Rom. 9:13. Cf. Howard F. Vos, *Genesis* (Chicago: Moody, 1982), p. 97: "Romans 9:10-12 makes it clear that God's sovereign choice was involved, a choice that had nothing to do with the relative merits of the twins, because the decision had been made before their birth."
94. Allen P. Ross, *Creation and Blessing* (Grand Rapids, Mich.: Baker, 1988), p. 439. Cf. Meredith G. Kline, "Genesis," *NBCRev*, p. 101: "By divine pre-appointment a place in the Abraham-Isaac succession was conferred on the younger of the struggling twins."
95. Walter C. Kaiser, Jr., *Toward an Old Testament Theology* (Grand Rapids, Mich.: Zondervan, 1978), p. 194.
96. Jewett, *Election and Predestination*, p. 31, note 1.
97. Th. C. Vriezen, *An Outline of Old Testament Theology* (Wageningen: Veenman & Zonen, 1960), p. 167, comments: "The Hebrew word for 'to hate' often means to scorn, or to rank something lower than something else, while 'to love' may mean to choose something and rank it higher than something else."
98. Ralph L. Smith, *Micah-Malachi*, WBC (Waco, Tex.: Word, 1984), p. 305. So also Joyce G. Baldwin, *Haggai, Zechariah, Malachi*, TOTC (London: Tyndale, 1972), pp. 222-23.
99. *The NIV Study Bible* note to Mal 1:3, p. 1425, reads as follows: "If Israel doubts God's covenant love, she should consider the contrast between God's ways with her and his ways with Jacob's brother Esau (Edom). Paul explains God's love for Jacob and hatred for Esau on the basis of election (Ro 9:10-13). God chose Jacob but not Esau."
100. John D. W. Watts, *Isaiah 1–33*, WBC (Waco, Tex.: Word, 1985), pp. 153-154.
101. Payne, *Theology of the Older Testament*, pp. 186-187, argues as follows. "Fundamentally, the saved status of this remnant group was due to their individual election . . . for our Lord

Himself spoke of them saying, 'Behold, I and the children whom Yahweh hath given Me' (Isa 8:18)."

102. Jewett, *Election and Predestination*, p. 48.

103. Joseph Addison Alexander, *The Gospel According to Matthew* (Grand Rapids, Mich.: Baker, reprint, 1980), p. 319. Cf. H. Bietenhard, "Please," *NIDNTT*, 2:819.

104. See J. Ramsey Michaels, *John, Good News Commentary* (San Francisco: Harper & Row, 1984), p. 233.

105. See the discussion by R. Tuente, "Lamb, Sheep," *NIDNTT*, 2:413.

106. George R. Beasley-Murray, *John, WBC* (Waco, Tex.: Word, 1987), p. 298. Carson, *Divine Sovereignty and Human Responsibility*, p. 188, observes in John 17 a "heavy emphasis on soteriological predestination."

107. Carson, *Divine Sovereignty and Human Responsibility*, p. 192.

108. F.F. Bruce, *The Acts of the Apostles* (Grand Rapids, Mich.: Eerdmans, 1952), p. 275.

109. Agreeing with this judgment, among others, are Donald Guthrie, *New Testament Theology* (Downers Grove, Ill: InterVarsity, 1981), p. 618, and J.I. Packer, "Determine," *NIDNTT*, 1:476.

110. Leon Morris, *New Testament Theology* (Grand Rapids, Mich.: Zondervan, Academie Books, 1986), p. 154.

111. P. Jacobs and H. Krienke, "Foreknowledge, Providence, Predestination," *NIDNTT*, 1:693.

112. John Murray, *The Epistle to the Romans*, NICNT, 2 vols. (Grand Rapids, Mich.: Eerdmans, 1959-65), 1:317.

113. So argues the respected exegetical scholar C.E.B. Cranfield, *The Epistle to the Romans*, ICC, 2 vols. (Edinburgh: T. & T. Clarke, 1975-79), 1:431.

114. F.F. Bruce, *Romans*, TNTC (London: Tyndale, 1963), p. 176. According to *BAGD*, "*Proginōskō*," p. 170, the verb in Rom 8:29 means to "choose beforehand." Murray, *Romans*, 1:317, affirms that *proginōskō* means to "forelove." Similarly Fritz Rienecker and Cleon L. Rogers, Jr., *LKGNT*, p. 743: "God's foreknowledge is much more than knowing what will happen in the future; it includes as it does in the language of the LXX (e.g., Num 16:5; Judg 9:6; Amos 3:2), His effective choice." Cf. Jacobs and Krienke, "Foreknowledge," *NIDNTT*, 1:693: "In Paul the verb *proginōskō*, 'foreknow, choose beforehand,' demonstrates the character of God's activity among men. It assumes the aspect of a personal relationship with a group of people which originates in God himself." Cf. R. Bultmann, "*Ginōskō*," *TDNT*, 1:715: "In the NT *proginōskō* is referred to God. His foreknowledge, however, is an election or foreordination of his people (Rom 8:29; 11:2) or Christ (1 Pet 1:20)." And C. Samuel Storms, *Chosen for Life* (Grand Rapids, Mich.: Baker, 1987), p. 85, adds, "God's foreknowledge is his special delight or gracious affection with which he views us. . . . A good synonym is 'forelove'."

The rendering of Rom 9:29 by modern NT versions is instructive. Consider the following translations:

Good News for Modern Man: "For those whom God had already chosen he had also set apart to become like his Son."

The Jerusalem Bible: "They are the ones he chose specially long ago and intended to become true images of his Son."

The New Testament: A New Translation (Moffatt): "For he decreed of old that those whom he predestined should share the likeness of his Son."

The New Testament: An Expanded Translation (Wuest): "Because those whom He foreordained He also marked out beforehand as those who were to be conformed to the derived image of His Son."

The New Testament: A Translation in the Language of the People (Williams): "For those on whom He set His heart beforehand He marked off as His own to make like His Son."

The Twentieth Century New Testament: "For those whom God chose from the first he did also predestinate to be conformed to the image of his Son."

New Living Translation: "For God knew his people in advance, and he chose them to become like his Son."

115. Jewett, *Election and Predestination*, p. 47, again underscores an important truism: "The doctrine of election . . . has not only a corporate but also an individual aspect. The elect are not only all those together whom God has chosen to be the objects of his grace and favor, but each one in particular."

116. Cranfield, *Romans*, 2:480.

117. Jewett, *Election and Predestination*, p. 133, concludes: "Obviously, the apostle is thinking of individuals as well as nations, since in the previous verse (9:12) he quotes the oracles to Rebecca before she gave birth to her sons (Gen 25:23). And the remark that he makes in the verse previous to that (9:11) is as forthright as it is awesome: he states that this oracle was pronounced not only before the children were born but before they had done good or evil, in order that (*hina* of purpose) the electing purpose of God might stand."

118. See the line of reasoning in Storms, *Chosen for Life*, pp. 76-85, and *The NIV Study Bible* note to Rom 9:13, p. 1719. For further evidence in support of the view of individual election to salvation, see John Piper, *The Justification of God: An Exegetical and Theological Study of Romans 9:1-23* (Grand Rapids, Mich.: Baker, 1983), pp. 34-54; Matthew Black, *Romans*, *NCBC* (Grand Rapids, Mich.: Eerdmans, 1981), pp. 131-132.; Murray, *Romans*, 2:13-21. Bruce, *Romans*, p. 188, affirmed: "Paul implies [that] when some receive the light and others do not, the divine election may be discerned, operating antecedently to the will or activity of those who are its objects."

119. *The NIV Study Bible* note to Rom 9:15, p. 1720, reads: "Paul denies injustice in God's dealing with Isaac and Ishmael, and Jacob and Esau, by appealing to God's sovereign right to dispense mercy as he chooses."

120. The verb *proetoimazō* ("prepare beforehand," here in the aorist tense) signifies "God's work of preparation arising from his free elective choice." S. Solle, "Ready, Prepare, Gird," *NIDNTT*, 3:118.

121. "Clark Pinnock's Response," in *Predestination and Free Will: Four Views of Divine Sovereignty and Human Freedom*, David Basinger and Randall Basinger, eds. (Downers Grove, Ill.: InterVarsity, 1986), p. 158.

122. Jewett, *Election and Predestination*, p. 43.

123. Cranfield, *Romans*, 2:589-90, interprets "knowledge of God" in Rom 11:33 ("Oh, the depth of the riches of the wisdom and knowledge of God!") as implying "God's elective love and the loving concern and care which it implies."

124. Jewett, *Election and Predestination*, p. 48.

125. The aorist middle *exelexato* (Eph 1:4) emphasizes the subject acting with respect to itself. As noted by B.F. Westcott, *Saint Paul's Epistle to the Ephesians* (Grand Rapids, Mich.: Baker, reprint, 1979), p. 8: "The middle voice emphasizes . . . the relation of the person chosen to the special purpose of him who chooses. The 'chosen' are regarded not as they stand to others who are not chosen, but as they stand to the counsel of God who works through them."

126. Jacobs and Krienke, "Foreknowledge," *NIDNTT*, 1:697, remark: "The word *prothesis*, 'plan,' serves to characterize God's activity in Christ as the fulfillment of an eternal purpose. It is one in which men do not have a say, either in time or in its intentions."

127. D. Mueller, "Will, Purpose," *NIDNTT*, 3:1016, refers to "The free decision of [God's] will which is prepared to carry it out."

128. Ibid.

129. See H.C.G. Moule, *Commentary on Ephesians, Cambridge Bible for Schools and Colleges* (Cambridge: Cambridge University Press, 1884), p. 48, who defined *eudokia* as God's "deliberate, beneficient resolve."

130. Jewett, *Election and Predestination*, p. 73.

131. Berkouwer, *Divine Election* (Grand Rapids, Mich.: Eerdmans, 1960), pp. 309-310. See also Jewett, *Election and Predestination*, p. 47. The liberation theologian Leonardo Boff, *Liberating Grace* (Maryknoll, N.Y.: Orbis, 1979), p. 88, helpfully affirms that "Though people are immersed in a sociological context, they nevertheless emerge as irreducibly individual."

132. *Martin Luther's Basic Theological Writings*, Timothy F. Lull, (Minneapolis: Fortress, 1989), p. xiv.

133. Donald Guthrie, *The Pastoral Epistles*, TNTC (London: Tyndale, 1957), p. 129.

134. B.F. Westcott, *Saint Paul's Epistle to the Ephesians* (Grand Rapids, Mich.: Baker, reprint, 1979), p. 8. Cf. L. Coenen, "Elect, Choose," *NIDNTT*, 1:534; cf. Rienecker and Rogers, *LKGNT*, p. 610.

135. Yet Klein, *The New Chosen People*, p. 44, asserts that "election and salvation are separate issues."

136. Edward G. Selwyn, *The First Epistle of St. Peter* (Grand Rapids, Mich.: Baker, reprint, 1981), p. 119. The important lexical authority, *BAGD*, p. 710, translates 1 Pet 1:2 as chosen "according to the predestination of God the Father."

137. According to J.A. Thompson, *Deuteronomy*, *TOTC* (London: InterVarsity, 1974), p. 95, "The demands of God, once rejected, became a hardening influence on Sihon's heart, so that he was unable to respond favorably to Israel's request."

138. Brunner, *Christian Doctrine of God*, 1:327.

139. William G.T. Shedd, *Commentary on Romans* (Grand Rapids, Mich.: Baker, reprint, 1980), p. 292. Charles Bigg, *The Epistles of St. Peter and St. Jude*, ICC (New York: Scribner, 1909), p. 133, rightly concludes that unconditional reprobation "is irreconcilable with the idea [or character] of God."

140. R.C. Sproul, *Chosen by God* (Wheaton, Ill.: Tyndale, 1986), p. 145.

141. Cranfield, *Romans*, 2:492

142. Davidson and Martin, "Romans," p. 1035.

143. Brunner, *Christian Doctrine of God*, p. 331

144. Charles Bigg, *A Critical and Exegetical Commentary on the Epistles of St. Peter and St. Jude*, ICC (Edinburgh: T. & T. Clark, 1902), p. 133.

145. Reinecker & Rogers, *LKGNT*, p. 673. Cf. U. Becker, "Hard, Hardened," *NIDNTT*, 2:156: "In the NT men who do not open themselves to the Gospel are described as hardened."

146. Jewett, *Election and Predestination*, p. 78.

147. Charles Haddon Spurgeon, *Lectures to My Students* (Grand Rapids, Mich.: Zondervan, reprint, 1954), p. 80.

148. See Jewett, *Election and Predestination*, pp. 129-31.

149. D. Mueller, "Will, Purpose," *NIDNTT*, 3:1018.

150. Sproul, *Chosen by God*, p. 196. Other authorities have noted that in context Paul had just requested prayer for all persons, especially for kings and those in authority (1 Tim 2:1-2). The phrase "all men" is said to refer to all *classes* of people whom God desires to save. Scripture, indeed, uses "all" or "every" to denote "all kinds of" (Luke 11:42; John 12:32; Acts 2:5; 10:12; Col 1:23; 1 Tim 4:4; 6:10). Augustine, for example, held that God elects to salvation all kinds of people, from kings to beggars, from wise men to fools (*Enchiridion*, 27). Thomas Aquinas, ST I.1, q. 19, art. 7, stated that Paul's words "can be understood as applying to every class of individuals, not to every individual of each class; in which case they mean that God wills some persons of every class and condition to be saved, makes and females, Jews and Gentiles, great and small, but not all of every condition." Guthrie, *Pastoral Epistles*, p. 71, noted that the text "speaks of God's consistent mercy towards all, without distinction of race, color, condition or status." See also Calvin, *Institutes*, III.24.16.

C H A P T E R   4

1. James Denney, *The Death of Christ*, R.V.G. Tasker, ed. (London: Tyndale, 1951), p. 174, wrote: "Scripture converges upon the doctrine of the atonement; it has the unity of a consistent testimony to a love of God which bears the sin of the world. . . . To Him bear all the Scriptures witness; and it is as a testimony to Him, the Bearer of sin, the Redeemer who gave His life a ransom for us, that we acknowledge them. This is the burden of the Bible."

2. For example, the late Southern Baptist theologian Dale Moody devoted only half a dozen pages to Christ's death in his systematic theology *The Word of Truth* (Grand Rapids, Mich.: Eerdmans, 1981). Likewise the important Roman Catholic theologian Richard P. McBrien discusses the cross in less than ten out of 1, 250 pages in his book *Catholicism*, 2 vols. in 1 (Minneapolis: Winston, 1981).

3. Emil Brunner, *The Mediator* (Philadelphia: Westminster, 1947), p. 436.

4. Irenaeus, *Against Heresies*, V.1.1; cf. ibid., V.21.1-3. Cf. Irenaeus, *Proof of the Apostolic Preaching*, 31: "Because death ruled in the body, it was necessary through the body that it should be done away with and man set free from its oppression."

5. Origen, *Commentary on Matthew*, XVI.8. Cf. Origen, *Commentary on Romans*, II.13; *Exodus Homily*, VI.9; *Against Celsus*, I.31; VII.17.

6. Gregory of Nyssa, *The Great Catechism*, 24. Cf. Gregory Nazianzus, *Orations*, 45.22.

7. John of Damascus, *The Orthodox Faith*, III.27; cf. ibid., III.1.

8. Gustaf Aulén, *Christus Victor* (London: SPCK, 1970), p. 4; cf. ibid., p. 55.

9. Anselm, *Cur Deus Homo?*, I.23.
10. Ibid., II.6; cf. ibid., II.7, 18.
11. J.I. Packer, "What Did the Cross Achieve?" *Tyndale Bulletin* 25 (1974):4.
12. Peter Abelard, *Sentences*, 23; cf. Abelard, "Exposition of the Epistle to the Romans," *LCC*, 10:283-284.
13. Faustus Socinus, *Praelectiones Theol.*, p. 591; cited by L.W. Grensted, *A Short History of the Doctrine of the Atonement* (Manchester: Manchester University Press, 1920), p. 287.
14. Horace Bushnell, *God in Christ* (New York: AMS Press, reprint, 1972), p. 216.
15. Ibid., p. 192; cf. ibid., pp. 212-13.
16. Ibid., pp. 247-48.
17. L. Harold DeWolf, *A Theology of the Living Church* (New York: Harper, 1953), p. 267. Cf. DeWolf, *The Case for Theology in Liberal Perspective* (Philadelphia: Westminster, 1959), pp. 77-80.
18. Hugo Grotius, *A Defense of the Catholic Faith Concerning the Satisfaction of Christ Against Faustus Socinus*, trans. F.H. Foster (Andover, Mass.: Warren F. Draper, 1889), p. 100.
19. John Miley, *Systematic Theology*, 2 vols. (New York: Hunt & Eaton, 1892-94), 2:168; cf. ibid., 2:169.
20. "The demerit of sin imposes no obligation of punishment upon the divine Ruler." Ibid., 2:178.
21. Ibid, 2:176. Cf. ibid, 2:95: "The vicarious sufferings of Christ are a provisionary substitute for penalty, and not the actual punishment of sin."
22. Ibid., 2:172.
23. Ibid., 2:181.
24. J. Kenneth Grider, "Atonement," *BDT*, p. 55.
25. J. Kenneth Grider, "Governmental Theory of the Atonement," *BDT*, p. 240. Cf. R. Larry Shelton, "Initial Salvation," *A Contemporary Wesleyan Theology*, Charles W. Carter, ed., 2 vols. (Grand Rapids, Mich.: Zondervan, Francis Asbury, 1983), 1:502-5.
26. Athanasius, *On the Incarnation of the Word*, IV.20.5. Cf. *Against the Arians*, I.60: "suffering in the flesh [the *Logos*] gave salvation to all."
27. Cyril of Jerusalem, *Lenten Lectures*, XIII.4.
28. James Arminius, *The Works of James Arminius*, 3 vols. (Auburn and Buffalo: Derby, Miller & Orton, 1853), 1:316. Thomas Watson, the first important Methodist systematic theologian, wrote: "Christ died for all men, so as to make their salvation practicable." *Theological Institutes*, 2 vols. (New York: Lane & Scott, 1851), 2:303.
29. Miley, *Systematic Theology*, 2:239. Cf. H. Orton Wiley, *Christian Theology*, 3 vols. (Kansas City, Mo.: Beacon Hill, 1952-53), 2:296: "Arminianism, with its emphasis on moral freedom and prevenient grace, has always held to the universality of the atonement."
30. Karl Barth, *CD*, vol. II/2, p. 123; vol. IV/1, pp. 222, 230-35.
31. Ibid, vol. IV/2, p. 46.
32. Ibid., vol. IV/1, p. 296.
33. Ibid., vol. IV/1, p. 486. Barth, ibid., immediately added: "His forgiveness repels chaos, and closes the gulf, and ensures that the will of God will be done on earth as it is in heaven. What, then, is the guilt of man, in the light of the fact that God encounters him in this way, as the One who pardons his sin?"
34. Ibid., vol. IV/1, p. 747. Cf. Karl Barth, *The Faith of the Church* (New York: Meridian Books, 1958), p. 91: "There no longer exists any object under the curse after what happened at Calvary. By taking over that curse Christ accomplished our acquittal." Cf. also *CD*, p. 774; vol. IV/1, p. 294; *Dogmatics in Outline* (New York: Philosophical Library, 1949), pp. 119-120.
35. Hendrikus Berkhof, *Christian Faith*, trans. Sierd Woudstra (Grand Rapids, Mich.: Eerdmans, 1979), p. 305. For the full discussion of Berkhof's position see the section, "Death and Reconciliation," ibid., pp. 299-307.
36. Ibid., p. 305.
37. Vincent Taylor, *Jesus and His Sacrifice* (New York: St. Martin's, 1965), p. 308. Cf. ibid., p. 309: Christ's sacrifice is "the perfect expression of his perfect penitence for the sins of men."
38. Clement of Rome, *Epistle to the Corinthians*, I.49.5; cf. ibid., I.7.4.
39. Ignatius, *To the Smyrnaeans*, 2; cf. *To the Trallians*, 2.

40. *Epistle of Barnabas*, 7.3; cf. ibid., 8:2, which describes Christ as the calf offered by God for slaughter.

41. *Epistle to Diognetus*, 10.2-5.

42. Cyril of Jerusalem, *Lenten Lectures*, XIII.33. Cf. ibid., XIII.18: "Jesus assumed the thorns to remove the condemnation."

43. Athanasius, *Incarnation of the Word*, XX.2; cf. XX.5; *Discourse Against the Arians*, I.60.

44. Augustine, *Reply to Faustus the Manichaean*, XIV.3. Cf. *On the Trinity*, IV.12-14; *On The Gospel of John*, XLI.6.

45. Augustine, *City of God*, X.20.

46. Ibid., XIII.11.15; cf. *Faith, Hope and Love*, 33.

47. Augustine, *City of God*, XVIII.49; *On the Gospel of John*, XXV.16, 18.

48. Martin Luther, *LW*, 26:288.

49. Aulén, *Christus Victor*, pp. 101-122.

50. John Calvin, *Institutes of the Christian Religion*, II.16.6. Cf. ibid., II.16.2: "Christ took upon himself and suffered the punishment that . . . threatened all sinners." Cf. ibid., III.4.26.

51. Ibid., II.16.5.

52. John Calvin, *Commentary on the Epistles of Paul to the Corinthians*, 2:242.

53. Calvin, *Institutes*, II.17.3. Cf. ibid., II.16.10: "Christ appeased God's wrath and satisfied his just judgment." Cf. ibid., II.17.4; III.4.26; cf. John Calvin, *Commentaries on the Catholic Epistles*, pp. 171-72.

54. Calvin, *Institutes*, II.16.7; II.17.5; III.4.30.

55. John Calvin, *Commentaries on the Epistles of Paul to the Philippians, Colossians and Thessalonians*, p. 159. Cf. Calvin, *Commentaries on the Catholic Epistles*, pp. 240-41.

56. Calvin, *Institutes*, II.17.2. Cf. ibid., III.6.3; III.11.8.

57. Calvin, *Institutes*, II.15.1-6. For an analysis of Calvin's development of the three offices, which would have a profound influence on later Protestant theology, see John Frederick Jansen, *Calvin's Doctrine of the Work of Christ* (London: James Clarke, 1956).

58. Benjamin B. Warfield, "Atonement," *Studies in Theology* (New York: Oxford University Press, 1932), p. 278. Warfield observed that the doctrine of vicarious sacrifice has been upheld by the major branches of the Christian church, e.g., the Greek, Latin, Lutheran, and Reformed.

59. See John Calvin, *Concerning the Eternal Predestination of God* (London: James Clark & Co., 1961), p. 106. A number of modern scholars conclude that Calvin upheld a twofold purpose in the Atonement. See James B. Torrance, "The Incarnation and 'Limited Atonement,'" *Evangelical Quarterly* LV.2 (April 1983):83-94; Tony Lane, "The Quest for the Historical Calvin," ibid., pp. 95-113; M. Charles Bell, "Calvin and the Extent of the Atonement," ibid., pp. 115-23; R.B. Knox, "John Calvin: An Elusive Churchman," *Scottish Journal of Theology*, 34 (1981):147-156. In his essay "The Quest for the Historical Calvin," p. 113, Lane comments that "Calvin was prepared to recognize *both* God's universal love for all mankind and his desire for all to repent and his purpose that some only should be saved. To the feeble human mind these are irreconcilable."

    R.T. Kendall, *Calvin and English Puritanism to 1649* (Oxford: Oxford University Press, 1979) argues that Calvin upheld a universal Atonement. He wrote, ibid., p. 13, that "Christ died indiscriminately for all people," adding that the Savior ascended and intercedes only for the elect who are saved. Christ's ascension and heavenly intercession renders the decree of election effectual. For Kendall, ibid., p. 212, scholastic Calvinism, including the Westminster standards, "represents a substantial departure from the thought of John Calvin."

    On the other hand, Paul Helm opposed Kendall's thesis as dividing the work of Christ. He wrote, "Calvin teaches that the death of Christ actually remitted sin, that such remission was for the elect, and that Christ intended to die for the elect." *Calvin and the Calvinists* (Edinburgh: Banner of Truth Trust, 1982), p. 30; cf. pp. 11, 14. Helm argues that Calvin was committed to a definite Atonement even though (prior to the Arminian controversy) he did not develop the doctrine explicitly.

60. John Calvin, *Commentary on the Epistles of Paul to the Galatians and Ephesians*, p. 157. In his commentary on 1 John 2:2 Calvin admitted to the truth of the Scholastic dictum that "Christ suffered sufficiently for the whole world but effectively only for the elect." *Commentaries on the Catholic Epistles*, p. 244.

61. John Calvin, *Commentaries on the Epistles to the Philippians, Colossians, and Thessalonians*, p. 148.
62. John Calvin, *Commentaries on the Epistle of Paul the Apostle to the Romans*, p. 211. See also Calvin's comments on Isa 53:6, John 1:29, John 3:15-16, John 4:42, and Rom 10:16 and in the *Institutes*, IV.14.7.
63. Calvin, *Institutes*, III.20.43. Calvin here echoes Luther's distinction between God's hidden and revealed will.
64. Ibid., III.21.6.
65. Ibid., III.21.5.
66. Ibid., III.14.11.
67. John Calvin, *Commentaries on the Prophet Ezekiel*, 2:247-248.
68. Herman Bavinck, *Our Reasonable Faith* (Grand Rapids, Mich.: Baker, 1977), p. 361, makes this point.
69. C.H. Spurgeon, "General and Yet Particular," *The Metropolitan Tabernacle Pulpit*, 63 vols. (Pasadena, Tex.: Pilgrim, reprint, 1969-80), 10:233. Cf. ibid., p. 230: "It has pleased God to put the whole race under the mediatorial sway of Jesus, in order that he might give eternal life to those who were chosen out of the world."
70. Charles M. Horne, *Salvation* (Chicago: Moody, 1971), p. 46. Cf. Walter A. Elwell, "Atonement, Extent of the," *ETD*, p. 99: "Paul had no trouble saying that God could be the Savior of all, in one sense, and of those who believe, in another sense."
71. Donald G. Bloesch, *Essentials of Evangelical Theology*, 2 vols. (New York: Harper & Row, 1978-79), 1:167.
72. Francis Turretin, *Institutio Theologiae Elencticae*, locus IV, q. 17, par. 5, quoted in *Reformed Dogmatics*, John W. Beardslee III, ed. (Grand Rapids, Mich.: Baker, 1977), p. 420.
73. Ibid., in Beardslee, *Reformed Dogmatics*, p. 421.
74. John Owen, "Death of Death in the Death of Christ," *The Works of John Owen*; William Goold, ed., 16 vols (Edinburgh: Banner of Truth Trust, 1965-68), 10:227.
75. Ibid., 10:214.
76 Arthur C. Custance, *The Sovereignty of Grace* (Phillipsburg, N.J.: Presbyterian & Reformed, 1979), p. 155.
77. Ibid.
78. Ibid., pp. 157-58.
79. In lieu of the phrase "limited atonement," Nicole prefers the concept "definite atonement" or "particular redemption." Christ died for the specific purpose of redeeming those whom the Father had given him. See Roger Nicole, "The 'Five Points' and God's Sovereignty," in James M. Boice, ed., *Our Sovereign God* (Grand Rapids, Mich.: Baker, 1977), pp. 31-33. Cf. Roger Nicole, "Particular Redemption," in James M. Boice, ed., *Our Savior God* (Grand Rapids, Mich.: Baker, 1980), pp. 165-78.
80. T.C. Hammond, *In Understanding Be Men* (London: InterVarsity, 1960), p. 115.
81. R.A. Torrey, *What the Bible Teaches* (New York: Fleming H. Revell, 1933), p. 144.
82. *The Oxford English Dictionary*, 12 vols. (Oxford: Clarendon, 1933), 1:539.
83. Geoffrey W. Bromiley, "Atone; Atonement," *ISBERev*, 1:353.
84. R. Laird Harris, "*Kāpar*," *TWOT*, 1:452-53. Cf. *BDB*, p. 497.
85. G. Lloyd Carr, "*Minḥāh*, *TWOT*, 1:515.
86. Gordon J. Wenham, *The Book of Leviticus*, NICOT (Grand Rapids, Mich.: Eerdmans, 1979), p. 65.
87. F.F. Bruce, *The Epistle to the Hebrews*, NICNT (Grand Rapids, Mich.: Eerdmans, 1990), p. 220.
88. Derek Kidner, *Psalms 1–72*, TOTC (Downers Grove, Ill.: InterVarsity, 1973), p. 106.
89. For convincing discussions that identify the servant of the Lord ultimately with the Messiah see Walter C. Kaiser, Jr., "*'ebed*," *TWOT*, 2:639-40; Jan Ridderbos, *Isaiah* (Grand Rapids, Mich.: Zondervan, 1984), pp. 366-373; and J. Barton Payne, *The Theology of the New Testament* (Grand Rapids, Mich.: Zondervan, 1962), pp. 254-57.
90. So Ridderbos, *Isaiah*, p. 484.
91. R.D. Patterson, "*sābal*," *TWOT*, 2:616.
92. Murray J. Harris, "Prepositions and Theology in the Greek NT," *NIDNTT*, 3:1180. Cf. F. Büchsel, "*lytron*," *TDNT*, 4:342-49; Nigel Turner, *Syntax* (Edinburgh: T. & T. Clark, 1963), p. 258; vol. III of J.H. Moulton, *A Grammar of New Testament Greek*.

93. Harris, *NIDNTT*, 3:1174, 1176.
94. Fritz Rienecker and Cleon L. Rogers, Jr., *LKGNT*, p. 471.
95. J. Gess, "Lamb, Sheep," *NIDNTT*, 2:411.
96. C.L.W. Grimm and J.H Thayer, *A Greek-English Lexicon to the New Testament* (New York: American Book Co., 1889), p. 50.
97. William B. Coker, "*pādāh*," *TWOT*, 2:716.
98. H. Vorlander, "Forgiveness," *NIDNTT*, 1:701.
99. C. Brown, "*lytron*," *NIDNTT*, 3:199. Cf. Leslie Mitton, *Ephesians*, NCBC (Grand Rapids, Mich.: Eerdmans, 1981), p. 52: "Its main significance is to suggest an entry into a new kind of freedom."
100. C.E.B. Cranfield, *Epistle to the Romans*, ICC, 2 vols. (London: T. & T. Clark, 1975-79), 1:202.
101. For developments of this interpretation see: Cranfield, *Romans*, 1:216-17; Leon Morris, *The Apostolic Preaching of the Cross* (Grand Rapids, Mich.: Eerdmans, 1965), pp. 184-202; George Eldon Ladd, *A Theology of the New Testament* (Grand Rapids, Mich.: Eerdmans, 1974), pp. 429-30; Donald Guthrie, *New Testament Theology* (Downers Grove, Ill., InterVarsity, 1981), pp. 467-70; and Colin Brown, "Reconciliation," *NIDNTT*, 3:151-60.
102. F.F. Bruce, *Epistle to the Romans*. TNTC (London: Tyndale, 1963), p. 107.
103. Alfred Plummer, *The Epistles of St. John* (Grand Rapids, Mich.: Baker, reprint, 1980), p. 35.
104. Rienecker and Rogers, *LKGNT*, p. 671.
105. H. Vorlander and C. Brown, "Reconciliation," *NIDNTT*, 3:166.
106. Cranfield, *Romans*, 1:267. Millard J. Erickson, *Christian Theology*, 3 vols. (Grand Rapids, Mich.: Baker, 1983-85), 2:815, affirms that in reconciliation man turns to God, "but the process of reconciliation is primarily God's turning in favor toward man." L. Berkhof, *Systematic Theology* (Grand Rapids, Mich.: Eerdmans, 1941), p. 373, observed that the subjective component of the sinner's reconciliation to God is secondary to the objective component of God being propitiated by Christ's death.
107. Rienecker and Rogers, *LKGNT*, p. 527.
108. H. Weigelt, "Clothe," *NIDNTT*, 1:315.
109. Anselm, *Cur Deus Homo*, I.1.
110. John Murray, *Redemption Accomplished and Applied* (Grand Rapids, Mich.: Eerdmans, 1955), pp. 9-18.
111. Ibid., p. 14.
112. Augustine, *The Trinity*, X.13.
113. F. F. Bruce, *The Epistle to the Hebrews*, NICNT (Grand Rapids, Mich.: Eerdmans, 1990), p. 76.
114. Rienecker and Rogers, *LKGNT*, p. 774. According to O. Bauernfeind, "*aselgeia*," *TDNT*, 1:490, the word means "debauchery" or "licensciousness," particularly gross sexual excesses.
115. *The NIV Study Bible*, p. 1099, n. on 2 Pet 2:1.
116. F.F. Bruce, *The Epistles of John* (Grand Rapids, Mich.: Eerdmans, 1970), p. 50.
117. Scripture indicates that there are degrees in God's love. That God does not love everyone in the same sense is clearly stated in Mal 1:2-3; Rom 1:7; 8:29; 9:13; Col 3:12; 1 Thess 1:4; 2 Thess 2:13.
118. A.H. Strong, *Systematic Theology* (Valley Forge, Penn.: Judson, 1907), p. 771.
119. Thomas J. Nettles, *By His Grace and for His Glory* (Grand Rapids, Mich.: Baker, 1986), p. 302.
120. Erickson, *Christian Theology*, 2:826.
121. Martin Luther, "Lectures on Galatians (1535)," *LW*, 26:176, 179.
122. D.M. Baillie, *God Was in Christ* (New York: Charles Scribner's Sons, 1955), p. 194, n. 1.
123. John Calvin, *Sermons on the Epistle to the Ephesians* (Edinburgh: Banner of Truth Trust, 1973), pp. 488-489.
124. Ibid., p. 483.
125. Calvin, *Institutes*, II.15.4.
126. Ibid.
127. Cited by Brian G. Armstrong, *Calvinism and the Amyraut Heresy* (Madison, Wisc: Univ. of Wisconsin Press, 1969), p. 167.

128. James Denney, *The Death of Christ* (London: Tyndale, 1951), p. 164.
129. Ibid., p. 173.

C H A P T E R   5

1. Pelagius, *On Nature and Grace*, 49.
2. Lyman Abbott, *What Christianity Means to Me* (New York: Macmillan, 1921), p. 137.
3. Ibid., p. 63.
4. Ibid., pp. 184-85.
5. Shailer Mathews, *The Gospel and the Modern Man* (New York: Macmillan, 1912), pp. 275-276.
6. Ibid., p. 184.
7. Wenzel Lohff, "Call to Faith," *Encyclopedia of the Lutheran Church*, J. Bodensieck, ed., 4 vols. (Minneapolis: Augsburg, 1965), 1:351.
8. Formula of Concord, "Solid Declaration," XI.15, in *The Book of Concord*, T.G. Tappert, ed. (Philadelphia: Fortress, 1959), p. 619.
9. Ibid., "Solid Declaration," XI.17., *Book of Concord*, p. 619.
10. Ibid., "Solid Declaration," XI.76, *Book of Concord*, p. 628.
11. Ibid., "Solid Declaration," XI.41, *Book of Concord*, p. 623.
12. Cited by Heinrich Schmid, *The Doctrinal Theology of the Evangelical Lutheran Church* (Minneapolis: Augsburg, reprint, 1961), p. 444.
13. Ibid., pp. 445-46.
14. Francis Pieper, *Christian Dogmatics*, 4 vols. (St. Louis: Concordia, 1950-57), 2:29.
15. Ibid., 2:30; cf., ibid., 2:24, where Pieper upholds "the Scripture truth that when God works through means, He can be resisted (Matt 23:37; Acts 7:51)."
16. Ibid., 2:400-401; cf. ibid., 2:403.
17. H. Orton Wiley, *Christian Theology*, 3 vols. (Kansas City: Beacon Hill, 1940-43), 2:344.
18. Ibid.
19. W.T. Purkiser, ed., *Exploring Our Christian Faith* (Kansas City: Beacon Hill, 1960), p. 273.
20. W.T. Purkiser, Richard S. Taylor, and Willard H. Taylor, *God, Man, and Salvation* (Kansas City: Beacon Hill, 1977), p. 429.
21. Ibid., p. 432.
22. William W. Klein, *The New Chosen People: A Corporate View of Election* (Grand Rapids, Mich.: Zondervan, Academie, 1990), p. 157. In fact, Klein relies heavily for support of his corporate view of election and calling on many liberal or mediating scholars, such as H. Wheeler Robinson, R. Schnackenberg, E. Schweizer, C.H. Dodd, J. Jeremias, E. Best, C.K. Barrett, A. Richardson, A. Oepke, etc.
23. Ibid., p. 146.
24. Ibid., p. 212.
25. Ibid., p. 107.
26. Anthony A. Hoekema writes convincingly as follows:

> If our condition by nature is as described [in these passages] it is obvious that we cannot in our own strength accept the gospel call. To ask people who are by nature spiritually dead, hostile to God, unable to understand the things of God's Spirit, and unable to submit to God's law, to respond favorably to his invitation to repent of sin and believe in Christ is like asking a totally deaf woman to answer your question or a totally blind man to read a note you have written. It is like standing on top of a roof and asking a man on the sidewalk below to fly up to join you. *Saved by Grace* (Grand Rapids, Mich.: Eerdmans, 1989), p. 82.

27. Augustine, *On the Predestination of the Saints*, 32. Cf. *Admonition and Grace*, 13.
28. Augustine, *Eighty-Three Different Questions*, q. 65.
29. Augustine, *On the Spirit and the Letter*, 60.
30. Augustine, *Eighty-Three Different Questions*, q. 68.
31. Augustine, *On the Predestination of the Saints*, 15.
32. Augustine, *On the Grace of Christ*, 15.
33. Augustine, *Confessions*, VIII.7.

34. Ibid., VIII.12.
35. John Calvin, *Institutes of the Christian Religion*, III.2.34. Calvin added in the same section: "as we cannot come to Christ unless we be drawn by the Spirit of God, so when we are drawn we are lifted up in mind and heart above our understanding. For the soul, illumined by him, takes on a new keenness, as it were, to contemplate the heavenly mysteries, whose splendor had previously blinded it. And man's understanding, thus beamed by the light of the Holy Spirit, then at last begins to taste those things which belong to the Kingdom of God, having formerly been quite foolish and dull in tasting them."
36. Ibid., III.24.8
37. Ibid., III.24.1. Cf. ibid., III.24.3: "we are illumined according as God has chosen us."
38. Charles Haddon Spurgeon, "God's Will and Man's Will," *Metropolitan Tabernacle Pulpit*, 8:185.
39. Augustus H. Strong, *Systematic Theology* (Valley Forge, Penn.: Judson, 1907), p. 790.
40. Ibid., p. 792.
41. J.I. Packer, "Call, Calling," *EDT*, p. 184.
42. Ibid.
43. L. Coenen, "Call," *NIDNTT*, 1:273.
44. Ibid.
45. Ibid., p. 274.
46. Ibid., p. 275.
47. Arthur C. Custance, *The Sovereignty of Grace* (Phillipsburg, N. J.: Presbyterian and Reformed, 1979), p. 292.
48. Arthur W. Pink, *The Doctrine of Salvation* (Grand Rapids, Mich.: Baker, 1975), p. 93.
49. J. I. Packer, "Call, Calling," ·*EDT*, p. 184.
50. See W. Grundmann, "*anankazō*," *TDNT*, 1:345.
51. R.E. Nixon, "Matthew," *NBCRev*, p. 843. The lexical authority *BAGD*, p. 242, comments that *eklektoi* is used "especially of those whom God has chosen from the generality of mankind and drawn to himself."
52. Simon J. Kistemaker, *Acts*, NTC (Grand Rapids, Mich.: Baker, 1990), p. 107.
53. Lewis B. Smedes clearly affirms the divine initiative behind Saul's reception of grace. Wrote he, "It is a gift. Paul ran from Christ; Christ pursued and overtook him. Paul resisted Christ; Christ disarmed him. Paul persecuted Christ; Christ converted him. Paul was an alien; Christ made him a member of the family." *All Things Made New* (Grand Rapids, Mich.: Eerdmans, 1970), p. 119.
54. Donald Guthrie, *New Testament Theology* (Downers Grove, Ill.: InterVarsity, 1981), p. 619, commented: "Both [Luke and Paul] knew that it was impossible to decline a command which had so clearly come from God."
55. Gordon H. Girod, *The Way of Salvation* (Grand Rapids, Mich.: Baker, 1960), p. 81.
56. Wilhelm Pauck, trans. and ed., *Luther: Lectures on Romans*, LCC (Philadelphia: Westminster, 1966), p. 247.
57. Ibid., p. 250.
58. *The NIV Study Bible*, Kenneth Barker, ed. (Grand Rapids, Mich.: Zondervan, 1985), note on Rom 8:28, p. 1718.
59. C.E.B. Cranfield, *Romans*, ICC, 2 vols. (London: T. & T. Clark, 1975-79), 1:69. F.F. Bruce, *The Epistle to the Galatians*, NIGTC (Grand Rapids, Mich.: Eerdmans, 1982), p. 80, agrees: "The verb *kaleō* is part of Paul's vocabulary for emphasizing the divine initiative in salvation."
60. J.I. Packer, *Knowing God* (Downers Grove, Ill.: InterVarsity, 1973), p. 37.
61. F.F. Bruce, *The Gospel of John* (Grand Rapids, Mich.: Eerdmans, 1983), p. 164. A superb exegete, Bruce insightfully adds, ibid., pp. 153, 156: "None at all would come unless divinely persuaded and enabled to do so. . . . Those who come to Christ come to him by the 'sweet constraint' of that grace."
62. Leon Morris, *The Gospel According to John*, NICNT (Grand Rapids, Mich.: Eerdmans, 1971), pp. 598-599. Cf. Merrill C. Tenney, "The Gospel of John," *EBC*, 9:131, who wrote: "'All men' . . . means that Christ draws men to himself indiscriminately, without regard to nationality, race, or status. Jesus' utterance was prompted by the presence of Greek Gentiles and should be understood by the setting of the occasion."
63. C.H. Spurgeon, "The Marvelous Magnet," *Metropolitan Tabernacle Pulpit*, 29:233.

64. F.F. Bruce, *Commentary on the Epistle to the Hebrews*, NLCNT (London: Marshall, Morgan & Scott, 1965), p. 209.
65. Martin Luther, *The Bondage of the Will* (Grand Rapids, Mich.: Eerdmans, 1931), sect. XXV, p. 73.
66. Pink, *Doctrine of Salvation*, p. 88.
67. Spurgeon, "The Marvelous Magnet," 29:238.
68. Hoekema, *Saved by Grace*, p. 85.
69. John Murray, *Redemption: Accomplished and Applied* (Grand Rapids, Mich.: Eerdmans, 1955), p. 88.
70. Ibid., p. 89.
71. C.S. Lewis, *Surprised by Joy* (New York: Harcourt, Brace & Company, 1956), p. 229.
72. Augustine, *Commentary on Psalm 69*, 6.
73. Augustine, *Sermon on St. John*, 26.2.
74. Hymn #498, *Psalter Hymnal* (Grand Rapids, Mich.: Christian Reformed Publications, 1987), author unknown.

C H A P T E R 6

1. Albrecht Ritschl, *The Christian Doctrine of Justification and Reconciliation*, H.R. Mackintosh, ed. (Clifton, N.J.: Reference Book Publishers, 1966), p. 101.
2. Ibid.
3. Ibid.
4. Ibid., p. 108.
5. John C. Bennett, *Christian Realism* (New York: Charles Scribner's Sons, 1947), p. 82.
6. John C. Bennett, "The Christian Conception of Man," in *Liberal Theology: An Appraisal*, David E. Roberts & Henry P. Van Dusen, eds. (New York: Charles Scribner's Sons, 1942), pp. 202-3.
7. Hugo Assmann, *Theology for a Nomad Church* (Maryknoll, N.Y.: Orbis, 1976), p. 38.
8. Gustavo Gutiérrez, *A Theology of Liberation* (Maryknoll, N.Y.: Orbis, 1988), p. 118.
9. Alfredo Fierro, *The Militant Gospel* (Maryknoll, N.Y.: Orbis, 1977), p. 235.
10. Ibid., p. 234.
11. Leonardo Boff, *Faith on the Edge* (San Francisco: Harper & Row, 1989), p. 38.
12. James H. Cone, *A Black Theology of Liberation* (Maryknoll, N.Y.: Orbis, 1986), p. 48.
13. John B. Cobb, Jr. and David Ray Griffin, *Process Theology: An Introductory Exposition* (Philadelphia: Westminster, 1976), p. 31.
14. Ibid.
15. Richard S. Taylor, "Historical and Modern Significance of Wesleyan Theology," in *A Contemporary Wesleyan Theology*, 2 vols., Charles W. Carter, et al., eds. (Grand Rapids, Mich.: Zondervan, 1983), 1:65.
16. William G. MacDonald, "'. . . The Spirit of Grace' (Heb. 10:29)," in *Grace Unlimited*, Clark H. Pinnock, ed. (Minneapolis: Bethany Fellowship, 1975), pp. 88-89.
17. Daniel D. Whedon, "Doctrines of Methodism," in *Wesleyan Theology: A Sourcebook*, Thomas A. Langford, ed. (Durham, N.C.: Labyrinth Press, 1984), p. 100.
18. John Wesley, "Working Out Our Own Salvation," *The Works of John Wesley*, 14 vols. (Grand Rapids, Mich.: Zondervan, 1958), 6:509.
19. Albert C. Outler, "The Wesleyan Quadrilateral—in John Wesley," in *The Wesleyan Theological Heritage*, Thomas C. Oden and Leicester R. Longden, eds. (Grand Rapids, Mich.: Zondervan, 1991), p. 25.
20. John Wesley, *Explanatory Notes on the New Testament* (London: Wesleyan-Holiness Book Room, n.d.), p. 9 (note on Matt 3:8). Cf. Wesley's sermon "The Repentance of Believers," *The Works of John Wesley*, Albert C. Outler, ed., 22 vols. (Nashville: Abingdon, 1984-93), 1:335-352.
21. John Wesley, "Salvation by Faith," *Works*, Outler, ed., 1:121. Cf. "Justification by Faith," ibid., 1:194ff..
22. Charles G. Finney, *Lectures on Systematic Theology*, J.H. Fairchild, ed. (Whittier, Calif: Colporter Kemp, 1944), p. 365.
23. Ibid., pp. 365-366.
24. Ibid., p. 374.

25. W.T. Purkiser, Richard S. Taylor, and Willard H. Taylor, *God, Man, and Salvation: A Biblical Theology* (Kansas City: Beacon Hill, 1977), p. 174.
26. Ibid., p. 424.
27. Ibid., p. 412, n. 6.
28. Peter Toon, *The Emergence of Hyper-Calvinism in English Nonconformity: 1689-1765* (London: Olive Tree, 1967), pp. 144-45.
29. Cited by Thomas J. Nettles, *By His Grace and for His Glory* (Grand Rapids, Mich.: Baker, 1986), p. 389.
30. Joseph Hussey, *God's Operations of Grace: But No Offers of His Grace* (London, 1707), p. 372; cited by Nettles, *By His Grace*, p. 390.
31. Lewis Wayman, *A Further Enquiry After Truth* (London: J. & J. Marshall, 1738), p. 51; cited by Nettles, *By His Grace*, pp. 103-4.
32. John Brine, *A Refutation of Arminian Principles* (London, 1743), p. 5; cited by Nettles, *By His Grace*, pp. 390-91.
33. Soren Kierkegaard, *Kierkegaard's Concluding Unscientific Postscript*, trans. David F. Swenson (Princeton, N.J.: Princeton Univ. Press, 1941), p. 539.
34. Ibid., p. 540. Cf. Ibid., p. 188: Faith is "absurdity held fast in the passion of inwardness." Cf. Kierkegaard, *Fear and Trembling and the Sickness Unto Death*, trans. Walter Lowrie (Garden City, N.Y.: Doubleday, 1955), p. 10: Faith operates "by virtue of the absurd, not by virtue of human understanding, otherwise it is only practical wisdom, not faith."
35. Paul Tillich, *Dynamics of Faith* (London: Harper, 1957), pp. 1, 2, 4, 8, *passim*; *Systematic Theology*, 3 vols. (Chicago: University of Chicago Press, 1951-63), 3:130. Cf. *Dynamics*, p. 32: "Faith is participation in the subject of one's ultimate concern with one's whole being."
36. Tillich, *Systematic Theology*, 3:134.
37. So Tillich, *Dynamics of Faith*, p. 11, referred to "the disappearance of the ordinary subject-object scheme in the experience of the ultimate, the unconditional."
38. Tillich, *Systematic Theology*, 3:223. Cf. Paul Tillich, *Biblical Religion and the Search for Ultimate Identity* (Chicago: University of Chicago Press, 1955), p. 51: "Faith is the concern about our existence in its ultimate 'whence' and 'whither.'"
39. Tillich, *Systematic Theology*, 3:131.
40. Ibid., 3:220.
41. Rudolf Bultmann, *Kerygma and Myth*, Hans Werner Bartsch, ed. (New York and Evanston: Harper & Row, 1961), p. 33.
42. Rudolf Bultmann, *Theology of the New Testament*, trans. Kendrick Grobel, 2 vols. (New York: Charles Scribner's Sons, 1951-55), 2:76.
43. Bultmann, *Kerygma and Myth*, p. 121.
44. Rudolf Bultmann, *Essays Philosophical and Theological*, trans. James C.G. Greig (London: SCM, n.d.), p. 48.
45. See Hugh Ross Mackintosh, *Types of Modern Theology* (London: Nisbet, 1937), p. 284.
46. Karl Barth, *CD*, vol. II/1, p. 155.
47. Ibid., p. 158.
48. Ibid., p. 155.
49. Ibid., p. 156.
50. J.I. Packer, *Evangelism and the Sovereignty of God* (Downers Grove, Ill.: InterVarsity, 1961), p. 27.
51. Martin Luther, *What Luther Says* (St. Louis: Concordia, 1959), p. 1210.
52. Cited by Bertram L. Woolf, *Reformation Writings of Martin Luther* (London: Lutterworth Press, 1952), p. 32.
53. Martin Luther, *A Compend of Luther's Theology*, H.T. Kerr, ed. (Philadelphia: Westminster, 1943), p. 33.
54. Luther, *What Luther Says*, p. 494.
55. John Calvin, *Institutes of the Christian Religion*, II.3.6.
56. Ibid., III.2.7.
57. Ibid., III.2.8.
58. Calvin wrote, ibid., III.2.33: "faith is a singular gift of God, both in that the mind of man is purged so as to be able to taste the truth of God and in that his heart is established therein." Moreover, ibid., III.2.35, "Christ . . . illumines us into faith by the power of his Spirit."
59. Ibid., III.2.33.

60. Ibid., III.3.1.
61. Ibid., III.3.2, 9.
62. C.H. Spurgeon, "Faith and Regeneration," *SEE*, 7:141.
63. Ibid., 7:135.
64. Ibid., 7:136.
65. Ibid., 7:135. George Whitefield (d. 1770), the Calvinistic Methodist, likewise insisted that by virtue of total depravity the human responses of repentance and faith are gifts of God's grace. Whitefield declared that we sinners could not come to God until "God . . . put his faith in us." "Neglect of Christ [is] the killing sin," cited in Stuart C. Henry, *George Whitefield: Wayfaring Witness* (New York & Nashville: Abingdon, 1957), p. 108.
66. Spurgeon, *SEE*, 7:139.
67. Millard J. Erickson, *Christian Theology*, 3 vols. (Grand Rapids, Mich.: Baker, 1983-85), 3:933.
68. Victor P. Hamilton, "*Sub*," *TWOT*, 2:909.
69. Hugh Anderson, *The Gospel of Mark*, NCBC (Grand Rapids, Mich.: Eerdmans, 1981), p. 70.
70. James A. Brooks and Carlton L. Winbery, *Syntax of New Testament Greek* (Lanham, Md.: University Press of America, 1979), pp. 55-56. Cf. Robert Hanna, *A Grammatical Aid to the Greek New Testament* (Grand Rapids, Mich.: Baker, 1983), p. 14.
71. R.K. Harrison, "Deuteronomy," *NBCRev*, p. 226.
72. Calvin, *Institutes*, III.3.20.
73. So J.A. Thompson observes, "In the case of Judah, deep-seated wickedness caused by centuries of schooling and repeated excursions into idolatry had made evil virtually a fixed feature of her life and behavior." *The Book of Jeremiah*, NICOT (Grand Rapids, Mich.: Eerdmans, 1980), p. 374.
74. We must thus disagree with Purkiser, Taylor, and Taylor, *God, Man and Salvation*, p. 424, who write that Acts 11:18 "is the astonished Judaizer's way of conceding that the awakening grace which makes repentance possible is *offered* to all men" (italics added).
75. Luther, *What Luther Says*, p. 759. Leon Morris, *New Testament Theology* (Grand Rapids, Mich.: Zondervan, 1986), p. 181, reflecting on Acts 5:31 and 11:18, writes: "we are not to think of repentance as a human virtue, worked up out of human resources. It is in some sense a gift of God."
76. Arthur C. Custance, *The Sovereignty of Grace* (Phillipsburg, N.J.: Presbyterian & Reformed, 1979), p. 290.
77. Albert C. Knudson, *The Doctrine of Redemption* (Cincinnati: Abingdon, 1933), p. 408.
78. John Calvin, *Commentaries on the Epistles of Paul to the Galatians and Ephesians*, p. 262.
79. O. Michel, "Faith," *NIDNTT*, 1:605. Similarly, R.V.G. Tasker, *The General Epistle of James*, TNTC (London: Tyndale, 1957), p. 68. Cf. Colin Brown, "Righteousness, Justification," *NIDNTT*, 3:370.
80. Note especially the aorist passive indicative of *charizo*, to "give graciously." H.C.G. Moule commented that "Faith in Christ is here incidently viewed as a gift of Divine grace." *The Epistle to the Philippians* (Grand Rapids, Mich.: Baker, reprint, 1981), p. 31.
81. Second Thess 2:13 reads, ". . . saved through the sanctifying work of the Spirit and through belief in the truth." I. Howard Marshall comments that "The mention of the divine action first may well imply that it is this which gives rise to faith." *1 and 2 Thessalonians*, NCBC (Grand Rapids, Mich.: Eerdmans, 1983), p. 207.
82. Calvin, *Institutes*, III.1.3.
83. Karl Barth, *God, Grace and the Gospel*, trans. James S. McNab (Edinburgh & London: Oliver & Boyd, 1959), p. 7.
84. Ernest F. Kevan, *Salvation* (Grand Rapids, Mich.: Baker, 1963), p. 110.
85. H. Orton Wiley, *Christian Theology*, 3 vols. (Kansas City: Beacon Hill, 1952-53), 2:364.
86. Calvin, *Institutes*, III.3.1.
87. John Murray, *Redemption Accomplished and Applied* (Grand Rapids, Mich.: Eerdmans, 1955), p. 113.
88. Charles C. Ryrie, *Balancing the Christian Life* (Chicago: Moody, 1969), p. 170.
89. Ibid., p. 176.
90. Ibid., p. 178.
91. Zane C. Hodges, *Absolutely Free!* (Dallas: Redencion Viva, 1989), p. 31.

92. Zane C. Hodges, *The Gospel Under Siege* (Dallas: Redencion Viva, 1981), p. 14.
93. Hodges, *Absolutely Free!*, p. 145; cf. p. 158. Here Hodges follows Chafer, who wrote: "Next to sound doctrine itself, no more important obligation rests on the preacher than that of preaching the Lordship of Christ to Christians exclusively; and the Saviorhood of Christ to those who are unsaved." Lewis Sperry Chafer, *Systematic Theology*; 8 vols. (Dallas: Dallas Seminary Press, 1948), 3:387.
94. Ibid., p. 18. G. Michael Cocoris, pastor of the Church of the Open Door in Los Angeles, holds that repentance is strictly a change in one's belief system. Repentance does not involve being sorry for sin, turning from sin, or altering one's behavior. Repenting of sin (Rev 9:20-21), he argues, means changing one's outlook on sin, in the sense of recognizing that sin is a heinous problem that only God can resolve. Thus "Repentance means a change of mind or attitude. It does not include tears or turning. It doesn't even necessarily deal with sin." *Evangelism: a Biblical Approach* (Chicago: Moody, 1984), p. 69.

The writers of the book *Christ the Lord: The Reformation and Lordship Salvation,* Michael Horton, ed. (Grand Rapids, Mich.: Baker, 1992), pp. 12, 102, 121, 129, 140, 146, accuse Ryrie and Hodges of being modern antinomian extremists and of teaching a doctrine of "lawless grace" (p. 71) by virtue of their claim that one can assent to true statements about Christ without ever intending to surrender to him or obey him.
95. A.W. Tozer, *I Call it Heresy*, Gerald B. Smith, ed. (Camp Hill, Penn.: Christian Publications, 1991), p. 13.
96. John R.W. Stott, "Yes," *Eternity* (September 1959):37.
97. J.I. Packer, *Evangelism and the Sovereignty of God* (Downers Grove, Ill.: InterVarsity, 1970), p. 89.
98. James M. Boice, *Christ's Call to Discipleship* (Chicago: Moody, 1986), p. 10; cf. ibid., p. 21.
99. John F. MacArthur, *The Gospel According to Jesus* (Grand Rapids, Mich.: Zondervan, 1988), p. 21. MacArthur added, ibid., p. 30: "The call to Calvary must be recognized for what it is: a call to discipleship under the Lordship of Jesus Christ. To respond to that call is to become a believer. Anything less is simply unbelief."
100. Ibid., pp. 162-63.
101. Ibid., p. 167.
102. Ibid., p. 178.
103. Ibid., p. 207.
104. John Calvin, *Commentaries on the Acts of the Apostles*, 2:246; cf. ibid., 1:464.
105. Finney, *Lectures on Systematic Theology*, p. 122.
106. Charles H. Spurgeon, "Self-Delusion," *Metropolitan Tabernacle Pulpit*, 8:581.
107. Charles Haddon Spurgeon, "Faith's Way of Approach," *SEE*, 7:169. Paul Cedar writes that while doing a Bible study on the word faith, "I contended that an appropriate Biblical definition for faith is 'active obedience,' and shared that God has called us to be His obedient servants. The initial response of those in the group was surprise and resistance. Like many of us, they had fallen into the self-centered lifestyle. They did not wish to be servants of anyone nor were they excited about the lifestyle of obedience. Instead they preferred for God to fall into the flow of their lives and to subscribe to their wishes. Of course, they were challenging one of the basic requirements of being a true Christian. To follow Jesus Christ as Lord in obedience and to serve Him is not an option for authentic Christian lifestyle; it is imperative." *James, 1 & 2 Peter, Jude, The Communicator's Commentary* (Waco, Tex.: Word, 1984), p. 148.
108. Gordon H. Girod, *The Way of Salvation* (Grand Rapids, Mich.: Baker, 1960), p. 116.
109. Eugene H. Peterson, *The Message: The New Testament in Contemporary English* (Colorado Springs: NavPress, 1993), p. 184.
110. Ibid., p. 195.
111. H. Bietenhard, "Lord," *NIDNTT*, 2:514.
112. Calvin, *Institutes*, III.3.20.
113. Os Guinness, *In Two Minds* (Downers Grove, Ill. 1976), p. 128.
114. Guinness, ibid., p. 127, writes as follows: "The problem for many people today is not that it is too difficult to believe but that it is too easy. It is hard for them not to believe, for they slip in and out of belief caressed by the changing breezes of cultural fashion. . . . One person

may become a Christian because to believe in Jesus is 'where it's at'. . . . When the group or the fashion changes, such people change too."

115. Dietrich Bonhoeffer, *The Cost of Discipleship* (London: SCM, 1959), p. 38.
116. Ibid., pp. 35-36.
117. Ibid., pp. 36-37, 43, 46.
118. Alister E. McGrath, *The Sunnier Side of Doubt* (Grand Rapids, Mich.: Zondervan, 1990), p. 27.
119. See Gordon R. Lewis and Bruce A. Demarest, *Integrative Theology*, 3 vols. (Zondervan, 1987-94), especially vol. 1, chap. 1.
120. McGrath, *Sunnier Side of Doubt*, p. 19.
121. Augustine, *Of True Religion*, XXIX.73.
122. Augustine, *Confessions* (Baltimore: Penguin, 1961), p. 116.

C H A P T E R   7

1. S.J. McKenna, "Pelagians and Pelagianism," *NCE*, 11:58.
2. Walter Rauschenbusch, *Walter Rauschenbusch: Selected Writings*, Winthrop S. Husdon, ed. (New York: Paulist, 1984), p. 85.
3. Ibid., p. 75.
4. Lyman Abbott, *The Evolution of Christianity* (Boston & New York: Houghton and Mifflin, 1893), p. 250.
5. Lyman Abbott, *What Christianity Means to Me* (New York: Macmillan, 1921), p. 141.
6. Gustavo Gutiérrez, *A Theology of Liberation* (Maryknoll, N.Y.: Orbis, 1973), p. 159.
7. Leonardo and Clodovis Boff, *Salvation and Liberation*, trans. Robert R. Barr (Maryknoll, N.Y.: Orbis, 1984), p. 65. The Boffs insist that the goal of liberation theology is "a fuller and more humane society, freed and liberated, a society of the freed." Cf. *Introducing Liberation Theology* (Maryknoll, N.Y.: Orbis, 1987), p. 93.
8. James H. Cone, *A Black Theology of Liberation* (Maryknoll, N.Y.: Orbis, 1986), p. 48.
9. Lewis S. Ford, *The Lure of God: A Biblical Background for Process Theism* (Philadelphia: Fortress, 1978), p. 64.
10. Ibid., p. 86.
11. Norman Pittenger, "Bernard E. Meland, Process Thought and the Significance of Christ," in *Process Theology*, Ewert H. Cousins, ed. (New York: Newman, 1971), p. 215.
12. Norman Pittenger, "The Divine Activity," *Encounter* 47.3 (Summer 1986):262.
13. Richard P. McBrien, *Catholicism*, 2 vols. in 1 (Minneapolis: Winston, 1981), p. 752.
14. Hermas, *The Shepherd: Visions*, III.3. Cf. *The Shepherd: Similitudes*, IX.16: "they descend into the water dead, and they arise alive."
15. Justin Martyr, *Apology*, I.66; cf. ibid., I.61.
16. Irenaeus, *Fragments*, 34.
17. Cyril of Jerusalem, *Prologue to the Lenten Lectures*, 16.
18. Augustine, *Sermon*, 213.8. Cf. *Enchiridion*, 120, which refers to baptism as "the sacrament of rebirth."
19. Augustine, *On Forgiveness of Sins, and Baptism*, II.43. Augustine spoke of baptism as "that laver of regeneration." *On Nature and Grace*, IV.
20. Augustine, *On the Gospel of St. John*, 80.3. Cf. *On Marriage and Concupiscence*, I.22.
21. Augustine, *Enchiridion*, 42. Cf. *Sermon*, 259.2: "We are born again in baptism so that we may receive the image of the Creator."
22. Thomas Aquinas, *SCG*, IV.58.4.
23. Ibid., IV.59.3.
24. Thomas Aquinas, *ST*, III, q. 69, art. 7. Cf. Aquinas, *SCG*, IV.59.4.
25. Aquinas, *ST*, III. q. 68, art. 2.
26. Ibid., II-II, q. 2, arts. 6-7.
27. Second Vatican Council, *Dogmatic Constitution on the Church*, II.16.
28. Gregory Baum, "Baptism," *Encyclopedia of Theology: The Concise Sacramentum Mundi*, Karl Rahner, ed. (New York: Crossroad, 1982), p. 77.
29. McBrien, *Catholicism*, p. 738.
30. Ibid.
31. Martin Luther, *LW*, 53:103.

32. *What Luther Says*, comp. Edward M. Plass (St. Louis: Concordia, 1959), p. 53. Luther added, ibid., p. 51, "The fact is that just because they are unreasoning and foolish, they are better fitted to come to faith than the old and reasoning people whose way is always blocked by reason, which does not want to force its big head through the narrow door."
33. Cited by Heinrich Schmid, *The Doctrinal Theology of the Evangelical Lutheran Church* (Minneapolis: Augsburg, reprint, 1961), p. 463.
34. Ibid., p. 464.
35. Dietrich Bonhoeffer, *Cost of Discipleship* (London: SCM, 1959), p. 206.
36. Francis Pieper, *Christian Dogmatics*, 3 vols. (St. Louis: Concordia, 1953), 3:264, 269-270.
37. *The Book of Common Prayer* (New York: Church Pension Fund, 1945), pp. 276, 280.
38. Edwin H. Palmer, *The Holy Spirit* (Grand Rapids, Mich.: Baker, 1958), pp. 83-84, typically wrote of "the great error that is so prevalent today in some orthodox Protestant circles, namely, the error that regeneration depends upon faith, and not upon God; and that in order to be born again man must first accept Jesus as Savior. . . . According to Scripture, faith does not precede and cause regeneration, but rather, regeneration precedes and causes faith. Regeneration is necessary before man can do a single thing that is spiritually good."
39. John Calvin, *Institutes of the Christian Religion*, III.3.9.
40. Ibid., IV.16.19.
41. Ibid., IV.16.17-20. Calvin added that "the truth of baptism is in them (i.e., infants of Christian parents)." *Treatises Against the Anabaptists and Against the Libertines*, Benjamin Wirt Farley, ed. (Grand Rapids, Mich.: Baker, 1982), p. 52.
42. John Calvin, "Catechism of the Church of Geneva," in *Calvin: Theological Treatises. LCC*, vol. XXII, trans. J.K.S. Reid (Philadelphia: Westminster, 1954), p. 133. Cf. Calvin, *Treatises Against the Anabaptists*, p. 49: "Baptism entails repentance, or the renewing of life, with the promise of the remission of our sins. Circumcision entails the same, no more, no less."
43. Calvin, "Catechism of the Church of Geneva," p. 135.
44. Calvin, *Institutes*, IV.15.1.
45. W.G.T. Shedd, *Dogmatic Theology*, 3 vols. (Grand Rapids, Mich.: Zondervan, reprint, n.d.), 2:508, n. 1.
46. Ibid., 2:528, n. 1.
47. Ibid., 2:514.
48. John Murray, *Redemption Accomplished and Applied* (Grand Rapids, Mich.: Eerdmans, 1955), p. 106.
49. Louis Berkhof, *Systematic Theology* (Grand Rapids, Mich.: Eerdmans, 1941), p. 485.
50. Richard S. Taylor, "Historical and Modern Significance of Wesleyan Theology," in *A Contemporary Wesleyan Theology*, Charles W. Carter, et al., eds., 2 vols. (Grand Rapids, Mich.: Zondervan, 1983), 1:65.
51. John Wesley, "Working Out Our Own Salvation," *The Works of John Wesley*, 14 vols. (Grand Rapids, Mich.: Zondervan, 1958), 6:509.
52. Charles Finney, *Finney's Systematic Theology*, J.H. Fairchild, ed. (Minneapolis: Bethany, 1976), p. 224. Finney asserted, ibid., p. 221, that God requires sinners to be active in regeneration, understood as an entire change of moral state or moral character.
53. Ibid., p. 235.
54. See Ernest F. Kevan, *Salvation* (Grand Rapids, Mich.: Baker, 1963), p. 60.
55. George Whitefield, "The Nature and Necessity of Our Regeneration or New Birth in Christ Jesus," in Timothy L. Smith, *Whitefield and Wesley on the New Birth* (Grand Rapids, Mich.: Zondervan, Francis Asbury, 1986), p. 67. Cf. "There are numbers that have been baptized when grown up or when very young that are not regenerated by God's Spirit, who will all go to one place [i.e., hell]." "All Men's Place," in *20 Centuries of Great Preaching*, Clyde E. Fant, Jr., and William M. Pinson, Jr., eds.; 13 vols. (Waco, Tex.: Word, 1971), 3:119.
56. Cited by Peter Toon, *Born Again: A Biblical and Theological Study of Regeneration* (Grand Rapids, Mich.: Baker, 1987), p. 159.
57. Charles Haddon Spurgeon, "Baptismal Regeneration," *The Metropolitan Pulpit*, 63 vols. (Pasadena, Tex.: Pilgrim Publications, 1969-80), 10:319. Cf. ibid., 15:403. Spurgeon shared his own testimony in the sermon "The Necessity of Regeneration," ibid., 54:583-84. "I was sprinkled when I was a child, but I know that I was not thereby made a member of Christ, a child of God, and an inheritor of the kingdom of heaven. I know that nothing of the kind took place in me, but that, as soon as I could, I went into sin, and continued in it. I was not

born again, I am sure, 'till I was about fifteen years of age, when the Lord brought salvation to my soul through the regenerating work of the Holy Spirit, and so I was enabled to trust in Jesus as my Savior."

58. Spurgeon, "The Simplicity and Sublimity of Salvation," *Metropolitan Pulpit*, 38:266.

59. See Spurgeon's sermons "Regeneration," *Metropolitan Pulpit*, 3:185-192 and "The Believer a New Creature," 15:397-408.

60. Spurgeon, "The Believer a New Creature," ibid., 15:401.

61. Augustus H. Strong, *Systematic Theology* (Valley Forge, Penn.: Judson, 1907), p. 809.

62. Millard J. Erickson, *Christian Theology*, 3 vols. (Grand Rapids, Mich.: Baker, 1983-85), 3:933.

63. William James, *The Varieties of Religious Experience: A Study in Human Nature* (London & New York: Longmans, Green & Co., 1928), pp. 79-90.

64. Ibid., p. 114.

65. George Eldon Ladd, *A Theology of the New Testament* (Grand Rapids, Mich.: Eerdmans, 1974), p. 216.

66. George Ladd commented, "The references to the baptism of households (Acts 11:14; 16:15, 31; 18:8) may . . . well designate only those of mature age who confessed their faith in Christ. It is difficult to believe that such passages mean that the faith of the head of the household sufficed for his children any more than it did for his relatives and slaves." *A Theology of the New Testament* (Grand Rapids, Mich.: Eerdmans, 1974), p. 350.

67. Rienecker and Rogers, *LKGNT*, p. 324, confirm that "The calling upon the Lord effects the washing away of sin."

68. See H.E. Dana and J.R. Mantey, *A Manual Grammar of the Greek New Testament* (New York: Macmillan, 1950), p. 104. Rienecker and Rogers, *LKGNT*, p. 267, comment that *eis* ("for," "because of") "could be connected with the command 'Repent.'" The sense of Peter's words then would be, "Repent—and be baptized every one of you in the name of Jesus Christ—for the forgiveness of your sins."

69. F.F. Bruce, *Commentary on the Book of the Acts, NICNT* (Grand Rapids, Mich.: Eerdmans, 1981), pp. 76-77.

70. Strong, *Systematic Theology*, p. 823.

71. John Calvin, *Commentaries on the Catholic Epistles*, p. 371.

72. Elmer B. Smick, "*Mûl*," *TWOT*, 1:495; cf. Peter E. Cousins, "Deuteronomy," *NLBC*, p. 293.

73. Gleason L. Archer, Jr., *Encyclopedia of Bible Difficulties* (Grand Rapids, Mich.: Zondervan, 1982), pp. 170-71.

74. Charles L. Feinberg, *Jeremiah: A Commentary* (Grand Rapids, Mich.: Zondervan, 1982), p. 220.

75. Ibid., p. 218.

76. Merrill C. Tenney, *John: The Gospel of Belief* (Grand Rapids, Mich.: Eerdmans, 1976), p. 87.

77. Bruce A. Ware, "The New Covenant and the People(s) of God," *Dispensationalism, Israel and the Church*, Craig A. Blaising and Darrell L. Bock, eds. (Grand Rapids, Mich.: Zondervan, 1992), p. 78, sums up an important sector of evangelical opinion by stating that the Spirit's ministry in the OT was "selective," "task orientated," and "temporary." Some Reformed theologians deny any restriction of the Spirit's ministry in the OT. Thus Willem A. VanGemeren, "A Response," ibid., p. 339, writes: "Was not the Spirit involved in the regeneration and sanctification of the Old Testament saints? Did they not experience internalization of the law of God (cf. Ps 37:31; 40:8)? Was not the Spirit involved in helping the Old Testament saints persevere in their longing for the day of redemption?"

78. Strong, *Systematic Theology*, p. 661.

79. Ibid., p. 662.

80. J. Wesley Bready, *This Freedom—Whence?* (New York: American Tract Society, 1942), p. 104.

81. Ibid., p. 96.

82. Paul Loeffler, "Conversion: Introduction," *The Ecumenical Review* 19.3 (July 1967):250.

C H A P T E R   8

1. Emil Brunner observes that the doctrine of union with Christ is the "center of all Calvinistic thinking." *Vom Werk des Heiligen Geist* (Tübingen, 1935), p. 38, cited by Lewis B. Smedes, *Union with Christ* (Grand Rapids, Mich.: Eerdmans, 1983), p. 31.

2. Augustus H. Strong, *Systematic Theology* (Valley Forge, Penn.: Judson, 1907), p. 795.
3. James S. Stewart, *A Man in Christ* (New York: Harper, n.d.), p. 147.
4. See Evelyn Underhill, *Mysticism* (London: Methuen, 1930), p. 420.
5. Pseudo-Dionysius, "The Mystical Theology," I.1, in *The Divine Names and Mystical Theology*, John D. Jones, ed. (Milwaukee: Marquette University Press, 1980), p. 211.
6. Meister Eckhart, "Sermon 84," in *Meister Eckhart: Teacher and Preacher*, Bernard McGinn, ed., *The Classics of Western Spirituality* (New York: Paulist, 1986), p. 337.
7. Meister Eckhart, "Sermon 44," in *Meister Eckhart: The Essential Sermons, Commentaries, Treatises, and Defense*, trans. E. Colledge and B. McGinn, *The Classics of Western Spirituality* (New York: Paulist, 1981), p. 56. Cf. "Sermon 99," cited in Underhill, *Mysticism*, p. 420: "I must be completely He and He I: so that this He and this I become and are one I."
8. Eckhart, "Sermon 6," in *Meister Eckhart: The Essential Sermons*, p. 188.
9. John Tauler, "Sermon 44," in *Johannes Tauler: Sermons*, trans. Maria Shrady, *The Classics of Western Spirituality* (New York: Paulist, 1985), p. 148.
10. Tauler, "Sermon 40," in *Johannes Tauler: Sermons*, pp. 141, 143.
11. John Tauler, "Sermon for Septuagesima Sunday," cited by Underhill, *Mysticism*, p. 84.
12. Henry Suso, "Book of Truth," 4, cited by Underhill, *Mysticism*, p. 424.
13. *The Cloud of Unknowing and Other Works*, trans. Clifton Wolters (New York: Penguin, 1978), p. 111.
14. Ibid., p. 141.
15. A.M.J. Kloosterman, *Contemporary Catholicism* (London: Collins, 1972), p. 111.
16. F.X. Lawlor, "Incorporation in Christ," *NCE*, 7:428.
17. Karl Adam, *The Spirit of Catholicism* (New York: Macmillan, 1955), p. 22.
18. Ibid., p. 19.
19. Ibid., p. 21.
20. Anthony J. Wilhelm, *Christ Among Us* (San Francisco: Harper, 1990), p. 193.
21. Ibid., p. 221.
22. David C. Steinmetz, *Reformers in the Wings* (Philadelphia: Fortress, 1971), p. 97.
23. John Calvin, *Institutes of the Christian Religion*, III.11.5-12; *The Formula of Concord*, art. III.
24. E.L. Mascall, *Christ, the Christian and the Church* (London: Longmans, Green & Co., 1946), p. 77.
25. Ibid., p. 109.
26. Ibid., pp. 80-81.
27. Ibid., p. 111.
28. Ibid., p. 94. Mascall added, "By baptism a man or woman is incorporated into the glorified humanity of the Word-made-flesh, and is made one with those others who have been likewise incorporated, thus becoming a member of the Church, which is Christ's Body." *Christian Theology and Natural Science* (New York: Ronald Press, 1956), p. 315.
29. Mascall, *Christ, the Christian*, p. 194.
30. E.L. Mascall, *Corpus Christi* (London: Longmans, Green & Co., 1965), p. 45.
31. Ernest F. Kevan, *Salvation* (Grand Rapids, Mich.: Baker, 1963), p. 46.
32. Herman Kuiper, *By Grace Alone* (Grand Rapids, Mich.: Eerdmans, 1955), p. 39.
33. L. Berkhof, *Systematic Theology* (Grand Rapids, Mich.: Eerdmans, 1941), p. 449.
34. John Murray, *Redemption Accomplished and Applied* (Grand Rapids, Mich.: Eerdmans, 1955), p. 165.
35. Ibid., p. 162.
36. Anthony A. Hoekema, *Saved by Grace* (Grand Rapids, Mich.: Eerdmans, 1989), p. 57.
37. Ibid., p. 64.
38. Lyman Abbott, *The Evolution of Christianity* (Boston & New York: Houghton, Mifflin & Co., 1893), p. 256.
39. Ibid., p. 255.
40. Ibid., p. 254. Abbott added that "History is but the record of the process of this evolution of the divinity out of the humanity." Ibid., p. 254.
41. Adolf von Harnack, *What Is Christianity?* (London: Williams & Norgate, 1912), p. 155.
42. Ibid., p. 168.
43. Shailer Mathews, *The Faith of Modernism* (New York: Macmillan, 1924), p. 176.

44. Shailer Mathews, *The Gospel and the Modern Man* (New York: Macmillan, 1912), p. 75.
45. Mathews, *Faith of Modernism*, pp. 100-101.
46. W.G.T. Shedd, *Dogmatic Theology*, 3 vols. (Grand Rapids, Mich.: Zondervan, reprint, n.d.), 2:534.
47. Ibid., 2:534.
48. Calvin, *Institutes*, IV.17.9.
49. Ibid., III.1.1.; cf. ibid., II.17.1.
50. Ibid., III.18.3.
51. Robert L. Dabney, *Lectures in Systematic Theology* (Grand Rapids, Mich.: Zondervan, reprint, 1972), p. 615.
52. Ibid., pp. 612-613.
53. Strong, *Systematic Theology*, p. 795.
54. Ibid.
55. See A.J.M. Wedderburn, "Some Observations on Paul's Use of the Phrases 'in Christ' and 'with Christ,'" *JSNT* 25 (1985): 83, 87. He observes, p. 87, that *en Christo* and *en Kyrio* "are not likely to be 'formulae,' but rather characteristic, and versatile, phrases of Paul's." See also Michael Parsons, "'In Christ' in Paul," *Vox Evangelica* 18 (1988):25-28.
56. Smedes, *Union with Christ*, pp. 15-25, 57, 65-66, etc., strongly emphasizes this dimension of "union with Christ." He does so, unfortunately, to the neglect of the subjective, experiential dimension.
57. See the discussion by Murray J. Harris, "Prepositions and Theology in the Greek New Testament," *NIDNTT*, 3:1192-93.
58. Donald Guthrie, *New Testament Theology* (Leicester: Inter-Varsity, 1981), p. 651. Parsons, "'In Christ' in Paul," p. 27, agrees: "It is best, then, that we maintain *both* the individual aspect which clearly should not be neglected, together with the corporate nature of being in Christ."
59. Smedes, *Union with Christ*, pp. 91-92.
60. Parsons, "'In Christ' in Paul," p. 37.
61. F.F. Bruce, *1 & 2 Corinthians*, NCBC (Grand Rapids, Mich.: Eerdmans, 1980), p. 207.
62. Guthrie, *New Testament Theology*, p. 654.
63. Smedes, *Union with Christ*, p. 58.
64. Augustine, *On Christian Doctrine*, III.16.
65. Augustine, *Homilies on John*, 26.1.
66. F. Godet, *Commentary on the Epistle to the Romans* (Grand Rapids, Mich.: Zondervan, reprint, 1956), p. 243.
67. Martin Luther, in Ewald M. Plass, ed., *What Luther Says* (St. Louis: Concordia, 1959), p. 498.
68. B.F. Westcott, *St. Paul's Epistle to the Ephesians* (Grand Rapids, Mich.: Baker, reprint, 1979), p. 10.
69. Shedd, *Dogmatic Theology*, 2:534.
70. John Eadie, *Ephesians* (Grand Rapids, Mich.: Baker, reprint, 1979), p. 41.
71. Calvin, *Institutes*, IV.17.8.
72. Murray, *Redemption Accomplished and Applied*, p. 167.
73. Cited by Mathews, *The Gospel and the Modern Man*, p. 297.

CHAPTER 9

1. Jaroslav Pelikan, *The Christian Tradition: A History of the Development of Doctrine*, 5 vols. (Chicago: University of Chicago Press, 1971-89), 4:139.
2. Dale Moody, *The Word of Truth: A Summary of Christian Doctrine Based on Biblical Revelation* (Grand Rapids, Mich.: Eerdmans, 1981), p. 328.
3. Peter Toon, "Justification," *New 20th-Century Encyclopedia of Religious Knowledge*, J.D. Douglas, ed. (Grand Rapids, Mich.: Baker, 1991), p. 474, comments: "justification never seems to have been a major issue for the Orthodox and Eastern churches and so they have little or nothing to contribute to this continuing debate."
4. *The Racovian Catechism* (1605), chap. V.8, cited in *The Polish Brethren*, 2 vols., G.H. Williams, ed. and trans. (Missoula, Mont.: Scholars Press, 1980), 1:222.

5. Albrecht Ritschl, *The Christian Doctrine of Justification and Reconciliation*, H.R. Mackintosh and A.B. Macaulay, eds. (Clifton, N.J.: Reference Book Publishers, 1966), p. 274.

6. Ibid., p. 70.

7. Lyman Abbott, *What Christianity Means to Me* (New York: Macmillan, 1921), p. 140.

8. Shailer Mathews, *The Gospel and the Modern Man* (New York: Macmillan, 1912), p. 182.

9. Shailer Mathews, *The Faith of Modernism* (New York: Macmillan, 1924), p. 91. Cf. Mathews, *The Gospel and the Modern Man*, p. 184: "The loving God of the universe will save a man who tries to live as Jesus did."

10. Norman Pittenger, *Cosmic Love and Human Wrong* (New York: Paulist, 1978), p. 102.

11. Norman Pittenger, *Freed to Love: A Process Interpretation of Redemption* (Wilton, Conn.: Morehouse-Barlow, 1987), pp. 68-71.

12. John A. Hardon, *The Catholic Catechism* (New York: Doubleday, 1975), p. 169.

13. Augustine, *Sermon*, 158.5. Augustine viewed the "righteousness of God" (Rom 3:21) as an objective genitive, i.e., "the righteousness, whose origin is in God, given to the sinner."

14. Augustine, *On the Spirit and the Letter*, 45. Cf. *On Nature and Grace*, 29. At the end of his essay *On the Spirit and the Letter*, 45, Augustine attested the objective dimension of justification: "the term 'They shall be justified' is used in the sense of, They shall be deemed, or reckoned as just, as it is predicated of a certain man in the Gospel, 'But he wanted to justify himself'" (Luke 10:29).

15. Augustine, *On the Spirit and the Letter*, 18-20. Cf. Augustine, *On Grace and Free Will*, 14.27: Justification includes not only the remission of sin, but also "that grace which makes it possible to fulfill the Law so that our nature is set free from the dominion of sin."

16. So Augustine, *Letter*, 194.14: "When God rewards our merits, he is actually rewarding his own gifts."

17. Augustine, *City of God*, XX.25; XXI.13, 16, 26; Augustine, *Enchiridion*, 69.

18. Hendrikus Berkhof, *Christian Faith* (Grand Rapids, Mich.: Eerdmans, 1979), p. 435, commented: "Though Augustine does not deny the imputation, all the emphasis for him (unlike Paul) is on the inner renewal that rests on it, thus on what we are accustomed to call 'sanctification.' This has become the common meaning in Roman Catholic theology." Alister E. McGrath, in his scholarly study of justification, refers to "the misleading interpretation given to the term 'justification' by Augustine." *Iustitia Dei*, 2 vols. (Cambridge: Cambridge Univ. Press, 1986-87), 1:60.

19. Augustine, *Admonition and Grace*, 9.23; Augustine, *On the Gospel of John*, XXVI.15.

20. Richard P. McBrien, *Catholicism* (Minneapolis: Winston, 1981), p. 423.

21. Ibid., p. 1248.

22. Ibid., p. 738.

23. Willard H. Taylor, "Justification," *BDT*, p. 298. John Wesley, "Minutes of Some Late Conversations," *The Works of John Wesley*, 14 vols. (Grand Rapids, Mich.: Zondervan, 1958), 8:277, added: "We do not find it expressly affirmed in Scripture that God imputes the righteousness of Christ to any." What God does, according to Wesley, is reckon their faith as righteousness, namely, forgiveness of sins and the removal of guilt.

24. Wesley, "Justification by Faith," *Works*, 5:57: "Least of all does justification imply that God is deceived in those whom he justifies; that he thinks them to be what, in fact, they are not; that he accounts them to be otherwise than they are. It does by no means imply that God ... believes us righteous when we are unrighteous."

25. Ibid. R. Larry Shelton adds, "God pronounces believers righteous and justifies them when they fulfill by faith-obedience the requirements of the covenant relationship." "Initial Salvation: The Redemptive Grace of God in Christ," in *A Contemporary Wesleyan Theology*, 2 vols., Charles W. Carter, ed. (Grand Rapids, Mich.: Zondervan, Francis Asbury, 1983), 1:494.

26. Richard Watson, *Theological Institutes*, 2 vols. (New York: Lane & Scott, 1851), 2:226. Cf. ibid., 2:215.

27. Ibid., 2:211; cf. ibid., 2:214. Watson defined "the righteousness of God" as God's "rectoral justice in the administration of pardon," which, of course, is not capable of imputation.

28. Charles Finney, *Finney's Systematic Theology*, J.H. Fairchild, ed. (Minneapolis: Bethany Fellowship, 1976), p. 322. Cf. ibid., p. 320.

29. Ibid., p. 333.

30. Ibid., p. 320.
31. See the critique of Finney's view of justification in B.B. Warfield, *Perfectionism*, Samuel G. Craig, ed. (Philadelphia: Presbyterian & Reformed, 1958), pp. 152-165.
32. Leonardo Boff, *Liberating Grace*, trans. John Drury (Maryknoll, N.Y.: Orbis, 1979), p. 152.
33. Ibid., pp. 185-86.
34. Clodovis Boff, *Theology and Praxis*, trans. Robert R. Barr (Maryknoll, N.Y.: Orbis, 1987), p. 122.
35. Ibid., p. 101.
36. Ibid..
37. James H. Cone, *God of the Oppressed* (New York: Seabury, 1975), p. 229.
38. Olin P. Moyd, *Redemption in Black Theology* (Valley Forge, Penn.: Judson, 1979), p. 153, agrees: "Justification in Black Theology is Black folks coming to know the impact of the justice of God in an unjust world-life situation."
39. Karl Barth, *CD*, vol. IV/1, p. 563.
40. Ibid., p. 36.
41. Hans Küng, *Justification: The Doctrine of Karl Barth and a Catholic Reflection* (Philadelphia: Westminster, 1981), p. 80.
42. Barth, *CD*, vol. IV/1, p. 492.
43. Ibid., p. 74.
44. Gustaf Aulén, *The Faith of the Christian Church* (London: SCM, 1954), p. 223. Cf. ibid., p. 297.
45. Ibid., pp. 172-173.
46. Ibid., p. 292. Cf. Gustaf Aulén, *Reformation and Catholicity* (Philadelphia: Muhlenberg, 1961), p. 63, where justification by faith is presented as a continuing redemptive activity of God mediated by the Word and sacraments.
47. Ibid., pp. 224-225, 228, 231, etc.
48. Martin Luther, *LW*, 34:337. Cf. ibid., 25:151.
49. Ibid., 26:232.
50. Ibid., 26:232; cf. ibid., 25:260.
51. Ibid., 27:228; cf. ibid., 25:258.
52. Ibid., 26:377-378.
53. Ibid., 34:183.
54. "Baccalaureate Theses," 10, in *Melanchthon: Selected Writings*, trans. C.H. Hill (Westport, Conn.: Greenwood, 1978), p. 17.
55. Philip Melanchthon, *Melanchthon on Christian Doctrine: Loci Communes* (1555), Clyde Manschreck, ed. (Grand Rapids, Mich.: Baker, reprint, 1982), p. 161.
56. John Calvin, "Sermon on Luke 1:5-10," *CR*, 46:23. Calvin also noted, *Institutes of the Christian Religion*, III.11.1, that justification is "the main hinge on which religion turns."
57. Calvin, *Institutes*, III.11.2.
58. Ibid., III.11.21.
59. Ibid., III.2.17; cf. ibid., III.4.27.
60. Ibid., III.11.6.
61. Ibid., III.16.1. Cf. ibid., III.11.1: By partaking of Christ we "receive a double grace"; namely, we are "reconciled to God through Christ's blessedness" and we are "sanctified by Christ's spirit."
62. Ibid., III.17.10. Cf. ibid., III.17.5.
63. J.I. Packer, "Justification," *EDT*, p. 595.
64. Ibid., p. 596.
65. Ibid.
66. See the discussion in Leon J. Wood, "Ḥāšab," *TWOT*, 1:330.
67. Harold G. Stigers, "Ṣādēq," *TWOT*, 2:752-755.
68. Fritz Rienecker and Cleon L. Rogers, Jr., *LKGNT*, p. 33.
69. Leon Morris, *The Apostolic Preaching of the Cross* (Grand Rapids, Mich.: Eerdmans, 1956), p. 260.
70. Edward J. Young, *The Book of Isaiah*, 3 vols. (Grand Rapids, Mich.: Eerdmans, 1965-72), 3:389. Cf. J. Ridderbos, *Isaiah, Bible Student's Commentary* (Grand Rapids, Mich.:

Zondervan, 1984), p. 47, who wrote: "It is a description in Old Testament terms of justification by grace alone."

71. Young, *Isaiah*, 1:77.
72. Ibid., 3:358.
73. F.F. Bruce, *The Epistle of Paul to the Romans*, TNTC (London: Tyndale, 1963), p. 80. Cf. Jack B. Scott, "*ᵉmûnāh*," *TWOT*, 1:52.
74. C.E.B. Cranfield, *The Epistle to the Romans*, ICC, 2 vols. (Edinburgh: T. & T. Clark, 1975-79), 1:202, concludes that *dikaiosynē theou* means "a status of righteousness before God which is God's gift."
75. See M.J. Harris, "Prepositions and Theology in the Greek New Testament," *NIDNTT*, 3:1182. Harris observes that *dia* with the genitive signifies "the instrumental sense, which marks the medium *through* which an action passes before its accomplishment."
76. F.F. Bruce observed, *Commentary on the Epistle to the Hebrews* (London & Edinburgh, 1965), pp. 208-209: "The first covenant provided a measure of atonement and remission of sin committed under it, but it was incapable of providing 'eternal redemption'; this was a blessing which had to await the inauguration of the new covenant."
77. Ralph P. Martin, *2 Corinthians*, WBC (Waco, Tex.: Word, 1986), p. 154. Cf. John Eadie, *Ephesians, Greek Text Commentary* (Grand Rapids, Mich.: Baker, reprint, 1979), p. 182.
78. S. B. Narramore, "Guilt," *Baker Encyclopedia of Psychology*, David G. Benner, ed. (Grand Rapids, Mich.: Baker, 1985), p. 486.
79. Paul Tournier, *Guilt and Grace* (New York: Harper & Row, 1962), p. 41.
80. Narramore, "Guilt," p. 488.
81. Tournier, *Guilt and Grace*, p. 66. Tournier furthermore, ibid., p. 69, defines "true guilt" as "disobedience to God or any dependence other than on God alone."
82. See David A. Seamands, *Healing for Damaged Emotions* (Wheaton, Ill.: Victor, 1981), p. 79. Cf. C.M. Berry, "Perfectionism," *Baker Encyclopedia of Psychology*, pp. 810-811.
83. Calvin, *Institutes*, III.17.5.
84. Ibid., III.17.10; cf. ibid., III.17.8, 15.

CHAPTER 10

1. The perfect passive participle of the verb *anagennaō* (to "regenerate") in 1 Pet 1:23 suggests that the action effected by the new birth is ongoing in Christians (in sanctification).
2. *The Racovian Catechism*, V.2, cited in *The Polish Brethren*, George H. Williams, trans. and ed., 2 parts (Missoula, Mont.: Scholars Press, 1980), 1:215.
3. Walter Rauschenbusch, *A Theology for the Social Gospel* (Nashville: Abingdon, reprint, 1978), p. 104.
4. William Adams Brown, *Christian Theology in Outline* (New York: Charles Scribner's Sons, 1911), pp. 420-423.
5. Typical of Catholic theologians, Karl Adam (d. 1966) states the case: "Justification is not . . . a mere external imputation of the righteousness of Christ. It is the communication of a true inward righteousness, of a new love which re-makes the whole man; it is sanctification." *The Spirit of Catholicism* (New York: Macmillan, 1955), p. 208.
6. Council of Trent, Session VI, chap 10.
7. Council of Trent, Session VI, canon 32. Cf. Trent, Session IV, chap. 16.
8. Ibid., Session VI, chap. 10.
9. Session XXV, "Decree Concerning Purgatory."
10. F.G.L. Van Der Meer, *The Faith of the Church*, trans. John Murray (London: Darton, Longman & Todd, 1966), p. 391.
11. Ibid., p. 407. Van Der Meer, ibid., p. 405, adds that the works of the Christian "are good works, pleasing in God's sight and meritorious because of an adequacy that belongs really to Christ but which becomes ours as well as his."
12. Ibid., p. 408.
13. Ibid.
14. Ibid.
15. Ibid., p. 515.
16. John Wesley, "Brief Thoughts on Christian Perfection," in *The Works of John Wesley*, 14 vols. (Grand Rapids, Mich.: Zondervan, 1958), 11:446.

17. Wesley, "Christian Perfection," *Works*, 6:15; cf. ibid., 6:19; cf. "A Plain Account of Christian Perfection," *Works*, 11:375-376.
18. Wesley, "The Great Privilege of Those That Are Born of God," *Works*, 5:227-228.
19. Wesley, "The Scripture Way of Salvation," *Works*, 6:46.
20. Wesley, "A Plain Account," *Works*, 11:367.
21. Wesley wrote the following in "The Great Privilege of Those That Are Born of God," *Works*, 5:227: "By sin I here understand outward sin . . . an actual, voluntary transgression of the law; of the revealed, written law of God; of any commandment of God, acknowledged to be such at the time that it is transgressed." Cf. "On Perfection," *Works*, 6:417.
22. Wesley defined sin proper as "a voluntary transgression of a known law." "A Plain Account," *Works*, 11:396. Concerning involuntary transgression of known laws of God, Wesley, ibid., said "you may call them sins, if you please: I do not."
23. Wesley, "The Journal of John Wesley," *Works*, 3:75.
24. See Kenneth J. Collins, *Wesley on Salvation* (Grand Rapids, Mich.: Zondervan, Francis Asbury, 1989), p. 119.
25. Wesley wrote, "I believe this perfection is always wrought in the soul by a simple act of faith; consequently in an instant. But I believe in a gradual work both preceding and following that instant." *A Plain Account of Christian Perfection* (London: Epworth, reprint, 1952), p. 112. Cf. "The Scripture Way of Salvation," *Works*, 6:46.
26. John Wesley, "Letter of Nov. 17, 1759," in *The Letters of the Rev. John Wesley*, John Telford, ed., 8 vols (London: Epworth, 1931), 4:327.
27. Charles G. Finney, *Principles of Sanctification*, L.G. Parkhurst, ed. (Minneapolis: Bethany, 1986), p. 52.
28. Charles G. Finney, *Finney's Systematic Theology*, J.H. Fairchild, ed. (Minneapolis: Bethany Fellowship, 1976), p. 362.
29. Ibid., p. 368.
30. J. Kenneth Grider, *Entire Sanctification* (Kansas City: Beacon Hill, 1980), p. 112.
31. Ibid., p. 27.
32. *Discipline of the Pentecostal Holiness Church* (Franklin Springs, Ga.: Board of Publication, Pentecostal Holiness Church, 1953), p. 13.
33. "Baptism in the Holy Spirit," *Dictionary of Pentecostal and Charismatic Movements* (Grand Rapids, Mich.: Regency Reference Library, 1988), p. 43.
34. "Statement of Fundamental Truths," in *The Constitution and Bylaws of the Assemblies of God* (Springfield, Mo.: Gospel Publishing House, 1985), art. 7, p. 107.
35. Stanley M. Horton, "The Pentecostal Perspective," in *Five Views on Sanctification* (Grand Rapids, Mich.: Zondervan, Academie Books, 1987), p. 131.
36. Ibid., p. 193.
37. Ernest S. Williams, *Systematic Theology*, 3 vols. (Springfield, Mo.: Gospel Publishing House, 1953), 2:258.
38. Ibid., 3:50; cf., ibid., 3:74.
39. J. Rodman Williams, *The Pentecostal Reality* (Plainfield, N.J.: Logos International, 1972), p. 25. Cf. J. Rodman Williams, *Renewal Theology*, 3 vols. (Grand Rapids, Mich.: Zondervan, Academie, 1988-92), 2:179, 198-207.
40. See the booklet, "Have You Made the Wonderful Discovery of the Spirit-Filled Life?" (San Bernardino, Calif.: Campus Crusade for Christ International, 1966).
41. J. Robertson McQuilkin, "The Keswick Perspective," in Melvin E. Dieter, Anthony A. Hoekema, et al., *Five Views on Sanctification* (Grand Rapids, Mich.: Zondervan, 1987), p. 160.
42. See Steven Barabas, *So Great Salvation: The History and Message of the Keswick Convention* (London & Edinburgh: Marshall, Morgan & Scott, 1952), pp. 55-56.
43. McQuilkin, "The Keswick Perspective," in *Five Views on Sanctification*, p. 167. Barabas, *So Great Salvation*, p. 107, described the Keswick position as "the doctrine of sanctification by faith."
44. McQuilkin, "The Keswick Perspective," p. 155.
45. Barabas, *So Great Salvation*, p. 84. Cf., ibid., p. 99: "A life of victory over conscious sin is the rightful heritage of every child of God."
46. Ibid., p. 115.

47. Charles G. Turnbull, *Victory in Christ* (Philadelphia: The Sunday School Times Co., 1959), p. 15.

48. Ibid., p. 16.

49. Ibid., p. 13.

50. Karl Barth, *CD*, vol. IV/2, p. 507. Cf. ibid., p. 505: "Justification and sanctification must be distinguished, but they cannot be divided or separated."

51. Ibid., p. 511; cf. p. 500.

52. Ibid., p. 516. cf. p. 514.

53. Barth, ibid., p. 503, defined sanctification as the act of God by which in "free grace He converts men to himself." Cf. *CD*, vol. IV/1, p. 101: Sanctification "is a form of the atonement, of the conversion of man to God accomplished and revealed in Jesus Christ."

54. Barth, *CD*, vol. IV/2, p. 518; cf. p. 511. That Barth understood sanctification within a purely objective framework is clear from his statement in ibid., p. 517: "As we are not asked to justify ourselves, we are not asked to sanctify ourselves. Our sanctification consists in our participation in His sanctification."

55. Ibid., p. 511.

56. Anthony A. Hoekema raised the question why in Barth's view God gives the Holy Spirit only to some Christians and not to all God's elect (or his covenant partners). Hoekema argued that in Barth's representation the Trinity is divided against itself. "Do the Scriptures give us the impression that there are elect people to whom the Holy Spirit is not given?" *Karl Barth's Doctrine of Sanctification* (Grand Rapids, Mich.: Calvin Theological Seminary, 1965), p. 22.

57. Barth, *CD*, vol. IV/2, p. 620.

58. Reinhold Niebuhr, *The Nature and Destiny of Man*, 2 vols. (New York: Charles Scribner's Sons, 1951), 2:100.

59. Leonardo Boff and Clodovis Boff, *Introducing Liberation Theology* (Maryknoll, N.Y.: Orbis, 1987), p. 93.

60. Jose Miguez Bonino, "Wesley's Doctrine of Sanctification from a Liberationist Perspective," in Theodore Runyon, ed., *Sanctification and Liberation* (Nashville, Abingdon, 1981), p. 63.

61 Gustavo Gutiérrez, "Liberation Theology and Proclamation," in *The Mystical and Political Dimensions of the Christian Faith*, C. Geffri and G. Gutiérrez, eds. (New York: Herder and Herder, 1974), p. 67.

62. James H. Cone, "Sanctification and Liberation in the Black Religious Tradition," in *Sanctification and Liberation*, p. 190.

63. J.I. Packer, "'Keswick' and the Reformed Doctrine of Sanctification," *Evangelical Quarterly* 27 (July-Sept 1955):27.

64. Augustine, *On Grace and Free Will*, 17.32.

65. Augustine, *On the Spirit and the Letter*, 65. Cf. *Against Two Epistles of the Pelagians*, III.7.19: "When we call the virtue of the saints perfect, to this very perfection also belongs the recognition of imperfection, both in truth and humility."

66. Augustine, *Faith, Hope and Charity*, 31.118.

67. So Klaus Bockmuehl, "Sanctification," *NDT*, p. 615.

68. John Calvin, *Institutes of the Christian Religion*, III.16.1. Cf. ibid., III.11.1: "Being partakers of Christ we grasp a double grace."

69. John Calvin, *The Epistles of Paul the Apostle to the Romans and to the Thessalonians*, David W. and Thomas F. Torrance, eds., (Grand Rapids, Mich.: Eerdmans, 1961), p. 181.

70. Calvin, *Institutes*, III.3.9. Calvin, ibid., III.6.5, emphasized that Christians' spiritual progress often is painfully slow: "weakness so weighs down the greater number that, with wavering and limping and even creeping along the ground, they move at a feeble rate. . . . No one shall set out so inauspiciously as not daily to make some headway, although it be slight. Therefore, let us not cease so to act that we may make some unceasing progress in the way of the Lord. And let us not despair at the slightness of our success."

71. Ibid., II.7.1.

72. Ibid., II.7.10. Cf. ibid., "the law is like a halter to check the raging and otherwise limitless ranging lusts of the flesh."

73. Ibid., II.7.12.

74. Ibid.

75. Ibid., II.7.14.

76. Ibid., IV.20.15.

77. Douglas J. Moo, "The Law of Moses or the Law of Christ," in *Continuity and Discontinuity*, John S. Feinberg, ed. (Westchester, Ill.: Crossway, 1988), p. 217.
78. Calvin, *Institutes*, III.3.10; cf. ibid., III.3.14: "we are purged by his sanctification in such a way that we are besieged by many vices and much weakness so long as we are encumbered with our body."
79. Ibid., III.6.5.
80. L. Berkhof, *Systematic Theology* (Grand Rapids, Mich.: Eerdmans, 1941), p. 532.
81. Ibid., p. 537.
82. Ibid., p. 543.
83. *The Golden Treasury of Puritan Quotations*, compiled by I.D.E. Thomas (Chicago: Moody, 1975), p. 141.
84. J.C. Ryle, *Holiness* (Grand Rapids, Mich.: Kregel, 1952), p. 21.
85. F.F. Bruce, *The Epistle of Paul to the Romans*, TNTC (London: Tyndale, 1963), p. 153.
86. Donald G. Bloesch, *The Christian Life and Salvation* (Grand Rapids, Mich.: Eerdmans, 1967), p. 123.
87. Charles M. Horne, *The Doctrine of Salvation* (Chicago: Moody, 1984), p. 73.
88. F.F. Bruce, *The Gospel of John* (Grand Rapids, Mich.: Eerdmans, 1983), p. 397, n. 18.
89. J.I. Packer, *Keep in Step with the Spirit* (Old Tappan, N.J.: Fleming Revell, 1984), p. 205.
90. So argue Everett F. Harrison, *Interpreting Acts* (Grand Rapids, Mich.: Zondervan, Academie, 1986), p. 146; Michael Green, *I Believe in the Holy Spirit* (Grand Rapids, Mich.: Eerdmans, 1975), pp. 136-139; D.A. Carson, *Showing the Spirit: A Theological Exposition of 1 Corinthians 12–14* (Grand Rapids, Mich.: Baker, 1987), p. 145; and Packer, *Keep in Step with the Spirit*, p. 204.
91. I. Howard Marshall, *The Acts of the Apostles*, TNTC (Grand Rapids, Mich.: Eerdmans, 1980), pp. 306-307.
92. Ibid., p. 308. Cf. Harrison, *Interpreting Acts*, p. 308.
93. Packer, *Keep in Step with the Spirit*, p. 206. Grant R. Osborne concludes that the manifestation of tongues in Acts "authenticated the addition of new groups to the church . . . for the sake of the Jewish Christians in Jerusalem." "Tongues, Speaking in," *EDT*, p. 1101.
94. Lewis Sperry Chafer, *Systematic Theology*, 8 vols. (Dallas, Texas: Dallas Seminary Press, 1947-48), 6:170.
95. *The New Brown-Driver-Briggs-Gesenius Hebrew and English Lexicon* (Peabody, Mass.: Hendrickson, 1979), pp. 1070-1071.
96. J. Barton Payne, "*tamam*," *TWOT*, 2:974.
97. Charles Bridges, *A Commentary on Proverbs* (London: Banner of Truth, reprint, 1968), p. 50.
98. *New Brown-Driver-Briggs-Gesenius Lexicon*, p. 1070.
99. Ibid., p. 449.
100. Bridges said concerning those who claim to be without sin: "Vain boasters these are, who proclaim their good hearts. But the boast proves, not their goodness, but their blindness. That man is so blind that he cannot understand his own depravity." *Proverbs*, p. 342.
101. R.E.O. White, "Sanctification," *EDT*, p. 971. Or according to R. Schippers, "Goal," *NIDNTT*, 2:65, "*teleios* signifies the undivided wholeness of a person in his behavior."
102. *The NIV Study Bible*, p. 1808, *ad loc.*
103. William S. Plummer, *Commentary on the Epistle of Paul, the Apostle to the Hebrews* (Grand Rapids, Mich.: Baker, reprint, 1980), p. 521.
104. Martin Luther, *What Luther Says*, compiled by Edward M. Plass (St. Louis: Concordia, 1959), p. 1317.
105. Charles C. Ryrie, *The Grace of God* (Chicago: Moody, 1963), p. 102.
106. Charles C. Ryrie, *Basic Theology* (Wheaton, Ill.: Victor, 1986), p. 303.
107. Lawrence O. Richards, *Expository Dictionary of Bible Words* (Grand Rapids, Mich.: Zondervan, 1985), p. 395.
108. Ibid. Richards adds that the law was not intended to guide the believer to a holy life. Indeed, ibid., p. 396, "We are not to look to the law to help us become the truly good persons God intends us to be."
109. Robert L. Dabney, *Lectures in Systematic Theology* (Grand Rapids, Mich.: Zondervan, reprint, 1972), p. 357.

110. See Greg L. Bahnsen, *Theonomy in Christian Ethics* (Nutley, N.J.: Craig Press, 1967), pp. 207-216; Bahnsen, *By This Standard* (Tyler, Texas: Institute for Christian Economics, 1985).
111. Calvin, *Institutes*, II.8.7.
112. Ryle, *Holiness*, p. xvi.
113. Stephen F. Winward, *Fruit of the Spirit* (Grand Rapids, Mich.: Eerdmans, 1981), p. 21.
114. Baxter, *New Call to Holiness*, p. 181.
115. Baxter, *New Call to Holiness*, p. 113.
116. Thomas à Kempis, *The Imitation of Christ*, Donald E. Demaray, ed. (Grand Rapids, Mich.: Baker, 1982), p. 103.
117. Ibid., p. 244.

C H A P T E R   1 1

1. K. Steur, cited by G.C. Berkouwer, *Faith and Perseverance* (Grand Rapids, Mich.: Eerdmans, 1958), p. 47.
2. Karl Rahner and H. Vorgrimler, eds., "Perseverance," *Theological Dictionary* (New York: Herder and Herder, 1965), p. 351.
3. P. De Letter, "Faith, Loss of," *NCE*, 5:804.
4. *The Catholic Encyclopedia*, Robert C. Broderick, ed. (Nashville: Thomas Nelson, 1987), p. 402.
5. J.J. Connelly, "Perseverance, Final," *NCE*, 11:154.
6. J.J. Connelly, "Confirmation in Grace," *NCE*, 4:152.
7. F.G.L. Van Der Meer, *The Faith of the Church*, trans. John Murray (London: Darton, Longman & Todd, 1966), p. 408.
8. Ibid., p. 345.
9. Berkouwer, *Faith and Perseverance*, p. 54.
10. James Arminius, *The Works of James Arminius*, 3 vols., trans. James Nichols & William Nichols (Grand Rapids, Mich.: Baker, reprint, 1986), 3:467.
11. Ibid., 2:725.
12. John Wesley, "Predestination Calmly Considered," *Works*, 10:257. Cf. John Wesley, "A Call to Backsliders," *Works*, 6:526. Wesley added with a note of sarcasm, "Letter, DCCCXLVI," *Works*, 13:116: "You see the blessed effects of unconditional perseverance! It leads the way, by easy steps, first to presumption, and then to black despair!"
13. John Wesley, "The Perseverance of the Saints," *Works*, 10: 285-97.
14. J. Kenneth Grider, *Entire Sanctification* (Kansas City: Beacon Hill, 1980), p. 146.
15. Ibid., p. 31.
16. Dale Moody, *The Word of Truth* (Grand Rapids, Mich.: Eerdmans, 1981), p. 356.
17. Stanley M. Horton, "The Pentecostal Perspective," in *Five Views on Sanctification* (Grand Rapids, Mich.: Zondervan, Academie Books, 1987), p. 192. Horton adds, ibid., p. 96: "Even children of the kingdom can be cast out."
18. Ernest S. Williams, *Systematic Theology*, 3 vols. (Springfield, Mo.: Gospel Publishing House, 1953), 2:259.
19. Ernest F. Kevan, *Salvation* (Grand Rapids, Mich.: Baker, 1963), pp. 89-90.
20. Martin Luther, *LW*, 26:94.
21. Ibid., 23:187.
22. *What Luther Says*, Ewald M. Plass, ed. (St. Louis: Concordia, 1959), p. 39.
23. John T. Mueller, *Christian Dogmatics* (St. Louis: Concordia, 1955), p. 436.
24. Ibid., p. 437.
25. A.T. Robertson, *Word Pictures in the New Testament*, 6 vols. (Nashville: Broadman, 1930-33), 5:186.
26. Donald G. Bloesch, *The Christian Life and Salvation* (Grand Rapids, Mich.: Eerdmans, 1967), p. 90.
27. Augustine, *Admonition and Grace*, 22; cf. ibid., 36.
28. Augustine, *On the Gift of Perseverance*, 41. Cf. ibid., 9: "assuredly, when that gift of God is granted to them . . . none of the saints fails to keep his perseverance in holiness even to the end."
29. Augustine, *Admonition and Grace*, 11 (31); cf. ibid., 12 (38).
30. Ibid., 13 (40); cf. *On the Gift of Perseverance*, 1 (1).

31. Augustine, *Admonition and Grace*, 7 (13).
32. John Calvin, *Institutes of the Christian Religion*, II.3.11.
33. John Calvin, *Commentaries on the Epistles to the Philippians, Colossians, and Thessalonians*, p. 69.
34. John Calvin, *Commentaries on the Epistle to the Hebrews*, pp. 135-140.
35. Charles H. Spurgeon, "Enduring to the End," *SEE*, 12:298-99.
36. Charles H. Spurgeon, "Perseverance in Holiness," *SEE*, 8:475.
37. Spurgeon, "The Final Perseverance of the Saints," *SEE*, 12:316. Cf. Spurgeon, "Perseverance in Holiness," *SEE*, 8:479: "If the grace of God has changed you, you are radically and lastingly changed."
38. Spurgeon, "The Final Perseverance of the Saints," *SEE*, 12:315.
39. Ibid., p. 314.
40. Karl Barth, *CD*, vol. II/2, p. 332.
41. Ibid., p. 329.
42. Karl Barth, *The Christian Life*, trans. Geoffrey W. Bromiley (Grand Rapids, Mich.: Eerdmans, 1981), p. 94.
43. Anthony A. Hoekema, *Saved by Grace* (Grand Rapids, Mich.: Eerdmans, 1989), p. 4.
44. Ibid., p. 237.
45. F. F. Bruce, *The Gospel of John* (Grand Rapids, Mich.: Eerdmans, 1983), p. 154.
46. Fritz Rienecker & Cleon L. Rogers, Jr., *LKGNT*, p. 454.
47. Augustine, *Confessions*, XI.31.
48. Berkouwer, *Faith and Perseverance*, p. 207.
49. Peter T. O'Brien, *Colossians, Philemon*, *WBC* (Waco, Tex.: Word, 1982), p. 69.
50. John Calvin, *The Catholic Epistles* (Grand Rapids, Mich.: Eerdmans, 1948), p. 426.
51. H.N. Ridderbos, *Paul: An Outline of His Theology* (Grand Rapids, Mich.: Eerdmans, 1975), p. 255.
52. A.T. Hanson, *The Pastoral Epistles*, *NCBC* (Grand Rapids, Mich.: Eerdmans, 1982), p. 157.
53. W. Bauder, "Fall Away," *NIDNTT*, 1:608.
54. Donald Guthrie, *New Testament Theology* (Leicester: Inter-Varsity, 1981), p. 608, wrote: "It is difficult to see how a true disciple, who has been possessed by the Spirit, could reach a state of mind to declare that Spirit to be evil, thus reflecting a hardened state."
55. The verb "seized with remorse" (aorist passive participle of *metamelomai*) here may mean no more than "wishing it were undone." Rienecker and Rogers, *LKGNT*, p. 81.
56. John MacArthur, *The Gospel According to Jesus* (Grand Rapids, Mich.: Zondervan, 1988), p. 99.
57. David J. Ellis, "The Gospel According to John," *NLBC*, p. 1325. Cf. Donald Guthrie, "John," *NBCRev*, p. 959.
58. Simon J. Kistemaker, *Exposition of the Epistles of Peter and of the Epistle of Jude*, *NTC* (Grand Rapids, Mich.: Baker, 1987), pp. 311-13, j Pet 2:20-22 returns to a discussion of the false teachers introduced in vv. 1-18a.
59. Thomas Hewett, *Epistle to the Hebrews*, *TNTC* (London: Tyndale, 1960), p. 107. Cf. Rienecker and Rogers, *LKGNT*, p. 681.
60. This interpretation—that Heb 6:4-6 represents a strong warning to Jewish believers against turning away from Christ and reverting to a Judaism incapable of conveying salvation—is preferred by interpreters such as B.F. Westcott, W. Manson, E. Kevan, D. Guthrie, T. Hewitt, H.W.G. Thomas, and H. Kent.
61. The alternative interpretation—favored by Calvin, Owen, Grosheide, Hughes, Nicole, and other Reformed—suggests that the experiences and qualities cited in Heb 6:4-5 and 10:26 describe people who were thoroughly exposed to the Gospel, who made a Christian profession, who looked outwardly like Christians, but who were not regenerated. Their renunciation of the Gospel and opposition to Christ put them beyond the sphere of repentance. What Hebrews describes, the argument goes, is similar to "blasphemy against the Spirit" (Matt 12:31-32) or the "sin that leads to death" (1 John 5:16). This interpretation, in addition to assigning to unbelievers the fairly clear language of Christian experience, must ascribe the complementary words in Heb 6:9-10 and 10:39 to a group (of believers) different from the people (unbelievers) described in 6:4-6 and 10:26-29.
62. Guthrie, *New Testament Theology*, p. 633.
63. Berkouwer, *Faith and Perseverance*, pp. 119-120.

64. Hoekema, *Saved by Grace*, p. 255.
65. John Gill, *A Body of Divinity* (London: Turner Lasseter, reprint, 1957), p. 578.
66. Augustine, *Commentary on the Psalms*, 59.5.

CHAPTER 12

1. K.F.W. Prior, *The Way of Holiness* (Chicago: Inter-Varsity, 1967), p. 128.
2. Henry Alford, *The Greek New Testament*, 4 vols. in 2 (Chicago: Moody, 1958), 4:255.
3. John Murray, *Redemption Accomplished and Applied* (Grand Rapids, Mich.: Eerdmans, 1955), p. 175.
4. Craig Blomberg, "Degrees of Reward in the Kingdom of Heaven," *JETS* 35.2 (June 1992):159-72.
5. Bernard Ramm, *Them He Glorified* (Grand Rapids, Mich.: Eerdmans, 1963), pp. 113, 115.
6. Ibid., p. 100.
7. Ibid., p. 135.
8. C.S. Lewis, *The Great Divorce* (London: Geoffrey Bles, 1975), pp. 66-67.

GENERAL

INDEX